LAWRENCE KOHLBERG

Consensus and Controversy

Essays in Honour of Lawrence Kohlberg

Falmer International Master-Minds Challenged

Psychology Series Editors: Drs Sohan and Celia Modgil

LAWRENCE KOHLBERG

Consensus and Controversy

EDITED BY

Sohan Modgil, PhD

Reader in Educational Research and Development
Brighton Polytechnic

AND

Celia Modgil, PhD

Senior Lecturer in Educational Psychology
London University

CONCLUDING CHAPTER

BY

Lawrence Kohlberg
Harvard University

The Falmer Press
A member of the Taylor & Francis Group
(Philadelphia and London)

USA   The Falmer Press, Taylor & Francis Inc., 242 Cherry
Street, Philadelphia, PA 19106-1906

UK   The Falmer Press, Falmer House, Barcombe, Lewes,
East Sussex, BN8 5DL

First published in 1986

Library of Congress Cataloging in Publication Data

Library of Congress Cataloging in Publication Data is
available

Main entry under title:
   Falmer International Masterminds Challenged: 1
   Lawrence Kolberg: Controversy and Consensus
LC 86-6361
ISBN 1 85000 025 5

Jacket design by Caroline Archer

Typeset in 10/12 Times
by Imago Publishing Ltd., Thame, Oxon.

*Printed in Great Britain by Taylor & Francis (Printers) Ltd,
Rankine Road, Basingstoke, Hants.*

Contributors

Dr Sohan Modgil *and* Dr Celia Modgil
Brighton Polytechnic *University of London*

Professor Robert Carter
Trent University

Professor Don Locke
University of Warwick

Professor Dwight Boyd
*Ontario Institute for Studies in
Education*

Professor Harvey Siegel
University of Miami, Florida

Dr Olivera Petrovich
University of Oxford

Dr Peter Tomlinson
University of Leeds

Dr Peter Kutnick
University of Sussex

Dr Roger Straughan
University of Reading

Professor Robert Kegan
University of Harvard

Professor Jane Loevinger
University of Washington

Dr Charles Bailey
Homerton College

Professor John Martin Rich
University of Texas at Austin

John Wilson
University of Oxford

Professor Edmund Sullivan
*Ontario Institute for Studies in
Education*

Professor James Leming
*Southern Illinois University at
Carbondale*

Dr David Gordon
Ben-Gurion University of the Negev

Dr Marion Smith
*Roehampton Institute of Higher
Education*

Dr Brian Gates
St Martin's College

Professor Robert Enright, Dr Daniel
Lapsley and Dr Leanne Olson
Wisconsin-Madison University

Dr Lea Pearson
Birmingham Psychological Services

Dr Helen Weinreich-Haste
University of Bath

Professor John Broughton
Teachers College Columbia University

Professor Mary Wilcox
Iliff School of Theology

Professor Donald Joy
Asbury Theological Seminar

Professor Carolyn Edwards
University of Massachusetts

Dr Ian Vine
University of Bradford

Professor James Rest
University of Minnesota, Twin Cities

Professor Charles Evans
William Woods College

Professor Lawrence Kohlberg
University of Harvard

Acknowledgments

The undertaking of this *Falmer International Master-Minds Challenged* Psychology Series was only possible in collaboration with the numerous distinguished contributors herein. We are greatly indebted to them for demonstrating their trust by accepting our invitation to join forces to provide statements of how Kohlberg's theory is seen in relation to particular disciplines.

The volume has been greatly enhanced by the recognition given to it by Lawrence Kohlberg, who increased our confidence in the project by kindly agreeing to write the concluding chapter. We thank Professor Kohlberg for his very kind and generous support and for his edifying contribution to the content.

We are further grateful to Falmer Press, a member of the Taylor & Francis group. We express our very sincere gratitude to Malcolm Clarkson, Managing Director, Falmer Press.

Sohan and Celia Modgil
July 1984

Contents

V MORAL JUDGMENT AND MORAL ACTION

VI MORAL DEVELOPMENT AND EGO DEVELOPMENT

VII MORALITY, REASON AND EMOTIONS

VIII MORAL EDUCATION

IX MORAL CURRICULUM

X RELIGIOUS EDUCATION

XI SOCIAL REASONING

XII MORAL REASONING AND POLITICAL ISSUES

XIII THEOLOGICAL EPISTEMOLOGY

In loving memory of
Piyare Lal Modgil

Part I: Introduction

1. Lawrence Kohlberg: Consensus and Controversy

SOHAN AND CELIA MODGIL

For nearly thirty years, Lawrence Kohlberg has amplified his cognitive-developmental theory of moralization which has become prominent in the analysis of moral development and its consequent application to moral education. From its early transmission, the theory has not been without its critics (Alston, 1971; Peters, 1971; Simpson, 1974; Weinreich-Haste, 1974; Tomlinson, 1975), but many would add further credence to Peters' view that Kohlberg's findings are of unquestionable importance. However, Peters' (1971) warning that 'there is a grave danger that they [Kohlberg's findings] may become exalted into a general theory of moral development', may be seen by some to have been fulfilled.

EXISTING ISSUES OF DEBATE

With the imminent publication of Kohlberg's long awaited three volumes and thus the availability of his works in a collected form, it would now seem appropriate for his work to receive directed, comprehensive analysis. Reviews of Kohlberg's first volume (Locke, 1981; Petrovich, 1982) and recent articles in the *Journal of Moral Education* highlight the necessity for further evaluation. Kohlberg's measurement and methodology, structural unity, the invariant sequence of development, cultural universality, the logical necessity of the sequence of stages, increasing cognitive and moral adequacy of the stages (see Locke, 1979); the relationship between religion and morality, the meaning of autonomy (Petrovich, 1982); lack of a significant role for the emotions in moral education (Rich, 1980); 'the illusion of Stage 6' (Locke, 1980); and the labelling of students (Bolt and Sullivan, 1980) are still in doubt.

1

CURRENT COUNTERACTION TO CRITICAL ANALYSES

To counterbalance the above, a Social Reasoning Scale, based on Kohlberg's model, has been incorporated in The British Ability Scales (Pearson and Elliott, 1980); moral education is considered to be best seen as the development of certain kinds of knowledge and reasoning rather than the cultivation of certain kinds of feeling (Bailey, 1980), and controversy discussion has been found to be related to both moral reasoning and tolerance in Ireland (Breslin, 1982). Other favourable analyses of Kohlberg's work have been included in Modgil, C. (1975, 1980) and Modgil and Modgil (1976, 1980, 1982 and 1983).

Additional to the publication of Kohlberg's major three volumes, Kohlberg, Levine and Hewer (1983) review the major philosophical and psychological assumptions pertaining to the theory, incorporating Kohlberg's present thinking together with reviewing and presenting a response to the major criticisms aimed at his work. While highlighting studies which give credence to Kohlberg's earlier statements, Kohlberg, Levine and Hewer acknowledge the considerable amount of revision and expansion of the theory which has been stimulated by the criticisms of other scholars. The domain of moral development has been enlarged and some theoretical constructs basic for relating judgment to action have been developed. It is not believed that the critics have discovered Kohlberg's work to be biased in any 'hard' sense of the word but that they have highlighted certain theoretical and methodological issues to which Kohlberg and his researchers need to be sensitive. Kohlberg *et al*. '. . . believe, in line with Weber (1949), Habermas (forthcoming) and others, that objectivity is a "moment" of scientific inquiry; that the essence or "truth" value of objectivity does not reside in some reified, permanent, or factual quality inherent in the object of inquiry, but is, rather to be found in and understood as a process of understanding which is the changing relationship between the investigator and what he or she observes.'

CONTINUING THE DEBATE: THE STRATEGY OF THE BOOK

The book's objective is the evaluation of elements of Kohlberg's theory from the perspectives of a range of areas of knowledge: philosophy; psychology, incorporating a range of approaches and emphases; education; curriculum studies; religious education; theological epistemology; social and political studies; cross-cultural research and research methodology. It aims to provide in one single source the 'crosscurrents and crossfire', thus clarifying the contribution of Kohlberg to the evolution of the understanding of moral development.

The volume provides theoretical analyses, supported by research, of aspects of Kohlberg's theory, presented predominantly either positively or negatively by *pairs* of distinguished academics representing particular areas of knowledge. The *paired* contributions have been exchanged, through the editors, to provide an opportunity for both parties to refute the 'heart' of the opposing paper. This would perhaps go some way towards Locke's (1981) prescription that 'what the study of moral development needs at this stage of its own development . . . [is] a wide-ranging approach to the facts which, for the moment, leaves their theoretical explanation open.' Further, it is hoped that this work will partly fulfil Petrovich's

(1982) hope (in response to Kohlberg's emphasis on his and his colleagues' changing and growing views) 'that this growth will continue so as to include an openness to the evidence outside Kohlberg's own framework.'

Although axiomatic, it would be expedient to emphasize that the labelling 'predominantly positive' or 'predominantly negative' implies that the writer of the predominantly 'positive' chapter agrees in the *main* with the theory but is not in *entire* agreement, therefore being allowed some latitude towards disagreement. Likewise, 'negative' chapters mean that contributors *predominantly* but not *entirely* disagree with the theory, therefore permitting some latitude towards agreement. The interchange of chapters therefore produces points of consensus and of controversy.

The difficulties in this ambitious debate project are not minimized. Although every attempt has been made to achieve precise matching of pairs, in exceptional cases one of the contributors within a matched pair has followed a 'middle course'. This established itself as a 'contrasting' enough pair to lend itself to the debate format of the book.

Although the editors dictated the generic topics to be debated, the contributors were free to focus on any inherent aspect or specialization of their own. Again, however, the consequent interchange of the chapters allows formulation of points of consensus and of controversy, therefore retaining the thrust of the debate.

The choice of the contributors was restricted to those who are objectively critical and who are knowledgeable about the theory. Some of the most publicized critics tend to have non-scientific axes to grind and their views and their polemics are well known. The scholarly value of the book could be seriously damaged unless the contributors have the desire and the capacity for the kind of intellectual honesty needed to come to grips seriously with the scientific, psychological and social issues raised by the theory.

CONTENTS OF EACH CONTRIBUTION

Robert Carter underlines the frequency with which Kohlberg confronts long-standing philosophical concerns. Kohlberg's attempts to avoid the charge of 'relativist' have recently led him to fortify his work with that of Jürgen Habermas. Although an exciting and fruitful elaboration of the Kohlbergian position, it is less than apparent precisely which *forms* of relativism have been addressed and rejected. Carter attempts to disambiguate the term 'relativism', and to show that, if anything, Kohlberg is, in fact, closer to at least one major form of relativist thought than ever before. If this is so, it may shed light on just where the source of disagreement lies between Kohlberg and those less convinced that the end of ethics is justice. Don Locke also pays tribute to the way Kohlberg has combined psychological evidence and philosophical argument and, further, educational practice. He likewise gives attention to Kohlberg's critique of ethical and cultural relativism and concludes that Kohlberg has provided not a refutation but an explanation of cultural relativism. Locke further gives attention to Kohlberg's use of philosophical terminology, to his attempt to derive an 'ought' from an 'is' by arguing that the later and higher stages of moral reasoning are also morally better and to Kohlberg's conception of a highest, ultimate stage of moral reasoning, Stage 6.

Starting with an articulation of some of the general ways in which Kohlberg's work indicates avenues for crossing the border between psychology and philosophy, Dwight Boyd also focuses on the problematic relationship of 'is' and 'ought' suggested by Kohlberg. Boyd then systematically pares away unsupportable interpretations of Kohlberg's claims on this issue, for example, that what is intended is any sort of direct move from developmental facts to normative 'ought'-claims, or a simple conflation of the theoretical perspectives of normative justification and psychological explanation. Going beyond what Kohlberg has articulated, a suggestion is made for the most positive and promising interpretation of Kohlberg's substantive intentions in his recent affirmation of a 'complementarity' between moral philosophy and developmental psychology. Harvey Siegel in similar vein argues that any attempt to justify judgments of moral adequacy on the basis of empirical psychological research findings must of necessity fail, since such findings are in principle incapable of justifying judgments of moral adequacy. It is concluded that, if educational efforts at advancing students along the sequence of stages are to be justified, they must be justified not in terms of psychology, but in terms of moral philosophical argument regarding the moral adequacy of ethical judgments.

Within the specific moral psychology orientation Olivera Petrovich, although critical of various empirical and theoretical points of Kohlberg's views, singles out for its novelty in psychological research on morality the issue of the relationship between religion and morality. Petrovich's view is that the added seventh stage of Kohlberg's theory is the most interesting part, with respect not only to Kohlberg's theory alone but also to the area of moral psychology as a whole. By introducing the seventh stage, Kohlberg acknowledges that moral development cannot, in the end, be explained exclusively by cognitive psychology mechanisms. Instead, he admits that a value stance is necessary in moral discourse and, more specifically, comes to the view that religion must play some part in moral development. Petrovich sees the possibility of distinguishing *two* types of Kohlberg's theory instead of regarding the seventh stage as simply an extension of his six-stage theory: religious and secular, representative of two fundamentally different world views. Such potential should be of substantial value in generating future research. Peter Tomlinson also emphasizes features relevant to moral psychology, looking critically at the structuralism of Kohlberg's cognitive-developmental approach. Further, he examines Kohlberg's phenomenalism and its emphasis on conscious processing. Finally, arising out of the previous two, consideration is given to what Tomlinson contends to be a somewhat confused under-use of psychological paradigms.

What is often referred to as 'the judgment/action issue' is concerned with a variety of logical and empirical questions to do with the relationship between moral reasoning and behaviour. Peter Kutnick portrays Kohlberg's early theory with respect to this relationship, the criticisms and consequent revision of theory together with empirical support. Overall, the chapter demonstrates the continuous stage of flux, development and redevelopment of the field relating moral judgment to moral action. Roger Straughan argues that Kohlberg's contribution in this area is limited by his methodological emphasis upon hypothetical ethical dilemmas. His account of moral action is scanty and his claim that 'maturity of moral thought should predict maturity of moral action' is open to various objections. Overall, Kohlberg's methodology and his failure to draw necessary conceptual distinctions produce an obscure and inadequate account of this issue.

With reference to the more specifically psychological concern of ego development and Kohlberg's theory, Robert Kegan, although having some misgivings
about Kohlberg's own explicit conception of the relationship between moral and
ego development, views Kohlberg's works as a whole as the single most original and
potentiating contribution to the understanding of the ego since Sigmund Freud.
This positive assessment is based primarily on the necessity of a constructivist
concept of 'structure' for the study of meaning-constitutive processes of personality
(i.e., ego). Jane Loevinger outlines the gradual evolution of Kohlberg's ideas about
ego development and its relation to moral development. She emphasizes the
difficulties of his conflicting conceptions but, in conclusion, likewise considers the
vitality now evident in the broad field of ego development to be due to Kohlberg's
energy, substantial contributions and catalytic effect.

Charles Bailey outlines the part played by justification in morality, together
with an account of the inadequacy of feelings and affections to provide justifications, which lend support to Kohlberg's claim that cognitive judgment should have
priority of consideration over observed behaviour and affective matters in deciding
the quality of a person's morality. Bailey, however, raises doubt about the claims
by Kohlberg concerning the motivating force of cognitive judgment and proposes
a theory of a necessary affective mainspring to derive the system. John Rich
elaborates further on the role of the emotions in morality and identifies two types of
emotions involved in moral judgment and action. Such findings are related to
Kohlberg's theory by indicating that once the conventional and post-conventional
levels find a place for character traits distinctive of each level, they will also secure a
functional role for emotions in moral judgment and action—their ethical importance would rest upon the cognitive moral development theory itself.

Within the context of moral education, John Wilson suggests that Kohlberg
and other developmentalists should make clear just what is being asserted under
the heading of 'development' or 'stages of development'. Kohlberg has shown
nothing about children's ability to understand reasons, but may have highlighted
(what we know already) particular regimes that affect children at different ages,
and hence affect their preferences for using or proffering reasons. Edmund Sullivan
enters into similar considerations in his criticism of the shortcomings of the
progressive ideology of our time in which he includes Kohlberg's work. Schools are
currently involved in enculturating the virtues of consumer capitalism. In facing a
crisis of legitimacy of the values held by the culture, we need a post-progressive
approach to values which must proceed on the assumption that values are already
assimilated unconsciously and must be made subject to a 'critical awareness'.
Kohlberg's more recent work on the moral atmosphere merits interest and
attention.

In consideration of the moral curriculum, James Leming continues the theme
of the substantial problems to be overcome in the real world of schools if any
widespread implementation of Kohlberg's ideals is to occur. Leming's paper traces
the evolution of Kohlbergian programmes from the original narrow focus on the
use of hypothetical moral dilemma discussions to stimulate stage advance to the
current just community approach where the emphasis is on social behaviour and the
development of collective norms. The second part of the paper is an assessment of
Kohlbergian programmes from a practical perspective, with an analysis of how the
programmes are received by students, teachers, administration and community and
how that reaction will affect Kohlbergian programmes' effectiveness and accept-

ance. David Gordon analyzes Kohlberg's just community approach to moral education which he shows to be based on his conception of the hidden curriculum. Kohlberg assumes the hidden curriculum to be related to social relations within the school and to be the most effective part of the school curriculum because of its pervasive consistency. It is argued that both of these assumptions are mistaken.

Marion Smith, in general support of Kohlberg's theory for the insights it provides for religious educators, concludes that, although the theory and method do not constitute all that religious educators look for in their treatment of moral questions, his contribution has so far not been fully exploited even though his perspective of man as a free and responsible moral agent is in accord with religious doctrine. Brian Gates expounds further on the theme of the inadequacies of Kohlberg's theory for descriptions of the development of religious thinking and religious education. In particular, Kohlberg begs questions about the moral teleologies of different religions, as also about the ways in which religion and morality mutually impinge. Because of these weaknesses Kohlberg is less adequately placed to make a productive contribution to religious education and even primary moral education than he might otherwise be. The English tradition of religious and moral education and school assemblies has some insights to contribute to the American scene.

From the social cognitive developmental perspective Enright, Lapsley and Olson argue on the basis of the Lakatosian philosophy of science that Kohlbergian moral development is a progressive scientific theory which is responsible for generating a host of important social cognitive developmental domains, such as legal development, interpersonal understanding, conventional reasoning and belief discrepancy reasoning, as well as for establishing an important theoretical link between role-taking and morality. Lea Pearson acknowledges the difficulty in identifying a specific area as usefully denoted by the term 'social reasoning', and discusses four areas that appear to have common elements of social reasoning, although essentially disparate activities with differing criteria of effectiveness: social skills training, educational applications, measurement or assessment and theories.

Helen Weinreich-Haste argues that the criticisms of Kohlberg's political assumptions have brought into sharp focus a much broader debate about the way developmental psychology deals with values, and that, on balance, Kohlberg's explicit affirmation of a link between ideology and morality is a positive not a negative feature. Weinreich-Haste examines empirical studies of the relationship between moral reasoning and political ideology and action, together with parallel work on cognitive-developmental approaches to the growth of social, political and economic thought. Her analysis concludes with a consideration of the relationship between individual reasoning and social and cultural experience, and how work stemming from Kohlberg's theory illuminates this. John Broughton argues that Kohlberg has placed his moral development theory squarely in the liberal tradition of social and political thought. However, the political precepts that he borrows from that tradition are highly questionable. First, his social evolutionism proposes non-rational criteria for the ordering of societies, disregards historical phenomena, confounds society and culture, and encourages a nationalistic cultural paternalism. Second, his reduction of the state to the transactional matrix of civil society depoliticizes social life by reducing the political to the moral. It also serves to conceal power and authority, protecting the latter from any examination of legitimacy, and limiting the possibility of dissent. Finally, his 'psychologization' of society reifies subjectivity in terms of naturally conflicting 'interests' and naturally exchangeable 'roles', unwittingly elevating to a principle the objectification and alienation of social relationships.

Mary Wilcox illustrates the direct application of Kohlberg's theory of stages of moral reasoning and social perspective to the field of theological epistemology. A six-year longitudinal research project at Iliff School of Theology has shown clear correlations among Kohlberg's stages, William G. Perry's epistemological model and theological concepts related to truth and images of the church. From a more critical stance, Donald Joy summarizes the critical responses of representative researchers and theologians to the work of Kohlberg, and further suggests some foundational contributions for religious education which lie embedded in structural development research. Joy then places his non-negotiable foundational concerns and charges against Kohlberg's work which revolve around: What is moral reasoning?; the 'naturalistic fallacy'; and, Who is the 'reasoner', a subject, an object or an agent?

Cross-cultural research is the only empirical strategy that can establish the universality of Kohlberg's system. Carolyn Edwards reviews the sizeable body of literature on moral judgment development in people from cultural groups outside the dominant culture. On three central criteria, it is argued, a tentative consensus can be reached. Ian Vine argues more strongly in relation to the provisos introduced by Edwards concerning the revision required at the higher levels/stages and that the system cannot and should not be used to compare adequacy of development between different cultural groups. While rejecting some of Kohlberg's ethical philosophy and liberal-democratic ideology, Vine sees his descriptive theory as having considerable heuristic value for illuminating the socio-political role which an individualistic rhetoric of justice and rights can play.

James Rest examines the research of the Kohlberg group in developing a method for scoring moral judgment. Four major decision points are discussed in terms of the options that Kohlberg chose and the advantages and disadvantages of the options taken. A brief summary of the validation research is given, along with future questions and needs. Charles Evans specifically focuses on numerous questions raised regarding the validity and reliability of Kohlberg's methodology, together with the way in which it is used.

Lawrence Kohlberg contributes the final chapter to the book.

REFERENCES

Alston, W. P. (1971) 'Comments on Kohlberg's "From is to Ought"', in T. Mischel (Ed.), *Cognitive Development and Epistemology*, New York, Academic Press.

Bailey, C. (1980) 'Morality, reason and feeling', *Journal of Moral Education*, 9, 2, pp. 114–21.

Bolt, D. J. and Sullivan, E. V. (1980) 'Kohlberg's cognitive-developmental theory in educational settings', *Journal of Moral Education*, 6, 3, pp. 198–205.

Breslin, A. (1982) 'Tolerance and moral reasoning among adolescents in Ireland', *Journal of Moral Education*, 11, 2, pp. 112–27.

Kohlberg, L. (1981) *The Philosophy of Moral Development: Moral Stages and the Idea of Justice*, Vol. I: Essays on Moral Development, London, Harper and Row.

Kohlberg, L., Levine, C. and Hewer, A. (1983) *Moral Stages: A Current Formulation and a Response to Critics*, Basel, Karger.

Locke, D. (1979) 'Cognitive stages or developmental phases/A critique of the stage-structural theory of moral reasoning', *Journal of Moral Education*, 8, pp. 168–81.

Locke, D. (1980) 'The illusion of stage six', *Journal of Moral Education*, 9, 2, pp. 103–9.

Locke, D. (1981) Review of *The Philosophy of Moral Development*, in *The Times Higher Educational Supplement*, 4 December, p. 16.

Modgil, C. (1975) Piagetian operations in relation to moral development. Unpublished MPhil Thesis, University of Surrey.

Modgil, C. (1980) The patterning of cognitive development in relation to moral maturity. Unpublished PhD Thesis, University of London.

Modgil, S. and Modgil, C. (1976) *Piagetian Research: Compilation and Commentary*, Vol. 6: The Cognitive Developmental Approach to Morality, Windsor, National Foundation for Educational Research.

Modgil, S. and Modgil, C. (Eds.) (1980) *Toward a Theory of Psychological Development*, Windsor, National Foundation for Educational Research.

Modgil, S. and Modgil, C. (Eds.) (1982) *Jean Piaget: Consensus and Controversy*, London, Holt, Rinehart and Winston.

Modgil, S. and Modgil, C. (Eds.) (1983) *Jean Piaget: An Interdisciplinary Critique*, London, Routledge and Kegan Paul.

Pearson, L. and Elliott, C. (1980) 'The development of a social reasoning scale in the New British Ability Scales', *Journal of Moral Education*, 10, 1, pp. 40–8.

Peters, R. S. (1971) 'Moral Development: a plea for pluralism', in T. Mischel (Ed.), *Cognitive Development and Epistemology*, New York, Academic Press.

Petrovich, O. (1982) Review of *The Philosophy of Moral Development*, in *British Journal of Psychology*, 73, pp. 313–16.

Rich, J. M. (1980) 'Moral education and the emotions', *Journal of Moral Education*, 9, 2, pp. 81–7.

Simpson, E. L. (1974) 'Moral development research, a case study of scientific cultural bias', *Human Development*, 17, pp. 81–106.

Tomlinson, P. (1975) 'Political education: cognitive developmental perspectives from moral education', *Oxford Review of Education*, 1, 3, pp. 241–67.

Weinreich-Haste, H. (1974) 'The structure of moral reason', *Journal of Youth and Adolescence*, 3, 2, pp. 135–43.

Part II: Moral Philosophy

2. Does Kohlberg Avoid Relativism?

ROBERT CARTER

The history of Western philosophy begins with the struggle between the relativists and sceptics on the one hand, and those who, with Plato and Socrates, search for some ground on which unchanging knowledge claims might be based. It was sometimes expressed as an attempt to find a stable basis for meaning, rather than to give up in hopeless intellectual and moral despair. Unless relativism could be shown to be wrong, the very enterprise of philosophy was doomed. This opinion is still widespread, and hence there is little to give surprise in Lawrence Kohlberg's insistence that he is *not* a relativist. Indeed, there are those at both ends of the cognitive spectrum just waiting to pounce at the least show of epistemic faltering. Those who view Kohlberg as a dangerous liberal argue that his emphasis on moral autonomy is licence, and that his insistence on form rather than the listing of specific moral rules is but a quieter species of subversion. On the other side, the scientific behaviourists, positivists and emotivists find him to be too rationalistically philosophical for his own good. They argue that the empirical evidence alone should be attended to, and questions of normativity become matters of linguistic and cultural convention, or straightforward operational definitions (for example, 'good' is what positively reinforces). Thus Kohlberg writes, 'Behaviourists and psychoanalytic theorists who believe that there is no logical or empirical validity to moral utterances, that they are simply emotive expressions, are throwing out the scientific baby with the emotional bathwater.'[1]

In what follows, I will applaud Kohlberg's attempt to walk between the extremes of moral authority and empirical classification, but I shall also argue that his constant enemy is not relativism in all its forms, but only in its sceptical or nihilistic senses. As I see it, Kohlberg is now more clearly in the camp of the constructive relativists than ever before, as the conclusion to his most recent book in reply to his critics amply demonstrates:

... that objectivity is a 'moment' of scientific inquiry; that the essence or 'truth' value of objectivity does not reside in some reified, permanent, or factual quality inherent in the object of inquiry, but is, rather, to be found in and understood as a process of understanding which is the changing relationship between the investigator and what he or she observes.[2]

This perspective is acknowledged to be heavily influenced by the work of Jürgen Habermas, as is the label he now willingly wears—'objective hermeneutics'. The open-minded modifiability of Kohlberg's project, due to the methodology of 'objective hermeneutics', is, to this writer, quite exciting and philosophically promising. But it brings into focus an ambiguity which has often gone unnoticed in Kohlberg's writings, namely the precise meaning of his claim that he is certainly not a relativist, but rather a 'methodological non-relativist'.[3] The point is all the more important since many of his more tradition-minded critics continue to brand him a relativist, as though to totally discredit him by that charge alone. In attempting to clarify what the term 'relativism' is more regularly used to mean, and in indicating which of these meanings Kohlberg wishes to reject as applicable to his own moral position, and which, if any, might apply, it will be useful to disambiguate this multi-faceted label.

THE SOPHIST AS RELATIVIST

The 'relativism' to which Kohlberg is evidently opposed is the view that conflicting ethical opinions are (all of them) equally valid or true. I shall call this position 'epistemological relativism'. The difficulty with this stance is, as Kohlberg observes, that 'acceptance of the idea that *all* values are relative does, logically, lead to the conclusion that the teacher should not attempt to teach any particular moral values ... The students of a teacher who has been successful in communicating moral relativism will believe, like the teacher, that "everyone has his own bag" and that "everyone should keep doing his thing".'[4] This brand of relativistic ethics is reminiscent of the main thrust of Greek sophistry. Thus, moral values are relative to the individual, or to the state, and the reason for this variability of opinion is that conflicting ethical opinions are equally valid (or equally invalid or ungrounded), and therefore it is the individual, or the group, or the state which decides which argument or position to make 'appear' to be the stronger, or the weaker. The art of sophistry is to make the (apparently) stronger argument appear to be weaker, and the (apparently) weaker argument appear to be stronger. In fact, no moral argument is justifiably stronger or weaker than any other. All are equal, and therefore the choosing of one of them is all that is at stake. It is little wonder that the legendary Cratylus broke with civilized tradition because of his recognition that such relativism was scepticism, and since there is no *reason* to choose one thing over another, the wise thing to do is to choose as little as possible. He sat nearly naked and unconventionally dirty in public view, wiggling his fingers as symbolic of the fact that to say anything is impossible, for everything is in flux. One statement— any statement—is as true or false as any other. Of course, epistemological consistency should have prevented him from deciding whether to wiggle his fingers or not, to take nourishment or not, to be clean or dirty. Thus, *epistemological relativism* inevitably gives way to either *'cultural relativism'* or *'personal relativism'*. In the former view, one does in Rome as Romans do, for in this way one gains what one would not otherwise obtain—the possibility of reputation, position, wealth, and protection. Or, one becomes a *'personal relativist'*, having concluded that whatever one thinks is moral *is moral* for you. Thus, the pathetic Thrasymachus of Plato's *Republic* announces wildly that justice is whatever is in the interest of the stronger, and his own bullish stand makes it clear that he will fight to become powerful.[5] Plato and Kohlberg are united in viewing all of these relativisms as making significant moral discourse and decision impossible, or at best a mockery! Indeed, Kohlberg recently (1984) defined 'ethical relativism as a philosophic doctrine ... [which holds that] there is no way for thoughtful persons to resolve their differences in moral values and judgments.' But there is another meaning of relativism which is not only more tenable, but which seems in line with the more modest assessment of Kohlberg's achievements and claims in his most recent replies. While it may matter not at all whether the label 'relativist' does or does not apply, the attempt to clarify his present position against this ongoing debate may prove helpful not only in handling his critics authoritatively, but in making even more clear the implications of his present stance.

PROTAGORAS

While Kohlberg uses Protagoras as the symbol of the kind of relativism which destroys meaningful ethical discussion and decision-making,[6] Plato found it impossible to take the great Protagoras lightly. Gregory Vlastos urges that this is because Protagoras had 'moral inhibitions', and refused to identify 'a life of pleasure with the good life'.[7] Protagoras, somehow, established epistemic and moral limits to the sorts of actions which are acceptable. If we are to take these moral conclusions seriously, then we cannot make of Protagorean sophistry a straightforward epistemological relativism. Allegedly valid moral distinctions were possible for Protagoras, although the ultimate grounds of those distinctions may themselves be, in some deeper sense, relative to human minds and human preferences. Man is the ultimate measure. Whether such a position was taken by the historical Protagoras may be impossible to know, and, in any case, this is not the place to work it out. It is enough to suggest that Kohlberg, like Plato, will have to wrestle with relativisms which are more compelling than those provided by the run-of-the-mill sophists, and possibly more in line with the philosophically sophisticated Protagoras. Take, for example, the view that maintains that one's most basic presuppositions, perspective, or framework are not themselves (wholly) justifiable, if justifiable at all, but are chosen or 'elected' as those values or starting-points without which no other values or significant stances of any kind would or could arise. I shall call such a position 'perspectivism'.[8] A compelling account of such a relativistic thesis is provided by Jack W. Meiland in a recent article. He identifies a form of relativism which '... holds that one's beliefs are relative to one's perspective, presuppositions, or framework and freely chosen by the individual rather than forced on him by his historical-cultural situation'.[9] Relativism of this type need not yield a complete scepticism, or even a paralytic subjectivism. To quote a recent and articulate statement of such a position, 'it is not that all beliefs are equally true or equally false, but regardless of truth and falsity the fact of their credibility is to be seen as equally problematic.'[10] While the choice of presuppositions, framework (or perspective) may be subjective, or personal, nevertheless 'once these presuppositions are chosen, the rest of one's intellectual activity can be quite objective. For, given these presuppositions, certain statements will be true. They will be true for *anyone* who adopts those presuppositions.'[11] The usual criticism of this position is that relativism is self-vitiating in that there would be no (objective) rational grounds for adopting one's presuppositions.[12] As Meiland argues, however, 'emphasis on this sort of rationality (or on any other sort, or on any sort of non-rationality either) is itself an ideology.'[13] Rationality, like morality itself, is a commitment to such values as logical consistency, generality and universalizability, and reversability, without which it would not matter what one did or thought. Such 'axioms' are 'starting-points', or, more candidly, assumptions from which the 'objectivity', or 'necessity', or 'morality' of the rest of the system follows. Thus, it is a mistake to conclude 'that every variety of relativism results in complete subjectivism at all levels of intellectual activity.'[14] Even more to the point, to assume that every part of every doctrine must rest on there being sufficient 'or conclusive' grounds for its adoption is not only to deny the ongoing development of all human knowledge, but is to fly in the face of Godel's great discovery in even as exact a science as mathematics, *viz.*, that no system has the capacity for self-justification; i.e., no system can justify itself by means of its own axioms. Such justification is possible only by means of a meta-theory, a theory which both embraces the original, and serves to justify that system from a position beyond it. But, in turn, the meta-theory cannot justify itself, and so a meta-meta-theory is required, and so on ... In this sense, the axiomatic beginnings of a system are *taken*, not given or proved. What serves as a partial establishment of their validity is the fruitfulness of the system built on them, and the degree to which its findings accord with the empirical evidence as understood. In this sense of relativism, it may be quite accurate to observe, with Protagoras, that man is the measure of all things, and yet to suppose, as did Protagoras, that there is a better and a worse to moral theorizing. Perhaps this was why Protagoras maintained to the end that he had something worthwhile to teach, although none of it necessarily final, or guaranteed by a source external to man himself.

KOHLBERG'S CLARIFICATION

When Kohlberg and his associates write that Kohlberg's moral development thesis is '*a rational reconstruction of the ontogenesis* of justice reasoning',[15] they are making abundantly clear that a specified collection of 'metaethical assumptions' were taken 'prior to research' because they 'helped us to orient ourselves to the empirical study of moral development as Justice reasoning.'[16] The point is then stressed that 'at a philosophical level these assumptions remain controversial, but their use has led to the discovery of empirical findings which seem to justify their continued use.'[17] Not only that, but it is pointed out that there is an additional set of assumptions that have been employed, *viz.*, *normative-ethical* assumptions: 'For example, our claim that a sixth and highest stage of reasoning defines morally adequate principles and that each higher stage is a movement toward fulfilling Stage 6 criteria for just resolutions of moral conflict constitutes one such normative-ethical assumption.'[18] Kohlberg's stage theory is 'a rational reconstruction' based on such normative-ethical and meta-ethical assumptions. For these reasons at least, Kohlberg agrees with Habermas that 'our theory and observations lie in this more interpretive vein',[19] i.e., as a hermeneutical approach more like history or literary criticism than positivistic science. Quite correctly, Kohlberg goes on to show that Habermas' insistence that the 'art' of hermeneutic interpretation requires that one participate in a 'conversation' with the observed (subject or written text), is evidenced in Kohlbergian interview technique where the interviewer must strive 'to take the role (perspective) of the other.'[20] Furthermore, in order imaginatively to assume the other's perspective, the interviewer must try to see through his own careful reconstruction of the interviewee's meanings and structural patterns of reasoning.[21] Such a method 'rests on the communicative and empathic stance of an interpreter, not on a positivistic stance of someone trying to classify and predict "behaviour" as distinct from meaning.'[22] Such interpretation is participatory, and, it would seem, value-laden in two senses. First, one must try to grasp the value perspective of the interviewee, and second, one must 'rationally' reconstruct what he/she sees from the normative hypothesis of stage development theory.

Kohlberg quotes Habermas at length in an attempt to further define their agreement about the necessity of value-laden interpretation:

> In some sense all interpretations are rational interpretations, an interpreter cannot but appeal to standards of rationality which he himself has adopted as binding for all parties including the author and his contemporaries. Such an appeal to presumably universal standards of rationality is, of course, no proof of the soundness of that presupposition.[23]

The passage does go on to say that we ought to proceed to investigate the 'conditions for validity of normative (or moral) expressions', but more relevant for our purposes is the emphasis on the assumptive character of even 'universal standards of rationality'. The assumption is required for the enterprise of reason to get underway, and pragmatically justified by its fruitfulness in living and research. But assumptive it remains. So it is that Kohlberg concludes that his 'theory is a rational reconstruction because it (a) describes the developmental logic inherent in the development of justice reasoning with the aid of (b) the normative criterion of Stage 6 ....'[24] Kohlberg even observes that the philosophical (and social scientific) underpinnings need not be 'proved' in order to be employed.[25] Thus Habermas and Kohlberg share a position midway between hermeneutic objectivism (we can all come to agree about the meaning of the text) and hermeneutic relativism (Gadamer's position, i.e., giving up the quest for any sort of objectivity and explanatory power). As Habermas says, while dropping the claim of objectivity in its hard, value-neutral sense, 'we wish to advocate the desirability and possibility of approaches which promise to generate some sort of objective and theoretical knowledge.'[26]

It might be well to pause here to make a little more evident what Habermas is attempting. His work on 'legitimate speech acts' is focused on those operative or implied general presuppositions of consensual speech acts which apply universally and necessarily to all possible instances of legitimate communication. The utterer of such a speech act implies four different types of validity claims: (1) that what he says is accessible and comprehensible; (2) that his 'propositional contents' and/or 'existential presuppositions' are true; (3) that he is being truthful; and (4) that it is right and appropriate for him to be communicating.[27] To speak genuinely or listen implies such an 'ideal speech situation', whether or not one comes up short in any actual speech act situation. Whatever defects are present, however, legitimate speech acts rest on the assumptions of the four validity claims noted. Any *de facto* consensus may not be a genuine or rational consensus, unless it fulfils these four criteria. But even if these conditions are fulfilled, one of the main sources of difficulty for the relativist remains: to assume the validity or truth of one's claims is not sufficient to establish their universal and necessary validity. Whereas Gadamer doubts that we can ever transcend a hermeneutic point of view, and thus are trapped within the 'hermeneutic circle' wherein what is proved is so only by virtue of the very propositions which constitute the possibility of proof in the first place, and are themselves the starting-points or assumptions of the point of view in question. Habermas tries to transcend the circle by eliciting from all possible circles those claims without which no claims, or circles, or communication of any sort would be possible. Nevertheless, even though analysis reveals what must be assumed for communication to be genuine, it is not clear exactly how we can establish an ideal-observer-type objectivity for the content of those validity claims. We must assume that what we say is true, in order to communicate ideally, but this in no way shows that what we assume is, in fact, true except from a perspective already within the circle of assumptions.

If this conclusion is correct, then we are left with the relativist's insight that one's fundamental values, beliefs, methodology and even one's understanding of reason's place in the scheme of things, are taken by us to be true, not given to us with that pedigree, and that they are *not* evidently universal or necessary, but only assumptive or traditional, or in some other way acceptable or even required by our point of view.

Even Ricoeur's observation that the hermeneutic circle 'constitutes a vicious circle only for analytic understanding, not for practical reason'[28] may be seen as being open to a relativist interpretation. The relativist, as with both Ricoeur and Habermas, must find an escape from totally indecisive and pathological paralysis, and one may well adopt what Gadamer calls 'the superiority of tradition'.[29] The circle is not broken theoretically, in this case, but only pragmatically. The relativist warns us not to confuse the one with the other. To be less than certain about one's attainment of truth is not necessarily to be indecisive about how one will act. Not to know that, in all the world, one has found one's most ideal romantic partner, makes one no less in love. The situational and assumptive nature of one's validity claims is not removed, but neither does this cause us to falter and abandon hope. Habermas' project is a noble and exciting one, but it is not actualized, and there are reasons to doubt whether it can be in the conclusive sense to which he aspires.

GROUNDS FOR CONFUSION

By now it should be apparent that much of the difficulty we are encountering results from the fact that the terms being used simply refuse to stay still. Opponents of relativism point to its nihilistic scepticism, while defenders of relativism warn that it is the only realistic alternative, since scepticism on the one hand, and absolutistic certainty on the other, are both untenable extremes. The only places left to stand are all of them between the extremes. But that includes nearly everybody: pragmatists, phenomenologists, most empiricists, many rationalists, etc. Yet Meiland is on target when he writes that it is regularly assumed that,

... only that which is purely objective or absolute is worth expressing and (what is a different thing) worth communicating. This assumption would, of course, rule out literature, art and music, poetry, and in general that expression of that subjective experience of the world which constitutes the greatest part of our lives and gives our lives their meaning and significance.[30]

But what stands firm as a distinguishing characteristic of any relativism is that the foundational starting-point or assumptions of the perspective in question are not themselves proved, or demonstrably supported by the system they ground. Whether they are in any other way supportable is the issue to which we now turn. Suffice it to say, however, that what a relativism does continue to maintain is that even the doctrine of relativity itself is only relative, else there is an unfortunate break in the key insight of the position, *viz.*, 'the connection between relativising factors (conceptual frameworks, socio-cultural conditions, values and the like), on the one hand and *all* intellectual thought on the other hand.'[31] More consistently, the relativist can waive such a dualistic theory of the intellect. Thus, the assumptions of our ethical system are relative!

IDENTITY VS. COMPLEMENTARITY

In 'From Is to Ought', Kohlberg argued that 'the scientific theory as to why people factually do move up from stage to stage is broadly the same as a moral theory as to why people should prefer a higher stage to a lower.'[32] This *identification* of the empirical findings with the normative rightness of the position is now softened to a 'complementarity thesis'.[33] The complementarity thesis abandons the claim that the 'normative adequacy of an ethical thesis such as Kohlberg's can be tested by or be shown to imply empirical truth claims.'[34] As was mentioned earlier in this essay, the admitted practice of rational reconstruction requires the composition of both meta-ethical and normative-ethical assumptions in orienting the researcher 'to the empirical study of moral development as justice reasoning'.[35] One cannot empirically expect to test a normative claim, for that would be to eliminate the distinction between the is and the ought, prescription and description, yielding an identity theory again, and thereby once more engendering the howls of philosophers who warn that normative claims require reasons other than non-normative or empirical ones. Description yields only description, and the stages would be but several different ways of looking at the normal world, were it not for the imposition of the normative claims of 'higher' and 'more adequate'.

Imagine, for example, the often heard instance of someone chafing at Kohlberg's claim that Stage 5 or 6 reasoning is 'better' than Stage 4 reasoning. 'What is so wonderful about justice and moral autonomy,' one might ask, 'in a world where people have lost the security and power of common goals, and can no longer work together?' Indeed, justice and moral autonomy are superior only so long as (1) you assume reason and systematic research capable of resolving moral perplexities to some extent at least, and (2) you do not suppose that moral norms have not been sufficiently revealed to finite man by a divine source, and (3) you are convinced that morality is primarily a matter of moral reasoning. On this third point, Kierkegaard may serve as one example of someone who assumed that moral reasoning (the Ethical stage) is intrinsically inferior to the Religious stage of Faith, at which, and only at which, matters can be resolved properly. Or, if Christian *agape* is invoked, all the reasoning in the world, without love, is next to nothing, and *agape*, even with modest systematic reasoning, yields all. Or consider the Zen master who becomes moral by meditation whereby he discerns the state of inner harmony, integration and peace, and endeavours to express this diligently in the countless situations of life. We may *retrospectively* claim that these people are *reasoning* morally, and even that they *display* justice reasoning. However, they have either transcended such reasoning (Kierkegaard), or have by-passed it by learning to love, or to be harmoniously receptive in identifying with another person in his or her unique situation. It may well be a just act, but an interview need *not* reveal that the state of morality was arrived at through moral reasoning at all. Furthermore, it may be, when justice and love, or justice and divine command are in conflict, that love, or religiosity must be given the nod.

On this point Thomas McCarthy, in a critical essay on Habermas (and Kohlberg) warns that it may be a grave mistake to view the lower stages as inferior, or as regressions. There is much to learn from cultures and individuals who slice the moral pie differently: 'This is not a matter of regression, but of dialogue—dialogue that is critical, to be sure, but not only on one side.'[36]

Now how is one to take a stand here? If Kohlberg speaks for justice, and Kierkegaard for God, the choice between them will depend on much more than we have discussed thus far. In other words, Stage 5 reasoning is better, and more adequate than Stage 4 reasoning if, and only if, justice is given higher standing normatively than something else, e.g., *agape*, religiosity, integration of self, etc. What makes it seem to be empirically obvious to Kohlberg that justice works better than love in moral decision-making is that he has argued at length, as have countless philosophers, that justice is a key, if not the defining element of ethical reasoning. Thus, if it is normatively the case that justice is the goal, then empirically whatever best approaches this norm will be 'more developed'. As Kohlberg himself has noted, it is the normative which informs and orients the empirical findings. Justice may well be but one of several key considerations in ethics, and it may well be impossible just now to say conclusively whether one, two, or more of them ought to be so considered.

TOWARD STAGE 7

What all of this *does not* amount to is that it is all *relative*, in the sense in which one flips a coin (heads for justice and tails for *agape*), in order to decide what position to hold, or to argue (normatively) that one is better than another. Sceptical relativism does extinguish the point of either philosophical inquiry, or empirical research. But a relativism which continues to inquire into the normatively better, the more humanly meaningful, the more loving or the more just is forced to settle for, at best, only somewhat convincing arguments, and, at that, only for some. Where I think we continue to go wrong in such discussions is that we hesitantly come to agree that the philosophical and normative do not admit of proof, and then go on to say what is, nevertheless, patently obvious to anyone who will look with an open mind. An 'open mind' means, in fact, that anyone who accepts my perspective, who holds my assumptions, who shares my value preferences, will come to the same conclusion if he is consistent. That is so. There is 'objectivity' within a system, as Meiland has pointed out. And this is not at all relative.

What can one do, then, to defend one's rock-bottom assumptions, i.e., to convince someone else of the validity of one's perspective? Reasons can be given only up to a point—namely, the point of one's basic assumptions or starting-points. Then, if you try to get another person to understand why you say what you do, and hold what you hold, you can only go back through your whole life-view, again and again in the hope of getting another to see things as you do. As R. M. Hare puts this,

> Thus, if pressed to justify a decision completely, we have to give a complete specification of the way of life of which it is a part.... If the inquirer still goes on asking 'But why should I live like that?' then there is no further answer to give him, because we have already *ex hypothesi*, said everything that could be included in this further answer.[37]

For someone to understand fully why someone holds the position that he or she does, it is necessary to 'initiate' that person into one's overall perspective, or *weltanschauung*. This is precisely what Stage 7 thinking is meant to supply. In other words, for Kohlberg to explain, and to philosophically justify his views on normative matters, he must weave a life-tapestry in which he tells us what his assumptions are, and why they are instrumental in bringing about (1) a life of the kind that he selects, (2) in accordance with specific moral requirements and boundaries, (3) in accordance with a vision of individual human development and (4) those social structures which he values. All of these are further imbedded in a metaphysics/ethics/religion which affords the widest context and support for one's strictly moral conclusions. A moral system is but one among several moral systems, which themselves are subsets of the set of more embracing speculative systems dealing with the cosmos and our place in it. Stage 7 is the fullest account which one can give of why one's moral assumptions make sense, given one's perspective on man, the cosmos, and (depending on one's view) God. No wonder that Kohlberg states that the haunting question, 'Why be moral?' just never goes away if one limits oneself to morality itself.[38] He adds that religion, or ethics (i.e., a cosmic perspective) is 'a conscious response to, and an expression of, the quest for an ultimate meaning for moral judging and acting.'[39] Religion, or ethics (i.e., Stage 7 thinking) supplies 'additional social-scientific, metaphysical or religious assumptions' necessary to help answer questions which morality itself cannot answer. Indeed, what Kohlberg seeks is 'support in reality, in nature taken as a whole or in the ground of Nature, for acting according to universal moral principles',[40] and, I would add, for the normative assumptions which yield those moral principles in the first place. In this sense, Stage 7 thinking is implied as necessary for the justification of *any* stage of moral thinking. The egoism of Stage 1 is philosophically understandable only when one tries the equivalent of a Stage 7 defence of it. But, of course, it is only with the personal maturation of the individual that the possibility of philosophical reasoning arises. Nevertheless, there is no reason to suppose that any of the stages have not been philosophically expanded and supported, even if unsuccessfully, over the long run of human history. Is Stage 3, for example, cultural relativism, where one does what the group, small or large, collectively determines?

As already observed, however, it is not just a matter of philosophical coin-flipping as to which of the 'relative' moral, religious, ethical, or metaphysical positions to choose. One must weigh the supporting evidence in favour of claims about human nature, human pleasure, social arrangements and invitations, man and his place in nature, etc. The work of philosophical analysis, making terms and positions precise, logical scrutiny, completeness of vision, and the keeping abreast of the empirical data available, is considerable. Then, however, when all of this has been more or less done, one must still arrive at a normative viewpoint which, while in accord with (i.e., complementary to) the facts, is still normatively interpretive of them such that one is now oriented as to where one ought to go, and what one ought to do. Normative interpretation of facts is at the heart, not the periphery, of all social scientific and natural scientific systems, and not just in the softer realms of the arts subjects. As rockbottom assumptions, however, these starting-points are regularly taken to be given by the empirical facts, rather than as taken by the observing participant in the act of 'interpretive' research. Indeed, only recently has it become apparent in physics that the observer necessarily 'disturbs' the data through the very act of observing it. Or perhaps it is safer to say that the only data there are, are 'disturbed' data, i.e., data which are object-affected-by-subject data. What makes Kohlberg so rewarding and rich amongst the social scientists has been and is his philosophical acumen and honesty. He has throughout his work assumed that philosophical inquiry will reveal a nest of assumptions at the heart of the sciences which only philosophy can adequately deal with. In doing so, he has often revealed the nakedness of many of his fellow social scientists, who work without the need for philosophical clothes (supposedly). It is precisely his steadfast philosophical integrity that has led him to the point of sharing the exact problems faced by philosophers. Chief among these, I would argue, is the epistemological difficulty named relativism, revealing that normative understanding runs only parallel to empirical findings, at best, and is itself only speculatively supportable through the articulation of world views. Even at that, however, the conclusions reached remain relative in that one not convinced to hold the same assumptions must be asked to hear the whole story over again as the only means of justification and defence. Perhaps Nietzsche, more often feared than applauded for his unmasking of the assumptive 'abyss' at the heart of all systems, was closer to the mark than is thought. As Danto interprets him,

> We perhaps will never achieve truth in the old correspondence sense of the term. We can hardly be expected to do so if we will always require some system of concepts, and if any such system is an Apollinian imposition upon ... chaos ... But ... [there is] a quite distinct and liberating sense of truth in which we could always say something truer than what we had said previously. Those sentences which are capable of carrying us conveniently over the chaos, even though they are absolutely erroneous, are true in virtue of their success. In this regard, whatever has so far worked is insofar true. But surely others can work too. There is room for system after system, for the most daring experimentations. Let us, then, experiment with truth, he would say, and see whether we are able to find a language and a philosophy better than the one we have.[41]

Perhaps, in the light of this passage and the interpretive path of this essay, it is now worthwhile to reflect again upon the words with which Kohlberg closes his volume of replies, and with which we began: '... objectivity is a "moment" of scientific inquiry.'[42] It is precisely this recognition of the importance of the changeable 'moment', and the realization of the subjectivity of the 'changing relationship between the investigator and what he or she observes' that cognitive (vs. nihilistic) relativism has been distinctive in maintaining. The sands of this wide middle path may fluctuate towards the nihilistic extreme, or towards the objective end of the scale. They are rarely swept to nihilism, or to absolutistic dogma, at least not for long. Kohlberg has done much to keep the sands blowing fruitfully between the extremes. And, like philosophers everywhere, it is little wonder that he sees less clearly through the storms than he would like. It is my judgment that the sand storms are real, and not merely Berkeley's dust of idle speculation. Kohlberg's methodological non-relativism is flanked by hermeneutic methodological relativism, as I have tried to argue. His new ally, Habermas, is not only unable to free him from the philosophic vagaries of relativism and the justification of normative foundations, but takes him into the very thick of the debate.[43] At all events, perhaps Philippa Foot's comment may help fix the point that yet another key philosophical issue is surrounded by at least as much confusion as clarity: 'The practical conclusion may be that we should not at the moment try to say whether moral relativism is true or false, but should start the work farther back.'[44]

If it is the mark of significant and vital work that long-standing issues of philosophical importance continue to be addressed and responded to, then Kohlberg's work stands very high indeed. His research serves as a catalyst for further inquiry, both on his own part, and on the part of others. It may well be that if future advances in moral understanding require both the empirical input of the psychological sciences, and the theoretical assessment of philosophical inquiry, then Kohlberg stands in a key position as one of the few able to search actively for the linkages between these disciplines. This, in itself, is no small achievement.

NOTES

1   Kohlberg, L., Levine, C. and Hewer, A., *Moral Stages: A Current Formulation and a Response to Critics, Ms.* (the manuscript copy I am using is soon to be available in published form, by S. Karger AG, Basel/New York), p. 118.
2   *Ibid.*, p. 300.
3   Kohlberg, L. (1981) *The Philosophy of Moral Development*, Vol. I, Essays on Moral Development, San Francisco, Harper and Row, p. 98.
4   *Ibid.*, p. 11.
5   Plato, *Republic*, 336b–338a.
6   Kohlberg, *Philosophy of Moral Development, op. cit.*, p. 3.
7   Vlastos, G. (Ed.) (1956) *Plato's Protagoras*, Indianapolis, Bobbs-Merrill, p. xiii.
8   Danto, A. (1965) *Nietzsche as Philosopher*, New York, Macmillan, p. 77.
9   Meiland, J. W. (1980) 'On the paradox of cognitive relativism', *Metaphilosophy*, 2, 2, p. 122.
10 Barnes, B. and Bloor, D. (1982) 'Relativism, rationalism and the sociology of knowledge', in Hollis, M. and Lukes, S. (Eds.), *Rationality and Relativism*, Cambridge, Mass., MIT Press, p. 23.
11 Meiland, *op. cit.*, p. 123.
12 *Ibid.*
13 *Ibid.*
14 *Ibid.*
15 Kohlberg, *Moral Stages, op. cit.*, p. 7.
16 *Ibid.*, p. 14.
17 *Ibid.*
18 *Ibid.*
19 *Ibid.*, p. 16.
20 *Ibid.*, p. 17.
21 *Ibid.*, p. 18.
22 *Ibid.*, p. 21.
23 *Ibid.*
24 *Ibid.*, p. 22.
25 *Ibid.*
26 *Ibid.*, p. 24.
27 McCarthy, T. (1978) *The Critical Theory of Jürgen Habermas*, Cambridge, Mass., MIT Press, p. 288.

28   As quoted in *McCarthy*, p. 192.

29   Ricoeur, P. (1973) 'Ethics and culture: Habermas and Gadamer in dialogue', *Philosophy Today*, Vol. 17, p. 165.

30   Meiland, *op. cit.*, p. 126.

31   *Ibid.*, p. 119.

32   Kohlberg, *Philosophy of Moral Development*, *op. cit.*, p. 233.

33   Kohlberg, *Moral Stages*, *op. cit.*, p. 25.

34   *Ibid.*

35   *Ibid.*, p. 14.

36   McCarthy, T. (1982) 'Rationality and relativism: Habermas' "overcoming" of hermeneutics', in Thomson, J. B. and Held, D. (Eds.) *Habermas: Critical Debates*, Cambridge, Mass., MIT Press, p. 78.

37   Hare, R. M. (1952) *The Language of Morals*, Oxford, Oxford University Press, p. 69.

38   Kohlberg, *Philosophy of Moral Development*, *op. cit.*, p. 134.

39   *Ibid.*, p. 135.

40   *Ibid.*, p. 137.

41   Danto, *op. cit.*, p. 98.

42   Kohlberg, *Moral Stages*, *op. cit.*, p. 118.

43   McCarthy, *op. cit.*, p. 72: 'In the face of these problems and open questions, Habermas would, it seems, be well advised to adopt a much more tentative and critical posture towards cognitive developmental theories than he has to date.'

44   Foot, P. (1982) 'Moral relativism', in Krausz, M. and Meiland, J. W. (Eds.) *Relativism: Cognitive and Moral*, Notre Dame, Ind., University of Notre Dame Press, p. 166.

3. A Psychologist among the Philosophers: Philosophical Aspects of Kohlberg's Theories[*]

DON LOCKE

Perhaps the most striking—and certainly to my mind the most impressive—aspect of Kohlberg's work is the way in which he has combined psychological evidence, philosophical argument and educational practice. As anyone who has trod the interdisciplinary path will testify, the way tends to be narrow and hard, exposed as it is to complaint, criticism and often enough hostility on all sides—especially from the philosophers, trained as they are to be supremely critical of their fellow professionals, let alone anyone foolish enough to venture into their territory from outside. So, since the tone of this chapter will be unremittingly critical—though not, I hope, hostile—I want to make it clear at the start how much I admire the attempt, as opposed to the achievement. Nor is that qualification intended to be snide. For one thing, it is always easier to be critical than to be creative, and finding fault in others is no great achievement either, unless you have something positive to offer in their place, which I do not. And for another, in philosophy criticism is the sincerest form of flattery: to be ignored entirely is the unkindest cut of all. Kohlberg's achievement, it seems to me, lies more in the questions he has raised than in the answers he has given. But in philosophy, where we still look unsuccessfully for answers to questions raised in the sixth century B.C., that may be achievement enough.

---

* This chapter borrows from, extends and in some places modifies my previously published criticisms of Kohlberg's work (Locke, 1979, 1980, 1981; other relevant publications are Locke, 1983a, 1983b, 1983c). The most philosophically relevant of Kohlberg's own publications are Kohlberg, 1971, 1973 and 1979. These are included in Kohlberg 1981 but, irritatingly, have been revised, and the second and third combined, without any indication either that or exactly where alterations have been made. I have not attempted to document these changes, always a difficult task in handling Kohlberg's various theories, but will cite both versions, with page references to the more recent (for example, 1971/1981, p. 101). For reasons of space, however, I have kept to a minimum quotations and references, both to Kohlberg's writings and to my own.

ISSUES OF TERMINOLOGY

Kohlberg is not a professional philosopher, and his arguments often lack philosophical sophistication. In addition he writes so diffusely and so confusingly—
sometimes to the point of inconsistency (cf. Shweder, 1982)—that it is often
difficult to be sure exactly what the argument is. It seems sometimes like an
extension of the principle that if you throw enough mud, some of it is bound to
stick: if you say enough about topics of importance, some of it is bound to be true,
perhaps even significant. Reading the collected 'philosophical' works (Kohlberg,
1981) is therefore a bit like reading the Bible: you can find support for just about
anything somewhere in its pages; but the truth and illumination you find there is
more likely to be a function of what you brought to it in the first place than of what,
if anything, is actually there.

One particular respect in which the novice in any field tends to betray himself,
thus attracting the scorn of those who like to think they know better, is the loose
use of technical terminology. Kohlberg is no exception, and his misuse of
philosophical vocabulary may account in part for the relative indifference with
which most philosophers greet his work. One obvious if harmless example, which
nevertheless I personally find extremely irritating, is the use of the word 'logical' to
give a claim a philosophical dignity and respectability it may not deserve (Kohlberg
sometimes uses 'philosophic' in the same way). The most striking instance,
admittedly more evident in some of Kohlberg's followers than in Kohlberg himself,
is in such phrases as 'the logical priority of life over property'. There is, of course,
nothing 'logical' about this priority, even supposing it exists. The adjective serves
only to pretend that a ranking which seems central to the Kohlbergian value-system
is somehow necessary or unquestionable. But even if most of us would in most
cases agree that people are more important than things, it by no means follows that
this is always or necessarily, let alone logically, the case: is a person who kills
another to protect his property, is someone who lays down his life to protect what is
his—or even to protect what is someone else's—necessarily mistaking the true
priorities? Of course these issues are arguable; but the point is that they need to be
argued. The use of the word 'logical' is no argument in itself, merely an attempt to
forestall it.

Another instance is Kohlberg's claim that his six stages of moral reasoning
possess an 'inner logical order', so that the sequence is therefore 'logically
necessary'. If this were actually the case there would, of course, be no need of
longitudinal studies stretching back over twenty-five years, or empirical evidence of
any other kind, any more than we need social surveys to discover that husbands
tend to be married, or that siblings are invariably related. If something is logically
necessary then it cannot coherently be denied, much less disproved: the denial is
incoherent because self-contradictory. What is needed to establish a logical
necessity, therefore, is a demonstration that its denial does reduce to the absurdity
of a self-contradiction. What Kohlberg seems to provide, instead, is empirical
evidence that his stages occur in the order he claims they have to, at which point
many philosophers will close the book and turn to other things.

Another more important example of this misleading use of technical terminology is contained in Kohlberg's labelling his Stage 6 'The Stage of Universal Moral
Principles'. A principle is best understood, in the dictionary's words, as a general

guide to action; principled behaviour and principled morality, similarly, will be behaviour and morality based on such principles. We can then, if we like, distinguish principles from rules as Kohlberg does: rules are concrete and specific, principles more abstract and general. Thus the Ten Commandments of the Old Testament are rules, whereas the 'new commandment' of the Sermon on the Mount, that we should love one another, is a principle. The danger, however— especially if we then insist, as Kohlberg does, that principles, unlike rules, do not admit of exceptions—is that these principles will become so remote from action as to provide no definite guidance one way or the other. It is often not at all clear what exactly is the 'loving' thing to do in a concrete situation; the Seventh Command- ment, on the other hand, is more explicit. At this point principles become no more than values and, notoriously, the same value can lead to opposite courses of action: both supporters and opponents of capital punishment, for example, like to base their case on an appeal to the sanctity of human life.

Moreover, principled behaviour is by itself no guarantee of morality; and in certain extreme cases principled behaviour can seem worse, morally less admirable, than unprincipled. It depends, of course, on what exactly the principles are: there are principles which people have been prepared to accept, even as moral principles, and to act on, which make those people profoundly immoral, moral monsters, in my eyes; they would have been better, more moral, human beings for being less principled (the issues here are well illustrated in Bennett, 1974). This has, of course, been a frequent criticism of Kohlberg's claim that 'principled' morality (Stages 5 and 6) is necessarily superior to conventional (e.g., Alston, 1971; Mischel and Mischel, 1976); and Kohlberg will presumably reply that this is not principled morality at all, but principled *immorality*: the principles on which such people act are not moral, and in particular not Stage 6, principles in the first place. But if the stress is now put on 'moral' rather than 'principle', we need to be told which principles are going to be the properly moral ones: the defining feature of principled morality is not having principles and acting on them, but having the right principles. As calling Stage 6 'The Stage of Universal Moral Principles' is intended to imply, the only genuine moral principles will be those at Stage 6—and even more confusingly, there turns out to be only one to those!

Yet on any familiar understanding of 'moral principle' there can be moral principles, principles and not just rules, appropriate to reasoning at other stages, and not just Stage 5 but even lower stages: for example, 'Respect authority', 'Always think of what others will think of you', or 'Be a loyal citizen'. Indeed, Kohlberg often speaks in just this way himself, even suggesting that each stage will have its own characteristic set of moral principles, though when he does 'principle' is sometimes put in scare-quotes. This leads, naturally enough, to the suggestion that so-called 'principled morality', Stages 5 and 6, is not so much separate from as a theoretical 'reflective' or principled extension of earlier stages (cf. Gibbs, 1977; Lutz Eckensberger has suggested, similarly, that Kohlbergian moral development actually follows a spiral path, with Stages 4½, 5 and 6 being more sophisticated versions of Stages 1, 2 and 3 (Eckensberger, 1981)). The pure Kohlbergian doctrine, however, is that the only real principles are those at Stage 6.

One possible source of confusion here lies in calling these principles 'univer- sal'. It has been argued by philosophers, most notably by Hare (1952, 1963), that principles have to be not general but universal. But this cannot be what disting- uishes Stage 6 principles from any others: if Hare is right about this, any principle has to be universal in form if it is to count as a principle at all, at whatever stage of reasoning it arises; if principles are to be identified by their form, as they tend to be by Kohlberg, we are in no position to rule any out on account of their content. There is, however, a possible ambiguity here, between principles which are universally applicable and principles which are universally acceptable. When Hare and others call moral principles 'universal', they mean that they must apply universally, irrespective of person, to all those who fall under their scope—in the way, that, for example, 'Monks ought to be celibate' is intended to apply to all monks, no matter who they might be, but not to those of us who are not monks. But obviously, principles can be universal in this sense of applying universally without being universal in the sense of being accepted by everyone. It is quite possible for people to have different, incompatible, sets of 'universal' principles, i.e., we each accept our own, but apply them universally to each other. That is precisely the way it is, when we engage in moral debate, over abortion, capital punishment, nuclear deterrence, and the rest.

Kohlberg believes, however, that when people reach Stage 6 there will be a particular set of moral principles—indeed, one single solitary principle, variously identified as justice, equality and respect for persons—on which all will agree, this being the stage of universal principles. In other words, what is distinctive about Stage 6 principles is not that they are universal in the sense of being universally applicable, as may be true for all principles, but that they are universally acceptable, acceptable to everyone who reasons properly about them. Of course Kohlberg can, if he wishes, define Stage 6 moral thinking in terms of certain principles, so that it will follow as a harmless tautology that anyone who thinks in that way will accept those principles. But what he is not entitled to do is to pass, without argument, from the relatively uncontroversial claim that moral principles have to be universal in the sense of applying indifferently to everyone who falls under them, to the highly contentious claim that, ultimately, there are universal moral principles in the sense of principles on which everyone can, and perhaps will, agree. This is precisely the step which is obscured by the apparent ambiguity of 'universal moral principle'.

But perhaps the most pervasive of these terminological problems in Kohlberg's work is his use of the notion of justice itself. Theories of justice have been at the forefront of much recent philosophical ethics, thanks largely to the influence of Rawls' monumental work in this area (Rawls, 1971). But what Rawls is dealing with, primarily, is distributive justice, more popularly known as social justice, and perhaps best summarized in the title of his less intimidating, more accessible 1957 essay, 'Justice as Fairness'. Another more traditional conception of justice, which its defenders often oppose to Rawlsian justice, is compensatory or retributive justice, which focuses on what people deserve, both good and ill, rather than on what they need. But notice that these and other conceptions of justice are particular moral conceptions, operating within a wider moral framework: Rawls, for one, is careful to make the point that his is a theory of justice only—and, indeed, only one conception of justice—not a theory of morality as such. However important justice considerations may be, to Rawls and to us, they are only a part of morality, not the whole.

But there is, also, a wider conception of justice, deriving, I suppose, from the use of that word (as translated into English) by the Socrates of Plato's *Republic*, where justice does seem equivalent to morality in the widest sense: the just man and the good man, the just action and the right action, will be one and the same. Obviously Kohlberg's use of the term is to be understood in this second, wider sense. I do not see, otherwise, how he can identify justice, equality and respect for persons, it being an elementary point about justice in the narrower sense that it tends to conflict with equality: justice requires treating people not equally but differently, according to their needs, their deserts, or whatever else the basis of justice might be held to be. Even Rawls, who puts equality at the very centre of his account of distributive justice, nevertheless puts great emphasis on a modification which he calls, precisely, the Difference Principle.

Now again this would not matter—Kohlberg may call it justice or morality, goodness or doogness, or whatever he pleases—provided that it does not mislead. But mislead it does, as we shall see, when Kohlberg, impressed either by Rawls' philosophical eminence or his geographical proximity, seeks to identify his Stage 6 with Rawls' theory of distributive justice.

CULTURAL AND ETHICAL RELATIVISM

I turn now from these terminological quibbles, which I hope to have shown not to be entirely quibbling, to Kohlberg's more substantive philosophical contributions, beginning with his critique of what Bernard Williams has called 'the anthropologists' heresy, possibly the most absurd view to have been advanced even in moral philosophy' (1972, p. 34), ethical relativism. The points which Kohlberg makes here (especially 1971/1981, pp. 106–14) are correct and familiar enough, though experience shows that they are points which need to be made again for each new generation of students, and, as Kohlberg himself documents, need making especially to those social scientists who meddle in moral matters. There is, for example, the failure to distinguish cultural relativism, the doctrine that different cultures in fact have different moralities, from ethical relativism, the (ultimately incoherent) doctrine that these different moralities are all equally valid, all equally correct. The fact that a particular culture's morality permits a certain practice, female circumcision for example, does not of course mean that that practice is morally correct, not even within that culture, but only that it is regarded as morally correct within that culture, which is not all the same thing. Morality, correctly understood, is not to be identified with different social moralities; on the contrary it is precisely something in terms of which different social moralities can, and sometimes should, be criticized. Again, there is the failure to distinguish between ethical relativism and moral toleration, in particular toleration of the practices of others, both cultures and individuals. You can insist that people ought to be allowed to act in accordance with their own moral convictions, at least up to a point, without thereby conceding (incoherently) that their convictions are as correct as your own very different ones. On the contrary, it is precisely the relativist who will have to approve of intolerance, in those cases where it is someone's belief (which, according to the relativist, will therefore be valid for him) that he ought to interfere in the practices and beliefs of other people and cultures.

But I will not rehearse all Kohlberg's points here: he makes them well enough himself. What I want to consider instead is his apparent rejection not just of ethical but of cultural relativism, on the grounds that there are moral universals, common to all cultures, despite their superficial differences (1971/1981, pp. 123–30). Here too Kohlberg is not alone. There is, for example, the argument that the apparent differences between cultures are in fact the results of the same fundamental principles or values being applied in different social, or even geographical, contexts. Thus the same concern to preserve social and family structures might result in polygamous marriage being immoral in one culture but not in another, as a result of the different social and familial traditions in those cultures. The Eskimos occasionally leaving their aged to die, similarly, might be the result of giving human life the same supreme value that we do, but applying it in a situation very different from our own. But this is not Kohlberg's position, as I understand it.

Admittedly it is hard to be sure: in the space of a mere two pages (1981, pp. 126–8) he writes, 'not only is there a universal moral form, but the basic content principles of morality are also universal', 'my findings lead me to conclude that there are differences in fundamental moral principles between individuals or between groups, differences in stage', 'my evidence supports the following conclusions: There is a universal set of moral principles held by people in various cultures, Stage 6 . . .', and 'My finding [is] that our two highest stages are absent in preliterate or semi-literate cultures'! Small wonder that he ends up citing a markedly relativist statement by Baier (1958) as an instance of 'modified or methodological nonrelativism' (1971/1981, pp. 159)! As I understand it, however, Kohlberg's position is that even if there are fundamental differences between different moralities, they nevertheless all share, first, some thirty basic moral categories (listed, for example, under the headings of Elements and Norms in 1981, p. 117), and second, the same six-stage developmental sequence. But for one thing Kohlberg does not succeed in demonstrating that these things are universal across all moralities; and for another, even if he did, they would seem to be evidence for cultural relativism rather than against it!

If we start with the alleged 'Universal Categories of Moral Judgment', there is first the point that different moralities must presumably have something, or some things, in common if they are to count as moralities in the first place. This much seems conceptually guaranteed. What needs to be shown, however, is what these common features are, and in particular that they are those listed by Kohlberg. At this point, no doubt, any philosopher worth his salt will offer to invent a 'morality' which lacks some or all of Kohlberg's norms and elements. But if cultural relativism is the issue, we need concern ourselves only with actual, existing moralities, not with philosophical fantasies; and it is at least plausible to maintain that any existing morality will in fact be concerned with such things as rights and duties, character and self-respect, consequences and fairness, property and truth. What we need, however, is evidence that this is so, that every existing morality does take all (or need it only be some?) of these features into account, and this Kohlberg does not provide. In the absence of evidence and cases, there is always the danger that, faced with a possible exception, Kohlberg will preserve his list by retreating into tautology, i.e., by refusing to accept as a genuine instance of morality any set of customs or expectations which fails to include those norms and elements which he has listed.

Moreover, in discussing the content of different moralities there is an important distinction to be drawn between the topic, or what those moralities are about, and the message, or what they say about it (Cooper, 1981). Even if it is the case that all existing—and even all conceivable—moralities deal with such things as the value of life, or erotic love and sex, it does not of course follow that these moralities are therefore the same, or even similar: the topic may be identical, but the message very different. Kohlberg himself is aware of this, making the point in terms of a distinction (which unfortunately jars badly with the standard philosophical use of this terminology in this area) between form and content: similarity of form, or of what I, following Cooper, am calling topic, does not guarantee similarity of content, or message. As regards the latter, Kohlberg, so far, seems to agree with the cultural relativist.

But these differences in message, he seems to say, are the result of applying different stages of moral thinking to the same topics or content areas; and these stages of reasoning are universal across cultures. But in what sense are they universal? Not in the sense that they can each be found in every culture: Stage 6, in particular, seems difficult enough to find in our own, let alone anywhere else. Rather in the sense that moral reasoning in different cultures will always be an instance of one Kohlbergian stage or another. But this too Kohlberg does not remotely prove: to show, much less merely to claim, that instances of Kohlbergian stages have been found, in the right developmental order, in every culture studied, is not of course to show, or even claim, that every moral judgment in every culture provides an instance of some Kohlbergian stage. So long as it is possible for there to be moral judgments which do not belong to a Kohlbergian stage (cf. Gilligan, 1982; Tomlinson, this volume, Chap. 7), it will be possible for there to be moralities which are not classifiable as instances of this stage reasoning or that, and therefore for there to be moralities whose differences cannot be attributed purely to differences in stage.

Moreover, even if it were the case that differences between different moralities were attributable to different stages of moral reasoning, this too would seem to count more in favour of cultural relativism than against it. For one thing, as Kohlberg himself seems to concede, moralities at different stages would still be different moralities. And for another, as he seems to forget, the various stages are explicitly identified not by content, the particular attitudes or opinions expressed, but by form, the sorts of consideration to which an individual appeals in making and justifying his moral judgments. So, as Kohlberg often insists, the reasoning stage might be the same and yet the particular judgments justified in that way very different. There is therefore no guarantee that individuals or cultures reasoning at a particular stage will agree in their moral judgments, and therefore in their morality. Indeed, it seems at least equally likely that they will not. What Kohlberg has provided, it seems to me, even accepting his claims at face value, is not a refutation but an explanation of cultural relativism, an explanation of the differences in morality between cultures and individuals.

FROM 'IS' TO 'OUGHT'

The most striking of Kohlberg's philosophical claims, the one which originally interested me in his work, is probably best summarized in the title of his deservedly classic paper, 'From *Is* to *Ought*: How to Commit the Naturalistic Fallacy and Get Away with It in the Study of Moral Development' (but note the subsequent concession that this is 'a little misleading, because it suggests that it derives a moral *ought* . . . from the *is* of psychological theory and research' (1981, p. 97)!). Not that Kohlberg is alone here either: the dominant orthodoxy in philosophy seems to have changed, as is the way with dominant orthodoxies, from accepting Hume's Law to rejecting it. But what is distinctive about Kohlberg's contribution is his claim to offer not philosophical argument but empirical evidence that you can, after all, get from facts to values.

The essence of his position is that later stages of moral thinking are not just later but higher, and not just higher but better. This is not the simple and obviously question-begging claim that later stages are higher and better just because they come later. It is rather the claim that what makes them later is what makes them higher and better: later stages replace earlier ones because they are more adequate, cognitively, and being more adequate cognitively, they are therefore more adequate morally as well. So in what does this cognitive adequacy consist?

The idea seems to be that at any particular stage in his development the individual will have a certain way of handling his moral experience, of dealing with the claims and conflicts which society and other people impose upon him. This will be his current stage of moral thinking. But new experiences, or more complex social interactions, or a more sophisticated understanding of what those interactions involve, may generate claims and conflicts which he cannot resolve in the accustomed way, and he will therefore be forced to develop a more sophisticated and more effective way of handling his moral environment, and so move to a higher stage of moral reasoning. Thus cognitive conflict and its resolution provide an explanation not merely of why people move from stage to stage in the first place, but of why they develop through these particular stages in this particular order. Or, in the Piagetian jargon which Kohlberg sometimes favours, the increasing differentiation and integration of the higher stages ensures the maintenance of an equilibrium, defined as a balance of assimilation and accommodation, between organism and environment. Moreover, it is because the higher stages are more integrated and more self-consistent that they are more adequate not only cognitively but also morally: it is because higher stages are better able to reconcile moral claims and resolve moral conflicts that they are both later and better. This, then, is how we can get from an 'is' to an 'ought'.

But what this argument needs, first of all, is evidence that people do indeed move from stage to stage in order to escape cognitive conflict. In fact the evidence, such as it is, is that faced with conflicting arguments at a particular stage, people actually prefer to move *towards* that stage, even if it involves moving down not up (Turiel, 1966)! What is also needed, more fundamentally, is some demonstration that, and how, moving up a stage does enable the individual to resolve the moral conflicts left unresolved at the earlier stage. What Kohlberg actually provides, however, is an account of how each stage is philosophically and morally more sophisticated, showing a greater understanding of what morality is and involves, a greater insight into the nature and range of moral issues, and in particular a more accurate grasp of the formal features of moral judgment, such as universalizability and prescriptivity, or the correlativity of rights and duties. But the idea that this will make it easier to solve moral problems is surely absurd. On the contrary, an increased awareness of and insight into morality is likely to make moral conflicts *more* complex, more difficult to resolve, not less. The Stage 2 'instrumentalist' who solves his problems by appealing to what is most in his personal interest, while allowing that others are equally entitled to pursue their own interest as best they can, may well find moral issues easier to solve than someone agonizing over individual rights and social utilities at Stage 5.

Nor can it be argued that the later stages are more moral in the sense that this increased, more philosophical, insight into and understanding of morality will make it more likely that individuals recognize, and therefore do, what is actually the right thing in the particular situation. At least no-one will argue it who actually knows some moral philosophers! And the cynical will expect the reverse: that the more sophisticated our moral thinking, the more sophistical it is liable to be; that given man's enormous capacity for hypocrisy, self-deception and special pleading, the more adept we will be at finding some way of avoiding those claims and duties which happen not to suit us. Tolstoy, for one, thought that a simple moral consciousness was more likely to be pure and holy; and who is to say that he was wrong? Even if we do not go that far, we might at least notice that one familiar consequence of a heightened moral awareness is a sort of moral paralysis: the more complex the issue, the more difficult it may be to decide to be sure what is right, and the more difficult it becomes even to be able to do anything about it; we agonize, we dispute, but we do nothing. Moral philosophy, and moral psychology, become a substitute for action.

Thus the later and higher stages may be more adequate, both cognitively and morally, in the sense that they involve a better understanding of what, cognitively, morality involves. But I can see no grounds for believing either that they are more cognitively adequate in the sense that they better enable the solution of moral problems and difficulties, or that they are morally more adequate in the sense that they are somehow morally preferable. I think I might even prefer a world of Stage 3 reasoners, motivated by interpersonal concerns of caring, trust and loyalty, even if their basic motivation is to be liked by others in their turn, not only to a world of Stage 4 advocates of law and order, but even to a world of Stage 5 social utilitarians or Stage 6 lusters after impartial justice. Kohlberg's emphasis on the intellectual, cognitive, aspects of morality explicitly belongs in the rationalist ethical tradition stemming from Kant. But this approach has always had its critics who see morality as a matter more of interpersonal feelings and human sympathies than of formal principles of justice; and to these have been added, more recently, those who see this exaltation of intellect over emotion as a sexist preference for stereotypically male values over female (for this point as it applies to Kant, see Blum, 1982, and more generally 1980; for its possible application to moral development, see Gilligan, 1982).

STAGE 6: MORAL THINKING

We come now to the philosophical and moral apogee of Kohlberg's system, the *ne plus ultra* of moral thinking, the stage than which there is no higher, Stage 6: 'The Claim to Moral Adequacy of a Highest Stage of Moral Judgment'. For if the motive force behind moral cognitive development is cognitive conflict, the need to resolve problems and dilemmas arising in the moral domain, then the highest, most adequate stage of moral thinking, if there is one, will be the one which finally resolves all moral problems and conflicts; and this, apparently, is what Stage 6 is and does. Admittedly, in thus treating Stage 6 as the ultimate form of moral reasoning I am deliberately ignoring the mystical and mysterious Stage 7, Kohlberg's 'Cosmic Law—Agape' orientation. This, it seems to me, is an aberration. Kohlberg himself describes it as metaphorical, yet also suggests that it is needed to resolve conflicts and questions arising at Stage 6, which effectively undermines whatever case there is for treating Stage 6 as separate from, and preferable to, Stage 5. Stage 6, I have argued elsewhere (1980), is an illusion; but Stage 7, I believe, is a delusion, apparently created by the need to get the moral emotions of love, forgiveness and compassion back into the picture without returning to the allegedly inadequate Stage 3. But I confess I am unqualified to discuss Stage 7. I simply do not understand it.

This brings me to a major difficulty for those who would criticize Kohlberg's stages, and Stage 6 in particular. It is an important aspect of the theory, for which there is evidence in the research (Rest, 1973), that the various stages can be properly understood only by those who are at, above, or on the point of moving to, the relevant stage. This puts the critic in a position reminiscent of those who would criticize Freudian psychoanalysis. Just as the psychoanalyst may tell his critic that his criticisms are due to repressed hostility towards the father-figure Freud, and show only that he is himself in need of psychoanalysis, so the Kohlbergian may tell the critic of Stage 6 that his objections are due to a failure to appreciate what Stage 6 reasoning actually is, and show only that he is not there yet, indeed not even ready for it. So whether I understand even Stage 6 reasoning is, apparently, not for me to judge; but what is clear from Kohlberg's published writings is that he does not understand it either.

In fact it is always mildly amusing to notice, in discussions of Kohlberg's work, the implicit and sometimes explicit assumption that we, at any rate, are all Stage 6; and this despite the fact that the number of people credited with Stage 6 reasoning by the theory itself, especially in its revised form, is vanishingly small. The approved techniques for determining people's level of moral reasoning now provides no way of identifying those who might actually be at Stage 6; we have to rely instead on a familiar Roll of Honour of moral exemplars who typically include Socrates, Lincoln and Martin Luther King (the most striking omission is Jesus of Nazareth, despite possessing the one obvious qualification for inclusion, that of meeting an unnatural and untimely death on account of your convictions). Yet it seems that these saints and heroes have been chosen more for their reputation than from any clear evidence that their moral thinking belongs to Stage 6. Lincoln, for one, allegedly thought that the freedom of a slave would not justify the death of a single white soldier (or is this perhaps what is meant by the logical priority of life over property?); Socrates, for another, thought that obedience to the law was so much more important than human life that even when provided with an opportunity to escape he preferred his own death to a breach of his society's laws (Kohlberg himself (1981, p. 42) ranks the relevant judgments as Stage 5); and Martin Luther King, despite being prepared to break the law for a moral cause, nevertheless believed that the law must be upheld, and that those who break it, however nobly, must be prepared to accept the moral and legal consequences (the implication for the Heinz dilemma being that, having stolen the drug and saved his wife's life, Heinz should then deliver himself up for judgment and accept the punishment that he deserves). These do not seem to me typical Stage 6 responses; but to be sure we need to know what exactly Stage 6 is.

The appeal to authority aside there seem to be three ways of attempting to identify Stage 6 moral thinking: the first is by reference to those particular values and decisions which, from time to time, Kohlberg ascribes to the Stage 6 moral thinker, most notably the intrinsic value of human life, regardless of whose it is, and independently of personal affections and attachments; the second is by reference to his notion of justice as reversibility; and the third is via his attempt to identify this latter notion with that of his Harvard colleague John Rawls. Of these the second seems the most fundamental: the argument should presumably be that an adequate understanding of justice as reversibility will lead us both to those particular values and decisions which Kohlberg regards as Stage 6 solutions and to Rawls' principles of justice. More exactly, it should lead us to those values and solutions via Rawls' theory of justice. We will see, however, that this argument needs a distinction, which Kohlberg himself does not draw, between two quite different types of reversibility: this is one, but only one, reason why I claim that he does not himself fully understand his own Stage 6 (to be fair, I did not notice this distinction either, when I wrote my 1980 article. The need to draw it was brought home to me partly by helpful conversations with David and Stephanie Thornton, partly by reading Kohlberg, 1979).

The basic idea behind reversibility seems to be Hare's notion of universalizability (1952, 1963): Kohlberg's attempt to distinguish the two (1973) seems based on a misunderstanding of what universalizability as commonly understood by philosophers, actually is. At its simplest, universalizability is the idea that if we are to be consistent our moral judgments must apply equally to everyone who falls under them, regardless of who they are or how that judgment affects them, in the way that 'Monks ought to be celibate' applies to anyone and everyone who is a monk but not otherwise (Kohlberg appears to think that if this judgment were universalizable it ought to apply to everyone even those who are not monks!). This means in particular that we must be prepared to apply our moral judgments to ourselves as well as to others, and to others as well as to ourselves. In short, we must be willing to reverse them, to make the same moral judgment even when we are, so to speak, on the receiving end. If our moral judgments are not reversible in this way, then we are insincere or inconsistent or both. Either way they are not genuine, not properly, moral judgments.

This therefore means, as Hare and Kohlberg both insist, that in order to ensure that our moral judgments are properly reversible as they ought to be, we must put ourselves in the position of those others in relation to whom we make those judgments, and see whether we really would be prepared to accept those judgments as applying to us, if we were in their position instead of ours. And as both Hare and Kohlberg again insist, this is by no means easy to do. Indeed, for Kohlberg the gradual development of this capacity for role-taking is a prime ingredient in the development of specifically moral cognition. But if we can only do it, it seems to both Hare and Kohlberg that this technique may provide a way of resolving moral conflicts and dilemmas. For any solution which I come up with by imagining myself in the position of all the affected parties in turn, and then deciding which judgment, if any, I am prepared to reverse, i.e., prepared to apply no matter what my own position might be, will apparently be the same as what anyone else would come up with too, if they also imagine themselves in the position of every party in turn, and try to find a single judgment which is reversible over all. Kohlberg's name for this technique is 'ideal role-taking', or more recently and more memorably, 'moral musical chairs': 'In moral musical chairs there is only one "winning" chair, which all other players recognize if they play the game, the chair of the person with the prior claim to justice' (1979/1981, p.199).

Thus Kohlberg's argument appears to be that the formal requirement of reversibility can provide us with what we need for Stage 6 reasoning: a moral judgment on which all Stage 6 reasoners can agree, a moral judgment which will therefore provide the correct solution to the particular moral problem. But this argument is, as it stands, completely unsuccessful: reversibility of this sort will not guarantee a moral judgment on which everyone who is prepared to reverse their judgments can agree; it will therefore not provide us with a moral judgment which is correct; and even if it did provide us with a judgment on which everyone could agree, it still would not follow that that judgment was correct! Notice too that reference to the *prior* claim of justice: it implies, rightly as we shall see, that it is not reversibility as such, but something else, which determines the winning chair.

There is first of all the question whether, in any particular moral situation, there will always be one and only one properly reversible judgment, one on which everybody can therefore agree, provided only that they are prepared to reverse whatever judgments they make. Certainly Kohlberg seems to assume that there is. In the Heinz dilemma, for example, he claims that the wife would be able to reverse her judgment that Heinz should steal the drug, i.e., she would still think it right even if she were in the druggist's position. But the druggist, according to Kohlberg, cannot reverse his judgment: 'Presumably ... if it were his life at stake, the druggist would be rational enough to prefer his right to life over his property and would sacrifice his property' (1973/1981, p. 198). Yet this is only Kohlberg's presumption: suppose, instead, that the druggist were sufficiently irrational—or, if you prefer, sufficiently enamoured of private property or, more plausibly perhaps, sufficiently respectful of the laws of the land—that he *was* prepared to reverse his judgment, i.e., he would not want someone to steal, even if it were his life that was at stake. More plausibly still, suppose in Kohlberg's other example of the 'mercy-killing' dilemma, that a woman dying slowly in great pain asks her devout Catholic doctor to end her life for her. The woman is prepared to reverse her judgment: she would be prepared to take such a patient's life, if she were a doctor. But the doctor, equally, is prepared to reverse his judgment, that he should not kill her: even if he were himself in such pain, he still would not want someone to commit a mortal sin on his behalf. In these cases, and many another, we can have two—and more—different, conflicting judgments, both of which are reversible and therefore perfectly genuine, sincere moral judgments. It is therefore a mistake to assume that if a judgment is acceptable no matter which position we imagine ourselves occupying, it will therefore be acceptable no matter who imagines himself in those positions. It is a merit of Hare's account of universalizability that he recognizes, as Kohlberg does not, that different universalizers might be willing to universalize (or reverse) different, incompatible moral judgments, and so arrive at different, conflicting solutions to the same moral problem.

But if reversibility cannot guarantee a moral judgment on which everyone who is prepared to reverse their judgments can agree, neither can it guarantee a moral judgment which is correct, the right solution to the particular moral problem. For one thing, different, conflicting judgments cannot both be true, on pain of self-contradiction. For another, moral judgments can obviously be perfectly sincere, yet still mistaken: there may, for example, have been those Nazis who would have been prepared to go to the gas chambers themselves, had they turned out to be Jews; but even this degree of commitment to their convictions would not have meant that their moral judgment, that Jews ought to be exterminated, was correct. What has happened, I suspect, is that Kohlberg has confused the claim that a correct moral judgment will have to be reversible, with the claim that a reversible moral judgment will have to be correct. The former is, of course, true; but it is the latter he needs for his argument; and it, alas, is false.

Finally, even if we could reach agreement, by appealing to reversibility or anything else, it would not necessarily follow that the resulting judgment was therefore correct. Agreement does not guarantee truth, in ethics or anything else: agreement does not show that slavery is right any more than it shows that the world is flat. Admittedly, truth in ethics may be so difficult to determine, if it even exists, that agreement is all we can get. Agreement may therefore be better than nothing; and as we shall see later, there may even be cases where the right solution *is* whatever solution people manage to agree on, i.e., *any* solution, provided only that everyone accepts it. But in general, agreement is not truth, and an agreed solution is not necessarily the right one. Suppose, for example, that Heinz and his wife are, as befits citizens of that anonymous country in Europe, dutiful law-abiding citizens who would never regard themselves as justified in stealing, no matter what the cost to themselves. In that case it would be the druggist's judgment which all parties can reverse, and therefore agree on. Is it therefore the right solution, even in this instance?

No doubt Kohlberg will respond by saying that what matters is not actual agreement by the actual parties to the situation, but ideal agreement: not what judgment the actual parties are actually willing to reverse, but what judgment a rational person would be willing to reverse, a judgment, therefore, on which all rational persons can be expected to agree. But how are we to determine which judgment this is? One strategy, often favoured by Kohlberg himself, is simply to take it for granted that certain values and solutions will be obvious to everyone who thinks about them, and will therefore be acceptable to all: 'Utilitarianism, we intuitively feel, is unempathic . . .'; 'Few will intuitively accept . . .'; 'Intuitively, we feel . . .'; 'Presumably the druggist would be rational enough . . .'; 'Any rational person . . .'; 'By any philosophic definition . . .'. But intuitions are no argument, and it is at this point that Stage 6 moral reasoning seems to become nothing more than the solutions favoured by Kohlberg himself (cf. Alston, 1971; Harman, 1983), so that Stage 6 becomes no more than Kohlberg's own personal Stage 5. True, Kohlberg claims to have evidence that all Stage 6 reasoners do in fact agree on the solutions to moral dilemmas. But this is presumably because only those who come up with the right solutions will be classified as Stage 6 in the first place: if Stage 6 is supposed to be the stage at which all conflicts are resolved, there obviously cannot be conflicting solutions involving Stage 6 reasoning! Moreover there is no obvious way of establishing, by reference to reversibility alone, that life is more valuable than property, or any of the other values by which Kohlberg himself likes to solve the dilemmas he sets us. What provides this agreement for all rational people, if it exists, is not reversibility but something else, for example, the *prior* claim of justice.

Thus Kohlberg's other strategy, in attempting to find a basis for rational agreement in ethics, is his appeal to John Rawls. Rawls' theory of justice (1958, 1971) is based on a conception of parties in an original position, contracting behind a veil of ignorance. Personally I like to think of this in terms of a group of unassigned souls sitting on a cloud waiting to be born, and trying to decide what sort of society they would prefer to be born into. They know what sort of thing they are going to be, viz., human beings, with all the ills that human flesh is heir to; but they do not yet know who they are going to be. They will therefore choose whatever form of society will be best for them whoever they might turn out to be, whatever role they might come to occupy in it. So, on the principle that the way to ensure the fairest possible cutting of the cake is to warn, in advance, that the resulting pieces will be assigned at random, whatever form of society they eventually come up with will be the best, the fairest, the most just, that they can devise. It is from this general conception that Rawls proceeds to derive his detailed principles of justice.

Now the crucial difference between the parties to this original position, behind the veil of ignorance, and the parties to a Kohlbergian dilemma, is that Rawls' parties do not yet have any interests, desires, attitudes or opinions of their own: they have to decide, in effect, what should happen—and in particular whose interests, desires, etc. should be over-ridden—without knowing which set of interests, desires, etc. is going to be theirs. This is what ensures that any decision they make will be a disinterested, fair and impartial one: as both Rawls and Kohlberg note, Rawl's theory has as much in common with the 'ideal spectator' theory of Adam Smith as with theories of the social contract. And since this decision is disinterested, fair and impartial it will also be a decision on which all parties can agree, provided that they too are willing to be disinterested, fair and impartial in just the same way. Thus Rawls' device of the original position and the veil of ignorance seems to provide precisely what Kohlberg, and Stage 6, are seeking, viz., a just solution on which everyone can agree, provided only that they are prepared to reason in a just and impartial manner.

Notice, however, that this solution to Kohlberg's problem is arrived at entirely without benefit of reversibility. Indeed reversibility, so far from leading us to Rawls' solution, seems to lead us away from it: the fact that the actual parties to an actual situation are or are not willing to reverse a particular judgment has no bearing on whether or not that judgment would be chosen in Rawls' original position; it is even possible that the parties to an actual situation *are* willing to agree on a particular reversible judgment, without that judgment's being the one that would be chosen in the original position. For example, it seems likely that, in the original position, not knowing which sex we will turn out to be, we will decide that the sexes should have equal status: that is why sexual discrimination is unjust, on Rawlsian principles. But there are many couples where both parties are prepared to make and reverse the same judgment, that the wife should be the husband's loving and dutiful servant: the wife is willing to accept that role, and so is the husband, if he imagines himself in his wife's position. Reversibility here leads us astray: the fact that a judgment is agreed between parties who are willing to reverse their judgments does not mean that it is therefore the right one, on Rawlsian principles or anyone else's.

At this point, however, we need to draw the distinction which I mentioned earlier, between two types or levels of reversibility which I will call simple reversibility and ideal reversibility (there are, in fact, four forms of reversibility which ought to be distinguished, but I do not have space to discuss them all here). Simple reversibility consists in being prepared to accept and apply the same moral judgment, no matter how it might affect you personally. Reversibility in this sense is necessary if a judgment is to be genuine, sincere and consistent, moral judgment in the first place; and it is this sort of reversibility which Kohlberg has in mind when he asks, for example, whether Heinz's wife can reverse her judgment or whether the druggist can reverse his. But as we have seen, reversibility in this sense is no guarantee either of agreement or of truth: different people may be willing to reverse different judgments, i.e., still be prepared to accept them if they were in each other's positions; and different, conflicting judgments cannot all be true.

Ideal reversibility, on the other hand, consists in being prepared to accept and apply the same moral judgment not only whatever position you end up in, but also whatever position you start out from. Unlike simple reversibility, ideal reversibility therefore involves forgetting your own tastes and preferences, and asking instead whether there is any judgment you would be willing to accept even if you had somebody else's tastes and preferences in place of your own, assuming that they too were looking for a judgment which they could accept whatever their tastes and preferences might be. And this is, of course, precisely the situation of the parties in Rawls' original position, who do not yet know what their own tastes and preferences are going to be. Thus ideal reversibility is equivalent to Rawls' original position. It is this sort of reversibility which Kohlberg has in mind when he attempts to identify his position with Rawls, via a notion of ideal role-taking; but reversibility in this sense is not, like simple reversibility, a formal feature of moral judgments, necessary if a moral judgment is to be genuine, sincere and consistent, in the first place. It is, rather, a requirement imposed on moral judgments in order to ensure a form of impartial, 'rational' agreement.

But although ideal reversibility will lead us to Rawls' original position, it will not necessarily lead us to Rawls' principles of justice. For one thing, Rawls' derivation of his principles from the original position is blatantly question-begging: 'We want to define the original position so that we get the desired solution' (1971, p. 141). For another, Hare, from what is in effect the same position, prefers a form of Utilitarianism, viz., Preference Utilitarianism, or what I have called the Principle of Equal Interests (Locke, 1980). Moreover, even a judgment accepted by the parties in Rawls' original position does not necessarily provide the correct solution to a moral problem. Suppose, for example, that in the original position we are asked to decide whether people with two eyes should be obliged, wherever possible, to give one to those who are blind: there could, perhaps, be an annual lottery to decide which among the sighted are to surrender one eye to a national eye bank. Since we do not yet know whether we will be blind or sighted it seems at least likely that we will prefer to be sure of having one eye at least. Certainly the details of Rawls' argument, which I will not rehearse now, seem to imply that that would be the rational decision. Does it therefore follow that we sighted ought to give up one eye, transplants permitting, to those who are blind, i.e., that we actually do wrong if we do not? This is not, incidentally, an objection to Rawls' theory of justice, for that, explicitly, is a theory of distributive justice only, and not, as Kohlberg tries to make it, a theory of morality in general. What the example shows, rather, is that even if giving up one eye might be the just or fair thing to do—it *would* be fairer all round, if those without sight were given some—it is not necessarily morally required. There is more to morality than just justice; a solution to a moral problem might be just or fair in Rawls' sense, and still not be correct.

There is, finally, a more fundamental objection. This argument, the appeal to

ideal reversibility and the original position, rests, as we have seen, on a requirement of rational agreement. The underlying conception seems to be that articulated
most explicitly in Baier's *The Moral Point of View* (1958): the function of morality
is to find impartial, mutually acceptable solutions to conflicts of individual interests,
solutions on which all parties can therefore be expected to agree, provided they are
looking for impartial, mutually acceptable solutions to their problems. But
agreement, not even ideal agreement, does not necessarily guarantee truth. We
need to distinguish the claim that a correct solution will be one on which rational
people ought ideally to agree, from the claim that a solution on which rational
people can agree must therefore be the correct one. Indeed, Kohlberg seems
uneasily aware of this himself: it is significant that when he makes the claim that the
right principles or solutions are those which all rationally moral people would or
could accept (1981, p. 193), he puts the word 'right' into scare-quotes.

THE LIFEBOAT DILEMMA

The arguments in the last section are complex and abstract. They can, however, be
illustrated more concretely by an example provided by Kohlberg himself, in the
revised (1981) version of 'Justice as Reversibility'. A raft, or lifeboat, contains
three men but can support only two. One is the captain who can row and navigate;
another is a young man, strong and healthy, who can row but not navigate; the
third is an old man with a broken shoulder, who can neither row nor navigate.
Without the captain the chances of the other two surviving are nil; without the
young man they are only 50/50; but without the old man they are four out of five. So
who, if anyone, should go overboard; or should they perhaps draw lots?

Let us begin, once again, with simple reversibility: is there any solution to this
problem which any, or even all, of the parties is prepared to accept, even taking
into account what it would be like to accept that same solution if he were in each of
the other's situations? The answer has to be that we do not and cannot know, not
without being told much, much more about these three people (it could take a
novel at least). What does seem clear, however, is that there is any number of
different judgments which different people might be prepared to reverse in that
situation: I can easily imagine someone saying that they ought to draw lots, and
being prepared to accept that judgment whatever position he imagines himself in;
but I can also imagine someone saying that they ought to sacrifice the old man, and
being prepared to stick with that judgment even when he imagines that he is the old
man; I can even imagine the old man saying it himself (his name might be Oates);
and I can imagine someone deciding that the only judgment which he personally
can reverse, after all this ideal role-taking, is that they should all die together, since
that way none of them takes responsibility for the death of any other (these
possibilities are dramatically illustrated in Puka, 1976). And as well as imagining all
these things, and more, I can also imagine it being the case that all three parties
happen to agree about some one or other of them, i.e., that there is one
judgment—it need not always be the same judgment—which they are all willing to
reverse. It doesn't have to happen, but it could.

Now it may be that, like Kohlberg, you think that one of these judgments is the
right one, the correct solution to their moral dilemma. But if you do, it cannot be
because it, and only it, is reversible: which judgment is reversible, if any, will

depend on who is doing the reversing, i.e., on how the story is told. One person may be prepared to reverse one judgment, another another, and neither might be yours, or Kohlberg's. Nor can it be because it, and only it, is acceptable to all parties who are prepared to reverse their judgments: there may be no such judgment—even if all parties are prepared to reverse their judgments, they might be prepared to reverse different ones—and even if there is, it still might not be the one which you, personally, want to endorse.

So, in desperation, we turn from what the actual parties to the actual situation might or might not agree, to the solution which, ideally, rational parties ought to agree on. The Utilitarian solution, apparently, would be to sacrifice the old man, since that maximizes the probable ultimate good. The Rawlsian solution, according to Kohlberg, would be to draw lots, since that is the fairest. More exactly, sacrificing the old man conflicts with Rawls' difference principle, which states that inequalities are justified only if they operate to the advantage of the worst-off (i.e., eliminating those inequalities would make the worst-off even more worse-off), whereas picking on the old man is an inequality which further disadvantages the one who is already worst-off. At this point, however, Kohlberg miscalculates the odds (he forgets that, if it is a lottery, it might still pick the old man, or for that matter the captain): the average chances of the old man surviving, if there is a lottery, are only 17 per cent; but they rise to 50 per cent if, instead, the young man is thrown overboard. Thus the Difference Principle seems to require sacrificing the young man! And even if we forget about the Difference Principle and return to the original position, it is still not at all obvious that a lottery would be the right solution. Imagine that you are one of three souls waiting to be incarnated as the people on the raft, but without knowing who it will be: you have to decide now, impartially, what should be done. I suppose you might opt for the lottery, on the grounds that that gives you a chance whoever you turn out to be; but equally you might prefer that the old man be sacrificed, even if he turned out to be you, on the grounds that viewing it impartially, not knowing who you will be, that increases your chances of survival overall (averaged out, your chances are almost twice as good if the old man goes, than if you rely on the lottery). What this seems to show is that even the original position, ideal reversibility, does not guarantee a unique, correct and rationally acceptable answer to every moral problem. But, as we have seen, it is not intended to: Rawls' theory is not a theory of morality in general but of distributive justice in particular, and that is not what is at issue here.

But perhaps, like me, you do not think that there is one right judgment, a correct solution, in a case of this sort. This seems to be one of those situations, hinted at earlier, where any judgment, any solution, will be the right one, provided it is one that all the parties can agree on. Perhaps they cannot agree, in which case if we want to say that there is a right judgment, a correct solution, it can only be because we impose our own values on their situation. But if, in a situation like this, they can agree on something among themselves, then that surely is the right solution for them. And if another group of mariners in a similar predicament agree on a different solution, then that different solution is the right one for them. To insist that there must be a correct solution, the same for everyone—much less to seek to impose a 'correct' solution, by appealing to impartial standards of rationality—seems in this instance to be a mark of moral simplicity, not moral sophistication. If Kohlberg's claims for Stage 6 moral reasoning, for justice as reversibility, were correct, that would be a proof not of its cognitive superiority but of its cognitive inadequacy, its inability to deal adequately with the real variety and complexity of moral problems.

REFERENCES

Alston, W. (1971) 'Comments on Kohlberg's "From *is* to *ought*"', in T. Mischel (Ed.), *Cognitive Development and Epistemology*, New York, Academic Press, pp. 269–84.

Baier, K. (1958) *The Moral Point of Veiw*, Ithaca, Cornell.

Bennett, J. (1974) 'The Conscience of Huckleberry Fin', *Philosophy*, 88, pp. 123–34.

Blum, L. (1980) *Friendship, Altruism and Morality*, London, Routledge and Kegan Paul.

Blum, L. (1982) 'Kant's and Hegel's moral rationalism: A feminist perspective', *Canadian Journal of Philosophy*, 12, pp. 287–302.

Cooper, N. (1981) *The Diversity of Moral Thinking*, Oxford, Clarendon Press.

Eckensberger, L. (1981) 'On a structural model of the development of stages of moral development', unpublished paper presented at MOSAIC 1981, Liverpool.

Gibbs, J. (1977) 'Kohlberg's stages of moral judgment: A constructive critique', *Harvard Education Review*, 47, pp. 43–61.

Gilligan, C. (1982) *In A Different Voice: Psychological Theory and Women's Development*, Cambridge, Mass., Harvard University Press.

Hare, R. (1952) *The Language of Morals*, Oxford, Clarendon Press.

Hare, R. (1963) *Freedom and Reason*, Oxford, Clarendon Press.

Harman, G. (1983) 'Justice and moral bargaining', *Social Philosophy and Policy*, 1, pp. 114–31.

Kohlberg, L. (1971) 'From *is* to *ought*: How to commit the naturalistic fallacy and get away with it in the study of moral development', in T. Mischel (Ed.), *Cognitive Development and Epistemology*, New York, Academic Press, pp. 151–235.

Kohlberg, L. (1973) 'The claim to moral adequacy of a highest stage of moral judgment', *Journal of Philosophy*, 70, pp. 630–46.

Kohlberg, L. (1979) 'Justice as reversibility', in P. Laslett and J. Fishkin (Eds.), *Philosophy, Politics and Society*, Fifth Series, Oxford, Blackwell, pp. 257–72.

Kohlberg, L. (1981) *Essays on Moral Development, Vol. 1: The Philosophy of Moral Development*, San Francisco, Calif., Harper and Row.

Locke, D. (1979) 'Cognitive stages or developmental phases? A critique of the stage-structural theory of moral reasoning', *Journal of Moral Education*, 8, pp. 168–81.

Locke, D. (1980) 'The illusion of Stage Six', *Journal of Moral Education*, 9, pp. 103–9.

Locke, D. (1981) 'The principle of equal interests', *Philosophical Review*, 90, pp. 531–59.

Locke, D. (1983a) 'Doing what comes morally: The relation between behaviour and stages of moral reasoning', *Human Development*, 26, pp. 11–25.

Locke, D. (1983b) 'Moral reasons and moral action', in H. Weinreich-Haste and D. Locke (Eds.), *Morality in the Making: Thought, Action and the Social Context*, Chichester, John Wiley and Sons, pp. 111–24.

Locke, D. (1983c) 'Theory and practice in thought and action', in H. Weinreich-Haste and D. Locke (Eds.), *Morality in the Making: Thought, Action and the Social Context*, Chichester, John Wiley and Sons, pp. 157–70.

Mischel, W. and Mischel, H. (1976) 'A cognitive social-learning approach to morality and self-regulation', in T. Lickona (Ed.), *Moral Development and Behaviour: Theory, Research and Social Issues*, New York, Holt, Rinehart and Winston, pp. 84–107.

Puka, W. (1976) 'Moral education and its cure', in J. Mayer (Ed.), *Reflections on Values Education*, Ontario, Canada, Wilfred Laurier, pp. 47–86.

Rawls, J. (1958) 'Justice as fairness', *Philosophical Review*, 67, pp. 164–94.

Rawls, J. (1971) *A Theory of Justice*, Cambridge, Mass., Harvard University Press.

Rest, J. (1973) 'The hierarchical nature of moral judgment: A study of patterns of comprehension and preference of higher stages', *Journal of Personality*, 41, pp. 86–109.

Shweder, R. (1982) 'Liberalism as destiny', *Contemporary Psychology*, 27, pp. 421–4.

Turiel, E. (1966) 'An experimental test of the sequentiality of developmental stages in the child's moral judgments', *Journal of Personality and Social Psychology*, 3, pp. 611–18.

Williams, B. (1972) *Morality* Harmondsworth, Penguin Books.

Interchange

CARTER REPLIES TO LOCKE

Locke begins the second part of his chapter by remarking that Kohlberg's reasons for and rejection of *ethical relativism* 'are correct and familiar enough, though experience shows that they are points which need to be made again for each new generation.' Rightly, Locke observes that ethical relativism is the '(ultimately incoherent) doctrine that these different moralities are all equally valid, and equally correct.' Oddly enough, he concludes his crisp and telling critique of Kohlberg by saying to each of us that 'perhaps, like me, you do not think that there is one right judgment, a correct solution' to the lifeboat example, and that 'to insist that there must be a correct solution, the same for everyone ... seems in this instance to be a mark of moral simplicity.'

I think Locke is correct in arguing that Kohlberg is unable to provide the necessary evidence to show that Stage 6 reasoning yields a single correct solution to specific moral problems. But, then, how do we distinguish Locke's own solution from the position of the ethical relativist whom he cites with disapproval? Is he not forced to conclude that there are numerous solutions to moral dilemmas like the lifeboat example which are 'all equally valid'? If he resists such a conclusion, then it can only be because he wishes to rule out certain sorts of answers as being somehow inferior to others, perhaps on grounds similar to those advanced in Kohlberg's analysis of lower-stage reasoning, e.g., the egoism of Stage 1. Be that as it may, the point is that Locke *will* accept more than one answer as morally correct, or a right solution to a moral dilemma. Indeed, so will I. But why take it out on the relativist?

Perhaps there is an answer to this, somewhat along the lines of distinctions elaborated on in Chapter 2. If one thinks of a radical relativism (a self-defeating position akin to scepticism) where any answer is as good or bad as any other, then one has ample grounds, philosophical and human, for taking a dim view of relativism. On the other hand, if one's relativism is of the sort where it is possible to hold any one of several conceptual schemes, each of which is more or less internally consistent, impartial rather than biased, and comprehensive in scope, then one can talk of a 'right decision' only from within the specific moral viewpoint or system being adopted. Thus, in saying that one cannot determine a single, universal and absolute moral principle or moral answer, one need not mean that there are no criteria of better or worse at all. Locke doubtlessly agrees with this conclusion, yet he does so without seeing the relativistic leanings of his own position. Could it be that this is the result of his (and Kohlberg's) incorrectly identifying what it is that he objects to about relativistic positions? Consider the lifeboat again. What would a 'wrong answer' consist of? It would be an egoistic, or a selfish response, I suggest.

39

Picking the old man up, and heaving him overboard would serve as an illustration. Adequate answers have to take into account all of those affected by a decision, and must do so *impartially*. Imaginative reconstruction of the wishes, feelings, hopes, etc. of all concerned must occur, and the results be dealt with impartially, as though by a fourth party looking on from Locke's cloud above. And one can understand Kohlberg's stages as ways of charting the progressive expansion of imaginative and accurate empathizing, from the selfishness or ego-centredness of Stage 1, to the awareness of the need to cultivate the good-will of at least one other person of Stage 2, to the peer group orientation of Stage 3, to focus on community or nation (Stage 4), to the broadening of the social-contract and eventual universalization of Stages 5 and 6, to the embracing concern for all that is, i.e., the cosmic perspective of Stage 7. This last perspective, which Locke admits he doesn't understand, is the perspective from the cloud (akin to Spinoza's recommendation that we see things from the aspect of eternity), but with a clear proviso: the impartiality of the view of the whole must be infused with a love of, or caring about, that whole of things. Locke is right in noting that Kohlberg seems to be adding at Stage 7 what should have been present in his system all along: caring. Had Kohlberg been clearer in his treatment of the place of caring-feeling-compassion in his theory, he would likely have been able to chart the increasing capacity for genuine fellow-feeling together with the more abstract and cognitive skills required by and evidenced in moral reasoning. At Stage 7, selfishness is not only unacceptable, it is now impossible, for one is inextricably interconnected with all things. One is also impartial, in that one now wants the best for all of those involved in a moral decision, for one now cares for them (ideally) as one cares for oneself. Learning to care for oneself is but the first stage in the long development in moral sensitivity and imagination.

The trouble is that we can't put the various parts together, quite. We wish to avoid sceptical relativism, but everyday experience makes abundantly clear that moral dilemmas admit of conflicting and seemingly equally right moral solutions. Absolutism is too strong a pattern to impose, scepticism too weak. Similarly, we must care, but we must do so fairly or impartially. To care too much about some things at the expense of others is the formula for bias, while to over-compensate for this by focusing on justice and fairness can be to exclude love and caring altogether. Concern for the consequences of actions is also not enough, for results must be linked with moral principles and justice considerations, however good or bad they are in other respects. But to chain oneself to principles and justice considerations may well require an action which does not appear to bring about particularly desirable results. Locke's warning concerning relativism may well need to be revised to apply to ethics in general: one should warn each new generation about hasty generalizations, nihilistic or absolutistic, and focus instead on that myopia which we demonstrate as human beings, which places us somewhere between blindness and 20/20 moral vision. To this extent, I agree with Locke that 'an increased awareness of and insight into morality is likely to make moral conflicts *more* complex, more difficult to resolve, not less.' However, it is not clear to me that it is Kohlberg's claim that he makes moral judgment either easy *or* easier. His claim is that Stage 5 and 6 reasoning is more adequate, not that it makes morality easier. Indeed, the stage analysis is designed primarily to interpret moral reasoning, not to serve as a brain-insertable computer-chip which eliminates moral tension. What Kohlberg provides is considerable assistance in our journey from moral blindness (and insensitivity), to a perspective from which one can see with a bit more clarity whatever is not immediately under one's own nose.

LOCKE REPLIES TO CARTER

In order to decide whether Kohlberg is a relativist, we have first to decide what a relativist is, and as Professors Carter and Kohlberg amply demonstrate, this is none too easy to do. Professor Carter identifies the form of relativism which Kohlberg is particularly anxious to avoid as 'the view that conflicting ethical opinions are (all of them) equally valid or true'. The objection is that this leads 'logically' (see my chapter) to the conclusion that no-one—a teacher least of all—is entitled to impose their values on anyone else: we each of us have our own bag, and must be allowed to do our own thing. But, first, the objection to this form of relativism is that it is simply incoherent: if the opinions that abortion is morally unacceptable and that abortion is morally permissible, for example, are both equally true, then it follows that abortion is both moral and immoral, as blatant a breach of the law of non-contradiction as you might reasonably hope for. And, second, what follows is not Carter's conclusion but the opposite: if all ethical opinions are equally valid then if someone believes that he ought to impose his views on other people, and even that he ought to enforce them by threats and punishment if needs be, then he will be right to believe it, and therefore ought to do so.

What Carter and Kohlberg are objecting to, I think, is not ethical relativism of this sort, but what might better be called ethical anarchism, the idea that no moral opinion is better than any other, and hence that none has any claim to be taught or inculcated in preference to any other. But while not so obviously self-contradictory, this view still seems inconsistent: the essence of a moral belief or attitude—as opposed to a purely personal taste or preference—is that it is something which you think matters, which you want others to agree with you about and act upon. The remark, 'This is a moral matter, but you can think or do whatever you like about it' is virtually self-defeating: it seems to deny precisely what it asserts.

What would be consistent is what I would rather call amoralism, i.e., the denial of morality, a refusal to make moral judgment, leaving it instead to each person to do as he pleases. But this, too, is less easy to hold than it may seem. The standard justification is that it is wrong for one person to pass judgment on another, let alone to attempt to enforce his personal views on someone else's behaviour. But this, all too clearly, is itself a moral position: 'You should never make moral judgments' is, like 'All generalizations are false', simply self-refuting.

Nor do I find any clearer the form of relativism which Carter does ascribe to Kohlberg, viz., 'perspectivism'. Of course anyone who has moral opinions has, thereby, a point of view, a perspective on the topic in question. But this is true of anything: morality, science, or the height of Mount Everest. As I once heard Bernard Williams reply to the objection 'But that is just your opinion': 'I am not in the habit of saying things which are not my opinion.' What has to be shown, of course, is that it was *just* his opinion, that a moral perspective is only a perspective and nothing more. That is certainly not a view which, I would have ascribed to Kohlberg myself.

Postscript

DON LOCKE

The inevitable delay between writing and publication has meant that this chapter was out of date before it even appeared. When I wrote it I had not been able to read Kohlberg, Levine and Hewer (1983), a much more substantial piece of work than the repetitive and sometimes contradictory *Philosophy of Moral Development* on which this chapter is largely based. Since Kohlberg there modifies his position in a number of respects, a few further comments are in order.

One thing on which he has evidently not changed his mind is his rejection of cultural as well as ethical relativism, though the argument (pp. 72–5) seems to me to demonstrate more clearly than ever that it is not, in fact, a refutation of cultural relativism, but rather an explanation of why it occurs. On the other hand, Kohlberg does now recognize a difference between morality in general and justice in particular, and even that it is a mistake to identify the two. Prompted by the work of Carol Gilligan, he is prepared to allow a morality of care, benevolence and special relationships, different from but not opposed to the morality of universal and impartial justice. But justice is still primary — 'justice is the *first* virtue of a person or society' (p. 92) — and a morality of care or benevolence should be seen as supplementary to it (p. 21). Moreover, the 'central minimum core' of morality consists in 'striving for universal agreement in the face of more relativist conceptions of the good' (p. 93) such as Gilligan's, and at one point Kohlberg even repeats his earlier claim that 'virtue is not many but one and its name is justice' (p. 18; another example of this tendency to have it both ways occurs on p. 122, where a denial that Kohlberg has ever stated that males have a more developed sense of justice than females is immediately followed by an explanation of why the difference exists!). Admittedly Kohlberg does concede that this preference for impartial justice over personal obligations and responsibility is a controversial normative claim. But as Tomlinson argues in Chapter 7 of this volume, the main argument for focusing on justice in particular, and making it the core of morality, seems to be that that is where the theory works best! What Kohlberg has still to learn from Gilligan's work, it seems to me, is that moral conflicts can arise *within* individuals as well as between them, and there is if anything even less reason to hope that these conflicts must have some universally valid solution as demanded by principles of 'justice'.

Similarly Kohlberg now makes much more modest claims for Stage 6, at one point even 'dropping . . . the claim that such a stage answers most moral philosophic problems' (p. 64). Instead, Stage 6 is merely a 'theoretical construct' required by the theory; and Rawlsian justice is just one possible model of what Stage 6 justice reasoning might be. But Kohlberg's actual use of Rawls — 'justice as reversibility' — remains as confused as before, and the criticisms made above still apply.

The major change, however, is that Kohlberg has reversed his attempt to derive an 'ought' from an 'is'. Originally he had suggested that we might use the facts of moral development to show that one form of moral reasoning is philosophically, and therefore morally, more adequate than another. Now he wants to use the philosophical adequacy of the different stages to explain the psychological development. But what is not clear is *why* he wants to make this change, when everything else remains in place: Kohlberg continues to see moral development as based on cognitive conflict, and continues to insist that, in developing towards Stage 6, development consists in finding more and more adequate, more and more acceptable, solutions to moral problems. If that is so, the original argument from an 'is' to an 'ought' — more accurately, from an explanation of why the stages are cognitively or psychologically better to an explanation of why they are morally or philosophically better — still stands, though still subject to the same criticisms. Reading between the lines, what seems to have happened is that Kohlberg has only recently recognized what the Naturalistic Fallacy — or more accurately Hume's Law — actually is, and has thought, 'Good Heavens, I can't be doing *that*!' But that was precisely what he was doing and, as I said above, that was precisely what originally seemed most philosophically striking in this striking attempt to marry moral psychology and moral philosophy.

REFERENCE

KOHLBERG, L., LEVINE, C., and HEWER, A. (1983), *Moral Stages: A Current Formulation and a Response to Critics*, Basel, Karger.

Part III: Interface Between Developmental Psychology and Moral Philosophy

4. The Oughts of Is: Kohlberg at the Interface between Moral Philosophy and Developmental Psychology

DWIGHT R. BOYD

A strong tradition within modern academic thought, almost a sacred cow, has been the separation of the various 'disciplines' of inquiry. Put in the more precise terms of one of the leading exponents of this view, there are different 'forms of knowledge' through which we apprehend and attempt to understand reality around us and our experience within it. These forms of knowledge are differentiated in terms of unique and, for the most part, irreducible concepts, logical structures, testable expressions, and ways of testing claims, roughly illustrated, for example, by the differences between what a chemist and an historian does, or between what a psychologist and a philosopher does, in their respective 'fields' of academic endeavour.[1] Thus, in addition to the institutional boundaries which now circumscribe the actual practice of inquiry within existing academic institutions, there are also, supposedly, good reasons for recognizing and respecting the boundaries. Anyone crossing one of the boundaries thus does so at the double risk of trespassing on the fiercely-defended institutional territory of colleagues and failing to make sense (or to be convincing) to those on *both* sides of the boundary. Lawrence Kohlberg surely must be placed among the courageous few who have flaunted this tradition and taken these risks. For twenty-six years his work has refused to take the boundary between psychology and philosophy as an impenetrable given, but rather, has consistently suggested that some ways of crossing the boundary not only make sense, but are also both necessary and mutually beneficial to the respective disciplines.

One plausible explanation for why Kohlberg's work has, in general, been so

43

fecund is that he has not shied away from making claims strong enough to provoke others to take seriously the issues to which his claims are addressed. One example of such claims has been his assertion that his stages are culturally universal. Until very recently this claim has so clearly outstripped the evidence for it that one had to take it not just with a grain, but a shaker of salt. However, John Snarey's recent, systematic review of forty-three studies (seven of which are longitudinal) in twenty-six countries (representing a reasonable cross-section of types of cultures and levels of development and urbanization) concludes that these studies provide striking support for the underlying assumptions of Kohlberg's claim for cross-cultural universality, though they also, in Snarey's analysis, suggest kinds of possible biases at the upper end of the stage sequence, especially with regard to traditional folk societies and non-middle-class settings.[2] Thus, although the evidence is as yet not entirely conclusive, and although Kohlberg may in the end need to weaken some aspects of his universality claim, the nature and range of studies needed to evaluate the claim adequately has now apparently reached a reasonable confidence threshhold. More to the point of this paper, I submit that much of this interesting research might never have been conducted had not Kohlberg gone out on a limb for years with this claim, *and* had he not couched his rationale for this limb in terms of an alliance of both empirical and philosophical points.[3]

The response to the strong cross-cultural universality claim has been primarily on the empirical side, partly because the philosophical points were always drawn from standard, 'safe' positions of well-known philosophers, but also because the fact that they were being allied with empirical support was always left so understated as to escape much philosophical attention. However, Kohlberg has not shied away from also making strong claims on exactly this theme of alliance in such a form as to draw the attention of the philosophical side, as evidenced most succinctly in his now famous title, 'From *Is* to *Ought*: How to Commit the Naturalistic Fallacy and Get Away with It in the Study of Moral Development'.[4] Such a title is more than enough to raise the hackles of any philosopher with a conservative view of the notorious is-ought gap. With a few notable exceptions,[5] the response from the philosophical side to the proposed alliance has been less productive than that of the empirical psychologists. The responses have usually taken the flavour either of a sharp growl that here is yet another of those naive psychologists who does not realize that moral conclusions cannot be simply 'read off' the empirical facts of development (often in such a form as to suggest that the critic never read past the offending title) or of a well-argued and detailed insinuation that we must be placed on philosophical alert because here is an uncommonly sophisticated psychologist who is either getting entrapped in his own bad arguments or trying to sneak one by us.[6] In contrast to either of these two kinds of response, this paper will be oriented toward what might be said on the positive side of Kohlberg's claims about the connection between developmental psychology and moral philosophy.

As Jürgen Habermas has recently described this aspect of Kohlberg's work, 'Kohlberg's declared intentions are at the same time risky and relevant—they challenge anybody who does not mutilate either the social scientist or the moral and political philosopher in themselves.'[7] Explicating what these intentions are will be a major task of this paper, a large part of the problem being due to the vagueness which characterizes Kohlberg's claims and arguments on this issue, through which he has attempted to make good the claim of his title, 'From *Is* to *Ought*: How to Commit the Naturalistic Fallacy and Get Away with It in the Study of Moral

Development'. In order to lay the framework for this analysis I will first identify some general kinds of connections between developmental psychology and moral philosophy suggested by Kohlberg's work, connections which are for the most part relatively uncontroversial, but nonetheless extremely important for a full appreciation of Kohlberg's work. Then, building on this, I will engage in some exegesis of Kohlberg's statements concerning the focused relationship of 'is' and 'ought' in the context of a developmental framework. Due to the vagueness and unfinished nature of Kohlberg's thinking on this topic, this exegesis will very soon extend into the task of trying to articulate possible lines of thought which seem to be the promising directions of interpretation of Kohlberg's intentions, even if in the end it goes beyond what Kohlberg has clearly said. In all of this it should be noted that I do not intend to address questions related to the soundness of Kohlberg's empirical claims or to the justifiability of his normative philosophical position. Rather, I shall assume the acceptance of both, and the reader's acquaintance with them, in order to explore the nature of the relationship between these two kinds of concerns within Kohlberg's work.

APPROACHES TO THE BORDER

I will start by drawing attention to a series of very broad, basic, interrelated points of connection between psychology and moral philosophy which Kohlberg's work manifests or suggests—more or less open or clandestine border crossings, if you will. Although they all could be contested, the series starts with a relatively safe crossing clearly manifested within Kohlberg's work (though nonetheless important for the fact that so many people now safely travel back and forth via this clearly marked route), and then proceeds with progressively more risky and less clearly mapped crossings.

The first point of connection consists of an assumption which Kohlberg makes as a necessary condition of the psychological study of *morality*, an assumption which clearly situates his area of inquiry astraddle the boundary between psychology and philosophy. In criticizing the lack of progress in the past fifty years of child psychology, Kohlberg identifies the assumption implicitly: 'In my own area, moral development, the epistemological blinkers psychologists have worn have hidden from them the fact that the concept of morality is itself a philosophical (ethical) rather than a behavioral concept.'[8] What he means here is that intentionality is an essential characteristic of the area of experience which we identify as 'moral' and therefore any psychological account of this area of experience cannot just examine pieces of behaviour, but must also include the understandings and intentions of the psychological subject as moral agent. As he puts it, 'By insisting on the cognitive core of moral development, I mean ... that the distinctive characteristic of the moral is that it involves active *judgment*, as Alston (1968) seems to me to have clearly demonstrated from a philosophical point of view.'[9] 'To be "moral" an act must at least involve a moral judgment, a judgment of "ought" by the actor.'[10] As Blasi notes, this assumption of Kohlberg's, that 'without judgment, an action, no matter how beneficial, would not be moral',[11] clearly locates his work outside, and in opposition to, the 'prevalent view' characteristic of the psychological study of morality.

According to the prevalent view ... moral action is essentially irrational and is different from morally neutral action only in terms of specific content categories (helping, obeying, etc.) or in terms of the social function served by morality, for example, of enhancing social cohesion .... Perhaps the most important functions of cognition are not recognized in research on moral functioning, namely, the creation of meaning and the determination of truth. The moral meaning, in fact, is considered to be already present in the action tendencies and to be objectively determined either by their function for the individual and for the species or by arbitrary conventions. The question of truth is regarded as irrelevant in this context.[12]

From the perspective of this most prevalent view within psychology, the boundary separating psychology and philosophy is then not just something like the border between two nations, but more like the millions of miles of vacuum separating two planets—since philosophy can be fairly characterized as concerned precisely with 'the creation of meaning and the determination of truth'. But from Kohlberg's point of view, the way in which moral meaning is constructed and truth (or moral correctness) is determined is exactly what we need to study psychologically. The assumption that how a piece of behaviour is conceptualized by a moral agent is crucial to the understanding of it as moral, and the assumption that the nature (form) of the justification given for a particular moral act can be separated from an external description of the act, are both core assumptions shared by moral philosophy and by moral psychology as construed by Kohlberg.[13] For Kohlberg, the psychological study of the child as moral agent necessitates viewing the 'child as moral philosopher'.

The second point of connection widens and extends the first: Kohlberg assumes that a psychologist seeking to understand the development of moral judgment in human subjects should use for conceptual tools the philosophically differentiated categories of such judgment:

Moral judgments refer to *moral meanings in the world*—rules, laws, states of justice. Because of this, our basic terms for analysis come not from psychology but from philosophy and sociology. The basic moral terms reflect categories of moral experience, the dimensions shared by all moral experiences. They are in the realm of moral experience what the categories of space, time and causality are in the realm of physical experience. This is what we mean when we say the cognitive-structural approach implies the child is a moral philosopher, someone concerned with the fundamental categories of meaning.[14]

In his research programme since 1958, the way in which Kohlberg has sought to operationalize his intention to examine the psychological development of such 'categories of moral meaning' has changed several times.[15] The consistent motivation behind those changes (often puzzling and frustrating to critics not involved in the programme) has been the dual, boundary-crossing requirements of both (1) unambiguously identifying the way in which a subject structures moral meaning, that is, clearly separating the content of particular moral judgments from the form of the justification offered by a person for those judgments, and (2) doing so in such a way that the method could be used by other researchers while meeting psychometric standards of reliability and validity. Thus what has changed has been not only the actual terms of analysis but also how the terms are related to different ways of interpreting moral judgment interview data. Within the current system, which apparently satisfies both requirements,[16] the categories of analysis are identified as 'Orientations', 'Elements', 'Norms' and 'Issues', in decreasing order of abstractness.[17] All of these carry weight within the actual scoring methodology, but my point here can be made by focusing on how the category of 'Element' was

generated. Although the eventual aim was a reliable method for making psychological claims about how moral judgment manifests itself and develops within a human
being, the starting-point was apparently philosophy. As Colby *et al.* say,

> In beginning to identify and define the Elements, we turned to basic philosophic categories in
> ethics which define types of normative moral philosophies .... Thus our first division is between
> deontological reasons, principles or philosophies and teleological reasons, principles or
> philosophies.[18]

Within these gross divisions are finer distinctions not exactly made by philosophers
explicitly, though congruent with the different kinds of deontological and teleological
theories, identified as the four orientations—'Normative Order', 'Fairness', 'Utilitarianism' and 'Perfectionism'.[19] But for Kohlberg's purposes a further subdivision
into Elements is necessary:

> We may see fairness, for example, as a general orientation, but the ways in which one defines
> 'fairness' is important. 'Fairness as equality' is quite a different concept from 'fairness as reward
> for merit.' The distinction is an important one in moral philosophy, as it is in moral judgment
> assessment. The finer distinctions that we make within the Orientation are the Elements ....
> The Elements represent distinctions within the Orientations that made sense logically and
> philosophically and made a difference empirically.[20]

The boundary-crossing aspect of Kohlberg's work is clearly identified in the last
claim in this passage, but it would seem to have been viewed mainly from the
philosophy side. However, in answering the question why the more content-laden
categories, 'Norms' and 'Issues,' are necessary if the Elements give us such fine
distinctions among kinds of moral reasons, Colby *et al.* also focus on the same
boundary crossing from the psychology side:

> The reason is that we are concerned with concrete moral judgments. We are not trying to
> measure an individual's abstract philosophical positions, but rather what is going to make a
> difference when that individual is faced with an actual moral choice. An individual could read
> Mill or Kant or Rawls and state what sound like principles. But unless such 'principles' help them
> resolve moral conflicts, then what they are saying amounts to empty phrases. A person may say,
> 'I'm a Utilitarian, I believe in the greatest good for the greatest number.' But that does not help
> us much in determining that person's stage of moral reasoning. What we care about is how s/he
> makes moral judgments when his/her Utilitarianism is actually applied to values in conflict.
> Morality is a matter of choice and decision. It is not just a matter of using abstract words like
> 'justice.' It concerns the actual use of concepts like 'justice' when an individual makes a choice. It
> is through the Issues and Norms that we define the choice.[21]

Thus Kohlberg uses the highly differentiated categories of moral philosophy, but in
such a way as to be useful in the psychological explanation of how humans develop
and use their capacity of understanding the nature of moral conflicts.

The third kind of connection uses empirical results from this unique stance in
psychology to bulldoze new crossings into philosophy, or at least to set the survey
stakes that invite the bulldozing to be done. Up to this point a critic might note that
the influence across the border has been mostly one-way—philosophical assumptions and conceptual differentiations inform and permeate Kohlberg's empirical
methodology (although the suggestion noted above that some of the philosophically cherished beliefs do not always function in actual moral judgment, even that of
philosophers, is in itself a significant counter-offering). However, the relationship is
considerably altered when Kohlberg approaches the border with his supply train of
empirical findings. Even if those critics are right who argue for either a revision of

the upper end of the stage sequence or a loosening of the claims made for the nature of positions held to be 'post conventional',[22] the evidence for the invariant sequence of stages at least through Stage 4, and perhaps through Stage 5, is now quite strong.[23] If one accepts the soundness of these empirical claims, even in their most qualified formulation, that moral philosophy can proceed entirely uninfluenced is hard to countenance. Indeed, Kohlberg has staked out the rough direction for two different routes that philosophers might use to be open to the influence of his empirical findings. Both routes offer new perspectives on how moral philosophers reflexively conceive their philosophical tasks; I cannot do the required spadework to develop either of them here, but I want to outline them in such a way as to make a naive philosophical stonewalling of the border more difficult and less acceptable.

The first route challenges most directly the work of modern analytic philosophers, though it could be extended to approaches less exclusively oriented to language analysis. As Kohlberg puts it succinctly:

> . . . ordinary-language moral philosophers, particularly formalists such as Hare, think their task is to analytically define and clarify ordinary . . . moral language. If the form of ordinary moral language is, however, qualitatively different from that of the language of a normative ethical philosopher, the problem is different.[24]

The 'problem is different' (one might also say, 'far more difficult') because, if this philosophical method aims to uncover and clarify different facets of moral meaning as expressed through our shared language, then it matters very much that we share not only words, but also our underlying structures of moral understanding in whose service those words function. But this is exactly what Kohlberg's findings contest! Indeed, it is not simply the problem that the use of the 'language of a normative ethical philosopher' may be somewhat different from that of 'everybody else', but, more radically, that the patterns of use of the (non-philosopher) 'ordinary persons' themselves vary qualitatively. In short, the range of intended referents of the 'we' in ordinary language analysis (as in 'by "X" we obviously do not mean . . .') cannot simply be left unspecified by philosophers if Kohlberg's empirical claims are sound. To make this concrete, let me suggest that studies could be designed that would reveal substantive limits to a philosophical move as standard as the 'open question test' for the acceptability of definitions of moral terms, such as 'right'. That is, philosophers just assume that when such a test is applied to any 'inadequate' definition, such as '"right" means whatever is approved by the mores of one's society', then *everyone* who is being clearheaded and rational (and perhaps 'thinks about it a little bit') will be convinced of its inadequacy. On the contrary, if Kohlberg's findings are sound, and if one carefully tailored definitions to the stages, I would hypothesize that not only would *not* everybody be convinced but also one could predict (from a prior knowledge of subjects' predominant mode of moral judgment) who would fail to be convinced by the application of the test to which definitions.[25]

The second route hinted at by Kohlberg is much more dangerous (there are vicious currents of circular argument and vacuous claims all along the way that one can easily fall into) but, at the same time, much more important because it goes straight to the nerve centre of the philosophical domain. Illuminating it with the strongest searchlight, one might argue that if the developmental claims are sound, then the traditional philosophical view of justification must be modified. That is, what one attends to and finds convincing within morally justificatory engagements changes developmentally, and any attempt to give a thorough justification of a moral position can never stand completely 'outside' this fact. This is *not* to say that good moral reasons can be reduced to developmental facts, but rather, that viable conceptions of justification cannot be independent of those facts. Kohlberg puts it this way:

> Another implication of our stage psychology for moral philosophy is that arguments for a normative ethic must be stepwise .... There is no one line of argument for Stage 6 (or Stage 5) morality, but only a family of arguments that move from one stage position to the next.[26]

And in what I take to be an example of something philosophers need to keep in mind if they are not to fail to miss this route, Kohlberg makes the following observation:

> From my developmental perspective, moral principles are active reconstructions of experience; the recognition that moral judgment demands a universal form is neither a universal *a priori* intuition of humanity nor a peculiar invention by a philosopher but, rather, a position of the universal reconstruction of judgment in the process of development from Stage 5 to Stage 6.[27]

What Kohlberg seems to be suggesting here is that the very criteria that philosophers use to identify genuine instances of 'justifying a moral judgment' are themselves emergents of a developmental process—and something that changes throughout the stages of that process.

This raises in a much more unavoidable way than was true up to this point the spectre of the 'is/ought' problem. I will then return shortly and focus on this issue for the remainder of the paper. First, however, I think it important to note that there are some philosophers already trying to develop this route across the border. Thus, for example, consider the even broader epistemological thoroughfare argued by Stephen Toulmin:

> ... we can hope to keep philosophical and empirical questions about knowledge and learning entirely separate only if we can regard the *empirical application* of our cognitive concepts as something unchanging. To the extent that the criteria of application are in fact variable from stage to stage in the human life cycle—to the extent that *what we count* as 'knowing,' 'recognizing,' or 'understanding' varies, as between an infant and a newly speaking child, an adolescent, and a fully mature adult—that attempt will once again fail .... We do not have *unitary and invariant* criteria for judging the cognitive skills of human beings, regardless of age or stage, normality or deficit, but rather our criteria are determined, in any particular context, with an eye to those variables.[28]

It seems to me that Kohlberg's suggestive remarks about 'stepwise' justification are quite congruent with Toulmin's direction here. I suppose, also, that one could design studies, parallel to those suggested on the open-question test, that would cast doubt on the implicitly transcendent claims made for the status of some criterion of what is to count as 'justifying', for example, the 'generalization test'. Even if clear-headed, rational (and given the opportunity to 'think about it a little bit'), some subjects, I would hypothesize, would indeed accept some consequences of applying the generalization test to their moral position, which philosophers would argue 'could not' be accepted.

THE BARRIER OF THE 'IS/OUGHT' GAP

As I anticipated above, I will now turn to the more focused issue of the relationship between 'is' and 'ought' and how Kohlberg's comments on this relationship might best be interpreted and developed. The claim that our philosophical understanding of justification might have to be modified if Kohlberg's empirical claims are true, in short, that our sense of what *counts* as a good moral reason might in some way be contextualized by the facts of development, raises immediate and strong worries about the nature of the relationship being suggested. The relationship between statements of fact and moral judgments, between description and prescription, between describing and evaluating, between explanation and justification—in short, between 'is' and 'ought'—is commonly thought of as a 'gap' across which it is impossible to travel. One might say that it is seen as the moat which protects the castle of our moral claims from being overrun by the multitude of changeable contingencies. Although apparently non-existent within much of the historical tradition lying behind contemporary ethical views, e.g., in Aristotle or Aquinas,[29] since Hume at least the moat has been dug to the depth and breadth that it has been credited with the capacity to swallow up a whole range of well-developed moral theories, as well as many of the (philosophically) unsophisticated views implicit in moral 'common sense'. There have been, of course, some heroic attempts to leap the moat, or at least to show how one *can* jump from 'is' to 'ought', but it is commonly thought that most, if not all, have either fallen short or shown only that there are some narrow places in the moat caused by additions to the castle of pure 'moral' claims (and the jumps have thus really started from within the castle's grounds, while appearing to come from the side of 'is').[30] However, as evidenced by the two noted routes that Kohlberg has staked out for crossing the border from psychology to moral philosophy, it is clear Kohlberg's intentions are such that require the moat somehow to be bridged. The question is, what is the nature of the bridgework which might support these proposed routes, while at the same time not vitiating the function of the moat? More specifically, what is it about developmental psychology that leads Kohlberg to suggest that the bridge can be built?

A necessary preliminary to exploring these questions is to get a clearer picture of the moat. There are many different descriptions possible, which in turn require different kinds of bridge constructions. Indeed, the most common description usually takes a form something like 'you cannot derive an "ought" from an "is",' or 'no set of factual premises alone can yield a moral (ought) conclusion.' In this case, the very manner of describing the moat is almost tantamount to necessitating its unbridgeability. The problem here is that 'derive' and 'yield' are almost always interpreted as requiring that *deduction* is the *only* available argumentative form for the bridge—an unstated but highly contestable assumption.[31] That is another story, not necessary to complete here. However, it does serve to point up the fact that it matters very much how the problem is described as to whether or not it might be seen to have an answer, one to which Kohlberg's work might contribute. The description which I will be working with is much looser: '"ought"-claims are not reducible to "is"-claims', when what this is intended to convey (and the moat to represent metaphorically) is the belief that a moral (ought) perspective must provide some prescriptive 'leverage' to criticize whatever description of existing conditions is thought to hold true. That is, the way in which 'ought'-claims must differ from 'is'-claims describing existing states of affairs is located in their function and power to guide us in *criticizing* some aspect of what is currently the case, with an eye toward *changing* it for the better. The question can now be refined to how do Kohlberg's work and claims bear on this belief? In what follows I will run through a series of possible answers to this question, in what seems to me an increasing order of interpretive plausibility, and at the same time, an increasing order of suggestive incompleteness. However, I also want to note here that even if the elaboration of what seems to me the most plausible direction of interpretation of Kohlberg's intentions fails, in the end, to satisfy, a good share of the border-crossing nature of Kohlberg's work sketched in the previous section would not thus be vitiated.

Interpretation 1—Certainly Not Reductionism

The first, and least plausible, position which Kohlberg, as a psychologist, might take on the 'is/ought' difference is simply to deny it through a scientific reduction of 'ought'-claims to some kind of 'is'-claims, in a way which relegates 'ought'-claims to the status of unnecessary epiphenomena. On this view, the castle is some kind of mirage or figment of our imagination—if we proceed in that direction with the appropriate empirical tools, no moat will ever stop our progress because it will be filled in with explanatory accounts of how we just thought there was a castle. I will assume that what I said above (see p. 45) clearly rules out this interpretation, and no more needs to be said here, other than to reiterate that for Kohlberg the characterization of his theoretical orientation as 'cognitive' entails (in part) a focus on 'the definition of the subjects' structure in terms of the *meanings he or she finds in the world*', and that 'moral judgments refer to moral meanings in the world.'[32]

Interpretation 2—Clearly the 'Is' of (an Assumed) 'Ought'—But That's Not All

The second possible interpretation of Kohlberg's position on the relationship between 'is' and 'ought' might be to reduce it to that which is necessarily assumed by any *developmental* psychological theory. That is, insofar as 'to develop' is to change in some way deemed appropriate or positive, and insofar as Kohlberg conceives of what he is doing as describing how moral judgment 'develops' in the human subject, then there must be some normative standard (loosely, an 'ought') built into his empirical methodology. Indeed, Kohlberg clearly acknowledges this point:

> Not only are the moral judgments we score normative judgments, but our theory, upon which our scoring system is based, is itself normative in nature. While we have argued against classifying persons into evaluative 'boxes,' our scoring procedure does not specify a value-neutral attitude toward the moral judgments of subjects. On the contrary, our method and our theory presuppose a stance toward the greater or lesser moral rationality of the moral judgments being interpreted. Thus our stage interpretations are not value-neutral, they do imply some normative reference. In this sense our stage theory is basically what Habermas calls a 'rational reconstruction' of developmental progress. Our theory is a rational reconstruction because (a) it describes the developmental logic inherent in the development of justice reasoning with the aid of (b) the normative criterion of Stage 6 which is held to be the most adequate (i.e., most reversible) stage of justice reasoning.[33]

The description of the theory as a 'rational reconstruction of developmental progress' is a notion I will return to shortly. Similarly, it should also be noted both that Kohlberg no longer claims empirical verification of Stage 6 and that he seems to be broadening his conception of what might be included in Stage 6 (thus now seeing Rawls' model of justice as 'an instance' or example).[34] However, the relevant point here is that some notion of Stage 6 is clearly seen as the 'normative' criterion that 'aids' or organizes the empirical methodology which aims at explaining moral development. Thus one *could* say that the only 'is/ought' relationship which Kohlberg's work manifests is the one acknowledged here, namely, the assumption of an 'ought'-orientation and then an exploration of how human subjects learn, in progressive stages, to look at the world successfully through that particular 'ought'-orientation. However, although this must be part of the picture, and would surely constitute by itself a significant undertaking (relevant to both psychology and philosophy, and certainly to education), it cannot be the whole story. If one stopped here, then one would have to ignore the fact that Kohlberg has apparently intended and tried to say something far more controversial directly about the 'is/ought' relationship, and these claims cannot easily be reduced only to the above relationship. To these claims I now turn.

Interpretation 3—Surely Not a Naive Move from 'Is' to 'Ought'

A third possible position on the 'is/ought' relationship which we must eliminate as a legitimate interpretation of Kohlberg's view has already been mentioned in the introductory section of this paper. That is, one might infer (and many critics have done so, without *any* argument[35]) from the title of Kohlberg's central paper on this topic, 'From *Is* to *Ought*: How to Commit the Naturalistic Fallacy and Get Away with It in the Study of Moral Development', that Kohlberg advocates some naive move from the fact ('is') that people do change their moral judgment patterns in the order laid out by the stage sequence to the moral ('ought') conclusion that the identified end point of the sequence, Stage 6, is morally correct or justified. Although mistakes of this sort can probably be found in psychology, to accuse Kohlberg of it necessitates either ignoring or explaining away Kohlberg's explicit recognition of the need to avoid this kind of move. True, with some candour, Kohlberg does admit that 'my chapter ["Is to Ought"] weaves uneasily through many forms of the naturalistic fallacy, treating some as genuine fallacies, and others not',[36] and both the 'many forms' and the 'uneasy weaving' provide a not inconsiderable difficulty for even a sympathetic interpreter. However, it seems to me incontestable that Kohlberg decidedly identifies variations on the form under consideration in this section as a position which he is not taking:

> . . . there are two forms of the naturalistic fallacy I am not committing. The first is that of deriving moral judgments from psychological, cognitive-predictive judgments or pleasure-pain statements, as is done by naturalistic notions of moral judgment. My analysis of moral judgment does not assume that moral judgments are really something else, but insists that they are prescriptive and *sui generis*.[37] The second naturalistic fallacy I am not committing is that of assuming that morality or moral maturity is part of biological human nature or that the biological order is the better. . . .
>
> Science . . . can test whether a philosopher's conception of morality phenomenologically fits the psychological facts. Science cannot go on to justify that conception of morality as what

morality ought to be . . . . Moral autonomy is king, and values are different from facts for moral discourse. Science cannot prove or justify a morality, because the rules of scientific discourse are not the rules of moral discourse.[38]

When Kohlberg asserts that 'moral autonomy is king, and values are different from facts for moral discourse', I take him to be affirming the description of the 'is/ought' distinction in much the same way as my description above (p. 50). There is then, even on his view, clearly something across which a bridge needs to be constructed. Indeed, even if it can be argued that in the context of specific arguments Kohlberg sometimes fails to attend adequately to this difference, e.g., when he asserts that 'it is a simple matter of fact that middle-class children are advanced on measures of moral age development',[39] his core position seems clear, and these slips might be argued to be mistakes on his own view.

Moreover, it seems clear that Kohlberg wants to go on to say something about the 'is/ought' relationship in addition to this fundamental and clearly acknowledged difference between 'is' and 'ought'. Thus it seems to me that any philosophical critique which sets out to show that all of Kohlberg's arguments can be reduced to committing this basic error which he himself acknowledges as such is probably dependent on the question-begging assumption that there *is* nothing more that *can* be said about the matter.[40] But to make this assumption as an extension of the recognition of *some* difference does not seem warranted even *within* philosophy. As Kai Nielsen has put it recently:

Fifteen to twenty years ago it was orthodoxy in analytical philosophical circles to claim that for all their other differences Hume and Moore were right in agreeing that in no significant sense can we derive an ought from an is. At present there is no orthodoxy or even anything like a dominant view and, given our current understanding of how language works and our understanding of moral and ideological discourse, we could not reasonably remain content with old orthodoxies or take the question to be as straightforward as it was often thought to be.[41]

It is thus in the spirit of keeping the question open, while at the same time acknowledging that any naive move from 'is' to 'ought' has already been ruled out, that I turn to consider two further, more positive, directions that Kohlberg might intend.

Interpretation 4—Perhaps 'Ought' as 'Isomorphic' with 'Is'—But How?

In '*Is to Ought*' Kohlberg makes several direct positive claims about the relationship between 'is' and 'ought'. Some of the variation in how he articulates these claims is shown in the following quotations:

(a) The third form [after the two noted above which he rejects] of the naturalistic fallacy, which I *am* committing, is that of asserting that any conception of what moral judgment ought to be must rest on an adequate conception of what it is. The fact that my conception of the moral 'works' empirically is important for its philosophic adequacy. By this I mean first that any conception of what adequate or ideal moral judgment *should* be rests on an adequate definition of what moral judgment *is* in the minds of people.[42]

(b) The scientific theory as to why people *do* move upward from stage to stage, and why they factually *do* prefer a higher stage to a lower, is broadly the same as a moral theory as to why people *should* prefer a higher stage to a lower.[43]

(c) ... an ultimately adequate *psychological* theory as to why a child does move from stage to stage, and an ultimately adequate *philosophical* explanation as to why a higher stage is more adequate than a lower stage are one and the same theory extended in different directions.[44]

Although this does not exhaust the kinds of positive claims suggested, I am focusing on these first because a brief look at what Kohlberg says about them (both in the original paper and recently in *Moral Stages*[45]) is needed to clear away possible positions which could be confused with his other, more promising claims.

Part of the possible confusion arises because Kohlberg leaves all of this very vague and only suggestive, with little explanation of what he might mean. Thus, with regard to the first claim above, (a), Kohlberg says very little and simply slips it in immediately before his discussion of (b) as if it were some sort of introduction. If I understand (a) correctly, however, this cannot be the case. Rather, it seems to me that either it is not an instance of the naturalistic fallacy at all or it refers to something more substantive which should not be confused with a definitional matter. That is, on the one hand, this passage might be saying only that any adequate normative theory of morality must in fact *be* about morality. This is, of course, true, but it raises a conceptual issue, not a matter of empirical fact; indeed, it brings to mind Kohlberg's own claim about the conceptual cause of the inadequacy of other pyschological orientations toward the study of morality noted above (see p. 45). On the other hand, if one focuses on the sentence 'the fact that my conception of the moral "works" empirically is important for its philosophic adequacy', then exactly *what* it means for a conception of the moral to work empirically, and, if it does, *how* this fact might be important for a claim of philosophical (i.e., *moral*) adequacy, needs to be explained. But the explanation cannot be (and in fact the brief one Kohlberg gives here *is* not) anything close to a definitional matter. Rather, it anticipates a more substantive claim different from at least a surface interpretation of either (b) or (c), and I will thus leave further discussion to the following section.

What then might be said about (b) and (c)? In what seems to be intended as an explanation of (b), Kohlberg recapitulates an earlier claim that there is a kind of 'isomorphism' between moral judgment viewed developmentally and normative moral argument:

> ... although psychological theory and normative ethical theory are not reducible to each other, the two enterprises are isomorphic or *parallel*. In other words, an adequate psychological analysis of the structure of a moral judgment and an adequate normative analysis of the judgment are made in similar terms.[46]

This 'isomorphism' apparently refers to the claim that there is a 'correspondence' or 'mapping' relationship between the basic criteria used in the respective spheres:

> Both psychological and philosophical analyses suggest that the more mature stage of moral thought is the more structurally adequate. The greater adequacy of more mature moral judgment rests on structural criteria more general than those of truth value or efficiency. These general criteria are the *formal* criteria that developmental theory holds as defining all mature structures, the criteria of differentiation and integration. Now, these formal criteria (differentiation and integration) of development map into the formal criteria that philosophers of the formalist school have held to characterize genuine or adequate moral judgments.[47]

In short, the claim is that '... the *formal psychological* developmental criteria of differentiation and integration, of structural equilibrium, map into the *formal moral* criteria of prescriptiveness and universality.'[48]

Without trying to explain or evaluate the alleged parallel between differentiation and prescriptivity, and between integration and universality,[49] I think we can see that there are two different possible interpretations of what Kohlberg might be wanting to get at here. The first amounts to the claim that from the point of view of developmental psychology what the maturing moral subject does and what the moral philosopher does are essentially the same cognitive activity, the same orientation toward the construction of moral meaning and determination of moral truth, carried on at different levels of abstraction. Indeed, the very criteria that the moral philosopher articulates as necessary for a convincing moral 'ought'-claim are themselves a result from, and a reconstruction of, the philosopher's own activity as moral agent, the activity which is the direct object of analysis by moral developmental psychology.[50] In examining these claims of Kohlberg, Habermas makes the same point in terminology I will be using below:

> [According to Kohlberg's 'constructivist concept of learning'] subjects who move from one stage to the next should be able to explain why their judgments on the higher level are more adequate than those on the lower—and it is this line of the layperson's natural moral reasoning which is reflectively taken up by moral philosophers. This affinity is due to the fact that both the psychologist's subjects and the moral philosopher adopt the same performative attitude of a participant in practical discourse. In both cases, the outcome of moral reasoning, whether it is an expression of the layperson's moral intuition or the expert's reconstruction of it, is evaluated in the light of claims to normative rightness.[51]

On this interpretation, then, the claim here is not making any direct positive statement about the 'is/ought' relationship, but is rather a point similar to that already made above (see pp. 48ff.) concerning how developmental psychology can affect our conception of philosophical activity.

There is, however, another interpretation which is far less innocuous for the issue at hand. As it is stated, (b) would seem not so much to be making a claim about some sort of basic affinity between the moral meaning-making of the developing subject and the moral philosopher. Rather, it seems to be a statement about the relationship between a 'scientific theory' about stage change and a 'moral theory' about why higher stages are better. The relationship between the two is then claimed to be that they are 'broadly the same'. Habermas has labelled this interpretation (of both (b) and (c)) the 'identity thesis', and he rightly points out that this blurs an important distinction.

> The psychological theorist's attitude and type of claim are however, different [from that of the psychologist's subject or the moral philosopher]. Psychologists appropriately conceive of their subjects' learning process in terms of how the subjects would criticize lower-level judgments and justify higher-level judgments; but they, contrary to the subjects (and to their reflecting alter ego, the moral philosopher), describe and explain these judgments in a third-person attitude so that the outcome of *their* own reasoning is exclusively related to claims of propositional truth.[52]

I would agree with Habermas that especially (b) 'blurs' this important distinction (though as we will see below in the last section, I also think Habermas overstates the point in the last clause of this passage). But it is important to be clear that it is a distinction which Kohlberg himself *intends* to maintain, for as I have already noted above (p. 53), he explicitly acknowledges that 'science cannot prove or justify a morality because the rules of scientific discourse are not the rules of moral discourse.' Indeed, in Kohlberg's recent response to this criticism by Habermas he strongly agrees with the aim of avoiding the blurring of the distinction between the two theoretical perspectives, and repudiates any 'identity thesis' claim: 'The isomorphism claim we now renounce states that the normative theory as to the greater adequacy of each stage *is the same thing* as an explanatory theory of why one stage leads to another.'[53]

Certainly I think it is important that Kohlberg has now cleared up an ambiguity in his earlier claims that could lead to attributing a much stronger 'is/ought' connection to him than he wants to claim. On the other hand, except for the description of the two kinds of theory in (b) as '*broadly* the same' ('broadly'?), I think there is very little evidence that the 'identity thesis' was ever intended—especially given the explicit disavowals already cited. Indeed, although Habermas cites both (b) and (c) as evidence for the 'identity thesis', I think there is an important difference in (c) that Habermas misses. And because it can be seen as congruent with the subsequent analysis of what Kohlberg *is* claiming, I shall focus on it very briefly. The point is that in (c) the relationship between the two theoretical perspectives, psychological and philosophical, is *not* characterized as 'broadly the same', but rather as 'one and the same theory extended in different directions.' This could be, of course, interpreted as some sort of 'identity', as, for example, in the picture of one line extended in different directions from some point. However, I think the following metaphor is closer to what Kohlberg might have been trying to say here. Consider a perfect sphere placed equidistant between two mirrors equal in all relevant properties. And let us take the sphere itself as the object of theoretical attention, say, the phenomenon of moral judgment by human subjects, and the reflections of it in the mirrors to be theoretical accounts of the object. Then it would seem that if one were in exactly the right observing position, the reflections would look 'one and the same'. However, there would still be *two* reflections, 'extended in different directions', which could not be reduced one to the other. The over-stated case that there is *no* commonality between the two, *no* perspective from which one can view both without distorting the nature of at least one, is suggested to us by our 'normal' (discipline-promoted) disposition of getting into the position to have a close-up look at one reflection . . . and then looking over our shoulders and remarking how different the other 'must be'. A suggestion as to how Kohlberg's way of looking at moral judgment might constitute a sort of mediating position between two kinds of theoretical perspectives must now be considered. What follows will thus aim at an interpretation of what might be *behind* Kohlberg's vague 'isomorphism' claim, one which is not reducible to either interpretation of this claim offered above, nor open to the problems noted with regard to the second.

Interpretation 5—Plausibly, a Kind of 'Complementarity' between 'Is' and 'Ought'

In addition to criticizing Kohlberg for blurring the distinction between psychological accounts of the 'is' of moral development and philosophical or 'natural' moral reasoning about 'ought,' Habermas has offered a more positive interpretation of Kohlberg's intentions. Habermas calls this interpretation the 'complementarity thesis', claiming that Kohlberg 'rightly insists' on this relationship of psychological and philosophical theories:

> This 'complementarity thesis' states the case more adequately than the identity thesis does. The success of an empirical theory which can only be true or false may function as a check on the normative validity of hypothetically reconstructed moral intuitions. 'The fact that our conception

of the moral "works" empirically is important for its philosophic adequacy.' It is in this way that rational reconstructions can be put on trial or 'tested,' if 'test' means an attempt to check whether pieces complementarily fit into the same pattern. In Kohlberg, the following is the clearest formulation: 'Science, then, can test whether a philosopher's conception of morality phenomeno-logically fits the psychological facts.' Science cannot go on to justify that conception of morality as what morality ought to be ...'.[54]

As Kohlberg now accepts the distinction between the two theses, 'identity' vs. 'complementarity', and clearly affirms the complementarity interpretation,[55] it is important to try to elaborate more fully the nature of the connection being asserted.

In order to clarify how within a developmental theory such as Kohlberg's, psychology and philosophy might be 'complementary' (or how a psychological account of the 'is' of moral development might 'complement' a philosophical account of the 'ought' of moral judgment, and *vice versa*), it is necessary first to get a clearer picture of the nature of Kohlberg's empirical methodology—why, in short, he refers to his theory (following Habermas) as a 'rational reconstruction of developmental progress'.[56] Although there are substantive problems which I cannot go into here,[57] the essential point is that within Kohlberg's approach, empirical data are generated by one person (the interviewer) assuming an 'interpretive' or 'hermeneutical' stance *vis-à-vis* another person (the subject)—or at least this is the paradigmatic case underlying the approach. What this means is that the theoretical orientation of the interviewer's task is likened to that of interpretation, which 'rests on trying to come to agreement *with* another member of a speech-community who is *expressing his or her belief about something* in the world.'[58] In outlining how this orientation is manifested in his cognitive-structural approach, Kohlberg makes the following points:

> The first meaning of cognitive for us is that observations of others are made phenomenologically; i.e., by attempting to take the role of the other, to see things from his or her conscious viewpoint. Second, we mean by cognitive the fact that interviewing and scoring are acts of 'interpreting a text' around some shared philosophic categories of meaning. Insofar as each of us has been through the moral stages and has held the viewpoint of each stage, we should be able to put ourselves in the internal framework of a given stage. To understand others, to put oneself in the framework of others, is to be able to generate from their statements other statements that they can or do make from this framework, not because we are imposing upon them a framework to predict future speech acts but rather because we can organize the world as they do; i.e., for the moment we can share their meanings.[59]

Presented with a series of moral problems, or 'dilemmas', which invite the expressing and justifying of normative ought claims toward the solution of the problems, the subject is placed by the interviewer into what Habermas calls the 'performative attitude'.[60] But, given the interpretative stance of the interviewer outlined above, to some extent the interviewer *must also* assume this performative attitude. The stages that result from an analysis of the data so generated are then structural descriptions of the 'pattern of connections within the subjects' meaning', or the 'set of relations and transformations',[61] of the 'shared philosophic categories of meaning' identified as relevant by the end point of the stage sequence *performatively claimed by the interviewer*.[62] As Kohlberg puts it,

> The complementarity thesis to which we still subscribe makes the ... claim that an adequate psychological theory of stages and stage movement presupposes a normative theory of justice; first, to define the domain of justice reasoning and second, to function as one part of an explanation of stage development. For instance, the normative theoretical claim that a higher

stage is philosophically a better stage is one necessary part of a psychological explanation of sequential stage movement.[63]

The last sentence in this passage is, I believe, a more careful statement of what Kohlberg intended to convey in (b) (on p. 53 above), but which he overstated in terms of the different theoretical perspective being 'broadly the same'.

However, what Kohlberg now acknowledges more clearly in his acceptance of Habermas' characterization of the developmentalist's view of the 'is/ought' relationship as one of 'complementarity' is that, in order to give a full psychological explanation of the developmental progress through the stage sequence, the psychologist must adopt a perspective and utilize concepts and truthfulness checks which are 'external' to the interpretive stance which facilitates the reconstruction of qualitative changes in how the performative attitude in justice reasoning is manifested. As I noted above (p. 55), Habermas points out that the psychologist must at this point assume and be restricted to an 'objectivating' or 'third-person' attitude, one that seeks to explain the data in a way which meets the relevant standards of propositional truth claims. In Kohlberg's words,

> the psychological theory adds explanatory concepts in its explanation of ontogenesis, such as mechanisms of cognitive conflict, which are not reducible to the concepts of the normative philosophic theory.
> Thus, the empirical verification of the psychological stage theory does not directly confirm the normative validity of theories of justice ....[64]

In short, what this appears to me to leave room for is exactly the sort of difference between 'is' and 'ought' which preserves the 'critical leverage' of normative moral judgment.

What, then, does the 'complementarity thesis' come down to? There seem to be two ways in which it might be cashed out. One of them, primarily negative, is that which both Kohlberg and Habermas seem to be adopting. Although this way has some plausibility for some degree of doubt, or at an extreme level of 'ought', I believe it also could be interpreted as vitiating the difference between 'is' and 'ought' which we have just seen reaffirmed in Kohlberg. I will first examine this interpretation, and then, once again in the spirit of keeping the question open, I will briefly suggest a more positive interpretation which looks promising and avoids the problems.

First of all, as we have seen above (pp. 56–7), Habermas states the strength of the complementarity thesis in a negative mode: 'The success of an empirical theory which can only be true or false may function as a *check* on the normative validity of hypothetically reconstructed moral intuitions'; i.e., 'rational reconstructions can be *put on trial* or "*tested*".'[65] This claim is offered as the best interpretation which Kohlberg now clearly reaffirms: '... *falsification* of the empirical hypotheses of our psychological theory would, we believe, *cast doubt on* the validity of our normative theory of justice. In this sense, psychological findings can provide indirect support or evidence justification for the normative theory, although that theory also still requires philosophic or normative grounding....'[66] The problem here is that neither Kohlberg nor Habermas explains what is meant by phrases such as 'function as a check', 'put on trial or "tested"', or 'cast doubt on'. There are some senses which would perhaps yield a relatively unproblematic claim. Thus, to put it in Kohlberg's terms, if the 'doubt' that is 'cast on' one's sense of the rightness of a normative theory of justice is read as just '*some* doubt', rather than '*sufficient* doubt to reject', then the relationship suggested seems credible.[67] That is, it would mean simply that one might be reasonably motivated to rethink one's normative position, to examine its justification even more carefully, if empirical data indicated that human subjects showed no indication of developing in that direction, but instead, offered at a mature level a form of judgment fundamentally at odds with one's own position. But this would seem to me to amount to a much weaker relationship between psychological fact and normative 'ought'-claims than is suggested by 'complementarity'.

Similarly, I suppose also at some very extreme level this negative thesis must be true. That is, if one's normative theory levied extremely stringent 'oughts'—as in 'one ought *never* to act in one's own self-interest but always and only in the interest of the other'—then psychological evidence that humans do not appear ever to function this way would, indeed, 'cast doubt on' the normative validity of the theory, perhaps even considerably more than just '*some* doubt'. As philosophers are always fond of saying, 'ought implies can', and it is at least conceivable that psychology could establish something very close to 'cannots' for human beings. But this would again yield a much weaker sense of 'complementarity' than Kohlberg seems to be driving at.

On the other hand, for 'sufficient' doubt, or for anything less than these 'extremely stringent "oughts"', the danger is that this negative formation of 'complementarity' runs the risk of cutting the ground out from under the 'critical leverage' which our concept of 'ought' supplies. If negative empirical results relevant to some aspect of the psychological theory (such as the failure of a predicted developmental change within specified natural or experimental conditions) were seen as fundamentally threatening to the normative validity of the moral theory, then 'ought'-claims lose their unique power. On the sense of the 'is/ought' distinction with which I have been working, 'ought'-claims function to 'cast doubt on' the legitimacy or acceptability of the facts of the case, not the other way around. Moreover, although this is a complex question going beyond what I can deal with here (and probably necessitating a discussion of whether Kohlberg's research programme is progressive or regressive in Lakotosian terms), it seems to me that Kohlberg has shown little evidence of having his faith shaken in the normative validity of Stage 6, even though the empirical evidence has yet failed to verify its existence, and indeed the upper end of the sequence seems lacking in some cultures.[68] Rather than rejecting the normative position identified as Stage 6, he is more inclined to discuss what might be changed in our educational efforts, and why certain cultures might be lacking in sufficient social interaction, to effect a change in conditions such that people *would in fact* evidence the approved normative position. But this is not a criticism. Rather, the observation is meant to suggest that Kohlberg does indeed affirm the legitimate function of the normative 'ought' and thus the negative interpretation of the complementarity thesis, if I have understood it correctly, is difficult to maintain.

How might the complementarity thesis be given a more positive interpretation which avoids this problem? What it requires, I believe, is going back to the interpretive stance of the developmental psychologist outlined above. It seems to me that this stance is not entirely restricted to the attempt to understand from inside the way the other (subject) is determining moral meaning and rightness. Rather, as suggested by the earlier metaphor of the equidistant mirrors reflecting views of a common object, there is a sense in which it must also be 'extended in the different direction' of explanation. That is, as we saw above, in order to generate the data which facilitate the reconstruction of the ontogenesis of justice reasoning, the Kohlbergian interviewer must provisionally adopt the performative attitude along with the subject, to understand from the inside the subject's way of making and justifying 'ought'-claims of normative rightness in the context of certain kinds of moral problems. As Habermas explains this orientation, 'The performative attitude allows for a *mutual* orientation toward validity claims (such as truth, normative rightness, and sincerity), which are raised with the expectation of a "yes" or "no" reaction (or a quest for further reasons) on the part of the hearer.'[69] Assuming an interpretive stance, then, entails a mutual (both interviewer and subject) adopting of this performative attitude,[70] and the stages of moral judgment are coherent, consistent, and relatively stable patterns which can be reconstructed through this method. However, a simple description of these different patterns so determined does not fully constitute a developmental theory such as Kohlberg's; rather, what is also required is an account of how they are hierarchically ordered and why people change from one to the next. Part of this task will involve making predictions about what will happen in a variety of conditions and then utilizing the appropriate scientific methodology to test those predictions for truth, procedures which, as we have already noted above (p. 58), require restricting one's stance to an 'objectivating' or 'third-person' stance. However, it does not seem to me that *all* of this task can be so described; and thus, as I suggested above, Habermas may have overstated the case when he implies that the psychologist's orientation in this task of explanation is limited to *only* an objectivating attitude concerned with propositional truth alone.[71]

The point is this: the developmental psychologist is required not only to 'interpret' how a person is making and evaluating 'ought'-claims, but also to 'interpret' why a person would *change* their way of making and evaluating 'ought'-claims and why this change is systematic in a particular direction. Why is there change from '*X*' to '*Y*', say from Stage 3 to Stage 4, and not *vice versa*? Explaining this kind of change cannot be done solely from an objectivating attitude; to do so would be to give up the unique strength that this theory starts with, namely, the view of the subject as a constructive moral agent. Rather, in asking the general question, 'why do/did ... change from X to Y?', the psychologist must also assume mutuality with other subjects as a place holder in this question, thus also at the same time asking, 'why do/did *I* change from X to Y?' Thus part of a developmental psychological explanation of change *itself* requires the psychologist to adopt the performative attitude along with the subject, though now with regard to truth-claims rather than rightness-claims. But note that the '*X*' and '*Y*' in this task are not states of affairs, but rather, ways of making and evaluating 'ought'-claims, themselves derived through the assumption of an interpretive stance, and the *change* from '*X*' to '*Y*' is one about which it is appropriate to (and about which the subject *does*) make 'ought'-claims. Thus the developmental psychologist must also ask, along with the subject, 'why ought I change from "*X*" to "*Y*"?' In order to *make sense* to humans as moral agents, the psychological explanation of moral development must include the performative examination of this 'ought' question. Conversely, in order to be grounded in psychological reality, the justifiable normative position must be compatible with a performative examination of the 'is'-questions of change which account for how such a normative position can be manifested in human subjects. Although the direction of the theoretical perspectives of psychology and philosophy cannot be reduced to each other, neither alone gives us a whole picture of the phenomenon in common, moral judgment. Yet *how* they can complement each other is suggested by the common factor of the assumption of the performative attitude with regard to the different kinds of questions that have to be asked of the human subject experiencing moral development.[72] It is, I believe, this bi-dimensional, correlative adoption of the performative attitude by the developmental psychologist that best explains what lies behind the 'complementarity thesis' intended by Kohlberg. And it is also, finally, a rough blueprint for the work of constructing a bridge across the 'is/ought' gap at the border between development psychology and moral philosophy.

NOTES

1   P.H. Hirst, (1972) 'Liberal education and the nature of knowledge,' in R. F. Dearden, *et al.* (Eds.) *Education and Reason*, London, Routledge and Kegan Paul, pp. 15–16.
2   J. R. Snarey, (1985) 'Cross-Cultural Universality of Social-Moral Development: A Critical Review of Kohlbergian Research', *Psych. Bulletin*, 97, 1, p. 202.
3   See his often-repeated arguments against relativism, for example, in L. Kohlberg, (1971) 'From *is* to *ought*: How to commit the naturalistic fallacy and get away with it in the study of moral development,' in T. Mischel (Ed.), *Cognitive Development and Epistemology*, New York, Academic Press, pp. 151–235. This paper has been reprinted in L. Kohlberg (1981) *The Philosophy of Moral Development*, San Francisco; Calif., Harper and Row, pp. 101–89; and subsequent references to this paper will be to this source.
4   *Ibid.*
5   For example, see R. F. Kitchener, (1980) 'Genetic epistemology, normative epistemology, and psychologism,' *Synthese*, 45, pp. 257–80.
6   Instances of the former are legion, good examples being I. E. Aron (1977), 'Moral philosophy and moral education: A critique of Kohlberg's theory,' *School Review*, pp. 167–217; R. P. Craig (1978) 'Some thoughts on moral growth', *Journal of Thought*, 13, pp. 21–7; and S. Benhabib, 'The methodological illusions of modern political theory: The case of Rawls and Habermas', *Neue Hefte für Philosophie*, Vol. 21. An example of the latter is H. Siegel, (1981) 'Kohlberg, moral adequacy, and the justification of educational interventions', *Educational Theory*, 31, 3–4, pp. 275–84.
7   J. Habermas (1983) 'Interpretive social science vs. hermeneuticism', in N. Haan, *et al.* (Eds.) *Social Science as Moral Inquiry*, New York, Columbia University Press, p. 262.
8   Kohlberg, 'From *is* to *ought*', *op. cit.*, p. 102.
9   *Ibid.*, p. 136.
10 A. Colby, J. Gibbs, L. Kohlberg, B. Speicher-Dubin, and D. Candee, *The Measurement of Moral Judgment*, Vol. I: *Moral Stages and Their Scoring*, Cambridge, Cambridge University Press, in press, p. 14.
11 A. Blasi (1980) 'Bridging moral cognition and moral action: A critical review of the literature', *Psychological Bulletin*, 88, 1, p. 4.
12 *Ibid.*, p. 3.
13 There are, of course, exceptions to this within philosophy. But I think it is an accurate characterization of at least mainstream Western philosophy.
14 A. Colby *et al.*, *op. cit.*, p. 7.
15 *Ibid*; also see L. Kohlberg (1976) 'Moral stages and moralization: The cognitive-development approach', in T. Lickona (Ed.) *Moral Development and Behavior: Theory, Research, and Social Issues*, New York, Holt, Rinehart and Winston, pp. 31–5.
16 A. Colby, *et al.*, *op. cit.*; also see A. Colby, *et al.* (1983) 'A longitudinal study of moral development', *Monographs of the Society for Research in Child Development*, 48, pp. 1–106.
17 I hasten to add that these labels are *not* self-explanatory but defined idiosyncratically within the scoring system, with, e.g., 'Issues' and 'Norms' apparently referring to the *same* nine basic 'values', but used at different levels of interpretation.

18   A. Colby, *et al.*, *The Measurement of Moral Judgment*, *op. cit.*, p. 59.
19   *Ibid.*, pp. 59–60.
20   *Ibid.*, p 62.
21   *Ibid.*, p. 73.
22   See J. R. Snarey (1985) *op. cit.* for the former argument; and see J. C. Gibbs (1979) 'Kohlberg's moral stage theory. A Piagetian revision', *Human Development*, 22, pp. 89–112 for the latter argument.
23   J. R. Snarey, *op. cit.* and A. Colby *et al.*, 'A longitudinal study of moral judgment', *op. cit.*
24   Kohlberg, 'From *is* to *ought*', *op. cit.*, p. 182.
25   Obviously for this to work one would have to be far more sophisticated in how the definition was couched—i.e., it would have to sound natural as well as express the relevant core idea.
26   'From *is* to *ought*', *op. cit.*, p. 182.
27   *Ibid.*, p. 181.
28   S. Toulmin (1971) 'The concept of "stages" in psychological development', in Mischel, T. (Ed.) *Cognitive Development and Epistemology*, Academic Press, p. 41; R. Halstead has made a similar argument in 'Cognitive structures and forms of knowledge', in I. Steinberg, (Ed.) (1977) *Philosophy of Education 1977*, Philosophy of Education Society, pp. 203–14.
29   A. MacIntyre (1981) *After Virtue: A Study in Moral Theory*, Notre Dame, Ind.: University of Notre Dame Press.
30   For the classic collection of such attempts and critiques of them, see W. D. Hudson, (Ed.) (1969) *The Is/Ought Question: A Collection of Papers on the Central Problem in Moral Philosophy*, London, Macmillan; for a more recent review, see K. Nielsen (1979) 'On deriving an ought from an is: A retrospective look', *Review of Metaphysics*, 32, pp. 487–514.
31   T. D. Perry (1976) *Moral Reasoning and Truth: An Essay in Philosophy and Jurisprudence*, London, Oxford University Press; see also, D. Boyd, (1984) 'The principle of principles', in J. L. Gewirtz, and W. M. Kurtines, (Eds.) *Morality, Moral Development, and Moral Behavior: Basic Issues in Theory and Research*, New York, John Wiley and Sons. For a different implication of viewing justification as not equivalent to deductive argument, see K. Witkowski (1975) 'The "is-ought" gap: Deduction or justification?' *Philosophy and Phenomenological Research*, 36, pp. 233–45.
32   L. Kohlberg, C. Levine and A. Hewer (1983) *Moral Stages: A Current Formulation and a Response to Critics*, Basel, Switzerland, Karger, p. 12.
33   *Ibid.*, pp. 13–14.
34   *Ibid.*, pp. 60–4.
35   See, for example, Aron (1977) *op. cit.*
36   Kohlberg, 'From *is* to *ought*', *op. cit.*, p. 105.
37   Depending on how this is interpreted, it might or might not reduce to 'Interpretation 1' above.
38   Kohlberg, 'From *is* to *ought*', *op. cit.*, pp. 177–8.
39   *Ibid.*, p. 111; I am indebted to Cynthia Crysdale for drawing this argument to my attention.
40   See, for instance, Siegel (1981) *op. cit.*, pp. 275–84.
41   K. Nielsen, (1979) 'On deriving an ought from an is: A retrospective look', *Review of Metaphysics*, 32, pp. 487–8.
42   Kohlberg, 'From *is* to *ought*', *op. cit.*, p. 178.
43   *Ibid.*, p. 179.
44   *Ibid.*, p. 104.
45   Kohlberg *et al.*, *Moral Stages*, *op. cit.*
46   Kohlberg, 'From *is* to *ought*', *op. cit.*, p. 180.
47   *Ibid.*, p. 135.
48   *Ibid.*, p. 180.
49   One of the best efforts at this that I know of is found in Siegel (1981) *op. cit.*, pp. 279–80.
50   For another, more detailed statement of this claim, see D. Boyd and L. Kohlberg (1973) 'The is-ought problem: A developmental perspective', *Zygon*, 8, 3–4, pp. 358–72.
51   Habermas (1983) *op. cit.*, pp. 265–6.
52   *Ibid.*, p. 266.
53   Kohlberg *et al.*, *Moral Stages*, *op. cit.*, p. 16.
54   Habermas (1983) *op. cit.*, pp. 266–7. The quotation is from the passage quoted above from Kohlberg, see p. 52–3 and Note 38.
55   Kohlberg *et al.*, *Moral Stages*, *op. cit.*, pp. 15–17.
56   See passage quoted on p. 51 above, cited in Note 33.

57 For a discussion of some of them, see Habermas (1983) *op. cit.*

58 Kohlberg *et al.*, *Moral Stages*, *op. cit.*, p. 11.

59 *Ibid.*, pp. 11–12.

60 See Habermas (1983) *op. cit.*

61 Colby *et al.*, *The Measurement of Moral Judgment op. cit.*, p. 6.

62 In what way and how much the necessary assumption of a guiding normative framework within a 'developmental' theory qualifies the interpretive nature of moral judgment interviewing is a problem in much need of further discussion. It is clearly one dimension of the critique C. Gilligan (1982) is offering of Kohlberg's work in *In a Different Voice: Psychological Theory and Women's Development*, Cambridge, Mass, Harvard University Press.

63 Kohlberg *et al.*, *Moral Stages*, *op. cit.*, p. 16.

64 *Ibid.*

65 See note 54, my emphasis.

66 Kohlberg *et al.*, *Moral Stages*, *op. cit.*, p. 16, my emphasis.

67 I am indebted to Andrew Blair for bringing this point to my attention.

68 Snarey (1985) *op. cit.*

69 Habermas (1983) *op. cit.*, p. 255.

70 The interview is not completely 'mutual', of course, because the interviewer is almost exclusively in the role of the 'hearer', whereas the subject is kept almost exclusively in the role of the one uttering and attempting to redeem validity claims of rightness. Still, it *is* mutual in the sense that in order to generate useful data, the interviewer *must* genuinely attempt to *understand* the claims and justifications offered by the subject. One cannot help but wonder what would be the outcome of a more completely mutual 'interview' methodology, if it were possible. However, that the general claims for the stages are not vitiated by this problem is suggested very strongly by studies of dialogue, such as that of M. W. Berkowitz, J. C. Gibbs, and J. M. Broughton (1980) 'The relation of moral judgment stage disparity to developmental effects of peer dialogues', *Merrill-Palmer Quarterly*, 26, 4, pp. 341–57.

71 See p. 55 above, and Note 52.

72 I think that this does make sense of what Kohlberg may be after; and *perhaps*, though I am less sure, this may also be close to what Habermas means when he says rather cryptically, 'Finally, the relation of mutually fitting together suggests that the hermeneutic circle comes to its full closure only on the metatheoretical level' Habermas, (1983) *op. cit.*, p. 267.

ACKNOWLEDGEMENT

I would like to express my appreciation to Dr Charles Levine for many helpful discussions on the topic of this paper.

5. On Using Psychology to Justify Judgments of Moral Adequacy[1]

HARVEY SIEGEL

Research in moral education has been dominated for two decades by the work of Lawrence Kohlberg. A crucial feature of Kohlberg's conception of moral education is his view that we ought to help students to move through natural stages of development; and his attempts to foster moral development in the schools are attempts to facilitate the attainment, by students, of the highest stage of moral development it is possible for the students to reach.[2] Such intervention in schools is justified, according to Kohlberg, by his claim that higher stages of development are more adequate, morally, than lower stages. That is, for any given Stage S, Kohlberg claims that S is more adequate morally than the prior Stage $S-1$. Kohlberg claims that his empirical research helps to substantiate the claim to moral adequacy of higher stages of development; this is why he has devoted so much attention to the question of whether or not he has committed the naturalistic fallacy in his argument for the moral adequacy of higher stages.[3]

It seems clear that intervention in the schools in order to promote moral development through the stages can be justified only if Kohlberg is correct that higher stages are more adequate morally than lower stages.[4] Thus the claim to moral adequacy of higher stages plays a crucial role in Kohlberg's conception of moral education, both theoretically and in terms of practice—that is, in terms of intervention in the schools. However, as has been recently pointed out, the argument that Kohlberg puts forth in defence of the claim to moral adequacy of higher stages has never been subjected to serious scrutiny.[5] In this paper I will examine that argument. In particular, I will be concerned to investigate the way in which Kohlberg uses his psychological research findings to support the claim to moral adequacy. I will argue that the claim to moral adequacy of higher stages is not supported by Kohlberg's empirical findings, and consequently that Kohlbergian interventions in the schools to promote development through the stages are unjustified.[6] More generally, I will argue that judgments of moral adequacy must themselves be justified by appeal to considerations of a moral philosophical sort, and cannot be justified on the basis of empirical psychological research findings. Since no judgments of moral adequacy can be justified on the basis of empirical research, it follows *a fortiori* that Kohlberg's claim to moral adequacy of higher stages cannot itself be so justified. And since Kohlbergian educational interventions are themselves dependent for their justification on the claim to moral adequacy of higher stages, the failure of Kohlberg's argument to justify the latter constitutes a failure to justify the former as well.

In the penultimate section of this paper, I will argue that this result can be generalized: educational interventions as such cannot be justified by empirical research findings. Empirical research, while central to the planning and execution of educational interventions, is impotent with respect to the justification of those interventions.

WHAT ARE THE RESEARCH FINDINGS?

Kohlberg has reviewed his research in several publications. Here I shall briefly enumerate the major results. First, Kohlberg claims to have uncovered 'natural stages' of moral development: people generally progress through specifiable approaches to moral situations. These approaches are characterized not in terms of particular values or moral positions, but rather in terms of the form of moral reasoning engaged in. The stages, Kohlberg claims, are universal—that is, they are gone through by all people, irrespective of culture or society; and they are invariant—that is, they have a unique sequence, and people never violate the order of the stages by attaining a higher stage without first passing sequentially through lower ones. The stages constitute 'structured wholes', or as Kohlberg puts it, 'total ways of thinking, not attitudes toward particular situations.'[7] There are six stages, divided into three levels: the preconventional, conventional, and postconventional stages. Nevertheless, whatever stage a person does reach, that stage is only reached after passing through the sequence of prior stages.

Kohlberg's empirical findings have been reported in a number of publications; consequently I will refrain from reviewing them in any more detail here.[8] His findings have been criticized on empirical grounds in a number of places.[9] Here, however, I am not concerned to question the empirical adequacy of Kohlberg's research. Rather, I am concerned with a different question, namely: given Kohlberg's empirical results, to what extent do they support his argument for the moral adequacy of higher stages? It is to this question I now turn.

THE ARGUMENT FOR MORAL ADEQUACY

How does Kohlberg seek to use his research findings to justify his educational intervention programmes? He does not simply declare that what is, is what ought to be; that whatever the facts of moral development are, we ought to encourage continued (and intensified) development along those lines. This, as Kohlberg recognizes, would be an unjustifiable move, and a straightforward commitment of the naturalistic fallacy.[10] Instead, Kohlberg formulates an argument that proceeds as follows:

(a) Higher stages are more adequate *psychologically* than lower stages.
(b) There is a *parallelism*, or *isomorphism*, between the proper characterizations of the psychological and the moral adequacy of the stages.
(c) Therefore, higher stages are more adequate *morally* than lower stages.

While difficulties with the above argument centre on step (b), it is important for an understanding of the argument to be clear on step (a) as well. Hence I begin with it.

(a) In What Sense Does Kohlberg Claim That Higher Stages Are More Adequate Psychologically Than Lower Stages?

The argument begins with Piaget's work in cognitive development. Kohlberg accepts and works within the general perspective of cognitive-developmental psychology, which holds that people progress, from birth to 'cognitive maturity', through various levels, or stages, of development. The stages are marked off from each other by a general appraisal of integration, differentiation, and problem-solving or conflict-resolution ability, the higher stages being more capable of resolving cognitive conflict than the lower stages.[11] As we have seen, the stages are invariant, in that people generally move in the same direction: from relatively little conflict-resolution ability to increasingly refined resolution ability. This ability is termed (by Piaget) 'adaptiveness' (on the biological model), so that the higher, more integrated and differentiated stage is the more adaptive stage. Within this framework of developmental psychology, the more adaptive stage is the stage which better handles and resolves cognitive conflict, and so is the 'better' or 'more adequate' stage. Each stage is

> a structure which, formally considered, is in better equilibrium than its predecessor ... each new (logical or moral) stage is a new structure which includes elements of earlier structures but transforms them in such a way as to represent a more stable and extensive equilibrium.[12]

A structure which is in equilibrium is able to resolve problems which a disequili-brated structure cannot. Thus, equilibrium is related to problem-solving capability: the more equilibrated a cognitive structure is, the more able it is to resolve problems. Moreover, more equilibrated structures are more differentiated and integrated than less equilibrated structures. Thus equilibrium, differentiation, and integration are formal criteria by which the psychological adequacy of stages is judged. The more equilibrated, differentiated, and integrated a stage (or 'cognitive structure') is, the more adequate it is, psychologically.[13]

Kohlberg extends this general conception of psychological adequacy into the area of morality by conceiving of moral reasoning as a cognitive problem-solving endeavour: 'the sphere of morality or moral principles, we define as principles of choice for resolving conflicts of obligations.'[14] Moral deliberation, then, is simply a subset of the set of cognitive deliberations. As such, moral reasoning can be measured and 'staged', like any other reasoning, according to criteria of differentia-tion, integration, equilibrium and conflict-resolution ability: a more adequate psychological stage can solve problems better than a less adequate stage. Problem-resolution ability improves as one's cognitive faculties become more sophisticated and complex in the interaction with one's environment. That is to say, one's cognitive faculties become more adaptive, are better suited to resolving cognitive conflict, as one gains fluency in integrating and differentiating information. The criteria of differentiation and integration are the formal measures of cognitive adaptiveness and psychological adequacy, in that the higher level of differentiation and integration marks off the higher or more adequate cognitive stage. As Kohlberg says, 'These combined criteria, differentiation and integration, are considered by developmental theory to entail a better equilibrium of the structure in question. A more differentiated and integrated moral structure handles more moral problems, conflicts, or points of view in a more stable or self-consistent way.'[15] Higher stages of moral reasoning, then, Kohlberg claims, because they are more differentiated and integrated, and so are more satisfactorily equilibrated and able to resolve moral conflicts, are more adequate psychologically than lower stages of moral reasoning.

(b)   In What Sense Is There an Isomorphism between the Characterizations of Psychological and Philosophical Adequacy of Higher Stages?

It is extremely difficult to pin Kohlberg down on this question. Nevertheless, the isomorphism plays a crucial role in the argument for the moral adequacy of higher stages. Consequently, we shall be concerned to delineate and assess this 'isomorphism claim' in the bulk of the remainder of this essay.

　　　Kohlberg asserts the claim in many places. For example, he writes that

> while psychological theory and normative ethical theory are not reducible to each other, the two enterprises are isomorphic or *parallel*. In other words, an adequate psychological analysis of the structure of a moral judgment, and an adequate normative analysis of the judgment will be made in similar terms. The logical relations between stages represent indifferently the structure of an adequate theory of moral judgment development, or the structure of an adequate theory as to why one system of moral judgment is better than another.[16]

What is the nature of this parallelism or isomorphism? How does it function in the argument for moral adequacy? And how do Kohlberg's empirical research findings support the isomorphism claim, and so the moral adequacy claim? Investigation reveals that Kohlberg actually provides an argument with three separable strands, all of which attempt to fill out the isomorphism claim. For ease of presentation, we may call these strands of the argument for moral adequacy the *structural adequacy* strand; the *mapping* strand; and the *explanation* strand. We will take these in order, our aim being to see how, or if, they either separately or jointly legitimate the isomorphism step (step b) of Kohlberg's argument for the moral adequacy of higher stages of development.

(i)   The Structural Adequacy Strand

We have seen earlier that certain formal properties of cognitive structures, namely integration and differentiation (and so equilibrium), are taken by cognitive-developmental psychology to be criteria of psychological adequacy. We have also seen that such adequacy extends, according to Kohlberg, to moral structures or patterns of moral reasoning, so that moral structures can also be evaluated in terms of psychological adequacy. The structural adequacy strand of the isomorphism argument simply extends the developmental conception of psychological adequacy to judgments of moral adequacy as well: because stages of moral reasoning have formal characteristics (integration, differentiation, etc.), those stages which are more adequate formally or structurally, and so more adequate psychologically, are *ipso facto* more adequate morally. That is, structural criteria of adequacy constitute criteria of moral as well as psychological adequacy:

> Both psychological and philosophical analyses suggest that the more mature stage of moral thought is the more structurally adequate. This greater adequacy of more mature moral judgments rests on structural criteria.... These general criteria are the *formal* criteria developmental theory holds as defining all mature structures, the criteria of increased differentiation and integration.[17]

Moral judgments are more 'mature' morally, then, insofar as they are more structurally adequate. Does such moral maturity constitute moral adequacy? Kohlberg acknowledges that the mere 'fact' of structural adequacy cannot by itself constitute an argument for moral adequacy,[18] and that to argue that a higher stage is more adequate morally simply because it is more adequate structurally would be to commit a version of the naturalistic fallacy. The structural adequacy strand, as Kohlberg recognizes, thus does not by itself validate the isomorphism claim. Kohlberg extends this strand of the argument by interweaving it with the 'mapping' strand; to this we now turn.

(ii)   The Mapping Strand

Kohlberg continues the just-cited passage as follows: 'These formal criteria (differentiation and integration) of development map into the formal criteria which philosophers of the formalist school have held to characterize genuine or adequate moral judgments.'[19] Here we reach the crux of the isomorphism argument. Kohlberg argues that his account of the psychological adequacy of higher stages of moral development *maps into*, or is *isomorphic* or *parallel* to, criteria of moral adequacy which are independently justified on philosophical grounds. At this point we need to examine both the nature of the mapping or isomorphism relation, and the philosophical justification of formal criteria of moral adequacy to which Kohlberg appeals.

First, let us consider the mapping relation. Just how do formal criteria of psychological adequacy map into formal criteria of moral adequacy? What are the criteria of moral adequacy Kohlberg appeals to as being isomorphic to criteria of psychological adequacy? They are the criteria of *prescriptivity* and *universalizability*:

> What we are claiming is that developmental theory assumes formalistic criteria of adequacy, the criteria of levels of *differentiation* and *integration*. In the moral domain, these criteria are parallel to formalistic moral philosophy's criteria of *prescriptivity* and *universality*. These two criteria combined represent a formalistic definition of the moral, with each stage representing a successive differentiation of the moral from the nonmoral and a more full realization of the moral form.[20]

Kohlberg claims, then, that developmental psychology's formal criteria of differentiation and integration map into, respectively, moral philosophy's formal criteria of prescriptivity and universalizability. Moral judgments become increasingly differentiated as they progress through the stages, and so are more adequate psychologically; such increasingly differentiated judgments are also, Kohlberg argues, increasingly prescriptive in that moral judgments become increasingly independent of factual considerations relevant to such judgments. For example, as one makes moral judgments concerning the worth of human life, while moving up through the stages, one's judgments become increasingly prescriptive in that

> the moral imperative to value life becomes increasingly independent of the factual properties of the life in question. First, the person's furniture becomes irrelevant to his value; next, whether he has a loving family, and so on. (It is correspondingly a series of differentiation of moral considerations from other value considerations.)[21]

Similarly, the psychological criterion of integration maps into the moral criterion of universalizability:

> Corresponding to the criterion of integration is the moral question of universality, which is closely linked to the criterion of consistency, as formalists since Kant have stressed. The claim of principled morality is that it defines the right for anyone in any situation.[22]

Thus, higher stages of moral judgment are more adequate psychologically in that they are more integrated; they are also more adequate morally in that they are more universalizable. Universalizable judgments are more integrated than non-universalizable judgments in that they 'fit' (integrate) everyone into an over-arching system of judgment: by treating everyone alike, all are integrated into 'principled morality,' and none has special consideration that others lack.[23]

There are some obvious difficulties with certain aspects of the 'mapping' relation. For example, is it the case that moral judgments which are less differentiated (lower stage judgments) are less prescriptive? It is difficult to see why this is so. A lower stage judgment (e.g., 'Don't kill Jones, because she has good furniture') may be undifferentiated in that the worth of Jones as a person is not distinguished from the worth of Jones's furniture, but the judgment is nevertheless fully prescriptive.[24] However, I will refrain from the pursuit of such difficulties in order to turn directly to our central concern, namely: how (if at all) does Kohlberg's isomorphism claim contribute to the establishment of the claim to moral adequacy? That is, given (for the sake of argument) the 'parallelism' between differentiation and integration on the psychological side of adequacy of moral reasoning, and prescriptivity and universalizability on the philosophical side of adequacy of moral reasoning, how does the parallelism contribute to the establishment of the moral adequacy of higher stages of development?

The first thing to note is that the formal criteria Kohlberg appeals to as criteria of moral adequacy—universalizability and prescriptivity—are controversial, philosophically. That is to say, these are not generally recognized as legitimate criteria of moral adequacy; non-formalists (e.g., utilitarians or egoists) need not and would not recognize them as *bona fide* criteria of moral adequacy. The appeal to a formalistic meta-ethical position needs to be justified. Kohlberg rightly points out that formalists generally recognize these criteria.[25] But this does not justify the adoption of a formalist meta-ethics. Further argument is needed,[26] which Kohlberg does not provide.

More importantly, even if such argument were forthcoming and successful, what would be shown? It would be shown that formalism is a correct meta-ethical position, and so that the formal criteria of adequacy of moral judgment favoured by formalists—prescriptivity and universalizability—are indeed correct criteria of moral adequacy. This would be shown on philosophical, not psychological grounds; as Kohlberg acknowledges, while psychological study may help isolate formal criteria of moral adequacy, such criteria must be justified, or defended, on philosophical, not psychological, grounds.[27] So, the legitimacy of formal criteria of moral adequacy would be established independently of psychological considerations. Thus, if the claim to moral adequacy is correct—that is, if higher stages of moral judgment are indeed superior, morally, to lower stages, that moral fact is independent of the psychological fact (if it is one) that higher stages are psychologically superior to lower ones. The claim to moral adequacy, then, if it is defensible, is so only because the stages, as they ascend, better satisfy criteria of moral adequacy established independently of the psychological facts of moral development.

What role, then, can the isomorphism claim play in the argument for moral adequacy? Contrary to Kohlberg, it seems that the answer is 'none'. The fact (if it is one) that there is a parallelism between psychological and moral criteria of adequacy is, strictly speaking, irrelevant to the claim to moral adequacy. If higher stages are indeed more morally adequate than lower stages, then they would be so even if the facts of moral development were different than Kohlberg claims they are. Suppose people developed differently than Kohlberg's research indicates— suppose, that is, they developed through a random sequence of stages, or that they developed sequentially from Stage 6 through Stage 1, or that development was not universal so that people had different sequences of development from one another—if the claim to moral adequacy could be justified, we would still have to say that Stage 6 was morally superior to Stage 5, Stage 5 to Stage 4, and so on. In short, the evaluation of the moral adequacy of stages of moral reasoning and judgment is independent of the psychological facts of moral development, and those psychological facts are irrelevant to the establishment of the moral adequacy of the stages. Kohlberg is correct that the higher stage is more morally adequate than a lower stage only if the formalist criteria of moral adequacy on which he relies can be substantiated (as he recognizes, independently of the psychological data he amassed); but if those criteria can be substantiated, the psychological data he has amassed do not contribute to the argument for the claim to moral adequacy.[28]

(iii)   The Explanation Strand

As we have just seen, the structural adequacy strand and the mapping strand of the isomorphism claim fail, either separately or jointly, to establish that claim. The third strand of the isomorphism argument, the explanation strand, construes the isomorphism between psychological and philosophical adequacy as concerned with the ability of Kohlberg's theory to explain movement through the stages: 'the reasons which justify the judgments derived from one stage over those derived from the preceding one also figure in the explanation why a person moves to this stage from the preceding stage.'[29] So the isomorphism between psychological and philosophical adequacy has to do with reasons for stage change doing double duty: on the one hand, they explain why a person moves from stage to stage; on the other hand, they account for the moral adequacy of the move. This latter is done by showing that the later stage (moved to) is superior, according to the formal criteria of prescriptivity and universalizability, to the earlier stage (moved from). How is the former accounted for? Kohlberg suggests that we explain why people in fact move through the stages in terms of their ability to perceive the higher stage as the more adequate (in that it better satisfies formal criteria of psychological adequacy). People (perhaps unconsciously) recognize as superior those patterns of reasoning (which they can comprehend) which are most differentiated and integrated, and they prefer such patterns. The patterns are more adequate psychologically in that they are more differentiated and integrated; because of the mapping relation, they are also more prescriptive and universalizable. Hence that which justifies the higher stage as more morally adequate—its formal characteristics—also explains why people progress through the stages. They progress through the sequence of stages because in fact they prefer the highest stage (most adequate psychologically in terms of formal characteristics) they can comprehend. Isomorphic formal properties thus both justify and explain the movement through the stages. As Kohlberg puts it,

> an ultimately adequate psychological theory as to why a child does move from stage to stage, and an ultimately adequate philosophical explanation as to why a higher stage is more adequate than a lower stage are one and the same theory extended in different directions.[30]

Let us suppose that Kohlberg's explanation of stage change in terms of perceived formal (psychological) adequacy is satisfactory. Would this finding, coupled with the isomorphism between this explanation and the formalist account of moral adequacy, contribute to the establishment of the claim to moral adequacy of higher stages of moral development? Again, the answer is 'no'. For even if Kohlberg is correct that people progress the stages because they prefer the stage which more adequately satisfies the formal psychological criteria of differentiation and integration, the moral preferability of higher stages still rests on independent substantiation of the formal moral criteria of prescriptivity and universalizability. If it turned out that people preferred stages which were not more adequate psychologically, while the isomorphism between formal psychological and formal moral criteria was preserved, then the explanation of children's preferences for (psychologically) less adequate stages, while no longer isomorphic to the philosophical account of the moral justifiability of higher stages, would in no way challenge that philosophical account. Conversely, if Kohlberg is correct that people prefer stages which are more adequate psychologically, while the isomorphism between psychological adequacy and moral adequacy could not be sustained, then the explanation of children's preferences for (psychologically) more adequate stages would not in and of itself constitute an argument for the moral adequacy of those preferred (psychologically more adequate) stages. In other words, if on philosophical grounds we could conclude that higher stages are more adequate morally than lower stages, such a conclusion would be sustained even if the psychological facts of development, and the psychological explanation of those facts, were not 'isomorphic' or even compatible with that conclusion. Which is to say simply that the moral adequacy of higher stages is independent of the explanation of movement through the stages. While the parallel Kohlberg draws between the psychological explanation of movement through the stages and the philosophical justification of that movement is ingenious, that psychological explanation, like the psychological facts explained, is irrelevant to the determination of the moral adequacy of the stages.[31]

We are forced to conclude that neither the three strands of the isomorphism claim, nor Kohlberg's research findings or explanation of those findings, contributes to the establishment of the claim to moral adequacy of higher stages of moral development. Kohlberg's argument for the claim to moral adequacy (sketched earlier) is simply a *non sequitur*: it is not clear that step (b) is correct; even if it is, step (c) simply does not follow from (a) and (b). If (c) (the claim to moral adequacy of higher stages) is correct, it is correct independently of (a) and (b), and depends on philosophical substantiation of the adequacy of the criteria of moral adequacy Kohlberg appeals to.

THE ARGUMENT RE-APPLIED: GILLIGAN AND THE DEVELOPMENT OF 'WOMEN'S MORALITY'

The same point can be made with respect to the moral psychology of Kohlberg's colleague and critic, Carol Gilligan. Gilligan has criticized Kohlberg's research, in particular his longitudinal studies, for involving only male subjects, and for generalizing what she claims is male moral experience to females as well. In fact, Gilligan claims, female moral experience is radically different from male moral experience, in that while men develop a morality of justice, women develop a morality of care; while men view moral conflict as a conflict of rights, women view it as a conflict of responsibilities; and while men strive in their moral judgments to achieve autonomy, independence, and detachment, women seek to retain in their moral judgments a central place for contextual considerations, dependence on relationships, and attachment to their social situations.[32] Gilligan argues for women's alternative conceptions of self and morality largely on the basis of her own psychological research, and sees her work mainly as a contribution to the psychology of development which calls to our attention the fact that women's conceptions of self and morality develop differently from men's, and the fact that developmental theorists have by and large frustrated a proper understanding of development by generalizing from males to persons, by ignoring the developmental patterns of women, and by offering as a result conceptions of development which are inadequate, one-sided, and incomplete.

As with the above discussion of Kohlberg, I have no bones to pick with the results of Gilligan's research. Let us grant that women do in fact develop conceptions of self and morality as Gilligan describes. What follows for morality? That is, what follows for our judgments concerning the rightness of the conceptions and judgments women develop and make? I want to argue that, strictly speaking, nothing follows: the fact that women develop a morality of care and concern does not justify or demonstrate the rightness of such a morality, any more than the fact that men develop as Kohlberg describes justifies or demonstrates the rightness of that morality. In Gilligan's case, as in Kohlberg's, judgments of moral adequacy must be justified independently of the facts of development.

It must be emphasized that Gilligan sees her work as contributing mainly to psychology, not moral philosophy; in general she refrains from arguing that, since women conceive morality as she describes, their judgments are therefore correct or justified on that ground. (Although Gilligan is not always careful in this regard: she writes, for example, that she hopes her work 'will offer a representation of their [i.e., women's] thought that enables them to see better its integrity and *validity* ...',[33] thus suggesting that women's conceptions of morality are somehow self-validating.) In this respect Gilligan acknowledges the autonomy of judgments of moral adequacy from the vagaries of the psychology of development. And this, I have argued, is as it should be, since judgments of moral adequacy must be justified independently of the facts of psychology. It no more follows that a moral judgment arrived at *via* a developmental process which enhances considerations of care and concern is for that reason more adequate morally than a judgment which fails to honour such considerations, than that a moral judgment of Kohlberg's Stage 4 is more adequate morally than a judgment of Stage 3 because of the developmental scheme that Kohlberg has drawn attention to. In either case the justification of claims of moral adequacy must be had in terms other than those which focus on the facts of development.[34]

THE ARGUMENT GENERALIZED: EMPIRICAL RESEARCH IS IMPOTENT WITH RESPECT TO THE JUSTIFICATION OF EDUCATION INTERVENTION

We have seen thus far that Kohlberg's research findings concerning natural stages of moral development do not contribute to the justification of the claim to moral adequacy of higher stages, and so of the moral education intervention programme he has initiated. The argument for the moral adequacy of higher stages is unsuccessful; in addition, the isomorphism claim, central to the argument for moral adequacy and also to Kohlberg's way of relating his research findings to his educational intervention programme, does not justify the latter, as Kohlberg hopes. There can be no good argument, based on psychological evidence, for the moral adequacy of higher stages of development, but it is this sort of adequacy that is necessary for the justification of Kohlbergian educational interventions. If higher stages are indeed more adequate morally than lower stages, this must be shown by moral argument, and psychological data are strictly speaking irrelevant to such argument. If, on the other hand, higher stages are not more adequate morally than lower stages, any programme which seeks to facilitate movement through the stages is without justification.[35]

These results, if correct, raise a troubling question: how can any moral education intervention be justified? I have suggested elsewhere that educators have certain obligations to students and that among these obligations are the obligations (1) to help students reach moral maturity (in part) by inculcating specific habits, dispositions, and skills necessary for mature moral thinking and acting; (2) to treat students with respect as persons; and (3) to help students become self-sufficient and competent to guide rationally their own lives.[36] Moral education intervention, on this view, is justified on the same grounds as all educational intervention: namely, in terms of our obligation to help students to become rational persons. We are obliged to, and so justified in trying to, help children become rational persons; because being rational involves (in part) being moral, we are likewise obliged to, and so justified in trying to, help children become moral. That is, we are obliged to develop, and are justified in developing and implementing moral education interventions, insofar as these programmes are genuine attempts to realize the just-mentioned goals. While this brief sketch needs to be greatly expanded, the general approach here suggested seems to me to be the only way education interventions can be justified.[37]

I hasten to reiterate that my remarks concern all educational intervention, not just moral education intervention, for justification of the latter is simply a special case or subset of the former. Consider, for instance, the justification of reading programmes; that is, educational interventions designed to improve students' reading skills. It is of course correct that empirical research on information processing of the written word would be relevant to the design and execution of such programmes. But does research serve to justify such programmes? No. It does not for the same reason that research concerning, e.g., effective torture techniques, would not justify efforts to help students become effective torturers. In both cases the intervention must be justified independently of research; though of course once justified, research is clearly relevant to the planning and execution of the intervention. We do not justify teaching students to read on grounds of the nature of information processing; rather, we justify educational interventions to facilitate reading on the grounds that it is in some sense *good* for students to be able to read (I would argue that it is good for students to become proficient readers because it facilitates their achievement of self-sufficiency and rationality),[38] then turn to information processing (and other) research to see how best to organize the intervention. Thus it is not the case that only in the realm of moral education intervention is empirical research impotent with respect to justification. Such impotence is universal.

Appeal to the results of educational (or psychological) research to justify educational intervention, then, appears to be doomed to fruitlessness. For the results of the present investigation seem clear: however disconcerting it may be to empirically minded sorts, educational intervention simply cannot be justified by the results of educational research. For, as argued earlier, such research is, strictly speaking, irrelevant to the justification of those interventions.

Of course this does not mean that educational research is otiose. Quite the contrary. While educational research may not serve to justify educational interventions—in our extended example, Kohlberg's research findings concerning 'natural stages' of development do not justify moral education programmes designed to hasten students' progress through the stages—there is still much that educational research can do. If, for instance, Kohlberg is right that the highest stage of moral development is the morally most adequate stage of moral reasoning (despite the fact that his own argument to that end we found wanting), then we would naturally turn to appropriate research to find out how best to facilitate the attainment by the student of that form of moral reasoning. This might involve, for example, research aimed at developing ways of getting children to skip stages—a possibility even Kohlberg must recognize, since his evidence for the invariance of sequence of moral stages refers to 'merely the untutored response to social interactions during the maturing years.'[39] Likewise, if my view that educational intervention is justified in terms of our obligation to help students become rational persons is correct, we would naturally turn to appropriate research to find out how best to facilitate the attainment by the student of the knowledge, skills, traits, and dispositions which constitute the embodiment of our conception of rational persons.[40] In any case, educational research will direct our efforts to realize our goals, and clearly plays a crucially important instrumental role in our conceiving and executing of educational interventions. Nevertheless, such research is not to be expected to justify those interventions. For this, educational theorists and researchers alike need to look beyond the results of research.

CONCLUSION

In the previous section I have concentrated on a ramification for practice of this paper's central contention, namely that the justification of educational interventions is independent of the results of research. But the central contention does not directly concern (educational) practice; it is rather a point about the relationship between (developmental) psychology and moral philosophy. That relationship, I have argued, is, however rich it may be in other respects, thoroughly impoverished in the respect I have been focusing on: judgments of moral adequacy must be justified independently of psychological information regarding the origins and development of such judgments. Neither Kohlberg nor anyone else can justify judgments of moral adequacy by appeal to the facts of development.

NOTES

1   Portions of this paper borrow heavily from my 'Kohlberg, moral adequacy, and the justification of educational interventions', *Educational Theory*, 31, Summer/Fall 1981, pp. 275–84. I am grateful to that journal and its editor, Ralph C. Page, and to the University of Illinois, for permission to reuse that paper here.

2   Although Kohlberg has of late become more pessimistic about the chances of getting students to reach the highest (post-conventional) stages. See L. Kohlberg, 'Educating for a just society: An updated and revised statement', in B. Munsey (Ed.) (1980) *Moral Development, Moral Education and Kohlberg*, Birmingham, Al: Religious Education Press, pp. 455–70. Kohlberg has also given up the view that 'moral stages can provide the sole basis for moral education.' See L. Kohlberg, 'From is to ought: How to commit the naturalistic fallacy and get away with it in the study of moral development', in T. Mischel (Ed.) (1971) *Cognitive Development and Epistemology*, New York: Academic Press, pp. 151–235.

3   Kohlberg (1971) 'From is to ought', *op. cit.*, and Kohlberg (1973) 'The claim to moral adequacy of a highest stage of moral judgment', *The Journal of Philosophy*, 70, pp. 630–46.

4   As Kohlberg himself acknowledges. See Kohlberg (1971) 'From is to ought', *op. cit.*, pp. 153–4. See also W. Alston, 'Comments on Kohlberg's "From is to ought",' in Mischel (1971) *op. cit.*, pp. 273ff.

5   See F. E. Trainer (1977) 'A critical analysis of Kohlberg's contributions to the study of moral thought', *Journal for the Theory of Social Behaviour*, 7, pp. 41–63. The question is raised, but dealt with only briefly, by D. Locke (1974) 'Cognitive stages or developmental phases? A critique of Kohlberg's stage-structural theory of moral reasoning', *Journal of Moral Education*, 8, pp. 168–81, esp. pp. 178–80.

6   I hasten to point out the limited nature of my criticism. There is much of value in Kohlberg's work: his psychological data and theory are themselves of great interest; and he is to be especially commended for bucking the relativist pull of contemporary social science. See Kohlberg (1971) 'From is to ought', *op. cit.*, pp. 155–63, esp. p. 159. It is only Kohlberg's argument for the claim to moral adequacy that I wish to challenge in this paper.

7   Kohlberg, *ibid.*, p. 169.

8   *Ibid.*, pp. 163–80 and 195–6; Kohlberg (1969) 'Stage and sequence: The cognitive-developmental approach to socialization', in D. A. Goslin (1969) (Ed.) *Handbook of Socialization Theory and Research*, New York: Rand-McNally, pp. 347–480; and Kohlberg (1971) 'Stages of moral development as a basis for moral education', in C. M. Beck *et al.* (Eds.) (1971) *Moral Education: Interdisciplinary Approaches*, New York: Newman Press, pp. 23–92, reprinted in Munsey (1980) *op. cit.*, pp. 15–98.

9   See especially W. Kurtines and E. B. Greif (1974) 'The development of moral thought: Review evaluation of Kohlberg's approach', *Psychological Bulletin*, 81, pp. 453–70; D. C. Phillips and J. Nicolayev (1978) 'Kohlbergian moral development: A progressing or degenerating research program?' *Educational Theory*, 28, pp. 286–301; and Trainer (1977) *op. cit.*

10 Kohlberg (1971) 'From is to ought', *op. cit.*, p. 222; L. Kohlberg and R. Mayer (1972) 'Development as the aim of education', *Harvard Educational Review*, 42, pp.449–96.

11 Witness, for example, Kaplan's discussion: 'Insofar as development occurs in a process under consideration, there is a progression from a state of relative undifferentiatedness to a state of increasing differentiation and hierarchic integration.' In R. Kaplan (1967) 'Meditations on genesis', *Human Development*, 10, p. 83. For Kohlberg's use of the concepts, see, for example, Kohlberg (1973) *op. cit.*, pp. 635–8.

12 Kohlberg, *ibid.*, p. 632. I refrain here from raising questions concerning the ontological and epistemological status of 'cognitive structures'.

13 See D. Boyd and L. Kohlberg (1973) 'The is-ought problem: A developmental perspective', *Zygon*, 8, pp. 361–2. The above is an extremely brief and superficial account of the role equilibrium plays in Piaget's theory. For a fuller treatment, see J. Piaget (1971) *Biology and Knowledge*, Chicago, Ill., University of Chicago Press; and J. Piaget (1977) *The Development of Thought: Equilibration of Cognitive Structures*, New York, Viking. Helpful secondary sources are J. H. Flavell (1963) *The Developmental Psychology of Jean Piaget*, New York, D. Van Nostrand; and H. G. Furth (1969) *Piaget and Knowledge: Theoretical Foundations*, Englewood Cliffs, N. J., Prentice-Hall.

14 Kohlberg (1971) 'From is to ought', *op. cit.*, p. 215.

15 *Ibid.*, p. 185; see also p. 195.

16 *Ibid.*, p. 224, emphasis in original. See also pp. 154, 176–7, 180–1, 184–5, and 223; Kohlberg (1973) 'The claim to moral adequacy', *op. cit.*, p. 633; Kohlberg (1971) 'Stages of moral development', pp. 46–7, 70; and Kohlberg and Mayer (1972) 'Development as the aim of education', *op. cit.*, p. 484.

17 Kohlberg (1971) 'Stages of moral development', *op. cit.*, p. 46, emphasis in original. The same passage also appears in Kohlberg (1971) 'From is to ought', *op. cit.*, p. 184. See also Kohlberg and Mayer (1972) 'Development as the aim of education', *op. cit.*, pp. 458–9, 477, and 483–4; Boyd and Kohlberg (1973) 'The is-ought problem', *op. cit.*, p. 366; and B. Puka, 'Kohlbergian forms and Deweyan acts: A response', in Munsey (1980) *op. cit.*, pp. 446–7.

18 Kohlberg (1971) 'From is to ought', *op. cit.*, pp. 195–6.

19 *Ibid.*, p. 184; Kohlberg (1971) 'Stages of moral development', *op. cit.*, p. 46.

20 Kohlberg (1971) 'From is to ought', *op. cit.*, pp. 216–17, emphasis in original. See also p. 224.

21 *Ibid.*, p. 185; Kohlberg (1971) 'Stages of moral development', *op. cit.*, p. 47.

22 Kohlberg (1971) 'From is to ought', *op. cit.*, pp. 184–5; Kohlberg (1971) 'Stages of moral development', *op. cit.*, pp. 46–7.

23 See here Kohlberg (1973) 'The claim to moral adequacy', *op. cit.*, pp. 633–42; also Puka (1980) *op. cit.*, pp. 446–7.

24 See Alston (1971) 'Comments', *op. cit.* especially p. 277; Trainer (1977) *op. cit.*, p. 50.

25 Kohlberg (1973) 'The claim to moral adequacy', *op. cit.*, p. 641.

26 See here Alston (1971) 'Comments', *op. cit.*, pp. 276–7. Specific challenges to Kohlberg's formalism are made by Munsey, Aron, and Rosen in their articles in Munsey (1980) *op. cit.* See also Trainer (1977) *op. cit.*, p. 49.

27 Kohlberg (1971) 'From is to ought', *op. cit.*, pp. 195–6.

28 It is perhaps worth pointing out that Rawls, a formalist Kohlberg relies on heavily in his argument for a formalist meta-ethical position, acknowledges that the philosophical superiority of any substantive ethical view cannot be settled on the basis of psychology: 'I assume that the final stage, the morality of principles, may have different contents given by any of the traditional philosophical doctrines we have discussed. It is true that I argue for the theory of justice as superior, and work out the psychological theory on this presumption; but this superiority is a philosophical question and cannot, I believe, be established by the psychological theory of development alone.' J. Rawls (1971) *A Theory of Justice*, Cambridge, Mass., Harvard University Press, p. 462n.

29 Boyd and Kohlberg (1973) *op. cit.*, p. 367.

30 Kohlberg (1971) 'From is to ought', *op. cit.*, p. 154. See also pp. 180–3; Kohlberg (1971) 'Stages of moral development', *op. cit.*, pp. 47–8; and Kohlberg (1973) 'The claim to moral adequacy', *op. cit.*, p. 633. For a critical discussion, see Alston (1971) 'Comments', *op. cit.*, pp. 273–7.

31 For a general discussion of the irrelevance of psychological information to philosophical justification (especially of knowledge-claims), see H. Siegel (1980) 'Justification, discovery, and the naturalizing of epistemology', *Philosophy of Science*, 47, pp. 297–321.

32 Cf. C. Gilligan (1982) *In a Different Voice: Psychological Theory and Women's Development*,

Cambridge and London, Harvard University Press; Gilligan (1977) 'In a different voice: Women's conception of the self and of morality', *Harvard Educational Review*, 47, pp. 481–517; and Gilligan (1979) 'Women's place in man's life cycle', *Harvard Educational Review*, 49, pp. 431–46.

33   Gilligan (1982) *In a Different Voice*, *op. cit.*, p. 3, emphasis added.

34   Cf. the fine discussion of the problem of the justification of the claim to moral adequacy as it manifests itself both for Gilligan and for Kohlberg in O. J. Flanagan, Jr (1982) 'Virtue, sex, and gender: Some philosophical reflections on the moral psychology debate', *Ethics*, 92, pp. 499–512.

It is perhaps worth mentioning Kohlberg's most recent comments on the claim to moral adequacy. In his (1982) response to Flanagan ('A reply to Owen Flanagan and some comments on the Puka-Goodpaster exchange', *Ethics*, 92, pp. 513–28), Kohlberg addresses Flanagan's criticism of his (i.e., Kohlberg's) arguments for the moral adequacy of higher stages. In the course of his discussion, Kohlberg grants the central thesis of the present discussion, namely that psychological research cannot settle questions of moral adequacy: 'Psychological findings and theoretical explanations of stage movement do not, of course, constitute direct proofs of greater moral adequacy of higher stages of moral reasoning, which must be justified in the language of moral philosophy and not just the language of psychology if we are to avoid the naturalistic fallacy' (p. 523; cf. also p. 525). However, while acknowledging this inability of psychological evidence to secure judgments of moral adequacy, Kohlberg continues to argue for the justification of such judgments in terms of isomorphism, for example by noting that 'The *normative* theorists' efforts to justify these rational reconstructions are theoretically complementary to the developmental psychologists' explanatory theories for why there is movement from stage to stage' (p. 525, emphasis in original), and by arguing that 'To explain these findings psychologically is to engage in a normative-theoretical-rational reconstruction of stages or of theories to which they are related' (p. 525). Thus Kohlberg wants to have his cake and eat it too. To the extent that he holds that 'psychological findings ... do not ... constitute direct proof of greater moral adequacy of higher stages of moral reasoning', he is abandoning the claim that his psychological research constitutes justification of the claim to moral adequacy (unless he thinks that it constitutes *in*direct proof or *partial* justification, a possibility he does not articulate or argue for). But to the extent he holds that the efforts of philosopher and psychologist are 'theoretically complementary'; that the psychologist *qua* psychologist contributes to the justification of claims of moral adequacy; and that the psychological theorist's explanation of stage change is *normative* as well as theoretical; to that extent he re-embraces his effort to justify judgments of moral adequacy in terms of psychological research.

35   This latter point is well made by M. Scriven. See M. Scriven (1976) 'Cognitive moral development', in D. Purpel and K. Ryan (Eds.) *Moral Education: It Comes With the Territory*, Berkeley, Calif., McCutchan, pp. 313–29.

36   H. Siegel (1980) 'Critical thinking as an educational ideal', *The Educational Forum*, 45, pp. 7–23; Siegel (1980) 'Rationality, morality, and rational moral education: Further response to Freeman', *Educational Philosophy and Theory*, 12, pp. 37–47, especially sections 7, 8, and 10; and Siegel (1978) 'Is it irrational to be immoral? A response to Freeman', *Educational Philosophy and Theory*, 10, pp. 51–61.

37   I have tried to fill out this conception of education and moral education in the papers cited in note 36; see also I. Scheffler (1973) 'Moral education and the democratic ideal', in his *Reason and Teaching*, New York: Bobbs-Merrill, pp. 136–45; I. Scheffler (1973) 'Concepts of education: Reflections on the current scene', in his *Reason and Teaching*, pp. 58–66, especially pp. 62–4; H. Jones (1974) 'The rationale of moral education', *The Monist*, 58, pp. 659–73; and Scriven (1976) *op. cit.*, p. 318.

38   For a powerful challenge to the idea that reading (and, more generally, literacy) is a necessary prelude to rational thinking, see J. R. Martin (1979) 'Thinking and literacy', *Thinking*, 1, pp. 44–51.

39   Scriven (1976) *op. cit.*, p. 320.

40   See Siegel (1980) 'Critical thinking', *op. cit.*

Interchange

BOYD REPLIES TO SIEGEL

Siegel's paper represents the only sustained attempt that I know of (besides my own) to interpret and evaluate Kohlberg's claims about the relationship between moral philosophy and developmental psychology. In this effort Siegel evidences a detailed examination of what Kohlberg has said on the issue, offering both a good sampling of Kohlberg's actual claims and a creative framework for the difficult task of analyzing the meaning of those claims. Arguing, quite correctly, that the use of a theory such as Kohlberg's to guide educational interventions must be justified, Siegel investigates 'the way in which Kohlberg uses his psychological research findings to support the claim to moral adequacy', viewing this support of moral adequacy as a necessary step in any such justification. The essence of Siegel's argument is, I believe, the assumption that there *is* no way in which psychology (either facts or explanation) can increase our confidence in the justifiability of some moral position, combined with an attempt to show that all of Kohlberg's attempts to suggest any such notions must therefore reduce to confusion, to a failure to keep in sight the fundamental difference between 'is' and 'ought'.

In contrast to other, more superficial critics, Siegel starts with a clear recognition that Kohlberg understands and intends to avoid any naive move from 'is' to 'ought' in his discussion of the moral adequacy of the higher stages. As Siegel puts it:

> He does not simply declare that what is, is what ought to be; that whatever the facts of moral development are, we ought to encourage continued (and intensified) development along those lines. This, as Kohlberg recognizes, would be an unjustifiable move, and a straightforward commitment of the naturalistic fallacy.

This sort of acknowledgment clearly is a necessary, positive first step toward any thorough attempt to elucidate what Kohlberg might be trying to say. However, *given* this acknowledgment, one must then wonder about the nature of the rest of Siegel's argument. What is he trying to do? Throughout the paper Siegel suggests that Kohlberg's educational efforts are in question because his attempts to justify the moral adequacy of the higher stages of moral judgment (which would shape the aims of such educational efforts) fail because they are (somehow) based on appeal to psychological facts. The rhetorical effect of stating his conclusion in this way is at odds with the above-noted acknowledgment: it suggests that Kohlberg sees no need for independent philosophical justification for the moral claims guiding his educational efforts, but instead, depends entirely on some sort of 'is'-'ought' move. This is, at best, misleading. Note that the issue here is *not* whether Kohlberg has successfully defended his moral claims on philosophical grounds, but rather, whether his understanding of what is needed and his efforts at fulfilling this requirement can be reduced to whatever he says about how psychological evidence might somehow complement such philosophical argument. I think the answer is clearly 'no'. Moreover, if Siegel's interest is *really* how well Kohlberg has justified his educational aims, then I think it odd that he does not even consider the variety of things Kohlberg has said to this point. That Kohlberg's arguments may still be lacking certainly may be true, but this is *not*—contrary to Siegel's suggestion—because he depends only on whatever he can get out of his psychological findings.

This worry about Siegel's point is not something that emerges only by concentrating on the periphery of his claims; on the contrary, the same problem is clearly manifested in Siegel's own summary of the problem which concerns him. Thus, at the beginning of the paper Siegel anticipates what will structure his analysis in the following way:

> . . . Kohlberg formulates an argument that proceeds as follows:
> (a)   Higher stages are *psychologically* more adequate than lower stages.
> (b)   There is a *parallelism*, or *isomorphism*, between the proper characterizations of the psychological and the moral adequacy of the stages.
> (c)   Therefore, higher stages are more adequate *morally* than lower stages.

The first thing to be noted here is that this is *Siegel's* way of synthesizing Kohlberg's argument; Kohlberg has never formulated—and I suggest, *would* never formulate—his argument in this way. And Siegel offers no evidence that he does. Second, and this confirms my worry noted above, Siegel's synthesis implies that the only kinds of reasons Kohlberg recognizes for claiming that 'higher stages are more adequate *morally* than lower stages' are those summarized in (a) and (b). Again, as long as one interprets (a) and, in particular, (b) as simple factual claims—as Siegel does in this paper—and connects them to (c) with a simple deductive 'therefore', one can only be engaged in trying to show that Kohlberg contradicts his own explicit disavowel of exactly this sort of 'straightforward commitment of the naturalistic fallacy.' Just *how* psychological facts and/or explanations might be related to a normative moral positions in some way that is not reducible to this straightforward deduction is what Kohlberg clearly is trying to explore. Siegel seems to miss this entirely, insisting instead on *reducing* any such exploration to trying to show how a psychological fact can 'in and of itself' constitute an argument for moral adequacy. In short, whereas Siegel views the relationship between developmental psychology and moral philosophy in terms of the one-sided sexual metaphor of how '*impotent*' empirical research is with respect to justification, Kohlberg, it seems to me, is working with the more promising metaphor that a generative relationship requires an integration of what both sides have to offer.

SIEGEL REPLIES TO BOYD

Boyd's discussion is very helpful and informative. He does us a great service by systematically considering alternative interpretations of Kohlberg's 'isomorphism thesis'. I regret that space permits only a very brief and cursory response to Boyd. I limit my remarks to two central issues: Boyd's contention that if Kohlberg is right that conceptions of justification are themselves stage-bound or psychologically dependent, then moral philosophy must be altered; and his discussion of the 'complementarity thesis'.

THE PSYCHOLOGICAL ROOT OF CONCEPTIONS OF JUSTIFICATION

Boyd first addresses himself to general connections between moral philosophy and developmental psychology, and in doing so suggests that if Kohlberg's empirical evidence for the invariant sequence of stages through Stage 4 is sound (and Boyd regards the evidence as 'quite strong'), then the view 'that moral philosophy can proceed entirely uninfluenced is hard to countenance.' Boyd offers two ways in which the invariant sequence of stages might influence moral philosophy. The second (I foreswear here consideration of the first) is that '. . . if the developmental claims are sound, then the traditional philosophical view of justification must be modified', for '. . . what one attends to and finds convincing within morally justificatory engagements changes developmentally, and any attempt to give a thorough justification of a moral position can never stand completely "outside" this fact.' Boyd argues that this shows that 'viable conceptions of justification cannot be independent of those [i.e., developmental] facts', and suggests 'that the very criteria that philosophers use to identify genuine instances of "justifying a moral judgment" are themselves emergents of a developmental process—and something that changes throughout the stages of that process.'

   Suppose it is true that 'what one attends to and finds convincing within morally justificatory engagements changes developmentally.' Does it follow that 'viable conceptions of justification' depend on such developmental facts? No. Grant that there are developmentally-bound conceptions of justification, such that what a Stage 1 reasoner finds compelling justification differs from what a Stage 2 reasoner finds compelling. The psychological facts to which Boyd points establish that there are such rival conceptions of justification—justification, we might say, is stage-relative. We might say this, but it would be misleading to say so. For what is stage-relative are *conceptions* of justification, not justification. What constitutes *adequate* justification, or our best theory of justification, is settled on epistemological, not psychological, grounds; alternative stage-bound conceptions of justification no more relativize justification to stages than alternative conceptions of, for example, cause, time, or space relativize those notions. The evidence of alternative, stage-bound conceptions of, for example, space, is compelling. But we do not for this reason relativize our conception of space. Instead, we evaluate alternative conceptions with reference to physical theory. Similarly, alternative conceptions of justification are evaluated with reference to epistemological theory. So the fact that there exist stage-bound conceptions of justification does not relativize justification or show that our *epistemologically preferred* account of justification is dependent on factual developmental considerations. Consequently Boyd has not shown that developmental psychology influences moral philosophy in the way suggested. Conceptions of justification may well be stage-dependent; the *adequacy* of those conceptions is not.

IS, OUGHT AND COMPLEMENTARITY

In considering the various ways in which Kohlberg may be interpreted as suggesting a connection between 'is' and 'ought', Boyd acknowledges that, both from his view and from Kohlberg's, morality is independent of the facts of psychological development in the specific sense that 'science cannot prove or justify a morality' (Kohlberg) and that '"ought"-claims are not reducible to "is"-claims' where this means that the moral perspective provides 'prescriptive leverage' to criticize actual states of affairs (Boyd). This is important, for it grants the main point that some of Kohlberg's critics (myself included) seek to establish, namely that psychological facts concerning development cannot serve to *justify* moral claims.

(Boyd suggests that I and others question-beggingly assume that there is no other way in which 'is' can be related to 'ought.' But this is not right. What I do claim, and argue for (and so do not assume), is that from the point of view of epistemological theory the most pressing question is that of the possibility of justification of ought-claims on the basis of is-claims. This is the reason that I and others focus on the question of justification. No one denies that there may be other connections between developmental psychology and moral philosophy—though many deny that these other connections might be such that psychological facts turn out to have justificatory force with respect to moral claims.)

Boyd then grants the central point regarding the inability of developmental psychology ('is') to justify morality ('ought'). He contends, however, that there is nevertheless a way in which the gap between 'ought' and 'is' might be bridged. This way involves the 'complementarity thesis'.

What is the complementarity thesis? According to Boyd, in a Kohlbergian interview (the source of data) the subject is placed in a 'performative attitude', for the subject must articulate and defend her moral positions and reasoning. The interviewer, however, must assume an 'interpretive stance' *vis-à-vis* the subject in order to grasp properly the subject's remarks; consequently the interviewer too must assume the performative attitude. Both interviewer and subject adopt the performative attitude, and this is the root of the complementarity.

(Kohlberg suggests that complementarity clarifies the way in which normative theory serves to explain stage development: 'For instance, the normative theoretical claim that a higher stage is philosophically a better stage is one necessary part of a psychological explanation of sequential stage movement.' But this is false, and does not alleviate the difficulties with the 'explanation strand' of Kohlberg's argument for isomorphism discussed in my article. There could be many explanations of stage movement besides the one Kohlberg notes, most obvious of which is that the subject *mistakenly believes* that 'a higher stage is philosophically a better stage.' And in any case, Kohlberg's argument here *presupposes* a normative theory, which is used to explain psychological facts, and so is a case of normative considerations contributing to scientific explanation, not the other way around— and so is not a case of psychology contributing to the justification of moral claims.)

Boyd rejects what he refers to as the 'negative interpretation' of the complementarity thesis—rightly, I think—on grounds of difficulties with the idea that psychology provides a 'check' on moral theory. He then seeks to develop a 'positive interpretation' of the thesis. This positive interpretation is, unfortunately, somewhat obscure. It hinges on the fact that both subject and interviewer adopt the performative attitude. Boyd writes that:

... the developmental psychologist is required not only to 'interpret' how a person is making and evaluating 'ought'-claims, but also to 'interpret' why a person would *change* their way of making and evaluating 'ought'-claims and why this change is systematic in a particular direction.... Explaining this kind of change cannot be done solely from an objectivating attitude; to do so would be to give up the unique strength that this theory starts with, namely the view of the subject as a constructive moral agent.

This claim seems to me false. The psychologist can explain stage change from an 'objectivating attitude', while fully honouring the subject's status as 'a constructive moral agent'. For example, the psychologist may explain stage change by noting that the subject regards (either correctly or mistakenly) the later stage as more adequate than the earlier stage. False belief, as well as true belief, may serve in the psychological explanation of belief and action; such explanation, moreover, can be perfectly objective.

Boyd demurs, pointing again to the necessity of the psychologist's adopting the performative attitude: '... the psychologist must ... assume mutuality with other subjects ..., thus also at the same time asking "why do/did *I* change from X to Y?"' But Boyd argues that 'X' and 'Y' here are stages about which it is appropriate to make 'ought'-claims. Hence: '... In order to *make sense* to humans as moral agents, the psychological explanation of moral development must include the performative examination of this "ought" question.' I confess that I have difficulty following this argument. Boyd is suggesting, I think, that in order to explain why Jones has moved from Stage 1 to Stage 2, the psychologist must herself answer why she herself believes that Stage 2 is normatively superior to Stage 1. But this is false. The psychologist might have any normative view whatsoever regarding the relative merits of the stages, and still explain Jones' stage change in terms of Jones' normative and psychological convictions and features. Thus it is not clear why the psychologist must adopt the 'performative attitude', where that means giving up the 'objectivating attitude', in explaining stage change.

So it is not clear that the psychologist must, in the relevant sense, adopt the 'performative attitude'. She must, perhaps, while interpreting subjects during interviews; but it is not clear that that same attitude must be adopted when theorizing about, or explaining, stage change. Boyd has, I think, failed to distinguish between the psychologist's task of understanding subject responses, on the one hand, and the task of constructing a theory to explain subject responses and stage change, on the other. 'Interpretation' may be required for the first task, but Boyd has offered no reason for thinking that it is similarly required for the second.

Thus this version of the complementarity thesis is not as yet established. And even if it were to be established, it still would not follow that psychological information would be relevant to the justification of moral claims or theory. Nevertheless, the 'positive interpretation' of the complementarity thesis is provocative, and I wish to urge Boyd to develop it further—and I congratulate him for his effort to make sense, in a novel way, of Kohlberg's exceedingly obscure position regarding the relationship between developmental psychology and morality.

Part IV: MORAL PSYCHOLOGY

6. Moral Autonomy and the Theory of Kohlberg

OLIVERA PETROVICH

On an earlier occasion I had made several brief comments concerning Kohlberg's theory and research as presented in his first volume, *The Philosophy of Moral Development*.[1] The comments were, largely, about various points of disagreement with Kohlberg's views, empirical as well as theoretical. In addition to this, an equally controversial part of Kohlberg's system was singled out for its novelty in psychological research on morality and I assessed it as the most interesting part of his book. The part in question dealt with the issue of the relationship between religion and morality from the psychological point of view. In order to consider the relevance of religion to morality, Kohlberg has extended his six-stage theory to the seven-stage one. Since the move is novel for contemporary psychology, and since it entails a few other important issues related to both the psychology and philosophy of morality, my intention in this chapter will be to consider the meaning and implications of this part of Kohlberg's theory by examining the rationale for Kohlberg's introducing it. This, in turn, calls for a re-examination of some of the basic assumptions upon which the cognitive-developmental theory of morality rests, first and foremost, of the concept of autonomy. Kohlberg's Stage 7 has been conspicuously absent from the majority of references to his theory made by psychologists and other followers of his work, presumably because of their failure to see any major relevance of the added stage to the main theory. In contrast to this, my view is that the added seventh stage is the most interesting part not just with respect to Kohlberg's theory alone but also with respect to the area of moral psychology as a whole. Thus, the argument that follows will be pursued along two lines: first, that the concept of autonomy as used in moral psychology is untenable and needs to be redefined. Second, and this follows from the previously stated insufficiency of the notion of autonomy as a defining principle of morality, that our methodological and theoretical approach to the study of morality requires a radical change that would allow for an objective account of evaluative presuppositions made in any research on morality.

Before I come to suggest the continuing relevance of Kohlberg's theory despite some of its ineradicable shortcomings, I shall try to explore some of the reasons why the notion of autonomy epitomizes the fundamental weakness of the cognitive-developmental theory of morality, and of Kohlberg's theory more specifically. A suitable way to examine the status of the concept of autonomy is by tracing its origins in philosophy, notably Kant's, as well as the distortions it underwent in subsequent interpretations, especially in psychology. Although neither Kohlberg nor other psychologists discuss the concept of autonomy as in any way problematic, I hope to show that it is precisely the lack of an exact conceptual and operational definition of autonomy in moral psychology which is the cause of the majority of difficulties facing the cognitive-developmental approach to morality. It will be demonstrated that while the concept of autonomy has several noticeably different meanings in philosophy, related to different aspects of morality, in psychology the same concept has been used to signify a global, general notion of mature moral development. My argument will be that the concept of autonomy, as applied to psychology, requires a radical reappraisal if it is to be of any use in research and theory on moral development. To introduce the argument succinctly, the Kantian definition of autonomy as a property of legislating reason makes sense only in conjunction with Kant's conception of reason. Since the empirical psychological definition of reason differs fundamentally from the Kantian notion of reason, it follows that the very concept of autonomy in moral psychology must be reinterpreted in accordance with Kant's original understanding of it, or modified so as to be applicable to the science of psychology, or abandoned altogether. After having suggested what seems to me to be the only meaning that the concept of autonomy can legitimately have in experimental psychology, we shall try to see whether this revised notion of autonomy in psychology is actually sufficient as the defining principle of morality. Basically, it will be argued that autonomy in moral judgment is a necessary prerequisite for moral development; however, its claim to sufficiency as a criterion of mature morality is highly questionable. It is at this point that Kohlberg's modified, i.e., seven-stage, theory has the potential of becoming an interesting attempt at superseding the limits of the standard cognitive-developmental model in moral psychology. In other words, by introducing the seventh stage, Kohlberg acknowledges that moral development cannot, in the end, be explained exclusively by cognitive psychological mechanisms. Instead, he admits that a value stance is necessary in moral discourse and, more specifically, comes to the view that religion must play some part in moral development. Even though Kohlberg's idea of religion is peculiar, it nevertheless serves the purpose of demonstrating that an adequate theory of moral development ought to take into account the factor of religion. In this I see the possibility of distinguishing *two* types of Kohlberg's theory instead of regarding the seventh stage as simply an extension of his six-stage theory. These two potential types of Kohlberg's theory could be seen to represent two fundamentally different world views: religious and secular. I must make it clear, however, that this way of looking at Kohlberg's theory has never been suggested by Kohlberg himself.

In my concluding remarks I shall emphasize that Kohlberg's theory remains a controversial model due to a number of serious flaws. Notwithstanding this, I am inclined to perceive within it a potential to suggest a model that should be of substantial value in generating future research based on some ideas genuinely novel in this field. Such an evaluation of Kohlberg's theory is certainly, to some extent at least, due to the fact that at present there is no other, equally comprehensive yet more adequate model to replace it. And if his theory succeeds in nothing more than contributing to the shift of emphasis in current empirical research, its role will be fulfilled.

THE CONCEPT OF AUTONOMY IN PSYCHOLOGY: ITS MEANING AND ORIGIN

In contrast to philosophy where, as we shall see later, attempts have been made to distinguish several aspects of the concept of autonomy, psychologists have used the same concept with a single and rather general purpose to signify mature moral development. This stretchiness and flexibility in referring to 'autonomy' makes it difficult to group systematically all extant usages of it and to isolate that which could be regarded as the crucial feature of mature morality. Nevertheless, I shall try to review cursorily some of the most common ways of referring to autonomy, mainly from the works of Piaget and Kohlberg, followed by some examples from more recent sources, so as to bring to light what psychologists have in mind when using it.

On the whole, it is possible to distinguish the following major categories of reference to, or criteria of, autonomy in psychology. (a) An *individual* is morally autonomous if independent of any external influences, especially of adult authority. He has an autonomous conscience which is in reciprocal relationships with others and feels 'from within the desire to treat others as he himself would wish to be treated' (Piaget, 1965, p. 194). According to Kohlberg, an autonomous individual is characterized by an ability to make moral judgments and to formulate his own moral principles rather than to conform to moral judgments of the adults around him. Moreover, he is able to create laws rationally *ex nihilo* (1981, p. 153). (b) *Standard*, rule, principle, law or value is said to be 'autonomous' if it is internal to the child's own conscience (Piaget, 1965) and if 'the mind regards as necessary an ideal that is independent of all external pressures' (*ibid.*, p. 194). In Kohlberg's view, moral principles are autonomous when they have 'validity and application apart from authority of the groups or people who hold them' (*ibid.*, p. 17). Equally, human value or reason is autonomous if and when it does not depend on anything else including the 'respect for God and God's authority' (*ibid.*, p. 21). (c) General *attitude to rules*, laws, etc., can be heteronomous, semi-autonomous, or autonomous, according to the manner with which an individual relates to moral standards. Piaget holds that heteronomy means obedience to the adult, semi-autonomy is an advance towards obedience to the rule itself, albeit incomplete since the rule is still seen by the child as imposed from outside rather than as the 'necessary product of the mind itself', whereas true autonomy appears when the child 'discovers that truthfulness is necessary to the relations of sympathy and mutual respect' (*ibid.*, p. 194). (d) Heteronomy and autonomy are seen as distinct *types of morality*, autonomy being synonymous with the ethics of mutual respect whereas heteronomy represents the morality of duty (Piaget, 1965). According to Piaget, autonomy is equivalent to the rule of justice since the notion of justice emerges gradually, through social relationships 'in almost complete autonomy' (*ibid.*, p. 196). Kohlberg's view is similar to this, that is, autonomous morality is morality of justice and it is exemplified by Stage 6 in his theory of moral development. Kohlberg also speaks of a particular course or level of development as autonomous or 'postconventional', as one that reaches a 'higher form of reciprocity which we call "equity" ...' (1981, pp. 281–2). Finally, (e) the *domain of morality* is regarded as autonomous since it has 'its own criteria of rationality' (Kohlberg, 1981, p. 169).

Besides Piaget and Kohlberg, other psychologists have used the concept of autonomy in basically the same way, that is, as a label for mature moral development, without any specification as to the aspect of morality to which the concept refers. Among the more recent examples of the concept's application are: an 'individual, autonomous morality' is opposed to an imposed morality of the adult world (Weinreich-Haste, 1982, p. 182); 'autonomous thought' is contrasted with an 'heteronomous stage' (*ibid.*, p. 184); autonomous morality is recognized as 'true' morality (*ibid.*, p. 186) and is the result of a 'movement from heteronomous to autonomous thinking' (*ibid.*, p. 187); 'heteronomous moral belief' is associated with the notion of immanent causality as opposed to an 'autonomous moral belief' which is characterized by chance contiguity explanations (Karniol, 1982, p. 813); an autonomous individual is capable of acting on his own judgment and, at the same time, of being 'self-controlled and law-abiding' (Weinreich-Haste and Locke, 1983, p. xv); autonomy is an essential precondition of the 'equal dignity ... of *all* individuals' (Vine, 1983, p. 34).

In addition to attempts such as these to define autonomy positively, some authors have tried to show the concept's untenability. Thus, Emler regards the very idea of autonomy as a typical product of Western culture which 'has the ontological status of the tooth fairy and the Easter bunny' (1983, p. 59). Equally disapproving is Breakwell, on the grounds of man's being strongly influenced by his social group so that, 'it is questionable whether an individual ever acts as an "autonomous" agent' (1983, p. 232).

The grouping above is by no means exhaustive and precise since no great precision is possible due to an obvious overlapping between most of the examples given. Its sole purpose is to provide some basis for a critical examination of the meaning of autonomy in moral psychology. We shall see later, however, that it is expedient to reduce it further to a smaller number of categories so as to render them parallel to those discussed by philosophers.

One of the helpful ways to understand the nature of an event is to look at its history and, in the case of autonomy as a foundation stone of the cognitive-developmental theory of morality, I believe it is very noticeably so. First, we shall look at the concept's beginnings in psychology and, subsequently, at its origins in philosophy.

Since its introduction into psychology in 1932 in Piaget's book, *The Moral Judgment of the Child*, the concept of autonomy has been used extensively and in a number of different senses, a situation which precludes proper communication between researchers in any area. Although my primary task is to consider the theory of Kohlberg, much of what I have to say applies not just to Kohlberg but to the cognitive-developmental theory of morality as a whole, of which he is the best-known representative today. Since Kohlberg's use of the concept of autonomy does not differ from that of Piaget's in any major sense,[2] frequent references will be made to Piaget as well as to Bovet, to whom Piagetian theory owes a lot. Moreover, in my judgment, re-examination of the concept of autonomy in its complete surroundings is necessary in order to understand the logic of Kohlberg's implicit dissatisfaction with his six-stage theory and the subsequent extension of it into the seven-stage one.

Although there have recently been some attempts to dissociate the theories of Piaget and Kohlberg (for example, Weinreich-Haste, 1982), Kohlberg's theory is essentially Piagetian, as he himself claims: 'My own work on morality started from Piaget's notions of stages. . . . Inspired by Jean Piaget's (1948) pioneering effort to apply a structural approach to moral development, I have gradually elaborated over the years a typological scheme . . .' (1981, p. 16). Kohlberg insists on his Piagetian underpinning in many other places, such as, 'In the area of logic, Piaget holds that a psychological theory of development is closely linked to a theory of normative logic. Following Piaget, I claim the same is true in the area of moral judgment' (*ibid.*, p. 133), or, 'In Piaget's theory, which I follow . . .' (*ibid.*, p. 145), and so on. Another important influence that Kohlberg acknowledges is Kant: 'my theory and Rawls's grew out of the same roots; Kant's formal theory in moral philosophy and Piaget's theory in psychology' (*ibid.*, p. 192). We shall see later, when comparing some of their views, how faithful Kohlberg's theory has been to its allegedly Kantian roots.

It is doubtless correct to say that many of Piaget's ideas derive from the philosophy of Kant; all the same, his ideas about moral development of the child, and especially about his autonomy, have been influenced more strongly by Bovet than by Kant. Indeed, Piaget repeatedly acknowledges his debt to Bovet: 'we do not hesitate to declare that this article by P. Bovet was the true begetter of our results' (1965, p. 377).

In his book, *The Child's Religion* (1928), Bovet set out to explain the origin of the religious sentiment in the child, as opposed to that in the society, according to the fashion dominating anthropological circles of the time. (Before this work, Bovet had been known for his studies of imageless thought and similar experiments characteristic of German psychology, in particular of the Würzburg school.) Bovet's approach was, as he called it, a 'genetic standpoint' which enabled him to arrive at a conclusion that both the religious sentiment and respect for the moral rule derive from the child's respect for his parents who are perceived by the child as endowed with all the divine perfections. This assumption that respect for moral rules originates in interpersonal relationships, not in reason, led Bovet to reject Kant's doctrine of respect as 'psychologically insufficient' (*ibid.*, p. 134). In addition to his use of the 'genetic approach' method, Bovet found support for his rejection of Kant in what he took to be the view of St Thomas Aquinas, that is, 'The respect a man has for a precept develops naturally from the respect he has for the one who gives it' (*ibid.*, p. 132). The trouble with this reference to Aquinas, however, is that Bovet apparently misunderstood who the giver was according to Aquinas. Surely, it was God and not man. Aquinas held that the moral law was placed in a metaphysical setting from the very beginning and man was able, by reflecting, to discern the fundamental tendencies and needs of his nature (Copleston, 1982; also Joyce, 1923).

Although it is not quite clear whether Bovet himself used the word 'autonomy',[3] his emphasis upon respect between individuals as the mechanism of moral development was fully endorsed by Piaget who identified its two forms following Kant's terminology as heteronomy (unilateral respect) and autonomy (mutual respect). It is important to make it plain that Bovet's conclusions about the child's pre-ordained progression from the condition of being utterly overwhelmed by the sheer presence of grown-ups to his becoming gradually noticed and respected by them, were not based on any direct empirical observations but, instead, on letters from friends and acquaintances, private conversations, adults' reminiscences from their childhood, and the like. Here I quote just a few examples of the sort of 'evidence' Bovet used: 'When I was little (four years, or perhaps three and a half years old), a correspondent writes to me, we lived in a two-storied house . . .' (*ibid.*, p. 29), or, 'A lady of our acquaintance remembers well her repugnance, as a child, for the idea of a Heavenly Father, who alone was completely good . . .' (*ibid.*, p. 40) or, in the next sentence Bovet writes, 'The following account is even more precise. A mother speaks of her little girl, who, at a rather early age—six years—had slipped into a class . . . .' Much as this is not an occasion for going into greater detail about Bovet's theory and the ideas that had influenced him most obviously, it should be stressed that his theory is impregnated with speculations about the child's mind that match only the bizarre descriptions of the primitive mind produced by European anthropologists and other social thinkers of the late nineteenth and early twentieth centuries, to some of whom Bovet and Piaget refer frequently and with great esteem (for example, Durkheim, Frazer, Freud, Lang, Lévy-Bruhl, Spencer, Taylor). According to Lévy-Bruhl, for instance, an essential characteristic of the primitive mind is its confusion between external reality and internal thought (see Piaget, 1977, p. 110). Echoing this, Bovet writes that, 'The child's world of ideas is pre-logical; in it thought is sustained and animated by feeling' (1928, p. 31), whereas Piaget finds the 'analogies between the child and the primitive at every step' (1977, p. 110). Such presuppositions about the mind of primitive man have been convincingly repudiated by distinguished anthropologists. For example, in his critical review of such erroneous theories of primitive man and his religion, Evans-Pritchard singles out the *Introduction to the History of Religion* by F. B. Jevons (1896) and describes it eloquently as 'a collection of absurd reconstructions, unsupportable hypotheses and conjectures, wild speculations, suppositions and assumptions, inappropriate analogies, misunderstandings and misinterpretations, and especially, in what he [Jevons] wrote about totemism, just plain nonsense' (1980, p. 5).

In contrast to anthropology, however, similar unqualified assumptions about the nature of the child's mind have never been systematically repudiated in psychology.[4] Instead, research is still being generated to test some Piagetian ideas of this kind (for instance, immanent justice).[5] What is important to bear in mind is that the assumption fundamental to such research is that the young child is unable to differentiate himself from the external world, between the physical and psychological, the real and imagined, and the like. In Piaget's terminology, the child is a 'realist' who, 'in almost every domain . . . tends to consider as external, to "reify" as Sully put it, the contents of his mind' (1965, p. 184). This childhood realism, Piaget believed, is a natural and spontaneous tendency of child thought which can be of two types, general and moral, the latter being equivalent to heteronomy. A crucial implication of the child's confusion between the physical and the moral law (*ibid.*, p. 405) is his lack of rationality and, consequently, in the sphere of moral development, his inability to reason autonomously, since autonomy is a distinctive property of rational beings. Hence, the cognitive developmental theory of morality holds that moral development consists in the development of both rationality and moral autonomy, the latter being strictly dependent upon general cognitive development.

It is necessary to reiterate that the major difficulty of the cognitive-developmental theory of morality is that it is based upon certain conjectures for which there has never been sufficient evidence to justify their persistence in psychology. One could say, therefore, that in many ways Bovet's and Piaget's conceptions of the child's mind and of his understanding of the world, including morality and religion, are, to use Evans-Pritchard's expression, 'a monstrous mosaic', composed of all else save experimental evidence.

THE CONCEPT OF AUTONOMY IN PHILOSOPHY

In this section I look at some philosophers, mostly contemporary, whose views are rarely, if ever, mentioned by psychologists, despite their being directly relevant to the area of moral psychology. In the next section we shall examine Kant's views on the topic according to a non-standard interpretation of his ethical theory. In doing so I hope to mitigate the bias pervading the cognitive-developmental approach to morality caused by a selective attitude among psychologists when referring to philosophical sources on morality.

Originally, Kant defined autonomy as 'that property of the will by which it gives a law to itself (irrespective of any property of the objects of volition)' (1938, p. 59). 'This legislating', Kant wrote, 'must exist potentially in every rational being and must be able to arise from his will' (*ibid.*, p. 52).

On the basis of the majority of interpretations of Kant's formulation of autonomy, it is possible, on the whole, to distinguish three dominant modes of reference to it: the *individual*, the *standard*, and the *domain of morality*.[6] In addition, some authors distinguish between the autonomy *in* ethics and the autonomy *of* ethics (Macquarrie, 1967). Each of these can also be approached from either a descriptive or an evaluative point of view, which is in practice rarely done and has been the cause of considerable misunderstanding.

According to the first meaning above, an autonomous individual is a rational cause of his actions whose will follows the universal law freely (Paton, 1983) or, who rationally imposes upon himself the moral law or the categorical imperative (Hebblethwaite, 1981), and when he makes his own decisions of principle by adopting the principles of those who have given them to him in the past (Hare, 1972). In theological ethics, an autonomous agent is defined in negative terms, i.e., as being free from moral subordination to anything other than himself and not seeking or accepting divine assistance (Woods, 1966).

As to the moral standard criterion, philosophers define autonomy as guidance by one's own moral principles. In contrast to the criterion of the individual, the emphasis here is on the standard itself which, if autonomous, should not depend on any external factors or ulterior motives but should be valued for its own sake. On the definition in theological ethics, moral standard is autonomous in the sense that it does not require any metaphysical foundation.

Finally, the domain criterion judges morality to be independent of all other domains, such as history, social customs, science, or religion. As an autonomous discipline, morality is said to have a form and structure of its own, as well as unique concepts that are irreducible to concepts of the empirical sciences, especially psychology, or of metaphysics (Ewing, 1961; Macquarrie, 1967).

THE CONCEPT OF AUTONOMY AND KANT'S THEORY OF TRANSCENDENTAL IDEALISM

Here I turn to an interpretation of Kant's moral theory which seems to be particularly interesting with regard to the forthcoming argument. According to L. V. Baldacchino, it is essential to see Kant's moral theory as inseparable from his theory of transcendental idealism, which claims that our perception of the spatio-temporal world ultimately depends upon a non-empirical supersensible reality[7] which *is* independently real but is neither spatial nor temporal (1976, p. 7).

In Kant's view (1938), human reason is unconditionally autonomous since it is neither caused nor determined by any factors external to itself. The autonomy of reason means, therefore, independence of reason from the world and its natural laws. Such autonomy is possible, in the first place, because of reason's being part of the unconditioned or transcendent realm. In addition to the transcendent component, human reason includes a sensible component which belongs to the perceptual world. Those areas of human personality that are not partakers of transcendent reason are heteronomous for they are governed by natural or physical laws. Since human reason is imbued with various passions and desires, it cannot perceive the moral law in its perfect freedom or autonomously. In other words, although the moral law is situated in reason, it is usually experienced as an external constraining command or imperative. Notwithstanding this, human reason is capable of being autonomous in virtue of its being part of transcendent reason and, as such, it can promulgate the moral law since the law is contained within reason as an *a priori* principle. As an *a priori*, absolutely non-contingent moral principle, the categorical imperative is a principle of the supersensible. Its essence is in its form, not its content, since it originates in reason alone rather than in experience. As Baldacchino emphasizes, this *a priori* origin of the categorical imperative in pure reason is the ground of its universality so that all specific moral laws can be derived from it. Consequently, Kant's aim was to establish 'the moral law not as an alien authority compelling from without, but as an ideal self-imposed as part of our transcendental constitution as rational human agents' (*ibid.*, pp. 79–80). According to Kant, therefore, the supersensible is present *in* the rational will of a moral agent and a corollary of this presence is the awareness of the authority of the moral law which leads at most to the 'knowledge *that* a supersensible being exists' (*ibid.*, p. 108).

Another interesting part of Kant's moral theory has to do with his belief in man's utter dependence on God or the supersensible for the realization of moral goodness. One of his arguments is that the '*practical possibility* of achieving the absolutely necessary demands of the moral ideal which is logically possible for man can be counted upon only by "postulating" the existence of God and personal immortality' (after Baldacchino, p. 31; see also, Körner, 1955; Paton, 1983). As Baldacchino argues further, postulating the *idea* of man's striving toward the achievement of the highest good as requiring the existence of God can be regarded as equivalent to the idea of God's ultimate *purpose* in creating the sensible world.

To summarize Kant's moral theory as relevant for our discussion of autonomy, human reason *as* a partaker of the supersensible is the source of freedom and the moral law. According to Baldacchino's interpretation of Kant, 'the possession of reason can indeed be regarded as analytically bringing with it the consciousness of its fundamental principle of operation' (*ibid.*, p. 76). From this it follows that the self-legislating function of the moral agent does not imply his *creating* the moral law but only his *imposing* upon himself the law inherent in his reason. A similar understanding of autonomy has been suggested by other philosophers, for example, Mitchell, who writes, 'Autonomy requires that the standards used shall be, in some sense, the judge's own standards; not, however, in the sense that he must have invented them; only in the sense that he must have rationally accepted them' (1980, p. 153).

A CRITIQUE OF THE CONCEPT OF AUTONOMY IN PSYCHOLOGY

According to standard dictionary definitions, autonomy signifies a condition of self-governed existence and conduct, regulated by the laws inherent in a particular body, usually biological or political. The problem for psychology, then, is to determine the notion of autonomy that would be applicable to the nature of the psychological 'body', that is, a rational human being. In other words, we need a psychological answer to the question of what it means to be 'governed by one's own laws'.

As we have seen, none of the existing usages of the concept of autonomy in psychology is entirely satisfactory nor suited to the purposes of empirical research. Moreover, none of its usages by Kohlberg and other cognitive developmentalists is specifically cognitive. Nonetheless, of all the aforementioned notions or criteria of autonomy, by far the most important from the point of view psychology is that of the individual moral agent as the author of his decisions and actions. Paradoxically enough, this criterion has received no particular attention among psychologists who have used it interchangeably with other aspects of autonomy, notably the standard or principle criterion. I hope to show, however, that the moral standard criterion, albeit important and practically inseparable from that of the individual, must be regarded as secondary in the hierarchy of the psychologist's priorities. I ought to make it clear, however, that this, essentially psychological, reason for rejecting the standard criterion of autonomy in favour of the individual one, is different from that advocated by those who think that objective standards in morality do not exist (Perry, 1976). Among philosophers, on the other hand, the individual criterion of moral autonomy has elicited far greater interest. A particularly disputed one is that notion of autonomy whereby a reference is made to the self-legislating moral agent who, by implication, *invents* his own rules rather than accept them rationally *as* his own (see Adams, 1979; Anscombe, 1981; Ewing, 1973; Geach, 1981; Hare, 1972; Hebblethwaite, 1981; Mitchell, 1980; Quinn, 1975; Woods, 1966). This idea of 'legislating for oneself' has been declared absurd since it leads one to assume a voting procedure within one's own self, 'resulting in a majority, which as a matter of proportion is overwhelming, for it is always 1–0' (Anscombe, 1981, p. 27).

In psychology, as we have seen, the morally autonomous individual is generally defined as morally mature on account of his putative ability to formulate his own moral rules and to act on his own judgment. By contrast, the morally heteronomous individual is immature since he tends to abide by laws coming from outside and to act on command. However differentiated these two types of moral development may seem to be, the crucial psychological issue here is whether the individual (heteronomous) plays any part in subjecting himself to these external forces and, if so, what his motives are. It is important to note that any situation in which a normally intelligent individual is being dominated by some external forces does actually entail *some* participation of the individual himself so that, as Anscombe (1981) remarks, ultimately he *is* his own pilot, however obedient he may be. In other words, as long as a person is aware of what he is doing, it is, then, his decision to act in a particular way, say, to obey. Only if it turns out to be certain that he has no reason whatsoever for his judgment or action, could one say that he is probably governed from outside. That is to say, a truly heteronomous agent should not be able to perceive any worth in his judgments or actions other than their originating in an adult authority which prevents him from comprehending the moral import of a situation.[8] Although this possibility exists in principle, so far there has been no evidence to show unequivocally that the child is not making his *own* judgment. All that is available, however, is an inference on the psychologist's part imputing to the child a particular type of reasoning on the basis of the content of his judgment. Instead, the psychologist should strive to know why a person apparently acts on command: out of fear and some other ulterior motive, or out of respect for another person and agreement with the views of one whose commands he follows. Thus, it is commonly found in research reports that if a child mentions punishment or refers to an adult authority while trying to justify his judgments or actions, such response is taken to be indicative of the child's heteronomous morality. Such an inference is dubious, however, unless an attempt at clarification of the response's ambiguity be made. For one thing, the 'punishment' response may actually imply the child's understanding of the logic of a situation whereby he knows that whenever he does something naughty he is punished. That is to say, punishment is a *proof* that he was naughty and not necessarily a *reason* for seeing himself as naughty. By the same token, reference to an adult authority may simply mean that the child is expressing his approval of the statement pronounced by the authority and his mentioning it need be no more than an attempt to prove the validity of his judgments, not very different from an adult's referring to a distinguished authority in support of his particular opinion or theory. The point is that both our disagreement and our agreement with others could be justified by some defensible reasons unless it is clearly established that they are sheer parrotting. The current bias among researchers to over-estimate the significance of 'disagreeing' responses in young children as opposed to 'agreeing' ones which are believed to be heteronomous,[9] owes its origin to Rousseau's ideas about healthy and unfrustrated development, in which the child's rebellion against adults is of vital importance.

The act of consent *is*, therefore, autonomous since it has the authority of personal decision: it is the child himself who decides and chooses, however inarticulately, to act in a certain way. But the act of choosing itself is neither moral nor immoral; what makes it so is the reason, motive, or value chosen. Not all decision-making is moral although it is autonomous; thus, for example, an autonomous Nazi is morally worse than the obedient or heteronomous Nazi (Adams, 1979). To be sure, people's autonomous decisions need to be, and in practice are, judged by some existing criteria as morally acceptable or not. However, to assert that an individual is morally autonomous because of a particular principle adopted is, in fact, a value judgment, and it ought to be recognized that as such it lies beyond the immediate scope of the psychologist's competence. I shall revert to this later.

At this point I do not wish to go further in disputing the plausibility of not being autonomous while making one's own judgment, whatever its content may be. My sole purpose is to underline some important ambiguities pervading the cognitive-developmental approach to morality. It surely is a proper task for psychology to find out what the child actually means when he is trying to express himself, and a solution should be sought by means of empirical methods of investigation. No amount or depth of speculation can achieve this, and those psychologists who engage in philosophical debates at the expense of their immediate tasks are doing no service to their discipline. Besides, philosophers themselves are in need of solid empirical evidence to which to apply their minds and for this they rely, quite reasonably, on psychologists. As Anscombe (1981) points out, moral philosophy should not even be done until there is an adequate philosophy of psychology. We need a major advance in the methodology of studying morality as a cognitive function. While other areas of developmental psychology have undergone significant changes and methodological innovations, for example, techniques used for studying perceptual development in babies, methods of *verbal* investigation, most commonly used in research on moral development, have changed little since Piaget's work in the area. To illustrate this, we still lack precise knowledge of when to stop further questioning, i.e., when the subject has reached the point of 'necessity' or the limits of his reasoning capacity and has no other options to consider. It is highly unlikely, though, that this is going to coincide with his first utterance in response to the experimenter's question. What needs to be re-examined is the very approach to the individual as a cognitive being who is assumed to pass, in his development, through a series of progressive transformations from an initial lack of rationality and logic to a gradual overcoming of this and growing into a fully rational being. It is not surprising, therefore, that the young child as a moral subject is often treated as *a priori* unable to think about that which is beyond immediate words. However, there is a substantial amount of post-Piagetian research that demonstrates convincingly the young child's capacity for rationality and correct understanding of a variety of different phenomena (for example, Bryant, 1974; Damon, 1981; Donaldson, 1978; Flavell, 1977; Gelman and Gallistel, 1978; Johnson and Wellman, 1982; Petrovich, 1982, 1983; Starkey, 1983; Starkey and Cooper, 1980). Research on morality, too, has begun to produce data which run counter to basic presuppositions of the cognitive-developmental theory by showing that children do possess a capacity for mature moral reasoning provided certain conditions pertain, in the first place, that the test situation be commensurate with their general experience (Elkind and Dabek, 1977; Nelson, 1980; Shweder *et al.*, 1981; Wellman *et al.*, 1979).

The definition of autonomy in terms of moral standard is equally precarious in both philosophy and psychology. In psychology, the moral standard criterion requires that an autonomous standard be internal, rooted in the individual rather than external to him, in which case morality is heteronomous. Although this distinction may seem quite straightforward, the problem is that it actually conceals four possible meanings implied by the adjectives 'external' and 'internal', a confusion which should be of some interest to a research psychologist. For example, to say that a rule is external to the individual could mean either that (a) the rule exists objectively and apart from the individual's perception of it, such as it is understood in theological ethics, or (b) the individual conceives of it as something foreign to his own thought and beliefs. Conversely, an internal moral rule may imply that (c) the rule originates in the individual himself, i.e., is created by him *ex nihilo*, in the sense in which Kohlberg refers to it, or, it may simply mean that (d) the rule is accepted by the individual and henceforth regarded as his own. It is important to note that neither Kohlberg's nor Piaget's evidence brings out convincingly any of these alternative sources of the moral standard. Generally speaking, available evidence does not enable one to see whether subjects do indeed think that their moral rules differ intrinsically from other people's similar rules and are, thus, unique in virtue of their being invented by the subject himself, or whether they perceive the rules as something they have accepted, for some reason, as their own. Although this is an extremely interesting and important question for psychology and related disciplines, it is rather unfortunate that empirical psychologists have tended to be preoccupied with those meanings mentioned above which actually deal with the ontological status of the moral standard (a, c), and thus belong to philosophy, instead of focusing their attention upon the psychological side of the problem of how the individual relates a rule to himself and to what extent he is able to accept it as his own (b, d), as well as conditions under which this occurs. It is obvious, therefore, that in psychology the standard criterion collapses into the invdividual one, since it is the individual's perception of it that matters in the end.

Philosophers' objection to the use of standard criterion in discourse on moral autonomy is directed at the nature and status of moral standards. Even though all types of standards are necessarily elusive and arbitrary to some extent, this arbitrariness is not 'capricious', according to Woods (1966), nor does it imply that standards are absolutely independent and unrelated to any circumstances whatsoever. Furthermore, to call a moral standard 'autonomous' must be 'awkward' due to the standard's being devoid of any governing activities possessed by a moral agent in connection with his handling of a law. Instead, Woods suggests that the adjective 'autonomous' be applied to the moral standard only in the sense that the standard is independent of human will and as such cannot be set aside or abrogated (*ibid.*, p. 83). It is important that this proposal by Woods implies a distinction between various kinds of standards or laws with respect to their modifiability and, thus, obligatoriness. This view seems to be corroborated by empirical evidence which indicates that young children are able to distinguish between different kinds of moral rules, those that can be negotiated, i.e., social conventions, and those that cannot, i.e., genuine moral rules (Nucci and Turiel, 1978; Shweder *et al.*, 1981; Turiel, 1979), as well as between different forms of justice (Lerner, 1974). And according to a study by Peisach and Hardeman (1983), they seem to know very well that certain acts are wrong even if no-one finds out about them. On the whole, there seems to be reasonable support for the hypothesis that young children understand more about morality than they can express in an articulate manner (for example, Durkin, 1961; Mossler *et al.*, 1976; Shweder *et al.*, 1981).

An especially important problem in connection with the standard criterion of moral autonomy is the content of a particular standard, such as duty, justice or love, as well as the criteria for deciding on their adequacy in moral terms. This problem becomes exceedingly complicated by the fact that in the majority of cases an unequivocally evaluative standpoint is being taken by researchers in place of a descriptive one. For instance, Kohlberg's choice of the principle of justice as the supreme principle of morality is based on his idea of 'philosophic adequacy' of a particular reason and on its occurrence later in time (1981, p. 131). What is missing here, and in many other similar examples, is some indication as to the philosophy presupposed in defining the adequacy of an idea. Notwithstanding this, psychologists continue to operate on evaluative presuppositions when attempting to determine the form or structure of cognitive processes on the basis of the moral content of the reasons given. Similar criticism, though from a somewhat different point of view, has been made by Locke (1983) and Henry (1983). Yet, it goes without saying that the psychologist ought to give some account of his subject's moral values. This, however, needs to be distinguished and separated from a more strictly psychological analysis of autonomy. For, different philosophies of life embrace different values and moral principles, and the way psychologists are normally educated does not confer upon them a prerogative to decide which of these are morally more adequate than others. Thus, their primary task must be to find out whether someone's reasoning is guided by any principles at all and, if so, specify them. The evaluation of particular principles as moral is a different sort of task and, as I have already stressed, it lies beyond the immediate range of a psychologist's concerns.

Finally, a word needs to be said with regard to the third criterion of autonomous morality, that which applies to morality as a domain. Although independence of morality can be considered in its relationship with any area of human interest, it is by far most common to discuss it in connection with religion. Since the relationship between morality and religion is directly relevant for the seventh stage in Kohlberg's theory, more about it will be said when we come to that point. Here, it may be sufficient to mention that although a number of philosophers explicitly admit that morality has an integrity of its own, they nevertheless question the belief in the primacy of moral values over all other values, especially religious, as well as man's self-sufficiency in matters of morality (Ewing, 1961, 1973; Hebblethwaite, 1981; Mitchell, 1980). Instead, these thinkers emphasize the origin of our existing morality in a Judeo-Christian value system and argue for the necessity to consider these original values as part of our moral constitution.

In view of the problems associated with the concept of autonomy, it seems appropriate to raise the question of its usefulness in psychology. In my opinion, 'autonomy' as a psychological construct seems to be faced with three possibilities; (1) to be restored to its original meaning in the context of Kant's theory of transcendental idealism; (2) to be given a meaning and application restricted to the cognitive processes of decision-making alone; or, (3) to be abandoned altogether.

The first possibility must be envisaged due to the fact that there is a fundamental difference between Kant's notion of reason and that of the psychologists, including Kohlberg. As I have tried to show, Kohlberg's conception of reason is Piagetian rather than Kantian, in the sense that it is essentially materialist, based on biological and evolutionary ideas, whereas Kant's is metaphysical, grounded in his theory of transcendental idealism. Thus, it follows that the capacity for autonomy is a distinctive function of Kantian reason; the psychological reason is devoid of this legislating potential without allowing, at the same time, for a certain degree of anarchy since, on this view, freedom in legislating has nothing by which to be restrained. Hence, Kant's dictum that the will is free because it is subject to the moral law must sound paradoxical to the psychologist. The psychologist's reason, in view of its dependence both structural and functional on the individual's experience with the environment is, according to Kant, actually heteronomous. In Kant's view, heteronomy is a type of morality that exists side by side with autonomous morality; it is a morality that falls short of the ideal morality characteristic of the transcendent component of human reason and can never be transformed into it. On the other hand, psychologists regard heteronomy as a stage in moral development which necessarily precedes that of autonomy. For example, according to both Kohlberg and Piaget, all laws are initially perceived by the child as originating outside himself, more precisely, in the society of adults. This suggests that moral principles can only be contingent and empirical, rather than necessary and universal. To elucidate this point Kohlberg writes that moral judgments and norms 'are to be ultimately understood as constructions of human actors that regulate their social interaction' (1981, p. 134). In contrast to this, Kant's view is that such laws and principles whose origin is in the social character of the individual are an example *par excellence* of heteronomy where the law is sought in the property of objects outside reason itself, in this case in social relationships and interactions. Consequently, it seems compelling to conclude that Kant's notion of autonomy, as a purely rational, *a priori* function of reason, cannot be applied, without some major distortions, to empirical psychology which is based upon a materialist philosophy. Although one could have some sympathy for this option, it is not realistic to seek room for it in experimental psychology.

Finally, it must be conceded that Kant's conception of human reason as composed of both natural and transcendent elements is a somewhat strained separation between the two. This may be particularly unacceptable to the psychologist who is familiar with the problem of separating the effects of different psychological functions, say, cognition and perception, emotion and motivation, etc. All the same, the important point is that Kant's theory of moral autonomy does not suffer from an incoherence which is inherent in the psychological account of moral autonomy.

As for the third possibility facing the concept of autonomy in psychology, the prospect of completely abandoning it does not seem likely simply given the extent to which it has become part of standard technical discourse on morality and moral development. It remains, therefore, to examine more closely the second option, since a redefinition of the concept of autonomy in terms of cognitive processes appears to be most practical and viable for psychology.

Confining the use of the concept of autonomy to the process of decision-making has an important advantage in that it enables us to retain an accustomed notion that will now have a precise definition and so meet the elementary requirements of professional research and comprehensible theorizing. However, this solution entails certain important disadvantages. First, it confronts moral psychology with the problem of providing sufficient justification of her status as a science. In other words, if the psychology of moral development is to be reduced to the task of merely finding out whether one *thinks for oneself* while making moral judgments, the dilemma arises as to whether psychology will be able to meet the expectations of any science, such as furnishing explanations and making predictions regarding observed phenomena, since all the information available in this case would be a diagnosis of one's ability to engage oneself in a process of 'one's own' thinking. It seems, therefore, superfluous to argue for the need to know the *result* or outcome of one's thinking in order to assess its maturity or adequacy. This, however, *is* an evaluative judgment. A judgment of this kind is particularly vulnerable in the sphere of morality where criteria for evaluation do not have an objective empirical status, nor are they easy to identify or to achieve agreement about. The only solution to this problem seems to be in clearly specifying the presuppositions and criteria used by researchers when assessing one's morality. It certainly should not be assumed that psychologists are neutral when conducting research on morality and drawing conclusions from it. Indeed, as Haan puts it, 'morality cannot be investigated without researchers taking a moral position' (1982, p. 1096) or, as Kohlberg similarly asserts, 'there is no philosophically neutral starting point for the psychological study of morality' (1981, p. 98).

Another disadvantage of determining the meaning of autonomy in psychology by confining it to the individual's capacity for decision-making is that it inevitably leads to some form of moral relativism since all that matters on this criterion is that my choice of a moral principle be mine regardless of its content. Still, the menace of moral relativism implied by this criterion, which Kohlberg rightly strives to avoid, could be alleviated in the same way as when dealing with the problem discussed above, i.e., by taking account of the evaluative component present in, and interfering with, the descriptive one. In other words, a precise specification of presuppositions and criteria employed by researchers would allow for the separation of the two aspects of moral judgment, as yet largely confounded: (1) evaluating the cognitive process and, (2) evaluating its product. While the former is an obvious task for the moral psychologist, the latter is not his immediate responsibility, nor indeed, is it desirable that he pass value judgments on his subjects' moral reasoning. This is not to say, however, that values should have no place in a psychological account of morality. On the contrary, values are bound to come up since moral judgments *are* about values and the psychologist evidently must somehow deal with them. But, to leave this task entirely to intuition, by not specifying any objective criteria to be used, means to practise a non-scientific psychology. Our current approach to research on moral development needs to be modified so as to include a requirement that *all* data observed be recorded and accounted for, including those values that were not envisaged by a particular research design. This applies especially to values of religious character occurring in morality which, as I shall try to illustrate shortly, typically do not get any attention in research on moral development. Such a modification in our approach to the study of morality would ultimately create the possibility of structuring two distinct types of moral theory based on two distinct sets of values: religious and secular. An important consequence of this separation within the currently existing theory of moral development would be that, according to the individual criterion of moral autonomy, both religious and secular morality would have to be accepted as equally autonomous so far as rational human beings are concerned. For, what distinguishes religious from secular morality are not different cognitive processes but different values to which cognitive processes are applied. It is no use closing our eyes to the fact that both of these frameworks are value-laden and it is therefore not legitimate to operate within the secular and present it as value-free.

In view of all that has been said so far, it appears that moral psychology as an empirical science cannot be value-free or, if it is to be so, then it must remain within the scope of judging as a cognitive function. Consequently, psychologists should either withdraw from the area of morality because it necessarily presupposes value judgments, or else they ought to recognize that certain values and metaphysical standpoints are being assumed and so need to be specified according to the requirements of scientific objectivity. Notwithstanding this, I should like to underline that the psychologist's primary task, that of dealing with the decision-making aspect of autonomy, is not insignificant nor redundant in moral psychology. On the contrary, considering some of the major methodological problems in the area, this task ought to be of primary concern to an empirical psychologist.

SHADOW OF RELIGION IN MORAL PSYCHOLOGY AND KOHLBERG'S STAGE 7

As we have seen, by merely redefining the concept of autonomy so as to make it a meaningful tool in empirical psychology, no major advance in the theory on moral development can be expected since this move still does not enable us to evaluate one's *moral* maturity. In order to have such a model, a more radical amendment to the cognitive-developmental theory of morality is needed. As I have argued, this would involve, in the first place, an acknowledgment of the inevitability of values and metaphysical presuppositions as well as an objective statement of criteria to be used in studying moral development. Kohlberg's theory is the only one which makes this recognition explicit by postulating Stage 7 in the development of moral reasoning, whose crucial feature is that it introduces the factor of religion in morality. In order to understand better the significance and implications of this added stage, it will be useful to look at some of the reasons which led Kohlberg to admit the necessity of going 'beyond' morality in order to explain it more adequately.

One of the major reasons for Kohlberg's positing of the seventh stage is his implicit dissatisfaction with the original six-stage theory as a model to explain the universal development of rational morality. In other words, since moral agents are rational beings, they have certain cognitive demands, such as asking the question 'Why be moral?' which, apparently, cannot be answered by the cognitive structure of Stage 6 alone. As a result, Kohlberg admitted that 'such a morality uniquely "requires" an ultimate stage of *religious* orientation and moves people toward it' (1981, p. 344, my italics). Evidence that led Kohlberg to reach this conclusion is neither substantial (Power and Kohlberg, 1980) nor certain since it is based on a disputable theory of faith development propounded by Fowler.[10] In addition, Kohlberg quotes his encounters with some unusual human histories and literary characters. But it is very likely that Kohlberg did have some more direct data on the relationship between religion and morality as a result of his subjects' spontaneous mentioning of religious notions while answering purely 'moral' questions.[11] However, Kohlberg's manner of dealing with such unplanned responses is in line with the general trend among moral psychologists to disregard this sort of responses or simply to treat them as immature. I shall try to illustrate this in a moment. For the time being, suffice it to say that whatever it was that moved Kohlberg into this direction, it has played an important role.

As for the true nature of Kohlberg's Stage 7, no more than a sketchy account of it can be given since its significance is more in its implications than in its present content. The language in which he describes it is figurative and poetical or, to quote

Kohlberg, 'the term is only a metaphor' (1981, p. 344) used to signify some 'cosmic' rather than 'universal' perspective on life and morality (*ibid*., p. 345). One of the major reasons for the unfinished character of the seventh stage is, as I have already stressed, its poor empirical foundation. Since Kohlberg did not do any systematic research into Stage 7, many interesting questions remain unanswered, for example, how would a Stage 7 person go about answering questions concerning the meaning and value of life. In all likelihood, his or her type of response would resemble that of a Stage 4 subject, that is, the value of life would be accounted for in terms of God. Another important reason for the incompleteness of the seventh stage seems to be Kohlberg's ambiguous, even ambivalent, attitude toward religion as relevant to morality. For example, although he quotes a recent nationwide survey in which a 'large majority of Americans stated that their morality was dependent on their religious belief', he nevertheless interprets this result as a 'subjective attitude' rather than an empirical finding, on the grounds that earlier studies of Hartshorne and May (1928–30) found no relation between 'experimental measures of honesty and type or amount of religious belief' (1981, p. 304). However, this early finding does not seem to be corroborated by more recent evidence, some of which indicates that there is an active relationship between morality and religion from childhood to adulthood (Hilliard, 1959) and, more specifically, in adolescents (Wright and Cox, 1967, 1971). Moreover, it has been found that religious training of young children leads to greater needs-oriented reasoning and less hedonistic reasoning (Eisenberg-Berg and Roth, 1980).

In spite of his recognition of the factor of religion in morality, Kohlberg nevertheless argues for the separation of religion from morality on the grounds that 'religious education has no specifically important or unique role to play in moral development' (1981, p. 304). The assumption from which Kohlberg proceeds here is that moral development chronologically precedes religious development so that the latter has nothing to contribute to the former. Apart from the fact that there is no satisfying evidence to support this claim, the important question is whether a research psychologist should endeavour to search for the roots of each or, rather, should he strive to understand the nature and dynamics of their relationship in a developing human being. For, the former is not only more difficult to answer, but an answer to it, even if possible, may not be particularly helpful, especially from an educational point of view. That is to say, an empirical observation that morality and religion are related to each other ought to be a sufficient ground for our trying to elucidate the nature of this relationship, since even Kohlberg has found that 'a considerable portion of a child's orientation to divinity ... is a moral orientation' (1974, p. 13). Furthermore, if Kohlberg is correct in asserting that there are some 'universal religious issues that all people attempt to answer' (1981, p. 308), then it follows that depriving them of such answers by adhering to a concept of education which is against any direct moral and religious instruction cannot be particularly moral in itself.

It is not possible to detect all the conceivable causes of Kohlberg's undecided opinion on the role of religion in moral development. In addition to the problem of insufficient empirical evidence, Kohlberg and moral psychologists in general lack some theological information which would seem to be necessary for dealing with a topic bordering on the two disciplines.[12] Finally, Kohlberg's selection of Kant's sources is also partly responsible for this uncertainty since it led him to the faulty conclusion that Kant's linking of morality with religion was 'uncertain and imaginative' (*ibid.*, p. 338), whereas it could be described as actually 'imperative' (see Baldacchino, 1976; Körner, 1955; Paton, 1983). In defence of Kohlberg, however, it needs to be conceded that Kant's views on the status of religion in philosophy, especially in ethics, could be interpreted equivocally since, as Mitchell says, Kant was not 'fully consistent in his rejection of metaphysics and covertly appealed to the concept of nature in his formulation of the categorical imperative' (1980, p. 27–8).

In spite of all the difficulties associated with Kohlberg's idea of the role that religion plays in morality, the fact is that he makes a remarkable step by approaching this question directly in an utterly secular moral psychology. Thus, another way to demonstrate the significance of Kohlberg's provisional Stage 7 is by looking at the prevailing attitude toward religion in morality among research psychologists. This is not only useful but, indeed, necessary, since it may provide some explanation and even justification for the incompleteness of Stage 7 and its failure, at present, to answer satisfactorily the questions it purports to answer.

Although there is, as we have seen, a certain amount of evidence that the moral and religious domain are perceived by human subjects as related, there are many more examples of researchers' bias against considering seriously their subjects' referring to religion in any form. Here, I shall only illustrate the point by mentioning a few examples. For one thing, it is usually impossible to see, on the basis of data reported, whether subjects in a particular study mention religion spontaneously or not. They apparently do sometimes, despite the fact that the typical research design on morality does not make room for this sort of question (for example, Jensen and Rytting, 1972; Percival and Haviland, 1978), even though the context of research is such that it makes it quite natural for such responses to appear (Chaikin and Darley, 1973; Fein and Stein, 1977; Haviland, 1979; Karniol, 1980). Most of these papers summarize research on the notions of justice and immanent justice, and some of the authors single it out as a curious finding that even in adults there is a certain 'mysticism' and 'superstitious belief' in justice (Haviland, 1979, and Fein and Stein, 1977, respectively). The problem with research of this kind is that its authors normally do not give any reasons for interpretations they provide, nor specify the criteria used for dealing with such responses in which a child mentions God or any other religious concept. In a recent study of my own (1983), the evidence shows convincingly that preschool children do attribute certain types of events to God exclusively and refer to God as an important agency in particular, well defined, contexts, nothing of which suggests presence of some superstitious and mystical beliefs. No phenomenon can be understood properly if certain ways of looking at it are regarded from the start as irrelevant and thus to be dismissed. What people think and believe about any matter should have the status of empirical data in psychological investigations. As I have already indicated, Kohlberg, too, is susceptible of this tendency to explain away that which does not fit his theory. For instance, he writes that, 'the functions of morality and religion ... have been seen in the world religions of Christianity and Judaism as intimately related' (1981, p. 321), but overlooks the fact that a vast majority of his subjects belong to these two world religions and does not try to pursue the character of this relationship even when brought up by a subject.

Despite the fact that a number of thoughtful criticisms of Kohlberg's theory have been expressed so far, no radically new perspective on moral development has emerged. However diverse these criticisms may have been, there is a vantage-point from which they all look alike. Paradoxically enough, it was Kohlberg himself who has pointed to a genuinely different perspective by providing some *clues* to solutions of problems in moral development research hinted at by his Stage 7. I emphasize the word 'clues' in order to avoid a suggestion that something more than a hint has been given by Kohlberg. However, in view of the present situation concerning theory and research on moral development, this contribution on Kohlberg's part is not small. And, although his modified or seven-stage theory is in need of much revision and further development, it nevertheless possesses some important features: it broadens the scope of moral psychology, it helps redress the balance in research and, finally, in virtue of its novelty, it has some heuristic potential. Of course, none of this will be possible as long as psychologists continue to ignore its existence.

ACKNOWLEDGMENTS

I would like to thank Dr L. V. Baldacchino for his kind permission to quote some parts of his thesis. I also thank Professor Basil Mitchell for a helpful discussion about some of the ideas expressed here.

NOTES

1   See *The British Journal of Psychology* (1982), 73, pp. 313–16.
2   The only difference between Piaget and Kohlberg with regard to autonomy is the age at which it occurs, i.e., at around 10 to 12 years, according to Piaget, and much later in adolescence or even adulthood, according to Kohlberg. This is to be attributed to the age difference between their respective samples.
3   See Piaget (1965) *The Moral Judgment of the Child*, pp. 101–3.
4   Although Vuyk in her Vol. I of the *Overview and Critique of Piaget's Genetic Epistemology 1965–1980* writes that, 'It is indeed astonishing how many critics still use Piaget's early books without trying to find out whether he has changed his point of view or not' (p. xii), she has apparently avoided the problem by focusing on those works of Piaget in which he *has* changed his views. However, I have not been able to find, in either of her two volumes, any reference to, for example, morality, autonomy, religion, Bovet or Durkheim, all of which feature prominently in Piaget's early works dealing with the child's understanding of the physical and moral domain. My conclusion is, therefore, that there *are* still parts of Piaget's system which neither Piaget nor his followers have changed so that most of his assumptions from the early works remain at the foundation of his theory.
5   Immanent justice is defined by Piaget as the child's belief in 'the existence of automatic punishments which emanate from things themselves' (1965, p. 250).
6   According to Helm's classification, it is possible to distinguish four meanings of autonomy: (1) an adult-like, proper decision-making process; (2) an autonomous person's action as morally pure or altruistic; (3) an autonomous moral agent as fully conscientious in his acting, or, as the sole moral authority of his 'authentic' action; and, (4) motives for action as autonomous if actions are performed for their own sake (1981, pp. 5–6).
7   According to Baldacchino, the concept of 'the supersensible' is an ontological concept which is used synonymously with the concept of 'the unconditioned' which is epistemological in nature (1976, p. 33). Both 'the supersensible' and 'the unconditioned' refer to a non-contingent real existence with causal powers, an 'assumption' which 'entails the conception of this being as possessing understanding and will ...' (*ibid.*, p. 209).
8   This would be most likely to occur in connection with those morally relevant situations with which the child is unfamiliar due to his limited experience, for example, adultery, treachery, and other forms of moral evil absent from the child's general experience.

9 Even though Kohlberg points out that protest in itself is neither virtuous nor vicious and that what matters is the knowledge of the good behind it, he nevertheless asserts, 'Protesting is a sure sign of being at the most mature moral level ...' (1981, p. 45).

10 For a summary of Fowler's theory see Kohlberg (1981), pp. 323–36.

11 For instance, in answering Kohlberg's question, 'Should the doctor "mercy-kill" a fatally ill woman requesting death because of her pain?', some of his subjects mention God explicitly as a reason for a particular action (1981, pp. 20–1).

12 Kohlberg repeatedly confuses certain directly opposing notions, such as, pleasure with divine reward (p. 322), state laws with God's laws (p. 153), theistic with pantheistic religions (p. 322) or, makes a reference to the book of Job which is not quite accurate in that it ignores the final outcome of the character's suffering (p. 322).

REFERENCES

Adams, R. M. (1979) 'Autonomy and theological ethics', in *Religious Studies*, 15, pp. 191–4.

Anscombe, G. E. M. (1981) *Ethics, Religion and Politics*, The Collected Philosophical Papers, Vol. III, Oxford, Basil Blackwell.

Baldacchino, L. V. (1976) *Reason and the Supersensible: A Study in Kant's Use of the Concept of the Unconditioned in Moral and Perceptual Experience*, PhD Thesis, London, Birkbeck College.

Baldacchino, L. V. (1980) 'Kant's Theory of Self-Consciousness', *Kant-Studien, Philosophische Zeitschrift der Kant-Gesellshaft*, 71, Jahrgang, Heft 4, pp. 393–405.

Bovet, P. (1928) *The Child's Religion*, London, Dent.

Breakwell, G. (1983) 'Moralities and conflict', in Weinreich-Haste, H. and Locke, D. (Eds.) *Morality in the Making*, New York, J. Wiley and Sons, pp. 231–44.

Brett, G. S. (1921) *A History of Psychology*, Vol. III, London, G. Allen and Unwin.

Bryant, P. E. (1974) *Perception and Understanding in Young Children*, London, Methuen.

Chaikin, A. and Darley, J. (1973) 'Victim or perpetrator? Defensive attribution of responsibility and the need for order and justice', *Journal of Personality and Social Psychology*, 25, pp. 268–75.

Copleston, F. C. (1982) *Aquinas*, Harmondsworth, Penguin Books.

Damon, W. (1981) 'Exploring children's social cognition', in Flavell, J. and Ross, L. (Eds.) *Social Cognitive Development*, CUP, pp. 154–75.

Donaldson, M. (1978) *Children's Minds*, London, Fontana/Collins.

Durkin, D. (1961) 'The specificity of children's moral judgments', *Journal of Genetic Psychology*, 98, pp. 3–14.

Duska, R. and Whelan, M. (1977) *Moral Development: A Guide to Piaget and Kohlberg*, Dublin, Gill and Macmillan.

Eisenberg-Berg, N. and Roth, K. (1980) 'Development of young children's prosocial moral judgment: A longitudinal follow-up', *Developmental Psychology*, 16, 4, pp. 375–6.

Elkind, D. and Dabek, R. (1977) 'Personal injury and property damage in the moral judgments of children', *Child Development*, 48, pp. 518–22.

Emler, N. (1983) 'Morality and politics: The ideological dimension in the theory of moral development', in Weinreich-Haste, H. and Locke, D. (Eds.) *Morality in the Making*, New York, J. Wiley and Sons, pp. 47–71.

Evans-Pritchard, E. E. (1980) *Theories of Primitive Religion*, Oxford, Clarendon Press.

Ewing, A. C. (1961) 'Autonomy of ethics', in Ramsey, I. (Ed.) *Prospect for Metaphysics*, London, G. Allen and Unwin, pp. 33–49.

Ewing, A. C. (1973) *Value and Reality*, London, G. Allen and Unwin.

Fein, D. and Stein, G. M. (1977) 'Immanent punishment and reward in six and nine year old children', *Journal of Genetic Psychology*, 131, pp. 91–6.

Flavell, J. H. (1977) *Cognitive Development*, New Jersey, Prentice Hall.

Geach, P. (1981) 'The moral law and the law of God', in Helm, P. (Ed.) *Divine Commands and Morality*, OUP, pp. 165–74.

Gelman, R. and Gallistel, C. R. (1978) *The Child's Understanding of Number*, Cambridge, Mass., Harvard University Press.

Gelman, R. and Spelke, E. (1981) 'The development of thoughts about animate and inanimate objects:

Implications for research on social cognition', in Flavell, J. H. and Ross, L. (Eds.) *Social Cognitive Development*, Cambridge, CUP.

Haan, N. (1982) 'Can research on morality be "scientific"?', *American Psychologist*, 37, 10, pp. 1096–104.

Hare, R. M. (1972) *The Language of Morals*, Oxford, Clarendon Press.

Hastings, J. (Ed.) *Encyclopedia of Religion and Ethics*, Vol. III, Edinburgh, T. and T. Clark.

Haviland, J. M. (1979) 'Teachers' and students' beliefs about punishment', *Journal of Educational Psychology*, 71, pp. 563–70.

Hebblethwaite, B. (1981) *The Adequacy of Christian Ethics*, London, M. Morgan and Scott.

Helm, P. 'Introduction', in Helm, P. (Ed.) *Divine Commands and Morality*, OUP, pp. 1–13.

Henry, R. M. (1983) 'The cognitive vs. psychodynamic debate about morality', *Human Development*, 26, pp. 173–9.

Hilliard, F. (1959) 'The influence of religious education upon the development of children's moral ideas', *British Journal of Education*, 19, pp. 50–9.

Jensen, L. and Rytting, M. (1972) 'Effects of information and relatedness on children's belief in immanent justice', *Developmental Psychology*, 7, pp. 93–7.

Johnson, C. N. and Wellman, H. M. (1982) 'Children's developing conceptions of the mind and brain', *Child Development*, 53, pp. 222–34.

Joyce, G. H. (1923) *Principles of Natural Theology*, London, Longmans, Green and Co.

Kant, I. (1938) *The Fundamental Principles of the Metaphysic of Ethics*, New York, D. Appleton-Century Company.

Karniol, R. (1980) 'A conceptual analysis of immanent justice', *Child Development*, 51, pp. 118–30.

Karniol, R. (1982) 'Behavioral and cognitive correlates of various immanent justice responses in children: Deterrent versus punitive moral systems', *Journal of Personality and Social Psychology*, 43, 4, pp. 811–20.

Kohlberg, L. (1974) 'Education, moral development and faith', *Journal of Moral Education*, 4, 1, pp. 5–16.

Kohlberg, L. (1981) *The Philosophy of Moral Development*, Vol. I, San Francisco, Harper and Row.

Körner, S. (1955) *Kant*, London, Penguin Books.

Lerner, M. J. (1974) 'The justice motive: "Equity" and "parity" among children', *Journal of Personality and Social Psychology*, 29, 4, pp. 539–50.

Locke, D. (1983) 'Doing what comes morally. The relation between behaviour and stages of moral reasoning', *Human Development*, 26, pp. 11–25.

Macquarrie, J. (Ed.) (1967) *A Dictionary of Christian Ethics*, London, SCM Press.

Mitchell, B. (1967) *Law, Morality and Religion in a Secular Society*, Oxford, OUP.

Mitchell, B. (1980) *Morality: Religious and Secular*, Oxford, Clarendon Press.

Modgil, S. and Modgil, C. (1976) *Piagetian Research: Compilation and Commentary*, Vol. VI, Windsor, NFER Publishing Company.

Murphy, R. (1979) *An Overture to Social Anthroplogy*, New Jersey, Prentice-Hall.

Nelson, S. (1980) 'Factors influencing young children's use of motives and outcomes as moral criteria', *Child Development*, 50, pp. 869–73.

Nucci, L. P. and Turiel, E. (1978) 'Social interactions and the development of social concepts in preschool children', *Child Development*, 49, pp. 400–7.

Oxford English Dictionary, The Shorter, Vol. I, 3rd ed., Oxford, OUP, 1975.

Paton, H. J. (1983) *The Moral Law*, London, Hutchinson.

Peisach, E. and Hardeman, M. (1983) 'Moral reasoning in early childhood: Lying and stealing', *Journal of Genetic Psychology*, 142, pp. 107–20

Percival, P. and Haviland, J. M. (1978) 'Consistency and retribution in children's immanent justice decisions', *Developmental Psychology*, 14, pp. 132–6.

Perry, T. (1976) *Moral Reasoning and Truth*, Oxford, Clarendon Press.

Petrovich, O. (1982) 'Animism in young children', Poster presented at the meeting of the Developmental Section of the British Psychological Society, Durham.

Petrovich, O. (1983) Unpublished research on 'artificialism' in children's thinking, Department of Experimental Psychology, South Parks Road, Oxford OX1 3UD.

Piaget, J. (1953) *The Origin of Intelligence in the Child*, London, Routledge and Kegan Paul.

Piaget, J. (1965) *The Moral Judgment of the Child*, London, Routledge and Kegan Paul.

Piaget, J. (1977) *The Child's Conception of the World*, St Albans, Paladin.

Power, C. and Kohlberg, L. (1980) 'Religion, morality and ego development', in Fowler, J. and

Vergote, A. (Eds.) *Towards Moral and Religious Maturity*, Morristown, N. J. Silver Burdett, pp. 343–72.

Quinn, P. L. (1975) 'Religious obedience and moral autonomy', *Religious Studies*, 11, pp. 265–81.

Shweder, R. A., Turiel, E. and Much, N. C. (1981) 'The moral intuitions of the child', in Flavell, J. H. and Ross, L. (Eds.) *Social Cognitive Development*, Cambridge, CUP, pp. 288–305.

Starkey, P. (1983) 'Early numerical competencies', Paper presented at the meeting of the Developmental Section of the British Psychological Society, Oxford.

Starkey, P. and Cooper, R. G., Jr. (1980) 'Perception of numbers by human infants', *Science*, 210, pp. 1033–5.

Turiel, E. (1979) 'Distinct conceptual and developmental domains: Social convention and morality', in Keasy, C. B. (Ed.) *Nebraska Symposium on Motivation, 1977*, Vol. 25, Lincoln, University of Nebraska Press, pp. 77–116.

Vine, I. (1983) 'The nature of moral commitments', in Weinreich-Haste, H. and Locke, D. (Eds.) *Morality in the Making*, New York, J. Wiley and Sons, pp. 19–45.

Vuyk, R. (1981) *Overview and Critique of Piaget's Genetic Epistemology 1965–1980*, Vols. I and II, London, Academic Press.

Weinreich-Haste, H. (1982) 'Piaget on morality: A critical perspective', in Modgil, S. and Modgil, C. (Eds.) *Piaget: Consensus and Controversy*, London, Holt, Rinehart and Winston, pp. 181–206.

Weinreich-Haste, H. and Locke, D. (1983) 'Introduction', in Weinreich-Haste, H. and Locke, D. (Eds.) *Morality in the Making*, New York, J. Wiley and Sons, pp. xiii–xix.

Wellman, H. M., Larkey, C. and Somerville, S. (1979) 'The early development of moral criteria', *Child Development*, 50, pp. 869–73.

Wilshire, B. (1969) *Metaphysics: An Introduction to Philosophy*, New York, Pegasus.

Woods, G. F. (1966) *A Defence of Theological Ethics*, Cambridge, CUP.

Wright, D. (1972) 'The psychology of religion—A review of empirical studies', Bulletin of the Association for Religious Education, Extended Supplement 1.

Wright, D. and Cox, E. (1967) 'A study of the relationship between moral judgment and religious belief in a sample of English adolescents', *Journal of Social Psychology*, 72, pp. 135–44.

Wright, D. and Cox, E. (1971) 'Changes in moral belief among sixth form boys and girls over a seven year period in relation to religious belief, age and sex differences', *British Journal of Social and Clinical Psychology*, 10, pp. 332–41.

Wright, J. (1981) 'Morality and Hebraic Christian religion', *Journal of Moral Education*, 11, 1, pp. 32–40.

7. Kohlberg's Moral Psychology: Any Advance on the Present Stage?

PETER TOMLINSON

Appearing for the opposition in a debate-structured collection on the work of Lawrence Kohlberg makes it encumbent upon me to declare my appreciation, before saying anything else, of the importance and usefulness of his massive and systematic contribution to the developmental psychology of morals. Amongst these positive aspects various major features may be mentioned. One is the sheer scale of this pioneering and sustained onslaught on a domain of basic human interest, which his work has brought to the forefront of 'respectable' psychological concern. Another is the rare interdisciplinarity of approach. This includes not only the concern to make clear its axioms, assumptions, definitions and methodological principles, without taking all of these for granted in the mode of the average traditional psychologist, but also the attempt to interrelate the philosophical, psychological and sociological aspects involved. A further commendable feature is the long-term development of Kohlberg's views, following where the data seemed to lead and revising aspects of the theory on that basis. Finally, one can point to the combination of theoretical and practical concerns: Kohlberg's interest in moral and social education, for example, is long-standing.

Of course, even these praiseworthy features are not without their less fortunate side-effects. For instance, mastering the Kohlberg contribution is all the more difficult because of its grand and diverse scale and the ongoing revision, together with delays in the publication of important material, has caused frustration when people attempted to do so. However, none of us is perfect.

Such features and any critical assessment need to be considered in a larger (and more detailed) perspective of the whole contribution, including its history. I have offered such a review elsewhere (Tomlinson, 1980), and readers will also certainly profit from the scholarly but readable Handbook chapter by Rest (1984). Given that the whole of the present book is devoted to aspects of Kohlberg's work, my contribution will necessarily be much more focused here, restricting itself to features relevant to moral psychology. An interim definition of moral psychology is: an understanding of the phenomena and processes involved in an individual's moral activity. Of course, one cannot cleanly separate psychological aspects from other sides of the Kohlberg contribution, such as its philosophical and meta-ethical assumptions, but these will be the concern of other pairs of chapters in this book and my own focus will remain on individual processes. Even within this focus my scope demands a further limiting of attention to those aspects which, in my opinion, need alteration or revision. Whilst a considerable number of specific points will be raised, they will be encountered in the pursuit of the following major themes. First, a critical look at the *structuralism* of Kohlberg's cognitive-developmental approach, which is certainly central to his work and informs a number of the aspects I find problematic. Next a more specific topic: Kohlberg's *phenomenalism* and its emphasis on conscious processing. Thirdly, and arising out of the previous two, consideration of what I shall contend to be a somewhat confused under-use of *psychological paradigms*, whose correction would be consistent with certain, if not all, of Kohlberg's other basic insights.

Given the rolling nature of the Kohlbergian contribution, it is fortunate that a current formulation of its major features has just been published (Kohlberg, Levine and Hewer, 1983). The present chapter will therefore make considerable reference to this very clear recent statement. My critical comments will be grounded in references to a variety of psychological sources, including an as yet largely unpublished six-year longitudinal study in which I and my colleagues have attempted to check both the developmental and the phenomenological validity of Kohlberg's claims (see Tomlinson, 1983, for a preliminary account).

KOHLBERG'S COGNITIVE STRUCTURALISM

Kohlberg's cognitive stage structuralism lies at the heart of his work and leads to a variety of difficulties. By 'cognitive stage structuralism' I mean that Kohlberg takes as axiomatic the late Piagetian view of intellectual competence as the deployment of an organized set (*structure d'ensemble*) of logical operations and intellectual development as the successive acquisition, in an invariant order, of a series of increasingly complex and adequate structures or *stages* of cognitive competence. The focus of Kohlberg's application of this perspective has been the notion of justice, so that Kohlberg, Levine and Hewer (1983) succinctly summarize the theory as 'a rational reconstruction of the ontogenesis of justice reasoning.'

As I have noted before (Tomlinson, 1980) and as Rest (1984) has also highlighted, the axiomatic status of Kohlberg's cognitive structuralism is revealed rather strikingly when one considers at all closely the nature of the revisions made to the formulation of the stage sequence. For whereas one might naively have expected the enterprise to be one in which Kohlberg studied the changing types of moral judgment encountered with increasing age of subject and happened to find that these changes seemed best characterized in terms of an invariant sequence of organized social perspectives, the emphasis has definitely been otherwise. Kohlberg has made it very clear (for instance, in the recent scoring manual) that the mid-seventies revisions in conceptions of the stages were undertaken, as Rest (1984, p. 202) puts it: 'on the basis of how well the data generated conform to strict stage expectations (no reversals in longitudinal data, minimal stage mix, no stage skipping).' These changes also had the effect of removing sex difference tendencies in moral stage scores.

The situation is therefore more a case of Kohlberg *defining* cognitive development, with Piaget, as progress through an invariant sequence of mental organizations, then turning to morality and *defining* that (again with Piaget) as deontological justice. Kohlberg, Levine and Hewer are disarmingly frank in citing the reason for this:

> Following Piaget's lead, Kohlberg thought that justice reasoning would be the cognitive factor most amenable to structural developmental stage analysis insofar as it would clearly provide reasoning material where structuring and equilibrating operations (e.g. reversibility) could be seen. (1983, p. 92)

To be fair, one should add that there were further, meta-ethical considerations involved, including Kohlberg's acceptance from Hare of a Kantian emphasis on prescriptiveness and universalizability in moral judgment. Kohlberg was also concerned 'for cultural and ethical universality in moral judgment' and 'a cognitive or "rational" approach to morality' (Kohlberg, Levine and Hewer, 1983, p. 93). And to anticipate, I shall suggest below that if universal descriptions are what the psychologist is after, then relatively formal developmental structures are perhaps the most one can hope for. However, Kohlberg's particular structuralist emphasis leads to certain problems, to which we now turn.

(1) Definition and Scope of Kohlberg's Moral Psychology

As we have just seen, Kohlberg's study of moral development has been anchored very firmly in the study of thinking about social or distributive justice. However, when Kohlberg, Levine and Hewer (1983, p. 17) assure us that 'we have always tried to be clear that Kohlberg's stages are stages of justice reasoning' we are, I think, entitled to retort that this is indeed a concise description and that it is a pity that it wasn't used, from the outset, in preference to such expressions as *moral* development. For there is clearly more to moral life than moral reasoning and thus there is more to a moral psychology than the specification of what is cross-culturally universal in the development of justice reasoning.

This issue is in essence a definitional or philosophical one and I shall therefore not attempt to treat it at any length. It must receive some attention, nonetheless, not just because definitional aspects are of paramount importance, as Kohlberg has so frequently emphasized, but also because the deployment of his own social justice deontology has seriously restricted the moral-psychological relevance of his contribution.

As writers on morals typically agree (cf. Frankena, 1973; Wilson, 1967; Rest, 1984; Wright, 1971), morality is concerned with virtually all aspects of human action, not just with particular facets or subprocesses therein. Kohlberg would not disagree. In spite of using expressions such as 'moral development' in a number of his article titles, the content of these contributions has made it clear that although the development of justice reasoning is his central focus, he is nevertheless interested in questions regarding, say, moral action and the moral effects of social atmospheres.

But my complaint is actually more specific. Namely, given that moral reasoning is defined by Kohlberg as that concerned with the social justice of action prescriptions and thus moral action as action informed by such considerations, then this legislates out of consideration a good deal which one might have expected to be treated under a moral psychology. If an action arises, for instance, out of some strong and explicit first-order conviction concerning what one ought to do in specific circumstances (e.g., not deliberately spilling human blood), then unless further explicit considerations of a distributive nature are forthcoming, this should not qualify for Kohlberg as a moral action, i.e., something which his moral psychology ought to help understand. Given that this is a definitional point, all that one can demand is consistency. In that case one is inclined to refer to Kohlberg's preferred philosophical influences. Hare (1952), for instance, held that moral judgments are not just prescriptive and universalizable, but also over-riding. Likewise, Kant's practical reason was concerned with a rational formulation of the categorical *imperative*, which would be the response to one of his famous three original questions, namely: 'What *must* I do?' Doubtless over-ridingness is a formal feature that has informed Turiel's (1980) work on moral vs. conventional issues and has allowed Gilligan (1982) to focus on abortion decisions as worthy moral topics. Kohlberg, Levine and Hewer's (1983) response to their work appears a somewhat ambivalent effort to have things both ways. On the one hand, they accept that 'Gilligan's "personal" morality *is* part of the moral domain' (p. 27, italics theirs), though on the other hand they believe that 'our own conception of stages of moral reasoning must remain centred on justice.' And yet this 'does *not* lead us to postulate two generalized moral orientations, justice and care, as it does for Gilligan' (p. 25, italics theirs). They go on to contend that claims regarding the moral domain should be grounded in philosophical analysis and corroborated by psychological evidence, and that neither Turiel nor Gilligan has provided either philosophical rationale or evidence of a structural stage development in their sorts of stages. My reply would be that (a) another look at Hare might be instructive on the first count and (b) on the second, why should Gilligan, Turiel, or anybody else need cognitive stage structures when they don't necessarily start with Kohlberg's structuralist definitions and meta-ethical assumptions? Perhaps this cognitive conflict will yet lead to further equilibration on Kohlberg behalf. The importance of this definitional point will be further indicated by its relevance to a number of the more specifically psychological issues raised in what follows.

(2) Evidence for a Structured Organization of Moral Reasoning Operations

The Piagetian or 'hard' cognitive stage concept which Kohlberg seeks to apply in the justice reasoning domain involves four criterial attributes: qualitative differences, invariant developmental order, unitary organization of thought processes (*structure d'ensemble*), successive hierarchical integration and displacement by later stages. Thus Kohlbergian interest has been directed towards the form rather than the content of moral reasoning. This has been expressed by saying that Kohlberg is interested in 'justice operations' such as equality and reciprocity, which are seen as 'interiorized actions of distribution and exchange which parallel logical operations of equality and reciprocity [in the physical content domain]' (Kohlberg, Levine and Hewer, 1983, p. 95). Both types of operation are said to enable equilibration, this referring in the moral sphere to the balancing of conflicting value claims.

The applicability of the Piagetian hard-stage conception to cognitive development raises a whole host of issues, whatever the content area (cf. Brown and Desforges, 1979). On a somewhat restricted point of terminology, the above quotation surely reveals that the operations concerned are logical operations whatever the content domain: calling them 'justice operations' as opposed to logical operations (for physical content) has always seemed to me to be somewhat misleading. More seriously though, one might on the one hand admire Kohlberg's creative application of Piagetian logico-mathematical analyses to the domain of interpersonal prescription, or on the other hand doubt the wisdom of grounding himself in equilibration, that most nebulous of Piagetian notions (cf. Sullivan, 1967)—indeed, Kohlberg seems to have given the term a more straightforward meaning in terms of reversibility of value perspective than it had in its original physical content setting.

The establishment of sequentiality of the stages has received the lion's share of attention, with general agreement that the case is pretty firm up to Stage 4 at least. I shall therefore leave this developmental issue largely out of consideration, returning to it briefly in a different connection later in the chapter. For the moment I should like to look at a central feature of stages (cf. Piaget, 1972) that has wide significance for an integrated moral psychology, namely the notion of a structured organization of thought operations or *structure d'ensemble*.

When Kohlberg, Levine and Hewer (1983) mention this criterial attribute of the Piagetian stage concept they remark, 'The implication is that various aspects of stage structures should appear as a consistent cluster of responses in development' (p. 31). That is, a Piagetian stage is not simply another specific response, but an organization of a variety of subcompetences that are definitive of the stage. The concrete operational stage, for instance, is defined in terms of classification, seriation and conservation, with Piaget claiming that reversibility is a central theme. Evidence required for the structural organization aspect of the unity of a stage would appear to include synchrony of acquisition of the various constituent operations. Now although Kohlberg does talk of the justice operations of reversibility, reciprocity and equality, I would agree with Rest that the precise nature of the new logical operations defining each stage is not made very clear, nor 'how the variety of characteristics used to score each stage logically cohere and relate to the new operation' (Rest, 1984, p. 200). In Kohlberg, Levine and Hewer (1983, pp. 100–3) we find an account of how the forms of reciprocity vary with the changing social perspectives that have been emphasized as central to the revised version of the stages. Thus reciprocity considerations and social perspectives are not separable, since the one must apply to terms supplied by the other. Furthermore, equality and reversibility are not elaborated as further independent strands, rather they seem to be involved in what Kohlberg *et al.* call reciprocity. What we do not in any case appear to have been furnished with as yet are clear definitions and assessment procedures for tapping a variety of discernible justice operations, with data on the synchrony of their acquisition and development as minimal evidence for the *structure d'ensemble* feature of hard stages of justice reasoning. What we usually get instead when the question of evidence for organized structures is raised is, surprisingly, mention of the tendency of subjects to use a single dominant stage across different content areas of specific moral issue (compare, for instance, statements made on pp. 31 and 34 of Kohlberg, Levine and Hewer). But in reality this sort of data relates more to the assumed predominance of structures in thinking, and begs the question of definition and assessment of the element operations thereof.

(3)   How 'Moral-Psychologically Powerful' Are Justice Structures in Practice?

If we set the appropriate type of distributive justice dilemmas, such as Kohlberg's, then it is likely that we may elicit reasoning illustrating 'justice structures', and we may even be able to define a range of such operations and show by such methods a respectable coherence, as called for under the last point. The question arises, however, as to how far such structures are actually used in subjects' everyday moral activities. Every psychological paradigm must face the question as to what, in any given piece of relevant action, it is to treat as the functional units of process. Even the old-fashioned behaviourist had to specify the 'functional stimulus'. Insofar as the approach is cognitive, the question relates to the units of representation and the operations interrelating these and thence generating action. In the Kohlbergian-Piagetian stance the answer is clear: primacy is given to the social perspective and logical/justice operations of deontological or prescriptive balancing.

Before challenging that primacy as a general psychological truth, I ought perhaps to indicate that I have personally found Kohlberg' social distributive formalism useful in my own decision-making—but then perhaps that has more to do with my being a Western male with a Roman-Catholic upbringing and a philosophical training.

Meanwhile, however, it is relevant to point out that there is a good deal of evidence that the appropriate psychological units of analysis are pretty specific in many people. At a general cognitive level, for instance, the content effects found by Wason and Johnson-Laird (1972) challenge the primacy of formal-logical structures in deductive reasoning, and in Piagetian research Brown and Desforges' (1979) review concludes that the amount of *décalage* found amongst Piagetian tasks is embarrassingly high for a theory stressing abstract general structures in thinking. Within the domain of moral judgment research, investigators such as Haan (1978) have proposed stage models framed in more concrete terms than Kohlberg's, and Gilligan (1982) and Kitwood (1980) have emphasized much more specific aspects of relationships as the key elements in moral decision-making.

This issue as to the 'phenomenological validity' of stage structures is by no means easy to tease out, especially when Kohlberg, apparently eschewing his phenomenalism claim (see below), treats us in Kohlberg, Levine and Hewer (1983, pp. 95–101) to an account of how justice considerations can be seen to be implicit in moral orientations other than those explicitly focusing on distributive justice. Thus there is said to be implicit use of the 'equality operation' by the utilitarian orientation. Reciprocity and equality are 'more or less implicit' in the normative order orientation. And in the perfectionist orientation 'failing to show responsibil-ity to one's fellow man' is deemed to be an implicit use of an equality orientation. One feels that some kind of stretching and compromising is going on here: Kohlberg's emphasis on conscious reasoning processes is being modified in the interests of assimilating what has at least been thought of as an alternative perspective to the ethics and meta-ethics of the justice perspective. Such a move is hardly value-free (even if I happen to be somewhat sympathetic to it), but it is not my brief to pursue its philosophical-definitional aspects.

At all events, at the psychological level Haan (1978) certainly claims systematic evidence in favour of her scheme as opposed to Kohlberg's regarding people's everyday moral thinking. More recently, Veronica Esarte-Sarriés, Helen Krarup and I have attempted to analyze written and interview data from a six-year British longitudinal study of some eighty adolescents in order to assess the phenomenological validity of Kohlberg's approach. The main way in which we have done this was to attempt to 'raise ourselves using Kohlberg's bootstraps'. That is, we attempted to grade the scorability of basic evaluative thought-units and thematic groupings thereof in terms of the clarity with which one could attribute a particular Kohlbergian stage (revised version) to them. Thus, if the response virtually 'jumped out of the manual', i.e., had all the characteristics described of a given stage, then it would be termed a P-level score at that stage. Thus a P5 means a very *pure* instance of Stage 5. An S-level (*satisfactory*) score was awarded where things were less clearcut, but there were still sufficient features to allow the definite identification of a given stages unambiguously. An I-level (*impression*) stage score was given where although the response might be interpretable as generated by more than one stage, between which it was thus ambiguous, there were features, (e.g., content features) that might tend to be associated easily with a particular stage. In other words, an I5 means that the response is, strictly speaking, unscorable, though a zealous but unthorough Kohlbergian (if that isn't a contradiction in terms ...) would give it a Stage 5. Finally comes the U or *unscorable* category. We thus have a cumulative ordering of scorability in which the P level meets the conditions of the S and I levels, and the S level meets those of the I level. The inter-rater reliability was satisfactorily high.

In the present connection it is of interest to note that the percentages of thematic chunks scorable at the S level or better (i.e., S or P) were as shown in Table 1, where occasions one to five refer to annual responses to written forms of the 'Heinz and the drug' and 'Heinz the escaped convict' dilemmas over a six-year period (the second year was missed out). In the final year a face-to-face Kohlberg interview was carried out using the drug and Joe dilemmas, as well as an interview based on the method pioneered by Kitwood (1980), in which respondents talk about value-related activities from their own lives, prompted by such descriptions as: 'when someone I knew did something I thought was wrong'.

We have not yet systematically analyzed the nature of the I-level and

Table 1. *Percentages of Evaluative Themes at S and P Levels of Scorability*

	Story	
Occasion	Drug	Convict
Written: 1	22	22
2	33	35
3	38	30
4	34	32
5	40	44
Kohlberg interview	52	33 (Joe)
Kitwood interview	9	

Unscorable chunks in our data, but the initial impression is that whilst many of them are simply too brief, there are others that are either inarticulate or expressive of themes which just do not indicate clearly a particular level of social perspective as a basis in prescriptive decisions. These latter often seem to involve unmediated, first-order content values which are apparently unqualified by much comparison with other aspects or perspectives in the situation, for example, 'the druggist shouldn't refuse the drug because that's what drugs are for—curing people.' I realize that I am hereby indulging in more or less the opposite game to Kohlberg's subsumption of every moral perspective under the deontological justice approach through appeal to 'implicit' tenets. Nevertheless, it is noteworthy that the rather low percentages of clearly Kohlbergian stage-scorable (at least S-level) units in Table 1 relate largely to written responses to the *Kohlberg instrument itself*, with its interview form only achieving some 50 per cent clear scorability. For the Kitwood interview data on prescriptive judgments concerning own real-life content the proportion was very low indeed, at around 10 per cent. At the very least, these data ought to give pause to a theory which contends the virtually exclusive power of its distributive justice structures as functional units in *all* people's moral psychological processing.

This is perhaps a convenient place to make brief comment on a psychological aspect of Kohlberg, Levine and Hewer's (1983) treatment of Gilligan's 'alternative' ethic of care and responsibility, given that I have already highlighted some ambiguity in Kohlberg's contentions in this respect. One strand offered by Kohlberg *et al.* (*ibid.*, p. 21) is that 'special obligations of care presuppose but go beyond the general duties of justice, which are necessary but not sufficient for them.' This is clearly not a value-neutral statement, but I will leave that sort of issue to the philosophers. Kohlberg goes on to say on the same page: 'We believe that what Gilligan calls an ethic of care is, in and of itself, not well adapted to resolve justice problems; problems which require principles to resolve conflicting claims among persons, all of whom in some sense should be cared about.' My own preference would be to talk of the justice *aspects* of moral decision-making, which may involve more than justice, as has been argued and will be further contended below. However, whilst I would agree that even in various psychological respects one does need to deal with the distributive aspects of a problem (for example, to avoid feelings of inconsistency), it may be the case that some people simply do not, but instead assimilate some or all of their moral deliberations to a relatively unstructured ethic of person-oriented care or whatever. In this respect and on our own evidence, I suspect that Gilligan's women subjects are but the well-documented tip of a rather large iceberg whose bulk includes both sexes.

(4)   Where in Principle Could Justice-Structures Get Us Psychologically?

Although Kohlberg's emphasis on the formal-structural properties of moral reasoning has been maintained from his earliest writing to the most recent, it is also clear that there has been some evolution in readiness to relate form and content. In the earlier, 'extreme Platonic' period (for example, Kohlberg, 1971) the stages were said to be a matter of formal perspective and, as such, entirely neutral with respect to the content of particular decisions within particular dilemmas. Putting it crudely, it was not what you decided that mattered, so much as the stage perspective you used in so deciding, whence Peters' (1971) complaint that if he was lying in the gutter having been mugged, the stage level of his assailant would not be of very great concern to him. . . .

Currently (Kohlberg, Levine, and Hewer, 1983, pp. 49–51) it is recognized that formal stage features involving completeness or complexity of perspective tend to be correlated with particular decision contents and their active implementations. This is said to be the case both in terms of stages, with Stage 5 subjects tending to agree on particular courses of action in given dilemmas, and in terms of the more recently introduced notion of substages. The 'more equilibrated' substage B with its fairness orientation is likely to make particular decisions more in line with Stage 5 reasoning than the A substage, which is oriented to rules or pragmatics. And the higher stages and substages are also more likely to carry out their decision. It seems to me that this rather Cartesian view stressing the importance of the clarity of cognition for its broader effectiveness is (a) plausible and (b) entirely consonant with Kohlberg's heavy, if often implicit, emphasis on cognitive consistency as a basic human motive. Insofar as consistency does not hold such a central place, the point may lose considerable power. However, leaving further comment on that to the later section on psychological paradigms and models of the person, I should like to focus for the moment on what psychological yield there might be in knowing the stage and substage a person brings to bear upon a given decision.

A useful illustration of some of the issues involved here is provided in Kohlberg's own latest offering, where he comments on the difficult situation of Gilligan and Murphy's (1979) 'philosopher 2' in which 'the husband of the woman with whom he was having an affair was uninformed of this fact.' Philosopher 2's dilemma was 'whether I should call the guy up and tell him what the situation was', thus respecting what he held to be the husband's right to truth, or whether to refrain from so doing since his lover felt overwhelmed by other pressures and unable to face the additional stress of informing her husband of the affair at that time, saying she would do so at a more peaceful time. Kohlberg responds that the justice operation of reversing perspectives could enable to philosopher to see that sanity preservation is logically prior to and thus more important than truth-telling (the sanity in this case being that of the woman, not that of either of the men in the situation).

A first comment which seems required is that Kohlberg's version of justice as reversibility or 'moral musical chairs' here seems to equate with 'least common desirables should rule', so that, extrapolating further, anyone in such a situation who seriously threatened suicide as a deterrent should be acceded to. Putting it conversely, even the avoidance of death can hardly be assumed absolutely prior to any other value: it may be sad, but not irrational, for a person to prefer death to certain other forms of continued existence. A person's values are *their* values, and that is where value judgments originate. This is one of the basic points of Hare's prescriptivism. A reversible justice calculus such as Kohlberg's therefore requires attention to particular values and their priority order, which may vary across both persons and issues.

However that may be, from a psychological point of view it is clear that the philosopher in Gilligan and Murphy's example did not carry out the calculation suggested by Kohlberg and that a very heavy role has to be attributed to the particular value weighting of the alternative specific options in the situation. In this sense, Kohlberg is getting himself into the sort of difficulty traditionally associated with utilitarianism, namely how to measure value or happiness. It is not just utilitarians who have implicit justice problems, as Kohlberg contends, but also *vice versa*. And since the philosopher did not work out the justice aspects of his dilemma, but nevertheless did operate in a particular way (that is, did not inform the husband, who found out inadvertently), we would tend to conclude that a different orientation governed his action, most apparently his caring attitude towards the woman.

From this we can learn that both form (distributive equality) and content (particular values) are co-essential even where one simply seeks to enter content values into the justice equation, and that on occasion the over-riding factor is one or more particular values of especial importance to the decision-maker. A realistic moral psychology must acknowledge this. There is, however, a corollary which works somewhat in Kohlberg's favour. Namely, if value content is idiosyncratic and we are seeking to characterize moral development generally, then the development of a sequence of structures corresponding to the formal features of universal social reality may be the best we can expect. Of course, this does not salvage the completeness of the cognitive-structural developmental approach as a moral psychology, it rather lets us see the nature of its incompleteness and what is needed to supplement it.

KOHLBERG'S PHENOMENALISM

Amongst the philosophic assumptions of Kohlberg's approach is that of phenomenalism. We are given a very clear definition of what this means: 'The assumption of phenomenalism is the assumption that moral reasoning is the conscious process of using ordinary moral language' (Kohlberg, Levine and Hewer, 1983, p. 69). This definition is consistent with much of Kohlberg's other writings over a long period. He has long stressed the idea of conscious reasoning, both as the source and the basis for characterizing action and as the process of resolving cognitive conflicts engendered by lower stages and thus of upward progression (cf. Kohlberg, 1969, 1971).

Whilst one can agree that moral action is by definition purposive, this is hardly to say that it is based on conscious thought at all times. The idea of unconscious thought is hardly new, and Freudians are not the only psychologists to believe in it. As long ago as 1926 Wallas was talking of unconscious 'incubation' in problem-solving and more recently cognitive skills psychology has taken on board the notion of automatized processing (see Welford, 1968). Work such as that by Dixon (1971) and Norman (1976) offers direct evidence for unconscious cognition. In short, a virtually medieval, dualistic model of the person, in which conscious thought deliberately determines all action, is now seen to be quite unrealistic. Modern cognitive psychology (see Lindsay and Norman, 1977, for instance) shows how most, typically complex, purposive human activities could not be performed on this basis. A similar set of objections to the currency of thought being construed as purely verbal could also be mounted (see, for instance, Cohen, 1983), and one is in any case surprised to find a Piagetian defining thought as verbal in the first place. Not that any of this makes the assessment of moral or any other form of cognitive processing any easier, but then a psychology nowadays hardly starts with the measurement operation.

But there are in addition a number of ambiguities and possible inconsistencies in Kohlberg's treatment of the nature and role of moral thought processes. For instance, having defined his phenomenalism assumption as indicated above, Kohlberg nevertheless also talks of implicit tenets, for instance, the 'implicit' justice structures within utilitarian viewpoints. More strikingly he says: 'So far we have discussed moral action as though it were always preceded by deontic or responsibility judgments. In fact, this may not be the case' (Kohlberg, Levine and Hewer, 1983, p. 52). He goes on to allow that things may occur more in the manner emphasized by Piaget, who placed a primacy on systematic action coming first and possibly being followed by a *prise de conscience* or conscious realization of its nature. There is some tension here with the phenomenalism assumption. But then Kohlberg cites evidence of links not between systematic (but unreflective) action and eventual reflective-conscious thought, but between reasoning about real-life situations and reasoning about hypothetical dilemmas, so that we remain in the realm of relatively explicit thought. Thus the main emphasis seems to be on conscious verbal processes, as mentioned at the beginning of this section, but there appears to be some inconsistency and something of a mixing of different psychological models. We now turn in the final section to Kohlberg's use of psychological paradigms.

KOHLBERG'S USE OF PSYCHOLOGICAL PARADIGMS

Central to any psychology are the ways in which it models the elements and processes in the individuals it studies. This tends to boil down to the way it uses existing psychological concepts and paradigms. In this respect it seems to me that whilst Kohlberg makes an exemplary attempt to specify his conceptual resources, he does so in terms of a somewhat restricted and ageing set of paradigms, and treatment of the problems they yield leads him into certain ambiguities and inconsistencies, some of which have already been encountered.

Let us start with what Kohlberg thinks of as available resources. Even in the latest treatment by Kohlberg, Levine and Hewer the choice seems to be limited to the traditional trio of Behaviourism, Psychoanalysis and Cognitive-Developmental Structuralism, though there is also occasional mention of Psychometrics. As we have seen, Kohlberg's own clear preference is for the Piagetian structuralist version of cognitive developmentalism, and this offers him both advantages and disadvantages.

Amongst the advantages is the fact that at least in relation to the other two paradigms, cognitive structuralism is non-reductionist, particularly with respect to the judgmental/reflective aspects towards which philosophers have had an 'occupational bias' (Kleinberger, 1982). Another is that the particular nature of the claimed stage sequence, with selfishness low in the scale, together with the relatively 'natural' conception of development, allows Kohlberg to have things both ways, offering a moral education which looks like achieving what is wanted, yet not doing so by indoctrinatory means (Kohlberg, 1978). A third advantage is that the relatively broad and impressive nature of the viewpoint means that considerable flexibility is left for dealing with particular issues and applications as they arise. However, the tightness with which Kohlberg maintains certain features of the structuralist paradigm appears to raise problems when he also seeks to import certain aspects of other views.

One of the most general difficulties of cognitive-structural developmentalism lies in the distinction between competence and performance. There are at least two versions of this distinction: (a) a Chomsky-type distinction between an idealized general repertoire of operations needed for operating in a given domain (competence), for example, the deep structure of language or the basic justice structures of social distribution, on one hand, and their realization (performance) in a given case, on the other hand; (b) a particular person's range of capacities (*their* competence) and the actualization or instantiation of that competence in a given activity (performance). It is not always clear which Kohlberg means. But what these two distinctions share is that one cannot directly access competence, one can only witness what is done, that is, a performance, and perhaps infer from that to competence. To think otherwise is a category error (Ryle, 1949).

Much of Kohlberg's writing, emphasizing the role of cognition, awareness, choice and intentionality of moral action derives the benefit of version (b) of the distinction: no crude determinism here! But there are respects in which he seems to give up this distinction and take on the reductionism of 'the opposition'. Various strands are discernible.

A first relates to measurement. In Kohlberg, Levine and Hewer (p. 37) we find the firm statement that 'Kohlberg's current assessment instrument and interview method taps a subject's competence rather than his or her performance....' It is interesting that the statement immediately continues: '... by providing probing questions that *attempt* to elicit the upper limits of the subject's thinking' (italics mine). This almost reminds one of the psychometric positivism according to which IQ tests were said by true believers to tap directly a person's potential. Kohlberg's statement hardly needs comment, except perhaps that one thought that the rise of cognitivism had precisely saved us from this sort of dangerous simplism.

Secondly, the 'Platonic rationalism' espoused by Kohlberg means that a person is held to use the highest stage he or she is capable of. To know (how to reason about) the good is to apply that capacity. The implication is that the only motive known to cognitive-structural man is the love of consistency and cognitive balance. (One wonders about Dr Goebbels and other sophisticated instrumentalists....) True, there was a point in the history of Kohlbergian research when the competence-performance distinction was called on to perform an important role, when Kohlberg and Kramer (1969) contended that the regressions of high school Stage 5s to Stage 2 in their college years were merely 'functional' regression. As such, this seemed a reasonable view, though it would have brought problems for other aspects of Kohlberg's rationalism. Subsequently, however, this explanation was revised in favour of a purer reformulation of the stages, with much made of a possible transition 'stage' (4½), which seems to have swung back to 'rationalist determinism', with improved assessment making the identification of performance with competence even more confident.

A connected issue concerns the nature of the stage sequence. It is beyond my scope to go into this complex topic, and the interested reader is referred to Rest's very thorough (1979) discussion. The particular aspect I am thinking of here does, however, deserve some mention, namely, the fate of earlier stages. According to Kohlberg, later stages displace earlier ones by building hierarchically upon and integrating them. However, Levine (1979) has pointed out that a variety of models of stage development is possible and he favours a 'non-displacement, additive-inclusive' model in which earlier stage structures remain available for use. Only thus, contends Levine, can we preserve the competence-performance distinction and allow the study of influences on different levels of performance. Kohlberg's very brief reply to this (Kohlberg, Levine and Hewer, 1983, p. 152) does not seem to me to deal with the central issue, and his use of terms like 'optimal competence' is at best puzzling and at worst damning. The data yielded by our longitudinal research referred to earlier have alerted us to a further inconsistency in this domain. Not only did we find that our respondents were capable of using different stage arguments across various answers, but we also found that they would use different stages in a connected way within the same response. For instance, they might offer a five-ish argument for stealing the drug because of everyone's right to life, and then add the Stage 2 thought that in any case the druggist would make more money if he priced his drug at a realistic level: perhaps not 'of the world', but definitely 'in the world', as the pious used to say. In other cases it was the higher stage that was mentioned as a lesser consideration and in still others the respondent merely registered his or her confusion as between two different stage arguments. This suggested to us that Kohlberg's citing of high percentages of stage use of a given level as evidence of the power of the stage structures has rather led him into a somewhat crude psychometricism of cognitive traits (in this case stages). One had thought that cognitive man was a creature capable of thought, that is, of juxtaposing internal representations and schemata, though this issue reminded us of the potential inflexibilities of a cognitive structural model.

It seems fair to conclude, therefore, that without taking away from the creative and persistent contribution made by Kohlberg and his group, he is still labouring within a restricted set of rather old paradigms. As Rest (1984) has commented, Kohlberg has stayed with the cognitive units of Piagetian structuralism when there are now many other possibilities. Cognitive psychology has for a long time meant more than cognitive-structural developmental psychology, as a glance at a whole range of recent titles will show (for instance, Cohen, 1983). As Cohen has remarked, where the early cognitive psychologists in the information-processing tradition started by seeking the structures of human hardware and processing, they increasingly found that it was function, and varying function, that tended to determine processing and its nature. In other words, human psychological resources are very flexible and in a domain as rich as morality it is likely that many of them will be brought to bear. A moral psychology will likely need to be intelligently eclectic at this point in its history, and this probably means some compromise between aspects of the combined paradigms. As we have seen, the harsher pronouncements of cognitive-developmental structuralism seem to have got Kohlberg into some difficulties even regarding the selected range of aspects I have reviewed here.

The point is perhaps best brought home by considering a specific example. In the case of Gilligan's 'philosopher 2' and his 'dilemma of the fact', I have already pointed out that the contribution of justice structures is limited, even in principle. (One might also comment that a traditional utilitarian would surely have seen things rather differently from Kohlberg.) But applying a combination of paradigms would allow one to see very many more possibilities and get a better psychological understanding both of individuals' experiences and actions and of their social interrelations. Allowing the possibility of systematic unconscious regulation of action, for instance, it is quite possible that the philosopher's zeal for the husband's right to truth is (also) a convenient front for a more self-serving strategy. Again, focus on particular sensitivities might have oriented consideration towards the suffering that would be caused to the husband. In more complex vein, it is also likely that the woman's stress was being added to by her own internal conflict between approach (with respect to her lover) and avoidance (or informing her husband, which would to some extent free her). I have already suggested that Kohlberg's 'moral musical chairs' version of perspective-taking has built-in principles of dubious value: what *ought* to happen in such a situation is surely rather open. What *will* happen and why and how, in other words, the subject-matter of a moral psychological account, is perhaps even more arguable. Kohlberg's contribution so far should aid us to understand such cases, but it will do so more powerfully if integrated honestly and accommodatingly with insights from other paradigms, which tend to require some basic adjustments to the cognitive structural model of the person and moral processes. I therefore hope that there will be some advance on the present stage of Lawrence Kohlberg's work.

REFERENCES

Brown, G. and Desforges, C. (1979) *Piaget's Theory: A Psychological Critique*, London, Routledge and Kegan Paul.

Cohen, G. (1983) *The Psychology of Cognition*, 2nd ed., London, Academic Press.

Dixon, N. (1971) *Subliminal Perception: The Nature of a Controversy*, London, McGraw-Hill.

Frankena, W. K. (1973) *Ethics*, Englewood Cliffs, N.J., Prentice Hall.

Gilligan, C. (1982) *In a Different Voice*: Psychological Theory and Women's Development, Cambridge, Mass., Harvard University Press.

Gilligan, C. and Murphy, J. M. (1979) 'Development from adolescence to adulthood. The philosopher and the "dilemma of the fact"' in Kuhn, D. (Ed.) *Intellectual Development Beyond Childhood*, San Francisco, Jossey-Bass.

Haan, N. (1978) 'Two moralities in action context: Relationships to thought, ego regulation and development', *Journal of Personality and Social Psychology*, 36, pp. 286–305.

Hare, R. M. (1952) *The Language of Morals*, Oxford, Oxford University Press.

Kitwood, T. M. (1980) *Disclosures to a Stranger: Adolescent Values in an Advanced Industrial Society*, London, Routledge and Kegan Paul.

Kleinberger, A. F. (1982) 'The proper object of moral judgment and of moral education', *Journal of Moral Education*, 11, pp. 147–58.

Kohlberg, L. (1969) 'Stage and sequence', in Goslin, D. (Ed.) *Handbook of Socialization Theory and Research*, Chicago, Ill., Rand-McNally.

Kohlberg, L. (1971) 'From is to ought: How to commit the naturalistic fallacy and get away with it in the study of moral development', in Mischel, T. (Ed.) *Cognitive Development and Epistemology*, New York, Academic Press.

Kohlberg, L. (1978) Foreword to Scharf, P. (Ed.) *Readings in Moral Education*, Minneapolis, Minn., Winston Press.

Kohlberg, L. and Kramer, R. (1969) 'Continuities and discontinuities in childhood and adult moral development', *Human Development*, 12, pp. 93–120.

Kohlberg, L., Levine, C. and Hewer, A. (1983) *Moral Stages: A Current Formulation and a Response to Critics*, Basel, Karger.

Levine, C. G. (1979) 'Stage acquisition and stage use: an appraisal of stage displacement explanations of variation in moral reasoning,' *Human Development*, 22, pp. 145–164.

Lindsay, P. and Norman, D. A. (1977) *Human Information Processing: An Introduction to Psychology*, New York, Academic Press.

Norman, D. A. (1976) *Memory and Attention*, 2nd ed., New York, Academic Press.

Peters, R. (1971) 'A plea for pluralism', in Mischel, T. (Ed.) *Cognitive Development and Epistemology*, New York, Academic Press.

Piaget, J. (1972) 'Intellectual development from adolescence to adulthood', *Human Development*, 15, pp. 1–12.

Rest, J. (1979) *Development in Judging Moral Issues*, Minneapolis, Minn., University of Minnesota Press.

Rest, J. (1984) 'Morality', in Flavell, J. H. and Neimarck, E. (Eds.) *Carmichael's Manual of Child Psychology*, 4th ed. Vol. 1: Cognitive Development, New York, Wiley, pp. 172–277.

Ryle, G. (1949) *The Concept of Mind*. London: Hutchinson.

Sullivan, E. V. (1967) *Piaget and the School Curriculum: A Critical Appraisal*, Toronto, OISE.

Tomlinson, P. D. (1980) 'Moral judgment and moral psychology: Piaget, Kohlberg and beyond', in Modgil, S. and Modgil, C. (Eds.) *Toward a Theory of Psychological Development*, Slough, NFER, pp. 303–66.

Tomlinson, P. D. (1983) 'Six years in the moral lives of some British adolescents'. Paper presented to the Annual Meeting of the British Association for the Advancement of Science, University of Sussex.

Turiel, E. (1980) 'The development of social-conventional and moral concepts', in Windmiller, M., Lambert, N. and Turiel, E. (Eds.) *Moral Development and Socialization*, Boston, Allyn and Bacon, pp. 69–106.

Wason, P. and Johnson-Laird, P. (1972) *Psychology of Reasoning*, London, Batsford.

Welford, A. T. (1968) *Fundamentals of Skill*, London, Methuen.

Wilson, J. (1967) 'What is moral education', in Wilson, J., Williams, N. and Sugarman, B., *Introduction to Moral Education*, Harmondsworth, Penguin Books.

Wright, D. S. (1971) *The Psychology of Moral Behaviour*, Harmondsworth, Penguin Books.

Interchange

PETROVICH REPLIES TO TOMLINSON

Tomlinson's chapter is helpful in that it reiterates some important problems associated with Kohlberg's theory, this time in the light of more recent empirical evidence. Thus, I fully agree with Tomlinson in his criticism of Kohlberg's cognitive stage structuralism, an excessive focus upon *justice* reasoning while attempting to capture and describe *moral* development, an exaggerated emphasis on form vs. content in moral reasoning, etc. In fact, I would be even more critical than Tomlinson has been when it comes to some of the points just mentioned. However, my task on this occasion has been to evaluate that which I see as positive in Kohlberg's contribution to psychology and this in no way conflicts with the arguments put forth by Tomlinson. For that matter, our respective contributions to this volume could be seen as truly complementary rather than opposing since I discuss those aspects of Kohlberg's theory to which Tomlinson makes no reference at all, notably the notion of autonomy and Stage 7.

I also agree with some of Tomlinson's positive remarks about Kohlberg's achievements as, for example, the significance of his 'massive' work, its theoretical and practical concerns and the development of Kohlberg's own ideas. However, I am more reluctant than Tomlinson to recognize Kohlberg's approach as particularly 'interdisciplinary' or to admire Kohlberg's 'creative application' of the Piagetian model to his own research on morality. Instead, my view has been that a less selective philosophical stance on Kohlberg's part and a less rigid reliance on Piaget's model when dealing with his own data could have resulted in a far more adequate theory of moral development.

It seems to me more appropriate, therefore, to regard this postscript as a comment on Tomlinson's chapter rather than a reply to it since there is hardly anything in it I would wish to dispute.

TOMLINSON REPLIES TO PETROVICH

While I started my own chapter by distancing myself from the debate structure of this book, what I now have to say about Petrovich's contribution may sound like the pot calling the kettle black! Nevertheless, my general inclination is to express some surprise and comment that with friends like that, Kohlberg doesn't need enemies! For, in a nutshell, what Olivera appears to have done is to offer a contribution which can hardly be characterized as a defence of Kohlberg's psychology: the major portion of her chapter is devoted to exposing the problematic nature of the concept of moral autonomy, particularly as used by Piagetians including Kohlberg. The minor theme recommends more attention to the religious dimension. This, too, is somewhat in conflict with Kohlberg rather than supportive of him, for Petrovich is advocating a more important place for religious considerations just at the point when Kohlberg, Levine and Hewer are relegating the seventh cosmic-religious outlook to the second division of 'soft stages'.

What Petrovich's chapter does show is the breadth and depth of what a moral psychology must take into account. In terms of traditional subject delineations in the English-speaking world, this may be put alternatively by saying that an adequate moral psychology needs explicit connections of various sorts with other types of approach, especially philosophical, by which I mean analytical-definitional.

This is perhaps most clearly seen in the case of autonomy. I would certainly agree with Olivera that a lot is being taken for granted in typical psychological uses of that term. A critical appraisal that did justice to her analyses and explorations of that concept would require more effort and space than the scope of this response allows. I will therefore content myself by welcoming her initiative in turning the focus on to this central notion and by noting the complementarity of her treatment with the critiques offered by Trainer (1982). For my own part, I incline to the sceptical view Petrovich cites of Emler: it seems to me that autonomy is a peculiarly slippery term without a well differentiated and integrated conception of the person in interaction with environment, both personal and impersonal, to underpin it. The very term itself smacks of an internal-external separatism whose reification is increasingly recognized as limiting rather than enhancing psychological understanding. Rather than resolving scholastic disputes as to whether a given act is or is not autonomous, I suspect psychology would be better aimed at considering the range, nature and status of motives doubtless typically over-determining actions, and the processes and nature of such regulation within an overall interactive model of the person—though I concede that taking account of people's common sense, often all-or-no-autonomy notions might well be part of such an understanding.

Turning briefly to the religious theme raised by Petrovich, one has to agree that there is evidence that such a category does feature heavily in people's explicit accounts and justifications. Again, Trainer (1982) found typically swift reversion to the divine back-stop when he moved to meta-ethical issues, and recently a large-scale survey by Robert Towler at the University of Leeds concluded that religion forms an important part of the conscious outlook of a large majority of the population. To stay with this particular register, I must confess that the introduction of the seventh stage notion always seemed to me something of a *deus ex machina* whose critical examination raised more problems for Kohlberg's moral psychology than it solved (Tomlinson, 1980).

Petrovich thus rightly points to the Kohlbergian contribution, but also does a service in indicating two important areas where further development would be useful.

REFERENCES

Tomlinson, P. D. (1980) 'Moral judgment and moral psychology: Piaget, Kohlberg and beyond', in Modgil, S. and Modgil, C. (Eds.) *Toward a Theory of Psychological Development*, Slough, NFER, pp. 303–66.
Trainer, F. E. (1982) *Dimensions of Moral Thought*, Kensington, NSW: New South Wales University Press.

Part V: Moral Judgment and Moral Action

8. The Relationship of Moral Judgment and Moral Action: Kohlberg's Theory, Criticism and Revision

PETER KUTNICK

Meno: Can you tell me, Socrates, whether virtue is acquired by teaching or practice; or if neither by teaching or practice, then whether it comes to man by nature, or in what other way?

Socrates: You must think that I am very fortunate to know how virtue is acquired. The fact is far from knowing whether it can be taught, I have no idea what virtue is.

McLuhan: A Socratic dialogue is really a monologue with worshipful remarks interjected.

All three characters (Meno—the questioner, Socrates—the philosopher, and McLuhan—the social critic) play an essential role in Kohlberg's research generally, and more specifically in the relationship of moral judgment to moral action. From the simple question, to the self-seeking answer, to the critical overview, Kohlberg's theory has developed ('bootstrapped'), become more refined, responded to critics and stayed essentially the same. It is beyond the scope of this chapter to present the theory in total (see other chapters, and Kohlberg, 1958, 1969, 1976, and others). To clarify the moral judgment-moral action issue, this chapter will draw upon: selective psychological and philosophical underpinnings in the development of the theory; empirical support for the theory; criticisms; revision of the theory with recent empirical evidence; and will attempt to support the theory in the strongest terms possible by focusing on the monotonic evidence and a behaviour-by-stage analysis. In providing this chapter to support Kohlberg's view of the relationship of moral judgment and moral action, one must draw upon its history and reality; a full criticism will be left to others (see, for example, Straughan, this volume, Ch. 9; Locke 1983a, 1983b; Weinreich-Haste, 1983a; Kurtines and Greif, 1974).

TO BEGIN

The statement (and lay assertion) that moral judgment and moral action are one-and-the-same is both an oversimplification and a (Kohlbergian) monotonic statement of fact. It is an oversimplification in that the reader may not realize the depth of psychological and philosophical debate that continually rages about the statement. (The monotonic statement is discussed later in this chapter.)

As a psychological statement the argument may be framed as behaviourism versus cognitive development or moral development versus socialization. The classic and 'early' moral development study undertaken by Hartshorne and May in 1929 starts the debate. Their attempt to relate moral knowledge to moral behaviour consisted of providing many tests of lying, cheating, and stealing to 11,000 school-aged children in different activities of school work, home duties, contests, etc. They found a low positive correlation between an individual's behaviours in various situations and concluded with a 'doctrine of specificity'; the behaviourist dream, moral actions are learnt in specific situations and apply only to that situation. The behaviourist dream leaves a few problems though. Are moral actions simply actions repeated or neglected due to reinforcement patterns in life? If so, what makes the actions 'moral'? Presumably, we are speaking only of behaviours, there is no judgment factor. (But some social behaviourists—Aronfreed, 1969; Mischel and Mischel, 1976; and others—do acknowledge some 'cognitive mediating' or 'internalization' factor in moral development.) A second, and equally important, problem questions the difference between moralization and socialization. According to Kohlberg (1976) social learning theories assume:

1 Moral development is growth of behavioural and affective conforming to moral rules rather than cognitive-structural change.
2 The basic motivation for morality at every point of moral development is rooted in biological needs or the pursuit of social reward and avoidance of social punishment.
3 Moral development or morality is culturally relative.
4 Basic moral norms are the internalization of external cultural rules.
5 Environmental influences on moral development are defined by quantitative variations in strength of reward, punishment, prohibitions, and modelling of confirming behavior by parents and other socializing agents. (p. 48)

If one accepts current political doctrines on the 'rule of law' and the maintenance of conventions, then behaviourism provides insight and mechanisms of 'development'. But the personal ability to change and move towards an autonomous orientation is not accounted for in behaviourism, nor in psychoanalytic theory. Opening a psychological exposition on the relation of moral judgment to moral action, Kohlberg (1976) grounds himself in cognitive developmental theory (see Kohlberg, 1969) and identifies the following assumptions:

1 Moral development has a basic cognitive-structural or moral judgmental component.
2 The basic motivation for morality is a generalized motivation for acceptance, competence, self-esteem, or self-realization, rather than for meeting biological needs and reducing anxiety or fear.
3 Major aspects of moral development are culturally universal, because all cultures have common sources of social conflict, which require moral integration.
4 Basic moral norms and principles are structures arising through experiences of social interaction, rather than through internalization of rules that exist as external structures; moral

stages are not defined by internalized rules, but by structures of interaction between the self and others.

5   Environmental influences in moral development are defined by the general quality and extent of cognitive and social stimulation throughout the child's development, rather than by specific experiences with parents or experiences of discipline, punishment, and reward. (p. 48)

For Kohlberg, moral judgments arise from individual experience and actions and form the basis for further moral actions. His terminology of moral action necessarily involves moral cognition. Given that the individual develops in a stage-structural sequence, each stage has a unique cognitive orientation (form) which relates to perceived appropriate actions (content).

The philosophical and anti-positivist aspect of the theory involves the move away from culturally relative, quasi-obligatory preconventional and conventional levels of morality to a universal, deontic coherence of moral judgment and moral action. Kohlberg is one of the very few psychologists to integrate philosophical and psychological theory (see Lickona, 1976). He draws upon philosophers to support and clarify his arguments (including Rawls, 1971; Kant and others).

As in psychology, philosophers have adopted a range of explanations in their consideration of moral judgment and action. Straughan (1983, from Frankena, 1973) notes that theories range from externalist to internalist. Extreme externalists rarely consider a judgment factor, and base moral evaluations solely on actions. Extreme internalists consider moral judgments are always brought to fruition in moral action. Kohlberg, himself, has consistently identified with the Kantian position of rationalism (a moderate internalist position according to Straughan), hence moral judgments should focus our attention on people's conscious motives for deciding what they ought to do or refrain from doing (Kleinberger, 1982). At the highest level, actions are guided by moral decisions. At lower levels, actions accord with (limited) moral decision-making capabilities. Moral judgment is the only distinctively moral factor among all the factors which influence moral behaviour (Kleinberger, 1982). The essence of Kant's theory of morality is a progressive move from judgments based on retribution to judgments based upon justice. Kohlberg has further drawn upon the writing of Rawls (1971) to expand upon the meaning and appropriacy of justice.

Even with this strong philosophical backing, Kohlberg's theory is open to challenge due to the gap or 'weakness of will' between judgment and action (see Straughan); a point answered in the empirical studies showing a monotonic relationship between judgment and action. Kohlberg has also made use of Socratic, Platonic and Deweyian principles—but mainly in relation to programmes of moral education and moral atmosphere.

KOHLBERG'S THEORY: EARLY WRITINGS

It is beyond the scope of this chapter to recapitulate the totality of Kohlberg's theory of moral development (see Kohlberg, 1958, 1969, 1971; Weinreich-Haste, 1983a, and others). Yet several elements are essential to explain the relation of moral judgment to moral action. Hopefully the reader will forgive any redundant points in the effort to provide a background for the empirical verification of Kohlberg's theory.

Kohlberg's cognitive theory (1971) is in contrast to behaviourist, attitudinal and emotional research. He states that moral reasoning is a better test to predict moral action. A cognitive-developmental theory of morality is based upon each stage being a structured whole, following an invariant sequence, previous stages are integrated into succeeding stages in a hierarchical fashion. (An important, and often forgotten, corollary to the four main aspects of cognitive developmental theory states that preceding stages remain within the individual's cognitive repertoire, Kutnick 1983a. The individual is able to draw upon the preceding structures of thought and characteristic action schemes of earlier stages.) Higher stages more successfully differentiate moral obligations and moral responsibility from the non-moral. Higher stages differentiate the structure as opposed to the content of moral dilemma. Each higher stage is more predictive of moral action. As one rises in the moral hierarchy, the battle of conscience inhibitions become less. Here Kohlberg seeks to commit the *naturalistic fallacy* in moving from the subjective *is* to the objective *ought* at the postconventional level. Subjective relativism is swept away in the progression towards universal moral action. Philosophically, he has attempted to resolve the naturalistic dilemma with empirical evidence. Psychologically, as Weinreich-Haste (1983b) states, Kohlberg presents a double theory—one of cognitive development and one of morality.

Some further psychological clarification of the bases of Kohlberg's theory will help to illuminate aspects of the judgment-action problem. Kohlberg (1969) acknowledges that all development stems from the subject's interactions with the social and physical environment. Action is the basis for early cognition. Kohlberg (1976) clarifies that there are both cognitive and social perspective bases in moral development. Social perspective taking levels (see Selman, 1976, 1980) are necessary (but not sufficient) for the individual's movement through Kohlberg's first four stages (although it should be noted that social-perspective-taking may only be a social application of the logical-mathematical stages—see Duveen, 1984). Logical-mathematical stages, too, form a necessary but not sufficient base to moral development (for example: the reversibility of concrete operations is necessary for golden rule orientation of Stage 2; formal operational thought is necessary for a Stage 4 understanding of social systems beyond the concrete experience of the individual). In fact, Kohlberg (1971, p. 186) states,

> Our cognitive hypothesis is, basically, that moral judgment has a characteristic form at a given stage, and that this form is parallel to the form of intellectual judgment at a corresponding stage. This implies a parallelism or isomorphism between the development of the forms of logical and ethical judgment ... In a given stage, each aspect of the stage must logically imply each other aspect, so that there is a logical structure underlying each moral stage, but the isomorphism of cognitive and moral is not simply the application of a level of intelligence to moral problems.

This, perhaps, long-winded recitation of the cognitive aspects underlying morality is most important in the discussion of judgment and action. As Kohlberg (1984) notes, thought and action develop in a single track: 'Moral judgment causes action and arises out of action.' Schematically, judgment and action are related in two diverse ways: (1) Piaget (1932–65) discussed the Law of Conscious Realization (or the *prise de conscience*, 1976) in which actions precede and provide the experience upon which cognition is based—a sequence of action preceding thought characterizing the early logical-mathematical stages; and (2) the unique feature of formal operational schemes is that thought is no longer tied to the concrete here-and-now situation, and action is often shaped by thought.. Hence Kohlberg (1984) is quite clear in stating that 'moral judgment is necessary but not sufficient for moral conduct,' especially at the higher moral stages.

Before we can delve into the empirical support for Kohlberg's earlier writings, a further judgment-action relation should be mentioned. Moral development theory is not simply a presentation of philosophical/psychological problems posed in hypothetical dilemmas to adolescent Chicago males (Kohlberg's original sample). The relation of action to judgment and *vice versa* has implications for the promotion of moral development. Kohlberg's early writing (1968) referred to the child as moral philosopher, and he soon started practical (Socratic) classroom exercises for the development of morals in pupils (Blatt and Kohlberg, 1975; Colby *et al.*, 1977), and amongst prisoners (Kohlberg, Scharf and Hickey, 1975). Analysis of the effect of moral education led to a review of the Socratic method and discussion of the role of moral atmosphere (ritualized action relations) in moral judgment (to be discussed later).

EMPIRICAL SUPPORT FOR THE THEORY

In reviewing the type and amount of support that Kohlberg has received for his theory, the reader must be aware of the dictum—while the theorist may be full of merit, watch out for the 'ists' and 'ians.' Kohlberg certainly presents a substantial theory (measured by articles, chapters, books and controversies), of which Kohlbergians have variable grasp. This review will not necessarily sort out Kohlberg from the Kohlbergians. Rather, I shall briefly note: (1) support for the cognitive and social foundations of the theory; (2) support for the action/thought of development; and (3) support for the judgment/action thesis.

Numerous studies have supported, or at least correlated, the cognitive and social underpinning of the theory. Advancement from the preconventional levels (Stage 1, Stage 2) of judgment has been correlated with movement to concrete operational thought (Damon, 1975). Smith (1978) supports this correlation and suggests that logical thought develops much more widely by Stage 3, and various aspects of formal and concrete thought are found at that stage. Formal operational thought and principled moral reasoning (Stage 5) are correlated (Tomlinson-Keasey and Keasey, 1974). In an applied sense, Hook and Cook (1979) found that the use of equity theory (essential in the development of distributive justice) was related to ability to use formal operational thought. Role-taking, or its more cognitively refined form of social-perspective taking, has been correlated with moral judgment in 8 to 10-year-olds (Selman, 1971), in 5 to 6-year-olds (Selman, 1973) and in 11-year-olds (Moire, 1974). And, while Hollas and Cowan (1973) could find no correlation between logical thinking and role-taking, Smith (1978) actually poses a sequence of logical thinking and role-taking in moral judgment. Kurdek's (1978) review of the literature relating moral judgment to cognitive perspective taking found only inconsistent support for the hypothesis. Further support for the argument would require more specific evidence. In light of the variety of instruments used to acknowledge role-taking, Kurdek posed a necessary but not sufficient rationale to explain the findings of his review.

Why should this chapter include the cognitive and social cognitive bases to moral judgment? Aside from Weinreich-Haste's (1983b) view that moral reasoning may be limited by cognition and social cognition, this information is essential in discussing an action/judgment scheme (sequence). Piaget (1932–65) described actions (whether heteronomous rule application or cooperative manipulation of rules) which preceded cognitive/verbal awareness in children's moral behaviour/ judgment. This action/judgment sequence is known as the Law of Conscious Realization. The existence of the law has been supported by Breznitz and Kugelmass (1967) in their study of intentionality, where they state that 'the child actually uses intentionality long before he is conscious of the principle of intentionality, but that this may be a necessary condition in order for the principle to develop.' A study by Kutnick (1980) shows how patterns of interaction between child and heteronomous figures of authority (teachers and leaders) precede the child's cognitive recognition and acceptance of the role of authority. From this report on action/judgment, one must be aware that action and interactions (spontaneous and ritually patterned) are structured in the environment and form the basis for moral cognition.

At this point, one can make the assumption that action is closely tied to thought and judgment. Brown and Herrnstein (1975) present an oversimplified figural representation to show that moral actions do correspond to moral reasoning

Figure 1. *Brown and Herrnstein's Simplistic Depiction of Action-reasoning by Stage*

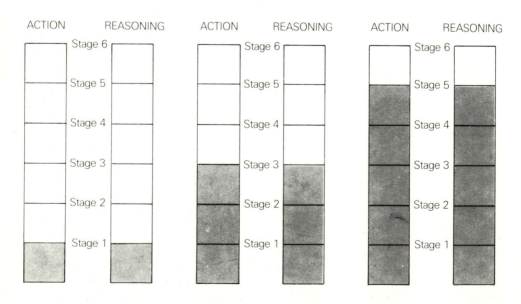

False over-simplified notion that moral reasoning and action are positively correlated: the more moral the thought the more moral the action.

(see Figure 1); although they viciously criticize the model for many valid reasons (to be discussed later). But, the actual model does receive support in the literature, especially in the monotonic relationship; that is, as one moves towards the higher stages of moral judgment, one's actions become more 'moral' (in a deortic sense) and the likelihood of them taking place becomes more reasonable. Krebs and Rosenwald (1979) found that moral stage predicted subjects' fulfilment of a verbal commitment to return questionnaires with surprising discrimination. Even at the lower stages one finds a judgment/action correlation. Saltzstein, Diamond and Belensky (1972) found Stage 3 subjects more likely to conform to group consensus in an Asch-type experiment than either Stage 2 (egocentric) or Stage 4 or 5 (systems and principled) subjects. More recently, Thornton and Reid (1982) tested the hypothesis that 'developmentally primitive attitudes will be associated with delinquent behaviour only to the extent that the behaviour in question is differentially evaluated at the different moral stages.' Their results supported the hypothesis that 'preconventional moral reasoning will be associated only with crimes in which the offenders believe they have a good chance of evading punishment.' Further, Gerson and Damon (1978) show that (non-Kohlbergian) levels of moral reasoning and action are consistent in preadolescent children's distribution of 'candy bars'.

While one expects judgment and action to be correlated at the higher stages, the studies cited should make the reader aware of the consistency of moral thought and action at earlier stages (often dominated by social convention). Undoubtedly the consistency is due to limitations of the concrete context and social/cognitive reasoning abilities. A teleological approach to moral development does not adequately account for the happenings at these lower stages. Kohlberg's increasing awareness of the effect of action upon judgment caused a move away from Socratic methods of moral education (Blatt and Kohlberg, 1975) to an acknowledgment of the role of (group and action-based) moral atmosphere in judgment. The emerging concept of the 'just community' stresses that atmosphere and relations of autonomy provide an action background for the development of higher moral stages (in communities, Reimer 1977; schools, Power and Reimer, 1978; and prisons, Kohlberg, Scharf and Hickey, 1975).

In the more focused teleological sense, Kohlberg's theory has received quite controversial support. Findings with reference to moral reasoning show that individuals unambiguously move from preconventional to conventional levels (see Turiel, 1969; and for a review of literature, Thornton and Thornton, 1983), and may progress to post-conventional (from Rest, 1975). But these findings stand against a background of previous social psychological criticisms based on group consensus (from Asch, 1952) and obedience to authority (from Milgram, 1974). Probably the most widely cited study relating thought to action is Haan, Smith and Block's (1968) 'Moral Reasoning of Young Adults'. In noting that activist youth maintain that there are moral necessities for their social-political protest, Haan *et al.* used Kohlberg's dilemmas, attitude sorts and biographical questionnaires to detect if the protestors were 'morally distinctive', and the 'nature and context of the socialization experiences associated with morality and its related behaviour'. Their results, although taken after the Free Speech Movement demonstration (and a large number of the sample being unassignable to a pure Kohlberg stage), showed distinctive backgrounds and behaviours at each of the three Kohlberg levels. There appeared to be a monotonic relationship between stage and action, with higher-stage individuals participating in sit-ins and being arrested. But a number of Stage 2 males participated in the same sit-ins and were arrested, causing a bimodel result. From this action similarity, one might suggest that Kohlberg's discussion on the distinction between form and content would provide insight into the difference between Stage 2 and Stage 5 or 6 thought, or there might have been a 'regression' to Stage 2 thinking in the transition from Stage 4 to Stage 5. Fiskin, Keniston and MacKinnon's (1973) research into moral reasoning and political orientation replicates the findings of Haan *et al.*, with higher moral stages adopting a more radical ideology and evidence of a Stage 2 regression. Perhaps the most convincing evidence of the moral-judgment-to-moral-action connection is the study by McNamee (1977). Working with the hypotheses that: (1) individuals at higher moral stages were more likely to act in a moral way; and (2) there was a relationship between level of moral reasoning about hypothetical dilemmas and behaviour in an experiment, McNamee asked subjects to participate in an experiment at an appointed time. As the subjects were being introduced to the experimenter, a stooge feigning a 'bad drug trip' sought help from the experimenter/psychologist. The experimenter replied that she had no experience with drugs and did not know what facility could help him. The subject had the choice of remaining an uninvolved observer or intervening. At the end of the encounter, the subject was administered a Moral Judgment Scale. Whether the subjects' answers only rationalized their previous behaviour or not, the results do appear very conclusive (see Table 1).

Table 1.   *Subjects Who Made a Helping Response at Each of Kohlberg (1972) Stages*

	Number	Percentage
Stage 2	11	9
Stage 3	29	28
Stage 4	17	38
Stage 5	24	68
Stage 6	5	100

Source: Adapted from McNamee (1977).

McNamee found people at most stages who *thought* they should help. Those who *did* help scored at high stages of moral reasoning. Those who *did not actually* help attributed the lack of action to the construal of experimenter-authority. The finding of a linear judgment-action relationship does contradict earlier work by Milgram and Haan *et al.* McNamee states that the significance of this study is the confirmation it provides for Kohlberg's theory that moral judgment predicts moral behaviour in a situation (by determining the interpretation of the situation and consequently the response to it). Additional judgment-action support for Kohlberg is found in studies of cheating by Schwartz *et al.* (1969), where there was less cheating at higher moral stages; and Krebs and Rosenwald (1979), in which subjects were asked to return personality questionnaires (replies are shown in Table 2). There is also evidence that higher moral stage reasoners are more likely to keep promises (Rest, 1979), and other studies have shown moral reasoning and prosocial behaviour to be associated (see Emler, 1983a, 1983b, for reviews).

Table 2.   *Reply Rate to Questionnaires by Stage (Percentages)*

Stage:	2	3	4	5
On Time	33	40	91	100
Late	0	33	0	0
Not at all	66	27	9	0

Source: Krebs and Rosenwald (1979).

Candee's (1976) American study relating Kohlberg's dilemmas to questions concerning judgment and responsibility in the Watergate break-in and My Lai massacre provides a clear summary of Kohlberg's theory of stage structure and moral choice. He states:

> Since structure and choice are conceptually independent, it had been thought that all arguments could be defended at any stage. However the logic of Kohlberg's theory of moral reasoning suggests that as the structure of moral reasoning develops, it leads to a single most just conclusion. (p. 1294)

In his discussion of results Candee states that individuals at higher moral stages:

> more often make decisions in moral dilemmas that are consistent with human rights and less often choose alternatives that were designed to maintain conventions or institutions. These findings are, at least partially, determinative of moral choice. Furthermore, since an observed pattern was in all cases monotonic, there is empirical support for Kohlberg's claim that at the highest stage of reasoning all persons, given the same information, should reach the same answer. (p. 1299)

The studies cited above provide empirical evidence of the monotonic relationship between moral reasoning and moral action. Moreover, there is a relationship between judgment and appropriately perceived action at the lower stages as well. The lower stage judgment/action correspondence may be explained by cognitive and social-cognitive processing capabilities of the subject, and moral atmosphere in an action/judgment scheme. If one applies research modes adopted from attitude measurement, there is a strong correspondence between moral development and Ajzen and Fishbein's (1973) levels of attitudes (from individual norm to social norm to personal norm, as discussed by Berndt, 1981 and Emler, 1983b).

CRITICISMS

Criticism of Kohlberg's theory, in particular the relation of moral judgment to moral action, comes from many angles. Philosophically, arguments focus on the problem of will, and questions such as the meaning and actuality of action. Possibly the most cited psychological criticism is attributed to Kurtines and Greif (1974), who queried methodological considerations and predictive validity of moral judgment to moral action. Other social psychologists have acknowledged the legitimacy of studies in moral conduct and moral reasoning, but ask if the two should be considered to be associated in any way. A major methodological critique queries the reality of hypothetical dilemmas and its relation to both actual dilemmas and moral action. Finally, there is a broad range of social and relational criticisms which focus on the structure of societal relationships and question if the individual has the ability to go beyond cultural relativism (to a universal morality). Kohlberg describes his theory as being in constant development, or 'boot-strapping,' and many of the criticisms are answered in his most recent revisions—which will be discussed: philosophical and then psychological criticisms.

Straughan (1983) provides the dilemma of an avid domestic gardener who, on one of the few autumn days available to work on the garden, has collected a large amount of dead leaves, twigs, etc. The obvious disposal method is to burn this material. But there is a breeze blowing in the direction of a neighbour's garden, where freshly laundered clothes have been hung to dry; a dilemma is created. Straughan's dilemma can be resolved at each of the Kohlbergian stages (from a Stage 1—is my neighbour bigger than I with a tendency to speak with fists; to.Stage 5—what is it to be a good and responsible neighbour given present needs and considerations). The various resolves between moral action and the real actions are termed as a 'problem of will.' The gap between justifying and motivating considerations may be influenced by weak or strong will. Hence, Straughan's suggestion that Kohlberg is neither an Internalist nor an Externalist, but a Moderate Internalist leaves the theory open to the following criticism: 'A moderate internalist believes that one ought to do X is to do X in the absence of countervailing forces.' Weakness or strength of will arguments do not ask why actions take place; the arguments rationalize why they do not take place. A creative amalgamation of will may be found in Habermas' (1979) fusion of action theory and reciprocity to the three levels of Kohlberg's theory. Incomplete and complete reciprocity characterizes the lower and higher stages at each Kohlbergian level, respectively recognizing forms of weakness and strength of will (or ego).

Locke (1983a, 1983b) involves himself with many problems of moral action. He attempts to avoid any simplistic definition of moral action, that is, action in accordance with the dictates of morality. (Kohlberg's teleological model holds that only Stage 6 actions can be moral, previous actions can only be quasi-moral.) But the layperson's understanding of moral action can vary between a broad definition (any action which may be interpreted as moral) and actions which are morally motivated; roughly Externalist and Internalist definitions respectively. And there are moral habits and rationalizations to be accounted for as well. Moral actions are generally far more expansive than Kohlberg allows. Locke also explores the schemes of action/thought and thought/action. Given a gap between thought and action, the gap may be found between theoretical and practical morality or between practical and actual morality. Kohlberg is aware of the first gap originally discussed by Piaget (which will be discussed in relation to Gilligan's and others' research). In relation to practical and actual morality, Locke queries how the individual can develop a Stage 6 notion of ought if the Law of Conscious Realization is in effect; if actions dominate practical thought, then moral conduct will be dominated by conventional or strongly ritualized activity. Locke's portrayal of the two gaps may be resolved by turning Kohlberg's theory on its head and stating that moral action will provide the key to moral thought; that is, actions may be seen to precede and follow from moral thought by reference to preoperational and formal operational schemes used by the individual.

Amongst the many psychological criticisms of Kohlberg's theory, Kurtines and Greif (1974) state that there is very low predictive validity from moral judgment to moral action. The evidence they cite includes (1) Haan *et al.*'s (1968) evidence of the Free Speech Movement Stage 2 males sitting-in; and (2) Fodor's (1972) study of delinquency and moral development which does not support Kohlberg. They also note that most research positively relating judgment to action has been underaken by Kohlberg or his colleagues and is not sufficiently independent. Some of these objections have been cited previously in this chapter, but more specific responses to the challenge are provided by Broughton (1978) (who challenges Kurtines and Grief's value orientation) and Kohlberg in his revised theory.

Brown and Herrnstein's (1975) social psychological challenge to judgment/ action represents the interface of social and developmental psychologies. They call the interface a paradox, and describe it in the opening to their chapter on moral conduct and moral reasoning:

> This is a chapter about a paradox. Students of the development of moral reasoning in children and young people have found that a great majority attains a conventional 'law and order' morality, which involves obeying the laws and trying to treat people decently. In the same research period, students of social psychology have outdone one another in discovering that in certain circumstances respectable young people are capable of deceitful conformity, vandalism, and indifference to life-and-death problems of strangers who ask for help, are capable even of endangering the lives of others. For the most part, the subjects in the developmental studies and in the social psychological studies were drawn from the same population—American young people, especially college students. Therein lies the paradox.
>
> The two kinds of psychologies—developmental and social—seldom read each other's work, and since their studies are described in different courses, the paradox has largely gone unnoticed. But if a young person believes in being lawful and decent, how can he sometimes lie, destroy property, ignore a threatened stranger, and be willing to endanger another's life?
>
> Actually, there is no paradox unless you make a certain assumption. You must assume that the way people think about moral issues determines the way they act. You must believe act and thought are normally in harmony. If you do not, then there is neither paradox nor even surprise in someone talking on the high road and acting on the low road. (p. 289)

Either there is no relation between moral reasoning and moral conduct or, minimally, the relationship is complicated by many other factors, according to Brown and Herrnstein. They draw upon a bank of social psychological literature to substantiate the claim that subjects rarely, if ever, act morally. The main studies include research by, or based upon: Milgram's (1974) obedience to authority, which did not show the monotonic relationship; Latene and Darley's (1968) bystander intervention, where it is relatively easy to avoid doing one's moral duty; Asch's (1952) strength of group consensus in the determination of behaviour; and Zimbardo (1969) on the effect of a 'releaser' and positive pleasure/reinforcement inherent vandalism. Brown and Herrnstein acknowledge the strength of a cognitive developmental theory of morality, but point to problems of regression (as in the Free Speech Movement data) and subject inability to act morally (although they may reason morally). These problems of inconsistency and regression are explained by citing 'complicating variables' (such as moral concern, moral responsibility, situation of authority, evidence of caring) and 'intervening variables' (of respectability, concern, etc.) respectively. Ignoring evidence of the monotonic relationship and using the structure/content split (to note that action alternatives are available to the subject at preconventional and conventional levels), Brown and Herrnstein state 'that a person at any moral stage can act in either of two opposing directions . . . two actions considered simply as behaviour, in the absence of any interpretation, cannot be ranked with respect to morality at all, but are simply morally irrelevant.'

Other social psychological criticisms of judgment/action come from Vine, Emler and Hogan. The criticisms appear to be aimed at Kohlberg's theory in general. Hopefully the reader will understand the relevance to the more focused judgment/action problems. Vine's (1983) two main concerns question the cognitive construction of the world and social realities therein. He acknowledges the cognitive and social perspectives inherent in Kohlberg's theory, but queries the dominance of rational/individualistic deontological justice concerns. Without a greater role for social experience (and only relying on logical and social-perspective bases), Vine states that the theory cannot account for action; social experience encourages and constrains. The contradiction Vine focuses upon is: action (human and social) is necessary for Stage 6, justice concerns can no longer predominate.

Emler voices two major concerns. First, he challenges Kohlberg's interpretation that low correlations in Hartshorne and May's studies show inconsistent evidence for moral character. Emler (1983c) draws upon the 0.2 correlation as evidence of consistency (although he criticizes the methodology of the Hartshorne and May studies). Further, there is consistent evidence that anti-social behaviour/character and moral conduct can be predicted using attitude measures. Emler concludes that evidence of moral character does exist, accounting for self-presentation and audience in a theory of moral pluralism. Second, Emler (1983b; Emler, Renwick and Malone, 1983) has also conducted studies relating Kohlberg moral stages to political orientation. Evidence generally supports a correlation of higher-stage scores to radical orientation. But, when Emler asked 'right-wing' and 'moderate' students to respond as if they were 'radicals,' they significantly increased their principled reasoning scores (using Rest's, 1975, Defining Issues Test). Emler *et al.* question whether variations in adult moral reasoning are a function of political position rather than developmental status.

A number of social psychological criticisms identify Kohlberg's theory as individualistic, rationalistic, liberalistic (see Hogan and Emler, 1978; Emler, 1983b). This critique challenges an overly cognitive view of development, which relies on abstract reasoning and the individual as the sole unit of moral analysis. Social experience and social influence are, thus, limited and a Western, male bias (as evidenced in Kohlberg's original Chicago sample) dominates the theory.

A further criticism questions the strength of research based on hypothetical dilemmas. Piaget was careful to differentiate practical and theoretical moralities (as discussed by Wright, 1983). Piaget's research differs quite substantially from Kohlberg's; Piaget worked with younger children and explored the social relational and logical bases of moral development. His theory was more social psychological: inherent in the theory is moral obligation to significant (parental and peer) others, with the action/judgment scheme of conscious realization. The judgment/action problem is not as salient for Piaget (as Kohlberg). But the movement from a practical morality (which weds thinking and obligation) to theoretical morality poses both a sequence of development and a challenge to moral development theory based solely on hypothetical (theoretical) dilemmas.

The practical-hypothetical critique is drawn upon by many researchers. Emler (1983b) points out that hypothetical dilemmas abstract the individual from real situations and subject responses may be oversimplifications (given many other competing variables in the 'real' situation). In a further analysis of her Berkeley study, Haan (1975) discussed the difference between hypothetical and actual moral reasoning. While Haan's study originally sought to compare moral (hypothetical) reasoning with political (actual) reasoning, she did state that there was no clear distinction between the two types; students interviewed actually discussed both types of reasoning as moral (see Weinrich-Haste, 1983b). Haan also found a large majority of subjects reasoned at different levels when questioned on hypothetical and actual dilemmas; 46 per cent score higher and 20 per cent lower when faced with actual dilemmas. For a large number of students, their participation coincided with a state of readiness and the disequilibrating situation caused a focusing and integration at a higher level.

A confusing distinction between practical and 'classical' moral judgment was found in a study by Leming (1981). Practical moral judgments were systematically lower than classical (hypothetical) judgments. The difference could be explained as tapping concrete situational thinking characteristic of practical judgment as opposed to the formal operational thinking necessary to many higher-stage judgments. Alternatively, Leming may have tapped a performance/competence divide, similar to findings by Kohlberg and colleagues in prison studies.

A final actual/hypothetical study is represented in research by Gilligan (Gilligan and Belensky, 1978). They explored actual and hypothetical decisions on abortion and morality. A rough correspondence between abortion and hypothetical thinking was found at all levels of moral reasoning. The discrepancies between actual and hypothetical reasoning could help to identify women undergoing transitions in thought, those who were stable, and those 'at risk'. Of greater importance, they found that a wide range of interpersonal concerns were integral in the formation of judgments: while justice was considered, concerns also included aspects of responsibility and caring.

BRINGING THE THEORY BACK TOGETHER; JUDGMENT/ACTION TODAY

Throughout the 1970s and 1980s, Kohlberg's general theory of moral development has been refined and clarified. The developments and implications of the theory are better described elsewhere (see, for example, Weinreich-Haste, 1983a). Kohlberg and colleagues are able to draw upon more extensive and longitudinal data. The original global and breakdown scoring has become more structurally based, providing more homogeneity and reliability and less variance in subject scoring. The result in scoring refinement has been a general depression in the higher stage scores with no-one reaching the ultimate Stage 6 (which remains an abstraction). Also, structural/developmental insights have shown that individuals who had been coded as regressing from Stage 4 to Stage 2 retain far more complex moral understanding than Stage 2 subjects; the regression more properly represents an incomplete stage progression from Stage 4 to 5; that is 4½ or 4/5. Another refinement in stage progression was the differentiation of A and B substages: A substages show greater heteronomous respect for rules and authority; B substages are more universalistic, prescriptive and reversible (with this differentiation, the researcher can identify subjects at lower stages making deontic choices as being those using a B orientation). For the most part, this bootstrapping refinement of theory has enhanced the post-conventional argument of the monotonic judgment-action relationship; the majority of this discussion is therefore centred on these findings.

Aside from Kohlberg's own reported early findings, his theory received specific support in studies such as Krebs and Rosenwald (1979) and Schwartz *et al.* (1969). A thorough review of the available literature by Blasi (1980) explored moral action to see if it were simply a 'luxury' or rationalization, or if it were significantly related to moral judgment. The review found: (1) studies of delinquents showed that they tended to use low levels of moral reasoning; (2) moral reasoning was positively related to 'real life' behaviour in six of twelve studies, with three negatively related studies; (3) moral reasoning and honesty were positively related in seven of seventeen studies, with seven negatively related; (4) moral reasoning and altruism were positively related in eleven of seventeen studies, with four negatively related; and (5) moral reasoning and conformity were positively related. Blasi provided a large amount of evidence for the monotonic judgment-action relationship, but qualified his findings by citing certain behaviours that were better related to reasoning, and IQ as a possible intervening variable. Blasi further speculated that the bridge from judgment to action was through responsibility; the individual's 'will to action' is aroused when one is obligated (in some way) to act.

Responsibility and caring appear essential in the judgment-action link. Gilligan and Belensky (1978)'s research on women undergoing abortion counselling showed shortcomings in Kohlberg's original work in that respect. Interpersonal and ongoing relational concerns of responsibility necessarily underlie moral reasoning; the subject appears more willing to participate in the appropriate moral action on that basis. Kohlberg's original male (adolescent) sample was not tested for responsibility, but one can imagine that his increase of sample pool and longitudinal results will support this inclusion.

Certainly Kohlberg and Candee's (1984) reanalysis of the Free Speech Movement and Milgram's obedience data, along with findings from McNamee, support the monotonic relationship and the role of responsibility in the judgment-action relationship. In rescoring data from the Free Speech Movement, Kohlberg and Candee found a strong monotonic relationship between moral reasoning and taking part in the sit-in (see Table 3a). They also found a monotonic relationship in reasoning and deontic choice (see Table 3b). In the reanalysis, the cause of the bimodal (e.g., Stage 2 males sitting in) result was partially explained by the additional Stage 4½ and B substages not accounted for in the original sample. The rescoring of the Milgram study showed the monotonic relationship of reasoning to action; those subjects who refused to participate scored at the higher stages and B substages (see Table 4). Scorers were unable to discover the role of judgments of responsibility in relation to the Free Speech Movement data. The Milgram data appear to divide between followers (of the experimenter) and those who perceived themselves in a position of responsibility for the victims, e.g., those who refused to carry on with the experiment. Results from the rescored Free Speech Movement and Milgram data, along with McNamee's study, suggest that within the higher stages of judgment, responsibility becomes more focused on the individual. There appears to be a monotonic increase in making judgments of responsibility consistent with deontic judgments of rightness.

Kohlberg and Candee actually identify a three-step process linking judgment to action:

Table 3a. *Kohlberg and Candee's Rescoring of the Relationship of Moral Stage and Sitting-In of the Free Speech Movement*

Stage:	3	3/4	4	4/5
Sit-in (percentages)	10	31	44	73
Total number at Stage	39	138	125	37

Table 3b. *Kohlberg and Candee's Rescoring of the Relationship of Moral Stage to Sitting-In, Controlling for Deontic Choice, Free Speech Movement*

	Choice											
	Right				Mixed				Wrong			
Stage	3	3/4	4	4/5	3	3/4	4	4/5	3	3/4	4	4/5
Sit in (percentages)	23	54	63	75	11	17	12	60	0	0	0	0
Total number at Stage	13	66	71	29	9	30	24	5	14	37	20	1

Table 4. *Kohlberg and Candee's Rescoring of Subjects Quitting Milgram Situation by Stage and Substage (Percentages)*

	Substage of Moral Reasoning			
	Stage 3	Stage 3/4	Stage 4	Substage totals
Substage A				
Quit	0	0	0	0
(N at Stage)	(2)	(6)	(1)	(9)
Ambiguous				
Quit	100	0	100	18
(N at Stage)	(1)	(9)	(1)	(11)
Substage B				
Quit	100	50	100	86
(N at Stage)	(1)	(2)	(4)	(7)
Stage Totals	50	12	83	
	(4)	(17)	(6)	(27)

1 making a deontic judgment of rightness or justice in a situation;
2 judging that the self is responsible or accountable in carrying out the deontic choice;
3 carrying out the action.

A monotonic increase in consistency between deontic judgment and responsibility judgment is reported in a study using hypothetical dilemmas of moral reasoning and responsibility undertaken by Helkama (1979). Higher stages, according to Kohlberg (1971), do become more prescriptive in that the individual is better able to differentiate between moral obligations/responsibility and non-moral considerations. Thus moral stage influences moral acts both through deontic choice and judgment of responsibility.

The studies cited above are based on hypothetical dilemmas linked to hypothetical and real moral decisions. A similar monotonic and consistent relationship also links hypothetical dilemmas and amoral actions (Schwartz *et al.*, 1969, found decreasing dishonesty with higher stages). In 'real-life' situations, Candee (1976; and Kohlberg and Candee, 1984) explored reactions to the My Lai massacre and the Watergate break-in. Candee (1976) showed that people's hypothetical moral judgments and real situational judgments progressed in a monotonic direction. In reviewing transcripts and media coverage from the courtmartial/trial of Lieutenant Calley, Kohlberg and Candee were able to show a monotonic relation of soldier's actions and their explanations: from Meadow's obeying officers and revenge for buddies Stage 2/3 orientation; to Calley's conventional 'good officer' Stage 3 orientation; to Bernhardt's refusal to shoot civilians Stage 4B orientation. The relationship between higher stages of moral judgment and action in My Lai was clear in the obligations (that Bernhardt) felt. Lower stages of reasoning were linked with action through 'quasi-obligation', taken on the basis of army group norms and hierarchical authority within a group moral atmosphere. Quasi-obligation and group moral atmosphere were characteristic of the testimony given by Watergate break-in participants too. Conventional (Stage 3 and 4) thought characterized much of the defendent's testimony. Reasons given for the break-in were adherence to the norms of one's reference group (e.g., Nixon's Re-election Committee) and to maintain the 'system' (Nixon's Government) as it stood. Thus, there is good evidence to support the monotonic relationship of judgment and thought, and consistency between level of thought and action in real-life situations.

From the monotonic support of Kohlberg's theory (reviewed previously) several philosophical questions are answered. First, there is evidence that individuals (minimally Western) do progress up the hierarchy of moral stages. Within each stage of judgment, there are stage-appropriate actions. These may take the form of (1) actions preceding conscious realization; (2) actions undertaken in adherence to subjectively relative quasi-obligations (to individual, group or system); and (3) universal moral actions initiated through judgments of moral reasoning and responsibility. Empirical evidence shows that individuals move from a relativist position of subjectivity to universal and objective moral good, the naturalistic fallacy. Previous questions concerning the gap between reasoning and actions (from Straughan) and breadth of actions which may be termed moral (from Locke) have been considered in the empirical studies cited. Kohlberg and Candee summarize their points on the judgment-action relationship as follows:

1   Higher-stage and substage B subjects are more likely to perform the moral actions.
2   Higher-stage and substage B subjects are more likely to judge the moral action as being right (deontic).
3   Higher-stage and substage B subjects are more likely to make a judgment of responsibility.
4   Reasons for not performing the moral actions may take the form of quasi-obligations.
5   There is greater consistency between moral judgment and moral action with increasing stage development.

From Kohlberg and Candee's summary, one may expect to find a pyramidlike

Figure 2. *A Proposed Model of Increasing Moral Judgment Moral Action Consistency/Responsibility with Development*

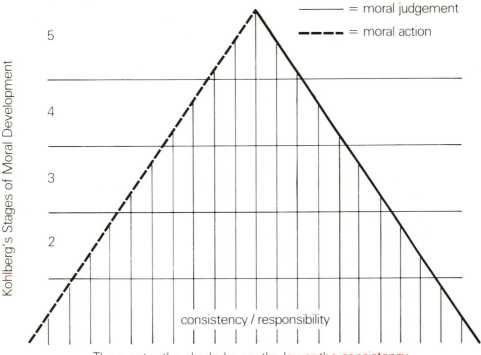

The greater the shaded area, the lower the consistency.

relationship between judgment and action shown in Figure 2, in preference to the bargraph presentation of Brown and Herrnstein (Figure 1).

Actually, a compromise between the polarity of the two Figures (1 and 2) would be a more realistic presentation of the judgment-action relationship. Remember that Kohlberg labels the action orientation of Stages 2, 3 and 4 as being due to quasi-obligations and moral atmosphere. Preconventional and conventional levels, then, have a consistency of judgment-action, albeit a consistent but immature relationship. Being careful not to confuse the structure-content argument and focusing on developing moral atmosphere research, one should make the 'immature' argument here.

From Kohlberg's early work with school and prison discussions, the role of social context and action has gained increasing prominence, both in the development and limitation of moral thought. It appeared obvious to apply Kohlberg's theory of moral development to schools; this would help fulfil moral education obligations of the education system. Children exposed to moral arguments above their own level of reasoning showed advancement ($\frac{1}{3}$ to $\frac{1}{2}$ stage) over a term (see Blatt and Kohlberg, 1975). Support for this type of study has been given by Rest (1976) and formalized into a discussion programme by Colby *et al.* (1977). But Blatt and Kohlberg found that enhanced moral reasoning did not carry over to moral behaviour (in tests of cheating). Maul (1980) also found that amount of experience, rather than grade level, enhanced moral development in an intensive education programme. Kohlberg's work in prisons (Kohlberg *et al.*, 1975) showed that moral reasoning may be enhanced, but prison culture drastically limited real-life reasoning; Kohlberg and colleagues criticized the role of the prison environment and suggested a 'just community' approach (that is, a democratic community with special living and social arrangements within a larger prison). A just community was based on the theory that gains in moral judgment had to be translated into patterns of action if moral development were to have a lasting effect. Applying the logic that a rigid and hierarchical environment limits reasoning (and hence action), Power and Reimer (1978) applied the just community approach in an alternative high school and noted a positive effect. A preconventional moral atmosphere (of prisons or traditional schools) limits: (1) development of moral reasoning by imposing rigid and ritualized patterns of action characteristic only of lower moral stages (a *prise de conscience* explanation of the effect of the hidden curriculum in teacher-pupil relations—see Kutnick, 1980); and (2) development of moral action by not providing an environment where deontic actions are acceptable or understood. A further example of the limiting effect of environment is described in Huston and Korte's (1976) survey of Western societies; a majority of these countries had no legislation to support any altruistic acts. But moral atmosphere does not always limit moral development. On the positive side, group moral atmosphere can enhance moral development, as shown in Reimer's (1977) study of the moral reasoning and actions of Israeli kibbutz children. Kohlberg suggests that moral atmosphere is a bridge between judgment and action. From the studies above, the bridge runs in two directions, serving either to limit or to enhance both judgment and action. The group/social context is a key determinant in moral development (according to Power and Reimer, who further argue for stages of 'collective normative values' and 'sense of community' characteristic of social environments). Accounting for the social context of moral development also adds a community orientation to Kohlberg's theory, meeting earlier criticisms of individualist and rationalist ideology (see Vine, 1983; Emler, 1983b).

SUMMARY

Any attempt to summarize Kohlberg's work on the relationship of moral judgment to moral action would follow a long and convoluted course. The essence of this chapter has been to portray the early theory, criticisms, revision of theory and empirical support. Here we shall bring together the main points.

　　Kohlberg's theoretical and empirical work has remained consistent over the last twenty-five years. Early limitations in the theory have been superseded in the development/refinement of theory and in meeting the challenge of his critics. The original statement that higher stages would become more prescriptive and, hence, more likely to dictate action has remained and been supported in the literature (on honesty/moral good and dishonesty/moral wrongdoing). One cannot define and explore moral action simply by behaviours exhibited; moral actions involve an internal or cognitive component. And the basis of the theory stresses that moral cognition both causes moral actions and arises out of moral action. Judgments move in a deontic direction towards what is morally right and obligatory (hence they become aretaically more sound or worthy of action). In committing this naturalistic fallacy, much attention and stress is put upon the monotonic relationship of judgment and action (ideally presented in Figure 2). With the refinement of the scoring system, Kohlberg and his colleagues have provided much empirical support for the monotonic relationship. Any specific figural portrayal of the judgment-action relationship must move beyond the simple bargraph of Brown and Herrnstein (Figure 1), but Figure 2 may not provide a complete picture. Kohlberg stresses that his theory explores the structure and not the content of moral judgments. The possible moral actions of the lower stages may be very diverse. (There is evidence of a Stage 2 response to the Heinz dilemma recommending either breaking into the chemist shop to help his wife, or not breaking in and protecting property.) The range of moral choice (of action) becomes smaller at higher stages and the individual assumes greater responsibility/consistency in relating judgments to actions. Figure 3 may be a fairer representation of the developmental process. This representation does move beyond the simple integration of judgment and action by interjecting judgment of responsibility; as one's level of reasoning rises, choice of action decreases and responsibility becomes more focused. Higher stages in the monotonic relationship are able to meet philosophic criticism by empirically showing a meeting of the objective (universal) and

Figure 3. *A Model of the Monotonic Relationship, Accounting for Range of Choice, Responsibility and Reasoning by Stage*

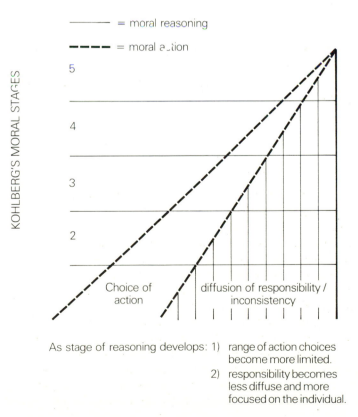

As stage of reasoning develops: 1) range of action choices become more limited.
2) responsibility becomes less diffuse and more focused on the individual.

subjective (relative). The psychological movement of deontic choice and increased responsibility by stage has been presented as a model of psychological function and sequence by Kohlberg and Candee following the format: (1) interpretation of the situation; (2) decision-making (deontic choice); (3) follow-through (moral and responsibility judgments); (4) follow-through (mediated by ego controls).

In stressing and seeking support for the monotonic relationship, Kohlberg appears to have given greater attention to higher stages (4 and 5) and correspondingly less attention to the lower stages and their relations to actions. Three problems arise from the emphasis on the higher stages: (1) incidents of low-stage individuals making deontic choices in preference to quasi-obligatory choices; (2) the various relations of action to judgment at lower stages incorporating the 'law of conscious realization' and 'moral atmosphere'; and (3) incidents of individuals capable of making higher judgments actually expressing lower-stage judgments and following through with corresponding actions.

The first problem has been explored in this chapter with reference to Kohlberg's addition of substage B in the revised scoring system. Individuals who made deontic choices but scored at low stages were most likely to be found at the B substage of their stage. Empirical support has been given in the rescoring of the Free Speech Movement and Milgram studies. A more contentious and difficult problem is to relate actions to judgments—generally throughout the moral stages or, minimally, to the three levels (preconventional, conventional, postconventional). This chapter has already reviewed the role of conscious realization (actions preceding cognitive awareness) in moral development, and Kohlberg has stated that judgments arise from and guide actions. But Piaget's 'law' is not characteristic of all logical-mathematical or moral stages. In relation to logical mathematical development, 'conscious realization' characterizes sensory-motor and preoperative stages. In Piaget's theory of moral development, conscious realization characterized the early adaptations of both morality of constraint and cooperation. In Kohlberg's theory 'conscious realization' is most characteristic of the preconventional levels. Concrete operations and formal operations (each with its own action-judgment scheme) characterizes the conventional and postconventional levels respectively. Figure 4 depicts a scheme and level description of the relation of judgment-action. Preoperational/preconventional action preceding judgment describes a child with cognitively limited understanding in a (perceived to be) controlled environment dominated by egocentrism, parental and hierarchical authority. Concrete operational/conventional activity dominates individual and group norms, backed by systematic sanctions; moral atmosphere is a key issue either in repressing moral thought to the practical norms of the group in the prison or enhancing group responsibility and promoting moral thought and action in the kibbutz. Formal operational/postconventional twists the action-judgment sequence to judgment-action. The individual is freed from concrete constraints to function at principled levels of thought and action—avoiding the tyranny of conventions. The notion of 'twist' is interesting because it counters logical/rationalist explanations of human behaviour, and is empirically supported.

The third judgment-action problem (that of making judgments at a lower level than the individual is capable of) can be handled by drawing points from the second problem. One can simply point out that this phenomenon may be explained as a performance-competence split; although one is capable, intervening variables do

Figure 4. *Action-Thought Schemes Depicted in Relation to Logical-Mathematical Stage and Moral Level*

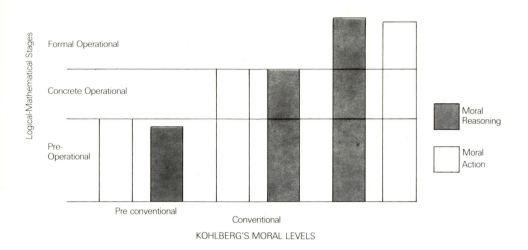

not allow the individual to use her/his full capabilities. This is a problem worthy of further social psychological exploration. Cognitively, all earlier stages remain in the individual's repertoire, hence we are able to draw upon them in appropriate circumstances. Moral atmosphere is just that circumstance which may depress or enhance moral judgment and/or action. Further, Kohlberg's use of hypothetical dilemmas provides situational conflicts. The stage analysis of answers provides certain characteristic ways in which the individual interprets rights and duties in that situation. The relation of hypothetical judgments to real judgments is mediated by the effect of moral atmosphere (as in prisons—Kohlberg *et al.*, 1975), and characterizes the individual's developmental/therapeutic situation (as in abortion decision—Gilligan and Belensky, 1978).

Overall, the field relating moral judgment to moral action is in a state of continuous flux, development and redevelopment. The multitude of subjects of which any reader must be aware include various theories in philosophy and psychology, theoretical and empirical research, descriptive research and research that promotes change. Kohlberg has been involved in all aspects of this field. His contribution has brought consensus and controversy. This chapter generally finds support for the naturalistic fallacy and the monotonic relationship. As the reader will judge (and perhaps act upon), there are still many further qualifications which must be made.

REFERENCES

Ajzen, I. and Fishbein, J. (1973) 'Attitudinal and normative variables as predictors of specific behaviours', *Journal of Personality and Social Psychology*, 27, pp. 41–5.
Aronfreed, J. (1969) 'The concept of internalization', in D. Goslin (Ed.) *Handbook of Socialization*

Theory and Research, Chicago, Rand McNally.

Asch, S. E. (1952) *Social Psychology*, Englewood Cliffs, N.J., Prentice-Hall.

Berndt, T. J. (1981) 'Relations between social cognition, non social cognition and social behaviour: The case of friendship', in J. H. Flavell and L. Ross (Eds.) *Social Cognitive Development*, Cambridge, Cambridge University Press.

Blasi, A. (1980) 'Bridging moral cognition and moral action: A critical review of the literature', *Psychological Bulletin*, 88, pp. 1–45.

Blatt, M. and Kohlberg, L. (1975) 'The effects of classroom moral discussion upon children's level of moral judgment', *Journal of Moral Education*, 4, pp. 129–61.

Breznitz, S. and Kugelmass, S. (1967) 'Intentionality in moral judgment: Developmental stages', *Child Development*, 38, pp. 469–79.

Broughton, J. (1978) 'The cognitive-developmental approach to morality: A reply to Kurtines and Greif', *Journal of Moral Education*, 7, pp. 81–96.

Brown, R. and Herrnstein, R. J. (1975) *Psychology*, London, Methuen.

Candee, D. (1976) 'Structure and choice in moral reasoning', *Journal of Personality and Social Psychology*, 34, pp. 1293–301.

Colby, A., Kohlberg, L., Fenton, E., Speicher-Dubin, B. and Leiberman, M. (1977) 'Secondary school moral discussion programmes led by social studies teachers', *Journal of Moral Education*, 6, pp. 90–111.

Damon, W. (1975) 'Early conceptions of positive justice as related to the development of logical operations', *Child Development*, 46, pp. 301–12.

Duveen, J. (1984) From Social Cognition to the Cognition of Social Life: An Essay in Decentration. Unpublished doctoral dissertation, University of Sussex.

Emler, N. (1983a) 'Approaches in moral development: Piagetian influences', in S. and C. Modgil and G. Brown (Eds.) *Jean Piaget: An Interdisciplinary Critique*, London, Routledge and Kegan Paul.

Emler, N. (1983b) 'Morality and politics: The ideological dimension in the theory of moral development', in H. Weinreich-Haste and D. Locke (Eds.) *Morality in the Making*, Chichester, John Wiley and Sons.

Emler, N. (1983c) 'Moral character', in H. Weinreich-Haste and D. Locke (Eds.) *Morality in the Making*, Chichester, John Wiley and Sons.

Emler, N., Renwick, S., and Malone, B. (1983) 'The relationship between moral reasoning and political orientation', *Journal of Personality and Social Psychology*, 45, pp. 1073–80.

Fiskin, J., Keniston, K. and MacKinnon, C. (1973) 'Moral reasoning and political ideology', *Journal of Personality and Social Psychology*, 27, pp. 109–19.

Fodor, E. M. (1972) 'Delinquency and susceptibility to social influence among adolescents as a function of moral development', *Journal of Social Psychology*, 86, pp. 257–60.

Frankena, W. K. (1973) *Ethics*, Englewood Cliffs, N.J., Prentice-Hall.

Gerson, R. and Damon, W. (1978) Moral understanding and children's conduct,' in W. Damon (Ed.) *New Directions for Child Development*, Vol. 2: Moral Development. San Francisco: Jossey-Bass.

Gilligan, C. and Belensky, M. F. (1978) 'A naturalistic study of abortion decisions', in W. Damon (Ed.) *New Directions for Child Development*, Vol. 2: Moral Development, San Francisco, Jossey-Bass.

Haan, N. (1975) 'Hypothetical and actual moral reasoning in a situation of civil disobedience', *Journal of Personality and Social Psychology*, 32, pp. 255–70.

Haan, N., Smith, M. B. and Block, J. (1968) 'Moral reasoning of young adults: Political-social behaviour, family background and personality correlates', *Journal of Personality and Social Psychology*, 10, pp. 183–201.

Habermas, J. (1979) 'Moral development in ego identity', in *Communication and the Evolution of Society* (T. McCarthy, trans.), Boston, Beacon Press.

Hartshorne, H. and May, M. A. (1928–30) *Studies in the Nature of Character*, Vol. 1: Studies in Deceit; Vol. 2: Studies in the Organization of Character, New York, Macmillan.

Helkama, K. (1979) 'The development of the attribution of responsibility: A critical survey of empirical research and a theoretical outline.' Research Report, 3, Department of Social Psychology, University of Helsinki.

Hogan, R. and Emler, N. (1978) 'The biases in contemporary social psychology', *Social Research*, 45, pp. 478–534.

Hollas, M. and Cowan, P. (1973) 'Social isolation and cognitive development: Logical operations and role-taking abilities in three Norwegian social settings', *Child Development*, 44, pp. 630–41.

Hook, T. J. and Cook, T. D. (1979) 'Equity theory and the cognitive ability of children', *Psychological Bulletin*, 86, pp. 429–45.

Huston, T. L. and Korte, C. (1976) 'The responsive bystander: Why he helps', in T. Lickona (Ed.) *Moral Development and Behaviour*, New York, Holt, Rinehart and Winston.

Kant, I. (1949) *Fundamental Principles of the Metaphysics of Morals*, New York, Liberal Arts Press.

Kohlberg, L. (1958) The Development of Modes of Thinking and Choices in Years 10 to 16. Unpublished doctoral dissertation, University of Chicago.

Kohlberg, L. (1968) 'The child as a moral philosopher', *Psychology Today*, 2, 4.

Kohlberg, L. (1969) 'Stage and sequence: The cognitive developmental approach to socialization', in D. Goslin (Ed.) *Handbook of Socialization Theory and Research*, Chicago, Rand McNally.

Kohlberg, L. (1971) 'From is to ought: How to commit the naturalistic fallacy and get away with it in the study of moral development', in T. Mischel (Ed.) *Cognitive Development and Epistemology*, New York and London, Academic Press.

Kohlberg, L. (1976) 'Moral stages and moralization', in T. Lickona (Ed.) *Moral Development and Behaviour*, New York, Holt, Rinehart and Winston.

Kohlberg, L. (1978) 'Revision in the theory and practice of moral development', in W. Damon (Ed.) *New Directions for Child Development* Vol. 2: Moral Development, San Fransisco, Jossey-Bass.

Kohlberg, L. and Candee, D. (1984) 'The relation of moral judgment to moral action', in W. Kurtines and J. L. Gewirtz (Eds.), *Morality, Moral Behaviour and Moral Development: Basic Issues in Theory and Research*, New York, Wiley.

Kohlberg, L., Kelsey, K., Scharf, P. and Hickey, J. (1975) 'The just community approach to corrections: A theory', *Journal of Moral Education*, 4, pp. 243–60.

Kohlberg, L., Scharf, P. and Hickey, J. (1975) 'The justice structure of the prison—A theory and an intervention', *The Prison Journal*, 51, pp. 3–14.

Krebs, D. and Rosenwald, A. (1979) 'Moral reasoning and moral behaviour in conventional adults', *Merrill-Palmer Quarterly*, 23, pp. 77–87.

Kurdek, L. (1978) 'Perspective taking as a cognitive basis of children's moral development: A review of the literature', *Merrill-Palmer Quarterly*, 24, pp. 3–28.

Kurtines, W. and Greif, E. B. (1974) 'The development of moral thought: Review and evaluation of Kohlberg's approach', *Psychological Bulletin*, 81, pp. 453–70.

Kutnick, P. (1980) 'The inception of school authority: The socialization of the primary school child', *Genetic Psychology Monographs*, 101, pp. 35–70.

Kutnick, P. (1983a) 'Moral incursions into constraint', in H. Weinreich-Haste and D. Locke (Eds.) *Morality in the Making*, Chichester, John Wiley and Sons.

Kutnick, P. (1983b) *Relating to Learning*, Hemel Hempstead, Allen and Unwin.

Latene, B. and Darley, J. (1968) 'Group inhibition of bystander intervention', *Journal of Personality and Social Psychology*, 10, pp. 215–21.

Leming, J. S. (1981) 'Curricular effectiveness in moral/values education: A review of research', *Journal of Moral Education*, 10, pp. 147–64.

Lickona, T. (1976) 'Critical issues in the study of moral development and behaviour' in T. Lickona (Ed.) *Moral Development and Behaviour*, New York, Holt, Rinehart and Winston.

Locke, D. (1983a) 'Moral reasons and moral action', in H. Weinreich-Haste and D. Locke (Eds.) *Morality in the Making*, Chichester, John Wiley and Sons.

Locke, D. (1983b) 'Theory and practice in thought and action', in H. Weinreich-Haste and D. Locke (Eds.) *Morality in the Making*, Chichester, John Wiley and Sons.

McNamee, S. (1977) 'Moral behaviour, moral development and motivation', *Journal of Moral Education*, 7, pp. 27–31.

Maul, J. P. (1980) 'A high school with intensive education: Moral atmosphere and moral reasoning', *Journal of Moral Education*, 10, pp. 9–17.

Milgram, S. (1974) *Obedience to Authority*, London, Tavistock.

Mischel, W. and Mischel, H. N. (1976) 'A cognitive social-learning approach to morality and self-regulation', in T. Lickona (ED.) *Moral Development and Behaviour*, New York, Holt, Rinehart and Winston.

Moire, D. J. (1974) 'Egocentrism and the emergence of conventional morality in pre-adolescent girls', *Child Development*, 45, pp. 299–304.

Piaget, J. (1932) *Moral Judgment of the Child*, (trans ed.) Free Glencoe Press, 1965.

Piaget, J. (1976) *The Grasp of Consciousness* (S. Wedgewood, trans) Cambridge, Mass., Harvard University Press.

Power, C. and Reimer, J. (1978) 'Moral atmosphere: An educational bridge between moral judgment and action', in W. Damon (Ed.) *New Directions for Child Development*, Vol. 2: Moral Development, San Fransisco, Jossey-Bass.

Rawls, J. (1971) *A Theory of Justice*, Cambridge, Mass., Harvard University Press.

Reimer, J. (1977) A Study in the Moral Development of Kibbutz Adolescents. Unpublished doctoral dissertation, Harvard University.

Rest, J. (1975) 'Longitudinal study of the Defining Issues Test', *Developmental Psychology*, 11, pp. 738–48.

Rest, J. (1976) 'New approaches in the assessment of moral judgment', in T. Lickona (Ed.) *Moral Development and Behaviour*, New York, Holt, Rinehart and Winston.

Rest, J. (1979) *Development in Judging Moral Issues*, Minneapolis, Minn., University of Minnesota Press.

Saltzstein, H., Diamond, R. and Belensky, M. (1972) 'Moral judgment level and conformity behaviour' *Developmental Psychology*, 7, pp. 327–36.

Schwartz, S., Feldman, K., Brown, M. and Heingartner, A. (1969) 'Some personality correlates of conduct in two situations of moral conflict', *Journal of Personality*, 37, pp. 41–58.

Selman, R. (1971) 'The relation of role-taking to the development of moral judgment in children', *Child Development*, 42, pp. 79–91.

Selman, R. (1976) 'Social cognitive understanding', in T. Lickona (Ed.), *Moral Development and Behaviour*, New York, Holt, Rinehart and Winston.

Selman, R. (1980) *The Growth of Interpersonal Understanding*, New York, Academic Press.

Selman, R., Damon, W., and Gordon, A. (1973) 'The relation between levels of social role-taking and stages of justice conceptions in children 4–10', Paper presented to the Society for Research in Child Development, Philadelphia.

Smith, M. E. (1978) 'Moral reasoning: Its relation to logical thinking and role taking', *Journal of Moral Education*, 8, pp. 41–9.

Straughan, R. (1983) 'From moral judgment to moral action', in H. Weinreich-Haste and D. Locke (Eds.) *Morality in the Making*, Chichester, John Wiley and Sons.

Thornton, D. and Reid, R. L. (1982) 'Moral reasoning and type of criminal offence', *British Journal of Social Psychology*, 21, pp. 231–8.

Thornton, D. and Thornton, S. (1983) 'Structure, content, and the direction of development in Kohlberg's theory', in H. Weinreich-Haste and D. Locke (Eds.) *Morality in the Making*, Chichester, John Wiley and Sons.

Tomlinson-Keasey, C. and Keasey, C. (1974) 'The mediating role of cognitive development in moral judgment', *Child Development*, 45, pp. 291–8.

Turiel, E. (1969) 'Developmental processes in the child's moral thinking', in P. H. Mussen, J. Langer and M. Covington (Eds.) *Trends and Issues in Developmental Psychology*, New York, Holt, Rinehart and Winston.

Vine, I. (1983) 'The nature of moral commitments', in H. Weinreich-Haste and D. Locke (Eds.) *Morality in the Making*, Chichester, John Wiley and Sons.

Weinreich-Haste, H. (1983a) 'Kohlberg's theory of moral development', in H. Weinreich-Haste and D. Locke (Eds.) *Morality in the Making*, Chichester, John Wiley and Sons.

Weinriech-Haste, H. (1983b) 'Social and moral cognition', in H. Weinreich-Haste and D. Locke (Eds.) *Morality in the Making*, Chichester, John Wiley and Sons.

Wright, D. (1983) 'The moral judgment of the child revisited', in H. Weinreich-Haste and D. Locke (Eds.) *Morality in the Making*, Chichester, John Wiley and Sons.

Zimbardo, P. C. (1969) 'The human choice: Individuation, reason and order versus deindividuation, impulse and chaos', in W. J. Arnold and D. Levine (Eds.) *Nebraska Symposium on Motivation*, Vol. 17, Lincoln, Neb. University of Nebraska Press.

9. Why Act on Kohlberg's Moral Judgments? (Or How to Reach Stage 6 and Remain a Bastard)

ROGER STRAUGHAN

The subtitle is not my own invention. At a conference on moral development held at Leicester several years ago and attended by Lawrence Kohlberg and a number of his associates, an informal discussion group met one afternoon to consider precisely that topic. The wording has ever since summed up for me one of the most fascinating and neglected areas of Kohlbergian theory, which I shall attempt to explore further in this chapter.

What is commonly known as 'the judgment/action issue' is not really a single, unified 'issue' at all, but a rather messy collection of loosely linked problems with which philosophers, psychologists and others have long been concerned—ever since Socrates' provocative claim that to know the Good is to do it. Philosophers have busied themselves with questions about the logical relationship between moral judgment and moral action; the emotive, prescriptive and conative features of moral judgments; and the analysis of 'moral weakness' and 'bad faith'. More recently psychologists have tried to study the empirical relationship between 'moral cognition' and moral behaviour, and to propose theoretical interpretations of that relationship.

These general concerns have given rise to a host of more specific problems, some of them highlighted by the design of the various psychological research studies and the assumptions lying behind them. Considerable difficulties have arisen in trying to reach agreement over what is to count as a moral judgment and how one is to know whether or not a subject has made one, and over what is to count as a moral action and how one is to know whether or not a subject has performed one.

The conceptual and methodological questions here are closely intertwined, but the logical priority of the former over the latter has not always been realized—we have to be reasonably clear about what it is we are trying to study before we try to study it. Misleading conclusions can easily be drawn by researchers who fail to respect this logical priority.

'The judgment/action issue' thus becomes an exceedingly complex matter, in that it is constituted by a variety of different problems of logically different kinds. All of these, however, stem from an apparently obvious feature of human life—namely that we all at times fail to do what we think we ought to do. This feature can be expressed in all sorts of ways; for example, by saying that human beings often fail to act upon their principles or to live up to their ideals, or that they are prone to moral weakness or weakness of will, or that they can at times reveal an inconsistency or gap between their moral reasoning and their behaviour. Various explanatory concepts have been used to account for this phenomenon, ranging from the theologian's 'original sin' through the commonsense notions of 'conscience' and 'character' to the psychologist's 'ego strength'. Attempts to define and explain the relationship between moral judgment and action, then, inevitably lead us into a conceptual minefield. It will be the contention of this chapter that Lawrence Kohlberg has not picked his way with sufficient care in this perilous area.

What has Kohlberg's contribution been here? It is an all-too-common criticism of Kohlberg that he is 'interested only in moral reasoning' and that his theory has nothing to say about moral *action*. A study of his extensive writings shows that this charge is not justified, yet the fact that it is so frequently levelled is perhaps not without significance. Kohlberg's predominant concern clearly *is* with moral reasoning, and it is certainly arguable that he has not said *enough* about moral action. Morality is by definition a practical business, for it is about what ought and ought not to be *done*. Of course, a person's reasons and justifications why it ought or ought not to be done are of great moral significance and interest, yet the very concept of morality becomes distorted, even incomprehensible, if undue emphasis is placed upon its 'judgmental' or 'theoretical' aspects. This fundamental point about the nature and function of morality is well underlined by Hare's comment: 'If we were to ask of a person, "What are his moral principles?" the way in which we could be most sure of a true answer would be by studying what he *did*' (italics in original).[1]

Kohlberg's basic approach to the study of morality, however, is in radical disagreement with Hare in this respect. According to Kohlberg, one finds out what a person's moral principles are (or whether he really has anything which Kohlberg would count as moral principles), not by studying how he actually behaves, but by analyzing and interpreting his verbal responses to a hypothetical dilemma. Yet, as I have argued elsewhere,[2] this hypothetical approach has important logical limitations, which make it an unreliable guide to what happens in 'real-life morality'. For example:

1   moral conflict comes to be construed exclusively as conflict between rival moral principles (such as truth-telling versus promise-keeping, or respect for property versus respect for life). This kind of moral conflict, however, is probably less common empirically and less central logically than is the clash between principle and inclination (when I judge that I *ought* to do *x*, but do not feel that I *want* to do *x*);

2   hypothetical dilemmas necessarily lack that first-hand immediacy which is an essential ingredient of genuine moral experience. In making a real-life moral decision, my motives, feelings, wants and emotions may run counter

to my hypothetical reasoning and judgments, which will often need to be modified if I actually find myself in such a situation. Direct emotional experience of a situation is a necessary condition of participating in it as a moral agent—and such participation is a very different activity from engaging in a hypothetical ethical debate about the Heinz dilemma.

Kohlberg's methodology, by its very nature, virtually equates moral agency with the making of judgments about hypothetical ethical dilemmas, and this orientation must impose severe limitations on what he can say about morality proper and the real-life business of moral decision-making. In this respect at least Kohlberg simply by-passes 'the judgment/action issue'. However, it would be unfair to suggest that Kohlberg totally ignores the problematic relationship between moral judgment and moral action, for he does occasionally in his voluminous writings address himself to this question. The remainder of this chapter will be devoted to a critical appraisal of this portion of his work.

Kohlberg's claim in brief is that the higher the stage of reasoning a subject is at, the more likely is he to act in accordance with his moral judgments, and that consequently 'maturity of moral thought should predict to maturity of moral action.'[3] This is because 'moral judgment determines action by way of concrete definitions of rights and duties in a situation.'[4] The evidence usually cited by Kohlberg to support this conclusion comes from experimental cheating tests, Milgram's obedience studies and an analysis of the Berkeley University sit-in.[5]

This account of 'moral action' is extremely scanty in comparison with the elaborate exposition and interpretation which characterizes Kohlberg's work on moral judgment. It is in my view inadequate and obscure in a number of respects; by examining these we may be able to clarify more precisely what is at stake in 'the judgment/action issue'.

(1) Drawing Conclusions from the Evidence

My first set of objections concerns the sort of evidence to which Kohlberg refers and the conclusions he tries to derive from it. The range of 'moral behaviour' on which he bases his generalizations is very restricted and hardly representative of our everyday experience. Decisions about whether or not to cheat or inflict electric shocks during psychological experiments or to join a university sit-in protest do not represent typical dilemmas with which most moral agents are faced. Indeed, it is doubtful whether the cheating test raises a *moral* issue involving *moral* behaviour in any significant sense at all. As Kohlberg himself says, '... the experimental situation is Mickey Mouse (it does not matter much whether one cheats or not), and ... it is fishy (the experimenter explicitly leaves the child unsupervised in a situation where one would expect supervision).'[6] This point is underlined by Hersh, Paolitto and Reimer: 'Experimental cheating tests ... are one step removed from real-life decisions. Subjects may not know that they are being observed for their cheating behaviour, but they do know they are involved in an experiment and may not attribute much importance to their actions.'[7] But the whole point about moral actions and situations is that importance *is* attributed to them and that they are *not* 'Mickey Mouse,' so why should Kohlberg think that he is investigating *moral* behaviour in such experiments?

To draw general conclusions about 'moral action' from such dubious examples, then, is quite unjustifiable. The moral domain covers a vast area, and it is a complex task to attempt to map out its main contours in terms of its characteristic form and content.[8] The meagre data on which Kohlberg bases his account of 'moral action' cannot begin to do justice to this complexity.

Furthermore, the data as presented cannot for the most part illuminate what Kohlberg appears to think they do, for in order to study the relationship between moral judgment and action we need to know (a) what the subject believed he ought to do, and (b) what he actually did do. Yet in the cheating tests it is *assumed* that subjects always think it wrong to cheat, and in the Milgram study it is *assumed* that subjects always think it wrong to inflict the electric shock; so the percentages which Kohlberg quotes are always of how many Stage X subjects *actually* cheated or gave the shock. But it is perfectly possible that many subjects do *not* believe they ought not to cheat or to give the shock, and are thus showing 'consistency' or 'strength of will' in acting upon their beliefs by cheating or giving the shock; this is particularly likely in the Milgram experiment, where many may believe they ought to keep to the terms of their contract and do what the experimenter asks them to do. Equally it is possible that some non-cheaters and non-shockers are showing 'inconsistency' or 'weakness of will' in *not* acting (because of some counter-inclination) upon their belief that it is morally *right* to cheat or give the shock in that situation. Kohlberg's percentages tell us nothing about all this, yet that is the information we need in order to clarify the relationship between judgment and action.

Kohlberg, then, fails to distinguish clearly enough between 'consistent action' (where subjects do what *they* judge is the right thing to do) and 'virtuous action' (where subjects do what is *generally considered* to be the right thing to do—by the experimenter at least). It is only studies of 'consistent action' which can help us unravel 'the judgment/action issue,' but unfortunately such studies seem to be conspicuous by their absence. Even the Berkeley sit-in analysis was based on *post-hoc* interviews, and asking students a year after the event why they acted as they did, and how they *now* think they perceived the situation *then*, is a very different procedure from trying to establish whether or not they acted as they believed *at the time* they ought to act.

As Kohlberg's data, therefore, can tell us little about either genuine moral action or consistency between judgment and action, his conclusion cannot be relied upon to throw much light upon the issue he claims to be tackling.

(2)   Choices and Reasons for Action

My second set of objections concerns a further failure on Kohlberg's part to draw essential distinctions and to specify precisely which aspect of 'the judgment/action issue' he is dealing with. This confusion is well illustrated in his article 'From Is to Ought', which concludes with a subsection entitled 'From Thought to Action'.[9] Kohlberg begins this subsection, as the title suggests, by discussing how to 'relate moral judgment to moral action' (pp. 226–8), placing his customary reliance upon cheating tests in arguing that 'maturity of moral thought should predict to maturity of moral action' (pp. 228–9). There are immediate problems here over how 'should' should be interpreted, and more seriously over what is meant by 'maturity of moral action' (other than that Kohlberg presumably approves of it); for as Blasi has commented, '... at present nobody seems to know the parameters by which to evaluate the degree of maturity specifically in moral action, independently of cognition'.[10] It is difficult to know what Kohlberg is talking about here, particularly as he has in the preceding paragraph stated that there is 'no valid psychological definition of moral behaviour', and that the only differentiating criterion is 'what the people involved think they are doing' (p. 228).

Leaving this difficulty aside, however, we soon find that Kohlberg is not really concerned with moral *action* at all but with moral *choice*, sliding into a discussion of the latter without appearing to realize that there is a crucial distinction to be drawn here, which lies at the very heart of the issue he is supposed to be analyzing. He writes, 'Prediction to *action* thus requires that the alternatives are ordered by a hierarchy related to the individual's basic structures. In the case of Stage 4, we could only predict how a subject would *choose* when social order stands clearly on one side and other values on the other, as in civil disobedience' (p. 230, my italics). As another example of how 'stage defines choice', he then refers to 'the principled subject's sensitivity to justice which gives him a reason to not cheat when "law and order" reasons have become ambiguous or lost their force.' The conclusion drawn in the following sentence is that 'moral judgment dispositions influence *action* through being stable cognitive dispositions' (p. 230, my italics).

This passage reveals serious confusion. There is one question about whether 'stage defines *choice*' (for example, does being at Stage 5 rather than 3 affect whether one decides that it is right or wrong to cheat, steal drugs for one's wife, etc.), and another question about whether 'moral judgment determines *action*' (for example, does being at Stage 5 rather than 3 affect whether one actually behaves as one believes one ought in cheating, stealing drugs for one's wife, etc.). These questions are logically distinct, and to blur that distinction is to miss the main point of 'the judgment/action issue'.

The confusion arises from the ambiguity of the notions of 'moral choice' and 'moral decision'. These can refer either to:

1   'judgmental', 'propositional' choices and decisions *that* it is right or wrong to cheat, steal drugs, etc., or to
2   'behavioural', 'action' choices and decisions *to* or *not to* cheat, steal drugs, etc.

It is this distinction which produces the possibility of 'weak-willed' behaviour, which in turn lies at the heart of 'the judgment/action issue', for it is normally considered a not uncommon feature of our moral experience to decide *that* we ought to do *x*, but to want for various reasons to do *y* rather than *x*, and consequently to decide *to* do *y* rather than *x*.

Why does Kohlberg ignore this distinction and say so little about the topic he claims to be investigating in this passage—'behaviour which is consistent with an individual's moral principles' (p. 228)? The explanation seems to lie in his failure to probe sufficiently deeply the concept of 'reasons for action'. Yet again there are crucial distinctions to be drawn here. In cases of 'weak-willed' behaviour what appears to be happening is that two different kinds of 'reason for action' are in conflict. The agent accepts that there are good reasons why he ought to do *x*, yet other reasons are operative upon him in the actual situation which lead him to do *y* instead. In other words he sees that factors *A*, *B*, *C*, constitute reasons which *justify* or *require* the doing of *x*, yet he fails to do *x* because factors *D*, *E*, *F*, constitute reasons which *motivate* or *incline* him to do *y*—or to put it more simply, we do not always want to do what we believe we ought to do. Reasons for action of a justifying kind, therefore, do not always provide us with reasons for action of a motivating kind.[11]

Kohlberg does not appear to recognize that these different kinds of reason for action can or should be distinguished. In the passage already quoted, in discussing how 'stage defines choice' he states, 'It is the principled subject's sensitivity to justice which gives him a reason to not cheat when "law and order" reasons have become ambiguous or lost their force', and immediately continues, 'We are arguing that moral judgment dispositions influence action . . .' (p. 230). But justice and law and order are *justificatory* considerations, and while these may well define the subject's 'judgmental' choice *that* it is wrong to cheat, they will not necessarily provide a *motivational* 'reason to not cheat' in the actual situation, where counter-inclinations may weigh more heavily when the chips are down.

This confusion between motivation and justification is evident elsewhere in Kohlberg's work. At one point he writes mysteriously of 'the motivational aspect of morality (as) defined by the motive mentioned by the subject in justifying moral action.'[12] At another he produces a table of 'motives for moral action' corresponding to each of the six stages.[13] Yet in none of these cases is Kohlberg really describing *motives* for *action*—that is, reasons which motivate a person actually to *act* in a certain way; what he is describing are verbal justifications of moral judgments—that is, reasons which a person gives to justify why he thinks that it is right to act in a certain way. Again we must conclude that it is Kohlberg's overwhelming methodological emphasis upon moral *judgment* which leads him to equate these fundamentally distinct kinds of 'reason for action'.

(3)   Rules and Principles

'Reasons for action' are also connected with a further oddity in Kohlberg's account, which concerns his view of rules and principles. Higher-stage subjects, who are allegedly more likely to act in accordance with their judgments than lower-stage ones, are said to reason in terms of principles rather than rules: 'morally mature men are governed by the principle of justice rather than by a set of rules'.[14] So principles appear to have a stronger, more reliable 'motivational power' than rules:

> The motivational power of principled morality does not come from rigid commitment to a concept or a phrase. Rather, it is motivated by awareness of the feelings and claims of the other people in the moral situation. What principles do is to sort out these claims, without distorting them or cancelling them out, so as (to) leave personal inclination as the arbiter of action.[15]

What precisely distinguishes a rule from a principle in Kohlberg's view? We are told:

> Justice is not a rule or a set of rules, it is a moral principle. By a moral principle we mean a mode of choosing which is universal, a rule of choosing which we want all people to adopt in all situations. We know it is all right to be dishonest and steal to save a life because it is just . . . We know it is sometimes right to kill, because it is sometimes just . . . There are exceptions to rules, then, but no exception to principles . . . A moral principle is not only a rule of action but a reason for action.[16]

This passage raises a host of questions, many of which fall strictly outside the scope of this chapter. Does Kohlberg, for example, grant too high and exclusive a status to 'the principle of justice', placing it at the apex of a Platonic hierarchy, where 'there are not many virtues but one', because 'the good is justice'?[17] Why can we not describe Stage 4 reasons as based on *principles* concerning the maintenance of law, authority and social order? Does Kohlberg really mean that moral principles are *universal* ('rules of choosing which we want all people to adopt in all situations') rather than *universalizable* in Hare's much more sophisticated sense? Who are the 'we' who all 'know' that it is sometimes all right to be dishonest, steal and even kill? Considerable strength of will is required to drop the pursuit of these tempting quarries.

There are, however, quite enough problems lurking in the principle/rule distinction as Kohlberg propounds it, and in the relevance he implies that it has for 'the judgment/action issue'. Kohlberg's distinction is obscurely expressed and is made no clearer by his description of a moral principle as a *rule* of choosing and also a *rule* of action; the distinction between a rule of action and a reason for action goes unexplained; and the ambiguity of 'choosing' and of 'a reason for action' is again ignored.

Let us try to dispel some of this conceptual murk. What characterizes a principle and distinguishes it from a rule (as we normally understand these terms) is not its content or its 'universality', but its function. Principles represent sets of highly general considerations which we *appeal to* in order to *justify* a particular course of action in a particular situation.[18] Rules on the other hand prescribe more specifically what is or is not to be done in that situation. In terms of content, therefore, there is room for possible overlap between rules and principles: truth-telling or promise-keeping, for instance, could count either as rules in situations where they function simply as prescriptions (as in the rules for witnesses in a court of law, summarized in the oath), or as principles if they are appealed to as a source of justification (as in an argument about the rights and wrongs of gazumping).

If principles, then, are essentially justificatory in nature, they do not have any *necessary* 'motivational power', for the reasons given in the previous subsection, and when Kohlberg claims that 'a moral principle is not only a rule of action but a reason for action', he can be referring only to a *justifying* 'reason for action' of the kind that is involved in the making of 'judgmental', 'propositional' choices and decisions. Principles cannot therefore be relied upon to bridge the judgment/action gap. We understand what is meant by expressions like 'he acted against his principles', and do not feel that we are talking logical or psychological nonsense when we use them. 'Having principles' is no guaranteed defence against succumbing to counter-inclinations. As Neil Cooper puts it, 'There is no necessary one-one correlation between the order of priority of a man's moral principles and the order of strength of his desires'.[19] This is because moral principles have a 'cool-hour' quality: 'a man's moral principles are those of his principles of action which in a cool hour he is least prepared to abandon belief in, however much he may be tempted to deviate from them in the heat of the moment'.[20] These important conceptual points show clearly why principles are an appropriate medium through which to describe some central features of Kohlberg's theory, for the discussion of *hypothetical* moral dilemmas is very much a 'cool-hour' activity. But it is in the heat of the moment that one has to choose or decide *to* act or *not to* act upon one's judgments, and here at the heart of 'the judgment/action issue' the role of principles becomes much more problematic than Kohlberg appears to realize.

CONCLUSION

My aim in this chapter has not been to show that Kohlberg is wrong in his claim that higher-stage subjects are more likely to act in accordance with their judgments than lower-stage subjects. Indeed, I have argued elsewhere that there are logical considerations which support this claim.[21] Kohlberg's suggestion that 'attention' correlates with 'strength of will'[22] could also be a fruitful one, and is again in accord with my own attempts at a logical analysis of 'weakness of will'.[23] (I have not referred to this aspect of Kohlberg's work in this chapter, as it appears unrelated to his basic, cognitive-developmental interpretation of 'the judgment/action issue'.)

What this chapter has shown is that Kohlberg pays scant attention to the complex relationship between moral judgment and moral action. He is prevented from getting to grips with these complexities, partly by the constraints of his 'hypothetical' research method and partly by the inadequacy and undifferentiated nature of his conceptual armoury. Whether or not 'cognitive definitions determine behaviour' as Kohlberg maintains, his own 'cognitive definitions' of moral agency, choices, decisions and principles have certainly determined and restricted his behaviour as an investigator of the moral domain.

REFERENCES

1 Hare, R. M. (1952) *The Language of Morals*, London, OUP, p. 1.
2 Straughan, R. (1975) 'Hypothetical moral situations', *Journal of Moral Education*, 4, 3, pp. 183–9. Also (1982a) *I Ought to, But . . .; A Philosophical Approach to the Problem of Weakness of Will in Education*, Windsor, NFER-Nelson, pp. 173–6
3 Kohlberg, L. (1971) 'From is to ought: How to commit the naturalistic fallacy and get away with it in the study of moral development', in Mischel, T. (Ed.) *Cognitive Development and Epistemology*, New York, Academic Press, p. 228.
4 *Ibid.*, p. 229.
5 See, e.g., Kohlberg, L. (1969) 'Stage and sequence: The cognitive-developmental approach to socialization', in Goslin, D. A. (Ed.) *Handbook of Socialization Theory and Research*, Chicago, Ill., Rand McNally, pp. 395–6. Also (1970) 'Education for justice: A modern statement of the Platonic view', in Sizer, N. F. and T. R. (Eds.) *Moral Education: Five Lectures*, Cambridge, Mass., Harvard University Press, pp. 77–9.
6 Kohlberg (1971), *op. cit.*, p. 229.
7 Hersh, R. H., Paolitto, D. P. and Reimer, J. (1979) *Promoting Moral Growth*, New York, Longman, p. 96.
8 See Straughan, R. (1982b) *Can We Teach Children to be Good?* London, Allen and Unwin.
9 Kohlberg (1971), *op, cit.*, pp. 226–32.
10 Blasi, A. (1980) 'Bridging moral cognition and moral action: A critical review of the literature', *Psychological Bulletin*, 88, 1, p. 8.
11 See Straughan (1982a), *op. cit.*, esp. Chs. 3 and 5.
12 Kohlberg, L. (1963) 'The development of children's orientation toward a moral order', *Vita Humana*, 6, p. 13.
13 Kohlberg (1969), *op. cit.*, pp. 381–2.
14 Kohlberg (1970), *op. cit.*, p. 70.
15 Kohlberg (1971), *op. cit.*, p. 231.
16 Kohlberg (1970), *op. cit.*, pp. 69–70.
17 *Ibid.*, p. 70.
18 See Peters, R. S. (1981) *Moral Development and Moral Education*, London, Allen and Unwin.
19 Cooper, N. (1971) 'Oughts and wants', in Mortimore, G. W. (Ed.) *Weakness of Will*, London, Macmillan, p. 197.

20 *Ibid.*
21 Straughan, R. (1983) 'From moral judgment to moral action', in Weinreich-Haste, H. and Locke D. (Eds.) *Morality in the Making*, Chichester, Wiley, pp. 125–40.
22 Kohlberg (1969), *op cit.*, pp. 396–7.
23 Straughan (1982a), *op. cit.*, esp. Ch. 6.

Interchange

KUTNICK REPLIES TO STRAUGHAN

To begin my reaction to Straughan's chapter, I should state that I am in general sympathy with his remarks. We both acknowledge that Kohlberg's theory is a valid and worthy attempt to understand morality and moral development from a theoretical and empirical view. We also agree that there are several weaknesses in the early empirical work which have detracted from the theory by limiting its conceptual frame to: (1) moral reasoning as opposed to moral practice; (2) hypothetical as opposed to real dilemmas; and (3) justificatory as opposed to motivating reasons for action. But progress towards resolving problems inherent in these three weaknesses has been made recently by Kohlberg and his colleagues. More fundamental disagreement between Straughan and me centres on Straughan's assertions that 'morality is by definition a practical business' and his limited differentiation between principle and rules. While I present the two points as separate disagreements, they both draw upon the Kohlbergian distinction between conventional and postconventional. I shall briefly expand upon these points.

LIMITATIONS IN THE EARLY THEORY

1   Moral Reasoning vs. Moral Practice.

In an ideal world, a moral developmental researcher would question (as Straughan suggests) 'what the subject believed he ought to do and what he actually did do', and follow this by asking what justification was given for the action. But the research has not progressed as far as that. In fact, even studies by Kohlberg (reanalysis of FSM and Milgram) and McNamee showing evidence of a monotonic relationship used an action-justification scheme; interviews were conducted after the act. Straughan is right to draw attention to this process as 'justification', for we do not know if the subject acted in accordance with established principle, or if the 'act' itself was the cathartic experience which forced the subject to develop further powers in reasoning. But, within Kohlberg's theoretical discussion of cognitive development (and in recent writings which have focused on moral atmosphere and conventional levels of morality) action plays a prominent role. Action is practice whether it precedes cognition (preoperational), coincides with cognition (concrete operational) or is informed by cognition (formal operational). In the enthusiasm to expand and expound Kohlberg's theory, many researchers have focused only on

158

postconventionality—their enthusiasm both limited their perception of action in moral development and created an overly cognitive interpretation to the theory.

2 Hypothetical vs. Real Dilemmas.

This is a serious problem in the theory. Hypothetical dilemmas do abstract the subject from immediate problems and lay the ground-work for the overly-cognitive interpretation. But there are positive correlations between moral and actual dilemmas (for example, see studies by Haan; Gilligan). And, if one *only* considers that the theory is about the monotonic relationship, formal and principled reasoning is an essential prerequisite in the justification of action. As an aside, an area of social psychological research which could add insight into the competence-performance (hypothetical-real) limitation is lacking in output and application; 'weakness of will' problems should be approached here and not particularly in cognitive developmental theory.

3 Justificatory vs. Motivating Reasons.

This overlaps with the previous limitations. Early research by Kohlberg did not allow for a separation of these reasons; cognitive disequilibrium was the motivating and reasoning force. Recent work by Gilligan does expand Kohlberg's original work by acknowledging judgment of responsibility and caring as central concerns in abortion decisions. Kohlberg now includes his understanding of judgments of responsibility as part of the monotonic process. With this addition to the theory, Kohlberg is able to differentiate between motivation and reasoning; but we should still not lose the distinction that both reasoning and motivation are qualified by stage development.

DISAGREEMENTS WITH STRAUGHAN

1 Morality Is by Definition a Practical Business.

As an assertion, I wonder if this statement can be justified. From a philosophical view it appears as an extreme form of Externalism. But, while one may read a morality into action, principles which inform action cannot always been seen by the lay observer. Destruction of property or coming to blows with a policeman may or may not be evidence of a simple disrespect for established order. These actions may or may not be informed by 'reason', such as the attempt to de-escalate nuclear tensions and make the world a safer place for humanity. There is a complex interaction between action and reason; simple assertions and practicalities only hinder our understanding.

2 Principles vs. Rules.

This is a fundamental distinction in Kohlberg's theory. To limit the distinction to 'function', as Straughan has, certainly limits morality to a 'practical business'.

Undoubtedly we could live in a conventional world where the 'rule of law' was obeyed to the extreme. The fundamental difference between principle and rule is that the former allows (or forces) individuals to go against rules/laws if they are perceived to be (in some sense) unjust. Principles do not simply 'justify' but inform action; and this is the difference between conventional and postconventional development.

In the exercise of validating Kohlberg's assertions on the relationship between judgment and action, several strengths and weaknesses in the theory have been reviewed. Only through dialogue and challenge can development take place. Kohlberg presents a theory which is in perpetual development. Recent research has provided evidence of the monotonic relationship. But it has also expanded the theory to include an element (motivational) of responsibility and caring and a broader conceptualization of action (in relation to judgment at lower stages and moral atmosphere).

STRAUGHAN REPLIES TO KUTNICK

I find it difficult, if not impossible, to attempt to 'refute' Kutnick's chapter, as requested, because he and I appear to be engaged in different enterprises and concerned with different questions. Perhaps it would be more accurate to say that we are tackling different aspects of 'the judgment/action issue' from different perspectives, starting from different methodological and conceptual assumptions— a point I shall exemplify in a moment. This disparity partly no doubt reflects the usual difficulties of communication which philosophers and psychologists often experience, even when discussing a common problem; in Kutnick's chapter, for instance, I do not understand his use of the philosophical term 'naturalistic fallacy'. Yet our two chapters are not merely an illustration of two people (or two disciplines) speaking different languages. Interestingly different intellectual stances and attitudes are being displayed, and in a book dealing with 'consensus and controversy' it may be worth devoting the bulk of my brief reply to outlining some of these.

The problem is at root a conceptual one. Kutnick, in his detailed evaluation of Kohlberg's work and of the various studies relating to it, implicitly accepts the validity and meaningfulness of a wide range of concepts which I find obscure and confusing. It is assumed that a clear, unequivocal, readily accessible meaning attaches to such expressions as (to take a random sample) 'cognitive mediating', 'deontic choices', 'subjectively relative quasi-obligations' and 'aretaically sound judgments', and also to such claims as 'moral cognition causes moral actions' and 'higher stages in the monotonic relationship show a meeting of the objective (universal) and subjective (relative)'. I suspect that it would not only be linguistically fastidious philosophers who find such language either incomprehensible or question-begging on the grandest of scales.

My basic objection to the conceptual repertoire of Kohlberg and the Kohlbergians, which Kutnick reproduces, is not that it lacks philosophical rigour and sophistication (though that charge could certainly be laid), but that it fails completely to do justice to our everyday moral experience and the language we have developed over several millennia to describe it. It is, for example, highly significant and to my mind amazing that in all the wealth of material presented by Kutnick on 'the judgment/action issue' not one mention is made of 'temptation' or (to put it slightly more technically) of 'counter-inclinations'. The motivational aspects of the potential gap between moral judgment and action and the notion of 'moral weakness' are totally ignored; instead, our failures to act upon our moral judgments are to be explained in terms of 'cognitive inadequacy'. But to focus so exclusively upon the 'cognitive' is to overlook those motivational factors which man has long seen as central to his understanding of why it is often hard to do what he believes he ought to do. What is more, it is perfectly possible, as I have argued elsewhere,[1] to include these motivational factors in a straightforward explanation of Kohlberg's findings to the effect that higher-stage subjects are apparently more likely to act upon their judgments than lower-stage subjects.

The Kohlbergian literature which Kutnick cites also adds weight for the most part to the other charges of conceptual ambiguity with which my own chapter is principally concerned. Reference is frequently made to moral 'choices' and 'decisions', usually without any attempt being made to distinguish between 'propositional' choices and decisions *that x* is right and 'behavioural' choices and decisions *to do x*, despite the fact that this distinction lies at the heart of (and indeed helps to create) the potential judgment/action gap. Likewise, little if any attention is paid to distinguishing between 'consistent action' (where subjects do what *they* judge they ought to do) and 'virtuous action' (where subjects do what is deemed by others—e.g., the experimenter—to be the right thing to do); in the report of McNamee's study, for example, we are told that those who did not actually help the stooge drug victim 'attributed the lack of action to the construal of experimenter-authority', but does this convoluted jargon mean that they believed at the time they *ought* to help or not? Kutnick's survey confirms my belief that data concerning 'consistent action' as such are as scanty as they are confused.

My conclusion, then, is that Kutnick has allowed himself to be led by the Kohlbergians into what I describe in my own chapter as a conceptual minefield, whereas my own approach has been to parade the perimeter, fieldglasses in hand, trying to spot and plot some of the more obvious mines. Which of us deserves the higher commendation for valour is open to question; no doubt exploring minefields is yet another operation which ideally requires consistency of judgment and action.

REFERENCE

Straughan, R. (1983) 'From moral judgment to moral action', in Weinreich-Haste, H. and Locke, D. (Eds.) *Morality in the Making*, Chichester, Wiley, pp. 125–40.

Part VI: Moral Development and Ego Development

10. Kohlberg and the Psychology of Ego Development: A Predominantly Positive Evaluation

ROBERT KEGAN

Despite various pronouncements upon ego development in his own work, Lawrence Kohlberg is not, nor has he claimed to be, an ego psychologist. Weighing his contribution to a subject not his own is thus properly more an inferential matter than an assessment of those productions he himself deems as contributions. Many psychologists, for example, now consider that Piaget's work makes an important contribution to the understanding of *emotion* (Cicchetti and Hesse, 1982; Chandler *et al.*, 1978; Harter, 1979; Cowan, 1978; Elkind, 1967; Tharinger, 1981; Kegan, Noam and Rogers, 1982; Greenspan, 1979; DeCarie, 1978) despite the fact that (1) Piaget himself did not take on the subject, limiting himself mostly to side-references and speculations, much as Kohlberg has done with the ego; and (2) most of what Piaget actually *did* say about emotion (e.g., emotion as energetics) is *not* what theorists such as those cited above take to be the source of his contribution to the topic; they are impressed rather by the usefulness of those ideas he *did* concentrate upon to the topic *they* are interested in. In other words, Piaget is taken as an important contributor to the understanding of emotion primarily because he exceeded himself in the study of cognition. In this essay, I take a somewhat similar view of the importance of Kohlberg's work on moral development for the study of ego development. Although Kohlberg has certainly been more interested in ego development than was Piaget in emotion, they share the attributes of (1) having opened a bigger door than they knew, and (2) being more impressive on a subject not of their own choosing at the implicit rather than at the explicit level. In fact, my own view is that while (1) Kohlberg's explicit conception of the relationship between moral and ego development is problematic, at best, and inconsistent with his basic premises, at worst; (2) Kohlberg's general body of work is so filled with promising implications for reconstructions and new connections in the field of ego psychology as to make it the single most original and potentiating contribution to the understanding of the ego since Sigmund Freud's.

This essay pays greatest attention to that aspect of Kohlberg's work which has the most significance for the study of the ego—a constructivist idea of structure and its development. I try to indicate how this idea addresses lacunae or unrealized aspirations in past or present conceptions of the ego within psychoanalytic and existential psychologies. I then try to suggest the way this central idea sheds new light on long-time concepts in ego psychology which Kohlberg himself does not explicitly address—namely, concepts of 'boundary', 'externalization, internalization, and projection', and 'observing ego'. With less elaboration I then turn to two other important contributions of Kohlberg's work for ego psychology, both of which arise out of the idea of structure: (1) a method of assessment that combines the strengths of systematic research and clinical sensitivity; i.e., is both intersubjectively rigorous and built upon idiographic processes of meaning-discernment; and (2) a conception of development that is both psychological and philosophic, hence explicitly relating the descriptive with the prescriptive, addressing issues of normativeness and the justification of goals in treatment or intervention. Finally, I indicate my misgivings about Kohlberg's explicit conception of necessary but not sufficient relationships between subsystems in personality each of which is believed to have its somewhat independent structural development.

Although Piaget is Kohlberg's intellectual father, Kohlberg is himself father to what might be called 'cognitive-developmental ego psychology'. As Piaget cannot be held responsible for what Kohlberg has done with him so Kohlberg is not responsible for the likes of Haan (1977), Selman (1980), Fowler (1981), Kegan (1982) and others; but the more explicit ego psychologies these theorists have developed are fundamentally indebted to Kohlberg's extension of Piaget's work on the mental constitution of the physical world to the mental constitution of the social-personal world.

Insofar as even the original Freudian conception of ego has had to do with *cognition*, *making sense*, *object-relating*, *reality*, it should always have seemed that Piaget's programme of work on cognitive development must have something to offer to ego psychology. This would seem to be especially so as time went on, since the psychoanalytic conception of the *motivation* for these processes has—from Hartmann to the present day—been a gradual movement away from an extrinsic, libidinally driven picture to a more intrinsic, meaning-oriented, relationship-oriented one. But it has taken more than a move by psychoanalytic theory to bring the possibility of fruitful interaction about; it has taken a move by cognitive-developmental theory as well. Kohlberg is responsible for this move. He demonstrated that the same intrinsically meaning-constitutive processes that Piaget posited for understanding how the mind organizes the physical world, had considerable power for understanding how the mind organizes the social-personal world. In doing so, Kohlberg lent a theretofore unachieved critical mass to the cognitive-developmental paradigm, touching off a reaction that may very well shed light on a number of the shadowy places in existing conceptions of the ego. Let us consider some of these lacunae and unrealized aspirations in psychoanalytic and existential ego psychologies.

PSYCHOANALYTIC EGO PSYCHOLOGY: THE ELUSIVE PRIMACY OF CONSTRUCTIVISM

Modern psychoanalytic theory, both through ego psychology and object-relations theory, has aspired to rid itself of the derivative, extrinsic view of the ego's processes of meaning construction which is so powerfully articulated in the work of Sigmund and Anna Freud. For the Freuds, the individual is primarily motivated by the desire to reduce or eliminate unpleasurable affect. By this reasoning the individual turns away from himself to the object (whether it be the object's representation as in primary process or the world of real objects as in secondary 'cognition') because his own system of warding off noxious experience has broken down. Object relations are thus formed extrinsically, a kind of necessary inconvenience never put better than in Freud's depiction of ego formation and reality orientation as an unavoidable 'detour' the psychic system must make to secure for itself the same peace it has desired since inception and which was much more efficiently obtained *in utero*. Similarly, Anna Freud believed the latency age child does not use abstract thinking because he does not *need* to; i.e., the defences he has are adequate to the task. Only with the resurgent drives of adolescence, she believed, is it necessary to construct the more complicated safety-preserving mechanisms such as intellectualization which *secondarily* bring abstract capacities into being. Ego development for the Freuds was thus essentially a by-product of a separate world with which it had little to do. Anna Freud likened this to a society's secondary gains of technological and scientific achievement during wartime. Sigmund Freud likened the ego to a clown in a circus, 'always sticking in its oar to make it look as if it has something to do with what is going on' (Freud and Jung, 1974, p. 404).

While modern psychoanalytic theories *espouse* an intrinsic motivation for processes of meaning coherence (Erikson, 1963; Fingarette, 1963) and object-relating (Winnicott, 1965; Fairbairn, 1962; Guntrip, 1968; Sandler and Sandler, 1978), the blunt truth is that they at worst conceal the libidinal motor inside a velvet glove, or at best are simply mute as to developing a conception of the ego's processes of meaning coherence and object-relating which will realize their aspirations. The history of psychoanalytic ego psychology since the Freuds is one of 'liberal revisionism' which does not finally call into question the basic psychoanalytic tenets which turn out not to be about drives alone, but the conception of the relation between *psychological development* and *meaning-constitution*, between *growing* and *knowing*. It should not be a surprise that undoing this knot would require someone who *shares* the modern psychoanalytic thinkers' convictions about a primary motivation toward processes of meaning coherence and object-relating but who does *not* share an investment in maintaining the psychoanalytic edifice. Kohlberg turned out to be that person.

Consider, for example, Erikson's brave and brilliant attempt to elevate Freud's theory of psychosexual development into a phenomenologically, existentially, and psychosocially oriented lifespan theory of personal processes of meaning coherence (1963, 1964, 1968, 1977, 1983). In Erikson's hands the mechanical, reductionistic, body-based 'anal stage', for example, becomes a system of meaning and world-coherence oriented to the issues of holding on and letting go in their fullest symbolic as well as literal sense. But this same elegant parallelism with the

Freudian system also betrays the impossibility of dignifying the individual's meaning-cohering processes with an original life of their own, since no activity of meaning-making brings the oral/autonomy meaning scheme into being, and its maintenance depends on no activity of meaning-making defending it, and no activity of meaning-making will bring about its reconstruction into a new meaning scheme. Oral Trust vs. Distrust develops into Anal Autonomy vs. Shame and Doubt, and the latter itself develops into Phallic Initiative vs. Guilt on the strength of a power *completely separate from the processes of meaning coherence*. Once the real work of the reassignment of an organically determined body-based mode of communication has taken place, Erikson is saying, new terms are set on what meaning-making shall be about. Fair enough; but hardly a theory of the development of processes of meaning coherence. Erikson's is a theory of the *consequences* for meaning coherence of presumed, wired-in reorganizations of psychophysiological energy.

Fingarette's (1963) less influential but highly creative effort to tie psychoanalytic ego psychology more directly to the processes of meaning constitution is similarly undermined. His failure is even more poignant than Erikson's because he more clearly aspires to a conception of ego organization as active processes of meaning-construal. He conceives growth processes in psychotherapy, e.g., as 'meaning reorganization' in opposition to the classical conception of uncovering 'hidden realities'. Introducing an explicitly constructivist notion of mental 'structure' (as opposed to psychoanalytic references to id, ego, superego structures), and an explicitly process-oriented conception of ego (as opposed to entity or state), Fingarette considers that a definition of anxiety 'must be cast in terms of *psychic structure* rather than psychic energy or perceived affect.... It is not primarily an affect, one among many affects, which the ego must master, rather it *is* ego-disintegration.... More precisely, where fundamental ego integrity is in process of becoming disintegrated relative to a prior state or organization we refer to the ego disorganization as anxiety. The context of these processes is set by the psychological *sine qua non*: the tendency toward psychic organization. Where it operates successfully we speak of ego; where it is threatened with central failure we speak of anxiety' (pp. 72–9). Longing for a truly constitutive ego, this becomes a Pisgah view of the Promised Land, for Fingarette, still tied to the Egyptian bondage of psychoanalytic biological determinism, cannot himself cross over into the new world:

> This conception fits neatly into the body of psychoanalytic theory. For example, we can now account very simply for the fact that the form of anxiety occurring in a particular situation is specific to the type of ego-integrity which is affected. For example, during the period when the primary ego orientation is phallic, significant disorganization of the ego is called 'castration anxiety'. Likewise, when the ego is predominantly oriented around the relationship to the sustaining mother, threats to the integrity of the ego are experienced as 'separation anxiety'. Thus as the individual moves through the crucial phases of life which challenge him to new self-integrations, there is always and inevitably the other aspect of this movement—the partial, temporary, or complete failure of the new and dominant pattern of integration of the self (p. 79).

Whoops! Constructivism is once again subordinated to a wired-in, biologically determined developmentalism. However much psychological distress may have to do with the state of meaning-disorganization, the 'primary ego orientations' themselves, the duration of a given system of meaning, and the processes that bring on *re*-organization are unrelated to meaning-making *or* anxiety (non-meaning-making). Continuity and change are at the behest of biology. Knowing and growing are separate realms.

What modern psychoanalytic ego psychologists *want* is a powerful theory to match their conviction that ego development is *intrinsically* about meaning-constitution, that some forms of conflict and distress are not only non-pathological, they are the very auguries of development itself. But what modern psychoanalytic ego psychologists *have* is a powerful theory of something else.

In demonstrating empirically that Piaget's conceptions about the mental organization of inanimate objects could be fruitfully applied to consider the mental organization of 'people objects', Kohlberg pointed the way to a solution to the problem of modern psychoanalytic ego psychology. He showed that in a broader realm of meaning-organization (moral development), a realm much closer to the concerns of ego psychologists, it made sense to consider *development* in terms *intrinsically* (not secondarily) related to meaning. In his most recent published reference to ego development (Snarey, Kohlberg and Noam, 1983), Kohlberg and his co-authors write:

> Ego development may be understood as the overall unity of the ego as it progressively reconstructs itself through a dialectical process in which the person 'makes sense' of his or her evolving relationship with others, the world, and life as a whole. Ego development thus includes the continuous redefinition of what is subjective and what is objective; on the subject side is an evolving self and on the object side is an evolving differentiation of one's natural, social, and ultimate environments. We believe that individuals strive for a general sense of self-consistency that encompasses the human striving for moral consistency (p. 305).

What makes a statement like this one different from similar espousals of an intrinsically-motivated constitutive ego is some thirty years of research leading to a still evolving, nonetheless powerful definition of a series of meaning-systems which have an entirely different character from those which come from neo-psychoanalytic ego psychology. Although Kohlberg's stages can be easily (and completely misguidedly) caricatured into Sunday-supplement, pop-psychology personality types, the 'stuff' of a given stage is actually no particular content, experience, motive, style, or attitude at all, but something quite abstract, a structure or underlying logic giving form to a person's experiences, motives, attitudes. In fact, the history of Kohlberg's ponderous, messy, and unconventional project, in which theory is continuously redrafted, is the story of better and better recognitions of the distinction between the contents of experience and the forms of experience. (The growth of the theory mirrors the ponderous, messy, organic growth of persons themselves, who grow by recasting what they have been taking as the form of their experience to the domain of content under the organization of a new form.)

Kohlberg's idea that ego development involves 'the continuous redefinition of what is subjective and what is objective' is reflected in his own moral stages, each of which defines a different subject-object distinction in moral knowing (see Kegan, 1982, pp. 46–72, for an explicit elaboration of this point). For example, at Kohlberg's Stage 3, the psychological category of 'differing points of view' can be reflected upon; the individual can organize, relate, hold simultaneously different points of view. Different points of view have become 'objects' or 'objective'; they can be manipulated. One result is that persons' moral knowing *can* construct the complex system of mutual reciprocity—thinking about what I want and another wants at the same time, for example; or thinking about another, thinking about me;

or doing unto others as I would have them do unto me. This morality of 'interpersonal concordance' which makes one susceptible to social expectation and conformity cannot *itself* be reflected upon or manipulated. Rather than that-which-*gets*-manipulated-or-organized (the 'object'), it is the very principle *of* organizing (i.e., subject).

Kohlberg's idea that the ego 'progressively reconstructs itself through a dialectical process' refers to the idea that the subject-object division reflected in any stage is itself part of an ongoing process which relativizes this dichotomy: the very principle of organization (what is 'subject') in Stage 3, for example, will become 'object' in Stage 4, when subtending the morality of interpersonalism gives rise to the psychological construction of *relationship-regulating* social system, institution and law.

Thus Kohlberg has not just extended Piaget by coming up with yet another set of stages for yet another domain, the social-personal rather than the physical-nonhuman. He has extended the power of Piaget's idea of 'genetic epistemology' to this bigger realm. Interestingly enough, the essence of this idea is very similar, in one sense, to Freud's—that biological processes and processes of knowing are linked. The reason psychoanalytic psychology cannot deliver on its aspiration for an intrinsically meaning-constructive ego is that Freud and Piaget have conceived radically different biologies. Freud's wired-in biology makes meaning-making a servant of biology. Piaget's open-systems, dialectical biology *makes processes of development and processes of knowing identical*. Kohlberg's theory elegantly suggests how the development of knowing, in a realm closer to that of the ego (i.e., moral meaning), is not the *consequence of* psychobiological development but is *itself* the process of psychobiological development. As development involves processes of 'differentiation and integration' (Werner, 1964) or 'emerging from embeddedness' (Schachtel, 1959) or 'globality to distinctness' or 'increasing differentiation of the organism from its environment', it is intrinsically about distinguishing self from not-self or subject from object. Hence any level of development or stage of development is *ipso facto* a subject-object relation, or logic or system of knowing. While it tells us nothing about the contents of a person's experience, it tells us how that experience will be shaped, how it will 'mean'. At the same time, any meaning system or underlying logic can be seen as part of a process, itself growing out of a past in which what is now object was once subject, and auguring a future in which what is now subject will become object of a new logic. By extending this Piagetian idea to a bigger realm, Kohlberg's general theory, and the gradual process of empirically filling it in, has pointed the way to a realization of a powerful conception of an intrinsically-motivated meaning-constitutive ego. He has suggested a new way to understand how processes of growing are inevitably about processes of knowing.

EXISTENTIAL EGO PSYCHOLOGY: CONSTRUCTIVISM WITHOUT DEVELOPMENT

Though psychoanalytic psychology has only gradually come to a conception of a meaning-constitutive ego, existential psychology (Lecky, 1945; Angyal, 1965; Maslow, 1954; Binswanger, 1963; May, 1958; Rogers, 1959), gestalt psychology

(Kohler, 1929; Wertheimer, 1938) and George Kelly's construct psychology (1955) have all shared the cognitive-developmental premise of constructivism. Kohlberg's theory of moral development represents the single most important contribution toward a collaboration between these psychologies and cognitive-developmentalism. These psychologies, just as does psychoanalysis, have an enormous amount to offer the cognitive-developmental paradigm which itself has many lacks; but that is not the subject of this essay. Kohlberg's work has helped to demonstrate that cognitive-developmental theory has to offer to these psychologies (1) a theoretically and empirically more articulate realization of their basic concepts, and (2) an understanding of a sequence of qualitatively distinct eras in the meaning-constitutive processes they study.

If Kohlberg's work brings constructivism to the psychoanalytic developmentalists, it brings developmentalism to the existential constructivists. Consider the thinking of Carl Rogers, at the heart of which we find an existential approach to the metaphors of twentieth century evolutionary biology. In contradistinction to the mechanistic and homeostatic conception of Freud, Rogers attends to what he regards as intrinsic processes of adaptation and growth. His first principle is the 'actualizing tendency':

> the inherent tendency of the organism to develop all its capacities in ways which serve to maintain or enhance the organism. It involves not only the tendency to meet what Maslow terms 'deficiency needs' ... [but] it [also] involves development toward the differentiation of organs and of functions, expansions in terms of growth, expansion of effectiveness through the use of tools, expansions and enhancement through reproduction. It is development towards autonomy and away from heteronomy or control by external forces. Angyal's statement could be used as a synonym for this term: 'Life is an autonomous event which takes place between the organism and the environment. Life processes do not merely tend to preserve life but transcend the momentary status quo of the organism, expanding itself continually and imposing its autonomous determination upon an ever-increasing realm of events' (Rogers, 1959, p. 196).

This actualizing tendency Rogers regards as the sole motive of personality; there are no separate systems with motives of their own. The tensions between defence and enhancement, for example, are integrated in a single system. There is presumed to be a basic unity to personality, a unity best understood as a process rather than an entity. This process, according to Rogers' conception, gives rise to the 'self', the meaning-making system with which the process is identified. Anxiety, defence, psychological maladjustment, and the processes of psychotherapy are all understood in the context of the efforts to maintain, and the experience of transforming, the self-system. Kohlberg's theory is quite compatible with these conceptions and elaborates them several steps further. Like Rogers he focuses on the 'organism-environment' relation, and, as previously discussed, seeks to work out the form-creating properties (meaning-constitutive properties) of any particular such relation. More than this, he proposes, and to a considerable extent has demonstrated, a regular history (at the formal level) to the processes of (in Rogers' words) 'transcending the status quo of the organism-environment relation'. Since the emphasis of Rogers' own definition is 'development', is it not crucial to know something about the history of these developments, about the differences as well as the commonality between an earlier moment in this history and a later moment, between an earlier transition and a later one; about regularities among people in this history if they exist, about the different 'selves' the actualizing tendency brings into being? (Rogers' descriptions of the changing self in therapy come close to suggesting it is basically one 'kind of self', or one moment in the history of development that requires therapy, namely the move from Stage 3 to Stage 4: 'from living only to satisfy the expectations of others, and living only in their eyes and in their opinions, he moves toward being a person in his own right' [1959, p. 310].)

In somewhat similar ways, gestalt psychologists and phenomenological psychologists (including Kelly), see the individual, as do Piaget and Kohlberg, as actively constructing meaning, but see no necessary relationship between the present organization of meaning and the last or the next. And most have no idea of qualitative transformations in the process of meaning-making by which the most basic principles of meaning-organizations are themselves altered. Kohlberg may be quite wrong in his theory, but at the very least he has made a powerful case for the worth of pursuing the question as to whether the meaning-constitutive processes these psychologies have long championed do not truly develop in the sense of evolving through qualitative eras according to regular principles of stability and change.

CONCEPTS IN EGO PSYCHOLOGY REVISITED[1]

Let us briefly consider the implications of Kohlberg's work for new understandings of a number of key concepts in ego psychology: *externalization/internalization/ projection*, *observing ego*, and *boundary*.

Consider two case vignettes (Kegan, 1982):

Alice is thirty years old, recently divorced, lives with her two children, and is concerned about the impact of her new sex life on her nine-year-old daughter. Is it wrong for her to 'have men to the house'? she asks the therapist. What does 'wrong' mean to Alice, we might wonder. 'I don't want to shock her,' she says of her daughter. 'I want so badly for her to accept me ... I'm afraid she could think I'm really a devil.'

Her daughter asked her if she'd made love to a man since her divorce and she had lied, saying no. 'And ever since that it keeps coming up to my mind because I feel so guilty lying to her because I never lie and I want her to trust me.'

Alice views the therapist as the source of answers to, and responsibility for, her moral questions: 'I have a feeling that you are just going to let me stew in it and I want more. I want you to help me get rid of my guilt feelings. If I can get rid of my guilt feelings about lying or going to bed with a single man, any of that, just so I can feel more comfortable ... I want you to say to go ahead and be honest, but I don't want the responsibility that it would upset her. I don't want to quite take the risk of doing it unless an authority tells me. I do not want to feel like I've caused any big traumas in the children. I don't like all that responsibility, feeling it could be my fault.'

Terry is fifteen years old, recently hospitalized in a psychiatric ward by her mother after her parents decided they could no longer deal with her. The final blow had come when her mother called school and discovered that her daughter had skipped that day. When Terry returned home at the appropriate after-school hour and was confronted with her mother's information, Terry flew into a rage at what she regarded as her mother's intrusiveness and demanded that her mother give her her bankbook so she could run away. When her mother refused, Terry took twenty dollars from her mother's purse and barricaded herself in her room. Her mother forced entry into the room. Terry escaped through a window and led her mother, assorted allies and eventually the police on a seven hour chase, which Terry gleefully reported in the hospital. On the checklist at admission Terry's mother describes Terry as 'bright,' 'egocentric,' 'narcissistic,' and 'manipulative'. Terry characterized her mother as 'stern,' 'stubborn,' 'nagging,' 'unwilling to compromise' and 'headstrong'.

In individual therapy, the therapist felt 'I could never establish a relationship with Terry. I wanted to talk with her about what she was feeling, but mainly she wanted to talk about how to maneuver in the hospital system, whether this or that would cause her to lose her privileges, how bad the food was. If I was nice to her, trying my best to establish a relationship of trust and support, she would just take advantage of me, or try to manipulate my concern for her. "If you really care about me you'll vote for my privileges." What was most important to her was getting her way, and it didn't much matter what other people wanted.' When it is discovered that she spoke to people outside the ward about people inside the ward (a violation of patient-patient agreements) and that she used 'unprescribed drugs' during a weekend pass (a violation of patient-staff agreements), the staff expells Terry from the community. They understand her behavior as hostile and acting out and they justify their own action on the grounds that she 'would not do the work of the ward,' 'was argumentative,' 'was disruptive,' 'was inciting to other patients,' and 'was a staff-splitter'.

While others regard much of Terry's behavior as violative of *their* moral valuing, it might also be important to hear and see that Terry spontaneously constructs her own predicament as one of moral victimization at the hands of others who 'are not fair': It's not fair for her mother to be checking up on her at school; it's not fair that her mother wouldn't give her her own bankbook; and, most of all, it's not fair that she has to be in the hospital: 'The only reason I'm in the hospital and my parents are home is they are over 21 and I'm not. They ought to be in here too, or none of us should be here. It's as much their problem as mine. We just can't get along.'

Although these vignettes confirm Szasz's view (1961) that underneath a 'clinical problem' one can usually find a 'moral problem', one is also struck by how *different* the moral worlds of Alice and Terry seem to be. A first implication of Kohlberg's work is that each even *has* something like a coherent, systemic 'moral world'; some might feel that Alice is guided by moral concerns (perhaps to a fault) but that Terry's behaviour is conspicuously *un*guided by moral concerns; some might feel that it is unlikely that generalizations based on one aspect of a person's life have any applicability to other aspects of that life, so that the notion of a common shape to moral meaning-making is unwarranted. But everyone is *some-where* in the process of development, and the implication of Kohlberg's work is that a level of development by definition amounts to a certain coherence in one's meaning-constituting (at least within a given domain, such as moral construing), and by definition amounts to *some* systemic form of moral meaning-making. We have neither the space nor the purpose in this chapter to demonstrate the generalizability throughout Alice or Terry's life of the moral developmental formulation we would make based on their construction of their presenting problems. Let us instead see what arises if we assume for a moment such generalization is warranted.

Alice may be at Kohlberg's Stage 3, but what does it really amount to if she is? Viewing Kohlberg's stages as structures of subject-object relationships formed in an ongoing process of meaning-constitutive development makes a diagnostic label like 'Stage 3' quite a bit more than Kohlberg's descriptive definition: 'What is right is living up to what is expected by people close to you or what people generally expect of people in your role. . . . Reasons for doing right are the need to be a good person in your eyes and those of others. . . . The social perspective involves an awareness of shared feelings, agreements, and expectations which may take primacy over individual interests. . .' (Kohlberg, in Lickona, 1976). While this description seems to fit Alice, Kohlberg's theory takes us quite a bit further than an outside description; it suggests the mental architecture that may be giving rise to this meaning for 'moral'. And this architectural 'plan' has implications for our understanding of long-time concepts in ego psychology (as well as for a clinician's treatment).

For example, it is common for clinicians to attend to the ways that Alice *projects* or *externalizes* aspects of her own psychological processes onto others, e.g., her therapist. She 'gives' him, psychologists might say, the part of herself that is consulted in the making of her decisions. Rather than being able to consult *herself* about such decisions, she *projects* this onto him. In the same way, other people's opinions of her are highly determinative of the way she feels about herself. Were she more able to consult herself, separate her own self-judgments from others, etc., she would be seen as less *externalizing*, more *internalizing*. Now to help suggest Kohlberg's contribution to this line of thinking let us briefly bring Terry into it.

From the Kohlbergian view Terry seems to be at Stage 2: 'What is right is following rules only when it is to someone's immediate interest, acting to meet one's own needs.... Reasons for doing right are to serve one's own interests or needs in a world where one recognizes others have their interests, too.... The social perspective involves an awareness that anyone has his own interest to pursue and that these conflict so that right is relative in the concrete individualistic sense' (Kohlberg, in Lickona, 1976). From a clinician's point of view it would not be surprising to attend to the way Terry also *projects* and *externalizes*, albeit in a different way. For example, Terry often talks about 'guilt', too, but unlike Alice, what Terry means by the word is not self-blame but an anxious anticipation of what real others will do, or not do, as a result of what she has done. This whole psychological situation is *external* in the sense that the crucial consideration is whether an actual other person will find out and do something. The domain of personally recordable subjective experience ('feelings') is moved from inside the self out onto the social arena of action, performance, manipulation, consequence and control; and it is so, such a formulation might go, because her own competing points of view are *projected* onto others who are then made into antagonistic holders of competing authority. Herself holding just one point of view, projecting the others, she lacks the self-reflexiveness that leads to the experience of one's subjective state or 'feelings'. Intrapsychically, this leads to the familiar concreteness and 'lack of insight'. Interpersonally, it leads to the lack of mutuality and need to control the other (since the other part cannot be 'controlled' internally).

So if it made sense to call Alice *externalizing*, it also makes sense to use the same idea to describe Terry, except for one thing: *every feature of Alice's* externality *would be considered* internal *with respect to Terry*! Were Terry to grow, we would imagine that her interpersonal and intrapsychic externalities would become internal. And what would that mean? In terms of social relations, it would mean she could construct mutually reciprocal relationships oriented to obligation and expectation on behalf of their maintenance, rather than oriented to instrumental self-benefit. Intrapsychically it would mean the capacity to experience and express feelings as self-referring subjective states (e.g., 'guilt' as a disjunction between different parts of oneself rather than between self and other). *But notice that both of these developments characterize Alice already and that in Alice we called them externalizing, not internalizing.*

What are the implications of Kohlberg's work, then, for the constellation of ideas signified by terms like 'projection', 'externalization', 'internalization'? (1) The very words 'projection' and 'externalization' are misleading. They suggest that something was once inside, and then, for some reason, was cast out, the usual explanation being that it was too anxiety-provoking to be held inside. Surely, some psychological processes are exactly of this sort. But there may be a whole set of psychological processes for which this is *not* a good accounting. What Alice and Terry 'externalize' *has never been inside*, Kohlberg's work implies, and the 'internalization' of what has been 'outside' will bring about a state of psychological organization which for each has *never* yet existed. In the case of Alice and Terry attending to such a change amounts to attending not to changes in emotion alone but to changes in *development*. What is projected is so, not because it was too difficult to hold it inside—a little like Anna Freud saying 10-year-olds don't think abstractly because emotionally they don't need to—but because it remains on the 'subjective' side of the subject-object balance. Terry cannot separate herself from her own needs and single point of view, Kohlberg's theory implies, because the logic of her own current developmental level leaves her embedded in, or subject to, her needs and interests. If this is so, it is very strange to refer to Terry as projecting or externalizing because Terry herself is doing neither. (2) Whatever we *do* call these processes by which others are confused with the self, a second implication of Kohlberg's theory is that there is a *systematic nature* to some or much of it. Rather than its being a random affair, or related to early childhood associations, it has coherent properties with respect to both a continuity of form across different aspects of an individual's life at any given time, and a regularity to the sequence of such forms across the life-history. (3) Finally, the whole idea of a dichotomy between 'externalizing' and 'internalizing' is relativized, since *a given level of psychological organization is only external relative to the developments that might follow*. The very same level of adaptation is *in*ternal with respect to the prior developmental level. Kohlberg's work implies that *everyone* is both externalizing and internalizing *in some sense*, and that clinicians would do far better in their efforts to understand patients by refusing to content themselves with a characterization like 'externalizing' alone. What we need to know is *which* externalization? and external *relative to what*? In other words, what we need to know is developmental level or stage, in order to appreciate both the constraints and the strengths of any developmental position. In fact, the very reason Alice's psychological situation is said to be not just *different* from Terry's, but *more evolved* (Stage 3 rather than Stage 2), is that Alice's externalization (her constraint) would amount to Terry's *growth*. The further implication of this line of argument is that even Terry's 'externalizing' (Stage 2) would look like the developmental achievement of internalization if we were to compare her psychology with someone at Stage 1.

The idea that everyone is both 'externalizing' and 'internalizing' *in some way* also suggests a new understanding of a related concept in ego psychology, that of *the observing ego*. Ego psychologists and modern clinicians, especially, use this idea to refer to that aspect of the person that can reflect on, or observe, the person's own psychological processes. The 'observing ego' is often thought of as the psychotherapist's ally in the therapeutic effort to help the person understand what is going on with him or her. It is not uncommon for clinicians to speak of the observing ego *quantitatively* ('He has very little observing ego') or *absolutely*, in the sense that one either has it or not ('There's no observing ego there to work with so insight-oriented therapy is out'). In contrast to these quantitative or dichotomous conceptions, Kohlberg's work implies that: (1) there is *always* an observing ego, and (2) its presence takes, not one, but several *qualitatively* different forms.

'Observing ego', in light of Kohlberg's theory, is a way of talking about the subject-object boundary, specifically what is there to be 'observed', i.e., what is object. Terry has the form of observing ego that permits her to know she has interests and needs persisting through time; there are 'things she wants'. She has no ability to reflect on the way her feelings and constructions of others are mediated by her embeddedness in her wants and interests. She would be unresponsive to the usual meaning of 'insight-oriented therapy' which has an unrecognized minimum developmental demand, but *not* because she has no observing ego, and *not* because she 'lacks insight'. She would be quite responsive to 'insight-oriented therapy' of a form commensurate with her capacity to have insight into what she wants and the implications of what others want for what she wants. Alice is able to be aware of her feelings as inner states but she is unaware of the systematic process by which she creates these feelings in herself. 'Observing ego' is, thus, neither a quantitative nor an absolute matter, but a qualitative one.

A somewhat similar thing can be said for the implications of Kohlberg's theory for the even more general idea of psychological *boundary*. In the existing ego psychology literature individual differences with respect to boundary tend to be looked at almost exclusively around a 'quantitative' continuum. In other words, the questions become: *How strongly* is the boundary between self and other maintained? *What constellation of defences* does the person have in order to maintain the boundary? *How flexible or rigid* are the boundaries? The question is never: *Which* boundary is being maintained? The orientation implies that there really is only one boundary and the only important questions have to do with whether or not it exists and how strongly it can be defended. The reduction of all boundary analysis to degree of defended differentiation derives from the lack of a *life-span developmental* perspective on self-other construction.

Nor does such a psychology completely yet exist. My contention is not that Kohlberg has given us a fully worked out constructive-developmental ego psychology; nor has he ever claimed to, nor did he set out to do so. That goal, and that work, has been taken up by others. But I do think, as I have tried to demonstrate here, that the seeds of such a psychology are to be found in Kohlberg's theory, and that it is from these seeds that the work of many who might be called 'constructive-developmental ego psychologists' has grown (Haan, 1977; Selman, 1980; Fowler, 1981; Kegan, 1982; Gilligan, 1982; Rogers, 1982; Hewer, 1983; Noam, 1984; Parks, 1980; Goodman, 1983; Basseches, 1984; Broughton, 1982; Souvaine, Lahey and Kegan, 1984; Kelley, 1983).

TWO FURTHER CONTRIBUTIONS: INTERPRETIVE ASSESSMENT AND EXPLICIT NORMATIVENESS

Space will only permit brief mention of two further contributions of Kohlberg's work to ego psychology, both of which are controversial and both of which I view quite positively. These are Kohlberg's method of assessing developmental position or stage, and Kohlberg's explicit address to the implicit normativeness of his theory; i.e., in what sense is a higher stage a better stage? Both of these contributions are a function of, and indicate Kohlberg's methodological and philosophical congruence with, his jointly constructivist and developmental view of *mental structure*.[2]

1. The essence of Kohlberg's long and multiform project to assess moral development amounts to repeated, and perhaps repeatedly improved, efforts to measure mental structure as directly as possible. His method of assessment (Colby, *et al.*, 1983a) and the many he has inspired,[3] share certain forbidding features: (1) they are expensive of time and money, all requiring at least an hour or more of a subject's time, administrable only on a one-interviewer-to-one-subject basis, and generally requiring transcription for data analysis; (2) they make considerable demands upon the interviewer's clinical sensitivity and upon both the interviewer's and the scorer's grasp of the psychological theory with which he or she is dealing. These non-accidental impracticalities increase the likelihood that the *act of measurement*—both the data gathering and the data analysis—will also be about *the engagement of the person's way of being* rather than merely a calculating or recording of their way of being.

Both Kohlberg's choice of interviewing activity and his unit of analysis are consistent with a central purpose of assessing structure. The form of the interview is actually identical to a Piagetian exploration of a child's construction of, for example, volume or quantity. Instead of introducing physical objects and exploring how they are organized, Kohlberg is introducing social objects and exploring how they are organized. The unit of analysis is a direct manifestation of how subject and object are distinguished, as opposed to some behaviour or verbal content probabil-istically associated with a given structure; i.e., structure is not *inferred from* the unit of analysis but *demonstrated in* the unit of analysis (Kohlberg, 1979; Noam, Kohlberg and Snarey, 1983; Hewer, 1982). Both these features—exploration (in the data gathering) and an identity between the data and phenomenon being assessed (in the data analysis)—distinguish Kohlberg's method from Loevinger's measure of ego development. Loevinger's sentence completion measure does not permit probing in the data gathering, and takes a 'sign' approach to data analysis (Kohlberg, 1979; Hewer, 1982). Kohlberg's approach attempts 'to pass with a minimum of interpretation from verbal expression or symbol to common structure . . . [dealing] in direct reflections, manifestations or showings of a structuring activity, *not* in indices or indirect signs' (Hewer, 1982, p. 5).

2. Ego psychology is a primary source for psychological practice, particularly various forms of 'mental health' practice. All practice is goal-oriented. A fun-damental question, as important as it is customarily neglected, is whether such goals are justified. How do we know they are not the arbitrary favourites of the practitioner's social class, gender, age, ethnic group? How do we know that well-intentioned 'practice' is not the unwitting exercise of power? The question of the justification of a practitioner's goals is not strictly speaking a psychological one, but a philosophical one. No framework for the study of the person which is only psychological can hope to address it. Any framework that *is* strictly psychological leaves its adherents to import an extra-theoretical source from which to justify the use of its understandings. This means the continual challenging and refining of one's own theory does not necessarily have any relation to an ongoing examination of the goals to which it is applied; it means the framework itself cannot generate an authority to enter the conversation about what uses are made of it; it means the question of goals and uses is outside the discipline. This is a situation fraught with danger.

Perhaps more than any other theorist in the constructive-developmental paradigm, Kohlberg shares with Piaget what the latter called 'the demon of philosophy'. Piaget never even regarded himself as a psychologist; as a result he created a whole new *kind* of psychology which amounts to *empirically grounded philosophy*. His studies of molluscs and children were in pursuit of the naturally-rooted forms and laws of how knowledge develops. In a sense, he was not really studying molluscs and children; he was studying epistemology. A similar thing can be said for Kohlberg. His framework is an empirically grounded way of 'doing philosophy', specifically 'ethics'. The philosophical heft of his contribution is not a function of extra-theoretical importations of Kant and Rawls upon whom he draws. Rather these thinkers are called upon to help him understand the phenomena which are intrinsically present in his programme of work. In modern terms Piaget and Kohlberg might be said to have developed a form in which philosophy is truly a 'social science'; from a more historical perspective, they might be said to have taken a step toward rescuing philosophy from two hundred years of increasing marginalization and restoring its role as a source for considering what we shall do and how we shall live. Kohlberg's contribution to ego psychology is a framework which *is* jointly philosophical and psychological and which *can* deal—in fact, insists upon dealing—with issues of the justification of one's goals simultaneously with issues of psychological processes.

That his framework forces these questions at all, quite aside from the merits of his answers, is itself a contribution. But the answers themselves are extraordinary. And they go back to his central contribution, the idea of *structure*. The criteria that justify *structural* development as itself a goal of practice are rooted in the naturally philosophical—or truth-oriented—quality of the structures *themselves*. This is the powerful sense in which the framework is jointly philosophical and psychological: not just the means of explanation, but *the phenomenon under examination* is itself psychological and philosophical. A given structure has a truth value, a degree of subjectivity and objectivity; the *colours* and *sounds* of any particular structure will vary for a myriad of reasons, including the influences of gender, class, age, ethnicity, and so on. But, theoretically at least, the criteria by which one structure is 'better' than another are blind and deaf to such colour and sound; structures are theoretically impartial, a matter of the form of organization, not what it is that is organized.

Kohlberg's methodological and philosophical contributions are evaluated in their own right elsewhere in this volume, but their specific contributions to ego psychology are clear. Methodologically, he has pointed the way to the possibility of directly exploring the structural features of an individual's meaning-constituting activity; he has done so by means of a discipline combining the strengths of quantifiable research (operationalization, intersubjectivity, replicability) and qual-itative, idiographic, hermeneutic analysis (case-by-case textual interpretation, identity between the data and the phenomena under investigation). By explicitly attending to the way structures of meaning constitute *natural philosophies* he has demonstrated the intrinsic relationship between a form of psychological develop-ment and philosophical adequacy; thus a 'constructive-developmental' ego psychol-ogy is suggested which avoids the twin deficiencies of arbitrary norms based on cultural, personal or professional conceptions of 'health', on the one hand, or an understandable dissatisfaction with a health-based normativeness which must then lead to normlessness on the other (see also Loevinger, 1976). Ego psychologies with arbitrary norms or no norms are equally inadequate guides to practitioners who ethically have no escape to the luxury of goal-lessness. The philosophical dimensions of Kohlberg's work suggest a non-arbitrary normativeness for ego psychology oriented not to notions of *health*, but to notions of *growth*. The implications of this for what 'mental health' interventions can and cannot be about, and for how the person in need of help is conceptualized, are staggering. They amount to nothing less than a full-scale challenge to metaphors of health/illness/treatment in response to the sometimes painful circumstances of an individual's growth and becoming.

KOHLBERG'S EXPLICIT CONCEPTION OF THE RELATION BETWEEN EGO AND MORAL DEVELOPMENT

The thrust of this essay has been that Kohlberg's chief contribution to ego psychology is to be found in his demonstration—a theoretically and emperically powerful demonstration—of a simultaneously constructivist and developmental conception of mental structure. He has shown us quite clearly, and with considerable discrimination, a sense in which the person is (1) *a maker of meaning*, whose (2) judging and experiencing comes under the influence of *a principle of organization* that at once orders experience holistically and systemically, and (3) at the same time is *itself vulnerable to development*; finally, (4) that this developmental process creates a common *sequence of* such *principles of organization*, each of which includes the last, all of which are describable at an abstract, content-less (i.e., formal) level.

But Kohlberg has done this through the study of a *specific kind* of meaning-making, the constructing of one's sense of right and wrong, 'moral judgment'. What has 'moral development' to do with 'ego development'? My own answer (Kegan, 1982), which may as yet be no more defendable than Kohlberg's, is that his specific stages manifest a structure (the subject-object distinction) which is more general or basic than a 'moral structure', i.e., is *the* basic structure being maintained and transformed in all cognitive-developmental stage descriptions, be they explicitly Piagetian (such as Selman's, 1980, or Fowler's, 1981, or Piaget's own, 1954); or not (such as Loevinger's, 1976, or that of Weinstein and Alschuler, 1984). Thus, I feel his greatest contribution to ego psychology comes at this implicit level, by which we are further let into the workings of a single basic motion in personality development, the evolution of subject-object relations. This single basic motion, which manifests itself in different domains of personality (cognitive, affective, interpersonal, intrapersonal) is what I would call ego, a definition that does not seem to me different from Kohlberg's own, cited earlier: 'an overall unity progressively reconstructing itself through a dialectical process in which the person "makes sense" of his or her evolving relationship with others, the world, life as a whole. Ego development thus includes the continuous redefinition of what is subjective and what is objective' (Snarey, Kohlberg and Noam, 1983, p. 305).

It is interesting what happens to this kind of a statement vis-à-vis Kohlberg's *explicit* conception. What happens makes the statement similar to Piaget's on emotion, that one cannot really separate emotion and cognition, that there are not 'cognitive objects' and 'affective objects', but one object; that cognition and emotion are different sides of a single phenomenon (Piaget, 1964). This statement, and Kohlberg's above, are truest to their theoretical convictions; but in their more explicit attentions to emotion or ego they seem to need to make them something quite separate from cognition or moral development, with a logic, role, or purpose all their own. The result in both cases, I believe, is that their explicit remarks are less illuminating than what we can infer from their basic programme of work.

For Kohlberg seems to have a different explicit answer to the question: What has moral development to do with ego development? He introduces the idea of rather independent strands of development that bear 'necessary but not sufficient' relationships to each other. Specifically, a given stage of social-perspective development requires, but is not guaranteed by, a given stage of cognitive-development; a given stage of moral development requires but is not guaranteed by a given stage of social-perspective-development; and, finally, a given stage of ego development requires but is not guaranteed by a given stage of moral development (Snarey, Kohlberg and Noam, 1983).

The idea of 'several related but differentiated lines of development within a multifaceted but unified ego', each line comprising 'a relatively circumscribed subdomain standing in asymmetrical relation to each other', each line 'characterized by a relatively distinct substructure' (Snarey, Kohlberg and Noam, 1983, p. 308) is problematic on several grounds: (1) 'Ego' seems to be receiving two definitions: is it a subdomain, one of several lines of development; or is it that which subsumes and unifies subdomains? (2) In the absence of some more explicit suggestion as to what unites the 'relatively distinct', 'relatively circumscribed' substructures, the model has difficulty holding onto the principle of unity and threatens to return us to a theory of multiple minds. In its own way this becomes not too different from the idea of 'relatively distinct' substructures such as ego, id and superego, each of which has its own motivations and purposes. (3) In the absence of some more explicit definition of the principles or meaning of 'structure' in the 'substructures', we are in danger of a much looser or vaguer appropriation of the concept than is consistent with the power of the general theory. What is a *moral* structure, as distinct from an *ego* structure? What does 'structure' mean used in this way? (4) In the absence of some more structurally explicit justification as to why one domain grows out of the last, the chain of necessary but not sufficient relations suggests a mechanical conception of personality processes that seems inconsistent with the paradigm's organicism. For example, the proposed model suggests that if an intervener wanted to facilitate ego development with three persons, all of whom were at ego stage X, he or she might attend differentially, depending on the subject's cognitive and moral development: if the subject were at moral stage Y the subject would be presumed to have the *capacity* to move to ego stage Y, and one might attend to the links between moral and ego realms; if the subject were at moral stage X, but cognitive stage Y, then we would have to attend to the links between cognitive and moral realms before we would be in a position to directly attend to the ego realm; on the other hand if the subject were at stage X in all three realms, then we would have to facilitate cognitive development to stage Y before attending to the links between cognitive and moral realms, and then finally to the original goal of facilitating ego development. The idea that these three persons with similar ego stages are also developmentally different in ways that are important and require recognizing is compelling. The idea in general that things go so neatly as this, or in specific that there is certainly one domain through which the process of change must enter, is not.

An alternative, holistic, unitary-structure conception of the relationship between realms is not without its own difficulties. While the best predictor of a person's level in any one domain may still be their level in any other domain, it is clear that persons are not always in perfect parallel in all domains. But the necessary-but-not-sufficient hypothesis, suggesting a statistical-descriptive approach to exploring the relationship, risks abandoning exploring what has been the central preoccupation of Kohlberg's paradigm since Piaget, that by which the parts are organized into a whole. Rather than relegating 'ego' to its own relatively circumscribed subdomain, I would think it would be preferable to explore, in clinical-developmental fashion (jointly quantitative and qualitative), the inner world of 'domain dysynchronies', for example, and the processes that work toward or against their integration. Do we really know enough about the general structure and process of meaning constitutive development to begin positing relatively independent substructures and their relations?

NOTES

1 A somewhat different form of this discussion first appeared in German in Noam and Kegan (1982).
2 A whole volume could be devoted to each of these topics, though fortunately both are well-discussed in a number of sources, Kohlberg himself being among the best of these. Re/assessment, see: Kohlberg, 1981; Hewer, 1982; Colby *et al.*, 1983a, 1983b; Kohlberg, Levine and Hewer, 1983. Re/normativeness, see: Kohlberg, 1971, 1973; Kohlberg, Levine and Hewer, 1983.
3 Selman's assessments of interpersonal understanding (Selman, 1980); Fowler's faith development interview (Fowler, 1981); Gilligan and Lyon's responsibility vs. rights interview (Lyons, 1981); Kegan's subject-object interview (Lahey *et al.*, 1984); Basseches' dialectical reasoning interview (Basseches, 1978); Broughton's natural epistemology interview (Broughton, 1975); Noam's stage-and-phase interview (Noam, 1983), Rogers' self-conception interview (Rogers, 1982).

REFERENCES

Angyal, A. (1965) *Neurosis and Treatment*, New York, Wiley.
Basseches, M. (1978) 'Dialectical operations'. Unpublished doctoral dissertation, Harvard University.
Basseches, M. (1984) *Dialectical Thinking and Adult Development*, Norwood, N.J., Ablex Publishing Company.
Binswanger, L. (1963) *Being-in-the-World*, New York, Basic Books.
Broughton, J. (1975) 'The development of natural epistemology in adolescents and young adults'. Unpublished doctoral dissertation, Harvard University.
Broughton, J. (1978) 'The development of concepts of self, mind, reality and knowledge', in W. Damon (Ed.), *Social Cognition*, San Francisco, Jossey-Bass.
Broughton, J. M. (1982) 'Cognitive interaction and the development of sociality: A commentary on Damon and Killen', *Merrill-Palmer Quarterly* 28, 3, pp. 369–78.
Chandler, M. J., Paget, K. F., and Koch, D. A. (1978) 'The child's demystification of psychological defense mechanisms: A structural and developmental analysis', *Developmental Psychology*, 14, pp. 197–205.
Cicchetti, D. and Hesse, P. (1982) 'Affect and intellect: Piaget's contributions to the study of infant emotional development', in R. Plutchik and H. Kellerman (Eds.), *Emotion: Theory and Research*, Vol. 2; New York; Academic Press.
Colby, A., Kohlberg, L., Gibbs, J., Candee, C., Speicher, B., Kauffman, K., Hewer, A. and Power, C. (1983a) *The Measurement of Moral Judgment: A Manual and Its Results*, New York, Cambridge University Press.
Colby, A., Kohlberg, L., Gibbs, J., and Lieberman, M. (1983b) 'A longitudinal study of moral judgment', *Monograph Society for Research in Child Development*.

Cowan, P.A. (1978) *Piaget with Feeling*, New York, Holt, Rinehart and Winston.

DeCarie, T. (1978) 'Affect development and cognition in a Piagetian context', in M. Lewis and L. Rosenblum (Eds), *The Development of Affect*, New York, Plenum.

Elkind, D. (1967) 'Egocentrism in adolescence', *Child Development*, 38, pp. 15–27.

Erikson, E. (1963) *Childhood and Society*, New York, Norton.

Erikson, E. (1964) *Insight and Responsibility*, New York, Norton.

Erikson, E. (1968) *Identity: Youth and Crisis*, New York, Norton.

Erikson, E. (1977) *Toys and Reasons*, New York, Norton.

Erikson, E. (1983) *The Life Cycle Completed*, New York, Norton.

Fairbairn, W. R. D. (1962) *An Object Relations Theory of Personality*, New York, Basic Books.

Fingarette, H. (1963) *The Self in Transformation*, New York, Harper and Row.

Fowler, J. W. (1981) *Stages in Faith*, New York, Harper and Row.

Freud, S. & Jung, C. G. (1974) *The Freud/Jung Letters*, W. McGuire (Ed.), R. Manheim and R. F. C. Hull (Trans), Princeton University Press.

Gilligan, C. (1982) *In a Different Voice*, Cambridge, Mass., Harvard University Press.

Goodman, R. (1983) 'A developmental and systems analysis of marital and family communication in clinic and non-clinic families'. Unpublished doctoral dissertation, Harvard University.

Greenspan, S. (1979) *Intelligence and Adaptation: An Integration of Psychoanalytic and Piagetian Developmental Psychology*, Psychological Issues Monograph 47/48, New York, International Universities Press.

Guntrip, H. (1968) *Schizoid Phenomena, Object Relations, and the Self*, New York, International Universities Press.

Haan, N. (1977) *Coping and Defending*, New York, Academic Press.

Harter, S. (1979) 'Children's understanding of multiple emotions: A cognitive-developmental approach'. Invited address presented to the Ninth Annual Symposium of the Jean Piaget Society, Philadelphia, 31 May–2 June.

Hewer, A. (1982) 'Structural developmental assessment'. Unpublished manuscript, Harvard University.

Hewer, A. (1983) 'From conflict to suicide and revival: Disequilibrium and requilibration in experience of psychological breakdown and recovery'. Unpublished qualifying paper, Harvard University.

Kegan, R. (1982) *The Evolving Self*, Cambridge, Mass., Harvard University Press.

Kegan, R., Noam, G. and Rogers, L. (1982) 'The psychologic of emotion: A neo-Piagetian view', in D. Cicchetti and P. Hesse (Eds.), *New Directions for Child Development: Emotional Development*, No. 16, San Francisco, Jossey-Bass.

Kelley, V. (1983) 'Ego development in men and women and psychotherapeutic self-understanding'. Unpublished doctoral dissertation, Yeshivah University.

Kelly, G. A. (1955) *The Psychology of Personal Constructs*, New York, Norton.

Kohlberg, L. (1971) 'From is to ought: How to commit the naturalistic fallacy and get away with it in the study of moral development', in T. Mischel (Ed.), *Cognitive Development and Epistemology*, New York, Academic Press.

Kohlberg, L. (1973) 'The claim to moral adequacy of a highest stage of moral judgment', *Journal of Philosophy*, 70, pp. 630–46.

Kohlberg, L. (1981) 'The meaning and measurement of moral development', The Heinz Werner Lecture Series, Vol. 13 (1979), Worcester, Mass., Clark University Press.

Kohlberg, L., Levine, C. and Hewer, A. (1983) *Moral Stages: A Current Formulation and a Response to Critics*, New York, Karger.

Kohler, W. (1929) *Gestalt Psychology*, New York, Liveright.

Lahey, L., Souvaine, E., Kegan, R., Goodman, R. and Felix, S. (1984) 'The subject-object interview: Procedures for its administration and assessment'. Unpublished manuscript, Harvard Graduate School of Education.

Lecky, P. (1945) *Self-Consistency*, New York, Island Press.

Lickona, T. (Ed.) (1976) *Moral Development and Behavior*, New York, Holt, Rinehart and Winston.

Loevinger, J. (1976) *Ego Development*, San Francisco, Jossey-Bass.

Lyons, N. (1981) 'Considering justice and care: Manual for coding real-life moral dilemmas'. Unpublished manuscript, Harvard University.

Maslow, A. (1954) *Motivation and Personality*, New York, Harper and Row.

May, R. (1958) *Existence*, New York, Simon and Schuster.

Noam, G. (1984) 'Marking time in the midst of the hardest movement: Adolescent borderline disorder in lifespan perspective', in K. Field and B. Cohler (Eds.), *Motive and Meaning: Psychoanalytic Perspectives on Learning and Education*, New York, Rup Publishing.

Noam, G. (1983) 'The stage-phase and style interview'. Unpublished manuscript, Harvard University.

Noam, G. and Kegan, R. (1982) 'Toward a clinical-developmental psychology', in W. Edelstein and M. Keller (Eds.), *Perspektivat und Interpretation*, Frankfurt, Suhrkamp Verlag.

Noam, G., Kohlberg, L. and Snarey, J. (1983) 'Steps toward a model of the self' in B. Lee and G. Noam, *Developmental Approaches to the Self*, New York, Plenum.

Parks, S. L. (1980) 'Faith development and imagination in the context of higher education'. PhD dissertation, Harvard University.

Piaget, J. (1954) *The Construction of Reality in the Child*, New York, Basic Books.

Piaget, J. (1964) 'Relations between affectivity and intelligence in the mental development of the child', in *Sorbonne Courses*, Paris, University Documentation Center.

Rogers, C. (1959) *Client Centered Therapy*, Boston, Mass., Houghton Mifflin.

Rogers, L. (1982) 'Developmental aspects of psychopathology: A preliminary study'. Unpublished qualifying paper, Harvard Graduate School of Education.

Sandler, J. and Sandler, A. M. (1978) 'On the development of object relations and affects', *International Journal of Psychoanalysis*, 59, pp. 285–93.

Schachtel, E. (1959) *Metamorphosis*, New York, Basic Books.

Selman, R. (1980) *The Growth of Interpersonal Understanding*, New York, Academic Press.

Snarey, J., Kohlberg, L. and Noam, G. (1983) 'Ego development in perspective: Structural stage, functional phase, and culture age-period models', *Developmental Review*, 3, pp. 303–38.

Souvaine, E., Lahey, L. and Kegan, R. (1984) 'Life after formal operations: Implications for a psychology of the self', in E. Langer and C. Alexander (Eds.), *Beyond Formal Operations*, New York, Oxford University Press.

Szasz, T. (1961) *The Myth of Mental Illness*, New York; Harper.

Tharinger, D. T. (1981) 'The development of the child's psychological understanding of feelings'. Unpublished doctoral dissertation, Department of Psychology, University of California-Berkeley.

Weinstein, G. and Alschuler, A. (1984) 'Self-knowledge development'. Unpublished manuscript, University of Massachusetts.

Werner, H. (1964) *Comparative Psychology of Mental Development*, New York, International Universities Press.

Wertheimer, M. (1938) 'Gestalt Theory', in W. D. Ellis (Ed.), *Source Book of Gestalt Psychology*, New York, Harcourt, Brace.

Winnicott, D. W. (1965) *The Maturational Processes and the Facilitating Environment*, New York, International Universities Press.

11. On Kohlberg's Contributions to Ego Development[1]

JANE LOEVINGER

There are more things in heaven and earth, Horatio,
Than are dreamt of in your philosophy. (Shakespeare)

Kohlberg's conception of the moralization of judgment has been hedged about almost from the beginning by the larger issue of maturation of personality generally. So much has been made of the moralization of judgment that it cannot be merely the trace of another concept, like, say, the child's conception of diagonality; it must have greater generality than that to justify the work done and the attention attracted. On the other side, only weak claims have been made for direct translation of moral judgment stage into any other realm. The strongest correlations of the measures of moral judgment are with intelligence, socioeconomic status, education, and age (Colby *et al.*, 1983), all equivocal in import. Those are the classic confounding variables in personality measurement. The burden of proving that a test is measuring a substantial component of personality becomes heavier rather than lighter in the face of such correlations.

My argument is that Kohlberg's model assumes a formal and rigid structure appropriate, if anywhere, only to a narrowly conceived concept. His claimed realm, however, is a wide one, by now encompassing all of ego development, with moral development as just one cell in the matrix of ego development. For that larger realm a stochastic model is more appropriate.

KOHLBERG'S WRITINGS ON EGO DEVELOPMENT

Kohlberg's ideas about ego development and its relation to moral development have evolved gradually. In 1964 he set forth the characteristics of his developmental

---

1 Lawrence Cohn and Augusto Blasi provided helpful comments, for which I am grateful, but the responsibility for this version is mine.

continuum and contrasted it with other psychological dimensions. Superego strength and ego strength were mentioned among the things moral development was not, but ego development was not mentioned (Kohlberg, 1964).

Shortly thereafter I tried to delineate the realm of ego development (Loevinger, 1966), a field I had been working in for a number of years. (Since that time we have exchanged ideas and manuscripts, and it can be assumed that we have been familiar with each other's main formulations, often in advance of their publication. However, references to ego development in Kohlberg's work do not necessarily refer to my version, nor do references to moral development in mine refer exclusively to Kohlberg's version.) Since then, Kohlberg has downplayed the issue of ego strength and repeatedly discussed the issue of the relation of moral development to ego development.

In 1972 Kohlberg stated that both cognitive and moral development are parts of ego development, but also, 'in general, attainment of a Piagetian cognitive stage is a necessary but not sufficient condition for the attainment of a parallel ego stage' (Kohlberg and Mayer, 1972/1981, p. 93); how to decide which ego stage corresponds to a given cognitive stage was not addressed. (Strictly speaking, when Kohlberg writes of parallel stages, he means corresponding stages.) Further, 'ego development is the psychologist's term for a sequence that must also have a philosophic rationale' (Kohlberg and Mayer, 1972/1981, p. 93).

In 1976 Kohlberg stated that ego development is a psychological, not a logical, dimension, and its levels are not structural stages, as are those of moral development. The unity and consistency of moral structures, defined by 'formalistic moral philosophy', are not characteristic of ego development. Further, there are no clear criteria for increased adequacy of successive ego stages, as there are for moral and logical stages. This position represents some change from the position in 1972; the hope of finding a 'philosophic rationale' for ego development has evidently faded.

Kohlberg summarized the relations of cognitive, moral, and ego development as follows:

1 Cognitive development or structures are more general than, and are embodied in, both self or ego structures and in moral judgment.
2 Generalized ego structures (modes of perceiving self and social relations) are more general than, and are embodied in, moral structures.
3 Cognitive development is a necessary but not sufficient condition for ego development.
4 Certain features of ego development are a necessary but not sufficient condition for development of moral structures.
5 The higher the moral stage, the more distinct it is from the parallel ego stage (Kohlberg, 1976, p. 53).

In 1981 Kohlberg stated, 'In our view, the ego comprises relatively circumscribed and self-contained subdomains, each possessed of a distinct structure, regardless of the functioning of a unitary ego' (Kohlberg, 1981, pp. 4–6). This statement foreshadows the fuller exposition of his recent joint paper (Snarey, Kohlberg and Noam, 1983) and vouchsafes that the latter represents his own views. It is, however, muddied by the phrase 'regardless of the functioning of a unitary ego', a confusion continued in the joint paper.

Snarey, Kohlberg and Noam (1983) present ego development as a matrix of subdomains. One axis of the matrix consists of three types of meaning-making, epistemological, moral, and metaphysical; the other axis consists of three types of environment, natural, social, and 'ultimate'. The stage theories propounded by

Kohlberg and his cohorts occupy the cells of the matrix, along with the stage theories of Perry (epistemological meaning-making about the social and ultimate environments) and, of course, Piaget (epistemological meaning-making about the natural environment). Thus not only is moral development governed by a rigid structure, all of ego development is rigidly, though differently, structured.

Elsewhere, Noam, Kohlberg and Snarey (1983) claim to have 'empirical support for our theoretical position that moral development is necessary but not sufficient for the parallel level of ego functioning.'

CRITIQUE

Kohlberg's writings on ego development evidently change from one year to the next. That is not necessarily inconsistency, since as knowledge increases, one has a right, even a duty, to change one's mind. There are, however, inconsistencies within sets of ideas that seem to belong together. Moreover, there is no clear path from data to the corresponding change in conception.

The first inconsistency is the following. Moral development and cognitive development have a symmetric relation to ego development and at the same time an asymmetric one. Ego development is the construct that includes both cognitive and moral development as instances, the symmetric case. Yet cognitive development is a necessary but not sufficient condition for ego development, at the same time that ego development is a necessary but not sufficient condition for moral development, the asymmetric case.

Currently Kohlberg appears to favour a contradictory asymmetric idea, namely, that moral development is a necessary but not sufficient condition for the corresponding stage of ego development (Noam, Kohlberg and Snarey, 1983). For me this idea strains intuitive understanding, but possibly one could concoct an explanation. However, the reversal from ego being necessary but not sufficient for moral development to moral being necessary but not sufficient for ego development, makes it impossible to claim logical necessity for the relation. If the relation is empirical, the supporting data for that strong claim should be collated and published, which has not been done.

Another inconsistency is vacillation between considering ego development as something more amorphous and less strictly structured than moral development versus having it strictly structured, at first in a way similar to moral development, later as a superordinate matrix, with its elements arranged in a definite number of rows and columns, all given labels out of a philosopher's lexicon.

Underlying the surface inconsistencies is a different problem: Kohlberg's complicated formulation has the airs and graces of precise logical and scientific thinking, whereas in fact it is an intuitive foray into a complex, almost inchoate field of knowledge. Had he expressed his ideas in the literary-philosophic-expository form that is his natural element, our differences would be minor.

In 1972, for example, he wrote that 'one pole of ego development is self-awareness; the parallel pole is awareness of the world' (Kohlberg and Mayer, 1972/1981, p. 93). This sounds like a precise, quasi-mathematical statement, yet one seeks in vain for the branch of mathematics in which poles can be parallel to each other, or even what mental image is called for. In fact, the quoted sentence is a bowdlerized version of Baldwin's 'dialectic of personal growth' (Baldwin, 1902, quoted in Kohlberg, 1969, p. 415).

The major example of false precision is the claim that stages in one sequence are necessary but not sufficient conditions for corresponding stages in another. The specificity of this claim lays his model open to the following criticisms (Loevinger, 1983a):

1 Since none of the elements of his matrix can be measured with any precision, specifying a mathematically exact relation among the dimensions or elements is premature.

2 As the authors assert a parallelism between the dimensions, they must have some way to match stages. Nothing precise about that matching is stated. They give hints: observation of logical parallels, parallels drawn by other theorists, age norms, parallels demonstrated empirically. Where are the age norms? Where are all the other parallels collated? If all kinds of evidence were drawn together, which they have not been, how should they be combined? Are there no differences of opinion or evidence? How should differences be resolved?

'Parallel' is one of Kohlberg's favourite words, apparently precise and mathematical in meaning, but in his usage ambiguous. Sometimes he asserts that stages are parallel, which I interpret to mean that the stages are corresponding ones in different dimensions. What does it mean to speak of dimensions, that is, sequences of stages, as parallel? In mathematics if two dimensions are parallel, one is redundant. Kohlberg evidently does not mean to say of two parallel dimensions that all the information in one is conveyed as well in the other. Does it mean anything more to say that moral stages are parallel to social perspective taking stages than to say that moral stages are parallel to the ordinal numbers 1 to 6 (or 5 or 7)? In Kohlberg's usage it seems to, but it is not easy to say exactly what the term signifies.

3 The nature of the fundamental structure of personality—ego development, if you will—is a profoundly unsolved problem. We can claim certainty about only fragmentary glimpses, and there is not universal agreement on those fragments. Yet Kohlberg and his colleagues have boldly carved this domain into neat, labelled rows and columns.

They are not the first to essay the task of providing a complete solution to the question of the basic structure of personality. If the other attempted solutions do not immediately come to mind, that is because no such solution has yet found wide acceptance. Cattell (1957), for example, has a 'Universal Index' of personality traits, not, however, universally accepted as such. Several other investigators have started large projects intending to use factor analysis to derive the ultimate structure of personality. The failure to publish results from some of those projects and the failure of others to achieve wide currency and acceptance testify to the difficulty of the project and the greater difficulty of persuading one's colleagues that one has succeeded. In the face of the limited success of major empirical projects, Kohlberg and his collaborators chose to pit their wits against the same problem with far less data and statistical paraphernalia.

Ego development, they say, has a definite structure consisting of nine sub-domains, each having as its own structure the stage model of Piaget (1968/1970). (Erik Erikson and Harry Stack Sullivan, 1953, the generally acknowledged pioneers in this field, are not accorded places in the matrix, nor am I, despite my two decades of work in the field. Sullivan, in fact, is not mentioned in the article. Thus the field of ego development they cede entirely to Piaget, Perry, Kohlberg, and Kohlberg's coterie.)

Another pervasive problem is Kohlberg's (1972) insistence on serving two masters, psychology and philosophy, or, as he has put it, 'Is' and 'Ought'. He proclaims that he is able to commit the classical naturalistic fallacy and get away with it. What Kohlberg has written about the naturalistic fallacy is profound and far from trivial. Most psychologists will agree with him that philosophic views of development can profit from psychological observation, but that is not the issue. Kohlberg demands that observable dimensions must also be precisely definable philosophically. That is a condition that the human race has not persuaded me that they are prepared to meet. I can only agree with his criticism of my work (Snarey, Kohlberg and Noam, 1983), that it lacks the normative component of his approach, that I am solely trying to determine what is, unrestricted by what ought to be.

AN ALTERNATIVE VIEW OF EGO DEVELOPMENT

Is Kohlberg really talking about ego development? Noone can copyright a term, particularly a term such as 'ego development', long in the public domain. It is difficult to trace the ancestry of the term, since there is a question which terms in other languages should be considered equivalent (Loevinger, 1976). Psychoanalysts have sought to make the term uniquely theirs, though Freud probably never used the term 'ego', on purpose, preferring terms from common speech, in this case *das Ich*, literally, 'the I'. When a term from common speech is appropriated for a new technical meaning, there ought to be some justification. What is Kohlberg's justification for use of the term? Since I cannot answer, I will instead present my own justification for claiming its use.

In proposing the term ego development for what is measured by our Sentence Completion Test (hereafter, SCT) (Loevinger and Wessler, 1970) and for what is covered by my monograph (1976), I argued that there were several justifications. As opposed to the psychoanalytic usage, the reasons were (1) that the psychoanalysts' usages are not mutually consistent, (2) that their major usage of the term applies only to the earliest developmental stages and leaves no term to describe later ego development, and (3) that the implication of Hartmann's (1939) usage, that the term applies only to the conflict-free sphere, is misleading if not actually erroneous. Erikson's (1950) usage, applying the term to development taking place throughout adolescence, is closer to our usage and incompatible with most other psychoanalytic usages, though rarely recognized as such by analysts themselves.

In positive terms, ego development was chosen to signify the overlapping domains of moral development, development of interpersonal integration, development of interpersonal relatability, some aspects of cognitive development, and so on because dimensions in all those domains, as sketched by Piaget (1932), Kohlberg (1964), Peck and Havighurst (1960), Sullivan, Grant and Grant (1957), Isaacs (1956), Harvey, Hunt and Schroder (1961), and others, had too many common elements to be altogether different or separable. In each case the sketch of the stage characteristics impinged on the purview of some or all of the others. No term of lesser scope appeared to be broad enough to cover the variety of manifestations of this multi-faceted, amorphous, yet psychologically convincing dimension.

At times I have wondered whether another term might have led to less confusion, such as, perhaps, development of the self. But that term has also been taken over by a school of contemporary psychoanalysts, advocates of an even more restricted theoretical approach than Hartmann's 'new psychoanalytic ego psychology', namely, Kohut (1971, 1977) and his cohorts. There are, moreover, reasons for keeping the term self for another and irreplaceable use, the self as subject (Blasi, n.d.).

The Brunswikian stochastic model (Loevinger, 1984) that has guided our work on ego development is as mathematically precise as Kohlberg's model; one could even argue that it is more faithful to the spirit of Piaget, who was first of all a naturalist. Our approach is relatively intuitive compared to test construction in the field of ability measurement, corresponding to the lesser predictability of personality manifestations than of ability manifestations. One would be hard pressed, however, to find instances even in ability measurement where the necessary but not sufficient relation holds in any context where the discovery is psychometrically useful and not redundant (Fischer and Bullock, 1981).

HARD CASES VERSUS HARD STAGES

Every typology or stage conception fits some cases beautifully but is difficult to apply to some other cases. The tests of a typology are how many cases it fits well and how it accounts for the other, hard cases.

Two versions of the Piagetian stage model have guided Kohlberg's work. The strong stage model, or, as he now prefers, the hard stage model (Kohlberg, Levine and Hewer, 1983), demands that each stage constitute a structured whole characterized by unity and consistency. This implies that the person's thinking will be manifested at one stage or two adjacent stages when observed across material of varying content. Since the formal organization of reasoning rather than the content defines the structure in hard stage theories, the distinction between structure and content of reasoning becomes crucial. (At this point their text gratuitously and erroneously likens my conception of structure to the psychoanalytic one—see Loevinger, 1983a.)

The weak, or soft, stage model allows for considerably more variation in the several manifestations of a stage. (One might wish, while he was filing a claim for the superior logic of his stages, that he had chosen more logical terms, such as rigorous versus stochastic stages.) In soft stages, they say, a structure is a hypothetical underlying entity that cannot be observed but only inferred from probabilistic signs; 'it cannot be logically abstracted from observations of a phenomenon' (pp. 34–5), which, they claim, hard stages can. Content as well as structure may be utilized as signs of underlying structure in soft stages. Thus there is no clear distinction between content and structure, and hence the distinction between competence or highest possible level (structure) and performance or characteristic or manifest level (content) is ambiguous.

They are here claiming, as Kohlberg (1981) has done previously, that

Kohlberg's Moral Judgment Instrument (hereafter, MJI) does not deal with signs or manifestations, as the Sentence Completion method of studying ego development does, but taps directly into the thing measured, namely, justice structures. I maintain, on the contrary, that the structure of thought cannot be reached directly by any transducer; it is always an inference. A person can, for example, give an answer just because they read the same kind of reasoning in a story or novel, even though it is beyond their level of spontaneous utterance. Also, a person may give a reason much lower than their functional level because of a recent infuriating experience, such as being asked to take a psychological test. Logically the claim that any test taps competence rather than performance is hard to substantiate. The tester always has to use some behaviour as the basis for the conclusions drawn. Only an act of faith or an act of inference can assure the tester that the behaviour is the best that the subject is capable of.

Kohlberg and his collaborators (Kohlberg, 1981; Kohlberg, Levine and Hewer, 1983; Snarey, Kohlberg and Noam, 1983) make much of the difference in measurement strategy between the MJI and the SCT. The MJI classifies a response at a given level only when it can be positively shown to have characteristics of that level. Correspondingly, the unit classified must be large enough to permit accurate classification, and the modal level of scored units characterizes the subject. For the SCT every response must be classified, whether it appears to give enough information to be pathognomonic of any stage or not. Correspondingly, the scored response can be brief, fragmentary, or otherwise ambiguous. Because many SCT responses are perfunctory and not telltale of the person's 'true' level of functioning, a more complicated scoring algorithm than the mode, namely, the set of ogive rules, is required. Roughly, the ogive rules give minimum weight to conventional responses, which are given a middle-level rating, a maximum weight to extremely high and extremely low responses.

These scoring strategies are appropriate to the corresponding transducers: the SCT uses a spontaneous, free set of responses, with no follow-up questions or opportunity to get at true or underlying meanings, whereas the MJI involves questioning the subject till the reasoning behind his responses is laid bare. In both cases, the raters' instructions are to interpret the meaning of the response at the level which the subject giving the response would recognize as his own meaning. However, these differences in measurement strategy do not necessarily imply corresponding differences in the variables measured, as Kohlberg seems to believe.

Kohlberg's method, adapted from the Piagetian *methode clinique* and used by most other members of the Kohlberg coterie, has the advantage of pushing the subject, presumably though not demonstrably, to this upper limit. However, the use of the mode as a scoring algorithm somewhat undercuts that reasoning, bringing the score again within the model of core functioning rather than maximum (see Loevinger, 1976, Ch. 9). The SCT, by contrast, accepts the spontaneous behaviour but weights extreme responses more heavily. Thus both methods use performance, both are based on a core functioning model, and both are weighted toward maximum performance (though that must be modified with respect to how the SCT ogive rules operate at the lowest stages). In short, the MJI uses a maximizing transducer but a typical algorithm, whereas the SCT uses a typical transducer but a maximizing algorithm.

The SCT rule to classify responses having no obvious relation to ego development has resulted in discovering many non-obvious but valid signs, many of which have become intelligible as they have been repeatedly confirmed and coordinated with other signs (Loevinger, 1979b, 1983b). Such discoveries, which have helped to shape and enrich our conception of ego development, are excluded by the ground rules of Kohlberg's manual (Colby *et al.*, 1983). We stake the major claim for the value of our version of ego development on this self-correcting process.

Finally, let us ask how far Kohlberg has substantiated his claim to having discovered hard stages. The chief data backing that claim are contained in Table 13 of Colby *et al.* (1983, pp. 29–34). Examining that table shows that approximately half the subjects (twenty-seven out of fifty-six, excluding three cases tested only on two occasions) have at least one sequence anomaly on Form A, B or C. A sequence anomaly is an occasion where a retest after three or four years yields a lower score than the previous test. Also, about half the cases (twenty-seven out of fifty-seven, excluding one case given only one form) have at least one major homogeneity anomaly. A major homogeneity anomaly I define as a full stage difference between any two of Forms A, B and C on a single testing occasion. Every case in the study has at least one minor homogeneity anomaly, that is, at least a half stage discrepancy between forms on at least one occasion.

Deviations from perfect sequentiality and deviations from perfect homogeneity are hard cases for their system. In handling those cases Colby, Kohlberg and their colleagues (1983) have used a line of reasoning that my colleagues and I have used (Loevinger, 1979a; Redmore and Loevinger, 1979), namely, that regressions on retesting after three- and four-year intervals were fewer than on retest after a two-week interval, hence could be accounted for by unreliability. That line of reasoning is appropriate to the SCT, since it is based on a stochastic model, but it radically undercuts the claim of Kohlberg's MJI to being based on a rigorous, non-stochastic model and having direct access to the variable measured. They have missed the fact that unreliability is the psychometrician's name for approximately what the Piagetian calls *decalage* and the Brunswikian calls the probabilistic texture of behaviour, the opposite of hard stages.

Indeed, the travail of Kohlberg, Colby and their collaborators through the many years and many editions of the scoring manual of the MJI testifies to how many such hard cases they must have encountered. Had there been no hard cases, earlier versions of the manual could have stood with minor refinements rather than leading to repeated introduction of radically new scoring principles in order to sustain the claim of perfect sequentiality.

Another indication that hard cases have been encountered is the several changes in the sequence of stages. First there were college students who apparently regressed from Stage 4 to Stage 2, an obvious violation of sequentiality. These students were then reclassified Stage 4½, an optional intermediate stage; an optional stage undercuts the conception of a rigorous stage structure in a different sense. Currently, however, that optional stage appears to be dropped. Examples of Stage 6 reasoning are now said to be rare or non-existent, but that has not stopped speculation about a soft Stage 7 (Kohlberg, Levine and Hewer, 1983). Nor is it clear how, if the stage sequence is a hard one, it turns into a soft stage at its zenith.

Another modification of the sequence is the definition of Substages A and B. Kohlberg and others have repeatedly declared that a major weakness of the SCT method is that it confuses structure and content, that content is not a reliable clue to structure. However, they now discover that subjects at Stage 5 choose the autonomous rather than the heteronomous resolution of their dilemmas more than 75 per cent of the time (Colby *et al.*, 1983). Thus they too find content a clue to structure. However, many persons below Stage 5 also make the 'right' or Stage 5 moral choice. The psychometric dilemma they handle by postulating substages. Those who make the better choice are classed as Substage B; they are said to tend also to use more structurally equilibrated and more formally moral reasoning, though no data are given to substantiate the correlation. The fact that there are two substages at each stage appears to reflect the fact that there are two choices to each dilemma.

Kohlberg's theories and generalities occupy a Platonic World of Forms, but his data, like all our data, dwell in the stochastic Real World, a fact glossed over in the frequent citation of general trends in data to be found only in theses, obscure journals or work in progress. Without seeing the actual data, one cannot ascertain to what extent the trends cited represent strict, invariable, one-to-one relations, as seems to be claimed, or only statistically significant trends.

Kohlberg and his colleagues agree with some critics of personality theory in admiring high correlations. For the critics, this entails gloating over the low correlations in many personality studies. For Kohlberg, it entails finding high correlations in some data, even at the expense of finding those high correlations with age and other confounding variables. In opposition to both, I have argued that a realm dominated by high correlations is unlikely to yield any new discoveries, that, with appropriate methodology, a realm of low correlations is potentially a source of new information (Loevinger, 1983b).

Kohlberg demands an *a priori* philosophic purity for the definition of stages, and he attempts to shoehorn the study of ego development into a logical straight-jacket. His claim to have discovered hard stages is meant to invoke an aura of ex- actitude to his conceptions. But the field remains obdurately complex. Rather than putting 'ego development in perspective' (Snarey, Kohlberg and Noam, 1983) as they claim, he and his colleagues have obscured ego development with impre- cisely used logical and mathematical terms.

CONCLUSION

Suppose we disregard as a temporary aberration Kohlberg's ambition to carve up ego development and apportion it to his inner circle. Let us, instead, look at the field as it existed prior to that attempt. No doubt the psychoanalysts will continue to think of it in their own terms, as will Habermas (1979), Ausubel (1952) and others who have adopted the term. In the absence of any compelling logical or empirical reason to do otherwise, I will continue thinking of the field as it appears to shape itself empirically.

Ego development is a field that covers much though not all of personality development. It does not include physical development, psychosexual develop- ment, or development of sheer intelligence (Loevinger, 1966). (The exclusion of intelligence already differentiates my version from that of Snarey, Kohlberg and Noam, 1983.) Neither Kohlberg's coterie nor the psychoanalysts have an exclusive claim to that vast territory.

Within the realm that remains, many topics have been explored developmentally, including interpersonal integration, friendship patterns, sense of self, modes of communication, and so on. In this broad field, which is ego development as I see it, Kohlberg's contribution has been magnificent. He has revolutionized the way many social scientists see moral development. His own work and that of his associates has enriched the field by cross-cultural data as well as many studies within our culture. Although some of those studies require replication and refinement, they have stimulated much interest and paved the way for more intensive studies.

Next in order of importance among Kohlberg's contributions has been to attract a stellar group of young investigators to the field, including many fine empirical scientists. Some of their studies were partly inspired originally by Kohlberg's work, but they can stand alone as substantial contributions.

Although I have reservations about the net effect of each researcher charting still another developmental sequence, seeking still another structure (Loevinger and Knoll, 1983), *in toto* these many sequences of stages provide us with a rich picture of the texture of personality development. With the vitality that the broad field of ego development now has, largely due to Kohlberg's energy, substantial contributions and catalytic effect, I am confident that a new generation of investigators will find new ways to integrate the growing insights into this vital area of psychology.

REFERENCES

Ausubel, D. (1952) *Ego Development and the Personality Disorders*, New York, Grune and Stratton.

Baldwin, J. M. (1902) *Social and Ethical Interpretations in Mental Development*, New York, Macmillan.

Blasi, A. (n.d.) 'The self as subject: Its dimensions and development', unpublished MS, University of Massachusetts, Boston Harbor.

Cattell, R. B. (1957) *Personality and Motivation Structure and Measurement*, Yonkers on Hudson, N.Y., World Book.

Colby, A., Kohlberg, L., Gibbs, J. and Lieberman, M. (1983) 'A longitudinal study of the development of moral judgment', *Society for Research in Child Development Monographs*, 48, 1, pp. 1–124.

Erikson, E. (1950) *Childhood and Society*, New York, Norton.

Fischer, K. W., and Bullock, D. (1981) 'Patterns of data: Sequence, synchrony, and constraint in cognitive development', in Fischer, K. W. (Ed.), *Cognitive Development*, New Directions for Child Development, no. 12, San Francisco, Jossey-Bass.

Habermas, J. (1979) 'Moral development and ego identity', in *Communication and the Evolution of Society*, Boston, Beacon.

Hartmann, H. (1939) *Ego Psychology and the Problem of Adaptation*, New York, International Universities Press.

Harvey, O. J., Hunt, D. E. and Schroder, H. M. (1961) *Conceptual Systems and Personality Organization*, New York, Wiley.

Isaacs, K. (1956) 'Relatability, a proposed construct and an approach to its validation', unpublished doctoral dissertation, University of Chicago.

Kohlberg, L. (1964) 'Development of moral character and moral ideology', in Hoffman, M. L. and Hoffman, L. W. (Eds.), *Review of Child Development Research*, Vol. 1, New York, Russell Sage Foundation, pp. 383–481.

Kohlberg, L. (1969) 'Stage and sequence: The cognitive-developmental approach to socialization', in Goslin, D. A. (Ed.), *Handbook of Socialization Theory and Research*, Chicago, Rand McNally, pp. 347–480.

Kohlberg, L. (1972) 'From *is* to *ought*: How to commit the naturalistic fallacy and get away with it in the study of moral development', in Mischel, T. (Ed.), *Cognitive Development and Epistemology*, New York, Academic, pp. 151–235.

Kohlberg, L. (1976) 'Moral stages and moralization: The cognitive-developmental approach', in Lickona, T. (Ed.), *Moral Development and Behavior*, New York, Holt, Rinehart and Winston, pp. 31–53.

Kohlberg, L. (1981) *The Meaning and Measurement of Moral Development*, Worcester, Mass., Clark University Press.

Kohlberg, L., Levine, C. and Hewer, A. (1983) *Moral Stages: A Current Formulation and a Response to Critics*, Basel, Karger.

Kohlberg, L. and Mayer, R. (1981) 'Development as the aim of education: The Dewey view', in Kohlberg, L., *The Philosophy of Moral Development*, San Francisco, Harper and Row, pp. 49–96 (original work published 1972).

Kohut, H. (1971) *The Analysis of the Self*, New York, International Universities Press.

Kohut, H. (1977) *The Restoration of the Self*, New York, International Universities Press.

Loevinger, J. (1966) 'The meaning and measurement of ego development', *American Psychologist*, 21, pp. 195–206.

Loevinger, J. (1976) *Ego Development: Conceptions and Theories*, San Francisco, Jossey-Bass.

Loevinger, J. (1979a) 'Construct validity of the sentence completion test of ego development', *Applied Psychological Measurement*, 3, pp. 281–311.

Loevinger, J. (1979b) 'Theory and data in the measurement of ego development', in Loevinger, J., *Scientific Ways in the Study of Ego Development*, Worcester, Mass., Clark University Press.

Loevinger, J. (1983a) 'On ego development and the structure of personality', *Developmental Review*, 3, pp. 339–50.

Loevinger, J. (1983b) 'Less is more: The value of low correlations', Presidential address, Division 24, American Psychological Association, Anaheim, Calif., August.

Loevinger, J. (1984) 'On the self and predicting behavior', in Zucker, R. A., Aronoff, J. and Rabin, A. I. (Eds.), *Personality and the Prediction of Behavior*, New York, Academic.

Loevinger, J. and Knoll, E. (1983) 'Personality: Stages, traits, and the self', *Annual Review of Psychology*, 34, pp. 195–222.

Loevinger, J. and Wessler, R. (1970) *Measuring Ego Development*. Vol. 1, San Francisco, Jossey-Bass.

Noam, G., Kohlberg, L. and Snarey, J. (1983) 'Steps toward a model of the self', in Lee, B. and Noam, G., *Developmental Approaches to the Self*, New York, Plenum.

Peck, R. F. and Havighurst, R. J. (1960) *The Psychology of Character Development*, New York, Wiley.

Piaget, J. (1932) *The Moral Judgment of the Child*, New York, Free Press.

Piaget, J. (1970) *Structuralism*, New York, Harper and Row (original work published 1968).

Redmore, C. D. and Loevinger, J. (1979) 'Ego development in adolescence: Longitudinal studies', *Journal of Youth and Adolescence*, 8, pp. 1–20.

Snarey, J., Kohlberg, L. and Noam, G. (1983) 'Ego development in perspective: Structural stage, functional phase, and cultural age-period models', *Developmental Review*, 3, pp. 303–38.

Sullivan, C., Grant, M. Q. and Grant, J. D. (1957) 'The development of interpersonal maturity: Applications to delinquency', *Psychiatry*, 20, pp. 373–85.

Sullivan, H. S. (1953) *The Interpersonal Theory of Psychiatry*, New York; Norton.

Interchange

KEGAN REPLIES TO LOEVINGER

After reading Loevinger's expectably alert criticism, reminding me of the many such occasions of her faithfully sceptical responses to Kohlberg and his associates, I am tempted to suggest that, like it or not, she has probably become a member of the coterie herself, so valuable a part has she played in the history of this highly collaborative programme. As her essay shows, she has certainly kept good track of its peregrinations; and as mine shows, you certainly don't have to go along with everything to be one of the gang.

Indeed, since I am in agreement with what may be Loevinger's chief explicit criticism here—the problematic nature of claims to 'necessary but not sufficient' relationships between different strands of personality development—I will use my brief space for rejoinder to what I take to be her chief *implicit* criticism—namely, a false impression of scientific precision which Kohlberg's language (even more, I gather, than his association with numerical trappings) promotes. Although there are ways in which Kohlberg must himself bear some responsibility for this (e.g., the 'necessary but not sufficient' business itself), I think fundamentally Loevinger's criticism betrays a misunderstanding of Kohlberg's very important, very defensible, mode of inquiry.

Although it strikes me as somewhat self-contradictory that Loevinger both attacks Kohlberg's rigidity and at the same time claims his 'natural element' is 'the literary-philosophic-expository form', her real problem seems to be in understanding the meaning of 'philosophy' in Kohlberg's social science. When she opposes philosophy and psychology, excluding the former from the domain of 'what is', she is missing not only Kohlberg's point, but also Piaget's, to whom she later claims her own approach is faithful. 'Kohlberg's demand that observable dimensions be definable philosophically', as she puts it, seems to Loevinger to bespeak some kind of naive faith in 'the human race'. But this 'demand' grows out of the same view that led Piaget to call the child a philosopher. In Kohlberg and Piaget's view, the 'philosophicalness' of a human's 'observable dimensions' is no *achievement* that the human race may or may not live up to; it is rather intrinsic to life itself. Development, Piaget and Kohlberg are saying, is inevitably 'philosophical'; the study of development is the study of a natural ethics, logic, epistemology; the demand that 'observable dimensions' be 'precisely definable philosophically' is really a demand that *developmental* observables be defined precisely, i.e., their underlying logic, epistemology or ethics be defined. Kohlberg's work is emphatically *not* a jointly philosophical and psychological analysis of a human phenomenon; it is an analysis of a phenomenon which is *itself* taken as simultaneously 'philosophi-

194

cal' and 'psychological'. The philosophy and psychology are 'in the phenomenon', and Kohlberg's work is a further step in the effort Piaget began to develop a new kind of social science—'genetic epistemology'—which might view developmental phenomena this way.

For the moment, it doesn't matter to me whether Loevinger thinks Kohlberg's step is a sure one or a faltering one, so much as she sees what path he is on. For her to claim that her assessment procedure and his, 'scientifically', have about the same status because each makes inferences about 'the thing itself' rather than directly exposing it, misses the whole point of different levels (or sizes of 'leap') in one's inference-making, which has been the very history of Kohlberg's ponderous research procedure. Of course his assessments make inferences. But what he is trying to do, each time he revises, is shorten the step from data to inference by spelling out more and more carefully the way the data express a structure that is intrinsically philosophical.

As I have tried to suggest, such analysis I believe leads to the subject-object relationship as the essence of philosophical structure intrinsic to development. Whether or not this is the case, the existence of *some* 'master structure' is implicit in both Kohlberg's and Loevinger's work. (Loevinger calls it a 'master motive' or 'master trait'.) It is this 'master structure' I believe that Kohlberg must be implicitly referring to when he speaks of stages (from different sequences) being 'parallel', a term which Loevinger understandably finds misleading. Ends of a pole (to help Loevinger with her visual image) will inevitably move through parallel routes if (1) they are ends of the *same* pole (the master structure) and (2) the pole itself *moves* through space (development is about the movement, or evolution, of this master structure). What Kohlberg and other structural-developmentalists are really suggesting in this talk of a 'parallelism' is not precisely that a given stage (of cognitive development, say) is *analogous* to a given stage (of moral development, say); rather that the relation between the two stages is *homologous*. An analogy involves *correspondence in function* between parts of *different structure and origin*; an homology involves a relation between parts having different functions but sharing a *common structure and origin*. As I tried to suggest in my essay, it is the help Kohlberg's work has been in our (still quite incomplete) understanding of this *common structure and origin* that may represent his most important contribution.

LOEVINGER REPLIES TO KEGAN

Loevinger considers that with respect to Kohlberg, the differences between the two chapters are minor and not very substantive, but that they differ radically with respect to psychoanalysis, where there is a new generation of theorists not acknowledged by Kegan. However, as Loevinger maintains that such a discussion is scarcely germane to the book, she is therefore willing to let her chapter stand as reply to his.

Part VII: Morality, Reason and Emotions

12. Kohlberg on Morality and Feeling

CHARLES BAILEY

The publication of Lawrence Kohlberg's first volume of essays on moral development[1] reminds me of one of the characteristics of this psychologist's writings that has always attracted me. This is Kohlberg's acceptance of the idea, surely correct, that accounts of psychological development in mental and moral abilities and attitudes must take account of justificatory arguments for supposing the development of certain characteristics to be more desirable than others. Kohlberg accepts this idea, not only for moral development, but for that whole range of developmental facilitation that we call education. Kohlberg favours what he calls a 'developmental-philosophic strategy for defining educational objectives' producing a 'theoretical rationale that withstands logical criticism and is consistent with, if not "proved" by, current research findings.'[2] He is absolutely clear that neutrally psychological observation and experiment cannot itself produce guidance for educators:

> A 'value neutral' position, based only on facts about child development or about methods of education, cannot in itself directly contribute to educational practice. Factual statements about what the processes of learning and development *are* cannot be directly translated into statements about what children's learning and development *ought* to be without introducing some value principles.[3]

On the other hand Kohlberg is not committed to an absolute separation of 'is' and 'ought', as he is at pains to point out in the well-known 1971 article.[4] 'Moral psychology and moral philosophy should work hand in hand,' he says, where this seems to mean that it is empirical investigation that shows people operating at different stages of moral judgment, but philosophical analysis that explains both why certain problems that ought to be handled by moral judgment makers cannot be handled at the lower stages, and why the later stages are justifiably called 'higher' or 'better' or 'more moral'.

197

With a theory of philosophical and psychological interaction of this kind it is not surprising to find another predominating characteristic of Kohlberg's work, namely the over-riding emphasis given to the place of cognitive acts of judgment as indicators of moral development rather than purely behavioural accounts of observed conduct or some kind of assessment of attitudes characterized as largely affective, feeling or emotive states. It is the central place of the notion of justification that produces this lack of surprise. From one perspective justification is recognized as necessary for constructing a proper theory of *development*, i.e., a theory of certain changes bringing about a *better* or *higher* state of moral judgment. From another perspective we have the recognition that justification, and especially the justification of conduct to oneself, is precisely what morality is all about. Briefly we can assert, for the moment, that justification must be a matter of reason, of cognition, and not a matter of affect or feeling. This proposition, of course, itself needs expansion and justification, and I shall return to this after a brief demonstration that Kohlberg is indeed emphasizing the predominance of cognitive judgment over the affective.

Kohlberg does not, of course, believe that the affective has no place in moral judgment or moral action. It is probably the case that all real moral judgments are accompanied by, if not impregnated with, affective mental states:

> The cognitive developmental view holds that 'cognition' and 'affect' are different aspects, or perspectives, on the same mental events, that all mental events have both cognitive and affective aspects, and that the development of mental dispositions reflects structural changes recognizable in both cognitive and affective perspectives. It is evident that moral judgments often involve strong emotive components, but this in no way reduces the cognitive components of moral judgment, though it may imply a somewhat different functioning of the cognitive component than is implied in more neutral areas.[5]

Kohlberg is even plainer towards the end of the 'From Is to Ought' article:

> I am arguing that moral judgment dispositions influence action through being stable cognitive dispositions, not through the affective charges with which they are associated.... Affective forces are involved in moral decisions, but affect is neither moral nor immoral. When the affective arousal is channeled into moral directions, it is moral; when not so channeled, it is not moral. The moral channeling mechanisms themselves are cognitive. Effective moral channeling mechanisms are cognitive principles defining situations.[6]

The picture is clear: it is to be cognitively structured judgment that both should and does move us to moral action; and where such cognitive structuring is rational, principled and altruistic, and autonomously undertaken by the agent, it is a higher form of moral judgment than where any or all of these characteristics do not obtain. This is in both a Piagetian and a Kantian tradition. Piaget saw the affective as a kind of neutral raw material:

> ... the child's behaviour towards persons shows signs from the first of those sympathetic tendencies and affective reactions in which one can see the raw material of all subsequent moral behaviour.[7]

But, like Kohlberg, he was quite clear that the quality of goodness could never flow from affect alone: 'As for sympathy, it has of itself nothing moral in the eyes of conscience. To be sensitive alone is not to be good; ...'[8] Kant argued for a morality in which we, as it were, free ourselves from the mechanisms of nature by subjecting ourselves to rational laws given by ourselves, the laws of practical reason.[9] Among the mechanisms of nature, of course, and especially for Kant, are the affections, feelings, emotions which *happen* to us 'under laws empirically conditioned' and give us no guidance in themselves as to what our moral duty is. The question of what to *do* about any issue of feeling or emotion can only be resolved, for Kant, Piaget and Kohlberg, by some act of cognitive judgment, preferably rational, autonomous and altruistic judgment. The tradition is clear and Kohlberg is solidly within it.

I said, a few lines back, that for Kohlberg it is to be cognitively structured judgment that both should and does move us to moral action. Note that this is to say two things and not just one. First, we say that for an act to be moral in a full sense it must derive from, and only derive from, a person's autonomous rational judgment. It is not enough for the act to look as if it derives from my own reason, it really must do so. This is to make a philosophical point which is, I believe, a correct one. I shall try to explain why I believe it to be correct in the next section. The second thing being said, however, is not a philosophical point but an empirical one, and I am not convinced that it can be asserted with quite so much confidence that it is our 'stable cognitive dispositions' that *actually do* move us to moral action. I shall discuss these motivational problems below (pp. 204–206).

THE PRECEDENCE OF JUDGMENT[10]

That the moral life is primarily a matter of judgment is evident from our commonsense view that it is only creatures capable of reflecting about what they ought to do that are capable of the moral life. It is not only the case that where we believe creatures incapable of such reflection we do not expect them to make moral judgments about, say, the behaviour of others. It goes further than that. If a creature cannot reflect about what ought to be done, it cannot reflect about what it should itself do. It is never, therefore, in a position to know whether what is done is what *ought* to be done or not; and because of this such a creature can never be praiseworthy or blameworthy in a technical, a prudential or particularly in a moral sense. Out of the context of reflection and judgment pieces of behaviour are neither moral nor immoral but mere happenings: part of the natural world but not of the world of morality.

Another thing about human moral agents that we know well enough from common sense, even if in this secular age we no longer quote St Paul, is that we do not always do what our reflective judgment tells us we ought to do, and we do not always refrain where our reflective judgment tells us to refrain. That there can be a disjunction between judgment and action, doing what I ought not and failing to do what I ought, is not so much a weakness of human moral life, as we understand it, as a defining characteristic of it. That a person can do what it seems to him the right thing to do, *or not do it*, is precisely what makes it meaningful to talk about moral or immoral action at all. It is for these reasons that we do not attribute moral agency to non-human animals. We do not, for the same reasons, attribute moral agency to *all* human beings. Newborn babies are not moral agents, i.e., they are not viewed as responsible, praiseworthy or blameworthy for their own actions. Even with adults, if we have reason to believe them incapable of reflective judgment we absolve them from moral responsibility, and most civilized countries recognize this in their laws.

Moral agents, then, are choosers in two senses: first, they must be capable, on reflection, of choosing what ought to be done and, secondly, knowing this, it must be possible for them still to choose to do or not do the act they themselves approve of. Put like this it seems odd that anyone should not behave in the manner they themselves approve of; but we all know that we are so capable, and we all know that this is the source of the more genuine forms of guilt.

The *primacy* of judgment rests on the fact that the second act of choice just indicated would not be possible unless the first act of judgment were possible. I cannot choose to do or not do what I ought to do *unless* I am capable of determining what I ought to do.

Determining, judging, what I ought to do is quite different from simply assessing what I feel like doing. Human beings do both these things, of course, but the claim here is that only the first is to do with morality. This is because of the connection between 'ought', 'reason' and 'justification'. Saying that I must do what I ought to do is equivalent to saying that I must do what I see there to be good *reasons* for doing, my actions should be *justifiable*. 'Doing what I ought to do' cannot translate into 'Doing what I feel like doing' precisely because, at least sometimes, doing what I feel like doing is exactly what I ought not to do.

It is worth spending a little more time on the relationship between morality, reason and justification. The justification of actions depends on the actions being set, and seen by the actor as being set, in a framework of considerations extending beyond the present and the particular. If a piece of behaviour is purely a response to the present and the particular, as presumably much non-human animal behaviour and at least some human behaviour is, we characterize it as *reactive* behaviour. A very wide range of organisms have their behaviour limited to reactions of an immediate kind. The response is to the immediately present and the directly particular stimulus or combination of stimuli. Such behaviours do not enter the dimension of justification at all, and therefore do not enter the dimension of morality. Certain happenings are simply followed by other happenings, and that is all there is to it.

Creatures capable of acting within a framework of justification then, that is, capable of considering their actions as justifiable or not, have to be able to present to themselves data of a relevant kind from beyond the present and the particular. 'Beyond the present' indicates considerations of a remembered or imagined kind. 'Beyond the particular' indicates that the particular stimulus, incident or happening can be categorized as a *kind* or *class* of happening, or as falling under *rules* or *principles* governing my responses to happenings of that kind. To do this, to fit happenings into these kinds of frameworks which we somehow carry in our minds is a large part of what we mean by *understanding* the happening. To understand a happening is to put it in relationship with the generalizable and the before and after, and we do this, of course, mainly by means of language. It is largely with language that we imagine, suppose, hypothesize, classify, reflect and judge, because it is largely with language that we shape principles, rules, generalizations and classifications. It is largely by means of language that we can relate an action or a belief, or a proposed action or belief, to supporting reasons, as we do when we say, 'I shall do this because *X*' or 'I believe this to be the case because *Y*'—'I shall give some money to Oxfam because they help to relieve suffering' or 'I believe in the historical existence of Jesus because of the supporting documentation of Josephus.' Justifying is thus an activity of creatures capable of certain kinds of cognitive and rational behaviour—capable, that is, of having their actions and beliefs *influenced* by the reasons; produced by their reflective and imaginative symbolizing, and presented to themselves. Morality is one branch of judging what is justifiable, particularly, but not solely, in our relation with others. It is thus very much a matter of cognition and understanding, and Kohlberg is right to characterize moral development in terms of changing cognitive structures rather than in terms of changing affective patterns, or even in terms of simple observed behaviour which might have been the outcome of urges, drives or other affective phenomena.

THE INADEQUACY OF AFFECT

The problem of considering further reasons why feelings and other affective phenomena cannot serve any justificatory role in the moral life, or act as any adequate indicator of a person's moral development, lies partly in the difficulty of classifying the great variety of conceptual differentiation in the affective area. A word like 'feelings' has a great variety of different connotations. Emotions have been the subject of much psychological and philosophical discussion; and notions like empathy and sympathy have also come under scrutiny as to exactly what has been picked out in human experience by such labels.[11] Some writers on morality and moral education have attached a good deal of importance, sometimes crucial importance, to affective considerations.[12] What follows, therefore, must be seen simply as a sketch of some of the difficulties.

A good example is provided by the idea of emotion. This is often used as a common label for the whole affective area, 'emotion' being seen as synonymous with 'feeling' and to be contrasted with 'reason' and 'cognition'. There has been considerable agreement among philosophers, however, that emotions can never sufficiently be characterized by feelings alone. A feeling is not even recognizable as, say, anger, fear or jealousy without a context of circumstances appraised as such, which gives sense to those characterizations. Non-referable feelings of general irritation, anxiety, discomfort on the one hand, and feelings of well-being or even elation on the other, are certainly experienced, sometimes in apparently inappropriate contexts, but these are only confusedly called emotions if the typical cases of emotion are supposed to be things like anger, fear or jealousy. In these named states the correct or incorrect characterization is determined not by an examination of the feeling, but by a rational appraisal of the context, of the circumstances.

In the moral sense it does not seem possible that emotions as such can be the basic determinants of what one *ought* to do. Take anger, for example. I appraise some situation with a certain kind of feeling accompaniment, and I call this being angry. That is, viewing a situation (say a man kicking a dog) makes me get excited, my blood pressure rises, my adrenalin flows, I sweat, I talk loudly—and so on. Now what has all this to do with morality? Not much, as far as I can see! The *moral* question is always whether I *ought* to be angry in these circumstances, whether my anger is appropriate. It is meaningful to ask about appropriateness in the case of emotions because the feelings do not just happen, they are the result of a certain kind of appraisal on my part which could have been otherwise. Emotions, like other behaviours, can be engaged in morally or immorally. They present occasions for moral judgment but cannot themselves *be* moral judgments. Whether I am appropriately angry can only be judged by the presentation of reasons, because the justification of anger, like the justification of other things, is a matter of reason.

Another affective phenomenon often associated with morality is that named 'sympathy'. Various characterizations of sympathy can be given,[13] but the one that appears most commonly to be in people's minds when the word is used is some kind of fellow-feeling or feeling of accord—a kind of affective agreement or identification. Morality can then be construed as acting out of sympathy,[14] and contrasted with acting out of duty. The latter is the working out, in a supposedly detached way, of what one ought to do; whereas the former is the warm, affective linking of oneself with the ends and the sufferings of another.[15] Duty is made to sound cold and inhuman; sympathy is made to sound the great shared human characteristic, the infinitely-to-be-preferred mainspring of morality.[16] Morality is to be seen, on this view, as the making of the sympathetic response, an affective and spontaneous rather than a worked-out response, a matter of the affections rather than of reason. Kohlberg, on this account, would be wrong to give primacy to rational, cognitive judgment.

There is, however, considerable difficulty in accepting this view. It is not that sympathetic feelings towards others, feelings of affection towards or accord with others, are not recognizable experiences that most people have at least some of the time; though like all affective states they are difficult to characterize with precision. It is what action should be taken as a result of having or not having these feelings that constitutes the problem.

If it were the case that feelings of sympathy were universal, that is, felt by all towards all for all of the time, then there might be a case for supposing that a deity or evolution had so engineered things that if we only heeded our proper feelings all would be well for all. We would know that what we ought to do was to act on our sympathies. But surely this is not the case? If I go by my feelings as they *actually* are, I find I have strong sympathetic feelings towards some people, weaker but still positive feelings towards others, indifference to yet others, and weak or strong negative feelings of hostility or lack of accord towards some few. Are we not honestly all like this? Is this not the normal state about the feelings of individuals? We cannot base a morality on the existence of these various and multitudinous shades of feeling. Rather, I need a morality that will help me deal with such variations of feeling. How I react to, relate with, those with whom I most easily feel accord is no test of my morality. The real test is how I react to those I am least in harmony with, those I positively dislike. Towards such as these I can only exercise a morality that is based on some rational and cognitive awareness of the worthiness of respect of all humankind: 'Love your enemies, bless them that curse you, do good to them that hate you . . . for he maketh his sun to rise on the evil and the good, and sendeth rain on the just and the unjust.'[17] The spirit of this great saying has to be a matter of intellectual and principled conviction or it can never be universal. Reason and principle can tell me my duty in a way that feeling can never do. Without that the moral world reverts to a world of my friends and my enemies, my tribe and the outsiders, in a way that surely characterized early historical and prehistoric times. Kohlberg is right to assume that as we can mark the moral development of mankind by the increasing sophistication and universalization of man's moral judgment, so can we mark the present-day moral development of individuals.

There are, of course, other kinds of affective states not clearly falling under the notions of emotions or sympathies. Urges, drives, whims, impulses and appetites are all characterized as feelings and appear to be mainly physiological. These, presumably, just happen to us. Of course I can put myself in a situation, or be put in a situation, where they are more rather than less likely to happen—there can be desire arousal and appetite arousal situations which I can seek or avoid. Nevertheless, these feelings are essentially natural happenings mainly beyond our control. The only connection they have with morality, so far as I can see, is that we have to judge rationally whether it is appropriate to respond to the feeling, seek to satisfy the urge or appetite, or not. The simple existence of a feeling of this kind can never tell me what to do. The moral problem is always of the order: given that I have an urge, desire or appetite, what should I do about it—try to satisfy it or try to resist it? Only some cognitive and rational appraisal of the circumstances in the light of some general and universal moral principle can tell me that. D. H. Lawrence urges the man contemplating a possible satisfaction of his sexual desires, 'Follow your passional impulse if it is answered in the other being,'[18] but surely he is wrong. He already introduces one consideration extra to the mere response to the 'passional impulse', namely that it should at least be 'answered in the other being', but most of us would want to say that there might well be other considerations as well, and see no reason why they should be ruled out in this arbitrary fashion. To be viewed in a moral dimension at all, a situation and its attendant feelings must always be rationally appraised. The mere presence of physiological desires, urges, drives and appetites only reminds us of our animality, and says nothing about our morality.

Yet other feelings that are sometimes connected with morality, and the last I shall consider, are those feelings some people claim to have which directly inform them of the rightness and wrongness of actions, feelings of approval and disapproval. We probably all have these feelings but they are very difficult to characterize. Some moral philosophers, the emotivists,[19] have claimed that these feelings, and possibly attempts to get other people to share them, are all there is to the essentially moral part of morality and moral discourse. Clearly Kohlberg does not share this view, and again I believe he is right not to.

Presumably the feelings we are now considering are awarenesses that cannot be put in the form of reasons, feelings of discomfort at the contemplation of some actions and of comfort at the contemplation of others. Some people refer to these feelings of discomfort as their consciences. The existence of these strange internal experiences is not to be denied. Their existence raises at least two interesting questions: what causes them, and what notice should we take of them as a guide to what is moral?

Causal explanations of these phenomena are legion and I only have space briefly to refer to some of the more significant. Freud, of course, has explained these non-rational and barely conscious rumblings of the superego by his theories of the introjection of parental values,[20] and Karen Horney brought out very clearly the harmful and destructive nature of these forces when not understood.[21] Eysenck and others have theories of early classical conditioning,[22] and Skinner has theories of operant conditioning or positive reinforcement,[23] all designed to explain feelings of discomfort and anxiety, or feelings of comfort and reassurance, when doing or considering doing certain things. Social psychologists, too, have indicated how we get feelings of anxiety when our judgments are too far removed from those of a significant group.[24] All these, it should be noted, are *causal* explanations, and it is very likely that there is some truth in all of them, none is logically excluded by the others and causes can, after all, be multiple. Such theories explain things that *happen* to us, how we come to have certain feelings under certain circumstances. If such theories are right, however, they also demonstrate that these feelings have nothing whatsoever to do with what I *ought* to do. Once understood as the non-rational, unconscious mechanisms that they undoubtedly are, they clearly present no reasons for doing one thing rather than another or for believing one thing rather than another, no real *justification* for action or belief, no real indication of the *quality* of a judgment. Unless, of course, the morally right is always to be construed as that which makes us *feel* the most comfortable and the least anxious—but that, surely, would be an odd morality.

So-called feelings of approval and disapproval raise other difficulties. Given that I have a certain feeling, how do I know, without additional reasons, that it is a feeling of approval or *dis*approval? Comfort is not the same as approval. Even nausea, or physical feelings of disgust, are not necessarily the same as disapproval. What characterizes a feeling as one of approval or disapproval? What is the difference between the feeling of disgust, nausea or discomfort that I have on seeing Fred torture the cat, and the very similar feelings I may have on seeing a veterinary surgeon perform a necessary operation on the cat? The difference is not to be discovered by a closer examination of my feelings, I suggest, but by a cognitive and rational consideration of the relationship of the circumstances to principles. The approval and disapproval flow from reason and not from feelings. What I feel about some action or contemplated action, if we are to stick to some distinctive characterization of 'feel', is neither here nor there as to whether the action is to be approved of or not. Feelings, once again, are part of the data to be dealt with, to be judged; and they therefore are nothing to do with the quality, the appropriateness, or the stage of development shown by the judgment that is brought to bear—the distinctively *moral* judgment.

To return to where all this started, then, Kohlberg comes out as correct, I believe, on those of his main basic presuppositions that I have been considering. He is right to recognize the necessity of philosophical, justificatory, considerations in determining the quality, the hierarchy, and indeed the nature of moral judgments; and he is right in maintaining the primacy of judgment over observed behaviour and affective considerations in the moral life and in the determination of its quality.

THE AFFECTIVE MAINSPRING

Kohlberg claims, I have said, 'that moral judgment dispositions influence action through being stable cognitive dispositions.'[25] I have accepted, and tried to support, part of this claim, but the empirical motivational claim remains to be discussed. Even if it is the case that moral judgment of a cognitive kind is a necessary precondition of the moral life, a necessary logical prerequisite of behaviour to be characterized as moral or immoral, does it then follow that such cognition is what moves us to action? There are two separate points to make about this.

The first point is the simple one that clearly the cognitive disposition does not *always* move us to appropriate action. If it did then immoral action would be impossible, since immoral action consists precisely in doing what my judgment tells me not to, or failing to do what my judgment tells me to do. But all of us, at some time or other, act immorally—we do what we ought not and we refrain from what ought to be done, even when the *ought* is determined by our own judgment. What is going on when this happens? Presumably the judgment arising from our cognitive disposition—the *moral* judgment—is overcome in terms of drive, motivational force, by some stronger disposition, of appetite, sloth, or whatever. Temptation is the old-fashioned terminology!

The second point is that even when the moral disposition, the cognitive judgment, *is* followed in action, it is difficult to demonstrate that the cognition, the reasoning, the judging, actually *causes* the action that is the moral action. In order to ensure that the motivation stemming from the judgment is stronger than contrary motivation stemming from appetite or whatever, it seems necessary to posit some kind of affective commitment *to* reason, *to* the results of one's own cognition. Such an affective commitment, a kind of caring about reason, is a human variable not much studied to my knowledge; but it makes a great deal of difference and helps to explain differences, not in the judgment itself, but in the disposition to *act* on the judgment and in the strength of guilt feelings when such judgments are not acted upon. Such caring about reason and judgment, such feelings as to the importance of reason and judgment, might go some way to explaining something else. Why do some people progress further along the Kohlbergian stages than others? There could be many reasons for this to do with child-rearing, education and the more generally pervasive social milieu. A likely hypothesis, though, is that the varying strengths of individuals' affective commitments to their own reasoning and cognition might have something to do with it. If I *care* about reason, and the attendant necessities of coherence and consistency, I am more likely to attend to dissonances and incongruities that appear in my present level of thinking, my present 'cognitive dispositions', and to seek a new and 'higher' stability. Even the proposed techniques of Kohlberg and his colleagues for the use of teachers depend upon the readiness of pupils to be disturbed by the provocation of such dissonances and incongruities.[26] What happens to the pupils who *see* the inconsistencies but are not *bothered* by them? Not all people capable of seeing inconsistencies are equally disturbed by such inconsistency; and that is one reason why equally clever people are not equally moral in their actions, or even in the quality of their moral judgments.

Whence comes this necessary care, such necessary affective concern for reason and one's own cognition? It is here that empirical research does not seem to help very much, and the work of Kohlberg and his colleagues does not seem to press into this kind of area. Yet care for reason, a sense of obligation[27] to one's own reasoning, seems to be the necessary affective mainspring which drives Kohlberg's whole system.

One can put together a mixture of reasonable conjecture, hints from child-rearing research, and something approaching logically necessary criteria to produce a probable theory of what has to happen to provide this affective mainspring which enables rational and autonomous cognition to be motivationally effective. I am not here attempting any kind of up-to-date survey of relevant research on this matter, though that would be an important task for someone. My empirical hints come from Klein[28] and Hoffman,[29] and my conjecture and criteria come from the nature of the case. The theory would run like this:

Reason has to gain, as it were, saliency. Rational cognition in the matter of understanding the physical world gets at least part of its saliency from the natural and hurtful hazard of getting things wrong. It pays to be somewhat rational about the material stuff and objects we encounter. Rational cognition in the matter of moral judgment, though mixed up with cognition of material things in its early stages, as Piaget has shown, soon emerges as something different. Often the comfortable thing to do is *not* what my rational judgment tells me to do. It does not always *pay*, in the normal and fairly immediate sense of that word, to follow my moral judgment. Against this, where can the saliency come from?

It is suggested that, as with other things, the saliency must be rooted in the child's affection, which in time adds to itself respect, for significant and broadly nurturant adults in the child's early life. Such adults could of course be parents or parent substitutes, but could include other family relations and also early teachers. Affection and respect is a necessary but clearly not sufficient condition for our purpose. The loved and respected adult must also be a model of human reason. That is to say, reason must be apparent in the adult's normal everyday behaviour; it must be the dominant mode, as it were; but it must also not come over to the child as mechanistic, non-yielding, always preprogrammed, absolutely predictable. Consistency and regularity are necessary, for that is what it is to be reasonable; but human flexibility is also to be signalled if the child's respect for his own fallible reason is not to be destroyed in its seedling form.

Such an adult, such adults, would control the whims and impulses of the child, but always rationally and humanely, and increasingly with explanations and reasons, with what Hoffman has called induction discipline, as contrasted with mere power assertion or love withdrawal.[30] Hoffman himself says that it may well be the case 'that the cognitive rather than the affective aspects of the parent's discipline are primary',[31] but what must be insisted on here is that there is a minimum at least of affective bond without which even the parent's cognitive and information-giving role would be sadly diminished.

Increasingly, Hoffman suggests, the adult must include in the reasoning and explanations given, attention to the existence, needs, purposes, pleasures and sufferings of other persons. This is not just a question of inducing concern for others, though there is nothing wrong if that is a consequence; it is more to do with extending the appropriate area in which reason should work. There is a sense in which it cannot be completely reasonable to be as rational as possible but always only in one's own interest.

Such attitudes, dispositions and behaviours, desirably manifested by parents and parent substitutes, would of course need to be continued by other adult contacts, especially the early teachers of young children who carry a heavy responsibility in this regard. Early teachers have a wider domain, a broader context, in which to manifest these desirable attitudes of eliciting warm respect from the child and radiating the necessary concern for reason. Their domain includes massive opportunities for rational routines, reasoned explanations, justifiable and explained rules and sanctions; and it unfortunately also provides, of course, countless opportunities for the manifesting of irrational and arbitrary talk and action.

What is clear, I believe, can now be summed up. Kohlberg is right, I have argued, to insist on the primacy of the rationally cognitive judgment as an indicator of moral quality, as distinct from immediately affective dispositions or observed behaviour. He is also right to insist on the desirability of such judgments moving moral agents to appropriate actions or forbearance. The motivating force of rational cognitive judgment, however, must depend partly on the opposing strengths of whim, impulse and desire, and partly—most importantly—on the strength of a person's affective concern for reason, on his or her sense or feeling of obligation to do what it is reasonable to do, or to believe what it is reasonable to believe. I have tried to hypothesize a desirable child-rearing scenario for generating and developing such a care and concern, without which all the Kohlbergian desirables will not occur.

NOTES

1 L. Kohlberg (1981) *Essays on Moral Development*; Vol. 1: The Philosophy of Moral Development, San Francisco, Harper and Row.
2 *Ibid.*, p. 49.
3 *Ibid.*, p. 64.
4 L. Kohlberg (1981) 'From is to ought: How to commit the naturalistic fallacy and get away with it in the study of moral development', in *Essays on Moral Development*, *op. cit.*, pp. 101–89.
5 L. Kohlberg (1981) *op. cit.*, pp. 139–40.
6 *Ibid.*, p. 187.
7 J. Piaget (1932) *The Moral Judgment of the Child*, London, Routledge and Kegan Paul, p. 405.
8 *Ibid.*, p. 395.
9 See Kant's (1909) *Critique of Practical Reason*, 6th ed., trans T. K. Abbott, London, Longmans, Green and Co., pp. 132–4.
10 Much of the material in the second and third sections is drawn from my (1980) article 'Morality, reason and feeling' published in *Journal of Moral Education*, 9, 2, pp. 114–21.
11 See, for example, E. Bedford (1967) 'Emotions', in D. F. Gustafson (Ed.) *Essays in Philosophical Psychology*, London, Macmillan; A. Kenny (1963) *Action, Emotion and Will*, London, Routledge and Kegan Paul; C. Bailey (1975) 'Knowledge of others and concern for others', in J. Elliott and R. Pring (Eds.) *Social Education and Social Understanding*, London, University of London Press.
12 See, for example, N. Bull (1969) *Moral Education*, London, Routledge and Kegan Paul.
13 See Bailey (1975) *op. cit.*
14 See P. Mercer (1972) *Sympathy and Ethics*, Oxford, Clarendon Press.
15 See R. S. Downey and E. Telfer (1969) *Respect for Persons*, London, Allen and Unwin, pp. 24–9.
16 See Bull (1969) *op. cit.*, pp. 79, 96 and 97.
17 Matt, 5:44–5.
18 D. H. Lawrence (1950) *Selected Essays*, Harmondsworth, Penguin Books, p. 239.
19 For a good account of emotivism see W. D. Hudson (1970) *Modern Moral Philosophy*, London, Macmillan, pp. 107–47, and the texts referred to there.
20 Brief but authoritative accounts can be found in R. Munroe's (1957) *Schools of Psychoanalytic Thought*, London, Hutchinson, esp. Ch. 5.
21 K. Horney (1939) *New Ways in Psychoanalysis*, London, Routledge and Kegan Paul.
22 H. J. Eysenck (1964) *Crime and Personality*, London, Routledge and Kegan Paul.
23 B. F. Skinner (1953) *The Science of Human Behaviour*, New York, Macmillan.
24 See, for example, the work described in M. Sherif and C. W. Sherif (1956) *An Outline of Social Psychology*, New York, Harper and Brothers, Ch. 8.
25 Kohlberg (1981) *op. cit.*, p. 187.
26 M. Blatt and L. Kohlberg (1971) 'Effects of classroom discussion on moral thought', in L. Kohlberg and E. Turiel, *Moralization Research, the Cognitive Developmental Approach*, New York, Holt, Rinehart and Winston.
27 I give a longer account of the idea of 'a sense of obligation' in my doctoral dissertation: (1974) *Theories of Moral Development and Moral Education: A Philosophical Critique*, University of London, Ch. 11.

28 J. Klein (1965) *Samples from English Culture*, Vol. 2; Child Rearing Practices. London, Routledge and Kegan Paul.
29 M. L. Hoffman (1970) 'Moral development', in P. Mussen (Ed.), *Carmichael's Manual of Child Psychology*, Vol. 2, New York, John Wiley and Sons, pp. 261–360.
30 *Ibid.*, p. 332.
31 *Ibid.*, p. 284.

13. Morality, Reason and Emotions

JOHN MARTIN RICH

Some recent educators have relegated emotions to a negligible role in moral education. Michael Scriven, for instance, says that affect is entirely subservient to a cognitive approach.[1] The emotions are the last supplement in the pedagogy of ethics, the 'icing on the cake'. Lawrence Kohlberg's cognitive moral development theory, while recognizing the emotions and other affective factors, does not provide a significant place for them.

This lack of emphasis on the emotions raises several questions. Do the emotions play a significant role in moral education and moral action? What relations, if any, do the emotions have to moral judgments? If a larger role for the emotions in moral education is warranted, can it be shown how the cognitive development approach could incorporate it, or must such a role be left to other theories of moral education?

THE COGNITIVE DEVELOPMENT APPROACH AND THE EMOTIONS

Kohlberg raises the question of whether values are relative or universal and indicates that his findings show culturally universal states of moral development. His theory, he claims, is both psychological and philosophical, and his findings generate a philosophy of moral education designed to stimulate moral development rather than teach fixed moral rules. His theory has been influenced by Dewey.[2] Kohlberg believes that a philosophic concept of morality and moral development is required, that moral development passes through invariant qualitative stages, and that moral development is stimulated by promoting thinking and problem-solving. Justice, Kohlberg holds, is the key principle in the development of moral judgment.

Kohlberg owes a great deal to Piaget's pioneering work;[3] he has sought to overcome the deficiencies in the latter's research by using a much larger sample that is more broadly based socially and is composed of equal proportions of popular and socially isolated children. Kohlberg also is concerned with general moral principles rather than, as with Piaget, simple virtues and vices. Kohlberg's study yielded six developmental stages allotted to three moral levels. Subsequent retesting of the group at three-year intervals has shown growth proceeding through the same stages in the same order.

A number of criticisms have been made of the developmental stages and the logical order of moral concepts in the stages themselves.[4] It is claimed that the stages need to be delineated more precisely: the distinction between Stages 5 and 6 is not clear; conceptual links can be found between Stages 2 and 5 that do not exist between 2 and 3; and possibly more advanced stages are needed, as well as fine calibration within the stages. It has also been suggested that the stages lack any necessary connection with moral action and therefore what has been provided are stages of general cognitive, rather than moral, development.

After failing to find Stage 6 subjects in Turkey, Kohlberg reduced the number of stages to five by making Stage 6 an advanced Stage 5 form.[5] Kohlberg also postulated the existence of a Stage 7 that involves contemplative experience of non-egoistic and non-dualistic variety.[6] But since no empirical evidence of this stage has been found, and since Stage 6 has been abandoned, Stage 7 can also be discarded from his theory.

The cognitive moral development theory recognizes that affectional factors may also enter into moral judgments, but that such judgments are primarily a function of rational operations. Moral development is a result of increasing ability to perceive social reality and to integrate social experience. A necessary—but not sufficient—condition for morality is the ability to reason logically. But the more important determinants of moral development are the amount and type of social experience and the opportunity to assume other roles and confront different perspectives.

Though moral judgment is influenced by such affective factors as the ability to empathize and the capacity for guilt, moral situations are defined cognitively.[7] In the case of 'will' (as in 'strong-willed' and 'weak-willed' persons), will is an important factor in moral behaviour but it is not distinctively moral; it only becomes so when informed by mature moral judgments. Moral judgment is the only distinctive moral feature in moral behaviour.[8]

One ostensible reason why emotions do not play a larger role in the theory is the historical tendency to view emotions as irrational forces. Kohlberg spends considerable time attacking irrational views.[9] He opposes irrational emotive theories of moral development such as those of Durkheim and Freud, and he also objects to Durkheim's and Dreeben's view that learning to accept rules and authority is a concrete non-rational process. These theories overlook the cognitive core of moral development.

The chief problem with Kohlberg's approach to the emotions, however, is to assume that emotions are irrational or non-rational forces in conflict with the cognitive core of moral development rather than developing a cognitive view of the emotions in relation to moral judgment.

A COGNITIVE VIEW OF THE EMOTIONS

It is generally believed that although animals may experience certain emotions, the range and complexity of human emotions is far greater. 'There is', says Wittgenstein, 'nothing astonishing about certain concepts only being applicable to a being that, e.g., possesses language.'[10] By learning to use a language humans gain skill in assessing their experiences and emotions. Emotions are learned within a linguistic context; as thinking is clarified so are the emotions as language is used to make statements about them (e.g., 'I feel sad'; 'I resent what he said').

Emotions involve feelings but not just feelings. There are innumerable feelings: itching, tickling, pain, dizziness, queasiness, and the like. It is appropriate to ask for reasons for the emotions but not for feelings (although we may at times ask for causes). Emotions are more closely tied to language and our evaluations of situations and can thereby be readily communicated even though metaphorical language must frequently be used. Feelings, more so than emotions, can be more specifically located in the body.

Emotions inform us and others what concerns us, what delights and frustrates us in carrying out our goals. Emotions tell us and others (when expressed overtly) what concerns us when we encounter difficulty in situations, as well as when we gain satisfaction and fulfilment. Whether a situation will evoke a particular emotion depends on the individual, his past experience, his interpretation of the situation, and how the situation may impede or facilitate the achievement of his goals.

Emotions can be rational or irrational depending upon the process of evaluation. Rational emotions are based on an accurate assessment of the facts in the situation, logically sound reasoning, and an ability to prevent those emotions which would immobilize insofar as goal achievement might become disproportionate and uncontrollable. In other words, if a student is anticipating taking a test the test may temporarily evoke fear, especially if the student has done insufficient preparation. But the student needs to assess the real dangers in the situation in relation to his academic goals, then determine the type and extent of study and review needed to put his plan into action. If the student still has disproportionate fear despite extensive and thorough preparation, then the fear is irrational and an impediment to goal achievement.[11]

MORAL EDUCATION AND THE EMOTIONS

Frankena states that the purpose of moral education is to bring about and maintain a moral social order in which each individual is, insofar as his native endowment permits, a morally good person and a fully developed moral agent.[12]

Certain emotions are involved in moral judgments and action. 'To make a moral judgment of an action, person, etc., is to judge the action by relating it to either a moral rule or moral ideal. Further, the judgment must be one that we believe we would publicly advocate.'[13] By moral action we mean an act based on a moral judgment, or one which has moral consequences even though a moral judgment was not involved.

Those emotions which are so involved are of two types: constitutive and regulative. Constitutive emotions are a necessary condition in ascribing accurately that a person has grasped a moral concept. When someone, for instance, fails to have remorse for voluntarily harming an innocent person, it would be reasonable to say that the individual has not fully grasped the concept of harm. Or if an individual commits premeditated murder and experiences no guilt for his act, then he is likely not to have a well-developed concept of murder. In these examples remorse and guilt are constitutive of the concepts of harm and murder.

How, specifically, can it be determined whether one has grasped a moral concept in terms of constitutive emotions? First of all, look to see whether appropriate constitutive emotions are present. As in the above illustrations, guilt and remorse are appropriate. Or, to take another example, we would expect a benevolent person not only to avoid wilfully harming another but to express the emotion of indignation when he observes someone harm or deny another his rights.

But if the constitutive emotions were present, why did they not prevent someone from performing the wrong act? In some cases they will do so, as when one is in the process of making a moral judgment. An individual, for instance, thinks of something he wants but recognizes that in order to obtain it he would have to harm another, and thereby with this recognition he begins to experience guilt. Thus if one knows what it means to harm another he will likely experience guilt when contemplating such harm, and the guilt may serve as a deterrent to such an act. It is true that for some people guilt may not be experienced very strongly or hardly at all in making this kind of moral judgment, and only arises subsequent to the act. It still shows, however, that such persons have a concept of harm and that it was only temporarily over-ridden by other considerations such as lack of self-discipline, unjustifiably enlarging the range of excuses, or by marking a mistake in moral reasoning. One may have a concept of promise-keeping but make some excuse why, say, a debt does not have to be paid, only to realize later that the excuse is unjustified and consequently suffer guilt which, in turn, may serve as a potent motivating factor in repaying the debt.[14]

A second way to determine whether a person has grasped a moral concept is by the absence of constitutive emotions in situations where ordinarily they could be expected to be present. An absence of appropriate constitutive emotion when committing a morally wrong act shows that the person does not fully have a concept of what is morally right in the situation or else has a concept but has mistakenly exonerated himself. (In some cases, however, a person cannot be held responsible but still experiences remorse. Thus he continues to assume personal responsibility even though he is publicly exonerated.)

A third way to determine whether a person has developed a moral concept is by observing if inappropriate emotions are expressed in certain moral situations. Inappropriate overt emotions can be considered morally callous or a case of moral deficiency. One does not express sorrow at the success of one's friends or joy when they die. Nor does one rejoice in the misfortunes of another or laugh at the sight of someone being denied his rights. In the former case of rejoicing, evidently the person lacks a concept of harm, as we would expect the expression of pity or remorse; and in the latter case, the person ostensibly lacks a concept of rights (or a particular right), as we would have expected an expression of anger, resentment or indignation.

Constitutive emotions, however, may do double-duty insofar as they are found in non-moral judgments. One may, upon conceptualizing an important personal ideal, experience remorse because of a failure to live up to it or remorse for a life not use wisely because of failure to achieve one's aspirations. Thus not all constitutive emotions enter into moral judgment.

Guilt, remorse and related emotions tend to be constitutive of what it means to learn a moral concept. Another class of emotions functions in a regulative capacity. These emotions, though various, are likely to be fear, anger, anxiety, pity and affection. Regulative emotions, in contrast to constitutive ones, are not a necessary condition in grasping a moral concept. They may influence moral judgments in desirable or undesirable ways. Fear, for instance, can enter moral actions in numerous ways. A person may anticipate the social consequences of his act, become fearful and, as a consequence, do the right thing. On the other hand, one judges that X is the right thing to do but becomes fearful of doing it because of a lack of moral courage or the like. Or Z should treat Y fairly but every time Z sees him it makes Z angry and, consequently, Z treats him unfairly. Or, let us say, Z believes that if he harms Y, then Y will retaliate, which in turn provokes fear and prevents Z from performing the act. But suppose Z knows that he can get away with the act without retaliation; he still does not perform the act because he grasps the concept of harm and apprehends how the act represents such a case. Prior to the act he may experience guilt which may in part preclude his performing the act. Thus while regulative emotions regulate only antecedently, constitutive acts may perform both regulative and constitutive roles by regulating antecedently, be constitutive of the moral judgment, and evoke appropriate emotions following the moral act.

In regulative emotions we have cases where Z, in considering not to repay a loan, becomes fearful and subsequently reconsiders his obligation. Although Z promised to help Y, he seriously considers not doing so, but each time he fails to act he becomes increasingly anxious and decides that he should keep his promise. Or Z is about to strike Y but suddenly takes pity on him and helps him instead. Although Z is not one who habitually keeps his commitments, he did so with Y because he developed a special affection for him. Z, for example, observed an elderly person being robbed. At first he thought it was none of his business, but suddenly he became angry and found himself intervening to stop the robbery. These illustrations, except in the case of guilt, show how regulative emotions operate in moral decisions.

However, the regulative emotions are less reliable in moral education because they can serve to prevent as well as promote moral action. And though the regulative emotions frequently prevent wrong acts, the constitutive emotions not only regulate but may rectify wrong behaviour.

Many different emotions have no role in moral education, as we have seen that constitutive emotions do double-duty and regulative emotions may help promote both right and wrong actions. Some emotions, moreover, do not have a direct role in moral education. Koestler speaks of 'self-transcending tendencies' in some emotions, such as in listening to Mozart, watching a great acting performance, and being in love.[15] He believes that a common denominator of these emotions is a sense of participation, identification, belonging as part of a larger whole which may be Nature, God, Mankind, Universal Order, etc. He says that these emotions produce a calming effect, contemplation and passive enjoyment. On the other hand, Koestler recognizes a 'self-assertive class of emotions' in which the ego is experienced as a self-contained whole and of ultimate value. He recognizes, however, that emotions can be mixtures of both types (as in the case of love).

Though the regulative and constitutive emotions previously discussed may usually be Koestler's self-assertive type, some, such as pity, may be of the self-transcending variety. Though not mentioned by Koestler, the latter type seems to enter into aesthetic valuation more than moral assessment and also may have some affinity with what Kant calls 'the sublime'.

Some readers may object that our position is not accurate because the emotions are not reliable guides to the rightness or wrongness of acts. One could have indignation because he believed that an act was wrong, whereas the act was not really wrong at all. Although one may believe his emotions are accurate indicators in moral situations, the person may still be wrong about the act itself. Thus, say the critics, emotions may serve to mislead and at times influence one to commit wrong acts. In the above example, however, one could have indignation as a result of an inaccurate appraisal of a situation and, consequently, the indignation is based on erroneous evidence, inapplicable or inappropriate principles, or failure to properly assess social consequences. One does not suddenly and impetuously become indignant for no reason and then act foolishly or harmfully; an inadequate or erroneous evaluation has been made and indignation is part of the total composite of how a person may evaluate a situation who concludes, say, that she has been unjustly treated. Though it happens in this case that the individual is mistaken, her indignation was part of the evaluation and not a prior cause.

Of course there are cases where a person's anger may precipitate rash action that she ordinarily would not engage in. And there are also times when one may not help a stranger in distress for fear of 'complications' and possible legal entanglements. Here, it would seem, are cases of regulative emotions which mislead and prompt wrong acts or inhibit right ones. Thus we do have instances of irrational emotions and emotions which have not been properly educated to a moral point of view—and this is a job for the moral education of the emotions.

We can illustrate how emotions are learned, using the examples of fear (a regulative emotion) and guilt (usually a constitutive emotion). Children, in gaining an understanding of their emotions, learn to label them correctly and respond emotionally to certain objects. A child has a primitive idea of language functions in learning to label things, limited to words and ostensive definitions. 'A child', says Wittgenstein, 'uses such primitive forms of language when it learns to talk. Here the teaching of language is not explanation, but training.'[16] The child gradually comes to see that 'the use of the word in *practice* is its meaning.'[17] More subtle distinctions are learned through increased experience. The child will learn that there are different language games and that a word may have a family of meanings.

Some emotions take objects (fear and anger) and some do not (dread and anxiety). How do children learn to respond emotionally to certain objects? They are taught, in the case of fear, that some objects are dangerous under certain conditions (e.g., glass) and others categorically dangerous (e.g., poison). Fears are built through conditioning, and as the child develops his judgment, he learns to distinguish situations where he need not be fearful when confronted with the formerly fear-producing object. It is not so much that the object itself is inherently fearful, but the words of warning which have been associated with the object.

Fear can also relate to a concept of harm. By learning which types of situations may have harmful factors, one can generalize in situations of the designated type that one may cause another harm if certain acts are performed. An individual may judge that what she is about to do may harm someone, and this evaluation immediately produces an anticipatory fear if the individual has previously accepted the imperative, 'Do not willingly harm another.' The fear acts as a brake. Without the emotion one has less incentive to abstain from the act, even though its absence does not preclude right action. The emotion only makes avoidance of the wrong action more certain.

Hoffman has shown in his theory of altruistic motivation how guilt develops.[18] The young child may know that the other is 'a victim' but is unable to distinguish between his own and the other's inner states, which is evident by the child giving the other what the child finds most comforting. At the second development level, that of role-taking, the child has acquired a sense that others have independent thoughts and feelings. The child is now far less egocentric and his response to the distress of others is more sophisticated, although it still is confined to the immediate situation. At the third level the child recognizes others as continuous persons with their own history and identity. By the pre-adolescent years the child can respond not only to transitory distress in others but also to what he imagines to be their general condition.

Guilt, for Hoffman, is a synthesis of sympathetic distress and awareness of being the cause of another's distress. Guilt may be aroused not only by acts of commission but omission. With the capability of foreseeing consequences, anticipatory guilt becomes a possibility. Guilt may also occur when one perceives the victim's plight as caused by action or inaction of others with whom he identifies (white civil rights activists in the US during the 1960s). Guilt may also be aroused over the stark contrast between the other's life and one's own (e.g., survivor's syndrome; upper middle-class youth *vis-à-vis* the poor). When the individual does not act (for whatever reason), he will typically experience sympathetic distress or will cognitively restructure the situation. Some emotions, such as guilt, are related constitutively to certain character traits.

CHARACTER TRAITS AND MORAL EDUCATION

This brings us to a critical juncture. It is my hypothesis (which I hope to demonstrate) that in order to relate the cognitive developmental theory to the emotions, some use must be made of character traits. Yet Kohlberg has renounced the character trait approach, referring to them as a 'bag of virtues'. A morality of principles is quite formalistic and could be acted upon for non-moral reasons. Good traits are needed to sustain the individual under the pressure of moral conflicts and the conflicts of principles. On the other hand, it would be difficult to know what traits to support without subscribing to certain moral principles. For instance, a disposition to do good and prevent harm is based on the principle of benevolence. Thus it seems that one could subscribe to a minimum of cardinal traits from which less important traits could be derived.

Kohlberg offers several objections to the character trait approach to moral education.[19] Arbitrariness exists in composing the list of virtues, depending upon the composition of committees to develop such a list, their agreements and inconsistencies. Virtue words are relative to cultural standards that are psychologically vague and ethically relative (e.g., the inability to agree on the meaning of 'self-discipline'). Moreover, to label a set of behaviours with a positive or negative trait does not in itself show that they are of ethical importance but represents an appeal to social conventions. Additionally, longitudinal research findings raise doubts whether childhood personality traits are stable or predictive over time and stages of development. Childhood traits, as used in Head Start, are not predictive of positive or negative adjustment. Research suggests that various character traits do not stand for consistent personality traits but are merely evaluative labels.[20] Thus, because of these shortcomings in the character trait approach, Kohlberg seeks a morality of principles. He defines a moral principle as 'a rule of choosing which we want all people to adopt always in all situations.'[21]

Kohlberg cites for support the landmark Character Education Inquiry in the late 1920s.[22] In the study 170,000 tests were administered to over 8000 public-school pupils between the ages of 11 and 16. The tests confronted children with the opportunity to cheat or with a conflict between their own good and that of others. They were, for example, given a chance to take money while they thought they were unobserved; to violate the time limit on a speed test; to cheat while grading their own papers; and to place dots in small circles while blindfolded without cheating.

About 7 per cent did not cheat at all, and about 4 per cent cheated at every opportunity; the vast majority acted honestly in some situations and dishonestly in others, and there was consistency in these patterns when the tests were repeated. This led Hartshorne and May, the principal investigators, to the rather startling conclusion that behaviour is highly specific, depending upon the specific case; there is no such thing as honest and dishonest children but only honest and dishonest acts. Thus little evidence was found of unified character traits or generality in moral behaviour. The concept of character based upon specific acts fits the stimulus-response theories of learning. Some other investigators have refined the data and corroborated the findings. Gross found that children who cheat in class in one type of situation do not do so in another.[23] And Stendler found that children who regard cheating as wrong in one situation are able to rationalize it in another.[24]

However, it is implausible that honesty in one situation cannot be generalized to other situations (and the same with other character traits); otherwise, it would be necessary to learn innumerable acts of honesty for each new situation one confronts. In practice, both generality and specificity can be found in human conduct. Low correlations could be rightfully expected from children, because of the lengthy period needed for socialization; adults, on the other hand, would more likely show consistency in moral virtues. Another study, which used the methodology of the Character Education Inquiry but observed adults rather than children, in situations that offered opportunity for apparently unseen cheating, found consistency in both honest and dishonest subjects, and a general trait of honesty was evidenced.[25] Thus, it can be concluded that character traits are less consistent, more situation-specific in children and more consistent and general in adults.

Kohlberg states that justice is the only moral virtue.[26] Justice or equality is the only principle for resolving claims; it requires that every person be treated impartially, that respect for persons be observed. Thus a moral principle is not only a rule of action but a reason for action.

Since the preconventional level is largely prior to the emergence of genuine moral judgment, our focus on character traits can be at the conventional and postconventional levels. Suggestive of a reconciliation of character trait theory and a morality of principles are Kohlberg's own motives for engaging in moral action.[27]

The conventional level begins by recognizing that the subject is motivated by anticipating others' disapproval and is likely to experience guilt in actual or imagined disapproval. This level is further differentiated by feelings of dishonour and institutionalized blame for failure of duty and by guilt from actual harm done to others. The person is now able to differentiate guilt for bad consequences from disapproval.

Guilt, remorse, and related emotions, as noted earlier, tend to be constitutive of what it means to learn a moral concept. Thus, in addition to the measures already employed to determine whether someone's development is at the conventional level, an additional test would be to determine whether the appropriate emotions were present. A second test to determine whether a person has grasped a moral concept is by the absence of constitutive emotions in situations where ordinarily they would be expected to be present.

The character trait typical of conventional level is conscientiousness. Conscientiousness arises from one's conscience in fulfilling one's duties; it is the attitude toward one's obligations and the manner in which they are fulfilled. One accepts the principle, 'Do one's duty'. A person must first accept something as his duty; then guilt will be experienced in two types of situations. The first type: 'D is an undesirable act (a violation of one's duty)—X did D.' And the second type: 'C is an obligatory act—X did not do C.' Thus guilt is a constituent emotion and arises over acts of commission and omission.

Although Kohlberg says that justice is the only moral virtue, it would appear that it is a moral virtue only for a Stage 6 person, because those at lower stages could not fully comprehend and act on the basis of justice. In contrast, conscientiousness is evidently the quintessential moral virtue for the conventional level.

Although justice is the character trait typifying Stage 6, two other character traits—compassion and benevolence—seem to be related to Stage 5; each of these has associated emotions. The virtue of compassion leads to the imaginative and emotional sharing of the distress or misfortune of another or others who are considered or treated as equals. The emotions associated with compassion are guilt, remorse, indignation and pity. It shows that one really has compassion whenever suffering remorse when harming someone. Thus remorse is compassion experienced when you consider yourself responsible or identify with someone else's suffering. One has accepted the principle: 'Do not willingly harm others' or 'Avoid causing others needless pain or suffering.' The emotions may be regulative insofar as an individual sees that another is being harmed; he may thereby become indignant or experience pity which in turn may lead to compassion.

Although compassion goes beyond the conscientiousness of fulfilling duties, it is not as positive as benevolence. Compassion is based on the perception of negative conditions and awaits those conditions before expression and action. Benevolence, on the other hand, is a positive trait that may prevent undesirable conditions from arising in the first place. One who is benevolent is desirous of the good of others, of a kindly disposition, charitable and generous. A benevolent person has a disposition to do what is right and good and to prevent harm; he accepts the principle: 'One should always try to do good and prevent harm.' The emotions associated with the trait of benevolence are guilt, and remorse, occasionally indignation, affection, joy and love. The benevolent person would experience guilt and remorse as constitutive emotions when doing wrong or failing to do what is good. His positive dispositions would be regulated in varying degrees and combinations by affection and love for others, and joy in doing good and helping others. And, in contrast to compassionate persons, benevolent persons do not wait for distress to arise but have a continuing disposition to be of help.

In summary, I have tried to demonstrate that the emotions should have a more important place in moral education and have outlined what this role should be. Those emotions involved in moral judgment and action were shown to be of two types: constitutive and regulative. These findings were related to Kohlberg's theory by indicating that once the conventional and postconventional levels find a place for character traits distinctive of each level, they will also secure a functional role for emotions in moral judgment and action. Thus Kohlberg's objection to the character trait approach could be overcome in this case because the traits would not be arbitrarily chosen or psychologically vague; moreover, their ethical importance would rest upon the cognitive moral development theory itself, and greater stability of each character trait would be achieved by recognizing that the trait is merely the patterned behavioural counterpart of the respective underlying principles in the conventional and postconventional levels. Thus by following those proposals, a rapprochement between the emotions and Kohlberg's theory could likely be achieved.

NOTES

1 M. Scriven (1975) 'Cognitive moral education,' *Phi Delta Kappan*, 56, pp. 689–94.
2 However, Kohlberg's universal ethical values, along with other aspects of his theory, differ from Dewey's views, which are transactional and situational.
3 J. Piaget (1965) *The Moral Judgment of the Child*, New York, The Free Press.
4 C. M. Beck *et al.* (Eds.) (1971) *Moral Education: Interdisciplinary Approaches*, Toronto, University of Toronto Press, pp. 355–72.
5 L. Kohlberg (1978) 'Revisions in the theory and practice of moral development,' *Moral Development, New Directions for Child Development*, 2, pp. 83–8.
6 L. Kohlberg (1973) 'Stages and aging in moral development—Some speculations,' *The Gerontologist*, 13, pp. 497–502.
7 L. Kohlberg and R. H. Hersh (1977) 'Moral development: A review of the theory,' *Theory Into Practice*, 16, pp. 53–9.
8 L. Kohlberg (1975) 'The cognitive-developmental approach to moral education.' *Phi Delta Kappan*, 61, pp. 670–7.
9 L. Kohlberg (1971) 'Stages of moral development as a basis for moral education,' in Beck *et al.* (1971) *op. cit.*, *Moral Education*, pp. 23–92.
10 L. Wittgenstein (1970) *Zettel*, Berkeley and Los Angeles, University of California Press, on p. 91e, 520.
11 J. M. Rich (1977) 'On educating the emotions,' *Educational Theory*, 27, pp. 291–6.
12 W. K. Frankena (1976) 'Moral education,' in K. E. Goodpaster (Ed.) *Perspectives on Morality: Essays by William K. Frankena*, Notre Dame, Ind., University of Notre Dame Press, pp. 161–8.
13 B. Gert (1973) *The Moral Rules*, New York, Harper and Row, p. 173.
14 I have dealt at length with the many forms of these excuses in moral decision-making in my 'Ryle and the teaching of virtue,' in I. S. Steinberg (Ed.) (1977) *Philosophy of Education*, Worcester, Mass. Hufferman Press, pp. 324–32.
15 A. Koestler (1967) *The Act of Creation*, New York, Dell.
16 L. Wittgenstein (1953) *Philosophical Investigations*, New York, Macmillan, No. 5.
17 L. Wittgenstein (1965) *The Blue and Brown Books*, New York, Harper Torchbooks, p. 69.
18 M. L. Hoffman (1975) 'The development of altruistic motivation,' in D. J. DePalma and J. M. Foley (Eds.) *Moral Development: Current Theory and Research*, Hillsdale, N.J., Lawrence Erlbaum, pp. 137–51.
19 L. Kohlberg (1981) *The Philosophy of Moral Development*, San Francisco, Harper and Row, pp. 78–81.

20 *Ibid.*, p. 299.
21 L. Kohlberg (1970) 'Education for justice: A modern statement of the Platonic view,' in N. F. and T. R. Sizer, *Moral Education: Five Lectures*, Introduction, Cambridge, Mass., Harvard University Press, pp. 69–70.
22 H. Hartshorne and M. A. May (1928–30) *Studies in the Nature of Character: Studies in Deceit* (Vol. I), *Studies in Service and Self-Control* (Vol. II), *Studies in Organization of Character* (Vol. III), New York, Macmillan.
23 S. M. Gross (1946) 'The effect of certain types of motivation on the "honesty" of children,' *Journal of Educational Research*, 40, pp. 133–40.
24 C. R. Stendler (1949) 'A study of some socio-moral judgments of junior-high school children,' *Child Development*, 20, pp. 15–28.
25 U. Bronfenbrenner (1962), 'The role of age, sex, class and culture in studies of moral development,' *Religious Education*, (July/August).
26 Kohlberg (1970) 'Education for justice,' *op. cit.*, p. 70.
27 Kohlberg (1981) *Philosophy*, *op cit.*, pp. 121–2.

Interchange

BAILEY REPLIES TO RICH

It is difficult to deal with all the points raised by Rich in the space available for my comments. I shall therefore concentrate on that part of his paper which seems to me of most significance, that is, the discussion of emotions or feelings as being both constitutive and regulative of moral judgment.

Two theses are involved:

1   Constitutive emotions are a necessary condition of ascribing accurately that a person has grasped a moral concept.
2   Regulative emotions may influence moral judgments and actions in desirable or undesirable ways.

These theses are used by Rich as a basis for his later arguments for a greater emphasis on the emotions and on the development of character traits in moral education. I shall not deal with Rich's contention that Kohlberg's framework could be altered to accommodate these ideas.

That emotions and feelings are *connected* with moral judgment and moral action is not denied by anyone, I believe. The point at issue is not the connection, but the priority; not the interrelationship, but the proper provider of the justificatory assertion that lies at the heart of moral agency. What is claimed in the Kantian, Piagetian, Kohlbergian tradition is that notwithstanding the presence and force of human feelings and emotions it is rational judgment, and only such judgment, that can provide justificatory claims, that can tell us what we *ought* to do. On this, as I have argued, I believe the essential propositions embedded in the tradition to be correct.

Since regulative emotions or feelings, as Rich points out himself, can act as much against appropriate moral action as in facilitation of it, the Kantian tradition must be right in saying that feelings alone cannot determine the appropriateness, the justification, of an action; only reason can do that. The regulative thesis, then, seems only to assert what we all agree, namely that emotions and feelings can and do move us to action. If the argument is that simply because of this we should encourage the development of emotions and feelings likely to move persons to appropriate moral action there are a number of objections:

1   It is never clear what in general terms these feelings are likely to be in a given situation. For example, in one situation anger might be an appropriate moral response whereas in another such an emotion might be inappropriate. Anger cannot therefore be encouraged as a general morally facilitating emotion. Surely the same applies to all feelings.

220

2 Some feelings which move us to action (love, friendship, sympathy) are notoriously difficult to cultivate towards all persons. They are always specific and limited in focus—I sympathize with Fred but I dislike Mary. The *moral* problem is one of generating respect for all persons, including those for whom I have feelings of dislike or even hatred.

3 To concentrate, as an educator, on the cultivation of feelings at, as it were, too early a stage in practical reasoning, gets dangerously near to indoctrination and manipulation. For example, the Schools Council Moral Education Projects in England use a mainly social psychology approach to moral education, seeking in part to develop feelings and behaviours of a considerate kind by encouraging rewarding social feedback. This is obviously dangerous unless in a framework of justificatory reason.

I have argued myself, in partial criticism of Kohlberg's position, that the whole moral enterprise does have to have an affective prime mover. But this has to be at a very general and presupposed level, namely, at the level of a presupposed affective commitment to reasoning and to the value of reasoning. This is an affective obligation, as it were, to do and believe what my own reasoning authorizes, and only that. Once such an affective obligation is genuinely felt, then notions of guilt have a more general and more rational explanation than those provided by the accounts of Freud or Eysenck. Any appeal to emotions at a level more superficial than this distorts the true nature of moral justification and betrays the rational autonomy of the moral agent.

Similarly there is some truth in what Rich says about emotions being constitutive of the understanding of moral concepts. If a person determines what he ought to do, and neither does it nor feels any guilt, then there is a sense in which such a person does not really understand the meaning of 'ought'. R. M. Hare pointed this out in his account of prescriptivism. Again, however, this is a very general point about the connection between certain general concepts of a prescriptive kind like 'ought', 'should', 'duty' and 'obligation', and it is much more doubtful that a similar constitutive necessity applies to notions like 'harm' and 'murder'. Space precludes more than counter-assertion: but it seems to me that it is perfectly possible to understand concepts like 'harm' and 'murder' without any particular feelings. What it is *not* possible to understand is what it means to say 'I *ought* not to harm people', or 'I *ought* not to commit murder' without *either* acting on these prescriptions *or* feeling guilty about acting against them. This in turn is connected with my remarks about the necessity of *feeling* a commitment to reason if reason is genuinely to oblige, genuinely to move to action.

In a nutshell: rational moral judgment *is* logically prior in the moral domain, as Kohlberg asserts; and such judgment *can* move to action, as Kohlberg asserts; provided always that there is some affective commitment to rationality itself. How to get this is something psychologists have told us little about, and the problem cries out for research.

RICH REPLIES TO BAILEY

Bailey capably presents one version of the reflective and judgmental side of morality. But though his moral agent reflects and judges, a hiatus exists with action, probably because an organism-in-the-environment is not envisioned. The reason why action does not flow from judgment is passed over by Bailey as less a weakness than a characteristic of moral life. Why this is the case, if it actually is such, is not fully explained. He asserts without demonstration that Kohlberg is right to characterize moral development in terms of changing cognitive structures rather than in terms of changing affective patterns. But if the two are much more closely connected than Bailey admits, then it makes sense to work out both conjointly. He does not want to accept the notion that morality involves what concerns us deeply in terms of ourselves and others because, for him, all moral judgments must be rationally justified; hence, not all such concerns can measure up to this test. Elevating rational justification to a supreme position may become an *ex post facto* rationalization, a type of dessicated formalism, if divorced from the affective life. Bailey appeals to common sense in assessing 'sympathy' rather than evaluate the many studies of altruistic behaviour. The reason Bailey cannot connect moral judgments and the emotions lies in an inadequate theory of the emotions, a theory little more sophisticated than that of the emotivists themselves.

Part VIII: Moral Education

14. First Steps in Moral Education: Understanding and Using Reasons

JOHN WILSON

What do educators normally do when they want to educate pupils in some subject, or discipline, or department of life? Since 'education' implies not just any change (or even 'development') in the pupil's thought and action, but a change by *learning*, towards more understanding, truth, knowledge or rationality, they have first to agree on how—in general terms—pupils *ought* to think about the area. They take it, for instance, that the pupils who want to learn science should not look in crystal balls, or slavishly follow the authority of Aristotle, but use the procedure and reasons incorporated in (to use a brief phrase) 'scientific method'. In history, they are not encouraged to give reasons such as 'An angel did it' or 'Whatever the facts, it must have been the wicked Jews plotting', but rather reasons that emerge from a consideration of certain kinds of (historical) evidence: documents, private diaries, and so on. In mathematics, it is not the shape of the numbers which is to count, but their value. And so on.

In some areas of education—morality, religion, politics and others—there is no public agreement about this, or at least no clear and well-defined agreement. The temptation then is to turn away from facing this first question—that is, the question: 'What procedures or methodology or types of reason are appropriate for this area?'—and instead to look, empirically rather than logically or philosophically, at what actually happens in children's minds. Such an enquiry might be entitled 'development', and (I suppose) asks some such general question as 'What is the natural course, or set of changes, or "development," of the child's thinking in this area?' By 'natural' I mean, roughly, what happens if children are not firmly and decisively taught otherwise: if there is no strong intervention from educators. I take it that the work of Piaget, for instance, like that of Kohlberg, attempts some sort of answer to this question.

There might, I suppose, be (perhaps there actually are) attempts to trace a child's 'natural development' in thinking about the physical world, or past events;

223

and this might be important for educators in science and history, since it would tell them (briefly) what they were up against, what certain types of pupils would find easy or hard to understand and act upon at certain ages or 'stages of development.' But, in fact, it is noteworthy that science and history have managed to establish themselves successfully—much more successfully than moral education—*without* teachers bothering themselves very much about such enquiries. Teachers in science and history know how their pupils *ought* to think: and they plug away, taking account of the peculiarities of this or that child who confronts them, in a fairly *ad hoc*, non-doctrinaire, trial-and-error way.

I do not of course deny the value of any proven generalizations that might help the educator, though I am not optimistic about establishing them. To take a personal example: I have, over the last twenty years, taught chess to over 1000 pupils, of varying ages and backgrounds. Certain features emerge: some like to be shown in detail how particular pieces move before venturing on a full-scale game, others find it easier to play at once; some like to have explanations beforehand, others learn in the course of play; some seem to find it hard to grasp the concept of a knight's move, others the concept of check-mate; and so forth. Occasionally one comes across a young Capablanca, who grasps everything at a very early age; occasionally one meets pupils who seem incapable of keeping all the rules in their heads however hard and long they try. Understanding and motivation (their 'natural' attitudes, personality, style of thought) are inextricably mixed here, and I at least would not claim to have established any fixed generalizations (or 'stages,' other of course than the strictly logical stages of, e.g., having to grasp 'check' before grasping 'check-mate') at all: none, that is, above the level of the banal or commonsense.

If anyone (like Kohlberg) sets out to produce such generalizations, it must at least be clear just what the generalizations are *about*, and how they bear on the task of actually educating pupils. It is here that I find Kohlberg's work—and, I should add, the work of all other developmental psychologists—entirely baffling. I do not understand, that is, precisely what he is trying to say: what the 'stages' are stages *of*, what counts as a stage, what is meant by saying that stages need (or need not) to follow each other in a certain order, and so forth. This makes it difficult if not impossible to criticize his work other than on grounds of intelligibility.

That, in fact, is what I shall try to do—briefly—in what follows; my purpose being, not so much to advance some thesis which is 'for' or 'against' Kohlberg's, but just to show some of the difficulties involved. In general I hope to show—what seems to me much more important than any particular point—that this area is an extremely complex and thorny one, such as can hardly be tackled except by a small team of interdisciplinary workers with excellent communications: a team which would have to include at least one philosopher possessed of something like J. L. Austin's ability, or at least his enthusiasm, in the establishing of distinctions and precise descriptions.

I shall be talking about reasons, and need to make clear what I take a reason to be. By 'a reason for' I shall mean, rather specifically, 'a proposition used to justify'; in this sense, X's being or being used as a reason for Y implies that the connection between X and Y is (or is taken to be) logical, not causal. In ordinary usage, 'reason' extends beyond this and often means 'cause'; but the distinction between the two—whatever terms we may use to mark it—is, at least *prima facie*, fairly clear. If I am asked why I smoke, I may attempt some kind of justification—'Because if I didn't I should lose my temper more often, which I think would be worse'; or I may simply offer a cause or explanation—'I'm an addict', 'Perhaps I was weaned too early', or whatever. (One difficulty in interpreting a person's responses to 'Why ...?' is this ambiguity. If someone says that he behaves in a certain way 'because all my friends do', 'because the Führer tells me to', 'because that's how I was brought up', or whatever, he may be offering an explanation rather than a justification. Actually, many people—certainly many children—are not fully aware of the distinction, so that their responses are systematically ambiguous in this way.)

I say 'is or is taken to be logical' to distinguish reasons in general from *good* reasons. If I do something when the Führer tells me to, believing that his telling me to *justifies* the action, I am certainly using a reason, but (we suppose) a bad one; it is different from my just being *motivated* by what the Führer says. (Here again we see the difficulty of distinguishing verbal responses which offer reasons from those which offer causes.) Good reasons are those which we take *actually* to justify, not just those which some person may take to justify. And there is a further complication, for anyone interested in moral education generally. We want pupils not just to have reasons, not just to have good reasons, but actually to be *moved* by these reasons; we want these good reasons to be the causes of their behaviour. Thus a programme of research which found that a certain kind of moral education (1) made pupils grasp good reasons, and (2) made them do right actions, would be insufficient; we want them to act *because of* the reasons. (On the difficulties of practical assessment here, see Wilson, 1973.)

There is also the question of what the reasons are reasons *for*. Traditionally philosophers have distinguished reasons for believing things from reasons for doing things ('practical reasoning'); and our own moral tradition strongly emphasizes action, deeds, as central to morality. Of course one may justify what one does: but there is also the possibility of justifying (i) what *other* people do or have done or may do, (ii) what one (or another person) *feels*, and even (iii) what sort of person one (or another) *is*. These have received very little attention either from philosophers (at least in the Kantian tradition) or from psychologists working in the moral area. So here is another ambiguity, which would profoundly affect the selection and presentation of stories or cases to children, and also their responses: as well as making sure that the responses represent reasons, are we to seek for reasons for *action*, or moral *verdicts*, or *attitudes*, or what?

Much more ought to be said about these and other difficulties; but perhaps I have said enough to venture on one—only one—particular area: that marked by the phrase 'understanding reasons'. Many people, not only Kohlberg and his followers, allege the impossibility of children at certain ages or 'stages' being able to understand certain kinds of reasons; just as other people, of course (like myself), allege the opposite. This cannot, obviously enough, be settled by empirical data alone: we have first to be clear what we are talking about. I aim here merely at drawing a few distinctions which should enable us to settle the question.

1 First and most clearly, there is a distinction between ability and motivation: between being able to *understand* a reason or some rational procedure, and *wanting*

to use it. No series of tests, interviews or observations which did not take this into account could determine whether a child understands a type of reasoning; for it might be the case that the child has understood in the past, or is immediately capable of understanding if it is explained to him, or does in fact now understand all right, but (for one reason or another) prefers not to go in for it. It has to be shown that the reason *makes no sense* to him. I understand (more or less) the kind of reasoning employed by Nazis and Samurai, but would not—even in an extended interview—wish to go in for it.

2 'Understanding reasons' is hopelessly vague: what might it mean? An initial distinction might be between (a) understanding *that* X is a reason for Y, and (b) understanding *why* X is a reason for Y. But we need a further distinction between (a(i)) understanding that X is or could be used as a reason (not necessarily a *good* reason) for Y, and (a(ii)) understanding that X is a *good* reason for Y ('a proper reason', 'really a reason', or whatever). Thus one could come to understand that being Jewish is, for some people (Nazis and others), a reason for meriting certain kinds of treatment; one would understand sentences like 'They put them into the gas chambers because they were Jewish.' Here 'because they were Jewish' is, as it were, a quotation; in Latin the clause would be in the subjunctive mood (*quod essent*), leaving open the possibilities that (I) they were not in fact Jewish, and/or that (II) their being Jewish was the reason that the Nazis believed to justify their action, but was not necessarily a good (genuine, proper) reason, and/or that (III) it was just the reason they gave (they didn't even think it a good reason). That is (a(i)): it includes, perhaps, all that need strictly be meant by 'understanding something as a reason'.

However, it is natural to press for (a(ii))— understanding something as a good (appropriate, etc.) reason—since we are primarily interested in those reasons children ought or might actually be induced to use in their own moral lives; we want first to know if they can understand them. There is of course a conceptual connection between thinking X a good reason for Y and, other things being equal or at least under some circumstances, actually using that reason. If someone never acted on what he had said were good reasons for acting, we might sometimes doubt his sincerity in having said it. But the connection is a loose one; once we have established what a person thinks are good reasons, it is a further question how far and under what conditions he actually uses them. Understanding X to be a good reason for Y is in principle separable from any particular commitment; I can grasp that in chess-playing there are (good) reasons why I should act in certain ways, without at all being committed to playing chess. What I come to grasp is, as it were, a hypothetical imperative: '*If* one wants to win at chess, then such-and-such is a reason for doing so-and-so.'

Note here that understanding a reason as good involves having *some* kind of justification for it, but not necessarily any intrinsic justification, as it were. That authoritative books on chess, or competent teachers of science, say that X is a good reason for Y is quite sufficient justification for my believing that X is a good reason for Y. I understand *that it is a good reason:* but not really why it is (for the reasons would be internal or intrinsic to chess and science, which—we suppose—I know little about). This point is independent of the point about commitment not necessarily being involved. I might be committed (in advance, as it were) to chess-playing, and hence willing not just to appreciate that the textbooks were authoritative and gave good reasons, but actually to *use* the reasons (because of my actual willingness to play chess).

Understanding that X is a reason for Y is, minimally, just a matter of *knowing the rule*, 'When X, then Y.' For instance, I may understand *that* litmus paper turning red is a reason for believing there to be acid; and I can even understand this *to be a rule* without understanding what litmus paper is or what acid is. Similarly I might say to a child, 'Learn this rule: when squiggles occur, make sure you sqump at once.' So far the child has learned something (if not much): he has learned the practical rule, 'When squiggles, then immediately sqump.' Perhaps one day he will come to know what squiggles are and what it is to sqump, and then the rule will be of more than theoretical or academic interest to him. Actually, with an additional input of information (even *ad hoc*), the rule can be most useful: 'When gipsies, run'—the child with this rule firmly fixed in its mind may be told on a special occasion, 'That's a gipsy', and then he runs.

3   Next, the child may *have the concepts* marked by X and Y as well as knowing the rule linking them. He may come to know what litmus paper and acid are. He becomes able, in principle, to *use* the rule by identifying instances of the concepts. He may still not be very good, in practice, at identifying litmus paper and acid; but at least he has the concepts of them—he knows what the words mean (just as I have the concept of an aardvark all right even though I have never seen one, and the concept of red even though I am red-green colour-blind).

4   Next—though this marks a sliding scale, not an absolute distinction—the child becomes more competent at *actually identifying* the items X and Y. He not only knows what litmus paper is, but can (perhaps) pick it out in the real world even when slightly disguised as something else (like picking out humans from androids). Here he not only has the concept, but is more or less able to identify instances.

5   Different again (and more to do with reasons): he not only understands the rule linking X and Y, and can identify X and Y in principle and in practice; he knows something (a little, or a lot) about *why* the rule holds, about why litmus paper turns red in acid, or—to move now gently into the more emotion-charged area of moral reasoning—why it is people's wants or interests that should count as a criterion for moral decision and action. *Why* it is, not just *that* it is: a very different thing. This too is a matter of more or less: one can understand a bit about why certain rules or procedures will solve equations or produce electricity, without understanding everything about why they do. Indeed, it is not clear that much sense can be attributed, at least in some cases, to saying that one understands *everything* about (say) electricity—one will have to know almost everything about the physical universe. ('Why "throw the switch and light comes on"?' 'Well, it, er, closes the circuit.' 'Why does closing the circuit produce light?' 'Well, you see, electrons move ...' 'Why do they move?'—we soon run out of answers, even if we are professors of physics.)

I turn now more directly to moral reasoning. The kind of reasoning we want children to understand, I take it, is of this form: There are people, and what you should do must be determined by their interests (not by, say, what someone tells you to do or what you feel like doing). What precisely is marked by 'interests' may be disputed: let us say, perhaps more simply, 'what's nice for people' or 'what's best for people'. Now (a) it is entirely clear, as in 2 above, that very young children could be taught that *this is the reason to use*, even if they did not understand what was meant by 'a person' and 'what's best for people'. They would be able (not necessarily willing) to *advance that rule*: and if another child said, for instance, 'I should do that because I was told to/all my friends do/that's what I felt like doing', they would be able to say, 'No, *that's* not the rule: the rule is, you must do what's best for people.' That may not be much, but it is something. Then (b), as in 3 above, they can be taught—one might simply say, told and made to memorize— what a person is, and what is meant by 'best for people' or 'nice for people'; so that in principle they know what these terms mean. Then they could at least say, 'Look I've got to do something [something important, if we are talking about morality] here: I know the rule is, "Do what's nice for people": but being very thick, or blind, or something, I don't know which of the things round here are people or what's nice for them. Could you please tell me—fill me in on the facts—and then I'll know what to do.' There is nothing very peculiar in this: imagine I have learned a rule that bismuth is best for dyspepsia; a doctor, in too much of a hurry, tells me that I have dyspepsia and then runs off: I go into a chemist (knowing the rule) and ask for bismuth. It is clear that knowing the rule counts for something, even if I do not know what dyspepsia and bismuth are. This works even for (a).

The unreality of these examples stems, surely, from the fact that even quite young children (a) can easily grasp—particularly if it is taught to them—the rule, and (b) do in fact understand, however roughly, what is meant by 'person' and 'what's nice (good) for people'. Their grasp of the concept 'person' is often, no doubt, tacit rather than conscious: that is, they might not be able to give a full and correct definition on the spot if asked. (Nor can most adults.) But they know well enough that mummy and daddy and brother Steve and the man who comes to mend the windows are in one class, and the cat, the furniture, and the windows are in another. They may get a bit muddled (for sentimental reasons, I think, rather than lack of intellectual grasp) about beloved dogs, or even about babies—though these are, indeed, borderline cases which have much exercised philosophers; but they know what a person is all right. If there were more borderline cases, as perhaps on Andromeda, it would be more difficult; but in this world persons are pretty clearly marked—not least by the fact that they *talk*, which is in fact quite a good criterion from the philosophical viewpoint. (And no child is tempted to think that parrots or tape-recorders are people.) They talk, and have feelings, and desires and a point of view. Since the child could hardly grow up normally, or at all, if he were not surrounded by persons from birth, it is hardly surprising that most children know what people are. And if we have a peculiar child who has not picked this up, we can *teach* him.

So, it seems, not only (a) and (b) but also (c)—in 4 above—the child can actually *pick out* people. Now what more does he need for a full sense of 'understanding moral reasoning'—that is, in essence, understanding the rule, 'When people, then do what's nice for them', and knowing both in principle and in practice what a person is? We cannot demand (5 above) a full knowledge of *why* that is the rule to follow, though no doubt it helps greatly with their moral education to know why; for to know *fully* why would take the child (or adult) very deep into moral philosophy, and even then there might be disputes (not everyone is totally persuaded by, just as not everyone even understands, this or that philo- sophical theory). Nor can we demand the factual and emotional knowledge and awareness which would, of course, help the child to know just what *was* in fact nice or good for people; that is desirable, but not part of what is meant by 'understand- ing a reason'.

It will be said, of course, particularly by 'developmentalists', that if a child 'just parrots' the rule, he does not really understand it; and that is (subject to the distinctions in 2 and 3 above) true. He has to grasp that it is *a rule*, not just utter the words; he has to utter the words and *mean* them, as parrots do not. But why on earth should he not? I might teach a child the rule: 'When it's full moon, go and find a hedgehog'; and he can understand *that* this is a rule, even if that is all he understands. Particularly if, as is surely the case, he knows what a person/full moon is and what is nice for people/what a hedgehog is, he cannot be accused of parrotting. He understands all right.

Now it will be said by 'developmentalists' that the child is not really to be placed in stage such-and-such (5? 6?) 'of moral reasoning', because his real reason for producing the rule is that his parents have told him to—'really' he is in the 'good boy' stage (or whatever). I would not know what to make of this, since I am not clear what the stages are stages *of*. But, if or insofar as they are supposed to be stages involving the *ability to understand reasons*, this objection misses the mark. For it is entirely clear that I can *understand* and produce, say, reasons for certain procedures in mathematics or science or anything else, simply because my father or teacher told me that those were the rules to follow. We have no temptation at all to say that the child understands no mathematics just because he does not understand the logical foundations of mathematics (perhaps in Russell and Whitehead) on which all else depends.

Nor is this point really relevant to—what we are not, anyway, centrally discussing here—the child's willingness to use the rules in practice. One could think of all sorts of anterior motivations for that. One person might think simply, 'Father told me to use that rule', another, 'It's in the Bible' (the Golden Rule); another, 'Well, the expert moral philosophers and moral educators seem to agree, and I trust them.' Of course it is *better*, from several points of view, if they understand something of the anterior reasons: they are more likely to appropriate the rule as genuinely their own, and anyway understanding things is always desirable. Actually the reasons behind the rule are such as any child *can* understand: *understand*, if not always sympathize with (and hence not always or even often act upon). 'How would you like it if other people were nice/nasty to you?' generalizes this, and in particular cases remarks like, 'She wants a turn too', 'They like cake too', and so on in practice—though they need stressing and generalizing, to make the point stick—give most children an adequate understanding. For these remarks are, as it were, symptomatic of a general rule or principle that people count equally (more technically, that moral judgments are universalizable; for a full-scale defence of this, see Hare, 1963, 1981; Wilson, 1971).

These points, or some of them, are apt to meet with some resistance in the area of morality or practical action; partly, I think, because of a grandiose or inflated view of what it is to have a reason for *doing* something (as against a reason for *believing* something). Let me repeat, perhaps parody, what I am trying to say by reverting to the parallel with games-playing. Suppose we thought it very important for children to perform competently at chess, just as (I take it) we now think it very important for them to perform competently at a certain kind of moral 'game'—that is, a system of thought and practice which accepts the equality of other people. Now it is surely quite clear that we could and perhaps should teach the child all sorts of rules, reasons and types of behaviour at quite a low level of understanding. The child could understand the rules, for instance, 'When you're white and opening the game, move your king's pawn', 'If you have to choose between posing the rook or the knight, lose the knight', and so on. In these and similar cases we should want to distinguish between (1) the child's knowing *that* such-and-such is the relevant reason—knowing, for instance, that it's because the rook is worth more that he ought to prefer losing the knight, not because the rook stands in the corner of the board: and (2) the child's knowing *why* the reason is a good one (why the rook is worth more, why P-K4 is a sound opening move for white). There is now a temptation to say that, if the child cannot do (2) as well as (1), he does not really understand anything at all; but this is false, as can here clearly be seen.

What Kohlberg has shown, I think, is nothing about children's *understanding* at all: certainly nothing about their powers of understanding if they were taught. He has shown, perhaps, that reasons which children—in some cultures—*prefer to offer in moral dilemmas*, when interviewed in a certain way, etc., tend to be of a certain kind, and tend to group themselves in a certain order of ages or stages. That is, surely, quite unsurprising in itself (though the details are not uninteresting). Children will, probably, in comparatively unstructured interviews (if not too contaminated), tend to prefer and use *those reasons which are most salient in the regime which controls them at that age/stage*. That has nothing to do with understanding, but with salience (I mean, the extent and force with which certain things are said and done in a regime). First the child is largely egocentric; then his parents have to tell him what to do by simple and direct commands; then he gets the idea of simple rules—not lying, keeping promises and so on; and thence to a more sophisticated reflection about the interests of people. The force of these regimes— which, incidentally, seem to be inevitable for any growing creature (that is why the general picture would cause no surprise to any parent)—naturally motivates the child, no doubt in obscure ways sometimes but in general for obvious causes, to *want to use*, and hence to produce in interviews, one or another broad class of reasons.

Something may perhaps be gained for moral education by highlighting the preferred reasons, if only because they highlight the regimes which produce them. If a child lives in a world where his behaviour towards other people is (inevitably) largely dictated by a series of sharp parental injunctions, we might reasonably conclude that—whatever might be gained in the long term by teaching him the general rule about others' interests—we could not reasonably expect him to *want* to think (even, if the point be pressed, to be *able* to think: not because of lack of cognitive grasp but simply because of the regime's pressure) in that style, because he is (as it were) conditioned to think differently: to obey orders, not to consider interests in a more reflective way. But that too, I suspect, parents and teachers know perfectly well already. Moreover, as I have hinted, it is far from absurd to teach children rules that they are unlikely to profit much from in practice, in the immediate future; we might wish to lodge the rules in their minds (rather like lodging the Ten Commandments in more religious days) so that they may bear fruit in the long term. I believe that the general rule about people's interests—however that may best be phrased both philosophically and pedagogically—ought to be firmly implanted, and the child encouraged to repeat and follow it when he can, as soon as he can understand it. What I hope to have shown above is that *that* kind of understanding does not demand intellectual sophistication.

ACKNOWLEDGMENT

My acknowledgments are due to the *Journal of Moral Education* (published at the NFER, Slough, Berks, UK) in which some of the material of this article originally appeared (*JME*, 9, 2, 1980).

REFERENCES

Hare, R. M. (1963) *Freedom and Reason*, Oxford, Oxford University Press.
Hare, R. M. (1981) *Moral Thinking*, Oxford, Oxford University Press.
Wilson, J. (1971) *Education in Religion and the Emotions*, London, Heinemann.
Wilson, J. (1973) *The Assessment of Morality*, Slough, National Foundation for Educational Research.

15. Kohlberg's Stage Theory as a Progressive Educational Form for Value Development*

EDMUND V. SULLIVAN

Since I was one of the first to write a critical analysis of Kohlberg's work, let me hasten to point out that I do not share the current distemper for 'progressive educational reforms', one of which I would characterize as Kohlberg's work on moral development. Therefore, I do not wish to give consolation to the 'new right' in educational thinking which tends to trivialize Kohlberg's immense contribution to moral discourse and practice. In order to commence with a discussion of Kohlberg's work for moral education, it will first be necessary to locate his work in the larger context of American educational philosophy.

If Kohlberg is a Piagetian in psychological matters, he is a Deweyan in educational ones. How is the question, 'Can values be taught?' handled from the point of view of progressive education? Dewey (1959) addressed the issue of the relationship of values to schooling quite succinctly:

> We have associated the term ethical with certain special acts which are labelled virtues and are set off from the mass of other acts, and are still more divorced from the habitual images and motives of the children performing them. Moral instruction is thus associated with teaching about these particular virtues, or with instilling certain sentiments in regard to them. The moral has been concerned in too goody-goody a way. Ultimate moral motives and forces are nothing more or less than social intelligence—the power of observing and comprehending social situations—and social power—trained capacities of control—at work in the service of social interest and aims. There is no fact which throws light upon the constitution of society, there is no power whose training adds to social resourcefulness that is not moral (Dewey, 1959, pp. 42–3).

From Dewey's progressive conception of the school, it is erroneous to attempt to separate values from intellectual development. In *Democracy and Education*,

*I would like to thank Allyn and Bacon, Inc. for permission to use extensive portions from a previous article entitled 'Can values be taught?' in a volume edited by M. Windmiller, N. Lambert and E. Turiel entitled *Moral Development and Socialization*. Copyright © 1980.

Dewey (1966) made note of a paradox that he saw when values and schooling were discussed. On the one hand, morality is identified with rationality; reason is set up as the faculty for critical deliberation in moral choices. On the other hand, morality and values are thought of as an area in which ordinary knowledge and intellectual skills have no place. Dewey saw this separation as having a special significance for value education in the schools. If valid, it would render such an enterprise hopeless by setting up the development of character as supreme, and at the same time treating the acquisition of knowledge and the development of understanding as something separate from character development. Dewey obviously saw the school as a moral and value-laden enterprise. There is therefore a rationale in Dewey's progressivism to have some reflection on values in the school.

In the context of progressive education and reform, Kohlberg's cognitive-developmental approach to values and values education is explicitly allied to Deweyan progressivism. Kohlberg and Mayer (1972) maintain that Dewey was a 'developmentalist' in terms of educational aims:

> The aim of education is growth or development, both intellectual and moral. Ethical and psychological principles can aid the school in the greatest of all constructions—the building of a free and powerful character. Only knowledge of the order and connections of the stages in psychological development can insure this. Education is the work of supplying the conditions which will enable the psychological functions to mature in the freest and fullest manner (Dewey, 1964).

Kohlberg's stages of moral development are claimed to be psychological stages of moral development which add flesh to Dewey's developmental bones (Kohlberg, 1971b, 1975). Kohlberg (1971b) suggests that his stages of moral development are a basis for developmental programmes in value education. Since they are formal stages, he claims that they get around the problem of indoctrination.

Specifically, Kohlberg aligns himself with Dewey, and reiterates, in contemporary terms, the 'progressive ethos':

1   That the aims of education may be identified with development, both intellectual and moral.
2   That education so conceived supplies the conditions for passing through an order of connected stages.
3   That such a developmental definition of educational aims and processes requires both the method of philosophy or ethics and the method of psychology or science. The justification of education as development requires a philosophical statement explaining why a higher stage is a better or a more adequate stage. In addition, before one can define a set of educational goals based on a philosophical statement of ethical, scientific, or logical principles, one must be able to translate it into a statement about psychological stages of development.
4   This, in turn, implies that the understanding of logical and ethical principles is a central aim of education. This understanding is the philosophical counterpart of the psychological statement that the aim of education is the development of the individual through cognitive and moral stages. It is characteristic of higher cognitive and moral stages that the child himself or herself constructs logical and ethical principles; these, in turn, are elaborated by science and philosophy.
5   A notion of education as the attainment of higher stages of development, involving an understanding of principles, is central to 'aristocratic', Platonic doctrines of liberal education. This conception is also central to Dewey's notion of a democratic education. The democratic educational end for all humans must be 'the development of a free and powerful character'. Nothing less than democratic education will prepare free people for factual and moral choices which they will inevitably confront in society. The democratic educator must be guided by a set of psychological and ethical principles which he or she openly presents to students, inviting criticism as well as understanding. The alternative is the 'educator-king', such as the behaviour-modifier with an ideology of controlling behaviour, or the teacher-psychiatrist

with an ideology of 'improving students' mental health. Neither exposes his or her ideology to the students, allowing them to evaluate its merit for themselves.

6   A notion of education for development and education for principles is liberal, democratic, and nonindoctrinative. It relies on open methods of stimulation through a sequence of stages, in a direction of movement which is universal for all children. In this sense, it is natural (Kohlberg and Mayer, 1972, pp. 493–4).

AN EXAMPLE OF A MORAL EDUCATION PROGRAMME

The discussions that follow are derived from earlier involvement by myself and my research associates as teachers in pilot courses in value education in both elementary and secondary schools (Sullivan and Beck, 1975). A major motive in our efforts at the elementary level was our desire to understand children's thinking on value issues during the middle years of childhood. Initially, the work of Piaget and Kohlberg was most informative. Our work was restricted mostly to students in the later elementary school years.

A key notion in all our work with students and teachers is 'structure'. The complexity of value questions and the uneasiness with which both teachers and students begin critical examination of value issues require, it seems to us, some ground rules and boundaries. Our approach has been to attempt to give students an initial sense of structure and order through what we call the 'principled discussion' method. We outlined topics for fifth and sixth-graders under the broad heading of 'human relations'. For each of the topics, we offered guiding questions for the discussion. At first glance this structure seems rigid, but in fact it allows ideas to be examined within a broad framework. We labelled this framework a mini-course in human relations, with the following content topics, each of which might occupy about two forty-minute periods:

1   Rules people have given us
2   The place of rules in society
3   Exceptions to society's rules
4   The individual's need for other people
5   Helping other people
6   The self and others
7   The place of law, judges, and police
8   The place of governments and other authorities
9   Law-breaking and the place of punishment.

In all, there are twenty topics suggested under this one unit. Children were given study notes on each of these topics to provide a structure and a sense of direction for the learning session or sessions.

Evaluation of our work in the elementary schools was both formal and informal. Of specific interest here is our formal evaluation procedure. Since we were interested in how children deliberate on moral issues, we found Kohlberg's work on moral reasoning directly relevant. In the fall of 1970, we interviewed forty-two students who deliberated on Kohlberg's moral dilemmas. These students were divided into two groups: (1) those who would participate in our mini-course in ethics (the experimental group); and (2) those who, as a group, were matched on age, IQ, and social-class status with the experimental group, but who did not participate in the mini-course (the control group). We assessed these students, using Kohlberg's moral dilemmas, over a two-year period at three intervals. A pretest was given to all the students before the experimental group started to work with value issues. The first post-test was given at the end of the course. The second or follow-up was given to both groups one year after completion of the course. These interviews were scored in order to determine the stage of each child's moral reasoning.

On the pretests, all the students were assessed as being at the preconventional level, and the two groups were similar on this account. Both groups at the first post-test showed an advancement toward conventional stages, but there was some indication that the experimental group was somewhat more accelerated in this development. Finally, in a post-test follow-up done a year after the mini-course was completed, the experimental group showed significantly higher levels of conventional reasoning (i.e., Stage 4 thinking).

Looking at the results more descriptively—that is, from the difference between the control group which showed some development in moral reasoning without formal help and the experimental group which participated in the twice-weekly discussions—we would say that both groups show a general developmental trend from predominantly Stage 1 thinking on the pre-test to predominantly Stage 3 thinking on the post-test. The differences between the two classes are seen in: (1) the emergence of Stage 4 reasoning in both the post-test and follow-up for the experimental class, while no Stage 4 thinking was apparent in the control group children; and (2) after the first year, the experimental children no longer responded at Stage 1 (external authority ... avoid punishment), but began thinking more at Stages 2 and 3. On the other hand, the control group children did not drop Stage 1 thinking as readily. As with the control group, the experimental group began with the same reliance on external authority structures (preconventional), but by the end of the first year these students had definitely swung to an orientation in which they began to think more independently, using ideas of fairness, reciprocity, and equal sharing. At the same time, a few students began thinking in the larger context of society.

Our work with adolescents preceded our elementary school efforts. The major part was carried out in two different secondary schools over a period of about four years. In the first school, one of our staff took over a third-year class in the humanities two days per week to discuss moral issues. Students at this age level are normally in what Kohlberg calls the conventional morality stage. For the most part, the issues raised in class were designed to produce reflection on moral conventions and to consider alternative, sometimes novel, solutions. Thus we encouraged what Kohlberg calls postconventional morality. During the initial meetings with the students, we had a direct discussion of moral theories and principles. The teacher structured the class much more at the beginning, then increasingly relinquished control of topics as the class progressed. The discussions were always informal, however, in a relaxed atmosphere. This class lasted for only one semester and we were not sure what we could accomplish in so short a period.

The class consisted of seventeen students who volunteered to participate in an 'experimental' ethics course. A matched comparison group (control) was assessed on moral reasoning at various times but did not attend the 'experimental' ethics course. Members of the experimental ethics class were encouraged by the teacher to discuss a number of topics. Although the following sequence was not rigidly adhered to, and side topics were introduced occasionally, the topics were in general as follows:

1. Some distinctive features of moral goodness
2. Myself and other people
3. An individual's need for other people
4. Acting out of moral reasons
5. The place of mixed motivations
6. The importance of spontaneity and single-mindedness
7. The place of moral principles and rules
8. The value of the act versus the value of the rule
9. Conscience
10. Justice, equality, and fairness
11. Developing mutually beneficial solutions
12. Moral diversity
13. The pursuit of happiness
14. An analysis of various virtues and vices.

Our purpose as educators would be to draw out those ideas that embodied a more critical attitude toward moral issues through asking questions and helping students to sustain this kind of thinking in discussion. Since most of our students were reasoning at the conventional level (Stages 3 and 4), we attempted for the most part to delve into the reasoning behind conventional norms, an understanding which we would typify as postconventional reasoning. At least from the point of view of moral reasoning, the results of our efforts can be seen in Figure 1.

When the ethics class ended, there seemed to be no detectable difference between the experimental group and the control group. At first we attributed this to the fact that the class was too short in duration. More informal interviews with students, however, made us think that we had accomplished more than was indicated by the Kohlberg moral judgment questionnaire. The students in the

Figure 1. *Mean Percentage of Stage 5 Usage for Each Group at Each Test Time*

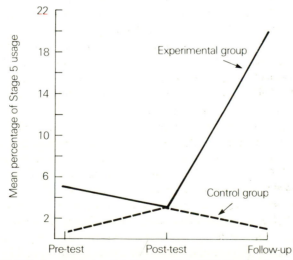

Reprinted with permission from Beck, Sullivan and Taylor (1972) 'Stimulating Transition of Postconventional Morality: The Pickering High School Study' *Interchange*, Winter, pp. 28-37.

ethics course seemed more reflective; their informal statements and evaluations of the course indicated a considerable amount of conflict which we felt was possibly growth-producing. In this light, the follow-up results were particularly intriguing. It would seem that the passage of time had tempered the feeling of conflict, and natural life experiences had produced opportunities for exercising some of the postconventional notions and skills gleaned from the classes. At any rate, the fact that the change that occurred was a Stage 5 change is reassuring, since it was in the direction of this kind of thinking that we had hoped to encourage our students.

After this initial effort in the secondary schools, we launched a full-scale effort for two semesters in another school. By this time we had devised an elementary ethics textbook for high school students and had identified other materials to bring to the classroom for discussion purposes. In our enthusiasm, both my associate, C. Beck, and I attended and conducted these classes; we also had some graduate students assisting us from time to time. At least from the point of view of Kohlberg's moral assessment, our efforts appeared to produce negligible results. The discrepancy between the results at this school and the one where we had previously been successful made us reflect on ways in which the two courses may have differed. First, the teaching format changed when we worked in the latter (unsuccessful) school, which we shall call School B. We used a structured textbook in School B that was not available when we worked at School A. Although the content was postconventional in orientation, it nevertheless reflected the initial interests of the teachers and not the students.

Notwithstanding some of our own mistakes, I have, after working with students in high schools for several years, come to the conclusion that the pervasive institutional life of the school as we know it impedes critical thinking. Our experience in the two high schools made us aware of the 'hidden curriculum' discussed by critics of the school. We became much more sensitive to how the structure of a school can implicitly encourage a certain kind of morality—to be more specific, an authoritarian, conventional one. Many of the efforts of individual teachers to help students toward a postconventional (Stages 5 and 6) level of moral development are frustrated by a school atmosphere and organization which constantly emphasizes lower-stage values and principles. Or, to put the point more positively, a school atmosphere and organization which exhibits postconventional features can greatly facilitate the development of students toward higher moral stages. Unfortunately, most school systems are run on broadly authoritarian lines. A relationship of mutual trust, respect and cooperation between student and teacher is extremely difficult to cultivate in such an environment. I will return to this issue in the final section of this chapter since it relates to a critique of 'liberal' experiments as exemplified in our own work.

The answer to the question, 'Can values be taught?' from a progressive view of education is 'yes', with some serious reservations. Those reservations, however, bring into question whether the school is now, or ever has been, an institution amenable to progressive reforms.

BEYOND PROGRESSIVISM BUT NOT 'BACK TO THE BASICS'

The work of Kohlberg is now being attacked by the 'new right' in educational circles. His major sin among many (see Sullivan, 1980) is his belief in an end point of morality which questions 'conventions'. He is also being taken to task for riding rough shod over the 'moral virtues' (see Kohlberg, 1971a). If one accepts that Kohlberg's work does not represent a complete moral theory, as I do, then these criticisms cannot be considered as fundamental. It would be more judicious simply to point out the theory's incompleteness and go from there. My major criticism of Kohlberg's work in the area of moral education, in reality, reflects my criticism of progressive education in general. It is to these criticisms that I will now turn. A critical look at progressive education does not, to my mind, open the doors to the 'back to the basics' movement; rather, one should be challenged to go beyond.

I would venture that the development of a post-progressive approach to values must proceed on the assumption that values are already assimilated unconsciously and now must be made subject to a 'critical awareness'. This approach to values proceeds from a frame of reference quite different from the liberal and traditional conceptions of value education. A post-progressive perspective starts with the assumption that our culture is in the thralls of a profound value crisis produced as a by-product of the development of advanced Western capitalism. Moreover, this crisis will not be alleviated to any appreciable extent by liberal reforms or by a return to the traditional virtues of a previous era (all the King's horses and all the King's men will not put Humpty-Dumpty together again). In fact, one can put the development of this problem at the door of liberal institutions and reforms.

It is not a question, from a postcritical perspective, of whether values can be taught. The school is now, and has always been, an institution immersed in values. In fact, it legitimates current societal values and consolidates and enculturates them for a new generation. If we are facing a value crisis, as I think we now are, it is a crisis of legitimacy of the values that our culture holds. It is a crisis of mass culture, embedded in the values of unending production and consumption—a set of values which is increasingly failing to merit the allegiance of the young, the poor and the disenfranchised. If one considers the school a legitimizing institution, then it follows that the schools are currently involved in enculturating the virtues of consumer capitalism. One of the functions of education is to provide individual competencies necessary for the adequate performance of social roles; education therefore is fundamental to the social stability and functioning of any society.

Bowles and Gintis have a blunt, but I would say accurate, way of illustrating this enculturation process with reference to work roles.

> The way in which workers come to have a particular set of work-relevant personality characteristics or modes of self-presentation requires a more searching analysis.
>
> We find the answer to this question in two corresponding principles, which may be stated succinctly as follows: the social relations of schooling and of family life correspond to the social relations of production.
>
> We have suggested above that the social relations of schooling are structured similarly to the social relations of production in several essential respects. The school is a bureaucratic order with hierarchical authority, rule orientation, stratification by 'ability' (tracking) as well as by age (grades), role differentiation by sex (physical education, home economics, shop), and a system of external incentives (marks, promise of promotion, and threat of failure) much like pay and status in the sphere of work. Thus schools are likely to develop in students traits corresponding to those required on the job (1973, p. 78).

Moreover, this process is replicated throughout the educational bureaucracy. This may be seen from Illich's somewhat less than flattering view of schooling:

School sells curriculum—a bundle of goods made according to the same process and having the same structure as other merchandise. Curriculum production for most schools begins with allegedly scientific research, on whose basis educational engineers predict future demand and tools for the assembly line within the limits set by budgets and taboos. The distributor-teacher delivers the finished product to the consumer-pupil, whose reactions are carefully studied and charted to provide research data for the preparation of the next model, which may be 'ungraded', 'student-designed', 'team-taught', 'visually-aided', or 'issue-centered' (1972, p. 59).

It is not possible to develop this theme in elaborate detail for this chapter, but I hope the quotes present striking illustrations of what is potentially a powerful hidden curriculum whose values are more or less unconsciously appropriated. In the context of education, the question of whether values can be taught must be looked at from at least two perspectives. First, if education is a process whereby an individual acquires his or her world view from society, we must first look at the process itself (Bowers, 1974). Second, as to the process, we understand socialization from a theoretical perspective, but there is little actual knowledge of the particular cultural assimilation that is actually being transmitted from the teacher to the student (Bowers, 1974). There is hidden curriculum of which we have little knowledge as to what assumptions and myths are being transmitted in classrooms and schools. I purposely used the quotes of Bowles and Gintes and Illich to provide for some readers a shock of awareness of the possible underside of a socialization procedure. Without this understanding of our own assumptions and myths, there is no way of assessing how they influence the psychic and social well-being of the individual who unquestionably internalizes them (Bowers, 1974). It is frankly difficult for educators to examine the mythical world they live in. (This reminds me of a statement attributed to Marshall McLuhan: I don't know who discovered water, but it certainly wasn't the fish.) The dominant assumptions about work, technology, consumption, success, progress, etc. are routinely transmitted in schools and classrooms without any concern about their validity or consequences (Bowers, 1974).

Consideration from a post-progressive perspective of whether values can be taught demands a new process of reflection about schools. In a sense it is a reflection on the water that we are swimming in—the covert or hidden curriculum:

The press of school routines shapes the student's sense of reality in a far more effective manner than the regular curriculum, but since this aspect of the school is seldom seen in political terms school boards and parents generally ignore it. Yet a case can be made that the school routines that make up the covert curriculum are regarded by teachers and school administrators as serving a more pedagogically important function than the academic curriculum. The strongest evidence supporting this generalization is that students are often dropped from school for exhibiting behaviour that challenges the routines of the school; they are seldom dropped, on the other hand, because they lack the intellectual ability to deal with academic curriculum. When viewed from this perspective, it becomes apparent that one of the chief functions of the academic curriculum is to serve as a vehicle for conditioning students to adopt the values of the school's covert curriculum. More importantly, when it is understood that traditional school subjects are used to teach values quite different from their officially stated purpose, there is no longer any reason to be mystified about why the school curriculum continues to be so uninteresting to students and irrelevant to what they need to learn. The irrelevance of the subject matter curriculum is necessary if the student is to learn the values and traits of docility upon which his academic survival and later his career as a worker depend.[*]

---

[*]Reprinted with permission from Bowers, C. A. (1974) *Cultural Literacy for Freedom: An Existential Perspective on Teaching, Curriculum, and School Policy*, Eugene, Oreg., Elan Books, pp. 62–3.

Let me now return to a criticism of my own work previously discussed in the section on progressive reforms. Recall specifically the difficulty we seemed to encounter in attempting to foster postconventional morality. The more one thinks about it, it becomes clear why it was difficult to encourage or stimulate postconventional morality. Such morality bucks a pervasive and hidden curriculum of schools which is embedded in fostering conventionality.

If anything, the high school consolidates conventional thinking if you consider the age range 15 through 18 years. We found (Sullivan *et al.*, 1975) on a sample of over 200 students from three high schools, that there was a model predominance of Kohlberg's Stage 3 thinking, with the beginning of Stage 4 and Stage 5 reasoning. It is easy to see why a course in value education simply will not work in encouraging reflective thought. The very structural life of the school is locked into a conventional set. In fact, even the discipline problems to which 'traditionalists' allude are not at a level of postconventionality, but more likely are of a preconventional kind. That conventionality is precarious can partly be attributed to the arbitrary nature of school convention. In our discussions with students, they clearly indicated their cynicism for what they felt was implied mindless conformity to school officials' dictums. The possibility of joint decision-making about school conventions is hardly ever considered by school officials, and students appear not to expect any part in that decision-making. Moreover, the conventional consensus of our culture is breaking down as I have already suggested, and this is reflected in school disruptions. Nevertheless, it strikes me that our high schools succeed all too well in enculturating conformity in most students and fail completely in an experiment in democratic living. The problem as seen from a postcritical perspective is simply that the schools are not, by their very nature in our society, programmed to enculturate a democratic process. Now however, the students do not appear to be wedded very strongly to the values implicit in the schools. This generation of students is coming into a post-industrial society and they are vaguely aware that the industrial model of the school and its hidden curriculum has precious little to offer them. The question, 'Can values be taught in the school?' can be answered 'yes', but it is becoming apparent that these values are dysfunctional.

There are no easy answers to our present problems. It is a cultural crisis. These types of resolution will not come from journeys 'back to the basics' or by liberal, piecemeal, social engineering—which I would judge my previously quoted work to be. A post-progressive perspective ultimately sees the situation as one needing transformation, which is, in essence, radical change. As one distinguished educator puts it:

> My concerns are with autonomy and reflectiveness and justice, with the kind of knowing that penetrates and transforms. The problems of curriculum, as I see them, must be confronted in the contexts of the technetronic society and its multiple systems of channeling and control. The pressures on the individual must be taken into account, along with the inequities that persist throughout the culture, the erosion of standards, and the collapse of trust. The capacity of the individual to feel himself to be a subject is linked for me, to his ability to conceptualize effectively, yes, and competently—the structures and forces that dominate the situations of his life. For these reasons, I find it extraordinarily difficult to think in terms of either/ors, to believe that humanism excludes competencies, or that competencies are, by definition, inhumane. Nevertheless, like John Dewey at the beginning of *The Child and the Curriculum*, I would say that the apparent dichotomy confronting us grows 'out of conflicting elements in a genuine problem—a problem which is genuine just because the elements, taken as they stand, are conflicting. Any significant problem involves conditions that for the moment contradict each other' (Greene, 1975, pp. 175–6).

In the above context, the recent work of Kohlberg on the moral atmosphere merits our interest and attention (Power and Kohlberg, 1980). It is in this recent work that Kohlberg chooses an attempt to encourage the practice of 'democratic decision-making' in the high school and then to assess its effect on the moral development of adolescents. This later work allows practice to inform theory rather than the opposite way around, which was characteristic of his earlier research on moral action. In the end, in spite of my criticisms of the theory on ideological grounds (Sullivan, 1977), it must be nevertheless reckoned as the most powerful research on moral discourse and practice in the last twenty years—no mean accomplishment.

REFERENCES

Bowers, C. A. (1974) *Cultural Literacy for Freedom: An Existential Perspective on Teaching, Curriculum, and School Policy*, Eugene, Oreg., Elan Books.

Bowles, S. and Gintis, H. (1973) 'I.Q. in the U.S. Class Structure', *Social Policy*, January/February.

Bowles, S. and Gintis, H. (1976) *Schooling in Capitalist America*, New York, Basic Books.

Dewey, J. (1959) *Moral Principles in Education*, New York, Philosophical Library.

Dewey, J. (1964) 'What psychology can do for the teacher', in R. Archambault (Ed.), *John Dewey on Education: Selected Writings*, New York, Random House.

Dewey, J. (1966) *Democracy and Education*, New York, The Free Press.

Freire, P. (1974a) *Pedagogy of the Oppressed*, New York, Seabury Press.

Freire, P. (1974b) *Cultural Action for Freedom*, Harmondsworth, Penguin Books.

Greene, M. (1975) *Curriculum and Cultural Transformation: A Humanistic View*, Cross-Currents, Summer.

Illich, I. (1972) *Deschooling Society*, New York, Harrow Books.

Kohlberg, L. (1971a) 'From is to ought: How to commit the naturalistic fallacy and get away with it in the study of moral development', in T. Mischel (Ed.), *Cognitive Development and Epistemology*, New York, Academic Press.

Kohlberg, L. (1971b) 'Stages of moral development as a basis for moral education', in C. Beck, E. Sullivan and B. Crittenden, *Moral Education: Interdisciplinary Approaches*, Paramus, N.J., Paulist Press.

Kohlberg, L. (1975) 'The cognitive-developmental approach to moral education', *Phi Delta Kappan*, 56, pp. 670–7.

Kohlberg, L. and Mayer, R. (1972) 'Development as the aim of education', *Harvard Educational Review*, 42, pp. 449–96.

Power, C. and Kohlberg, L. (1980) 'Religion, morality and ego development', in C. Brusselmans and J. Fowler (Eds.) *Toward Moral and Religious Maturity*. Monstown, N.J.: Silver-Burdett, pp. 343–72.

Sullivan, E. (1977) 'A study of Kohlberg's structural theory of moral development: a critique of liberal social science ideology', *Human Development*, 24, pp. 3532–76.

Sullivan, E. (1980) 'Can values be taught?' in M. Windmiller, N. Lambert and E. Turiel (Ed.) *Moral Development and Socialization*. Boston, Allyn & Bacon Inc.

Sullivan, E. V. & Beck, C. (1975) 'Moral education in a Canadian setting', *Phi Delta Kappan*, 56, pp. 697–701.

Sullivan, E. V., Beck, C., Joy, M. and Pagliuso, S. (1975) *Moral Learning: Some Findings, Issues and Questions*, Paramus, N.J. Paulist Press.

Interchange

WILSON REPLIES TO SULLIVAN

I am in broad sympathy with what Sullivan says, but it suffers from a number of (fairly characteristic) *idées fixes* which it is worth clarifying because they infest most of what psychologists and sociologists say about 'values' and 'education'.

1   The first is the idea that education is just another case of society pushing individuals around; as he quotes Bowers, 'a process whereby an individual acquires his or her world view from society.' That is not what 'educate' means. Educating people in (say) Nazi Germany or any other anti-rational society would precisely *not* mean any process of 'socialization' or 'enculturation' of that kind; it would mean (as it always does mean) a process of making people more reasonable (well-informed, understanding, aware, etc.) in certain areas—with the result, no doubt, that they might turn against their society.

2   This ties in with the idea, implicit in much educational writing, that we cannot avoid ideology. Sullivan takes some kind of stand in terms like 'progressive', 'post-progressive', 'critical thinking', 'democratic decision', and so on. But either (a) any of these values (whatever they may be) is just part of his, or our, or somebody's ideology, in which case why should there be any reason to promote it or research into it?; or (b) it is *for strictly logical reasons* necessary or desirable if people are to be educated, in which case these reasons must be made clear. (See Wilson and Cowell, 1983 on democracy.)

3   It also ties in with the idea, demonstrably naive, that schools and other institutions somehow pass on or transmit 'values', rather like infectious diseases, in some direct osmotic way to their pupils; if they are 'authoritarian' then the pupils have 'authoritarian' values, if 'democratic' the opposite, and so on. But (a) it is not clear what these terms are supposed to *mean*, and (b) if one has (say) democratic aims it does not follow one should use democratic methods. As a pupil, intense pressure, persuasion and sanctions were put upon me (in an 'authoritarian' way?) at school—for what? Not to conform uncritically, but precisely to *make* me 'critical', 'democratic', contra-suggestible, and so forth. Is that regime 'authoritarian' or 'democratic'? At this point the terms are clearly useless. (In my judgment, a great deal of the social background for effective moral education ought to be highly-structured, well-disciplined, strict, etc. *in order to* produce autonomous adults; whether true or false, that is an open question.)

243

Of course psychologists and even, I suppose, sociologists have their job to do; but what we want from them is not broad theories about development, or the way in which schools legitimize social values, or whatever. We want to know how to achieve goals in education which can be shown (by analytic philosophy or indeed common sense) to be reasonable and desirable. Thus the ability to discuss with other people is clearly educationally desirable; very well, how are we to promote this? What can psychologists and sociologists tell us about the most effective practical methods? Or, it seems to be a point of logic (not just of 'Kohlbergian theory') that other people's interests should count; that justice is a good thing. OK: as a mere philosopher I look to Sullivan *et al.* to tell us how to get pupils to grasp this and put it into practice. Educators have a particular set of journeys to make, and need particular information from the empirical disciplines—not just any information, and not theories, and particularly not ideologies (see Loukes *et al.*, 1983, Ch. 10).

REFERENCES

Loukes, H., Wilson, J. and Cowell, B. (1983) *Education: An Introduction*, Oxford, Martin Robertson.
Wilson, J. and Cowell, B. (1983) 'The democratic myth', *Journal of Philosophy of Education*, 17, 1.

SULLIVAN REPLIES TO WILSON

Although my own paper on Kohlberg and education takes a very different direction and is self-consciously political, it is not clear that my position on Kohlberg is antithetical to Wilson's. In fact, some of the minor caveats that he makes on Kohlberg are made in my own paper with a slightly different linguistic turn.

I find it interesting that Wilson maintains that Kohlberg has shown nothing about children's ability to understand reasons; rather his stages represent or highlight particular regimes that affect children at different ages, thus affecting their preferences for using or proffering reasons. Here I would venture that neither Wilson with his notion of *regimes* nor Kohlberg with his *stages* has made an adequate study of the *ecology* of moral judgments. It seems that the earlier work of Kohlberg on moral judgments (between 1958 and 1970) and Wilson's present position, locate the moral judgment as simply an individual's competence to venture moral judgments and reasons. Could not these regimes that Wilson speaks about be a result of the regimen of schooling itself as we now know it? It is here that I believe Kohlberg may have gone beyond Wilson when he ventured into the area of moral environments (i.e., Kohlberg's just community work). What is clearly absent in Wilson's paper is a deep sensitivity to the contextual nature of our moral universe. If we follow up Wilson's regimen idea, it is quite reasonable to ask, is this regimen generated by some age-related phenomena as he appears to indicate, or is it the result of the complex relation between the students' moral universe and the teaching-schooling context? If it is the latter, then much greater attention has to be given to the teacher as moral educator and not simply to the student as moral learner. This will short-circuit our proclivity simply to blame students for their moral turpitude; placing part of the onus for a moral universe on the process of schooling itself.

Part IX: Moral Curriculum

16. Kohlbergian Programmes in Moral Education: A Practical Review and Assessment

JAMES S. LEMING

The purpose of this chapter is to provide an appraisal of the work of Lawrence Kohlberg at the contact point at which his philosophical and psychological writings on moral development and moral education have been translated into educational practice in North America. The thrust of this evaluation will be formative rather than summative[1] in that Kohlberg's work in curriculum development is clearly 'in progress'. As work 'in progress' it is therefore as important to evaluate where his curricular ideals are heading as it is to assess where they have been.

The focus of this review will be decidedly practical. This position is adopted for two reasons. First, the theoretical writings of Kohlberg on moral development and moral education have been reviewed to the point of satiety. While much of this critical work has been insightful and appropriate regarding weaknesses or omissions in Kohlbergian theory, many of these critiques have either misinterpreted his thinking or assumed an overly restrictive interpretation. The purpose of this chapter is not to add to this dialogue since I am sure the other contributions to this volume will ably restate the many conflicting perspectives and interpretations which swirl around Kohlbergian theory. There is also a sense in which many of the criticisms of Kohlberg are now moot in the light of recent revisions in the theory, many of which were in part a direct result of his response to earlier critical reviews. My second reason for adopting a practical perspective is that if any curricular programme is to become an effective force in education it must develop as a result of practical activity.[2] It must gain acceptance in the eyes of those directly involved in the practice of education. For theory to move to practice the transition from academe to the real world of schools must be such that the end product, a curriculum or programme, is both attractive and satisfies a wide range of practical political, social and educational needs. It will be argued that at present the greatest obstacles to the success of Kohlbergian programmes lie in this realm of practical concerns. The history of educational reform lies littered with the corpses of elegant theories which for a variety of practical reasons have failed to have any lasting impact on life in schools. This paper will highlight the important practical issues which are relevant to the educational programmes of Kohlberg. It will become apparent in the course of this paper that the moral discussion approach of Kohlberg was built largely on theory without prior consideration of important practical issues. Kohlberg's own reflections on and revisions of his earlier educational programme indicate a move toward knowledge building and curriculum development based on the practical activities associated with the development of just communities in public schools.

Any appraisal of the work of a living scholar must, in the interest of relevance, attend to the latest formulation of his thinking. While earlier work may be of historical interest and serve to illuminate current thinking, an accurate assessment of a person's work demands contemporaneity. As a result the next section of this chapter will trace the evolution of Kohlbergian moral education programmes through 1983. In doing so it will be shown that many of the critical evaluations of his work are now dated.

EVOLUTION OF AN EDUCATIONAL PROGRAMME

In 1958 Lawrence Kohlberg completed his doctoral dissertation at the University of Chicago.[3] In his dissertation, based upon, but significantly extending, the work of Piaget,[4] Kohlberg presented his initial confirmation for a stage theory of moral development. Kohlberg's thesis presented an extension of the work of Piaget in that whereas Piaget was able to detect only two phases in moral development, Kohlberg hypothesized six stages. Piaget was reluctant to ascribe the formal properties of developmental stages to reasoning in the moral domain. Kohlberg hypothesized that the four properties of stages of cognitive development (qualitatively different, invariant sequence, structured wholes, and increasingly differentiated hierarchical integrations), as spelled out in Piaget's later writing,[5] applied equally well in the study of reasoning about moral questions. Also, whereas Piaget's observations regarding moral development had been limited to children between the ages of 6 and 12, Kohlberg's work, by inference at this point, carried the ideal of moral development well into adulthood.

Eight years after the completion of his doctoral dissertation Kohlberg published the first article in which he discussed the possibility of developmental moral education.[6] Whereas Piaget had not emphasized moral education much beyond the need for adults to diminish their own authority and exercise of constraint over youth and for schools to allow for more opportunity for cooperative behaviour on the part of students, Kohlberg's initial statement emphasized the need for teachers to engage in the presentation of genuine difficult moral conflicts and communicate with students in such a way that children are exposed to new cognitive elements. Kohlberg also emphasized the need for the teachers' developmental level of moral verbalizations to be matched to the developmental level of the child. The empirical basis of this first statement by Kohlberg rests on the work of Turiel,[7] which had demonstrated that children seem to accept and find comprehensible moralizing which is one stage above their own rather than one stage below or two stages above. No evidence is supplied in this initial statement by Kohlberg[8] that conflict accompanied by new cognitive elements will stimulate moral development. Evidence in this regard would await the appearance in 1969 of the dissertation of Moshe Blatt,[9] one of Kohlberg's doctoral students at the University of Chicago. Kohlberg attributes his interest and subsequent work in moral education to the inspiration of Blatt's work and refers to the finding that moral discussions can stimulate moral development as the 'Blatt Effect'. In Blatt's major studies classroom discussions of conflict-laden hypothetical moral dilemmas were held with junior and high school age youth for one semester.[10] In the course of the discussions teachers ensured that all students were exposed to 'plus one' moral reasoning, that is, reasoning at the next highest stage. At the end of the semester all students were retested for stage of moral reasoning, and those subjects in the experimental classes showed significant upward change when compared to the controls. Over the ten years following his original article on moral education Kohlberg presented and refined his views in a series of articles espousing the moral discussion approach.[11] This line of inquiry culminated in the real-world test of the Blatt effect in the Danforth Project.[12] In the moral discussion approach phase of the Danforth Project twenty social studies teachers from Boston and Pittsburgh were trained to conduct moral discussions in their classrooms. Although there was considerable variability in the results between classrooms, a substantial degree of change was shown in those classrooms that had the greatest range of moral stages, more discussion periods, and better use of teacher reasoning probes. A substantial number of other studies have also corroborated the existence of the Blatt effect. Four reviews of research on the Blatt effect report over forty studies in which the moral discussion approach produced significant stage advance in students.[13]

At present the following generalizations appear warranted regarding the moral discussion approach. The important conditions necessary to stimulate stage advance with the moral discussion approach are: (1) exposure to situations posing problems and contributions for child's current moral structure; (2) exposure to next highest stage; and (3) an atmosphere of openness and exchange. If the above conditions are present, evidence suggests that given a time frame of between one half to a complete academic year, discussing at least one moral dilemma per week, around one-third to one-half upward mean stage change will occur in the discussion groups. No change will be observed in control groups. Student stage change will be most pronounced in those groups in which student reasoning is a mixture of two or more stages and in which the teacher uses skilled Socratic probing. Also, while no change will occur without any one of these elements, it is not essential that the teacher supply them if the students supply them themselves.

In 1978, an article by Kohlberg appeared which signalled a shift in emphasis in his moral education programme.[14] This shift was marked by a movement away from the moral discussion approach toward the just community approach. This occurred, in part, because of practical difficulties encountered in the Danforth Project. As a result, the following statements concerning the nature of Kohlbergian programmes became dated.

1 The primary *goal* of public school moral education programmes should be principled moral reasoning.
2 The primary *method* of moral education is the stimulation of cognitive conflict through the discussion of moral dilemmas.

3 The proper *role* of the moral educator (teacher) is that of a Socratic facilitator not an advocate.

4 The proper content of moral education is hypothetical moral dilemmas.

Revisions in Theory and Practice

One mark of progressive theory building is the adoption of a position which is open to criticism and new experiences and perceptions. Unlike many educational theorists, Kohlberg has avoided a doctrinaire and dogmatic posture. Rather, he has revised, and continues to revise, his theory to account more adequately for experience and better explain the school's role in moral education.

The number of criticisms which were directed toward Kohlbergian theory was staggering. One bibliography lists over 100 between 1965 and 1981.[15] Kohlberg's post-Danforth revisions acknowledge the salience of many of these earlier criticisms, especially with regard to the need to incorporate within the theory attention to the content of moral reasoning and moral behaviour. Even though many criticisms were acknowledged by Kohlberg, no doubt the experience of attempting to translate theory into practice would have resulted in similar insights. Kohlberg acknowledges that the moral dilemma discussions which appeared to be such a powerful tool to researchers were of little or no significance to teachers and students. Zalaznick's observations (see below) pointedly present the student perspective.[16] The fact that one year after the Danforth Project evaluation only one of twenty teachers was still using moral discussion methods in the classroom speaks to the teacher's perspective. Undoubtedly, also of great significance was the realization that in the day-to-day life of school, there are experiences where teachers cannot avoid dealing with the content of moral reasoning and student behaviour. That is, incidents such as theft, drug usage, absenteeism, and the like may require a more forceful response on the part of teachers than the discussion of the problem.

These kinds of experiences and observations led Kohlberg to a broader vision of the proper goals and practices for moral education.[17] While Kohlberg's current position does not repudiate stage growth through the discussion of moral dilemmas, the new, broader emphasis marks a dramatic shift with regard to previous positions. Kohlberg's latest restatement of his position is embodied within the just community approach. Based upon the revisions discussed below, it will become apparent that many earlier criticisms of his work are now moot.

It is Kohlberg's current position that the teacher must become a socializer and advocate and move into the realm of indoctrination. This shift is primarily the result of the realization that real-world behaviour of students in the school must be dealt with and that moral educators can no longer wait until Stage 5, the developmental point at which moral thought presumedly leads to moral action. As a result of this realization, Kohlberg now holds that moral education can be in the form of advocacy or 'indoctrination' without violating the child's rights, as long as teacher advocacy is democratic and subject to the constraints of recognizing student participation in the rule-making and value-upholding process and recognizing the shared rights of teachers and students.[18] With this position Kohlberg corroborates Piaget's insights with respect to the critical role of the peer group in moral development. The role of moral educators is now seen as facilitating the functioning of peer group collective norms that are motivationally based on a strong sense of community. The focus of moral education now becomes group, rather than individual, development, and the major area of study and concern becomes group norms and expectations, something which Kohlberg says is neither internal consciousness nor external behaviour.

Just Community Approach

Because of the recency of the shift of attention from moral discussion to just community there exists far less published information on the approach. Wasserman's description of the operation of the Cluster School is the most complete,[19] and Power and Reimer's analyses are the best attempts to assess the nature of the outcomes of this approach.[20]

The Cluster School was an alternative high school within the Cambridge High and Latin School in which students and staff were given equal say over the operation of the school. A student-staff ratio of 10 to 1 existed, with the number of students being approximately seventy, selected from a lottery of volunteers to participate in this school within a school. At the heart of the school is the community meeting. At this weekly meeting real-life issues facing the school are discussed and decisions reached. Frequently these issues are moral in nature and, as Wasserman describes, standard moral discussion techniques were followed by staff. To this extent the just community approach represents 'old wine in new bottles', with the only difference being that the dilemmas are real-life rather than hypothetical. However, the focus on collective norms sets the emphasis of the just community approach apart from merely the facilitation of individual moral reasoning.

An important empirical question is what happens to students' 'morally speaking' as a result of their experience in a school-based just community. Reimer and Power studied this question through an analysis of the first four years of the Cluster School (1974–78).[21] The focus of their analysis was on the moral atmosphere of the school, and as a result was sociological rather than psychological. Specifically, they were concerned with the question of how norms come into existence and the process by which behaviour is brought into compliance with these norms. Reimer and Power see two parallel developments necessary for this to occur. First, they outline a sequence of phases of the development of collective norms within groups. These phases describe the development of group norms from a phase of norm proposal, to norm acceptance and expectation of compliance, to collective norm enforcement. Over the four-year period studied by Reimer and Power four normative areas emerged as of major importance within the school: social integration, respect for property (stealing), drug usage, and attendance (absenteeism). It was recognized that in the study of norms, basically constraints on behaviour, one also needs to understand the motivational basis by which individuals agree to act in accordance with the norms. This motivational dynamic was presented in terms of a sense of community characterized by mutual trust and care. Building mutual trust and care were seen as essential in that this sense of community was to provide the motivation for students to voluntarily put limits on their personal behaviour for the collective good.

It is reported that in three of the four normative areas collective norms developed and student behaviour was brought into compliance with these norms.

In one of these areas, drugs, no such norm emerged, and as Reimer and Power report, the fourth-year retreat of the Cluster School was a disaster, with widespread drug usage and physical fights over the issue.[22] The students had not seen the need for such a norm, and teachers had adopted advocacy positions which obviously had little impact. Also, as a result of the retreat it became obvious that the sense of community which had been evolving over the years was indeed very fragile.

The study of just communities is in its nascency, and it would be premature to judge the possibilities of this programme by the results achieved in one school. Clearly the shift in emphasis to social behaviour and the focus on collective norms are essential foci for a more complete approach to moral education. The results of the Cluster School raise many significant questions which will require additional study and reflection on practical experience, but as an expansion of the area of concern with respect to moral education it represents a promising development in Kohlbergian theory and practice.

Kohlberg's recognition that teacher advocacy is essential in moral education is an ideal that could radically reconstruct Kohlbergian programmes. Currently Kohlberg appears to limit the advocacy on the part of the teacher to advocacy of a sense of trust and mutual care and advocacy of a concern for fairness in issues facing the community. The problem, as demonstrated by the events in the Cluster School, is that on specific issues (e.g., drug usage) teacher views on what is in the interest of the school community are not shared by students. At this point what role should the teacher assume? Is it responsible to be a party to illegal activity? Should teachers step outside the collective norm framework and exercise authority and, if so, what effect would this have on the sense of community, collective norms and student behaviour? This is an exceedingly rich area for future inquiry, and one possibility would be for an incorporation of perspectives from social learning theory to account more adequately for the outcomes of experience.

Overall, Kohlberg's contribution to the study and practice of moral education is impressive on a number of accounts. First, his longitudinal study of the development of moral reasoning through stages is a highly useful tool for the understanding of moral communication. The research on the stages of moral reasoning is both empirically impressive[23] as well as an intuitively obvious reflection of reality to anyone who has spent time in schools talking to students of widely varying ages about moral questions. An understanding of the stages of moral reasoning is an invaluable tool for teachers wishing to engage in meaningful moral dialogue with students.

Second, there can be little question that the moral discussion approach results in stage growth. There exists no other approach to moral education which has been so systematically studied and found to yield such predictable results. If one cannot have confidence in this research finding it is hard to imagine any educational research one can have confidence in. If one sees the facilitation of advancement in moral reasoning as a valid goal for moral education, the Kohlbergian moral discussion approach provides a proven method.

Finally, Kohlberg's most recent formulation of the goals and methods of moral education, while not as well developed and researched at this time as his stage theory and moral discussion approach, represents a promising, rich, new juxtaposition of psychological and sociological insights. It holds forth the promise of a more unified perspective on moral education where concerns for collective norms, substantive moral content and democratic schooling are related to stages of moral reasoning.

PRACTICAL CONSIDERATIONS

The remainder of this paper will address what I see as the major practical issues which stand in the way of Kohlbergian programmes in moral education becoming a viable and continuing enterprise in public education in the United States. My observations in this regard will centre on the moral discussion approach. This perspective is taken because of the much richer body of literature upon which to draw. Since the discussion of moral dilemmas is also an integral part of the just community approach, to that extent these observations will apply equally to both approaches. For any reform to be successful to change the nature of schooling, it must be acceptable to a variety of constituencies. The benefits of the reform must clearly outweigh the costs. With respect to Kohlbergian programmes, I will analyze the perceptions and reactions of three critical groups: teachers, students, and administration/community.

The Teacher and Kohlbergian Programmes

The teacher plays a critical role in the implementation of any curriculum. The moral discussion approach makes special demands on teachers. It requires that teachers achieve an understanding of a complex developmental theory, that they demonstrate an array of new behaviours in the classroom and that they develop a commitment to the process of developmental education. This commitment is especially important in the face of society's expectations for academic success: room must be made in the curriculum for moral discussions. The purpose of this section is to examine the available evidence regarding the compatibility of teachers' world views, work conditions, and abilities with the moral discussion approach to moral education. How teachers respond to teacher training in moral discussion is a rich area of inquiry.

There is strong evidence to suggest that most teachers see moral education in terms of getting students to conform to certain acceptable standards of moral behaviour. Research with practising teachers suggests that when they are presented with alternative approaches to moral education, teachers will prefer approaches which place an emphasis on the obedience of students to accepted social norms.[24] Lortie, in his classic study *Schoolteacher*, found three kinds of responses among teachers when questioned about moral education: (1) about half stressed behavioural outcomes; (2) most references to moral outcomes stressed obedience and compliance; and (3) teachers saw themselves doing the work the family had failed to do.[25] There is reason to believe that for a significant number of teachers moral education is perceived as a means of social control and/or the socialization of youth into the existing normative structure of the school, community or society.

Given this perception of the goals of moral education, what happens when teachers are trained to do Kohlbergian moral education? The most insightful descriptive study in this regard is by Silver.[26] In 1977 a series of in-service workshops were held at Winston School, a co-ed college prep day school located in the Midwest. The workshops were conducted by a team from the Center for Moral Education, Harvard University. Teachers were instructed in the theory and practice of Kohlbergian moral education. Two years later Silver interviewed a sample (twenty-five of sixty) of the teachers who had participated in the programme regarding their perceptions about moral education, the unexamined assumptions underlying these meanings, and how these meanings had affected their classroom teaching. Silver found that while 80 per cent of the teachers reported a change in their thinking regarding moral education, they showed no concomitant shift in their teaching practices. The faculty at Winston School were well-educated, competent and highly experienced. As a group they were interested in ideas. It is usually the case that the more intellectually alive teachers are drawn toward approaches to teaching which involve intellectual challenge for themselves and their students. This makes the finding by Silver even more troublesome, and it is not an isolated one. Kohlberg reports that in the Danforth Project he and Fenton trained twenty teachers in the Boston area to use Blatt-type moral dilemma discussions in the classroom. One year after the study only one of the twenty teachers involved was doing moral discussions in the classroom. As Kohlberg succinctly stated, 'The operation was a research success but the educational patient died.'[27]

How does one account for the difficulty that traditional Kohlbergian moral education programmes have in becoming a continuing part of curriculum and teacher repertoire? Two related factors will continue to haunt efforts to incorporate moral education programmes into schools: teacher role definition and curricular press. As a rule most teachers see their primary responsibility as the transmission of a significant body of knowledge to their students. This knowledge, organized into a curriculum, is seen as essential to the students' future well-being and in the life of teachers there seems never enough time adequately to present this information. There exists substantial support within communities for the importance of this goal. As a result most teachers see little opportunity for moral discussions in their classrooms. Even if curricular press were not a factor in teachers' lives, we would still face the question whether teachers can be trained in such a way that they develop a lasting commitment to developmental moral education. I concur with Fullan's analysis that teachers will change their approach to teaching if and only if they perceive the change as of benefit to some problem which they face.[28] It is difficult to imagine a problem faced by teachers which would be ameliorated by moral dilemma discussions. In this regard Silver found that many teachers understood Kohlbergian theory and were favourably disposed toward it, but did not practise it due to perceived curricular press and irrelevance. He also noticed the intriguing phenomenon of teachers using moral discussion as just another way of enforcing school rules. The phenomenon of teachers transforming an innovation and thereby legitimizing existing practice was recently carefully documented in Popkewitz, Tabachnick and Wehlege's large-scale evaluation study of Individually Guided Education.[29] Their finding was that IGE reform in schools, while not significantly changing the schools, was used to give credence, by providing legitimation, to the existing school practices and norms that it was intended to change. As Silver points out, Kohlbergian programmes are not to be immune to this dynamic.

The above perspectives suggest that there are strong factors at work in the lives of teachers which make problematic Kohlbergian moral education programmes being adopted and implemented. At present the evidence suggests that teachers do not see the goals and methods of Kohlbergian moral education as essential or compatible with their lives as teachers.

If moral dilemma discussions as a method of moral education seem to offer formidable practical problems with regard to implementation, the just community approach appears to present almost insurmountable barriers. At least the moral discussion method is compatible with the concept of individual teachers in self-contained classrooms responsible for a given body of subject-matter. The just community experience, as described in the literature, requires structural reorganization of the school day to allow for more democratic functioning. To date, reports of the democratic experiments in secondary schools indicate it has been used largely in alternative school settings and primarily with alienated or disruptive youth. To this extent the approach has been successful and persisted because it solved a practical problem of a school system. To any careful observer of American education, however, it is intuitively obvious that the just community approach would create problems for most mainstream schools and would not significantly lessen any extant problem. For this valuable ideal not to be stillborn will require a major revolution in the thinking of teachers, administrators and community concerning the function of schooling. Today the response from the schools would be, 'It's not practical.'

If, for a moment, we assume that there exist no structural or role perception barriers to the implementation of Kohlbergian programmes we would still be left with the question, 'Can teachers be trained to implement such programmes?' The answer depends upon to whom one listens. It is obvious that from reports of the Danforth Project and from the myriad studies reporting the results of curricular interventions that teachers can be trained to be effective with the moral discussion approach. There exists a number of 'how to' methods books for those teachers who wish to learn on their own.[30] The Center for Moral Education at Harvard will also provide Kohlberg-trained in-service teams as well as summer institutes. In addition numerous courses on values education have sprung up at major and minor institutions. However, for training to be done well is a time consuming task. The institutes held in Cambridge, Mass. run for two solid weeks with each day a full day. Silver reports that the training programme at the Winston school consisted of a three-part, twenty-seven-hour in-service training course conducted by staff from the Center for Moral Education at Harvard University. Involved in this training was the analysis of teachers' taped discussions in classrooms.[31] Mosher estimates that, after the initial training, it takes an hour a week for approximately twelve weeks of audio and/or videotape review with the teacher to supervise adequately his/her progress in this area.[32] Obviously, training in Kohlbergian moral education is a time consuming and expensive proposition.

John Napier in two studies, one using pre-service teachers, the other using masters-level elementary school teachers, raises questions concerning teachers' ability to correctly stage score moral statements.[33] In both studies students were exposed to the Kohlberg theory and then asked to stage score a series of moral statements adopted from the Rest Defining Issues Test. Napier called this scoring intuitive in that teachers had not received training in scoring. Following this pretest students were given a self-training global scoring manual.[34] Subjects were then asked, after an appropriate interval, to stage score the same statements. Napier found in both studies no overall differences between intuitive and scoring guide stage scoring. It was also found that the teachers were incorrectly scoring on the basis of content rather than structure of moral content.

One cannot conclude from the Napier study that teachers are incapable of making accurate judgments concerning student stage of moral reasoning. The training the teachers received in the studies was superficial in that self-paced instructional materials were used. To stage score accurately is not learned easily—the Kohlberg sanctioned scoring workshop held annually at the Center for Moral Education involves two intensive weeks of training. Of course, teachers need not possess the level of sophistication in stage scoring required of developmental psychologists. It is possible to argue that the success of the Danforth Project would suggest that teachers can accurately recognize student stage responses and provide exposure to 'plus one' reasoning. However, it is equally plausible that the stage growth that occurred in this study and the other interventions was the result of naturally occurring stage differences rather than the teachers' awareness of those differences.

A related area of concern is teachers' ability to carry out Kohlbergian programmes in the classroom. This necessarily involves considerations regarding teachers' level of moral reasoning, as Kohlbergian moral education programmes require that teachers be able to understand student moral responses and to insure that students are exposed to the next highest stage of moral reasoning. These abilities in turn require that teachers be at an advanced level of moral reasoning. Clearly it would be most desirable if teachers were at the principled level, especially if they teach at the secondary or college level. If it were found that teachers were at a stage of moral reasoning lower than their students, the comprehension and preference studies[35] suggest that they would be limited in their understanding of student responses and thereby in their ability to insure plus one conditions.

What is the evidence on the stage reasoning of teachers? As a group are they sufficiently advanced to have the capacity for effectively carrying out Kohlbergian programmes? Giffore and Lewis found in a sample of Michigan teachers that the predominant stage orientations were 4 and 5A, with 43 per cent of the samples' reasoning at the principled level.[36] Consistent with this finding, Rest reports that among approximately 2500 college graduates 42 per cent of the samples, moral reasoning was at the principled level.[37] Wilkins, using a sample of Australian pre-service students, found the mean percentage of principled reasoning consistent with the above samples.[38] Bloom, however, using a sample of practising teachers, found that only about 30 per cent of their reasoning was at the principled level.[39]

While it is difficult to compare and interpret these findings, a few general observations seem warranted. Teachers' level of moral reasoning is similar to that of other college graduates, and generally college graduates' mean level of moral reasoning is significantly higher than that of school-age youth.[40] On a teacher-by-teacher analysis many teachers are sufficiently advanced to have the prerequisite ability to conduct effective moral discussions with school-age youth. On the other hand, the majority of teachers reason at the conventional level and many fall below the mean level of principled reasoning of high school students. It is these teachers who would seem to be incapable of leading effective moral discussions with youth until they have achieved a level of moral reasoning sufficient to understand correctly the stages and understand and control effectively the course of classroom discussion so as to maximize the potential for moral development. The question can also be raised concerning how teachers at the conventional level of moral reasoning would interpret the just community ideal, and whether they could participate in such a way to make a positive contribution. It would appear that anyone who failed to accept the concepts of individual rights within a democratic social setting would stand at odds with the ethos of the just community approach. It is obvious from my own experience in teacher education that around 25 per cent of existing teachers have failed to achieve Stage 5 thinking. Regardless of the excellence of the training programme, where teachers lag behind students in moral reasoning they cannot become effective Kohlbergian teachers. More likely than not, they will reject the goals of the programme.

To sum up, it would appear that there are a number of practical concerns associated with the role of the teacher in Kohlbergian programmes. First, even though Kohlbergian moral education appeals primarily to the more intelligent, creative, risk-taking teachers, it does not seem central enough to their existence as teachers to be incorporated voluntarily into their teaching repertoire. Second, for many teachers the enterprise moral education is perceived more from an inculca-tive than developmental perspective. Third, the time involved in training and supervision requires a major personal and financial commitment. Finally, even if the above issues could be surmounted, there would still exist the problem of the teacher engaging in self-immolation through ill-advised use of the approach. Witness the following description of what is perceived as model Kohlbergian moral education in the classroom. This event is reported by Sullivan as occurring as a part of the Danforth Project in the Brookline Public Schools:

> We began our discussions by examining sources of traditional moral roles, for example, parent authority, the law of the land, conscience, custom and public opinion, reason and revelation. In talking about parental authority as a source of moral rules, Jean argued:
>
> Jean: What difference does it make what rules your parents give you so long as you take them?
> Teacher: Because Adolph Eichmann's parents may have given him certain rules that might not be good moral rules.
> Jean: Yeah, but still the kid doesn't know what he's doing.
> Teacher: But I'm saying that a person can't rely on parental rules just because they are parental rules as being good moral guides.
> Jean: Because all it takes is one parent to tell you to kill or something. Then the next parent will say it.
> Teacher: What we're trying to do is to find some standard for making moral judgments. The idea of making judgments just on the basis of rules parents have given you may not be a satisfactory way. Different parents could give a lot of different rules and some of them might be better than others. You have to evaluate these parental rules by some standard.[41]

One does not have to live in a rural conservative area to break out into a cold sweat over the potential effect such discussions might generate for the school and moral education programme with parents' concern over the undermining of parental authority. Clearly, teachers would need not only technical skills but also practical judgment which would allow for moral discussions to be conducted as consistent with community values. As a former teacher who has used moral dilemmas in the classroom, it soon became obvious to me that political astuteness was equally as important as technical teaching skills to the effective integration of Kohlbergian strategies in the public schools.

Obviously student behaviour is an important concern to many teachers. Another practical question which must be asked concerns whether the goal of classical Kohlbergian moral education programmes—the stimulation of moral reasoning to higher levels—can be expected to result in any significant changes in student social behaviour. As discussed above, an underlying motivation for adopting moral education programmes is the expectation that they should result in positive changes in student behaviour. Analyses exist which suggest that a link between moral reasoning and behaviour should exist.[42] The evidence for this link is, however, of such a nature as to have little practical significance. In the most complete analysis of the empirical evidence to date, Blasi, while supporting a link between moral reasoning and behaviour, concedes that the evidence is ambiguous, conflicting and difficult to interpret.[43] Blasi sees the major problem in this regard to be the lack of an articulated and theoretically clear rationale for establishing expected relationships. Should such a rationale be developed and a link between moral reasoning and social behaviour be established, the practical question raised above would, however, continue to exist. For example, Masterson in a study with adolescents found a clear relationship between higher moral reasoning and such behaviours as friendliness, task orientation and support for classroom norms.[44] Bear and Richards, in a study with sixth grade youth, found that children who employ lower stages of moral reasoning display more conduct problems, and demonstrate more variability in conduct ratings as rated by teachers.[45] This line of research, since it deals with school-age youth in school settings, is clearly more relevant to the practical question being raised than studies which attempt to establish a relationship between principled thought and moral behaviour. Since principled moral reasoning is largely unattainable for public school-age youth, this latter type of data which is frequently cited to support the behaviour-thought link[46] is not of practical significance for most parents, administrators and teachers. Also, since the current line of research examines naturally occurring reasoning, rather than moral reasoning which is the result of an educational intervention, even conclusive findings in this regard would not meet the necessary conditions to have practical significance. It would still be possible for the identified relationship between moral reasoning and behaviour to be the result of a third underlying factor such as home environment. For research on this question to have practical significance it would have to satisfy the following conditions:

1   be conducted with school-age youth in a school setting;
2   compare social behaviour pre- and post-intervention;
3   assess behaviours seen as of practical significance to teachers, administrators and parents. This would require monitoring out-of-school behaviour as well as in-school behaviour;
4   show change in what adults perceive as a positive direction.

With regard to this last point, the evidence on student activism[47] suggests that the transition to postconventional reasoning may result in a transitional stage which is marked by moral relativism and political activism. It is highly probable that many of the individuals most interested in moral education would be unwilling to tolerate the antisocial impulses which evidence suggests might result if school-age children could be advanced beyond conventional reasoning.

While evidence regarding the above four points considered essential for practical significance is non-existent, recent revisions in Kohlberg's approach to moral education, most notably the just community interventions, offer considerably more hope. They offer more hope, however, predominantly because of a shift away from individual autonomous reasoning and a movement toward the individual placing himself within a social environment and acquiescing to its social norms. It would appear from a practical viewpoint that the outcomes of the just community approach are most consistent with the expectations frequently placed on moral education programmes. Also the life of such programmes, and therefore their success, would depend on these sorts of outcomes. Paradoxically, the feasibility of implementing such programmes poses far more formidable challenges than teachers holding moral discussions in their classrooms.

The Student and Kohlbergian Programmes

There is little question concerning the effect of Kohlberg's moral discussion programme on the moral development of students. Reviews of studies in which the moral discussion programme was implemented indicate convincingly that the programme has a significant effect on student moral reasoning, producing over the course of a semester or academic year betwen one-third and one-half upward stage change (see Note 13).

An important question which is relatively unexplored concerns the student reaction to participation in Kohlbergian programmes. That is, what do students 'think about' Kohlbergian programmes? As a result of being in such a programme do their attitudes change toward talking about moral questions? Do they 'buy' the stage concept and accept it as a significant educational goal, or do they see it as just another 'educational game'? One could argue that regardless of what students 'think about' Kohlbergian programmes, as long as moral development is facilitated, the approach is a valid one. However, it could also be argued that if the approach trivializes moral questions in the students' minds or creates a pattern of withdrawal from moral issues, then the collateral learnings are as important as stage growth. Historically one of the byproducts of the discipline-oriented post-sputnik curriculum development in the United States was a negative reaction on the part of students toward the revised subject-matter. Important to the long-term life of Kohlbergian programmes is the development on the part of students of a positive attitude toward moral curriculum. We have already seen that questions can be raised concerning teachers' acceptance of the moral discussion approach. Do students share this lack of enthusiasm?

The published evidence on this question is sketchy. I could locate only two sources, both students who had been participants in just community interventions.[48] The Kolber perspective is very positive and focuses on the affectively satisfying nature of the experience of participation in a just community. Kolber found the idea of living together and building a sense of community around the ideal of justice a rewarding experience. Kolber's perspective is a glowing one. Zalaznick, on the other hand, while concurring with many of Kolber's observations, has some serious concerns about the just community experience. Zalaznick discussed with his fellow students their impressions at the Scarsdale Alternative School. His overall view was positive primarily due to the emotional satisfaction engendered as a result of the closeness developed among students in their efforts to develop self-governance in the school. My own work in alternative schools confirms the observation that students find close relationships among peers and between peers and teachers very satisfying. An environment of caring is very attractive to many students when compared to a larger depersonalized school and social environment. This is especially true with regard to the more collegial teacher-student relationships which occur in more democratic settings.

Zalaznick and his fellow students expressed two major areas of concern. First is what Zalaznick refers to as moral intimidation. In spite of greater participation by students in the governance of the alternative school, students could sense that there was a purpose to the school that they could not influence. That is, students were aware that the goal to 'make us moral' had been planned out and students could not affect it. Students resented the fact that the school, in this regard, no longer belonged to them.

Zalaznick also notes the negative influence of developmental theory being shared with the students. The awareness of higher stages being better led to feelings of intimidation among lower-stage students and reactions of the sort, 'I'm Stage 2 and proud of it.' Students also reported resenting the feeling that they were being pushed to higher stages. Zalaznick also reported that students developed an awareness that there were right sides (higher-stage) and wrong sides (lower-stage) to moral issues. As a result of this awareness students seemed to close up cognitively and be no longer open to cognitive reorganization.

The second area of concern was labelled by Zalaznick as abuse of stage hierarchy. It was reported that students sensed that not only were there better 'contents' but also there were better or smarter students. It seemed as if to many students higher-stage learners had 'right' on their side. Related to this is what he refers to as a 'halo effect' in that students and teachers may see some students as of lower stage and of little potential.

There can be little question that many students find as satisfying expanded control over their lives in schools and the more open relationships developed in such an experience. In this regard the just community approach seems to be consistent with student needs. The moral discussion approach, however, seems to pose a serious problem in that it creates distinctions and distance between students and the perception that some are better than others. One of my most memorable experiences as a teacher was my ill-advised decision to let students know, after unrelenting insistence, their stage of moral reasoning. Most were stunned to the point of disbelief to find out that they were in fact much lower than they had imagined. Further moral discussions never had the spontaneity and openness following this event. My own personal experience and the perceptions of students as reported by Zalaznick raise the question of how open developmental educators can be with their students regarding the goals of moral education. Developmental moral education appears to have its own Catch 22. It appears that complete openness concerning stage hierarchy and more adequate ways of resolving moral dilemmas may have negative effects on students' feelings and resultant moral growth. On the other hand, failure to share the nature of the educational goals with students may create feelings of suspicion. Moral educators require openness from students, but can they defend not also being open with their students? The paradoxical possibility is that in order for teachers to be effective moral educators they must be dishonest or, at the very least, not open with their students.

School administration and kohlbergian programmes

Central to the success of any educational innovation would be the support of the administration of a school.[49] The purpose of this final section of the paper is to examine major concerns likely to be held by school administrators about Kohlbergian programmes. By inference, in this section, community attitudes will also be discussed, as school administrators serve at the will of the local community's elected school board and have the charge of carrying out their vision of quality education for the children of the community.

Two public school administrators, Thomas Sobol, Superintendent of Schools, Scarsdale, New York and Robert Sperber, Superintendent of Schools, Brookline, Massachusetts, have recently discussed their perspectives regarding the implementation of Kohlbergian programmes in public schools.[50] Both of these administrators speak from experience in that Kohlbergian programmes have been implemented in their districts. Both also represent districts known for excellence and innovation. Because of space limitations I will focus my discussion of Sobol's and Sperber's concerns on four persisting issues which administrators face: academic achievement, fiscal matters, programme evaluation, and community relations.

In the United States today the most important goal which the public expects schools to accomplish is to successfully teach the basic academic subjects. If Kohlbergian programmes are introduced, how will they affect the time spent and achievement gained in academic subjects? Room in the school day will have to be created. If, for example, the discussion of moral dilemmas is introduced in the English and US History curricula, what impact will this have, if any, on the academic achievement of students? Little information exists on this topic; however, the commonsense impression is that the less time one spends on traditional classroom activities, the less the student will learn. I realize that this is a simplistic view, but it is one which public school administrators must frequently face from community members.

There is some evidence to suggest that development in moral judgment is most difficult to achieve when the teacher and students have strong curricular priorities and the dilemmas discussed are defined by a given academic content.[51] This would suggest a degree of incompatibility between the goals of academic achievement and developmental moral education. No sound conclusions are warranted at this time, but this area is in need of resolution if administrators are to be able to throw their full weight behind such programmes.

Who will pay? There will likely be considerable expense incurred in implementing such a programme. Where will the money come from? US schools currently operate on very tight budgets. The 1983 summer Institute in Moral Development and Moral Education sponsored by the Harvard University Center for Moral Education carried a fee of $1100. Certainly one can begin a programme for much less per teacher; however, some expenses in terms of teacher training, curriculum development and materials are unavoidable. Where will those funds come from, and what will be the ramifications of either increasing local taxes or reallocating funds from more traditional areas?

Most school districts are willing to spend money if it can be shown that it results in a positive benefit to the students and educational programme. Can Kohlbergian programmes demonstrate such practical benefits to justify the expense? Most evaluations to date have focused on the development of moral reasoning. It is unlikely that one-third of a stage mean growth, while psychologically significant, would be perceived by the community to be of much educational significance. It is more likely that student moral behaviour could be the arena in which the programme were evaluated. Incidents such as drug usage by just community students, or discussions questioning parental authority, would have far more impact regarding programme evaluation than stage advance.

Ultimately all school administrators must keep peace with the communities they represent. It undoubtedly would be a sensitive and delicate task to win support for any moral education programme in today's political climate. Recently in the state of Illinois the State Superintendent of Public Instruction proposed that local schools should be teaching basic American values. The public outcry was so strong that he was forced to back down from what seemed, on its face, to be a safe proposal. The public's concern was that local control of schools would be abridged. Moral education is a definite 'buzz word' in American society. Its very mention inflames ordinarily calm and rational individuals. An awareness of this phenomenon has led some prominent Kohlbergians to remove the word 'moral' from their public discussions of the approach.[52] Instead of moral dilemma discussions we now have dilemma discussions. Moral education becomes civic education and the goals of Kohlbergian programmes are now focused on listening skills, social sensitivity, critical thinking and the like. While there can be little question concerning the perceived political astuteness of such 'moralspeak' (apologies to Mr Orwell), one remains with the question (posed above) about honestly sharing with students the purposes of the moral education programme: 'Can a programme thrive in a school if it cannot be open and honest with students and parents regarding its goals?'

The above concerns all pose very 'sticky wickets' which must be negotiated if Kohlbergians are to achieve the necessary administrative support. It will take as much hard work, dedication and brilliance by those in the educational trenches to implement Kohlbergian programmes as it did for Kohlberg and his associates to develop this exciting new promise for moral education.

NOTES

1 M. Scriven (1967) 'The methodology of evaluation', *AERA Monograph Series on Curriculum Evaluation, No. 1, Perspectives of Curriculum Evaluation*, Chicago, Ill., Rand McNally, pp. 39–83.

2 J. J. Schwab (1975) 'The practical: A language for curriculum', *Science, Curriculum and Liberal Education: Selected Essays*, I Wesbury and N. J. Wilkof (Eds.), Chicago, Ill., University of Chicago Press, pp. 287–321.

3 L. Kohlberg (1959) 'The development of modes of moral thinking and choice in the years 10 to 16', PhD dissertation, University of Chicago.

4 J. Piaget (1965) *The Moral Judgment of the Child*, New York, The Free Press.

5 J. Piaget (1971) *Biology and Knowledge*, Chicago, Ill., University of Chicago Press.

6 L. Kohlberg (1966) 'Moral education in the schools: A developmental view', *School Review*, 74, pp. 1–30.

7 E. Turiel (1966) 'An experimental test of the sequentiality of developmental stages in the child's moral judgment', *Journal of Personality and Social Psychology*, 3, pp. 611–18.

8 Kohlberg (1966) 'Moral education in the schools', *op. cit.*

9 M. Blatt (1969) 'The effects of classroom discussion on the development of moral judgment', PhD dissertation, University of Chicago.

10 M. Blatt (1969) 'Effects of classroom discussion' *op. cit.*, M. Blatt and L. Kohlberg (1975) 'The effects of classroom moral discussion upon children's level of moral judgment', *Journal of Moral Education*, 4, pp. 129–61.

11 L. Kohlberg (1971) 'Stages of moral development as a basis for moral education', *Moral Education: Interdisciplinary Approaches*, C. Beck, B. Crittenden and Edmund Sullivan (Eds.), Toronto, University of Toronto Press; L. Kohlberg (1973) 'Education for justice: A modern statement of the

Platonic view', *Moral Education: Five Lectures*, T. Sizer and N. Sizer (Eds.) Cambridge, Mass., Harvard University Press; L. Kohlberg (1975) 'The cognitive developmental approach to moral education', *Phi Delta Kappan*, 56, pp. 670–7; and L. Kohlberg and E. Turiel (1971) 'Moral development and moral education', *Psychology and Education Practice*, G. Lesser (Ed.), New York, Scott Foresman.

12 A. Colby, L. Kohlberg, E. Fenton, B. Speicher-Dubin and M. Lieberman (1977) 'Secondary school moral discussion programs led by social studies teachers', *Journal of Moral Education*, 6, pp. 90–111.

13 R. Enright, D. K. Lapsley, D. J. Harris and D. J. Shawver (1983) 'Moral development interventions in early adolescence', *Theory into Practice*, 22, pp. 134–44; J. A. Lawrence (1980) 'Moral judgment intervention studies using the defining issues test', *Journal of Moral Education*, 9, pp. 178–91; J. S. Leming (1981) 'Curricular effectiveness in moral/values education: A review of research', *Journal of Moral Education*, 10, pp. 147–64; and A. Lockwood (1978) 'The effects of values clarification and moral development curricula on school-age subjects: A critical review of recent research', *Review of Educational Research*, 4, pp. 325–64.

14 L. Kohlberg (1978) 'Revisions in the theory and practice of moral development', *New Directions for Child Development: Moral Development*, W. Damon (Ed.), San Francisco, Jossey Bass, pp. 83–7.

15 J. S. Leming (1983) *Contemporary Approaches to Moral Education: An Annotated Bibliography and Guide to Research*, New York, Garland Publishing, pp. 149–72.

16 E. Zalaznick (1980) 'The just community school: A student perspective', *Moral Education Forum*, 5, pp. 27–35.

17 L. Kohlberg (1978) 'Revisions in theory', *op. cit.*, L. Kohlberg (1980) 'High school democracy and educating for a just society', *Moral Education: A First Generation of Research and Development*, Ralph L. Mosher (Ed.) New York, Praeger Publishers, pp. 20–57.

18 Kohlberg (1978) 'Revisions in theory', *op. cit.*, p. 85.

19 E. Wasserman (1980) 'An alternative high school based on Kohlberg's just community approach to education', in Mosher (1980) *op. cit.*, pp. 265–78.

20 J. Reimer and C. Power (1980) 'Educating for democratic community: Some unresolved dilemmas', in Mosher (1980) *op. cit.*, pp. 303–20; and C. Power and J. Reimer (1978) 'Moral atmosphere: An educational bridge between moral judgment and moral action', in Damon (1978) *op. cit.*, pp. 105–16.

21 Reimer and Power (1980) 'Educating for community', *op. cit.*

22 *Ibid.*

23 A. Colby, L. Kohlberg, J. Gibbs and M. Lieberman (1983) 'A longitudinal study of moral judgment', *Monographs of the Society for Research in Child Development*, 48, 1, Serial No. 200.

24 L. E. Longstreth (1970) 'Values and teaching: A study of teacher beliefs', PhD dissertation, University of Colorado; S. L. Schulte (1982) 'A survey of attitudes toward moral education', DE dissertation, University of Toledo; and M. V. Wallace (1980) 'A survey of the attitudes of public high school teachers regarding moral education', EdD dissertation, Temple University.

25 D. C. Lortie (1975) *Schoolteacher: A Sociological Study*, Chicago, Ill., University of Chicago Press, pp. 111–14.

26 M. Silver (1982) 'Moral education and teaching: An interview study of teachers', PhD dissertation, Washington University.

27 L. Kohlberg (1980) 'High school democracy', *op. cit.*, p. 39.

28 M. Fullan (1981) 'School district and school personnel in knowledge utilization', *Improving Schools: Using What We Know*, R. Lehming and M. Kane (Eds.), Beverly Hills, Calif., Russel Sage.

29 T. S. Popkewitz, R. B. Tabachnick and G. G. Wehlage (1982) *The Myth of Educational Reform: A Study of School Responses to a Program of Change*, Madison, Wisc., University of Wisconsin Press.

30 J. B. Arbuthnot and D. Faust (1981) *Teaching Moral Reasoning: Theory and Practice*, New York, Harper and Row; R. E. Galbraith and T. M. Jones (1976) *Moral Reasoning: A Teaching Handbook for Adapting Kohlberg to the Classroom*, Minneapolis, Minn., Greenhaven Press; and J. Reimer, R. H. Hersch and D. P. Paolitto (1983) *Promoting Moral Growth: From Piaget to Kohlberg*, 2nd ed., New York, Longman.

31 Silver (1982) 'Moral education', *op. cit.*, pp. 38–41.

32 As quoted in R. Sperber and D. Miron (1980) 'Organizing a school system for ethics education', in Mosher (1980) *op. cit.*, p. 80.

33 J. D. Napier (1978) 'The ability of elementary school teachers to stage score moral thought statements', *Theory and Research in Social Education*; J. D. Napier (1978) 'The validity of preservice

teacher use of Kohlberg's issue stage scoring system', *Theory and Research in Social Education*, 6, pp. 16–30.

34 N. Porter and N. Taylor (1972) *How to Assess the Moral Reasoning of Students*, Toronto, Ontario Institute for Studies in Education.

35 J. Rest, E. Turiel and L. Kohlberg (1978) 'Relations between level of moral judgment and preference and comprehension of the moral judgment of others', *Journal of Personality*, 37, 3, pp. 20–30.

36 R. J. Griffore and J. Lewis (1978) 'Characteristics of teachers' moral judgment', *Educational Research Quarterly*, 3, 3, pp. 20–30.

37 J. Rest (1976) 'Moral judgment related to sample characteristics', Final Report to National Institute of Mental Health, Grant #8703 MH 24988, University of Minnesota.

38 R. A. Wilkins (1980) 'If the moral reasoning of teachers is deficient, what hope for the pupils?' *Phi Delta Kappan*, 61, pp. 548–49.

39 R. B. Bloom (1976) 'Morally speaking, who are today's teachers?' *Phi Delta Kappan*, 57, pp. 624–5.

40 J. Rest (1976) 'Moral judgment characteristics', *op. cit.*

41 P. Sullivan (1980) 'Moral education for adolescents', in Mosther (1980) *op. cit.*, p. 173.

42 D. Locke (1983) 'Doing what comes morally: The relation between behaviour and stages of moral reasoning', *Human Development*, 26, pp. 11–25; L. Kohlberg and D. Candee (1984) 'The relations between moral judgment and moral action', *The Psychology of Moral Development* L. Kohlberg (Ed.), New York, Harper and Row, pp. 498–581.

43 A. Blasi (1980) 'Bridging moral cognition and moral action: A critical review of the literature', *Psychological Bulletin*, 88, pp. 1–45.

44 M. Masterson (1980) 'The social behaviour of students at different stages of development', in Mosher (1980) *op. cit.*, pp. 188–202.

45 G. G. Bear and H. C. Richards (1981) 'Moral reasoning and conduct problems in the classroom', *Journal of Educational Psychology*, 73, pp. 644–70.

46 Kohlberg and Turiel (1971) 'Moral development and moral education', *op. cit.*, pp. 456–64, and Kohlberg (1971) 'Stages of moral development', *op. cit.*, pp. 74–81.

47 N. Haan, M. Brewster Smith and J. Block (1968) 'Moral reasoning of young adults: Political-social behaviour, family background and personality correlates', *Journal of Personality and Social Psychology*, 10, pp. 183–201.

48 W. Kolber (1981) 'Living in a just community: A student perspective', *Moral Education Forum*, 6, pp. 43–6; and E. Zalaznick (1980) 'The just community school: A student perspective', *Moral Education Forum*, 5, pp. 27–35.

49 C. Argyris (1962) *Interpersonal Competence and Organization Effectiveness*, Homewood, Ill., Dorsey; and M. D. Miles (Ed.) (1964) *Innovation in Education*, New York, Teachers College Press.

50 T. Sobol (1980) 'An administrator looks at moral education: An if I ask these things, will ye still call me friend?' *Educational Leadership*, 38, pp. 16–17; and R. Sperber and D. Miron (1980) 'Organizing a school system for ethics education', in Mosher (1980) *op. cit.*, pp. 58–82.

51 A. Higgins (1980) 'Research and measurement issues in moral education interventions', in Mosher (1980) *op. cit.*, p. 100.

52 E. Fenton as quoted by L. Kuhmerker (1980) 'From the editor's desk', *Moral Education Forum* 5, 1, p. 28.

17. Kohlberg and the Hidden Curriculum

DAVID GORDON

One can analyze Kohlberg's ideas about a moral curriculum from many different points of view. Most of these lead back to matters addressed in other chapters in this book. Thus I will limit myself to discussing Kohlberg's notion of a moral curriculum in relation to one concept only—the hidden curriculum.

The hidden curriculum features very prominently in those writings of Kohlberg and his co-workers which relate to the moral curriculum. It begins its Kohlbergian career in the article, 'The moral atmosphere of the school' (Kohlberg, 1970). This opens with the following marvellous passage:

> I have to start by saying that Philip Jackson is responsible for my paper, by which I mean he is 'to blame'. First he is responsible beacuse he invented the term 'hidden' . . . curriculum to refer to 90 percent of what goes on in classrooms. Second, he is responsible because he induced me to speak about the (hidden) curriculum when my only qualification to do so is that I have never studied it. While I have done plenty of observing of children in . . . classrooms, such observation has . . . not (been) in terms of the nature of classroom life and its influence on children. Third, he is to blame because he wrote a book defining the hidden curriculum on which I based this paper, and then he prepared a document . . . defining the (hidden) curriculum in a completely different way, leaving me holding the bag (p. 104).

My main thesis in this chapter is that, tongue-in-cheek formulation apart, this passage shows up the serious difficulties Kohlberg has with the notion of a hidden curriculum. His conception of the latter has been a major factor in shaping his view of how a moral curriculum should be constituted. As I regard his conception as mistaken or, better, as inexact, I would argue that he lays himself open to a number of telling criticisms of the moral curriculum he advocates. These criticisms all derive from different and, I think, more sophisticated approaches to the hidden curriculum.

I shall first sketch Kohlberg's approach to the hidden curriculum and try to show how it shaped his ideas concerning a moral curriculum. I will then contrast his approach with others and point out the criticisms of the Kohlbergian notion of the moral curriculum which follow from them.

KOHLBERG, DURKHEIM, THE KIBBUTZ AND THE JUST COMMUNITY

To start with Kohlberg was influenced by Jackson's (1968) characterization of the hidden curriculum in *Life in Classrooms* as three characteristics of classroom life with which children have to come to terms: crowds, praise and power. In later articles Kohlberg goes beyond these three characteristics (which, if I understand Jackson correctly, were only *examples* of items in the hidden curriculum), but he continues to see the hidden curriculum as related to *social relations* within the class and the school. Thus in his article, 'High school democracy and education for a just society', he writes: 'while the high school social studies curriculum teaches equal liberty and due process, the high school "hidden curriculum" (the governance and informal social relations of the school) teaches something very different' (Kohlberg, 1980, p. 36). The same view of the hidden curriculum is apparent in the writings of his students and co-workers (Wasserman, 1980, p. 269; Power, 1981, p. 5).

The above quote points indirectly to an important emphasis of the Kohlbergian approach: *the hidden curriculum is seen as extremely powerful, in particular with regards to its impact on moral development*. As Wasserman (1978) puts it: 'the hidden curriculum has a profound influence on the moral and civic education of students' (p. 164). It is precisely in connection with this point that Kohlberg's view of the hidden curriculum links up with another dominant strand in his thinking—his flirtation with the work of Emile Durkheim.

Durkheim's conception of the overpowering influence of society on consciousness would naturally be relevant to someone interested in moral development, because Durkheim stresses society's moral dimension. This moral dimension is so all-encompassing that society is, for Durkheim, the source even of our religious beliefs (Durkheim, 1965, p. 237).

In the 'moral atmosphere' paper Kohlberg is mainly concerned to show us the negative consequences of Durkheim's position. He sees this as leading to an indoctrinative, authoritarian form of socialization, and maintains that it is the Russian system of education with its stress on group conformity and pressure which has taken Durkheim's educational theory to its logical conclusion.

However in other writings we find Kohlberg relating to Durkheim's ideas in a rather different way. Perhaps the most important example is 'Cognitive-developmental theory and the practice of collective moral education'. This paper is concerned with moral education in an Israeli kibbutz, an education which impressed Kohlberg profoundly. He argues in effect that kibbutz education can be seen as an example of a non-indoctrinative, non-authoritarian application of Durkheim's ideas. Here Kohlberg is mainly concerned with Durkheim's emphasis on altruistic attachment to the social group. As he puts it:

> Durkheim holds that altruistic concern or sacrifice, like the sense of duty, is always basically directed toward the group rather than to another individual or to an abstract principle....

Accordingly, a central part of moral education is the sense of belonging to, and sacrificing for, a group. Says Durkheim (1961, p. 238), 'In order to commit ourselves to collective ends, we must have above all a feeling and affection for the collectivity ...' (Kohlberg, 1971, p. 355).

It is this feeling for the collectivity that Kohlberg found in kibbutz education.

While left-wing kibbutz theory of collective moral education is much like the theory of Durkheim and the Russians, when one enters a left-wing kibbutz and talks to the MADRICHIM (youth leaders) and the youth, one notes little emphasis on fixed rules, upon discipline and punishment, or upon respect for authority for its own sake.... The MADRICH is a consultant, not an authority, and orders are seldom given, speeches or lectures seldom made, voices seldom raised.... (However) underneath the informality of the MADRICH there is a considerable amount of iron, and this iron is based on the theory of collective education. By the theory of collective education I do not mean indoctrination into a collectivist ideology.... The iron of kibbutz education ... is not kibbutz ideology but the iron of the welfare of the peer group and of the kibbutz in which it is embedded.... (K)ibbutz education (is) guided by a theory of collective education running from Durkheim through the modern Russian psychologists. This theory stresses the psychological principle of using an adult-guided peer group which has collective responsibilities and collective sanctions ... (Kohlberg, 1971, pp. 358–60).

What appears to have impressed Kohlberg most about kibbutz education is that measures of moral maturity of kibbutz educated youth[1] seemed to indicate that kibbutz moral education was far more effective than Blatt's moral discussion approach (which has been derived directly from Kohlberg's research and theory). Blatt (Blatt and Kohlberg, 1975) had been interested in the effect of discussion of moral dilemmas on moral judgment. He developed a twelve-week programme which involved participation of students at varying stages of moral development (as defined by Kohlberg) in twice-weekly discussions of such dilemmas. In these discussions the teacher supported and clarified those moral arguments which were one stage above those expressed by the majority of the students. Blatt's findings were that this programme resulted in the class moving up on the average about one-third of a stage.

Kohlberg's study of kibbutz educated children suggested much more dramatic changes, and thus he concludes that 'total immersion through adolescence in the kibbutz is a much more powerful moral education environment than Blatt's limited discussion procedures' (Kohlberg, 1971, p. 369). The research related to a moral curriculum by the Kohlberg group over the last decade can be interpreted as a series of attempts to create a similar sort of non-indoctrinative 'total immersion' in other environments. This has led to the idea of transforming the school into a 'just community'.

One such example, and one in which Kohlberg was directly involved, was the Cluster School—an alternative school within the Cambridge High and Latin School. It consisted of approximately sixty-five students and six staff who met for classes (in English and Social Studies) and group meetings two hours a day. For the rest of the time students took classes in the main Cambridge High School. Once a week everyone participated in the community meeting which was run on the basis of discussion and majority rule, with all participants, staff and students, having one vote. The issues raised at the community meeting tended to be those of direct relevance to the students as individuals, and to the group as a community—drug use, thefts, disruptive behaviour, class cutting, grading, school rules (Wasserman, 1980, p. 268). These community meetings however were *not* simply examples of the usual type of democratic participatory activity so fashionable in alternative schools in the 1970s. The staff was expected to take an active role in ensuring that the discussions exemplified those characteristics which stimulate moral growth according to Kohlberg's theory, e.g., exposure to the next higher stage of moral reasoning, exposure to cognitive moral conflict (Wasserman, 1980, p. 269).[2] This community meeting was the most central aspect of the Cluster School *vis-à-vis* the notion of a just community. As Power (1981) puts it:

> The community meeting was the single most important event in the school. It served two general purposes: it was the arena for democratic decision-making and the major community building ritual. It was a ritual for community-building because at the community meeting Cluster members formulated and then reminded each other of their most basic ideals and beliefs as a school community. The representation of the community's norms, values, and basic ideals helped to strengthen them and thus strengthen the sense of community (p. 7).

A good deal of research has been published reporting the Cluster experience. I will not review this in any detail. Suffice it to say that the research certainly does seem to support the claim that a sense of community, in the sense of shared norms which reflected the values of justice and collective responsibility, did seem to develop, at least in part (Reimer and Power, 1980). What is important for us is that the Cluster School illustrates and encapsulates Kohlberg's conception of the hidden curriculum and its importance for moral education, a conception which has gradually moved the Kohlbergian moral curriculum from Blatt-like classroom discussions of hypothetical moral dilemmas to the hidden curriculum of a just community.

IS THE HIDDEN CURRICULUM LIMITED TO SOCIAL RELATIONS WITHIN THE SCHOOL?

Through linking the discussion in the previous section with the basic tenets of Kohlberg's cognitive-developmental approach to moral development, we can see that Kohlberg's just community approach is based on the following line of reasoning:

Assumptions:

1 The hidden curriculum is related to the social relationships that obtain within the school.
2 The hidden curriculum is the most pervasive and thus the most effective influence of the school on the student's moral development.
3 Moral development should lead toward the moral maturity of a principled sense of justice (Kohlberg, 1970, p. 121).

THEREFORE

Conclusion: Effective moral education entails transforming the school into a just community (in the sense exemplified by schools like the Cluster School).

Assumption (3) is associated with Kohlberg's psychological theory and educational philosophy and is discussed in other articles in this book. Therefore for brevity's sake I will regard it as unproblematic in the context of my analysis here. My focus is on the first two assumptions and I now turn to a critical discussion of them. In this section I will analyze assumption 1 and in the following sections I will analyze assumption 2.

Kohlberg's characterization of the hidden curriculum in terms of social relations is not uncontroversial. In the literature one can distinguish between three different types of definition of the term. The first divides school learning *outcomes* into two mutually exclusive groups: (1) academic learnings, which are associated with the manifest curriculum, and (2) non-academic learnings—attitudes, values, dispositions, certain social skills—which are associated with the hidden curriculum. I call this first approach the Outcomes Definition. The second definition focuses on the school *environment* which is divided into two mutually exclusive components—the 'cognitive' environment, on the one hand, and the physical and social environments, on the other. (I am assuming that the rather peculiar term 'cognitive environment' is sufficiently clear on the intuitive level to make it unnecessary to define it formally.) Then one of these components—the cognitive environment—is associated with the manifest curriculum, while the other—the physical and social environments—is associated with the hidden curriculum. This is an Environmental Definition of the hidden curriculum, and is clearly the approach Kohlberg adopted.

The third definition distinguishes between two *modes of influence*, a conscious, deliberate influence associated with the manifest curriculum and an unconscious, unplanned influence associated with the hidden curriculum. One example of this is the definition Jane Martin (1976) offers of the hidden curriculum: 'In sum a hidden curriculum consists of some of the outcomes or byproducts of learning ... particularly those states which are learned but not openly intended' (p. 137). I will call this sort of definition the Latent Influence Definition of the hidden curriculum.

Does it really matter how one defines the hidden curriculum? Is the choice of definition any more than a sterile philosophical game? I think it does matter for one absolutely central reason—*the three different approaches do not necessarily deal with the same phenomena.* For example, the kind of learning outcomes most writers on the hidden curriculum have been interested in can be the result of both latent or manifest influences, and of the impact of social, physical or cognitive environments.

How then should one decide between the competing definitions? In a previous article (Gordon, 1982) I proposed what I called the Pervasiveness Test as a criterion. This derives from the very brief but profound section on the hidden curriculum in Bloom's (1972) article, 'Innocence in education'. Bloom maintains that the hidden curriculum 'is in many respects likely to be more effective than the manifest curriculum' (p. 343). Why should this be so? He suggests that the reason is that the hidden curriculum is 'so pervasive and consistent over the many years in which our students attend school' (p. 343). In the next section I am going to point out some difficulties with Bloom's position. However, I would still maintain that any good definition of the hidden curriculum must acknowledge the partial truth at least of Bloom's claim. In other words, it must, minimally, give us some hint as to why the phenomenon subsumed under the term 'hidden curriculum' should usually be more consistent and pervasive than that which is taught in the manifest curriculum and should, in fact, differentiate between the two curricula on the basis of consistency and pervasiveness.

What I argued was that the Pervasiveness Test showed the Latent Influence Definition of the hidden curriculum to be far superior to the other two. Specifically when comparing the Environmental Definition (and limiting it to the social environment as Kohlberg does) and the Latent Influence Definition, the former can be seen to be far more limiting. Certain aspects of the social environment—the structural properties of the school as a social organization—*are* pervasive and consistent. However, so are certain aspects of the cognitive environment, in particular the deep structure of the school's formal curriculum. In other words, the Environmental Definition does not effectively separate the pervasive and consistent influences from the limited and fleeting ones.

On the other hand, the Latent Influence Definition does seem to effect this separation quite convincingly. The teacher as transmitter of the manifest curriculum has to take into account many conflicting factors in the classroom situation, and these factors are themselves continually in flux. There is no reason to suppose that his or her planned conscious solutions over time to these conflicting, changing demands of the situation will form a stable, consistent pattern. However, as unconscious transmitter of the hidden curriculum, his behaviour is determined largely by the nature of his personality, by his deeply held beliefs and by his role within the social structure of the school. These are far more likely to display a certain consistency over time.

Defining the hidden curriculum in terms of latent influence undermines Kohlberg's approach to the moral curriculum, for three reasons. First, and perhaps least importantly, it makes a lot of the writing of the Kohlberg school on the hidden curriculum sound linguistically odd. Sentences like: 'The need to make the hidden curriculum an atmosphere of justice, and to make this hidden curriculum explicit in intellectual and verbal discussions of justice and morality, is becoming more and more urgent' (Kohlberg, 1970, p. 122), are virtually incomprehensible when removed from the context of the special sense in which Kohlberg is using the term 'hidden curriculum'.

A second and related point is that conceiving the hidden curriculum as latent influence highlights the fact that Kohlberg's notion of a school as a just community is rather limiting, despite his talk about 'total immersion'. In particular, the Latent Influence Definition renders unimportant the whole notion of a planned moral curriculum, and in general of a school faculty planning activities to promote moral development. The argument is that irrespective of what is planned, the really important moral atmosphere of the school is going to come out in the *spontaneous* interactions of students and faculty. When schools like Cluster work, it is not because the community meeting or the lessons in English and Social Studies exemplify the pedagogical principles derived from Kohlberg's theory. Rather it is because these activities have been incorporated into a school whose faculty either constituted a just community anyway, or, through the work of Kohlberg and his co-workers *as organizational consultants* (and *not* as moral educators or consultants about moral education), have become such a community. And in this regard the published data from the research on schools like Cluster are very incomplete. We either are not told much about the general climate of the school (apart from activities like community meetings) and how this changed as a result of the Kohlbergian intervention, or else what we are told is presented more or less as an aside.

For example, from the articles by Mosher (1980) and Sperber and Miron (1980) it seems clear that the organizational climate and decision-making structures at Brookline High School (which had a similar programme to Cluster) and the way these were influenced by Mosher acting as a sort of organizational development consultant (Fullan, Miles and Taylor, 1980) are not typical of the average high school. Yet almost no attention is paid to the question of how important this climate and decision-making structure were for the Kohlbergian moral education programme that developed at this school.

The third problem the Latent Influence Definition of the hidden curriculum creates for the Kohlbergian approach is that it forces us to start paying attention to aspects of schooling that Kohlberg's stress on social environment had allowed us to ignore. Specifically, the cognitive environment regains the central place that it has for most educational philosophies. So, to take Cluster as an example: we must now address the question of the impact of the hidden curriculum of the *parent* school in those lessons the Cluster students took there. After all, Cluster students spent much more time at the parent school than at Cluster. So one can express considerable doubt about Kohlberg's claim that the activities at Cluster constitute an extensive involvement with a just community.

It seems to me that Kohlberg could try to counter this argument in at least two different ways. It will be instructive to examine these two possible counter-arguments, both of which fail, I think.

(a) Kohlberg could use the fact that although the Latent Influence Definition cuts across the social/physical/cognitive environment distinction, it would be absurd to claim that all three environments are *necessarily* equally important with regards to *every* item taught in the hidden curriculum. It may be that for a particular aspect of hidden curricular learning one of these environments is more salient than the others. Thus Kohlberg, while conceding that the Latent Influence Definition of the hidden curriculum is superior to the Social Environment Definition, could argue that with regard to moral development the social environment of the school is its most salient environment. Thus he could claim that its latent influence is far more important than the latent influence of (say) the cognitive environment.

On the face of it this is a very persuasive argument. It certainly seems that it can be upheld with regard to other settings that have interested Kohlberg, e.g., the kibbutz, and prisons (Kohlberg *et al.*, 1975). However schools are a different sort of setting, one whose cognitive component is, by virtue of the nature of education, totally compelling. This is so in general, and also when we consider moral education, as Purpel and Ryan (1976) have shown in their article whose title, 'It comes with the territory: The inevitability of moral education in the school', expresses the point I am making rather well. I could add that the hidden curriculum of the school's cognitive environment would seem to be central when considering an approach like Kohlberg's, which he characterizes as *cognitive* developmental.

(b) The second possible counter-argument could be derived from the last paragraph of Kohlberg's (1980) 'High school democracy' article.

> Our just community alternative school is not a kibbutz lifelong community, it is only a six-hour school. Our remedy of wider community volunteer projects is a weak solution in comparison to the kibbutz. It can be no more unless teachers, students, and parents are to live a common life as part of a larger intergenerational community. As a result, like Plato's republic, our just community school is as much an incomplete Utopian ideal as it is a reality. Its reality is sufficient, however, to engender in both students and teachers some of the aspirations and competences a just society requires (pp. 56–7).

The argument implied in this passage I would call the 'You Can't Be Perfect' Argument. In other words Kohlberg might concede that schools like Cluster would offer a better moral education if all aspects of the hidden curriculum (as well as the manifest curriculum, for that matter) were informed by the principles of a just community. However, one must be realistic and not utopian. The attempt at Cluster was not a complete realization of the just community, but it went some of the way in that direction—certainly more than the hypothetical moral dilemma approach which was the first Kohlbergian foray into the real world of the schools.

This argument rests on the belief, implied in so much[3] of Kohlberg's writings, that degree of success with regard to moral development is a simple, increasing function of the extensiveness of a moral curriculum. This belief is, I think, mistaken, because it itself rests on an over-simplified view of the pervasiveness of the hidden curriculum, a view already identified in the previous section as Kohlberg's assumption 2: i.e., the hidden curriculum is the most pervasive and thus the most effective influence of the school on the student's moral development. I now turn to the critical analysis of this assumption, an analysis which among other things will show up the flaw in the 'You Can't Be Perfect' Argument.

THE CONSISTENCY OF THE HIDDEN CURRICULUM

Bloom's (previously mentioned) concern with the pervasiveness of the hidden curriculum suggested two properties of that pervasiveness. (i) It is related to the hidden curriculum's consistency. The hidden curriculum is a homogeneous curriculum, its pervasiveness is one of *non-contradictory* messages. (ii) Consistent pervasiveness is a necessary and sufficient condition for a curriculum to be effective.

These two properties make up Kohlberg's assumption 2. Let us examine each of them separately. The *inevitable* linking of pervasiveness and consistency seems to me to be extremely questionable, considering the complexity and contradictory nature of modern culture. Schools are reflections of culture—this is the basis for preferring the Latent Influence Definition of the hidden curriculum—and thus in contradictory cultures the school's hidden curricula, at least in part, can be assumed to transmit contradictory messages. These contradictory messages will not be entirely amorphous in a structural sense. They will be organized within large, pervasive and consistent *message blocks*—to this extent Bloom is certainly correct. But the different blocks will often be contradictory.

Kohlberg himself supplies us with an example. Laura, one of the students at Cluster, has this to say:

> Cluster has signified that in this democratic school people should respect one another and care. That is what community is ... Cluster is a democratic school within Latin High School, but it is different than Latin. I'm not saying Latin teachers aren't fair. It's just you come in, the teacher is in front, saying 'Now you do this,' and you just listen. In Cluster, you come in and the teacher says 'How should we approach our lesson' and people try to work as one (Kohlberg, 1980, p. 36).

In such a situation we should not be surprised if the effects of the moral curriculum are less than we had hoped for. Laura's thinking on hypothetical problems is often Stage 4 (Kohlberg, 1980, p. 31), but when talking about her real-life plans and her beliefs about city ghettos, the government, etc., her thinking is at Stage 3.

What is interesting is that Kohlberg ignores the contradictory hidden curriculum as an explanation of Laura's lack of transfer of attitudes from the Cluster environment to the 'real' world. Remaining within the conceptual framework of his assumption 2 and its previously mentioned corollary that success of a moral curriculum is an increasing function of its extensiveness, he writes:

> Laura's moral and positive attitudes of participation in the democratic school, then, have not transferred to the larger civic world *in the absence of a parallel process of participation in the larger community*. Our conclusion is that a civic education for civic participation ideally should include two experiences: the direct democracy of a smaller school community found in the alternative school . . . and the experience of participation in the larger community . . . for the generalization of (fourth-stage) attitudes to a participatory attitude to the wider society (Kohlberg, 1980, p. 37; italics mine).

Unfortunately I do not think one can safely ignore the possibility of contradictory hidden curricular messages. This realization has two important consequences for Kohlberg's ideas concerning moral curriculum. First, to return to and to complete the discussion in the previous section—it shows up the flaw in the 'You Can't Be Perfect' Argument. We now see that we cannot say that a moral curriculum that covers (say) 70 per cent of school activity is better than a moral curriculum that covers (say) 50 per cent. It may be that the '70 per cent curriculum' is, to a large degree, undermined by a contradictory 30 per cent whereas the '50 per cent curriculum' might not be. Second, becoming aware of possible contradictory hidden curricular messages must result in a rethinking of how to derive a practical programme of moral education from Kohlberg's psychological theory of moral development.

However, the most important and bothersome consequence of the idea of contradictory hidden curricular messages is that it suggests the radical possibility that schools may not be suitable sites for moral education at all, unless their relationship with the wider society is completely redefined.

Kohlberg has argued eloquently for conceiving the school as a bridge to the wider society. However his concern has been with the 'moral' side of life, both in school and in general. Yet the school can only be the sort of bridge he envisages if its *general* hidden curriculum transmits the message that school is part of the real world. Among other things this means that the *image of knowledge* the school presents must stress the interconnections between theoretical knowledge and practical affairs. This was something Dewey (1964) (another thinker to whom Kohlberg continually alludes) understood very clearly. The problem is that modern work in the sociology of knowledge has shown that creating this connection is far more difficult than Dewey thought, and also far more difficult than creating the moral bridge Kohlberg is interested in.

Bernstein (1977) has probably made the most significant contribution to our understanding of this problem. One of his central concepts is the *degree of classification* of the curriculum. A curriculum with *strong classification* is one in which curriculum contents 'are well insulated from each other by strong boundaries' (p. 88). Such curricula (which are the most prevalent type, at least at the high school level) have two important properties relevant to our discussion. First, the strong boundary maintenance between contents carries over to the school knowledge/everyday knowledge boundary. In other words, educational codes (another term Bernstein uses) with strong classification transmit the hidden curricular message that the world of the school is divorced from the 'real' world. Such a hidden curriculum undermines the moral education of the just school community.

Could one not simply use Bernstein's conceptual scheme to advocate that we try to transform the school curriculum into one with *weak classification*? This would seem to be a necessary precondition for a viable Kohlbergian moral curriculum. Which brings us to the second property of educational codes with strong classification that Bernstein relates to, a property which unfortunately shows how utopian the above suggestion is: the strong classification of the school curriculum is the result of the structure of subject-matter guilds *within the universities*. In other words, the undermining hidden curricular messages are the result of forces *outside* the school itself. They are thus not amenable to change from within the school, but rather can only be changed through a drastic restructuring of the entire educational system.

THE EFFECTIVENESS OF THE HIDDEN CURRICULUM

Let me now turn to the second property of pervasiveness suggested by Bloom, and assumed by Kohlberg: consistent pervasiveness is a necessary and *sufficient* condition for a curriculum to be effective. Here I will be concerned with the sufficiency aspect of this proposed property. A recent paradigm shift of emphasis in work on the hidden curriculum has shown up a major flaw in this way of regarding pervasiveness. I am referring to what are called *resistance theories*. As has been shown by people like Giroux (1981), the fact that hidden curricular messages are not openly acknowledged by teachers does not mean that they cannot be spotted by the pupils. In fact, messages which imply or express dominant class hegemonic impositions often are spotted and resisted or rejected.

How is this related to Kohlberg's moral curriculum? In a brilliant critique of Kohlberg's theory of moral development, Sullivan (1977) has argued that Kohlberg's seemingly universalistic theory is, in fact, an example of liberal social science ideology which is characterized by blindness to the role of class consciousness. Sullivan points out that Kohlberg's position is essentially Kantian, and that Kantian formalism was considered by Marx and Engels as an abstract formalism implying a universality, but in fact masking a middle-class ideology.

From my point of view it isn't necessary to decide whether Sullivan is correct or not. What is important is that his argument has, at the very least, a surface plausibility. For this reason it would be perfectly understandable if working-class pupils were to interpret a Kohlbergian moral curriculum as an example of dominant class hegemony and thus were to reject it.

However, when one begins to consider this possibility, one also begins to interpret certain things that happen in the school in new ways. Consider the following incident that Kohlberg (1978) describes at Cluster:

> Together with the teachers I attempted to formulate theory in terms of the task of creating a new conception of a school community in addition to obtaining research data. Such a participant-consultant role has its perils.... At (one) community meeting, a student proposed a motion that 'there was too much of Larry Kohlberg's moral discussion in the school and that students should be morally developed before they get into high school.' She proposed beefing up the English skills curriculum so that students would be sure of making college. The motion passed, though moral discussion goes on at this school (p. 9).

Kohlberg interprets this as a difficulty which arises because of what he calls the 'psychologist's fallacy', i.e., the tendency for psychologists to assume that what is relevant, important and 'right' from the experimental perspective is also relevant, important and 'right' for the student and teachers in real-life school situations. As I understand it, the psychologist's fallacy is seen as an example of the communication gap that exists between the university ivory tower and the 'real' world, a gap that can be breached (in this case at least) if the psychologist displays empathy and flexibility.

On the other hand, the resistance theory perspective invites us to ask whether the student quoted above comes from a working-class background or not (Kohlberg does not supply us with this information), and if the answer is in the affirmative, to perhaps interpret her motion as an example of a *social class* communication gap. If this is so (either in this particular case or in similar ones that have occurred or can be envisaged), then Kohlberg's theory faces a far deeper implementation difficulty than the psychologist's fallacy.

CONCLUSION

Kohlberg's approach to moral education in general and his view of how the moral curriculum of the school should be constituted are undoubtedly major contributions to the field of moral education. What I have argued in this chapter, essentially, is that the Kohlbergian contribution could be even more substantial if it were not constrained by a limiting conception of the hidden curriculum. I have shown how this conception leads Kohlberg to underemphasize or ignore at least four aspects of the hidden 'moral' curriculum, viz., (1) its unplanned and unintended dimension; (2) its connection with the hidden cognitive curriculum; (3) its being constituted often by contradictory message blocks; (4) its being open to counter-hegemonic resistance. Although I have described these aspects of the hidden curriculum as undermining the Kohlbergian moral curriculum, I do not believe that they force us to regard Kohlberg's approach as totally misconceived. On the contrary, I think that recent developments in thinking about the hidden curriculum *can* be incorporated into the Kohlbergian framework. Thus, hopefully, my comments in this chapter can be regarded as constructive criticism and also as implying directions for future conceptual and empirical research.

NOTES

1 Actually the article relates to a specific subpopulation of kibbutz educated youth known as 'youth aliyah' students.
2 Nevertheless one should stress that at least one critique of Kohlberg's work (Aron, 1977) argues that the conceptual link between Kohlberg's theory and the educational practice ostensibly derived from it is not as clear as one would like it to be.
3 But not in all of it; cf., for example Kohlberg (1980, p. 36). Here, at least, he does mention the contradiction that at times obtains between the hidden and the manifest curricula.

REFERENCES

Aron, I. E. (1977) 'Moral philosophy and moral education: A critique of Kohlberg's theory', *School Review*, 85, 2, pp. 197–217.

Bernstein, B. (1977) *Class, Codes and Control*, Vol. 3, London, Routledge and Kegan Paul.
Blatt, M. M. and Kohlberg, L. (1975) 'The effects of classroom moral discussion upon children's level of moral judgment', *Journal of Moral Education*, 4, 2, pp. 129–61.
Bloom, B. S. (1972) 'Innocence in education', *School Review*, 80, 3, pp. 333–52.
Dewey, J. (1964) *Democracy and Education*, New York, Macmillan.
Durkheim, E. (1961) *Moral Education*, New York, The Free Press.
Durkheim, E. (1965) *The Elementary Forms of the Religious Life*, New York, The Free Press.
Fullan, M., Miles, M. B. and Taylor, G. (1980) 'Organizational development in schools: The state of the art', *Review of Educational Research*, 50, 1, pp. 121–84.
Giroux, H. A. (1981) 'Hegemony, resistance and the paradox of educational reform', *Interchange*, 12, 2/3, pp. 3–26.
Gordon, D. (1982) 'The concept of the hidden curriculum', *Journal of Philosophy of Education*, 16, 2, pp. 187–98.
Jackson, P. W. (1968) *Life in Classrooms*, New York, Holt, Rinehart and Winston.
Kohlberg, L. (1970) 'The moral atmosphere of the school', in Overly, N. V. (Ed.) *The Unstudied Curriculum*, Washington, D.C., Association for Supervision and Curriculum Development.
Kohlberg, L. (1971) 'Cognitive-developmental theory and the practice of collective moral education', in Wolins, M. and Gottesmann, M. (Eds.) *Group Care: An Israeli Approach*, New York, Gordon and Breach.
Kohlberg, L. (1978) Foreword to Scharf, P. (Ed.) *Readings in Moral Education*, Minneapolis, Minn., Winston Press.
Kohlberg, L. (1980) 'High school democracy and educating for a just society', in Mosher, R. L. (Ed.) *Moral Education: A First Generation of Research and Development*, New York, Praeger.
Kohlberg, L., Kauffman, K., Scharf, P. and Hickey, J. (1975) 'The just community approach to corrections: A theory', *Journal of Moral Education*, 4, 3, pp. 243–60.
Martin, J. R. (1976) 'What should we do with a hidden curriculum when we find one?' *Curriculum Inquiry*, 6, 2, pp. 135–52.
Mosher, R. L. (1980) 'A democratic high school: Coming of age', in Mosher, R. L. (Ed.) *Moral Education: A First Generation of Research and Development*, New York, Praeger.
Power, C. (1981) 'Moral education through the development of the moral atmosphere of the school', *The Journal of Education Thought*, 15, 1, pp. 4–19.
Purpel, D. and Ryan, K. (1976) 'It comes with the territory: The inevitability of moral education in the schools', in Purpel, D. and Ryan, K. (Eds.) *Moral Education: … It Comes with the Territory*, Berkeley, Calif., McCutchan.
Reimer, J. and Power, C. (1980) 'Educating for democratic community: Some unresolved dilemmas', in Mosher, R. L. (Ed.) *Moral Education: A First Generation of Research and Development*, New York, Praeger.
Sperber, R. and Miron, D. (1980) 'Organizing a school system for ethics education', in Mosher, R. L. (Ed.) *Moral Education: A First Generation of Research and Development*, New York, Praeger.
Sullivan, E. V. (1977) 'A study of Kohlberg's structural theory of moral development: A critique of liberal social science ideology', *Human Development*, 20, 6, pp. 352–76.
Wasserman, E. R. (1978) 'Implementing Kohlberg's "Just community concept" in an alternative high school', in Scharf, P. (Ed.) *Readings in Moral Education*, Minneapolis, Minn., Winston Press.
Wasserman, E. R. (1980) 'An alternative high school based on Kohlberg's just community approach to education', in Mosher, R. L. (Ed.) *Moral Education: A First Generation of Research and Development*, New York, Praeger.

Interchange

LEMING REPLIES TO GORDON

In Gordon's paper the just community approach is criticized because it is based on a narrow and unidimensional interpretation of the hidden curriculum. Gordon argues that in order to account for the pervasive and consistent nature of the latent curriculum and its effect on students one must go beyond a mere focus on planned social relations and include a much wider range of school phenomena such as cognitive elements and the spontaneous interactions occurring between faculty and students. While I can agree with Gordon's perspective that the concept of the hidden curriculum and its impact on students requires a multi-dimensional perspective, and also accept Gordon's characterization of Kohlberg's just community approach as placing the focus on social relations, I feel that in a number of instances he has misinterpreted and oversimplified Kohlberg's position. I also feel he is too rigid in his own interpretation of the hidden curriculum. Let me explain.

Kohlberg's rationale for the just community approach is more complex than Gordon's characterization; namely, it is a better, more effective way of stimulating principled moral reasoning. In Kohlberg's latest revisions (cited in my paper) there is a decided shift from an exclusive concern for stimulating stage growth to an equally explicit concern for fostering certain kinds of moral behaviour. The just community approach, with the evolution of a sense of individual and collective responsibility to adhere to agreed upon norms, has moved beyond an educational rationale concerned merely with principled reasoning to an educational approach concerned also with moral behaviour. An additional purpose of the just community approach is to counter what Kohlberg sees as rampant privatism in today's society and schools and to foster a sense of community and commitment to democratic governance based on justice. To this degree the just community approach is civic education in the best Deweyan sense. With both of these goals of the just community approach, the concern is for the solid attainment of a fourth-stage commitment of being a good citizen, that is, participating in the development of collective rules and adhering to those rules. The predominant goal of the just community approach is not, as Gordon suggests, the stimulation of principled reasoning through manipulation of the hidden curriculum. With the just community approach the norms which govern relations between students and staff are no longer 'underground' but rather are the data of interaction and reflection. In the late nineteenth century the traditional moral goals of schooling were driven underground by social and political shifts in the United States.[1] The just community approach attempts to reverse that phenomenon and bring the hidden curriculum out into the open and subject it to public examination. To say that the just community approach is merely an attempt to harness the hidden curriculum in the service of facilitating stage growth in moral reasoning is a gross oversimplification of the principles guiding its practice. Of course when looking at any school experience academics can divine layer upon layer of hidden meaning behind the overt practices, and undoubtedly this is also the case with the just community programmes. What remains 'hidden' in just community settings is in need of explanation. The nature of this new hidden curriculum can best be found in the reflections of those most affected by it—the students. It is relatively unimportant what we academics see in the hidden curriculum when compared to the meaning derived from the schooling experience by the students themselves. There are fleeting glimpses in the literature of the perceptions of students and faculty, but like other interpretations of the hidden curriculum in schools, the evidence is largely speculative and lacking in well-grounded empirical evidence.

Finally, I think Gordon has been too monolithic in his interpretation of the hidden curriculum in general. Clearly the concept of a hidden curriculum involves both moral and non-moral dimensions. For example, the hidden curriculum conveys unexamined messages to children concerning punctuality, individual pursuit of academic achievement, neatness, and the like. Most of the time these concerns are non-moral in character. On the other hand, there are also clear moral concerns conveyed by the hidden curriculum. It appears entirely appropriate to me that the moral phenomena of schooling, whether hidden or explicit, reside primarily in the realm of student experiences in the social environment. Of course there are unexamined moral issues presented uncritically for student acceptance in textbooks, but there is reason to suspect that these are not very effective. For example, Ehman found in an analysis of existing research on political learning in schools that the most important determinant of political attitudes was not the cognitive curriculum but the classroom atmosphere.[2] Likewise in the Hartshorne and May[3] classic study on nature of character it was found that it was not the cognitive curriculum that influenced character; the only variable associated with the character of the students was the classroom ethos of individual teachers. Thus, I conclude that, not only conceptually but also empirically, there is reason to believe that the arena in which moral education should be conducted is appropriately that of participating in and making sense of group life. To this extent the just community approach has focused on the proper dimension of schooling to achieve its goals, and the evidence that it is achieving its ends, although nascent, is impressive compared to what we know regarding the effect of other dimensions of schooling (e.g., textbooks) on moral development.

NOTES

1 E. Vallance (1973) 'Hiding the hidden curriculum', *Curriculum Theory Network*, 4 pp. 1–6.
2 L. H. Ehman (1980) 'The American school in the political socialization process', *Review of Educational Research*, 50, pp. 99–119.
3 H. Hartshorne and M. A. May (1928–30) *Studies in the Nature of Character*, New York, Macmillan.

GORDON REPLIES TO LEMING

Considering that the ostensible structure of this book had defined my role as critic of Kohlberg's moral curriculum, I should welcome Leming's reservations about the practicality of Kohlberg's proposals. However, in fact, my response will attempt to defend these proposals against Leming's criticism. This is not as paradoxical as it first sounds. Leming and I have not really adopted opposing stances *vis-à-vis* the Kohlbergian curriculum. Our chapters have different things to say, but the tone—one of critical admiration—is similar. This critical stance is thus not negative across the board, and does not require acceptance of all criticisms of Kohlberg's work. In particular I do have difficulties with some of the points Leming has raised.

Leming's scepticism about the practicability of Kohlberg's ideas derives from certain assumptions about planned educational change. I will relate here to two of these, which seem to me to be questionable.

1 *Teachers implement innovations only if they are seen as answers to actual difficulties and problems they are facing.*

On this point Leming quotes Fullan, an important organizational development specialist. Nevertheless, the evidence is equivocal. Daft and Becker have shown that the schools which adopt innovations are *not* those facing difficulties,[1] but rather those that are functioning well, and feel free to try something new. I myself have also presented evidence which shows that changes are often adopted not as a response to difficulties but rather as a response to fashionable educational discourse.[2]

2 *It is easier to get a single teacher to adopt an innovation than it is to bring about structural changes in a entire school.*

In fact, teachers require the *support* of extensive school-wide structural and normative changes in order to persevere with innovations. Sarason, for instance, has argued that most attempts at planned change in the classroom fail because they do not take into account the school's culture.[3] One must distinguish between trying out an innovation and long-term adoption. Getting a school to try the just community approach may be more difficult than getting a single teacher to try the moral discussion approach in the classroom, as Leming claims. However, once one has overcome initial difficulties, a school which does try to build a just community may have a better chance of adopting this as a permanent feature of its culture than the teachers in the Danforth Project had of adopting the moral discussion approach as individual teachers.

In any event, pointing out the implementation difficulties of an educational theory does not necessarily constitute a criticism of that theory. All education theories need to be augmented by implementation strategies and need the help of professional change agents in order to influence the schools themselves. Practical difficulties become a criticism only if they can be shown to be insurmountable, or to require social changes that go beyond the school system itself. The difficulties Leming points out at the teacher level do not seem to me to be of this sort. On the other hand, the difficulties at the community level (and perhaps also at the administrative level) are, by definition, linked to the wider social context. Thus I do see a convergence of sorts between these parts of Leming's chapter and my own analysis of Bernstein's notion of weak and strong classification, and of Sullivan's critique of Kohlbergian theory.

One final unrelated comment of a semantic nature: Leming interprets teacher advocacy as some sort of indoctrination. This seems to me to be a very strange use of the term 'indoctrination'. None of the usual methods of distinguishing between indoctrination and education which have been developed in educational philosophy would regard teacher advocacy as indoctrinative, unless it prevented the students from rationally evaluating the positions put forward by either teacher or students.

NOTES

1 Daft, R. L. and Becker, S. W. (1978) *The Innovative Organization*, New York, Elsevier North-Holland.
2 Gordon, D. (1984) *The Myths of School Self-Renewal*, New York, Teachers College Press.
3 Sarason, S. B. (1971) *The Culture of the School and the Problem of Change*, Boston, Mass., Allyn and Bacon.

Part X: Religious Education

18. Religious Education

MARION SMITH

Religion is concerned with the meaning of existence for the individual, for society
and for the whole of creation. Such a meaning is transcendent because it goes
beyond the immediate and specific to final and ultimate meaning. Man's sense of
obligation to search for such ultimate meaning includes also the expression of his
relationship to what he understands as transcendent. His responses have throughout history been in the form of ritual actions, statements of belief (both narrative
and formal) and ideal standards of conduct between one human being and another.
The study of religion involves the investigation of such matters in one or more
religious traditions, either from curiosity about this human phenomenon, or from
interest in the individual's own tradition. Religious education in schools may be
interpreted as the encouragement of a sound and comprehensive study of reli-
gion(s) within the limitations of youthful immaturity and ignorance. Religious
education may also have the additional aim of fostering allegiance to one particular
religious tradition, or, at the least, of preparing the way for an adult commitment to
it, for it is now recognized that religious education has its most important phases in
adult life. Morality is part of the study of religion. Ideals of conduct in different
religious traditions may be considered or the values and standards upheld in the
individual's own tradition may be studied, in every instance as a reflection of man's
beliefs in ultimate meaning. The individual's capacity for moral reasoning will
affect the interpretation of moral issues and conduct.

KOHLBERG'S VIEW OF RELIGION

In two recent and important papers, Power and Kohlberg (1980) and Kohlberg and
Power (1981) discuss the relationship between religion and morality. They argue

that each is a distinct aspect of human experience, but that there are also ways in which they interpenetrate. Moral reasoning, according to Kohlberg, is the way in which a person decides conflicting claims between individuals, and decisions are made on the basis of a developing sense of justice. Religious judgment is defined as 'conscious reflection on that which provides ultimate reassurance and meaning for life' (Power and Kohlberg, 1980, p. 347). Into this category falls consideration of questions which go beyond immediate problems to more fundamental ones such as 'why exist?' and 'why act morally?' Religious judgment searches for a universal explanation, an ultimate reason for moral and all other activity, whereas moral judgment is concerned with the reasons to be marshalled for the solution of some particular issue. Morality is therefore an aspect of religious thought, included as one of its concerns.

A religious perspective contributes to the importance attached to morality, not by supplying moral prescriptions but by supporting 'moral judgment and action as purposeful human activities' (Kohlberg and Power, 1981, p. 336). Toulmin (1950, p. 219) is quoted with good effect: 'Ethics provides the reasons for choosing the right course, religion helps us put our hearts into it.' Religious affirmation expresses 'confidence in the ultimate significance of moral action' (Power and Kohlberg, 1980, p. 346). They refer to 'Why act morally?' as a limit question, that is, it arises at the boundary of moral reasoning, and it is religion which addresses itself to such questions.

Kohlberg postulated a 'Stage 7' (1973) to signify this religious orientation. Because the questions and conflicts which arise at Stage 6 are resolved by means of religion rather than by logic alone, Stage 7 is not to be regarded simply as an extension of the preceding series of moral reasoning stages. Kohlberg says he means Stage 7 to be taken as a metaphorical term. At the earlier Stages 1–5 the question, 'Why be moral?', can be given non-religious answers. For example, at Stage 1, it can be answered by an appeal to human authority and the avoidance of punishment. At Stage 2 motivation may be from self-interest, at Stage 3 from the desire for the approval of others, at Stage 4 from the concern to uphold society and to maintain a respected place within it, and at Stage 5 moral choices may be made to satisfy individual needs provided that others' rights and and welfare are protected. At Stage 6 moral choices are determined by universal principles of human justice, but it is at this point that the questions arise: 'why bother to work for justice in a world which is so obviously unjust?' and 'why bother when death cuts short our efforts?'

Kohlberg makes Stage 7 distinct, and describes it as having a religious orientation because these questions are not finally answered by logic or reasoning. Having faced ultimate meaninglessness as a possibility, the religious man turns from despair to faith in the worthwhileness of moral endeavour. In elaborating the characteristics of Stage 7, Kohlberg and Power (1981, p. 369) speak of its perspective as 'cosmic' and 'infinite' though they qualify their terms by saying that the attainment of such a perspective is a matter of aspiration, not possibility. For the individual there is a 'shift from centring on the self's activity and that of others, to centring on the wholeness or unity of nature or the cosmos' (p. 371), and there is an attachment which may be called 'love' as the reverse of the despair which has been faced and rejected. 'Love of the whole . . . supports us through experience of suffering, injustice and death' (p. 371). Morality is, therefore, given this ultimate grounding and significance, not lightly, but with personal commitment.

A second way in which religion and morality are related is through the self (Power and Kohlberg, 1980). It is the same self which asks questions about morality and questions about religion, and the answers have somehow to be integrated if the person is to be satisfied. If religion functions to support the ego, to give it a sense of ultimate worth, then, it is suggested, religion strengthens the self which is involved in making moral decisions. The effect is not, primarily, on the particular choice which is made, but on the effort of trying to make such a choice responsibly and then of attempting to carry the judgment into action. For example, a religious interpretation of life can renew a sense of moral purpose, or encourage in the face of injustice, and give reassurance that the struggle is not futile. Religion may also contribute towards greater sensitivity, and obligation if others are regarded as brothers.

Kohlberg's interest in religion has led him to collaborate with others whose special concern is with the relation between morality and religion, and his theory has also generated work which must be discussed in its own right in the next section of this chapter.

Power and Kohlberg (1980) have attempted a comparison of progress in religious thinking with progress in moral reasoning. They have used Kohlberg's moral dilemmas together with selected questions used by Fowler (1981) in his investigation of the development of faith (particularly those concerned with personal life history, with reasoning about life in the face of boundary conditions such as death, suffering and wonder, and with questions about specifically religious topics). Power and Kohlberg collected data from twenty-one subjects who, on previous scoring, had been distributed across Fowler's stages. They found that there was 81 per cent overall agreement between the moral stage used for the Fowler questions (i.e., religious thinking) and for the Kohlberg moral dilemmas. However, in Stages 1–3 there was 100 per cent agreement, and divergences at Stages 4 and 5 were such that moral reasoning could be one stage higher than that of religious reasoning, but never the other way round. In discussing their results, they comment that, at Stages 1–3, thinking about religion and morality is undifferentiated, and suggest that, from Stage 4, the inherent capacities for logical and systematic thought make it possible to distinguish one sphere from the other.

This evidence is interesting, and not necessarily inaccurate, although it is based on a small sample (for example, the 100 per cent agreement involves eight subjects). A much larger sample would make the pattern of progression, if such exists, easier to see. There are also reservations about the reliability of Fowler's scoring procedures (see below). Power and Kohlberg use this evidence to support their claim that 'moral judgment is a necessary but not sufficient condition for religious reasoning at least at the higher stages' (1980, p. 359).

Kohlberg and Power (1981; Power and Kohlberg, 1980) have constructed descriptions of parallel religious and moral conceptions stage by stage, stressing the 'theistic versions' (1981, p. 340). They have done so 'to illustrate how elements of moral reasoning are taken up in religious considerations' (1981, p. 343). Their data have been drawn from several sources: Kohlberg's own collection of responses to moral dilemmas where religion was introduced by the subject, Power's study described above, Fowler's data from his interviews on faith development, and Oser's (1980) formulation of stages of religious judgment. The following is a condensed account of the main characteristics at each stage if the question, 'why be moral?', is interpreted in religious terms.

At Stage 1 the judgment of what is right is determined by the word of a physically stronger adult or by God characterized in similar terms of superior and arbitrary strength. Intentionality, in God or man, is not recognized. At Stage 2, just as moral judgments are based on fair exchange, so it is assumed that God will give a fair exchange for appropriate prayer and religious practices. In this case, it is the form of moral reasoning which determines religious expectation. (We may note a problem here when it appears that God does not respond, or keep his side of the bargain. God is then found to be unjust and arbitrary. The consideration, though not the conclusion, is found, for example, in Psalm 10: 'Why dost thou stand afar off, O Lord? Why dost thou hide thyself in times of trouble?')

At Stage 3 meeting the community's expectations and receiving its approval determine moral judgments. In religious reasoning, God is perceived in personal terms, and man's actions are designed to please and win his approval. At Stage 4 moral judgments are made with a view to upholding the social order. God is the supreme being by whose laws the whole universe is upheld and governed, and man's part is to collaborate with and to uphold these laws. Stage 5 moral judgments are made with full acknowledgement of the importance of order, but with recognition also of the individual's right to make his own judgments according to conscience. God is understood as an 'energizer' supporting and encouraging autonomous moral action. (Is this what Rahner, 1978, p. 20, means when he defines transcendent experience in terms of the condition of possibility for the 'consciousness of the knowing subject that is co-present in every spiritual act of knowledge and the subject's openness to the unlimited expanse of all possible reality'?) At Stage 5 there is cooperation between man and God in creating a community in which each individual can be free and respected. Stage 6 is largely speculative but Kohlberg refers to the cosmic perspective, going beyond human concerns.

Such parallelism between religious and moral conceptualization requires additional evidence but it seems likely that this might be found. For example, there would be little difficulty in finding from biblical and other religious literature, material which matches each of the stages. It would be a profitable exercise to reflect upon the conception of God implied in many familiar religious statements, and provisionally to assign a stage to each. This stage conception is important at all levels of religious education, and there are implications for the presentation of religious ideas.

Cross-sectional interviewing and the combined religion/morality stage characteristics may suggest that people are at a particular stage for both dimensions, but the evidence points towards development in morality progressing ahead of religious development, as we should expect if religion concerns the totality of our existence. The stage development theory implies that certain theological notions are incomprehensible or have little meaning until a certain stage of moral reasoning is reached, and this is a commonsense view also. Conversely, it is a serious difficulty when moral judgment levels outstrip the level of preaching or teaching which is being offered. For example, a view of God presented in Stage 2 or 3 terms will appear inadequate to those who are firmly at Stage 4, or beyond, in moral reasoning. We cannot assume that religious conceptions will inevitably catch up with moral advances, expecially when religious pronouncements have the authority of the institution or its appointed ministers. A religious interpretation of life may then appear to have been outgrown. A mismatch between religious and moral statements could well account for those adults who, having 'given up' religion in adolescence, are found in middle-age to have incredibly childish views of what religion means to their contemporaries, whose religious conceptions have gone on developing along with their other capacities.

The relationship between Moral Education (ME) and Religious Education (RE) is therefore complex, and the work Kohlberg and his associates have begun in teasing out the precise details is significant for religion. The life-span aspect of moral development is also relevant, for, if it is normal for adults to continue to develop in moral judgment in response to the events and demands of their adult experience, then religious development, if it is to keep pace, must also show progression.

MORALITY AND EXPERIENCE

Assuming the relationship between morality and religion described in the previous section to be correct, progression in moral development will determine the possibilities for progression in religious development. This section examines more closely the role of experience in bringing about transitions between moral stages and outlines some implications for religion.

Throughout childhood development occurs more or less continuously and often rapidly in several dimensions, so that it is quite difficult to disentangle cognitive, social, moral and religious strands. It is hard to discover, with any precision, the effects on development attributable to enlarged horizons, such as the move beyond family to play group, to school(s), to clubs, and to the increased opportunities given for activities of many types involving sharing, cooperation, competition, leadership, rebellion and relationships with others of all ages. These are all potentially formative experiences, and most of us would take the view that a variety of such experiences provides the background for normal development in moral judgment.

Kohlberg (1973) considers that progression as far as Stage 4 conventional moral reasoning depends in large measure on cognitive factors, primarily on 'seeing' the greater adequacy of the structures of each stage in turn. Development is also dependent upon the more adequate perception of the social system which arises from role-taking ability. (This also has a cognitive base: see Selman, 1980.) Kohlberg has claimed that discussion of hypothetical dilemmas promotes stage transition. Although the individual is called upon to explain and to justify a viewpoint in the presence of others who suggest their own solutions and counter-arguments, the 'moral' experience is vicarious. The role of experience here in promoting transition is the creation of disequilibrium and cognitive conflict, resolved by accepting or forming reasons at a more complex but more adequate structural level (Blatt, 1973; Turiel, 1974; Rest, 1973).

According to the evidence (Kohlberg, 1973), Stage 5 principled moral reasoning does not occur until adult life, and it is suggested that it requires a different kind of experience from that which appears to bring about development in the earlier stages. A distinctive feature of Stage 5 is that principles, or ideals, are not just 'seen' cognitively as more adequate, for they are, by definition, not a social reality to which the individual can conform but constitute something which *ought* to be accepted as the norm. In addition, at Stage 5 the individual is determined to work from within the existing (though unsatisfactory) framework of conventional thinking while being at the same time committed to the principles or ideals which, in his view, would reform or at least improve society. The possibility of a specific personal experience being decisive or influential in transition to the principled level of moral reasoning (which in any case demands formal operations) has been proposed.

This line of argument has come partly from attempts to explain apparent regression in the stages of moral reasoning found among college students, and partly from the extended revision of scoring which is now made available in the *Manual* (Kohlberg, 1979). The revised scoring has shown that some of the early assessments of stage were too high, and this has been noticed by several researchers, including myself (Smith, 1978). In one much quoted study (Kohlberg and Kramer, 1969) it was found that 20 per cent of the sample who had (apparently) attained Stages 4 or 5 in high school regressed to a dominant Stage 2 during their second and third year at college, although by the time they were 25 they had again reached Stages 4 and 5, with a greater usage of Stage 5 than before. In 1969 the explanation referred to the situation of students trying to establish their identity away from home restrictions, with ego-development of primary importance. They had to learn how to use moral structures for their personal integration (1969, p. 116).

Some of the 1969 explanation remains valid, but the more important consequence of the problem of 'regression' has been the characterization of transitional Stage 4½ which is postconventional but not yet fully principled. The *Manual* (1979) describes the social perspective at Stage 4½ as of one who stands 'outside of society' but who is also making personal choices without commitment to society as a whole. An obligation to follow personal conscience is insisted upon, and this goes with a degree of tolerance for the conscience choices of others (at least hypothetically). There is relativism because as yet the several principles are not coherent or necessarily consistent with each other.

Erikson's concept of moratorium is used in explanation of the difference between the experiences of late adolescence or early adult life, and adult moral experience. The college student really has responsibility only for himself. For a short while it is possible for him to stand aside, while he reviews and considers the options he has among a wide range of values, and he can be experimental without too much concern about long-term consequences. From his observations and conclusions, says Erikson, the young person can construct his identity. This period of limited personal responsibility is ended when he takes on the normal adult responsibilities which involve sustained caring for the welfare of others and the experience of moral choices where the consequences are irreversible. In 1973 Kohlberg thought there was some evidence that reflection encouraged by structured discussion of moral issues promoted transition to Stage 5, though he acknowledged that students may enjoy their moratorium but not progress to Stage 5, just as many adults have moral experiences which do not alter their stage of moral reasoning.

For religious education the transitional Stage 4½ will normally be found at the point of higher education and professional training, and chaplains as well as lecturing staff can profit from understanding its characteristics. It is also worth the consideration of those responsible for clergy training, perhaps in the decisions to be made over selection of candidates, as well as in the approach to the content of courses. One example of the latter is the study of world religions. It has to be decided whether the material is being received simply as information (which could well be the case during school years) or whether the doctrines and beliefs are among the wide range of options tolerated by the relativism of Stage 4½ and even viewed as a possible personal choice.

Some empirical evidence has been provided by an associate of Kohlberg. Gilligan (Kohlberg and Gilligan, 1971; Gilligan, 1980, 1982a) studied the relationship between what are proposed as the ethical ideals in the resolution of hypothetical dilemmas and those when the moral dilemma is a real one. Her account is based on data collected from two separate studies. In the first, college students were interviewed at 19–20 years and again at 26, and they were asked to talk about events in their own lives which they had found to present problems of moral dilemma. In the second study the subjects were women who had to decide whether or not to have an abortion; they were also interviewed a second time a year later. Gilligan reports that 'when judgment was tied to action, thinking shifted to issues of responsibility and care, and the understanding of what these activities entailed also followed a developmental progression' (1980, p. 247).

In the discussion of hypothetical dilemmas, Gilligan suggests, it is easier to focus on the ethical issues and ideals involved, but when the dilemma is personal, other factors are significant. Gilligan remarks on the effects of the realization of power involved in taking a course of action which will have important consequences to the person taking the decision as well as to others, and also to the limiting circumstances which are the context of each individual's own situation. She refers to Niebuhr's (1963) discussion of responsibility, to the demands of finding 'the fitting response', and to the consideration of both a person's own position and the responses of the community as part of that total position. She also found that the subject's conception of self and of others affected understanding not only of social relationships but also of the identification of moral issues. She considers her work is an expansion of Kohlberg's research, first by tying together moral and ego development, and second by adding to the focus on justice the complementary ethic of care (i.e., the interdependence of the human community).

In another paper Gilligan (1982b) has claimed that two modes of moral reasoning are to be found among children. Boys' comments are oriented to justice and rights, whereas girls speak of care and response. She says that 'the contrasting images of hierarchy and web' derive from childhood experiences of inequality and interdependence and that these give rise to the ideals of justice and caring. If further evidence shows this to be correct, then there would be implications for the presentation of religious ideas, but such a marked distinction between the sexes is not yet completely established.

Another Harvard associate, James Fowler, has incorporated Kohlberg's moral reasoning stages into a comprehensive scheme of stages of faith (Kohlberg, 1974; Fowler, 1980, 1981; Smith, 1983a, 1983b). What Fowler has done is to bring together a number of developmental schemes, and from them construct a composite sequence of faith stages, where 'faith', in a short definition, means 'being-in-relation' to our ultimate environment (Fowler and Keen, 1978, p. 23). The theological exposition of faith is derived from Niebuhr (1963; Fowler, 1974), together with Smith (1979). (This is not necessarily religious faith, but mainly with that connotation.) The cognitive-developmental work of Piaget, Selman (1980) and

Kohlberg describes three facets of faith: (A) Form of logic, (B) Role-taking, (C) Form of moral judgment. Erikson's sequence of life-crises (stages) is also incorporated in the developmental survey of faith as it is conceptualized over a life-time. There are also four other facets of faith in Fowler's scheme: (D) Bounds of social awareness, (E) Locus of authority, (F) Form of world coherence, (G) Role of symbols (Fowler and Vergote, 1980, pp. 80–1).

Fowler's procedure is to invite his subjects to talk over their life histories, paying special attention to crises and turning-points. Some of these events will obviously include moral judgments. In addition, Fowler invites discussion of specifically religious topics. He has characterized six developmental stages, which he has labelled (1) Intuitive-Projective Faith, (2) Mythic-Literal Faith, (3) Synthetic-Conventional Faith, (4) Individuative-Reflective Faith, (5) Paradoxical-Consolidative Faith, (6) Universalizing Faith. The details of the stages are hypothetical constructions rather than the outcome of rigorous procedures of testing and analysis such as we have with Kohlberg's work. Fowler is at present turning his attention to the problems of scoring, and is also engaged in longitudinal studies designed to demonstrate development. His work is, naturally, of great interest to those concerned with religious education at all age-levels. It makes sense to suppose that the way in which religious doctrines, practices and symbols are understood changes along with intellectual, social and other aspects of development, as well as in response to particular events, whether these are part of the human lot or of a more personal kind.

Fowler's theory of faith-development as a series of transformations and reinterpretations of human representations of the meaning of existence contributes to our understanding of the phenomenon of conversion (to which he devotes a chapter: 1981, pp. 269–91). Theologians usually speak of conversion as a change of direction (a change of mind, *metanoia*), often assumed to be a once-and-for-all alteration, or even reversal, of previously held ideas and previous life-styles. Some also recognize that it is a life-time's occupation to complete this change of direction. Fowler, too, sees conversion as meaning a change of the contents of faith. His rather cumbersome definition is: 'Conversion is a significant recentring of one's previous conscious or unconscious images of value and power, and the conscious adoption of a new set of master stories in the commitment to reshape one's life in a new community of interpretation and action' (1981, pp. 281–2). This recentring occurs at each stage transition, and, in many cases, the apparent disintegration of previously satisfactory ways of thinking can cause considerable anxiety and disturbance. Fowler is pointing to a more complex understanding of conversion. It is possible to change orientation, goals and life-style in a religious conversion without changes in structures of thought, but every progression in faith is also a conversion. Fowler suggests that religious conversion may require a recapitulation (he calls it a backward spiralling) of previous faith stages so that all the earlier stages of faith are re-lived but with 'a re-grounding of (their) virtues and their reorientation in light of faith's new centre of value, images of power and decisive master-story' (1981, p. 289). This is an adaptation of Niebuhr's account (Fowler, 1974), but so far there are no empirical data.

A problem in the evaluation of Fowler's work is that details of scoring procedures are not as yet generally available (even though there are numerous accounts of his theory, and, perhaps premature, attempts to utilize it in religious education curriculum changes, for example, Groome, 1980). By Fowler's own admission, the data given in his book are 'in rough form' (1981, p. 323). There is evidence for related development in cognitive, social-perspective taking and moral reasoning development, dating as far back as Selman (1971a, 1971b; see also Smith, 1978) and incorporated in Kohlberg's stage and scoring descriptions in the *Manual* (1979). There is, however, no evidence that Fowler has taken account of this detail, for example, in discovering what level is reached in (F) Form of world coherence, or (G) Role of symbols when moral reasoning is not at the level compatible with cognitive attainment and social perspective. Howe (1979) suggests that development in aspects D–G (see p. 286 above) needs to be correlated with development levels in A–C. In any case, there are well-tried tests and scoring schemes available for these three. At present, Fowler's model arouses considerable interest, and some experimental use of it has been made, or is in progress (Gorman, 1977; Marshall, 1979).

Selman's contribution to Kohlberg's stage description has been mentioned above, and his work has also been used by Fowler. The way people see each other is a necessary element in resolving moral dilemma, and may even affect the delineation of the precise nature of the issue and determine the cast of the play itself. Human relations are also the concern of religion and not only in strictly moral issues. Selman's work is therefore significant for both morality and religion. In his developmental scheme (1980, p. 153) he prefers to speak of four levels, rather than stages, of social perspective. (Note that Fowler has, somewhat arbitrarily, 'extended' Selman's scheme by two further stages.) This cautious distinction derives partly from his finding that development is not altogether simultaneous across the domains he has examined (1980, p. 84): concepts of the individual, of close friendship, of peer-group organization and of parent-child relations. Unevenness in development attributable to inequalities of experience tends to disappear by about 11 years of age (1980, p. 207), but it is not yet clear whether a level 3 scoring, for example, in conflict resolution in the domain of friendship, is also found for the issues of punishment, and conflict resolution in the domain of parent-child relations. Further results from Selman's project may bear on the problem of whether scoring levels are affected by the subject-matter of the test dilemma, as Rest (1976) has suggested. The particular concepts Selman has chosen to investigate are of great interest to religion and to questions of authority and obedience (Smith, 1980).

The material discussed in this section reflects the fruitfulness of Kohlberg's theory in encouraging others (particularly former students and associates) to enlarge the subject of investigation beyond morality to the 'self' which is moral and which exists in a context of day-to-day events. This broadening takes Kohlberg's work into the sphere of religion in a different sense from morality as a religious concern.

SOME CRITICAL APPRAISALS

Those concerned with ME within the context of RE recognize that Kohlberg has provided a useful 'map of the terrain' and his stage descriptions are helpful in representing changes in moral understanding. It is not his fault if some have incautiously assumed he has prepared a complete 'catechetical kit' for ME and then found some gaps. In this section reference is made to a number of papers evaluating his work in the context of RE.

Philibert (1975a, 1975b) discusses aspects of Kohlberg's work which he considers of positive use in RE, providing that they are not taken to be all that is necessary. Philibert writes from a knowledge of medieval moral philosophy, and challenges Kohlberg's dismissive attitude to the 'bag of virtues' type curriculum. He argues that Aristotle's conception of virtue and the importance of habit have more in common with Kohlberg's position than Kohlberg has perhaps realized. In expounding Aristotle's views (and with additional support from Aquinas), Philibert shows that habit is not to be mistaken for the mere automatic repetition for its own sake, but is to be conceived of as a means by which an individual is able to achieve an optimum performance. He says (1975a, p. 463), 'Virtue is the maturation of human powers, through exercise, to the point where those powers are capable of attaining with facility the optimum performance of their operational potential'. Habit, is, therefore, the exercising of human abilities so that they not only develop strength but are, as it were, kept in good working order. Philibert points to mathematical skills as an example, where the goal is to have them in readiness to solve major problems.

One of Philibert's most useful points is the creative possibility in the practice of virtue. He uses the example of courage/fortitude and analyzes its acquisition, to show that it can never be conceived of as mere habit, as though there were always the same courageous act to be performed. In every instance where 'courage' would be an appropriate attitude, there must be a fresh consideration of the demands of the situation, the possible courses of action and their likely outcome, and other virtues may need to be involved, such as prudence, self-control and justice. These four are Aristotle's virtues whereas Kohlberg speaks only of justice, but Philibert is correct in recognizing that to carry a decision of justice into action, prudence, self-control and courage may all be required. It is in this way that Philibert argues that Kohlberg's concern with justice (and the stages of conceptualizing it are important) is too narrow for a complete programme of ME (within RE) and that there is a place for 'the practice of virtue' (i.e., habit forming) which is not in conflict with Kohlberg's developmental approach. For Kohlberg's description of progression uses terms such as increasing differentiation, integration, adaptation, the widening of concerns to include both self and others, so that the individual goes on to the fullest realization of his personal capacities, and this, says Philibert, is precisely what Aristotle meant by his 'maturation of human powers through exercise'.

Youniss (1973) points out that Kohlberg's view of man is much to be preferred to alternatives offered by some other psychologies. He mentions as examples the new humanistic view of man as essentially good and therefore to be left alone and Skinnerian behaviourism which is a 'too utterly mechanistic perspective on man' (p. 355). Some of Youniss' qualifications and reservations concerning Kohlberg's methodology have been clarified or answered since 1973, but he has a useful, if ironic, list of the demands made on the teacher who attempts to use the discussion methods Kohlberg suggests. He says the teacher must be a diagnostician in order to know the child's level; an inciter to know when and how to provoke; a true believer in development since the restructuring takes time and so needs patience; a sophisticated politican remaining credible and knowing when to intervene. These are, of course, necessary capabilities for teachers of most subjects, but they are worth rehearsing when ME (or RE) is often undertaken by those who are not trained teachers.

The advantages of the discussion of moral dilemmas are mentioned by several. Sholl (1971) finds it a valuable alternative to a typical adult 'right answer' approach to moral questions (often with the reinforcement of a notion that virtue will be rewarded). Haggett (1974) also gives qualified approval of discussion methods and a developmental approach towards ME. Bachmeyer (1973) notes the value of stage descriptions in improving the effectiveness of moral discussion and the discussions themselves as stimulating thought about moral issues, as an alternative to the type of ME which is a recital of moral traditions, or homilies, requiring agreement with the teacher's own views. Emswiler (1976), similarly, sees the advantages of an approach which encourages learning and discovery of our own answers to moral questions. He says, 'It is not as important to teach the entire credo and dogmas of our faith as to establish the bases for continuing development' (p. 626). All would agree that, from the point of view of religion, Kohlberg's ME programme is valuable but not complete. They also represent what O'Donohoe (1980) describes as the prevalent Catholic attitude to ME: it is not that 'content' is to be eliminated, but rather that people should be helped to handle it in a responsible and creative manner. Concern is with the person who acts, not simply with the action.

One of the most helpful and balanced assessments comes from Duska and Whelan (1977) who present a Catholic post-Vatican II treatment of moral development utilizing the insights of Kohlberg's research, and addressing themselves directly to questions of the relation between moral reasoning development and the moral authority assumed by the Church (and their arguments would apply to any denomination or religion which offers firm direction on moral questions). They describe the moral stages where a Christian perspective provides the content within Kohlberg's formal structure. (Their account resembles that of Power and Kohlberg, 1980, described above, but includes the role of the Church as both community and authoritative institution.) They indicate some of the models of God held at different stages, such as 'a biblical commander' or 'ultimate orderer', (p. 90). Where the Church has made pronouncements on specific issues, they point to the importance of developing the individual's reasoning about them. On the controversial question of the Church's supposed denial of individual conscience, they firmly quote from the papers on Vatican II to the effect that the post-conciliar Church is 'telling people that although it can give moral guidance, it cannot make up people's minds for them' (p. 91). People must take responsibility for their moral decisions. The 'crisis of faith' which so often accompanies the adolescent or young adult who is at Stage 4½ is seen as a desire for independence from the Church and all it stands for, parallel with the desire to be independent of parental restriction. This is regarded as a necessary position before there can be a return to the Church from free choice and as a mature adult. A wise and useful comment is made here in suggesting that a certain voluntary relinquishment of personal satisfactions may be needed in order to relate to others and to avoid lonely isolation.

McDonagh (1980), as a moral theologian, criticizes the 'individualist liberal character' of Kohlberg's work, and queries his concern with the development of the individual person as a moral agent. The particular emphasis of McDonagh's paper is the person-in-community, and he considers the need for group strategies and group responsibility to counter some of the major moral problems of the present century, such as racism, peace and war, population and starvation, conservation and pollution. He argues that the true growth of the self arises from self-transcendence in response to others, and that this 'mystery' is inaccessible to conceptualizing and verbalizing. With this in mind, he also finds Kohlberg's focus on justice too narrow, for it omits love, trust, vocation, the creative mystery of the person. Though he accepts human striving in morality, he insists on the response to others evoked by their presence as essentially gift. McDonagh also considers that Kohlberg's account of moral development understates or underestimates evil. Another area of criticism lies with the neglect of the role of action, for, he says, understanding of what we do is often only in the actual doing. Kohlberg's work is therefore regarded as inadequate at a number of points.

These criticisms would be substantial if it were being claimed that Kohlberg's theory and ME programme represented the whole of morality as this is understood within religion. From a developmental point of view, it is useless to expect appreciation of world problems on the scale McDonagh mentions (for example, the problems of Latin America in relation to self-centred consumerism and triviality) before the individual can grasp the meaning of 'society', and can move to a conceptualization of this in international terms. How would group strategies be devised, except by Stage 5 principled moral reasoners? The notion of self-transcendence is important in religious thinking, but it has already been shown that the conceptualization of 'self' is developmental, and its mystery is not denied because the way it is given is explored at different ages. Again, to speak of evil is to speak from religious commitment, and 'to struggle that good may prevail over evil' (p. 340) involves us in the question raised at the beginning of this chapter, and by Kohlberg himself, 'why act morally?'

Conn (1975) is appreciative of Kohlberg's work for moral and religious education and suggests how it could be even more valuable if the creative element in moral judgment received greater attention. The extreme relativism which Kohlberg reports of college students is said by him to be transitional towards a principled morality. (Conn does not refer to Kohlberg's Stage 4½.) However, Conn argues that there needs always to be some degree of relativism in our moral judgments if we are to do justice to the complexity of human reality, where problematic situations cannot be fully resolved by 'absolute, abstract and pre-determined answers'. He goes on to claim that the values of love, fidelity and honesty have to be applied to particular concrete situations with sensitivity and critical judgment. This is what Conn means by the creative response to a moral situation, and for him a fully human moral judgment needs this individual and personal application of principle. 'Extreme' relativism must certainly go if every-thing is not to be arbitrary, but a 'principled conscience ... exists and functions within the context of an enduring and valid relativism' (p. 222).

This attitude of constructing a moral judgment according to the complexities of a specific situation and not pronouncing, as it were, *ex cathedra*, is sound, and, to some extent, Conn is really turning around the possibilities of Kohlberg's theory for education rather than finding fault with it. In a subsequent paper (1981) he refers to critics who interpret Kohlberg's theory as inadequate because they wrongly suppose he has claimed to explain all of moral development. Conn himself has moved away from such a tendency by recognizing that Kohlberg has been dealing with a carefully defined aspect of morality. In this second paper, Conn answers one particular criticism—Kohlberg's insufficient attention to the affective side of moral consciousness—by pointing out that Kohlberg's theory 'often criticised as rationa-listic, is more deeply rooted in affectivity than is commonly recognised' (p. 34).

In elaborating his argument, Conn makes two main points. He says that, while it is true that the limitations of each stage are left behind as a more adequate structure is found, there are positive elements in each stage which are taken on in a more refined form. For example, the limitations of egocentrism are gradually overcome, so that there is 'a drive for self-transcendence in the moral realm' (1981, p. 37), but the concerns for fairness, intentionality, mutual relations, welfare and justice are preserved throughout the structural changes. Through all of them there is some sort of recognition of other selves having thoughts and feelings like our own. This awareness could be called 'empathy', which is the emotional side of role-taking. Conn quotes Kohlberg's comments on the cognitive and affective aspects of role-taking (Kohlberg, 1976, p. 49) and also mentions the attention Kohlberg has paid to the necessary development in social perspective as a prerequisite in moral reasoning. From this he concludes that affectivity is not absent from Kohlberg's theory.

These comments have all been from Catholic sources. On the Protestant front there are few examples to review. Perhaps one of the oddest supporters of Kohlberg is West (1978) who organizes biblical history into six consecutive periods in which the criteria for moral decision-making match Kohlberg's stages: Stage 1—the era from Adam to the Flood; Stage 2—the era from Noah to Jacob; Stage 3—the era of Joseph; Stage 4—the era of Mosaic law up to the time of Jesus; Stage 5—the era of Jesus' ministry; and Stage 6—the period following the Crucifixion and Pentecost. Such a scheme is innocent of modern biblical criticism and for all practical purposes is useless. The discussion of moral situations within the biblical narratives, however, can be useful and stimulating as Sholl (1971) has shown.

Kohlberg's theory in relation to the conception of immorality has been discussed by Joy (1980) from the evangelical position. He approves the theory because it assumes human accountability for moral choices, but he accuses Kohlberg of saying that immorality is no more than underdevelopment. In the Judaeo-Christian tradition, says Joy, immorality is 'deformed moral reasoning and behaviour', but he seems to be confused about the distinction between immaturity and immorality. Whatever the degree of cognitive complexity in moral reasoning (which Kohlberg describes) it is still possible to make conscious decisions which are believed to be morally right or wrong. The lower levels are 'less moral' only from a neutral perspective on the scale as a whole, which sees the greater comprehensiveness and objectivity of the higher levels. From the perspective of any individual involved in moral decision-making a relatively low level may still represent an advance on previous reasoning. Spidell and Lieberman (1981), adherents of the Church of Christ, have suggested that at each higher stage of moral reasoning development there is an increasing awareness of the scope of sin, and, correspondingly, differences in the interpretation of the doctrine of justification.

Dykstra (1980), Presbyterian, has mainly adverse criticisms to make about Kohlberg's theory, but his arguments imply that he has not understood it correctly. He seems to be under the misapprehension that moral maturity, for Kohlberg, is simply a matter of cognition. Dykstra says that moral virtue is not the single quality of justice which, further, is neither necessary nor sufficient for morality. For Dykstra, mature moral judgments (and actions) can be based on 'empathy and imaginal thinking'. It is difficult to understand how the cognitive can be ruled out altogether by Dykstra, even if he wishes to emphasize the role of sharing the feelings of others. Some cognitive development is required even to reach this level (Selman, 1980).

Kegan (1980) discusses the religious dimensions of cognitive or structural-developmental theories, including Kohlberg's. He owes something to Tillich and Niebuhr, as well as to his own Hasidic background. He points out that stage descriptions are reference points in the individual self's continuing process of composing meaning for existence. 'Persons are not their stages of development; persons are a motion, a creative motion, the motion of life itself' (p. 407). This is not a particularly new observation, though it is worth noting because critics of structural-developmental theory often do not realize the role of the stage descriptions. Kegan goes on to suggest that, from the religious perspective, any holding on to the meaning we have as though it were final, is a form of idolatry, because it is 'taking for ultimate what is only preliminary' (p. 421). The 'religious self' is called to leave one position of order and meaning in order to find one which is better, and reliance on this possibility is trust in the ultimate ground of being which continues to uphold the self throughout these transformations.

CONCLUSION

If Kohlberg's work is to be utilized for religion (either for religious studies or for religious education) it must not be considered narrowly as a tool, effective or otherwise, for the moral component of the curriculum. It is to be valued, first of all, as a type of psychological theory which acknowledges the freedom and responsibility of human beings and their attachment to a moral ideal which lies always ahead and beyond. Man experiences himself 'as a being in whom there is a difference between what he is and what he should be. The difference between what we simply in fact are and what we should be is primarily an experience which grounds our existence as moral beings' (Rahner, 1978, p. 407). Morality is therefore a matter neither of simple absolutes nor of social conditioning; though some religious viewpoints insist on both of these, mainstream opinion tends to hold that man, as a moral agent, must strive to find the proper course in the complexities of his daily life, and so rationality as well as intention are important. Such moral striving is life-long, and Kohlberg's theory shows the possibility for development and the refinement of moral understanding which can go along with the experience of the years. Morality certainly involves more than the analysis of a moral problem, and the investigations of those who have enlarged the scope of Kohlberg's work are beginning to give promising insights for RE.

It could be said that Kohlberg's direct contribution to RE so far is slight. This is not because of its unsuitability. It can only be explained by a widespread but surprising reluctance to accept structural-developmental theories of any kind. Institutional religion has frequently placed greater reliance upon instruction and training than on the individual's understanding of doctrines and their consequences for daily life. Teachers in state schools have often followed the same line or else have concentrated on information about religion(s) including statements of moral codes. The evidence suggests that by about 16 years of age (i.e., school-leaving age in the UK) many but by no means all pupils have acquired conventional moral reasoning. Therefore teachers of RE in day-schools cannot expect to find many progressing beyond this level. However, the evidence for the development of moral reasoning in adult life is a challenge to those responsible for adult religious education, and it is here that Kohlberg's work has much to offer.

REFERENCES

Bachmeyer, T. J. (1973) 'The use of Kohlberg's theory of moral development in religious education', *The Living Light*, 10, pp. 340–50.

Blatt, M. M. and Kohlberg, L. (1975) 'The effects of classroom moral discussion upon children's level of moral judgment', *Journal of Moral Education*, 14, 2, pp. 129–61.

Conn, W. E. (1975) 'Postconventional morality: An exposition and critique of Lawrence Kohlberg's analysis of moral development in the adolescent and adult,' *Lumen Vitae*, 30, pp. 213–30.

Conn, W. E. (1981) 'Affectivity in Kohlberg and Fowler', *Religious Education*, 76, pp. 33–48.

Duska, R. and Whelan, M. (1977) *Moral development: A guide to Piaget and Kohlberg*, Dublin, Gill and Macmillan.

Dykstra, C. (1980) 'Moral virtue or social reasoning', *Religious Education*, 75, 2, pp. 115–28.

Emswiler, J. P. (1976) 'Implications of developmental research on religious education methodologies', *Religious Education*, 71, 6, pp. 622–8.

Fowler, J. (1974) *To See the Kingdom: The Theological Vision of H. Richard Niebuhr*, Nashville, N.Y., Abingdon Press.

Fowler, J. and Keen, S. (1978) *Life-maps: Conversations on the Journey of Faith*, Berryman, J. (Ed.), Waco, Tex., Word Books.

Fowler, J. (1980) 'Faith and the structuring of meaning', in Fowler, J. and Vergote, A. (Eds.) *Towards Moral and Religious Maturity*, Morristown, N.J., Silver Burdett, pp. 51–85.

Fowler, J. (1981) *Stages of Faith: The Psychology of Human Development and the Quest for Meaning*, London, Harper and Row.

Gilligan, C. (1980) 'Justice and responsibility: Thinking about real dilemmas of moral conflict and choice', in Fowler, J. and Vergote, A. (Eds.) *Towards Moral and Religious Maturity*, Morristown, N.J., Silver Burdett, pp. 223–49.

Gilligan, C. (1982a) *In a Different Voice: Psychological Theory and Women's Development*, Harvard, University Press.

Gilligan, C. (1982b) 'New maps of development: New visions of maturity', in *American Journal of Orthopsychiatry*, 52, 2, pp. 199–212.

Gorman, M. (1977) 'Moral and faith development in 17 year-old students', *Religious Education*, 72, 5, pp. 491–504.

Groome, T. H. (1980) *Christian Religious Education*, London, Harper and Row.

Haggett, M. (1974) 'Do Catholics need moral education?' *The Clergy Review*, 59, pp. 681–7.

Howe, L. T. (1979) 'A developmental perspective on conversion', *Perkins Journal*, 33, 1, pp. 20–35.

Joy, D. M. (1980) 'Moral development: Evangelical perspectives', *Religious Education*, 75, 2, pp. 142–51.

Kegan, R. (1980) 'There the dance is: Religious dimensions of a developmental framework', Fowler, J. and Vergote, A. (Eds.) *Towards Moral and Religious Maturity*, Morristown, N.J., Silver Burdett, pp. 403–40.

Kohlberg, L. (1973) 'Continuities in childhood and adult moral development revisited,' in Baltes, P. and Schaie, W. (Eds.) *Life-span Developmental Psychology*, New York, Academic Press, pp. 179–204.

Kohlberg, L. (1974) 'Education, moral development and faith', *Journal of Moral Education*, 4, 1, pp. 5–16.

Kohlberg, L. (1976) 'Moral stages and moralisation: The cognitive developmental approach', in Lickona T. (Ed.) *Moral Development and Behaviour; Theory, Research and Social Issues*, London, Holt, Rinehart and Winston, pp. 31–53.

Kohlberg, L. (1979) *Standard Form Scoring Manual*, Centre for Moral Education, Harvard University.

Kohlberg, L. and Gilligan, C. (1971) 'The adolescent as a philosopher; The discovery of the self in a post-conventional world', *Daedalus*, 100, pp. 1051–86.

Kohlberg, L. and Kramer, R. (1969) 'Continuities and discontinuities in childhood and adult moral development', *Human Development*, 12, 2, pp. 93–120.

Kohlberg, L. and Power, C. (1981) 'Moral development, religious thinking and the question of a seventh stage', in Kohlberg, L. *Essays on Moral Development*, Vol. 1, London, Harper and Row, pp. 311–72.

McDonagh, E. (1980) 'Moral theology and moral development', in Fowler, J. and Vergote, A. (Eds.) *Towards Moral and Religious Maturity*, Morristown, N.J., Silver Burdett, pp. 319–42.

Marshall, R. B. (1979) 'Faith inquiry: An exploration of the nature and nurture of adolescent faith', *Perkins Journal*, 33, 1, pp. 36–50.

Niebuhr, H. R. (1963) *The Responsible Self*, London, Harper and Row.

O'Donohoe, J. A. (1980) 'Moral and faith development theory', in Fowler, J. and Vergote, A. (Eds.) *Towards Moral and Religious Maturity*, Morristown N.J., Silver Burdett, pp. 373–401.

Oser, F. (1980) 'Stages of religious judgment', in Fowler, J. and Vergote, A. (Eds.) *Towards Moral and Religious Maturity*, Morristown, N.J., Silver Burdett pp. 277–315.

Philibert, P. (1975a) 'L. Kohlberg's use of virtue in his theory of moral development', *International Philosophical Quarterly*, 15, pp. 455–79.

Philibert, P. (1975b) 'Some cautions on Kohlberg', *The Living Light*, 12, pp. 527–34.

Power, C. and Kohlberg, L. (1980) 'Religion, morality and ego development', in Fowler, J. and Vergote, A. (Eds.) *Towards Moral and Religious Maturity*, Morristown, N.J., Silver Burdett, pp. 343–72.

Rahner, K. (1978) *Foundations of Christian Faith*, London, Darton, Longman and Todd.

Rest, J. R. (1973) 'The hierarchical nature of moral judgment', *Journal of Personality*, 41, 1, pp. 86–109.

Rest, J. R. (1976) 'New approaches in the assessment of moral judgment', in Lickona, L. (Ed.) *Moral Development and Behaviour: Theory, Research and Social Issues*, New York, Holt, Rinehart and Winston, pp. 98–218.

Selman, R. (1971a) 'The relation of role-taking to the development of moral judgment in children', *Child Development*, 42, 1, pp. 79–91.

Selman, R. (1971b) 'Taking another's perspective: Role-taking development in early childhood', *Child Development*, 42, pp. 1721–34.

Selman, R. (1980) *The Growth of Interpersonal Understanding: Developmental and Clinical Analysis*, New York, Academic Press.

Sholl, D. (1971) 'The contributions of L. Kohlberg to religious and moral education', *Religious Education*, 66, pp. 364–72.

Smith, M. E. (1978) 'Moral reasoning: Its relation to logical thinking and role-taking', *Journal of Moral Education*, 8, 1, pp. 41–9.

Smith, M. E. (1980) 'Obedient sonship', *British Journal of Religious Education*, 2, 3, pp. 85–98.

Smith, M. E. (1983a) 'Developments in faith', *The Month*, 16, 7, pp. 222–5.

Smith, M. E. (1983b) 'Contemporary theories of psychological growth', in O'Leary D. and Sallnow, T. (Eds.) *Religious Education and Young Adults*, Slough, St Paul Publications.

Smith, W. C. (1979) *Faith and Belief*, Princeton, N.J.

Spidell, S. and Lieberman, D. (1981) 'Moral development and the forgiveness of sin', *Journal of Psychology and Theology*, 9, 2, pp. 159–63.

Toulmin, S. (1950) *An Examination of the Place of Reason in Ethics*, Cambridge, Cambridge University Press.

Turiel, E. (1974) 'Conflict and transition in adolescent moral judgment', *Child Development*, 45, pp. 14–29.

West, A. N. (1978) 'Biblical history as a progression through Kohlberg's moral stages', *Journal of Altered States of Consciousness*, 4, 1, pp. 23–36.

Youniss, J. (1973) 'Kohlberg's theory: A commentary', *The Living Light*, 10, pp. 352–8.

19. ME + RE = Kohlberg with a Difference

BRIAN GATES

From the perspective of Religious Education (RE) Lawrence Kohlberg (1971) has evident attraction as one of the exponents of an evolutionary sequence of child development who have been so influential in the last twenty years.[1] At a time when RE was under scrutiny and considered by many to be somewhat lacking in educational justification in public state provision,[2] it was helpful to be able to show that there is a rationality and coherent logical structure in children's religious development. Piagetian interpretation of a child's understanding of the world was seen to include not only concepts of space, time and place, but also those of morality and religion. This was the effect of the work of Goldman (1964) in the UK, Elkind (1964) and Peatling (1973) in the USA, and, in some degree, of Godin (1971) in Belgium and France.[3] The shift from sub-religious intuitional thinking, through the concrete 'flat-land' thought of middle childhood to more elaborated (and therefore genuine?) religious understanding was welcomed as a basis on which the teacher might order his/her otherwise confused approach to the matter of religious belief and behaviour.[4] Very similarly, Kohlberg seemed to provide a parallel account of stages of moral development that any teacher might refer to in understanding individual children in class.

In addition, from a background of Christian moral theology, Kohlberg could be seen as validating a new and contemporary version of an ancient tradition: a 'socio-psychological' equivalent of natural law.[5] For in his view there is a natural human givenness which betrays a recognizable pattern of moral development that is invariant in sequence and universal in provenance.[6] Again, this has been welcomed when much else in social science is shifting sands.[7]

The enormous interest in Kohlberg's work ensured that his account of six stages was widely disseminated even while refinements of the developmental continuum were still being made in the light of further longitudinal and cross-cultural study.[8] Although Kohlberg himself may now be even more careful than ten

295

or fifteen years ago to qualify the claims he makes about moral development, the basic shape of his assumptions about religion and morality, both separately and as they interconnect, has been consistent since 1958.[9] Without calling into question the total worth of Kohlberg's position, at several points it is less well grounded in common sense than it might be and accordingly more insensitive about the nature of RE than it need be.

In the pages that follow, four major areas of incompleteness will be identified: the empirical base; 'Where there's no will there's no way'; alternative religious outcomes; and religion within and without the bounds of morality. Finally, some reflections on religious and moral education are included which draw on particular experience in England and Wales.

EXPOSING WHAT IS MISSING

The Empirical Base

The care taken by Kohlberg to follow up his subjects over an extended period of time confirms that he recognizes how important it is that his theory is well earthed in ordinary human experience. This is all the more vital given the claim that natural humanity in its entirety has a moral direction which progresses with the interaction of psycho-genetic inheritance and social context. It is perhaps the more surprising therefore to discover that in several respects the base is open to question, as remarked elsewhere in the book. The evidence of 'regression' by subjects during the period of higher education is open to various interpretations;[10] this, and Kohlberg's recasting in recent years of the upper stages to the point of withdrawing Stage 6, if not also Stage 5, are unsettling in themselves.[11] Of greater threat, however, is the size of the data base invoked to support the predictive correlation of stage of moral development with actions performed.[12] It is a commonplace of the religious experience of mankind, as of Adlerian psychology, that it is the deeds that count more than the words: do the actions that crop up match earlier verbal declarations, or were these sown on the wind? There is a fundamental snag here, and since RE must needs be specially sensitive in respect of a much remarked human propensity for hypocrisy, we will return to it. For the moment, however, the point is registered that Kohlberg's own data may be too ambiguous to bear the weight of normative judgment attributed to them about the way the individual 'shapes up' towards moral and religious maturity.

Some doubt on Kohlberg's judgment is cast by empirical evidence from other sources as illustrated in the following three examples. The first comes from England in the 1960s and takes the form of children responding to such quotations as 'what does naughty/bad/wrong mean?'; 'what does being fair mean?'; 'telling lies/ bullying—what are they?'; 'is it wrong to tell lies/bully? If so, why?'. According to Williams (1969), who conducted the research with 790 children aged 4–18 years, responses fell into seventeen different modes which were in turn reducible to Peck and Havighurst's well established types: Amoral; Expedient (self-considering); Irrational-conscientious (self-obeying); Conforming (other-obeying); and Rational-altruistic (other considering). On Kohlberg's consecutive stage sequence there is a shift from amoral and expedient through role conformity to principled altruism.

According to Williams, however, all these different responses are found even in the youngest children and commonly a child answered him in more than one mode. Although a 'pecking order' may emerge in each child as s/he grows older, the different modes of thinking develop *in parallel*, initially prompted by situation-specific reactions of adults but later generalized to other areas. Thus, what the neighbours will think or a twinge of guilt may subsist alongside a generous altruism in the thinking of even the most mature of adults, and a 'primitive' altruistic reasoning may well occur in the young child.[13] Kohlberg (1971) admits as much from his own family experience in his 4-year-old son's vegetarian protest and sympathy for seals. But this is categorized as Stage 1 because associated with a parallel judgment that Eskimos deserve to be eaten because they kill animals. The subtlety of the child's response is missed, if the fellow-feeling and basic sense of justice can be crudely put down as Stage 1; in this particular instance it is perhaps less obviously an outrageous comment in the 'land of the buffalo burger' than it would be among Jains.[14] But RE sensibilities are also aroused by the issue of whether or not evidence from children indicates a capacity for altruistic thinking of a sustained kind in earliest years, in respect of both humanity and God. Williams indicates that the evidence is not irrefutably on Kohlberg's side in this.

A second example from England in the 1970s presses this particular point further. As part of a larger study on the development of beliefs and values in children and young people, Gates (1976) includes an analysis of a subsample of 310 children's (aged 6–16 years) responses to the questions, 'whom do you love?. . . Do you think you should love everybody (where you live . . . in your class)?. . . Why/why not?. . . How do you decide who to love?' Using the Williams' classification, the different modes are found across the entire age-range, with one exception. Curiously, other-obeying responses (invoking personal figures, society or peer group, or the law) were rarely given in this context, although they were more frequently used by the same boys and girls elsewhere in the interview. The few which were 'other obeying' took religious form: 'you're meant to love each other. *Meant by whom*? meant by God' (11-year-old girl with no formal religious association). 'In Islam it says even if the people are people you don't like, you should still have respect for them. We are really kind of brothers and sisters to everyone in that kind of way. *There is nobody you don't respect*? There are some I don't respect because they are bullies, but you still have to respect; that is what it says in Islam' (13-year-old Muslim boy). But not all the religious responses took this form, for instance, a 7-year-old Catholic girl: 'I love everybody in the world, even if they don't like me. They are God as well, they've got Jesus inside them—God the spirit.' Here the claim on her love comes simultaneously from within and without herself. Closer inspection of the relationship between religion and morality is yet to come, but alternative empirical data do not confirm that Kohlberg's stages are consecutive and invariant in sequence and confined in childhood years to instrumental hedonism or comfortable conformity.

The third example comes from South India early in 1980. It is in the form of an intensive study by Kalam (1981) of the religious and moral thinking of 150 individuals in the region of Chavakkad in the state of Kerala. In effect he achieves remarkable control of the religious variable in a non-Western setting, for his subjects share a common linguistic, cultural and political background, and similar economic status, yet there are three distinct religious groups involved: Mar Thoma Christians, Hindus and Muslims. The ages ranged from 8 to 80 and each group was evenly stratified into five age bandings. As part of Form A of Kohlberg's moral judgment interview, subjects were all presented with Indianized versions of the Heinz (now Raju) and other dilemmas. They were also taken through a semi-clinical interview schedule, adapted for intelligibility, but based on Fowler's (1981) approach to faith development. Responses on both tests were then scored by Kalam and independently by Colby on the moral and Fowler and his associates on the religious.

On philosophical grounds, Kohlberg holds the view that religion and morality are logically independent, though variously interrelated. In addition, he makes the empirical claim that the trans-culturally universal pattern of moral development is necessary for and prior to the relativities of religious development (Power and Kohlberg, 1980). Fowler shares Kohlberg's Piagetian heritage but puts forward the alternative claim that faith (ultimate horizon/personal centre of commitment) not only develops in a parallel series of stages, but *precedes* and is necessary for the moral stages. The result of Kalam's research is to cast empirical doubt on both their views. In half his sample Kalam finds complete agreement between moral and faith stages; of the other seventy-four, forty-one show a half-stage difference, twenty-one a full stage and twelve more than one stage. These differences are not confined to upper stages, but occur across the range of Stages 1 to 4 or 5. More disturbingly in this present context, forty-six reveal a higher religious than moral stage, twenty-eight a higher moral than religious. By implication Kalam goes on to question the validity of using the evidence of Power (1977) and Shulik (1979)—adduced by Kohlberg, or Mischey (1976)—adduced by Fowler, to support their respective views. Whereas in the case of his own research scoring was done by two different persons 'blind', in the other cases the same person(s) were responsible and privy to the entire scoring. In other words, the precedence of moral development over religious development, or *vice versa*, may relate more to scorer inclination than to a cognitively universal fact.

Kalam's study also repudiates the claim by Kohlberg to have changed successfully from content-dominated scoring procedures to criterion-based formal structure. Even with the carefully annotated Scoring Manual, Kalam argues that reference is still made to content or, if not, that arbitrary judgments occur. One instance of the difficulty of content-free scoring is illustrated by the response of an 8-year-old Muslim boy to the Heinz dilemma: 'give your (Heinz's) wife to the druggist, who will then give her the medicine and cure her so that he can have her as one of his wives.' By criterion reference scoring this may indicate someone at Stage 1/2: although technically the solution is found within the bounds of Islamic law, the wife becomes a 'bartered bride'. The boy went on to say, however: 'If you love your wife, you want her to live, somehow or other; you wouldn't want to keep her to yourself and let her die.' It is difficult to question that this is a cognitively satisfying response of a higher stage. Similarly, Kalam draws attention to Kohlberg's attribution of Eichman to Stage 1 rather than Stage 4 in his thinking when, *formally* the latter seems more appropriate.[15] The switch away from content would therefore appear to be a partial one.

Overall, the work of Kalam, as a moral theologian, directs its critical gaze to devastating effect at the empirical grounding of Kohlberg's and Fowler's theories. Thus a succession of questions generated by the sensitivities of Religious Education has the cumulative effect of creating scepticism that Kohlberg has really identified the proven shape of moral evolution in human beings as he had hoped.

'Where There's No Will There's No Way'

There are some versions of Moral Education which have as their priority the induction of children into well defined routines of behaviour. Outward conformity is at a premium; inward understanding appears to count for very little. Arguably, what is involved here is more 'socialization' of a particular kind than moral education. Indeed, it is one of Kohlberg's strengths, from an RE perspective, that he abhors conditioned learning as the main vehicle for moral education and instead places great stress on individual reasoning which may be sharpened by practice. Thus, dilemmas are a means not only of assessing the stage of an individual's moral development, but also of encouraging his/her further progress.

It would therefore be unfair to criticize the fact that Kohlberg uses Socratic dialogue as a technique for refining personal understanding and judgment. Indeed, in more recent writings, he has also set this in the context of the participatory role experience in democratically run cluster schools (Kohlberg, 1980); this is seen as a context for cultivating (he actually uses the term 'indoctrination') civic sense to combat a current mood of 'privatism' in society at large. With Power he has called attention to 'the social atmosphere of the school as an educational resource'. However, the medium throughout is exclusively verbal and from an RE perspective this would seem to be a mistake.

Basic beliefs and values are often verbally articulated, but they may also be nurtured, carried and expressed in gesture, image and example, in music, movement and visual art.[16] An approach to Moral Education or RE that lacks these enactive, iconic and imitative dimensions is impoverished, and the cluster school may well miss out on life if its priority is primarily cast in the following terms: 'the teacher's role is to facilitate the discussion and resolution of the conflict by encouraging students to speak thoughtfully, sharpening the points of disagreement, raising unexamined but important issues, and presenting ideas which challenge further enquiry.'[17] Learning to think clearly and critically is important but there is more to Moral Education than this.

It is not surprising in this light that Kohlberg has had to acknowledge a gap between the school (or prison) expression of a just community and the larger school or rest of society; societies operate not just at the diverse levels of moral sophistication, but in far more than just verbal currency. RE because of its appreciation of ritual, myth and image in the religious experience of mankind has to find Kohlberg wanting in these respects. Their contribution to the realm of moral experience has been remarked in disciplines ranging from anthropology and sociobiology to psychoanalysis,[18] and the artistic hearts that like an Iris Murdoch or a Maurice Sendak explore the sovereignty of good in more imaginative forms.

A restriction in Kohlberg's own perspective is also apparent in his reluctance to recognize that knowledge of what is good might not actually be translated into actions that are good. While respecting this persistent loyalty to Plato, RE is aware that by implication less respect is shown for the Hebrew tradition of humankind as fallen, a tradition replicated elsewhere in the world's great collection of creation stories, and translated theologically into a much misunderstood doctrine of original sin. The Pauline 'good that I know I don't do, the evil that I'd rather avoid I do instead' may not be a universally human experience, but it resonates for many.[19] In individual terms, it may be dealt with under the heading of weakness of will, more sociologically, as collective aberration and estrangement that inhibits action for good through structural pressures to the contrary.[20] Either form is a further reminder of the gulf between theory and practice mentioned above. Even if the adage, 'the shinier the halo the dirtier the feet', has got it wrong, RE has to say to Kohlberg: look again at the process by which words and intentions are transformed into actions. Not only is there an affective as well as a cognitive ingredient to which Kohlberg duly insists he does justice,[21] but there is also the matter of the connative. The actor's willingness and motivation are crucial, and Kohlberg pays less attention to them than an RE perspective would sense to be both appropriate and necessary.

Alternative Religious Outcomes

In spite of the widespread occurrence of the Golden Rule in different civilizations,[22] there is evident diversity in religion and culture, past and present. By virtue of his singular commitment to the principle of justice, however, and his insistence not only that moral precedes religious development, but that it does so in a unilinear way, Kohlberg shrinks reality. In effect he imposes a monochrome view of morality on an otherwise pluralistic universe. RE has its own experience of making the same mistake. There was a time when it enjoyed a confusion of identity with Christian education, and allowed privileges to be claimed for church authority that do not belong in public educational provision in an open society.[23] There has also been a temptation to define religion as 'theistic belief', when this religious tradition or that may even be sceptical of all talk of God or gods.[24] RE is the more wary then when a Kohlberg (or a Rawls) posits one particular model of morality.

This is not to deny that justice as a key concept figures throughout the religious experience of mankind. But the Islamic sense of justice as determined by Qur'an is qualified differently from Judaic or Christian justice, as also from Buddhist or Hindu. Again, other key concepts are just as important in the field of social ethics, or, for instance, that of love or 'agapeistic responsibility'. Indeed, such may be more morally constructive for solving a dilemma than the principle of distributive justice mathematically applied. Would the moral theologians from any of these traditions agree with Kohlberg that the drawing of lots for suicide is the most sensitive moral outcome from the dilemma in which a pilot, an old man and a young man are marooned on a raft with survival prospects fair if there were two of them, poor if three?[25]

The starting-point within a religious tradition may actually be antithetic to Kohlberg because the notion of Revelation, on some renderings, deliberately demotes the power of human reason. For instance, on certain understandings of the Bible, the Qur'an, or the Granth as the Word of God, any definition of true justice must derive exclusively from that one source. All other sources are human counterfeit. Religious and moral development alike must be moulded towards that scriptural norm.

On these views, Kohlberg's justice is, strictly speaking, irrelevant because its autonomous logic presumes to rule when it is seen as lacking the true authority to do so. Kohlberg may retort that this sounds very like Stage 3 reasoning, but if it is, and it is therefore judged to be rationally inferior, to change the mind of someone of this persuasion will involve their theological as well as moral transformation. Alternatively, Kohlberg will need to acknowledge that the source of true revelation and morality lies beyond reasons. Kohlberg may be unable to agree to this, but the position is held with deep conviction by religious believers of many complexions.

There is also another position within religious traditions with regard to the notion of revelation. Instead of seeing scripture and reason as incompatible, with the one overwhelming the other for either believer or sceptic, they are claimed to be complementary. Special revelation fulfils general knowledge; there is a natural religious and moral sense that is completed by the grace of God. Thus, Paul and Aquinas in the Christian tradition affirm that there is a basic sense of God and ought found generally in human experience.[26] Similar views are found within the Jewish tradition of the Noachic Covenant,[27] or in Islam with the Mu'tazilite recognition of right and wrong independently of the Qur'an itself, though underwritten by it.[28] In the Indian tradition, the emphasis is more on progressive enlightenment and stages of spiritual discovery than on special scriptural revelation, so that the questing path of salvation is often seen as quite compatible with rational enquiry. However, in all these cases, revelation and enlightenment, while not overturning reason, anticipate a process of personal transformation whose moral outcome will not be simply the rational autonomy of Western liberalism. For such an outcome, contrary to Kohlberg's theorizing, would actually be an unnatural law.

From such critical backgrounds as these, it is not surprising to find dissenting theological criticism of Kohlberg. For instance, some evangelical Christians are impatient with the way the individual is recognized as potentially authoritative, in wilful ignorance of the grace of God from beyond.[29] Similarly, some Catholics defer instead to the Roman magisterium as determinative source for both religious and moral education, although others are able to accommodate their Catholic faith to fit the Kohlberg framework.[30] A more radical critique is that of Dykstra (1981) who thinks that Christian ethics and education are not cognitive developmental but involve instead multi-dimensional moral growth. He contrasts the 'juridical' ethics of Kohlberg with what he terms 'visional' ethics—mystery-encouraging rather than problem-solving, for it is imagination, the vehicle of personal illumination, that transforms someone's character. He accepts Kohlberg's account of (the first) four stages of social reasoning, but claims that any outcome in moral virtue derives from other more imaginative sources.[31] Dykstra's view chimes well with an existentialist criticism which is suspicious of any well ordered sequence of human development. Kohlberg's 'conveyor belt' is far too predictable for the individual child or adult who may think or act discontinuously and so remain mysterious at heart.[32]

From a Jewish perspective, Rosenzweig (1977) seizes on Kohlberg's central concern with universal justice to advance the claim that they share the same priority for fostering progress towards it.[33] However, closer inspection indicates that similarity is more apparent than real. Comparing Kohlberg with modern and Reformed Jews, Chazan (1980) identifies fundamental incompatibilities. Irrespective of any 'natural law' connection, he says that contemporary educational provision by the non-orthodox Jew aims at reinforcing a sense of Jewish group identification and teaches a specific and substantive value system markedly different from Kohlberg's. Some of the teaching methods might alone be shared with him. As to the more orthodox tradition of Jewish education, because of its preoccupation with a very specific and definitive life-style, Chazan finds it very different from Kohlberg's stress on patterns of thinking. Kohlberg is interested in formal principles, whereas orthodoxy stresses the oneness of principles and Jewish tradition in an all-inclusive Jewish communal setting.

Similar points of difference can be identified from other religious traditions.

Even secularized versions of the world's religions have fundamental differences in expectation that derive from their distinctive theological and ethical resources.

Thus Kohlberg's understanding of moral development is the poorer from his not having recognized the different impacts that religion can have in its outward and inward manifestations. Where religion and revelation are viewed as different as chalk from cheese, then Kohlberg's ambitions for children's moral or religious development are almost certainly in conflict with those of the religious community. Where, however, they are viewed as complementary, the religious communities might still ask of Kohlberg that he show more sensitivity to their own theologically laden aspirations for children. RE, in turn, acknowledges the need for stage development talk to be open to outcomes differentiated by theologic, whether Christian or Hindu, Marxist or atheist.[34]

Religion Within and Without the Bounds of Morality

The sheer diversity of religions and world views creates serious difficulty for any approach to religion and ethics which wants to route them all to one particular destination—along the same path. In this Kohlberg has shared the Western insularity of much moral philosphy which has allowed itself the luxury of defining its terms of reference in substantial ignorance of other traditions of reflection and value elsewhere in the world.[35] References may have been made in passing to other world views, but even recently it is Spinoza or Santayana who are invoked for 'mystical pantheism' rather than the Indian religious tradition.[36] Thus not only is the cross-cultural base less than adequate in empirical terms, conceptually it is doubtful whether the actual diversity of religions and world views has been taken very seriously at all.

In this Kohlberg's understanding of the relation between religion and morality may itself be the root fault. He insists that the moral reference point comes first: in terms of the Euthyphro dilemma, good is good because it is and not because declared to be such by God. In this he is at odds with believers in a scriptural revelation which is propositionally prescriptive of right and wrong. He also fails to recognize the logic of more inductive theological positions. Because the very polarity built into this dilemma is taken as a starting-point, it is the more difficult for him to allow the position that goodness and godness may mutually coinhere, or, again, that there may rationally be claims 'both ways'—from justice or love on God, or from religious conviction on moral expression.

It is possible, however, to detect some hesitation in Kohlberg on this front. His postulation of a hypothetical Stage 7 may have been immediately occasioned by the Catholic context to which he was speaking (Kohlberg, 1974), but it also reflects his awareness that there is a nagging 'Why?' question to be answered in respect of any moral action. Why do right rather than wrong? Even if I have arrived at the elusive Stage 6 why does it matter? Why should I bother? At this juncture Kohlberg admits the relevance of fundamental assumptions and beliefs about the meaning of life. Curiously, they have been left to the end.

In subsequent writings explanation of Stage 7 has been limited. Latterly, however, he appears to admit that Stage 7 concerns may be in some sense continuous with each stage of moral development, and Fowler's work on stages of faith development is seen as providing the further explanation. Yet, as has already been remarked, there is a fundamental disagreement between them over whether religious or moral development has priority over the other. The concluding section of Kohlberg's statement on this question, written in conjunction with Power, is firm that stage of moral development places a ceiling on religious development. It is not at all permissive that stage of religious development, or mode of religious thinking, may open up a new stage, let alone whole avenues, of moral development.

In this Kohlberg's thinking may yet be open to change. For Power's appreciation of the religious dimension of knowing and being in which he follows Tillich and others[37] at least entails new recognition of a continuous relation of moral and religious wavelengths. Without conceding Fowler's claim that morality depends on faith (however broadly defined) and thereby abandoning notions of natural law and human autonomy, it is still possible to insist that religion contributes significantly to the content and context, grounds and bounds, of morality (Wallwork, 1980). Religion may not be the necessary or sufficient basis for ethics, but ethics without religion may not be sufficient either, and the necessity of ethics, like that of religion, is no less open to debate and doubt.

The phrase 'autonomy of ethics' may actually be misleading if it has the effect of adolescent posturing of ethics against religion, as though proving some substitute machismo virtue. 'Autonomy' as expounded by Riesman in *Lonely Crowd* has the positive connotation of independence and critical openness, as contrasted with sheepish conformity. However, as he stresses in the third edition, it can also appear narcissistic, self-centred, and even neurotic, lacking the communal warmth and sensitivity that may actually be an aspect of conformity.[38] Perhaps the term 'relative autonomy' would better serve their general interests if the relation between ethics and religion were each described as relatively autonomous. Thus an outcome that was relative to cosmic meaning (my own and others) might be admitted as common goal.

If indeed there is flexibility in Kohlberg's thinking on this general front, the popularized impression of a monorail to the sixth stage or seventh heaven will need to be re-made. How drastically will depend on the extent to which he may care to recognize divergent and convergent highways and byways by and along which men, women and children grow in moral stature, religious belief and unbelief.

WHAT ENGLAND HAS THAT KOHLBERG LACKS?

Throughout this chapter the term RE has been used in an English sense to connote a form of education which is different from Christian and other particularized forms of initiatory religious education, although complementary to them. This is a distinction that was systematically hammered out in the period 1965–80.[39] It acknowledges the importance of specific nurture in a faith being provided by a parent religious community, but it recognizes that such is out of place in a public educational system. Instead it sees the priority of the public school curriculum to be enabling boys and girls to become not just literate and numerate, but also 'religiate', so that they leave school having had the opportunity to understand and test religious belief and unbelief on their pulses, and knowing, at least at a preliminary level, their way around the religious experience of mankind.[40]

This development has been nourished in the face of the tensions of religious diversity: fifty or more years ago they were between different versions of Christianity and the 'Agreed Syllabus' tradition developed to provide a common biblical framework within which the disputants could feel their common interests were being served.[41] Now it is between different world religions, including secular humanism, and again a common framework has been sought,[42] this time more inclusive of other faiths.

The result is that unlike the USSR, England and Wales have a built-in opportunity for the exploration of basic ingredients of religious beliefs and ideologies, and opportunity for critical thinking about them.[43] Unlike the USA, it is not customary for reference to religious belief to be extensively bracketed out from public school. In principle, therefore, there is opportunity to examine both mainstream religious tradition and quite possibly to build immunity against more hazardous flowerings.[44]

From this RE perspective the question arises whether Kohlberg's position in compartmentalizing religion and ethics may in part be a rationalization of the great divide between church and state, between beliefs and values, in the American school system.[45] The unhappy consequence of it is that other skills and resources relevant from RE for moral education and development are neglected by him.

It may even be that in the English tradition of school assemblies, not understood as sectional acts of formal Christian worship, but open explorations and celebrations of the values, beliefs and identities that undergird the school as an educational community, there is experience for Kohlberg to draw on.[46] Here may be a means of enriching his cluster schools within schools to achieve the larger participation model of school-in-the-world for which he yearns.[47]

NOTES

1 Not to be confused with earlier developmental hypotheses such as G. Hall's 'ontogeny recapitulates phylogeny' or A. Gesell's 'age portraits'. The 'cognitive developmental' approach has stressed much more the interaction between subject and social context.

2 E.g., P. H. Hirst (1965) 'Morals and religion in the maintained school', *British Journal of Educational Studies*, 14, 1.

3 For summary analysis see: D. Elkind (1971) 'Development of religious understanding in children and adolescents', in M. Strommen (Ed.) *Research on Religious Development*, New York, Hawthorn Books, or B. E. Gates (1975) 'Readiness for religion', in N. Smart and D. Horder, *New Movements in RE*, London, Temple-Smith.

4 Cf. R. Goldman (1965) *Readiness for Religion*, London, Routledge and Kegan Paul, and Local Education Authority Agreed Syllabuses 1965–75.

5 For introduction to this tradition see A. P. d'Entrèves (1951) *Natural Law*, London, Hutchinson.

6 Kohlberg's cross-cultural data are limited in quantity, but evidence from Israel, Turkey and Taiwan encouraged him to advance the claim to have discovered this trans-cultural constant; cf. 'Moral and Religious Education and the public schools', in T. Sizer (Ed.) (1967) *The Role of Religion in Public Education*, Boston, Mass., Houghton Mifflin.

7 Cultural relativism which accepts the principle that humankind is utterly conditioned by time and place has emerged comparatively recently in the West—the 'Midas touch' turns all to history—whereas existence in the Indian tradition has been perceived as impermanent for thousands of years.

8 It is a moot point whether the funding and publicity were counterproductive. Certainly they guaranteed momentum, whereas a comparable venture in the field of Moral Education in Oxford sponsored by the Farmington Trust was cut at the quick of its development.

9 The year of completion of Kohlberg's Chicago PhD thesis: *The Development of Modes of Moral Thinking and Choice in the Years Ten to Sixteen*.

10 In the follow-up longitudinal study the seventy-five original boys became fifty; the reported

regression is predominantly related to changed social context.

11 It would appear that Stage 6 is now regarded as the preserve of select moral philosophers. Stage 4B is becoming the most commonplace goal instead.

12 Opting out of the S. Milgram 'volunteers for electric shock' experiment appeared to correlate with Stage 6 thinkers or Stage 2. Since Stage 6 is no longer considered realistic for most people, the emergent basis of predictive correlation suddenly disappears.

13 The question of validity of the notion of 'altruism' whether in human or animal kind is at the centre of major debate in sociobiology: cf. R. Dawkins (1976) *The Selfish Gene*, London; A. Montagu (Ed.) (1980) *Sociobiology Examined*, London, Oxford University Press.

14 The Indian emphasis on ahimsa (non-violence) reaches 'extreme' expression in the Jains who may even be wary of quenching living flame or breathing in a micro-organism that unwittingly could be killed.

15 So the manual: L. Kohlberg, A. Colby, J. Gibbs, B. Speicher-Dubin and C. Power (1980) *The Measurement of Moral Judgment*, Harvard Centre.

16 Cf. B. E. Gates (1982) 'Children prospecting for commitment', in R. Jackson (Ed.) *Approaching World Religions*, London, J. Murray.

17 Kohlberg and Power (1980) *op. cit.* p. 370.

18 Cf. S. Langer (1957) *Philosophy in a New Key: A Study in the Symbolism of Reason, Rite and Art* Boston, Mass., Harvard University Press.

19 Rom, 7:14–20.

20 Cf. R. Niebuhr (1932) *Moral Man Immoral Society* New York, Scribners and P. Tillich (1957) *Systematic Theology*, Vol. 2, London, Nisbet, Chs 13–15. The link between the traditional Christian notion of sin and the Hegel-Marx translation of it as 'alienation' is often overlooked.

21 Cf. W. E. Conn 'Affectivity in Kohlberg and Fowler', *Religious Education*, 76, 1, pp. 33–48.

22 Cf. E. G. Parrinder school textbooks: (1973) *Themes for Living: Man and God*, London, Hulton, and N. Bull (1971) *The Way of Wisdom Series III Rulers*, London, Longman.

23 Cf. B. E. Gates (1973) 'Varieties of RE', *Religion*, 3, 1; 'RE a proper humanism', *London Educational Review*, Autumn.

24 The point is most commonly made with reference to Theravada Buddhism; cf. N. Smart (1971) *Religious Experience of Mankind*, London, Fontana, p. 366.

25 Cf. T. Kalam (1981) *Myth of Stages and Sequences in Moral and Religious Education*, Lancaster PhD, pp. 198–201. Current address: Dharmaram College, Bangalore 560029, India.

26 Cf. Rom. 2:14, 15 and, for Aquinas, A. P. d'Entrèves *op. cit.*

27 Gen. 9:8–17 with all of human and animal-kind.

28 Cf. G. F. Hourani (1980) 'Ethical presuppositions of the Qur'an', *Muslim World*.

29 Cf. D. M. Joy 'Moral development: Evangelical perspectives', *RE*, 75, 2, pp. 142–51.

30 Cf. R. Duska and M. Whelan (1977) *Moral Development: A Guide to Piaget and Kohlberg*, Dublin, Gill and Macmillan; D. O'Leary (Ed.) (1983) *RE and Young Adult*, Slough, St Paul Publication Ch. 3.

31 On the theological front he appeals elsewhere to David Tracy's *Blessed Rage for Order* and *The Analogical Imagination*.

32 So B. Lealman (1983) 'The last step of reason?' *Journal of Moral Education*, 12, 2, pp. 104–10; cf. Fynn (1977) *Mr God, This Is Anna*, London, Collins.

33 Some parallels have been drawn between Kohlberg's casuistical analysis of subjects' statements and those of Rabbinic tradition on the one hand and Roman Catholic consistatorial courts on the other.

34 See F. Oser (1980) 'Stages of religious judgment', in C. Brusselmans *Toward Moral and Religious Maturity*, New Jersey, Silver Burdett, pp. 277–315; cf. J. L. Elias (1982) 'Ideology and RE' *Lumen Vitae*, 37; 4 pp. 382–95.

35 The field of comparative ethics is currently being opened up; cf. *Journal of Religious Ethic* and more particularly R. Hindery (1978) *Comparative Ethics in Hindu and Buddhist Tradition*, India, Banarsidass.

36 Power and Kohlberg (1980) *op. cit.*, p. 356 for religion and morality in Indian traditions; cf. N. Smart (1958) *Reasons and Faiths*, London, Routledge and Kegan Paul, Ch. 7.

37 Notably from philosophers of religion.

38 Riesman (1961) *op. cit.*, pp. xvii–xxi.

39 Cf. B. E. Gates (Ed.) RE Directory of England and Wales, Lancaster, RE Enquiry Service.

40 The term 'religiate' is coined to indicate that there is public evidence and experience to be understood irrespective of private belief on the part of the individual.

41 The Agreed Syllabus tradition is described in J. M. Hull (1975) 'Agreed Syllabuses, past presents

future', in N. Smart and D. Horder (Eds.) *New Movements in RE*, pp. 97–119.
42 The constitution of the RE Council of England and Wales includes representatives of professional teacher associations and of the main parent religious communities, including the British Humanist Association.
43 This was built into the Schools Council (1977) *Ground Plan for the Study of Religion*; by contrast, the Soviet system concentrates on induction into one particular ideology.
44 Arguably a Jonestown or an Iranian surprise take-over might better be anticipated/countered given effective RE provision in American state schools?
45 On the current prospect for teaching RE in American schools, cf. D. L. Barr and W. E. Collie (1981) 'Religion in the schools: The continuing controversy', *Church & State*, March, pp. 8–16.
46 J. M. Hull *School Worship: An Obituary*, London, SCM Press.
47 So 'Educating for a just society' in B. Munsey (Ed.) (1980) *Moral Development, Moral Education and Kohlberg*, Alabama, Religious Education Press, pp. 455–71.

REFERENCES

Brusselmans, C. (Ed.) (1980) *Toward Moral and Religious Maturity*, New Jersey, Silver Burdett.
Chazan, B. (1980) 'Jewish education and moral development', in B. Munsey, *Moral Development, Moral Education and Kohlberg*, Alabama, Religious Education Press, pp. 298–325.
Colby, A., Kohlberg, L., Gibbs, J. and Lieberman, M. (1980) *A Longitudinal Study of Moral Judgment*, Harvard, Center for Moral Education, unpublished paper.
Dykstra, C. (1981) *Vision and Character: A Christian Educator's Alternative to Kohlberg*, New Jersey, Paulist Press.
Elkind, D. (1964) 'The child's conception of his religious identity', *Lumen Vitae*, 19, pp. 635–46.
Elkind, D. (1967) 'Developmental psychology of religion', in A. H. Kidd and J. L. Rivoire, *Perceptual Development in Children*, London, University Press, Ch. 8.
Fowler, J. W. (1981) *Stages of Faith: The Psychology of Human Development and the Quest for Meaning*, New York, Harper and Row.
Gates, B. E. (1976) *Religion in the Developing World of Children and Young People*, Lancaster University, unpublished doctoral thesis.
Godin, A. (1971) 'Some developmental tasks in Christian education', in M. Strommen (Ed.) *Research on Religious Development*, New York, Hawthorn Books.
Goldman, R. (1964) *Religious Thinking from Childhood to Adolescence*, London, Routledge and Kegan Paul.
Kalam, T. P. (1981) *The Myth of Stages and Sequence in Moral and Religious Development*, Lancaster University, unpublished doctoral thesis.
Kohlberg, L. (1967) 'Moral and Religious Education and the public schools: A developmental view', in T. Sizer (Ed.) *The Role of Religion in Public Education*, Boston, Mass., Houghton-Mifflin.
Kohlberg, L. (1971) 'From is to ought: How to commit the naturalistic fallacy and get away with it in the study of moral development', in T. Mischel (Ed.) *Cognitive Development and Epistemology*, New York, Academic Press, pp. 151–235.
Kohlberg, L. (1971) 'Stages of moral development as a basis for moral education', in C. M. Beck, B. S. Crittenden and E. V. Sullivan (Eds.) *Moral Education: Interdisciplinary Approaches*, Toronto, University Press, pp. 23–92.
Kohlberg, L. (1974) 'Education, moral development and faith', *Journal of Moral Education*, 4, pp. 5–16.
Kohlberg, L. (1976) 'Moral stages and moralization: The cognitive developmental approach', in T. Lickona (Ed.) *Moral Development and Behaviour*, New York, Holt, Rinehart and Winston, pp. 31–53.
Kohlberg, L. (1980) 'Educating for a just society: An updated and revised statement', in B. Munsey (Ed.) *Moral Development, Moral Education and Kohlberg*, Alabama, Religious Education Press, pp. 455–70.
Kohlberg, L. and Power, F. C. (1980) 'Religion, morality and ego development', in C. Brusselmans (Ed.) *Toward Religious Maturity*, pp. 341–72.
Kohlberg, L. and Power, C. (1981) 'Moral development, religious thinking and the question of a seventh stage', in *Essays on Moral Development*, London, Harper and Row.

Mischey, E. J. (1976) *Faith Development and Its Relationship to Moral Reasoning and Identity Status in Young Adults*, Toronto University, unpublished PhD thesis.

Munsey, B. (1980) *Moral Development, Moral Education and Kohlberg*, Alabama, Religious Education Press.

Peatling, J. (1973) *The Incidence of Concrete and Abstract Religious Thinking in the Interpretation of Three Bible Studies*, New York University, unpublished PhD thesis.

Peck, R. F. *et. al.* (1960) *The Psychology of Character Development*, New York, Wiley.

Power, F. C. and Kohlberg, L. (1980) 'Religion, morality and ego development', in C. Brusselmans (Ed.) *Towards Moral and Religious Maturity*, pp. 343–72.

Riesman, D. (1961) *The Lonely Crowd*, New Haven, Conn., Yale University Press, Preface.

Rosenzweig, L. (1977) 'Towards universal justice: Some implications of L. Kohlberg's research for Jewish identity', *Religious Education*, 72, Nov.–Dec.

Rosenzweig, L. (1980) 'Kohlberg in the classroom: Moral education models', in B. Munsey (Ed.) *Moral Development, Moral Education and Kohlberg*, Alabama, Religious Education Press, pp. 359–80.

Shulik, R. and Kohlberg, L. (1980) *The Aging Person as Philosopher: Development in Adult Years*, Harvard Moral Education Centre, unpublished paper.

Tillich, P. (1963) *Morality and Beyond*, New York, Harper and Row.

Wallwork, E. (1980) 'Morality, religion and Kohlberg's theory', in B. Munsey (Ed.) *Moral Development, Moral Education, and Kohlberg*, Alabama, Religious Education Press, pp. 269–97.

Williams, N. (1969) 'Children's moral thought. Part I: Categories of moral thought; *Moral Education*, 1, 1; Part II: Towards a theory of moral development', *Moral Education*, 1, 2.

Interchange

SMITH REPLIES TO GATES

Gates has undertaken a difficult task in trying to write a mainly negative appraisal of Kohlberg's work in respect of religious education. Such an account, we might expect, would have to demonstrate that the theory is unreliable or that it is not relevant to religious education.

Three illustrations are offered which, Gates claims, cast doubt on the theory. Two of them (Williams, 1969; Gates 1976) report and categorize responses to questions. The underlying theoretical foundation is unclear, but it does not seem to be cognitive-developmental in the way that Kohlberg's is, with the demonstration of mental structures (e.g. classification, reciprocity) available at each level and constituting the hierarchical relations. Therefore Gates seems to go well beyond his evidence to claim that the invariant sequence of levels of reasoning is not confirmed. Was this actually being tested in a scientific sense?

The third illustration is doubtful evidence because, as stated in my account, Fowler's scoring procedures are still in a preliminary state, and Gates' account is unclear on the distinction between faith development and the development of religious reasoning. Statistical significance has not been stated and since the points of transition are important, the figures quoted tell us very little for a sample ranging from 8–80 years of age. To say that this piece of research has a 'devastating effect' on the empirical grounding of Kohlberg's theory is simply unjustified. Nor can these three pieces of evidence be counted as having any 'cumulative effect of creating scepticism'.

Gates criticizes Kohlberg's emphasis on words. Can anyone from a Judaeo-Christian tradition (and Islam is closely connected) be justified, though, in calling an emphasis on the verbal 'a mistake'? Revelation is primarily transmitted through 'the word'. Kohlberg is not, of course, setting up to be a teacher of religion, and so his concentration upon one medium of communication rather than another is not culpable.

A concern with moral development presupposes recognition that our moral conduct is all too often less than ideal. The religious doctrine of original sin expresses the acknowledgment that human frailty is unable to withstand the many social pressures and conditioning influences which together constitute human limitation. To pay attention to as many facets of a moral question as we can handle is recognition that the answers are not always self-evident, and to behave as though they were is perhaps an instance of immature egocentricity. The control of the will to carry out what conscience directs is obviously a discipline of another sort, but it is surely helped when our reason allows us no escape from seeing our duty.

Motivation is not neglected in Kohlberg's theory, and the relation of his work to religious commitment is bound up with a proper understanding of Stage 7.

For some people, it is said, adherence to revelation in sacred scripture is opposed to human reasoning about morality. Let us test this generalization through Islam and the Qur'ān. The Islamic conception of God is that he is creator of the universe; creation is an act of mercy (in giving man his existence) and an expression of orderliness. This order is exemplified not only in natural law but in the sense of moral order/disorder with which man is endowed. Justice is the maintenance and establishment of the orderliness proper to humanity. The Qur'ān gives few examples of what Gates calls 'propositionally prescriptive of right and wrong'. Hence Islamic law (which covers all aspects of life: religious, domestic, social and commercial) is derived from the highly intellectual processes of interaction between Qur'ān, the practice of the Prophet, the agreed practice of the community and analogical reasoning. (Much the same could be said of the Jewish Talmud. Likewise we know well the continued debate amongst Christians over major moral issues.)

This is not a Western view of Islam. The information comes from Muslim sources. It is hard to see how the use of the revelation of the Qur'an is at odds with Kohlberg's theory. Of course not every humble Muslim is able to grasp this way of putting things, but this is simply evidence of levels of understanding within any religion. This is a point well made by W. Cantwell Smith in *Faith and Belief.* Across religions, and across the generations in the history of the same religion, there are parallels in attitudes and understanding which support developmental theory. Each religion seems to exemplify the full range of stages.

Gates writes of religions 'in which religious and moral *development* alike must be moulded towards the scriptural norm' and that 'some Catholics defer to the Roman magisterium as determinative source for both religious and moral *education.*' In each case, he seems to take development and education to mean conduct, whereas Kohlberg's theory is to do with mode of understanding.

Some account needs to be taken of the point of calling Stages 3 and 4 'conventional morality'. This will be the adult norm and official teaching will naturally attempt to bring adults to this consensus. The small percentage of adherents who, in some issues, go beyond are the ones whose teaching, writing or example bring about changes in the religion as a whole. Their individual judgment grows out of the foundations of their faith. It is in this way that 'revelation' and 'reason' interact to produce, for example, the teaching of Aquinas (to whom Gates refers), but we know that examples of his stature are rare.

For these reasons we cannot accept the arguments offered for 'alternative religious outcomes'. A cognitive-developmental theory argues that, because of our common humanity, mental structures are found in an invariant sequence, but the effects of cultural environment will be seen in matters such as the furthest limits normally reached. In the present debate, Kohlberg's interpretation of autonomy (Stage 5) must be examined (rather than Riesman's) and it is quite inaccurate to speak of it without showing its close relation with the conforming attitudes of Stage 4.

Unfortunately, Gates leaves his definition of religious education to the end, but what is the precise meaning of being enabled to test religious belief 'on the pulses'? At least to Stage 4 the motivation to morality is not necessarily religious, and a researcher is not required to investigate morality only in a religious context.

The question to be asked of Kohlberg's work is whether it is relevant to religious education, not whether it comprehends the whole of it, and our conclusion remains affirmative.

GATES REPLIES TO SMITH

Smith's exposition of Kohlberg is characteristically sympathetic and well resourced. In this, she is able to draw on her own research applying Kohlberg's classification and also on the corpus of writings of Kohlberg and his colleagues. The two most substantial claims which she makes for him are that he illuminates our understanding of morality as itself a religious concern and that what he has to say about self and interpersonal relationships is also of potential significance for religion.

Part of the argument is compelling. Developmental psychology, following Piaget, is able to demonstrate that boys and girls tend to move from a more restricted form of reasoning in early childhood to a more elaborated mode in late adolescence and adult years. Insofar as individuals are able to be consistent in providing explanation of their understanding of themselves, others and the world around, it is reasonable to expect that their general cognitive development will be reflected in what they actually say. What is less clear is that the outward forms of verbal reasoning are fully able to express the range of meaning sensed from within by child or adult on any particular front. This point is well made in Kegan's use of the words 'dance' and 'creative motion' in preference to more static sounding metaphors of stage or level. Indeed, Kegan is quoted on this; the fact that Smith does so may indicate that she is sensitive about this issue. In other respects, however, she remains loyal to a tighter evolutionary format.

Thus she underscores the set sequence of stages, the way a stage determines a person's thinking, and the temporal priority of the moral stage over religious. For instance, from the portraits sketched from Kohlberg and Power, children may well find themselves thinking of God in terms of mercenary reward and punishment, or ready with criticisms or arbitrariness. By contrast, only the few who get to Stage 5 will be able to understand God as 'energizing' autonomous moral action.

Evidence to support this conclusion is questionable, however Smith herself appears to recognize the shaky quality of the data base used by Kohlberg and Power, and even more so by Fowler. But in citing a Psalm to illustrate the sentiments of Stage 2, she may not be recognizing that the psalmist's speculation, or indeed the Mosaic Decalogue, can all be interpreted by reasoning that corresponds to *each* of Kohlberg's stages. This simply indicates that different forms of moral reasoning exist and that they can be arranged in hierarchical order. It does not entail that all six occur in invariant sequence with little or no 'to-ing and fro-ing' by the individual between any or all the different modes. At what stage is the 6-year-old who speaks of Jesus helping her to decide to help someone, or who explains the giving of presents as to make his mum happy? Although Smith states plainly at one point that 'the lower levels are "less moral" only from a neutral perspective on the scale as a whole', it is easy to see how the language of Stages 1 and 2 can lead to the use of such terms as 'pre/sub-moral' or 'pre/sub-religious'. Because of the judgment that primary and elementary school children are to be expected on the first and second floor escalators of reasoning, they are at risk from such branding; loftier interests and exploring, which they might already be trying at, may go unnoticed. Godin's (1971) comment on Goldman is applicable here: hermeneutical reasoning capacity is not the same as symbolic sense—whether religious or moral.

Kohlberg's insistence on the principle that the moral must always precede the religious is reiterated by Smith. This is more incongruous for one with evident interests in Biblical scholarship than for Kohlberg. For while there are biblical examples of appeal to a moral sense that is to be read off from nature and history, there are also many passages where a theological notion such as the prophetic Day of the Lord is invoked to challenge attitudes and behaviour which is careless of others. This is not done 'heteronomously' but so that the conviction of wrong is provoked from within. By the same token, religious models in story, deed or visual emblem may possibly be understood ahead of or certainly simultaneous with perception of moral consequence.

It may be that Kohlberg's protracted scheme for moral and religious develop-ment has encouraged Smith to speak of adult education as the most important time for moral and religious development. Adulthood in the sense of three score years and ten is however not yet the common condition of mankind: the Western world and northern hemisphere can easily forget the child mortality rates and stunted lives that remain commonplace elsewhere. Because they are described as rarely reached, the majority of humankind is excluded from Stages 5 or 6. And yet without assuming human perfectibility, it may be that acts of altruistic care and compassion are within the potential of anyone, given the appropriate prompts. Here is proper ground for both RE and Moral Education to work on.

Unfortunately, Smith's rendering of RE as the factual study of the beliefs and doctrines of world religions, manifests the same lack of affection for the embodied ingredients of religious tradition which Kohlberg reveals for morality. Both might be surprised at the wonder and gratitude, or the tenderness and sorrow for another, that young children can share in rationally. There are vehicles for religious and moral development that teachers as well as Kohlberg would do well to seize on as a fairground for morality that can also be fun!

Part XI: Social Reasoning

20. Moral Judgment and the Social Cognitive Developmental Research Programme

ROBERT ENRIGHT, DANIEL LAPSLEY
AND LEANNE OLSON

It is our purpose in this chapter to show that Kohlberg's moral development theory and the cognitive developmental approach (Kohlberg, 1969) are alive and well. We shall do this by claiming that the Kohlbergian approach is responsible for generating a host of important social cognitive developmental domains, such as legal development, interpersonal understanding, conventional reasoning, and belief discrepancy reasoning, as well as for establishing an important theoretical link between role-taking and morality.

If one wishes to claim that a theory is viable and productive, how does one go about it? Do we rely on consensus and claim that it must be doing fine because so many people are interested in the domain or are employing interventions from a Kohlbergian perspective? If so, one might have seen alchemy as a viable scientific enterprise in centuries past because of the intense interest of its partisans. Do we rely on a psychometric analysis of the area as others (Kurtines and Greif, 1974; Broughton, 1978) have done? While the field may be psychometrically sound, it may be at the same time relatively unimportant. The problem, then, is to show that a domain of inquiry is both viable and important. How can this be accomplished?

We shall rely here on the philosophy of science, focusing on the methodological criteria proposed by Lakatos (1978) for the determination of whether a research programme is progressive or not. According to Lakatos (1978), it is possible to reconstruct scientific activity such that one can identify 'hard core' theoretical propositions such as Kohlberg's six-stage sequence that are protected from refutation by a 'protective belt' of auxiliary propositions such as environmental constraint in a cross-cultural context, the latter of which are subjected to empirical test. In addition, each research programme has a 'positive heuristic' which gives direction to the research. It consists of models or suggestions as to how to fortify the protective belt, how to account for anomaly, and importantly, how to anticipate new facts. A research programme is progressive only if it is capable of generating a series of content-increasing theories that consistently anticipate new facts, even though it may only be intermittently successful empirically.

Recently, Lapsley and Serlin (in press) have attempted to reconstruct along Lakatosian lines Kohlberg's cognitive developmental approach in general, and his theory of moral reasoning in particular, in order to assess its progressive or degenerative nature (e.g., Kohlberg, 1969). According to Lapsley and Serlin, the hard core propositions of the cognitive developmental approach involve, in part, the assumption that structural development must show stage-like features. The positive heuristic consists partly of the 'suggestion' to deploy ever more powerful stage models until empirical realities are accounted for, and partly of the suggestion to seek new domains of inquiry to which structural descriptions may be productively applied. If Kohlberg's cognitive-development approach can be shown to have heuristic power in that new domains are brought under its theoretical umbrella (i.e., are theoretically consistent with it), then the research programme can be said to be progressive, quite apart from the intermittent empirical success of the moral development theory itself.

The purpose of this chapter, then, is to determine just how progressive the heuristic machinery of the Kohlbergian cognitive-developmental approach is. We will proceed by considering those social-cognitive domains which seem indicative of consistent theoretical progress in our understanding of social knowledge. In addition, we will examine the implication of these theories for social education and clinical practice. We shall discuss the following domains: role-taking, legal development, interpersonal conceptions, conventional reasoning, and belief-discrepancy reasoning.

ROLE-TAKING

Our first domain, role-taking, pre-dates Kohlberg's system of moral development. George Herbert Mead as far back as 1934 popularized this cognitive skill, generally defined as 'stepping inside the other's shoes' and understanding his or her thoughts, feelings, or behaviour. It was not, however, until Kohlberg (1976) and Selman (1976a) synthesized role-taking and moral development that the stage sequence became refined and expanded. Table 1 lists all stage sequences of interest here.

There are several different role-taking sequences derived from scientific investigations (e.g., Chandler, 1973; DeVries, 1970; Feffer and Gourevitch, 1960; Kohlberg, 1976; Selman and Byrne, 1974). Social perspective-taking stages are generally conceived with progressively more complex coordinations of perspectives. On the lower levels, the person has difficulty coordinating his/her own perspective with that of another person. Eventually, the person can simultaneously coordinate both perspectives, move to a group perspective, and eventually to a coordination-of-groups or a systems perspective.

Because of the close correspondence between role-taking and moral stages, one may claim that the two domains are tautological. When you define one, you define the other, and, thus, one's claim that role-taking informs us to a greater extent about morality is illogical. Such a claim for tautology, however, is unfounded. Selman (1976b) reports correlations between role-taking and moral development as .47 with age controlled; it should be clear that this moderate

Table 1. Stages of Moral Development and Various Social Cognitive Domains

Moral Development	Role-Taking	Legal Development	Interpersonal Understanding	Belief-Discrepancy Reasoning
Stage 0 Premoral in that the other is not considered in moral decisions.	**Stage 0** Egocentrism. No differentiation of viewpoints.		**Stage 0** A close friend is equated with momentary physical interaction.	**Stage 0** The child does not realize he/she can judge disagreeing others.
Stage 1 Punishment and obedience orientation. The individual focuses on one other person, the authority, in order to avoid punishment.	**Stage 1** Subjective role-taking. The person realizes the other can think differently because both may have different data regarding a given situation.	**Stage 1** A legal right is only understood as something that an adult allows. That which is allowed is a legal right; that which is not allowed is not such a right.	**Stage 1** A close friend is defined by one-way assistance only (one perspective).	**Stage 1** The child rejects the contrary belief of the other person and negatively evaluates the discrepant other.
Stage 2 Relativism. The person helps other only to the extent that he/she will benefit.	**Stage 2** Self-reflective role-taking. The person can view the self from the other's viewpoint in a reciprocal perspective.		**Stage 2** A close friend is defined as someone who cooperates with you (two perspectives).	**Stage 2** The person declines to evaluate others in relation to their beliefs or thinks that people are good regardless of their beliefs (two perspectives).
Stage 3 Good boy/girl orientation. The person focuses on the group and adheres to the group norms in order to please others.	**Stage 3** A 'generalized other' perspective is taken in which the person can simultaneously and mutually consider the viewpoints of self and other, often in an infinite regress way.	**Stage 2** A legal right is confused with privileges associated with being nice or liked.	**Stage 3** A close friend is someone who mutually shares intimacy with you. The third person perspective or 'generalized other' emerges.	**Stage 3** The person realizes that an evaluation judgment about the disagreeing other is possible but only with more information about the other person and his/her beliefs. The person takes a plurality of perspectives on the disagreeing other, focusing on that person, the current beliefs held, and the consequences of those beliefs (multiple and systems perspectives).
Stage 4 Law and order orientation. The person focuses on the entire society and follows societal dictates to contribute to an orderly and functional community.	**Stage 4** Systems perspective. The person is aware that person A can influence person B, altering B's behaviour or thoughts. Interactive influences dominate here—groups influencing other groups or individuals influencing other individuals.		**Stage 4** Autonomous independence characterizes friendships. Friends are seen as open-systems susceptible to other's influences and changes. Certain combinations of personalities produce close friendships in one pair, but not in another.	
Stage 5 Principles orientation. The person adheres to abstract rules or principles, usually part of a social contract, that insure individual rights.		**Stage 3** A legal right is seen in terms of ethical principles. A legal right goes beyond authority's sanctions or privileges.		

relationship that shows only 22 per cent of variance overlap mollifies the tautology argument. Role-taking and moral development appear to be distinct domains.

It was not until Kohlberg (1976) and Selman (1976a) saw the rational connection between role-taking and moral development that Stage 4 role-taking was clearly described. Before then, the great majority of the work in the area ended on Stage 3 (see Enright and Lapsley, 1980). Further, it was Kohlberg's theory that postulated the necessary-but-not-sufficient link of role-taking with moral development. As one example, one could not advance, in theory, to Stage 3 in the moral realm without first having developed Stage 3 role-taking abilities.

Walker (1980) has empirically validated such a claim in an impressive intervention study. One group of fourth through seventh grade children was classified as Stage 2 moral and Stage 2 role-taking (group 1); another group was classified as Stage 2 moral and Stage 3 role-taking (group 2) at a pre-test. Because group 2 had the necessary role-taking prerequisite for growth to Stage 3 moral development, it was expected that this group would change to a statistically greater degree than group 1 on the moral realm following an intervention. All subjects were exposed to a brief moral development intervention. As expected, at post-test group 2 had progressed to moral Stage 3 to a significantly greater extent than group 1. The importance of such a work is that it more precisely defines how the moral educator must diagnose and intervene for successful moral change. The success of an intervention may well depend on how well social role-taking exercises are incorporated into the moral education curriculum.

In summary, moral development theory has led to an expansion of role-taking stages to Stage 4, to a more precise theoretical link between the two domains, and to more precise intervention strategies based on the necessary-but-not-sufficient condition assumption.

LEGAL DEVELOPMENT

How can someone be a child advocate without knowing children's concerns? If one wishes to protect children in a legal way, is it not best to involve them in the decisions affecting them? An adult's understanding of legal development, or children's and adolescents' understanding of the law, may help those concerned with children's rights.

Legal development is a rational derivative of Kohlberg's moral development sequence. Defined by Tapp and Kohlberg (1971), legal development is concerned with the child's conception of what the law *is*, not of what it *should be*. There are only three stages which correspond to Kohlberg's preconventional (moral Stage 1–2), conventional (moral Stages 3–4), and postconventional (moral Stages 5–6) levels, respectively (see Table 1). This sequence has been validated by Tapp and Levine (1974), Tapp and Kohlberg, (1971) and Melton (1980).

One problem with this sequence is that, to our knowledge, it has never been empirically distinguished from moral development. Because legal development asks, 'What *is* a right?' and moral development asks, 'What *should* the people's rights be in this dilemma?', the researchers have presumed them distinct. It should be obvious that such a presumption is a scientific question, not an axiom. We may be dealing with a moral tautology here, but future research may solve the mystery.

Regardless of this potential problem, Melton (1972) makes clear that children's conceptions of the law are usually that they have quite limited rights. This can get them into trouble in the legal world. For example, Grisso and Lovinguth (1979) asked juveniles to describe the meaning of the following portion of the *Miranda* warning: 'You do not have to make a statement and have the right to remain silent.' Although most accurately defined the right to remain silent, a full 60 per cent incorrectly replied that they must 'talk' if the authority so requests. This is a Stage 1 legal development conception which, clearly, is not in the juvenile's best interest. The need for legal education, based on the Kohlbergian sequence, may help such juveniles to better understand their rights. A higher-level legal conception would allow the youth to see that an authority's request is not a legal right.

From the social cognitive domain of legal development has come a four-step educational programme as outlined by Tapp and Levine (1974) and Levine and Tapp (1977). The most basic ingredient is the exposure to legal knowledge. Knowing one's basic rights may not increase one's complexity of thought, but it is the stimulus that may precipitate such discussion. Next is the basic Kohlbergian principle of mismatch and conflict. Exposing the individual to higher levels and ideas contradictory to his/her own views may stimulate more complex legal thought forms, as has been shown in the moral arena (e.g., Blatt and Kohlberg, 1975; Enright, Lapsley and Levy, 1983; Turiel, 1966). Participation is the third component which implies that the student of law should become behaviourally involved in the legal issues of school and community. Finally, there is legal continuity which primarily involves generalization. The student, through legal education, should come to realize that thoughts and discussions about rights go beyond the legal system and include parent-child, teacher-student, and peer-peer relations as well. The idea is to avoid the tendency to place 'rights' thinking into a narrow compartment.

Legal development, thus, has pointed out one particular way in which moral thinking can be applied. Youth's incomplete understanding of their Miranda rights is one important example here of how legal development can help juveniles. Legal development, in turn, has given back a great deal to moral development in the form of Tapp and Levine's rational, comprehensive educational model. The two domains are, thus, better off having known one another.

INTERPERSONAL UNDERSTANDING

With the moral development stages as analogies Selman (1980) has created a new social cognitive domain, interpersonal understanding. It involves a person's understanding of other people, friendships, peer groups and parent-child relations. A description of stages only within the friendship domain is provided in Table 1.

As can be seen in the table there is a close correspondence among the domains of role-taking, moral development and interpersonal understanding. For example, Stage 2 across all three domains involves cognitive reciprocity in which the other's and the self's views are simultaneously considered. As another example, on Stage 4 the person coordinates systems perspectives in all three domains. The systems perspective is applied to justice issues in moral development whereas systems are employed in understanding friendships in interpersonal understanding.

Interpersonal understanding has contributed two important ingredients to our understanding of social cognition: measurement and intervention. With regard to the former, the reliability properties of the interview assessments are strong. Inter-rater agreements are usually in the 90 per cent range (Enright, 1980; Selman, 1980) and the internal consistency reliability across dilemmas has been reported at .79 (Enright, 1980). Short-term stability has been reported at .61 (Brion-Meisels, 1977) and at .92 (Enright, 1980). It should be obvious that such reliabilities for interview procedures that tend to be somewhat idiosyncratic are impressive. Such rigorous attention to psychometric detail can be used as a model for moral development test properties which have been criticized not so much for their inaccuracies as for their absence (Kurtines and Greif, 1974).

As with the role-taking and moral link, interpersonal conceptions and moral development may be called tautological without the necessary convergent-discriminant analyses. Enright (1976) has shown the distinctions between the domains (.80 within interpersonal understanding, and in the range of .40 with Carroll's, 1974, moral scale based on Kohlberg's theory), thus exonerating the domain from the claims that it is a social cognitive imposter.

In the realm of education and clinical practice, interpersonal understanding has made some important strides. Using the model in two twenty-two-week interventions, Enright (1980) found that sixth graders' and first graders' under-standing of friendships can be improved. In the first study, sixth graders were randomly assigned to a cross-age teaching condition or to a control group. The experimental children ran interpersonal understanding groups for first graders. The sixth graders presented friendship dilemmas to their charges and then led discus-sions about the issues. At post-test, the experimental sixth graders were higher in both interpersonal conceptions and moral development than the control group.

In the second study, two first grade teachers used the interpersonal under-standing paradigm as the primary discipline technique in their classrooms. For instance, if a child has an argument with another, the teacher asked him about sharing, what that argument may do to the children's friendship, and how he could strengthen that friendship. For the first semester Class 1 engaged in this interven-tion; Class 2 served as the control. At post-test Class 1 was higher than Class 2 in both interpersonal understanding and moral development as defined by Damon (1977). During the second semester, once Class 2 began the intervention, the children here gained in both social domains to match Class 1. Interpersonal understanding provided the teachers with an effective and positive alternative to punishment in solving interpersonal altercations in the classroom.

Selman (1980) has further used the domain in a clinical setting where he helps those who have particularly difficult interpersonal problems to increase their complexity and subtlety of understanding other people. If we had only a moral domain rather than one describing friendships, the clinical interventions would likely be imprecise and, in some cases, inappropriate. The extension of moral development theory into this area has enhanced diagnosis and treatment. But, without moral development theory having already been in place, this domain might never have been generated.

SOCIAL CONVENTIONAL REASONING

As previously indicated, the heuristic machinery of the cognitive developmental approach bids us to articulate ever more powerful stage models and to extend them into uncharted domains of inquiry—all of this to be deemed a progressive research programme. If successful, this extension of cognitive developmental principles would yield a more differentiated and finely articulated description of social cognitive processes. Such is the case with the recent interest in delineating the domain of social conventional reasoning (Turiel, 1983; Smetana, 1983; Nucci, 1982). Social conventional reasoning is a domain distinct from moral reasoning proper, but it posits structural stage-like development in accordance with the strictures of Kohlberg's cognitive developmental approach. Conventional rules involve behavioural regularities; they are established through convention to regulate the actions of others in a social system. In addition, conventional rules are arbitrary and involve no prescription. It is a conventional rule, for example, for individuals not to eat food with their fingers, for children not to address teachers by their first name or to chew gum in class, or to talk without raising their hand.

Moral rules, on the other hand, are not arbitrary and do indeed involve prescription. They are not established through social consensus, but rather are obligatory, universally applicable and impersonal (Turiel, 1983). Rules which govern lying, stealing and aggression, for example, are *moral* rules, since violations of these rules affront ethical standards of conscience which exist apart from the press of consensus and convention. There is now substantial evidence that even very young children make the domain distinctions between moral and conventional rules (e.g., Nucci and Nucci, 1982; Smetana, 1981), and that conventional reasoning itself follows a developmental progression (Turiel, 1983), as Table 2 indicates. The social conventional stages were not rationally derived from the

Table 2.   *Stages of Social Conventional Reasoning*

Major Changes in Social Conventional Concepts
Stage 1 Convention as descriptive of social uniformity. Convention is not conceived as part of structure or function of social interaction. Conventional uniformities are descriptive of what is assumed to exist. Convention is maintained to avoid violation of empirical uniformities.
Stage 2 Negation of convention as descriptive social uniformity. Empirical uniformity is not a sufficient basis for maintaining conventions. Conventional acts are regarded as arbitrary. Convention is not conceived as part of structure or function of social interaction.
Stage 3 Convention as affirmation of rule system; early concrete conception of social system. Convention is seen as arbitrary and changeable. Adherence to convention is based on concrete rules and authoritative expectations. Conception of conventional acts is not coordinated with conception of rule.
Stage 4 Negation of convention as part of rule system. Convention is now seen as arbitrary and changeable regardless of the rule. Evaluation of the rule pertaining to a conventional act is coordinated with evaluation of the act. Conventions are nothing but social expectations.
Stage 5 Convention as mediated by social system. The emergence of systematic concepts of social structure occurs. Convention is seen as a normative regulation in the system with uniformity, fixed roles and static hierarchical organization.
Stage 6 Negation of convention as societal standards. Convention is regarded as codified societal standards. Uniformity in convention is not considered to serve the function of maintaining the social system. Conventions are nothing but societal standards that exist through habitual use.
Stage 7 Convention as coordination of social interactions. Conventions as uniformities that are functional in coordinating social interactions. Shared knowledge, in the form of conventions, among members of social groups facilitates interaction and operation of the system.

Source: Turiel (1978).

moral stages as were the other stage models here. Thus, the conventional stages cannot be directly and analogously compared with the moral stages in Table 1.

In two studies (Nucci and Turiel, 1978; Nucci and Nucci, 1982), for example, children were questioned about spontaneously occurring moral and conventional transgressions. The children were asked, 'What if there were no rule in the school about (the observed event), would it be all right to do it then?' The results indicated that approximately 80 per cent of the subjects at each grade felt that the social conventional act would be appropriate if no rule existed to prohibit it, while over 85 per cent of the children at each grade stated that the moral act would not be right even if there were no rule to prohibit it. These results support the view that the moral and conventional domains are conceptually distinct. Actions are evaluated within the moral domain on the basis of their intrinsic features, such as justice or harm, while conventional acts are evaluated in terms of their status as regulations within a social context (Nucci, 1982). This conclusion has been supported using standardized moral and conventional stimuli as well (e.g., Smetana, 1981). In general, then, actions within the conventional domain are judged as wrong only if a social rule or norm exists prohibiting the action, while moral transgressions are universally held to be wrong even in the absence of consensual norms.

As Table 2 indicates, reasoning about social conventional concepts is thought to follow a structural developmental stage sequence. As pointed out previously, the social conventional stage sequence is not presumed to be related to Piagetian logical development or to positive justice domains. However, since the stage features of conventional reasoning follow the strictures of structural developmentalism, it is possible to subsume this domain under the broad theoretical umbrella of the Kohlbergian cognitive developmental approach. In social conventional reasoning each successive level progressively coordinates '... increasingly broad aspects of the relationship between shared uniformities in social behavior and the organization of individual's interactions within social systems or collectives' (Nucci, 1982, p. 106). That is, the development of social conventional concepts involves the progressive understanding that conventions involve shared knowledge of uniformities, and that the uniformities serve to coordinate social interactions. The sequentiality of this stage sequence has been demonstrated by Turiel (1978), and replicated by Damon (1977) and Turiel (1983).

The importance of the social conventional domain lies in its productive capacity to generate novel conjectures concerning social reasoning, and in its educational implications. Concerning the former, it is proposed that the development of concepts about convention are structured by underlying concepts of social organization, rather than by concepts of equality and reciprocity. Further, it is proposed that the social conventional sequence is not linear, but involves oscillation between affirmation and negation of concepts of convention and social structure (Nucci, 1982). New lines of research will need to determine the extent to which the moral development sequence is conflated with the distinct domain of conventional reasoning, and the relation between Piagetian logical developments and the social conventional domain.

It is clear, then, that the extension of structural developmentalism into the social conventional domain has extended our understanding of social cognitive development, and that this extension is content-increasing. However, it also has challenging educational implications as well. According to Nucci (1982, p. 107), value instruction in the social-conventional domain would be aimed at getting students to 'comprehend the function of ... arbitrarily designated traditions for the maintenance of cultural organization and cultural continuity, while appreciating the ways in which variations in convention serve to define differing cultural patterns both across and within systems as a function of the shifting of consensual values over time.' The instructional methodology for advancing students to higher stages would be similar to instructional strategies in the moral domain, though curricular materials would be domain-specific in accordance with the view that development within each system is structurally independent. That is, moral instruction would focus on the effects of actions on others, while social conventional instruction would focus on aspects of social order and normative expectations (Nucci, 1982). According to Nucci (1982), to treat moral issues with reference to social convention (and *vice versa*) would constitute domain inappropriate instruction, and would diminish the likelihood that the intervention would stimulate development.

BELIEF DISCREPANCY REASONING

The newest social cognitive domain to appear is belief discrepancy reasoning (Enright and Lapsley, 1981). As with interpersonal understanding, legal develop- ment and conventional reasoning, the stage sequence was rationally derived from the basic moral development sequence. Belief discrepancy reasoning concerns the way an individual thinks about others who disagree with him/her. The sequence, thus, progresses from the simple to the complex. On the early stages, the individual is close-minded, thinking those who disagree with the self are bad people. This gives way to relativism, and finally to viewing people and their beliefs as interconnected systems. The other's belief, on this level, is a part of the person's entire psychological makeup and must be judged in this context. See Table 1 for a description of the stages relative to all other social cognitive domains discussed here.

As with the majority of other social cognitive domains, belief discrepancy reasoning can be discriminated from moral judgment. In a correlational study of belief discrepancy reasoning with Rest's (1976) moral judgment instrument, ninety-four ninth and twelfth graders, and college students were involved. The two measures shared only 14 per cent of the variance (the partial correlation, controlling for age, between the two instruments was .38, $p < .001$). On the other hand, the internal consistency reliability within belief discrepancy reasoning was .70. The two domains are distinctly different, measuring different aspects of social thought.

The importance of belief discrepancy reasoning is that it redefines the traditional conceptions of open-mindedness and closed-mindedness. Such con- structs as authoritarianism and dogmatism have been conceived in a bi-polar way for decades (see Adorno *et al.*, 1950; Rokeach, 1960). These early theorists presumed that closed-mindedness was a personality trait rather than a developing social cognitive ability. Thus, the notion of development or change once someone was diagnosed as closed-minded was rarely discussed. The scientific development of belief discrepancy reasoning, on the other hand, has given the clinician a stage blueprint for change and points the way in intervention toward increasing the closed-minded person's complexity of thought. After all, this new conception sees closed-mindedness as a low level of reasoning in a cognitive sequence.

The construct validity for belief discrepancy has been solid. The stage sequence in Table 1 has been validated with three different instruments on four different samples ranging from grade 1 in the United States to the elderly (see Enright and Lapsley, 1980; Enright, Roberts and Lapsley, 1983). Belief discrepancy reasoning has been related moderately to Piagetian logical development, has been discriminated from Rokeach's (1960) dogmatism scale, has been replicated in Africa, and has shown predictable development in a longitudinal sequence (Enright and Lapsley, 1981; Enright, Roberts and Lapsley, 1983; Enright, Lapsley, Franklin and Steuck, in press).

Without the basic Kohlbergian sequence as a guide, we may never have realized that the very popular closed-mindedness/open-mindedness construct is actually a cognitive and a developmental construct.

CONCLUSION

Using one of Lakatos's criteria for assessing progress or degeneration in a research programme, we must conclude that moral development theory is thriving. It has anticipated at least the four new social cognitive domains described here as well as new refinements in its ancestor role-taking. We are, of course, now left with quite a dilemma on our hands. By claiming vitality for a theory if it generates new theories, we may have opened the flood gates for many an unnecessary stage approach that we quickly catch and mount as 'important' and as needed new evidence. With our Lakatosian approach we could see all kinds of new domains generated in the name of 'progress': children's understanding of how a refrigerator works, adolescents' understanding of why their little brothers won't eat their peas, children's understanding of why adults prefer to eat apple pies rather than mud pies. In our quest to support the vitality of moral development, we just may end up reducing social thought to the absurd, to the trivial.

Such a fear can be overcome by carefully scrutinizing any new domain for its ultimate usefulness in theory or in practice. Surely a refinement of Stage 4 in role-taking is not a trivial enterprise for it informs us of a long hidden adolescent thought form in a domain going back at least to Mead (1934) and possibly to Baldwin (1906). The example of youth's misinformation about the Miranda warning speaks well to the need for intensive legal education. Given that discipline is a topic dear to all pedagogues, interpersonal understanding has led to a technique for humane discipline that is actually constructive in that it increases social thought complexity for the disciplined student. Finally, without a belief discrepancy domain, we would still conceive of closed-mindedness as a somewhat fixed personality trait and we certainly would not have knowledge of the thought form subsequent to open-mindedness. Stage 3 belief discrepancy reasoning informs us that a person may, in fact, negatively judge others subsequent to open-mindedness. On Stage 3 the person judges the other's belief as part of the other. This means getting to know the other very well before passing judgment. This means judging how the other's belief translates into behaviour, how it affects the other's beliefs generally, and how that belief fits into the other's overall personality. Only then does a Stage 3 reasoner pass judgment on the other based on his/her belief. To be able to reconstruct such a popular and traditional approach as dogmatism with

Kohlbergian cognitive developmental theory speaks well to the power of that theory.

Anyone making the claim that the Kohlbergian paradigm is degenerating must describe a new moral approach that has informed us regarding social cognition to an even greater degree than the Kohlbergian. It must account for refinements in children's thinking and any new stages that are higher than previously discovered ones. Further, it must demonstrate greater clinical utility than has any domain described here. We can foresee arguments pointing to domains of *equal* power, such as the social learning approach. But equality has never been known to overthrow a research programme, as Lakatos instructs. The Kohlbergian moral paradigm is, indeed, alive and well.

REFERENCES

Adorno, T., Frenkel-Brunswik, E., Levinson, D. and Sanford, R. (1950) *The Authoritarian Personality*, New York, Basic Books.

Baldwin, J. (1906) *Social and Ethical Interpretations in Mental Development*, New York, Macmillan.

Blatt, M. and Kohlberg, L. (1975) 'The effects of classroom moral discussion upon children's level of moral judgment', *Journal of Moral Education*, 4, pp. 129–61.

Brion-Meisels, S. (1977) *Helping, Sharing, and Cooperation: An Intervention Study of Middle Childhood*, Unpublished doctoral dissertation, University of Utah.

Broughton, J. (1978) 'The cognitive-developmental approach to morality: A reply to Kurtines and Greif,' *Journal of Moral Education*, 7, pp. 81–96.

Chandler, M. (1973) 'Egocentrism and anti-social behavior: The assessment and training of social perspective taking skills', *Developmental Psychology*, 9, pp. 326–32.

Damon, W. (1977) *The Social World of the Child*, San Francisco, Jossey-Bass.

DeVries, R. (1970) 'The development of role-taking as reflected by the behavior of bright, average, and retarded children in a social guessing game', *Child Development*, 4, pp. 759–70.

Enright, R. (1976) *An Experimental Analysis of a Social Cognitive Model Through a Cross-Age Training Program*, Doctoral dissertation, University of Minnesota.

Enright, R. (1980) 'An integration of social cognitive development and cognitive processing: Educational applications', *American Educational Research Journal*, 17, pp. 21–41.

Enright, R. and Lapsley, D. (1980) 'Social role-taking: A review of the constructs, measures, and measurement properties', *Review of Educational Research*, 50, pp. 647–74.

Enright, R. and Lapsley, D. (1981) 'Judging others who hold opposite beliefs: The development of belief discrepancy reasoning', *Child Development*, 52, pp. 1053–63.

Enright, R., Lapsley, D., Franklin, C. and Steuck, K. (in press) 'Longitudinal and cross-cultural validation of the belief discrepancy reasoning construct', *Developmental Psychology*.

Enright, R., Lapsley, D. and Levy, V. (1983) 'Moral education strategies', in M. Pressley and J. Levin (Eds.), *Cognitive Strategy Research: Educational Applications*, New York, Springer-Verlag.

Enright, R., Roberts, P. and Lapsley, D. (1983) 'Belief discrepancy reasoning in the elderly', *International Journal of Aging and Human Development*, 17, pp. 213–21.

Feffer, N. and Gourevitch, V. (1960) 'Cognitive aspects of role-taking in children', *Journal of Personality*, 28, pp. 283–396.

Grisso, T. and Lovinguth, T. (1979) *Juveniles' Definition of Legal Defense and Right to Silence*, Paper presented at the Meeting of the American Psychological Association, New York, September.

Kohlberg, L. (1969) 'Stage and sequence: The cognitive-developmental approach to socialization', in D. Goslin (Ed.), *Handbook of Socialization Theory and Research*, New York, Rand McNally.

Kohlberg, L. (1976) 'Moral stages and moralization: The cognitive developmental approach', in T. Lickona (Ed.), *Moral Development and Behavior*, New York, Holt, Rinehart and Winston.

Kurtines, W. and Greif, E. (1974) 'The development of moral thought: Review and evaluation of Kohlberg's approach', *Psychological Bulletin*, 81, pp. 453–70.

Lakatos, I. (1978) 'Falsification and the methodology of scientific research programs', in J. Worral and

G. Currie (Eds.), *The Methodology of Scientific Research Programs: Imre Lakatos Philosophical Papers*, Vol 1, Cambridge, Cambridge University Press.

Lapsley, D. and Serlin, R. (in press) 'On the alleged degeneration of the Kohlbergian research programme', *Educational Theory*.

Levine, F. and Tapp, J. (1977) 'The dialectic of legal socialization in community and school', in J. Tapp and F. Levine (Eds.), *Law, Justice, and the Individual in Society: Psychological and Legal Issues*, New York, Holt, Rinehart and Winston.

Mead, G. (1934) *Mind, Self, and Society*, Chicago, Ill., University of Chicago Press.

Melton, G. (1972) 'Teaching children about their rights,' in J. Henning (Ed.), *The Rights of Children: Legal and Psychological Perspectives*, Springfield, Ill., Charles C. Thomas.

Melton, G. (1980) 'Children's concepts of their rights', *Journal of Clinical Child Psychology*, 9, pp. 186–90.

Nucci, L. (1982) 'Conceptual development in the conventional domains: Implications for values education', *Review of Educational Research*, 52, pp. 93–122.

Nucci, L. and Nucci, M. (1982) 'Children's social interactions in the context of moral and conventional transgressions', *Child Development*, 53, pp. 403–12.

Nucci, L. and Turiel, E. (1978) 'Social interactions and the development of social concepts in preschool children', *Child Development*, 49, pp. 400–7.

Rest, J. (1976) 'New approaches in the assessment of moral judgment', in T. Lickona (Ed.), *Moral Development and Behavior*, New York, Holt, Rinehart and Winston.

Rokeach, M. (1960) *The Open and Closed Mind*, New York, Basic Books.

Selman, R. (1976a) 'Social-cognitive understanding: A guide to educational and clinical practice', in T. Lickona (Ed.), *Moral Development and Behavior*, New York, Holt, Rinehart and Winston.

Selman, R. (1976b) 'Toward a structural-developmental analysis of interpersonal relationship concepts: Research with normal and disturbed pre-adolescent boys', in A. Pick (Ed.), *Tenth Annual Minnesota Symposium on Child Psychology*, Minneapolis, Minn., University of Minnesota Press.

Selman, R. (1980) *The Growth of Interpersonal Understanding*, New York, Academic Press.

Selman, R. and Byrne, D. (1974) 'A structural-developmental analysis of levels of role-taking in middle childhood', *Child Development*, 45, pp. 803–6.

Smetana, J. (1981) 'Preschool children's conceptions of moral and social rules', *Child Development*, 2, pp. 211–26.

Smetana, J. (1983) 'Social-cognitive development: Domain distinctions and coordinations', *Developmental Review*, 3, pp. 131–47.

Tapp, J. and Kohlberg, L. (1971) 'Developing senses of law and legal justice', *Journal of Social Issues*, 27, pp. 65–91.

Tapp, J. and Levine, F. (1974) 'Legal socialization: Strategies for an ethical legality', *Stanford Law Review*, 27, pp. 1–72.

Turiel, E. (1966) 'An experimental test of the sequentiality of developmental stages in the child's moral judgment', *Journal of Personality and Social Psychology*, 3, pp. 611–18.

Turiel, E. (1978) 'The development of concepts of social structure: Social convention', in J. Glick and A. Clarke-Steward (Eds.), *The Development of Social Understanding*, New York, Gardener Press.

Turiel, E. (1983) *The Development of Social Knowledge*, New York, Cambridge University Press.

Walker, L. (1980) 'Cognitive and perspective-taking prerequisites for moral development', *Child Development*, 51, pp. 131–9.

21. Social Reasoning

LEA PEARSON

Social reasoning is not intuitively a clearly delineated area of psychological investigation. Four areas that appear to have common elements of social reasoning are discussed. These are social skills training, educational applications, measurement or assessment, and theories. These are seen as essentially disparate activities with differing criteria of effectiveness. Although they have problems in common these are not peculiar to the areas discussed. Various concerns of general applicability are highlighted but no specific area is identified as usefully denoted by the term 'social reasoning'.

It is difficult to contribute a chapter labelled as 'predominantly negative' without seeming to be just that. Moreover, the larger the output of any single person, and the larger the related theory, the greater the potential for criticism. It is inevitably easy to criticize the theory, its application, its assumptions, the evidence supporting it, from some standpoint or other. There would be no point unless it were worth the effort and recognized that constructive, or even negative, criticism may be a valid and ultimately productive activity, that if it is, it can only be so as a function of what is criticized. There is plenty of evidence in the biological sciences that parasitic activity can be a productive part of effective cycles!

In a volume devoted to the work of Lawrence Kohlberg it proved to be singularly difficult to write about 'social reasoning'. Any attempt to use either word as a keyword would certainly overwhelm the speediest reader. As a composite term, the two words are used infrequently, and the term denotes no specific model or investigation or activity or skill. Asking professional and academic psychologist colleagues—a desperate measure to find some starting-point—does not clarify matters. One set of items in the British Ability Scales (BAS) (Elliott *et al.*, 1979) is titled the Social Reasoning Scale. In the early stages of work on the BAS these items were concerned with moral reasoning. Both the type of items and the system of scoring were modified significantly for practical considerations; the final title reflects a need to signal something with a rather different approach to the Kohlberg dilemmas with which one began, not a connection with a different theory or model.

Social reasoning, at least as used by the BAS, is loosely derived from moral reasoning. It concerns judgments about social dilemmas which inevitably have

325

moral overtones, and may be indistinguishable from moral problems. The BAS is a set of psychometric measures. Pearson and Elliott (1980) suggested that there were indications that some of the research using Kohlberg's stages had application to the Social Reasoning Scale. Moral reasoning and attempts to measure this and social reasoning seem therefore to be relevant considerations, although these inevitably overlap with other chapters.

In contrast to academic approaches, or their modification as measures or tests, professional psychologists have long been concerned with individuals whose social behaviour is perceived by themselves or others as a problem. Social skills training incorporates elements of discussion, assessment, counselling which include elements of reasoning about social situations. While this approach—essentially a practical, professional problem-solving approach, $\simeq$ contrasts with an academic theoretical quest for knowledge, both, as indicated, involve assessment, and the particular problems that entails. Both approaches lend themselves to different sorts of generalization or broadening which leads to a further overlap. Any developmental model of acquisition is likely to be applied practically—often by educators who wish to ensure that normal acquisition takes place, or to accelerate this. Any effective strategy for solving individual problems runs a parallel risk—often by changing its emphasis on treatment to one on prevention. Social skills training is not only a strategy to help individuals or small groups, but a contender for mainstream curriculum. It is helpful to consider these different and varied applications separately, although they are not always easy to disentangle. The criteria for an effective model of human behaviour are very different from those for helping to solve individual problems; the criteria for effective tests or measures, and for curriculum innovation, are different again.

Because such different applications are supported or otherwise by different criteria, suggesting that one is invalid or inadequate may not entail the others being so. If psychology, academic and professional, worked on a simplistic deductive model, one false premise might have a domino effect. Professional psychologists are not able to refuse help because there is no perfect model—increasingly they are likely to see their evidence of effective treatment or intervention as data that valid models must describe or predict.

The remainder of this chapter highlights some relevant issues in social skills training, educational application, measurement or assessment, and theories.

SOCIAL SKILLS TRAINING (SST)

Social skills models seem to have derived rather roughly from perceptual and motor skill models. Argyle (1979) suggests such models are heuristically useful in drawing attention to the importance of feedback, and hence gaze, and in suggesting training procedures that may be effective through analogy with motor skills training. Ellis and Whittington (1983) suggest that the essence of SST is: 'an explicit and controlled attempt by the trainers to enhance the social skills of the trainees', using procedures which involve sensitization to significant features of social interaction, practice by the trainees of some elements, feedback regarding the practice, further practice in the light of feedback. Such an approach emphasizes observable behaviour, but Ellis and Whittington suggest that current trends are away from an applied behavioural model, towards including concern with aspects of social interaction that are not readily observable.

SST has been used for various purposes—chiefly to remedy deficits in notably unskilled groups or individuals, but also to provide specific skill enhancement for those whose work may require this, and to enhance or accelerate normal skills in childhood and adolescence. As remarked above, in this latter use some similarity with applications of moral reasoning is evident. Many of the points raised by writers in this area are paralleled by comments on moral reasoning. Schroeder and Rakos (1983), reviewing models of SST as a remedial activity, propose an interactional model that comprises assessment, overt and covert competence, behaviour in context, and a view of persons as influential in situations. McFail (1982) distinguishes between social skills and social competence. Social skills are defined as specific abilities which enable individuals to perform competently in specific social tasks; social competence is defined as the evaluation of an individual's performance by someone else, not something inherent in performance—and consequently subject to considerable variation or inter-rater discrepancies.

Deficits in skills have been identified in numerous populations—for example, adult psychiatric patients (Platt and Spivak, 1972), depressed college students (Gottlib and Asarnow, 1979) and suicide attempters (Patsiokas *et al.*, 1979). The cognitive skills of interpersonal problem-solving are similarly well documented and summarized by Shure (1981); McFail (1982) outlines similar decision skills; Trower (1982) discusses cognitive competences and expectancies.

Research studies of SST use a range of self-report questionnaires and (sometimes parallel) rating scales completed by teachers and others (for examples see Jesness, 1962) although these are less common in clinical practice.

As Furnham (1983) remarks, the 'meteoric rise in research and training in social skills over the past decade has not always been tempered by scholarly appraisal of social skills theory and therapy outcomes.' Most researchers in SST seem to derive their own definitions or modify those of previous researchers. Curran (1979) regarded 'social skills' as a 'mega construct' and has attempted to clarify some of the reasons for a wide divergency of definitions. Like many developments by professional psychologists the evidence of effectiveness is lacking or limited. At an unsophisticated level there are indications that it is practicable, acceptable to clients, welcomed by teachers and others. SST is apparently changing constantly, and currently emphasizing non-behavioural aspects, including cognitive strategies. It is difficult to envisage a major theory or model or its validation—it may not even be appropriate to envisage other than piecemeal developments for some time.

EDUCATIONAL APPLICATIONS

Both SST and versions of Kohlberg's work have been claimed to have an appropriate general role in the curriculum. Some educationalists (for example, Hargreaves, 1982) who write of the 'hidden curriculum' perhaps highlight that schools do train a range of attitudes, judgments, values whether or not they plan to do so. Enright (1981) describes a curriculum exercise in primary grades which is based on Selman's (1976) stages of interpersonal conceptions. This model shares with Kohlberg a stage sequence structure, but the teaching sequences also involve an SST approach deriving from Spivak and Sure (1974).

Various commentators on moral reasoning (for example, Duska and Whelan, 1977) suggest that Piaget and Kohlberg have established a developmental process—the next stage is to look at the educational applications. It seems patently obvious, at least in the UK, that such initiatives would be politically contentious. It could also be argued that even if educational administrators and advisers are prepared to accept innovation on little relevant evidence, psychologists should protect them from doing so. At a time of limited resources and considerable competition for space in the curriculum it might be appropriate to match educational problems with the resources that could be offered; it might also be relevant to investigate what teachers are prepared to teach, and what outcomes might be unacceptable.

MEASUREMENT OR ASSESSMENT

The BAS Social Reasoning Scale has little more data available than the rather speculative suggestions outlined by Pearson and Elliott in 1980. It seems likely that its use by professional psychologists is limited. The BAS was initially planned in the 1960s; a major psychometric measure incorporating twenty-three separate scales is a lengthy project and risks being something of a white elephant by the time it finally emerges on the market. In the last decade, educational psychologists in the UK have increasingly emphasized the use of criterion-referenced measures in an assessment through teaching model which provides a dynamic rather than static assessment of a child's learning (Pearson and Tweddle, 1984). It is difficult in this climate to advocate for individual assessment purposes a measure of social reasoning which gives a level only, and has little direct implication for teaching programmes. This scale, like the rest of the BAS, underwent a rigorous series of modifications and trials, and was standardized on 2356 children. Inter-scorer reliability was checked in a small-scale study with ten educational psychologists producing a coefficient of $> .8$. Technically, it is a well validated instrument for research purposes. However for a pre- and post-experimental measure it is probably too gross. Children and young people are assigned to a median level; 50 per cent of children in the standardization sample scored at level 1 or above at 5 years 8 months; at level 2 at 7 years 9 months, and at level 3 only at 18 years 5 months (extrapolated). Only sixteen youngsters aged between 14 and 17½ years scored at level 4.

The Social Reasoning Scale was developed specifically as a developmental measure of the breadth of social reasoning. It is straightforward to administer and cannot be modified by users. Its format shows a considerable change from Kohlberg's Moral Judgment Scale (MJS) which reflects the difficulties children have with the stories or dilemmas also reported by Ziv (1976). Ziv criticizes the MJS as the only psychological measuring instrument published without a publicly available administration and scoring manual. Wilson (1973) suggests that the changes in scoring criteria over the years limit the comparability of different studies. In early trial work on the BAS using MJS items it was apparent that educational psychologists could not use this consistently without training. Colby (1978) also suggests that it is likely that stage scores will be assigned to interview material in different ways in different studies. Rest (1976) highlights the practical difficulties of assigning subjects to stages because of the gradual acquisition process, and the instability of responses during transitional phases. Turiel (1975) demonstrated that the transition from Stage 4 to Stage 5 involves a phase of 'disequilibrium' in which responses cannot be classified as representing any given stage. Rest suggested that an individual's stage might be described in terms of a profile of percentage probability of responses at each stage. Kohlberg (1969) reports that on average only 47 per cent of a subject's responses are at his predominant level.

Technical improvements, with the help of hindsight, can always be suggested. A more fundamental criticism of the MJS as a measure is its interdependence with theory. Broughton (1978) points out the difficulties of simultaneously evaluating the truth of a theory and the validity of the instrument. Bergling (1983) makes a similar point, emphasizing that the verification of the theory entails the replication of the MJS in a final form on new data.

Apart from research purposes, most assessment of social (or moral) reasoning (or competence) appears to be informal, using self-report questionnaires, rating scales or observation schedules. Formal measures are, inevitably, too insensitive to measure change over a short period, or to lead to prescriptive teaching programmes.

THEORIES

Kohlberg's theory can be seen as the third major empirical exploration of moral development, being preceded by Piaget (1932) and Barnes (1894). In the twenty plus years since Kohlberg's theory was proposed there have been hundreds of empirical studies and a large number of papers discussing his theory. Other chapters in this book are concerned with this area; it is relevant here only to highlight some concerns that have fairly general implications and would therefore also be likely to apply to social reasoning. Essentially these concern claims made for the theory; the mismatch between the theory and particular models of man or morality or developments in current psychological thinking.

Bergling (1983) points out that no synthesis of research findings related to the theory has been published, and that the major findings of published research have not led to any formalized theory with postulates and well defined terms. Consequently the validity of the theory is still questionable. Broughton (1978) makes a similar general point in suggesting that although the empirical utility of the cognitive-developmental approach is demonstrable, the question of its truth has not yet been confronted.

One issue raised directly or indirectly by several commentators is the validity of the model of morality underpinning the theory. While Graham (1976) sees this as a welcome return to a psychology where the voluntaristic views of William James may be regarded with respect, where full moral values are conceptualized as a late development, Hamlyn (1978) declines to discuss in any detail the growth of moral understanding in the absence of a developed moral philosophy. He questions whether there is a progression, and what this is a progression towards. Tomlinson (1983) identifies, as many others have, a strong Kantian influence in the work of both Piaget and Kohlberg, and a related and unquestioning emphasis on judgment and reasoning involving rules and principles. Wilson (1973) suggests that Piaget,

Kohlberg and many others suffer from the defect of allocating uncritically and confusingly a particular context to morality. This seems an inappropriate criticism of Piaget (1932) who, as Wright (1982) points out, stressed the differences between theoretical and practical morality—judgments in theory will be 'devoid of pity and lacking in practical insight', whereas in practice sympathies and antipathies will be engaged 'for he is in the presence, not of isolated acts, but of personalities that attract and repel him.' Piaget suggested that practical morality is largely or partly intuitive, and may match poorly with theoretical morality some or much or all of the time. Kohlberg's central approach is less able to adapt to a binary approach.

The predication of such double systems is common although they vary widely. Russell (1978) sees moral considerations as optional—one can obtain a highly sophisticated level of moral judgment but also judge that moral considerations are unimportant or not as attractive as morally primitive alternatives in a given situation. Skemp (1979) suggests that parents inculcate in the child behaviour that is acceptable to the culture in which they are growing up—not stealing, not investigating the anatomy of playmates of the opposite sex. If this is a morality at all it is one based on obedience enforced externally by fear and internally by guilt. It is difficult to see this as a basis for the kind of morality that is based on the love of one's fellows.

Shotter (1979) postulates that the moral world is constructed unselfconsciously by its members in their exchanges, is then experienced by them as an external world, and exerts a coercive force upon them to think, perceive, act and communicate in its terms. Man has two major modes of social being—primary, immersed and unselfconscious; secondary, detached and selfconscious. This is particularly reminiscent of Ryle's (1949) statement that many people can talk sense with concepts, but not about them. Ryle is frequently quoted and not always to any clear purpose. It is arguable whether a dilemma of no great personal relevance necessarily calls for a detached and self-conscious response or talking about concepts, although a high-level response would use the secondary mode.

Tomlinson (1981) questions whether approaches such as Kohlberg's are sufficiently interactive; whether thought structures characterize the whole of a person's outlook on all issues. Peters (1971) suggests that justice is a difficult and abstract concept and could be replaced by concern for others which can also be a fundamental concept of morality.

The concept of intentionality, or the relative considerations of intentions and consequences, have been investigated, often with reference to Piaget's work. Wegner and Vallacher (1977) suggest that the omission of considerations of intentionality distinguishes young children's judgments from those of adults. Weiner and Peter (1973), examining judgments made by over 300 children between 4 and 18 years of age, found that distinctions between effort and performance, which they claim are analogous, showed no marked age trends. Chandler, Greenspan and Barenboim (1973) argue that the verbal presentation of dilemmas emphasizes consequence; using videotaped presentations children of 6 often take account of intentions. Gutkin (1972) suggested four successive stages in the appreciation of intention when intention and damage are varied systematically—damage only, mainly damage, mainly intention, intention only.

Other areas with equivocal findings include the interrelationship between moral reasoning and action (for example, Turiel and Rothman, 1972). While some relation between level and action is apparent, the evidence is not likely to convince a behaviourally inclined psychologist that an intervening reasoning variable is as efficient as observation.

Work by Kohlberg and De Vries (1969) and Kuhn *et al.* (1977) supported the hypothesis that a specific level of general reasoning ability is necessary but not sufficient for the equivalent level of moral reasoning to be attained. This is not supported by other studies. For example, Ainsworth and Bell (1974) found that at the early (sensory-motor) stages social reasoning may be more advanced than other deductive reasoning; Hopwood (1978) found that this was reversed by concrete operational stages.

Kohlberg (1971) claimed that the stages represent a logically necessary progression—Peters (1971) contests this; Alston (1971) points out that if one accepts this progression it does not entail any superiority of moral thinking in the later stages. Biggs (1976) quotes Kohlberg (1970) as stating that upward movement through the stages is justification that they should—Biggs also suggests that there is some (weak) empirical support, sufficient to ask whether school environments are likely to promote this. It seems reasonable to hope for greater clarity as to the status of moral stages before they are applied.

COMMENT

If there is an area of psychology concerning human behaviour or competence which can sensibly be distinguished from others and labelled as morality or values or social skills or social reasoning, this is likely to include psychologists in the activities discussed above, and probably in many others. Those who seek to develop theories will be particularly concerned to demarcate their areas, to ensure that such theories are compatible with other related theories, to test their descriptive and predictive powers. Those who seek to help individuals and groups will want to ensure they do so effectively using among other checks adequate pre- and post-assessment procedures, observed behaviour, structured feedback from clients and their families or care-givers. Those who seek to apply the theory or the intervention strategies for more general educational purposes may ideally wish to have a valid theory and proven effectiveness; however it is likely that administrators, teachers, parents will be less concerned with scientific validity, far more concerned with practical and political issues, possibly resentful of what might be perceived as a psychological prescription for morality or values. It seems likely that all such developments will be facilitated by precise and reliable measures.

Some implicit assumptions may also need to be investigated. Kitwood (1983) suggests that the implicit notion of consistency needs investigating. Inconsistencies, particularly in psychoanalytic case studies, are already well documented.

At present it is difficult to defend social reasoning as a useful term, or to state clearly what it denotes. At least on this interpretation it encompasses activities that are comparable on some dimensions, but quite markedly different on others. They happen to share certain problems—of agreed definition, of designing forms of assessment which are sensitive, and of proven reliability and validity, of uncertainty about their logical status, and perhaps also their political status. Those are shared with many other areas of psychology and other disciplines so are hardly defining characteristics.

REFERENCES

Ainsworth, M. D. and Bell, S. M. (1974) 'Mother-infant interaction and the development of competence', in Connolly, K. and Bruner, J. S. (Eds.), *The Growth of Competence*, London, Academic Press.

Alston, W. P. (1971) 'Comments on Kohlberg's "From is to ought"', in Mischel, T. (Ed.), *Cognitive Development and Epistemology*, London, Academic Press.

Argyle, M. (1979) 'New developments in the analysis of social skills', in Wolfgang, A. (Ed.), *Non-verbal Behaviour: Applications and Cross Cultural Implications*, New York, Academic Press.

Barnes, E. (1894), 'Punishment as seen by children', *Pediatric Seminary*, 3, pp. 235–45.

Bergling, K. (1983) *Moral Development—the Validity of Kohlberg's Theory*, Acta University Stockholmiensis, Stockholm, Stockholm Studies in Educational Psychology.

Biggs, J. B. (1976) 'Schooling and moral development', in Varma, V. P. and Williams, P. (Eds.), *Piaget Psychology and Education*, London, Hodder and Stoughton.

Broughton, J. (1978) 'The cognitive-developmental approach to morality: A reply to Kurtines and Greif', *Journal of Moral Education*, 7, pp. 81–96.

Chandler, M. J., Greenspan, S. and Barenboim, C. (1973) 'Judgments of intentionality in response to videotaped and verbally presented moral dilemmas: The medium and the message', *Child Development*, 44, pp. 315–20.

Colby, A. (1978) 'Evolution of a moral development theory', *Moral Development New Directory for Child Development*, 2, pp. 89–104.

Curran, J. (1979) 'Pandora's box re-opened? The assessment of social skills', *Journal of Behaviour Assessment*, 1, pp. 55–71.

Duska, R. and Whelan, M. (1977) *Moral Development*, Dublin, Gill and Macmillan.

Elliott, C. D., Murray, D. J. and Pearson, L. S. (1979) *The British Ability Scales*, Windsor, NFER-Nelson.

Ellis, R. and Whittington, D. (Eds.) (1983) *New Directions in Social Skill Training*, London, Croom Helm.

Enright, R. D. (1981) 'A classroom discipline model for promoting social cognitive development in early childhood', *Journal of Moral Education*, 11, pp. 47–60.

Furnham, A. (1983) 'Research in social skills training: A critique', in Ellis, R. and Whittington, D. (Eds.), *New Directions in Social Skill Training*, London, Croom Helm.

Gottlib, I. and Asarnow, R. (1979) 'Interpersonal and impersonal problem-solving skills in mildly and clinically depressed university students', *Journal of Consulting and Clinical Psychology*, 47, pp. 86–95.

Graham, D. (1976) 'Moral development: The cognitive developmental approach', in Varma, V. P. and Williams, P. (Eds.), *Piaget Psychology and Education*, London, Hodder and Stoughton.

Gutkin, D. C. (1972) 'The effects of systematic story changes on intentionality in children's moral judgments', *Child Development*, 43, pp. 187–95.

Hamlyn, D. W. (1978) *Experience and the Growth of Understanding*, London, Routledge and Kegan Paul.

Hargreaves, D. H. (1982) *The Challenge for the Comprehensive School*, London, Routledge and Kegan Paul.

Hopwood, D. (1978) 'An investigation of causal schemata in ability, effort and kindness attributions of performance', Unpublished thesis, University of New York.

Jesness, C. F. (1962) *The Jesness Inventory*, California Youth Authority, Report No. 29.

Kitwood, T. M. (1983) *The Study of Persons and their Values*, Issues in Educational Research VIII, Western Australia; Institute for Educational Research.

Kohlberg, L. (1969) 'Stage and sequence: The cognitive-developmental approach to socialism', in Goslin, D. A. (Ed.), *Handbook of Socialisation: Theory and Research*, New York, Rand McNally, pp. 347–480.

Kohlberg, L. (1970) 'Stages of moral development as a basis for moral education', in Beck, C. and Sullivan, E. (Eds.), *Moral Education*, Toronto, University of Toronto Press.

Kohlberg, L. (1971) 'From is to ought', in Mischel, T. (Ed.), *Cognitive Development and Epistemology*, London, Academic Press.

Kohlberg, L. and De Vries, R. (1969) 'Relations between Piaget and psychometric assessments of intelligence', in Laratelli, C. (Ed.), *The Natural Curriculum*, Urbana, Ill., University of Illinois Press.

Kuhn, D., Langer, J., Kohlberg, L. and Haan, N. (1977) 'The development of formal operations in logical and moral judgment', *Genetic Psychology Monographs*, 95, pp. 97–188.

McFail, R. (1982) 'A review and reformulation of the concept of social skills', *Behavioural Assessment*, 4, pp. 1–33.

Patsiokas, A., Clum, G. and Luscumb, R. (1979) 'Cognitive characteristics of suicide attempters', *Journal of Consulting and Clinical Psychology*, 47, pp. 478–84.

Pearson, L. and Elliott, C. (1980) 'The development of a social reasoning scale in the new British Ability Scales', *Journal of Moral Education*, 10, pp. 40–8.

Pearson, L. and Tweddle, D. (1984) 'The formulation and use of behavioural objectives', in Fontana, D. (Ed.), *Behaviourism and Learning in Education*, Edinburgh, Scottish Academic Press.

Peters, R. S. (1971) 'Moral development: A plea for pluralism', in Mischel, T. (Ed.), *Cognitive Development and Epistemology*, London, Academic Press.

Piaget, J. (1932) *The Moral Judgment of the Child*, London, Routledge and Kegan Paul.

Platt, J. and Spivak, G. (1972) 'Social competence and effective problem-solving thinking in psychiatric patients', *Journal of Clinical Psychology*, 28, pp. 3–5.

Rest, J. R. (1976) 'New approaches in the assessment of moral judgment', in Lickona, T. (Ed.). *Moral Development and Behaviour: Theory Research and Social Issues*, New York, Holt, Rinehart and Winston, pp. 198–218.

Russell, J. (1978) *The Acquisition of Knowledge*, London, Macmillan.

Ryle, G. (1949) *The Concept of Mind*, London, Hutchinson.

Schroeder, H. E. and Rakos, R. F. (1983) 'The identification and assessment of social skills', in Ellis, R. and Whittington, D. (Eds.), *New Directions in Social Skill Training*, London, Croom Helm, pp. 117–90.

Selman, R. (1976) 'A structured approach to the study of developing interpersonal relationship concepts: Research with normal and pre-adolescent boys', in Pick, A. (Ed.), *X Annual Minnesota Symposia on Child Psychology*, Minneapolis; Minn., University of Minnesota Press.

Shotter, J. (1979) 'Men the magicians: The duality of social being and the structure of moral worlds', in Chapman, A. J. and Jones, D. M. (Eds.), *Models of Man*, Leicester, The British Psychological Society.

Shure, M. (1981) 'Social competence as a problem-solving skill', in Wise, J. and Smye, M. (Eds.), *Social Competence*, New York, Guildford Press.

Skemp, R. R. (1979) *Intelligence Learning and Action*, New York, John Wiley.

Spivak, G. and Sure, N. (1974) *Social Adjustment of Young Children: A Cognitive Approach to Solving Real-Life Problems*, San Francisco, Jossey-Bass.

Tomlinson, P. (1981) *Understanding Teaching—Interactive Educational Psychology*, London, McGraw Hill.

Tomlinson, P. (1983) 'Piagetian psychology of moral development—some persisting issues', in Modgil, S., Modgil, C. and Brown, G. (Eds.), *Jean Piaget: An Interdisciplinary Critique*, London, Routledge and Kegan Paul.

Trower, P. (1982) 'Towards a generative model of social skills: A critique and synthesis', in Curran, J. and Monti, P. (Eds.) *Social Skills Training: A Practical Handbook for Assessment and Treatment*. New York: Guilford Press.

Turiel, E. (1975) 'The development of social concepts mores customs and conventions', in De Palma, D. J. and Foley, J. M. (Eds.), *Moral Development: Current Theory and Research*. New Jersey: Lawrence Erlbaum Associates, pp. 7–37.

Turiel, E. and Rothman, G. R. (1972) 'The influence of reasoning on behavioural choices at different stages of moral development', *Child Development*, 43, pp. 741–56.

Wegner, D. M. and Vallacher, R. R. (1977) *Implicit Psychology*, New York, Oxford University Press.

Weiner, B. and Peter, N. (1973) 'A cognitive-developmental analysis of achievement and moral judgments', *Developmental Psychology*, 9, pp. 290–309.

Wilson, J. (1973) *The Assessment of Morality*, Windsor, NFER.

Wright, D. (1982) 'Piaget's theory of practical morality', in Bryant, P. (Ed.), *Piaget, Issues and Experiments*, Leicester, British Psychological Society.

Ziv, A. (1976) 'Measuring aspects of morality', *Journal of Moral Education*, 5, pp. 189–201.

Interchange

ENRIGHT, LAPSLEY AND OLSON REPLY TO PEARSON

Is Einstein to blame for the bomb? Is Darwin to blame for godless hedonism? Is Marx to blame for totalitarian, oppressive 'Marxist' regimes throughout the world today? Must a creative theorist stand accused of the erroneous derivations of the disciples, or even the casual followers of the leader? These questions must be placed at the heart of Pearson's argument. Her ideas are accurate in assessing the state-of-the-art in social skills training, educational application, measurement and theory in the area of social reasoning *as she defines the term*. The problems presented, however, are not the onus of Kohlbergian theory.

Consider, for instance, social skills training. This often derives from social learning theory, not cognitive developmental. That the field 'has not always been tempered by scholarly appraisal of social skills theory' is not Kohlberg's burden. The domains are similar in that morality and social skills both concern interpersonal issues, but the underlying philosophies differ. That terrorists blow up a bus in the name of Marx is not a blot on *Das Kapital*. Marx did not advocate terrorism.

Pearson is probably accurate in claiming that Kohlbergian curriculum would be 'politically contentious' in the UK. We, however, should not see this as a blight on Kohlbergian theory or even on Kohlbergian education. Political opposition is not the final arbiter on the quality of an idea. Did we condemn Darwin's theory when the celebrated Stokes monkey trial turned in favour of the prosecution? Look at today's politics. A recent US court ruling decided in favour of Darwin and against creation. Politics can be fickle.

In measurement, indeed, it may be that the BAS Social Reasoning Scale is 'rather speculative'. This is for Elliott, Murray and Pearson to tidy up. It has little import for the *moral* development research programme. That Kohlberg's instrument is cumbersome is a more valid criticism by Pearson. Kohlberg's, however, it not the only assessment device we have, as Rest has pointed out for a decade. It is rarely considered a vilification of the *theory* of intelligence now that the measurement of it has exploded to include weak and strong instruments. Were we left with only an inefficient, quick-test of IQ, then we have a legitimate complaint.

In turning to Kohlbergian theory, it may be that 'the question of its truth value has not yet been confronted.' Must we remind the reader that Einstein's theories are still being tested? Some of his far-reaching views of time and space are only now being validated. Is it a fatal flaw if the research pieces are slowly glued together? This is occurring in Kohlbergian theory before our eyes, as this volume attests.

Finally, we must ask: What is the alternative? If we dismiss the Kohlbergian idea because it has not yet clearly defined its link to social reasoning, do we take up a different theory? None exists. Do we stop asking the question? Few would stand for such anti-intellectualism. Kohlberg's is one of the few clues to unlocking the secrets of the social reasoning world. Let us accept Kohlbergian theory, along with its imperfections, until a greater super-sleuth comes along better to solve the mysteries.

PEARSON REPLIES TO ENRIGHT, LAPSLEY AND OLSON

The basic postulate of this paper, that the Kohlbergian moral paradigm is alive and well, is irrefutable. Indeed, the extensions described are attractive developments in their own right. If the paradigm facilitated the work reported, it is at one level justified. Nevertheless, one is left with some disquiet. The paradigm is limited by the largeness of its scale. It is also inviolate until an equivalent alternative is produced. It seems self-evident that the Kohlberg model would have to be forsaken before that could happen—one is aware of the impracticality of an equivalent paradigm being developed and at the same time uneasy that only such a development could displace the present theory.

One feels a similar unease about the early emphasis on heuristic power in finding new compatible domains as the major validation, and the recognition much later in this chapter that an additional mechanism is needed to avoid trivializing this. Perhaps that is knocking down straw men, anyway—a more interesting question is how wide a range of non-trivial compatible domains can be digested before the theory risks seeming so general as to be trivial in a different sense—self-evident, tautologous? Is it acceptable to include other skills or judgments which are usually acquired incidentally—semantics, non-verbal problem-solving? Can this be demarcated from traditionally taught attainments—mathematics, reading, etc.? If everything people do can be fitted to a three or four or five or six-stage sequential model, what have we discovered; what implications for problem-solving, remediation, education can such a general model have?

I am left with some doubts about the practical implications of macro-models; my internal concerns are not diminished—perhaps the nature of large-stage models is conducive to some inconsistency. An example I omitted from my chapter is the use of cross-cultural validity as a vindication—together with specific references to cultural practices. Perhaps there are distinguishable levels of interactions between individuals and theories. If the individual, whether naive or sophisticated, both sees theories as essential and wants them to be specific as well as general, and is also concerned that they should not be more prone to verification than falsification, then I will admit to being stuck at that level.

Part XII: Moral Reasoning and Political Issues

22. Kohlberg's Contribution to Political Psychology: A Positive View

HELEN WEINREICH-HASTE

I have in my possession a pledge dated October 1969, drawn up by students and faculty at Rutgers*. 'I will oppose any unjust war my country may undertake. I consider it my right and duty to judge the morality of my government's actions. I commit my personal energy to the creation of a peaceful and humane society.' This pledge expresses three things: a statement of moral principles about a political issue, a statement about the relationship between the individual's moral position and government policy, and a statement of intended moral action within a political context. It is typical of North American campus rhetoric in the period of the Vietnam War.

Analyzed from the perspective of Kohlberg's theory, the pledge reflects at least Stage 5 moral reasoning; lower-stage thought does not include the idea that it is a person's *right and duty* to question the government. The key rhetorical issues in the pledge, justice, rights and humanitarianism, are central concepts of American liberal democracy; they are also central to Kohlberg's theory of *morality*.

The flowering of political radicalism in the 1960s and early 1970s produced a rich harvest of research on the relationship between moral reasoning, political ideology and political action; indeed, Kohlberg's theory of moral development virtually supplanted personality models in the explanation of youth dissent. But the relationship between moral development and politics is not confined to cataloguing the moral stage of campus dissenters. In this chapter, I will consider five areas in which I consider that Kohlberg's work on moral development has made a major contribution to the study of politics. Some of these contributions are direct, some are indirect. I shall first consider the criticisms of Kohlberg's political assumptions, his explicit identification of his theory of moral development with liberalism, and his relative lack of attention to social and historical factors in the construction of individual moral perspectives. I shall argue that this particular critique has brought into sharp focus a much broader debate about the way developmental psychology

---

*My thanks for this to Howard E. Grvber

deals with values, and that on balance, Kohlberg's explicit affirmation of a link between ideology and morality is a positive not a negative.

I shall then look at empirical studies of the relationship between moral reasoning and political ideology and action. Thirdly, I shall look at parallel work on cognitive-developmental approaches to the growth of social, political and economic thought. Fourthly, I shall consider the ways in which the work of Kohlberg and his associates on participatory democracy and 'just communities' in schools and prisons can be seen as studies of the micro-political environment. Finally, I will consider the wider social and political context and the relationship between individual reasoning and social and cultural experience, and how work stemming from Kohlberg's theory illuminates this.

THE CRITIQUE OF LIBERALISM

Bias-hunters come in two forms. The first kind want their science value-free, and their accusations identify forms of subjectivism in theory and methodology; the second kind recognize that social science cannot (and should not) be value-free, but want an explicit and sophisticated exposition of the sources of value and of the influences of culture and history on theory building and interpretation. Kohlberg originally threw down a gauntlet in 1971 in his paper 'From Is to Ought', in which he affirmed that the psychological development of individual moral reasoning paralleled the philosophical progression towards universal ideas of justice and liberal democracy; he has subsequently written further elaborations of this viewpoint. In doing this, he upset both kinds of bias-hunter.[1]

Kohlberg argued that liberalism implies social evolution in parallel with moral evolution; this means progression towards greater justice, to relations based on social contract, and towards individual autonomy in rights and decision-making. He argued that history confirms this view; 'The agonisingly slow but relatively consistent trend towards greater justice, civil rights and racial equality is one of the many historical indicators of the directionality of a democratic system towards carrying its original premises of justice beyond the boundaries accepted by the founders of the system. Indeed, the major moral crises of the past 20 years have represented conflicts between universal justice and the boundary-maintaining demands of the society-sustaining morality.'[2]

This quotation clearly links moral judgments *about* justice with social and political policies concerned with the *establishment* of justice. Applying a moral judgment to a social situation becomes translated into policies and laws which effect justice: the polity is by implication therefore the aggregate of individual moral concern. This position is stated even more explicitly by one of his followers (Candee):

> The importance of Kohlberg's sequence lies in the fact that morality is at the very crux of political philosophy. While Kohlberg avoids an exact definition of morality, he does characterise it by the concept of justice, loosely defined as 'giving each person his due'. But this is also the main purpose of political systems. Their existence ideally serves the function of distributing the goods and services of society in a just manner.[3]

Kohlberg is avowedly expressing a liberal point of view which makes very explicit assumptions about the primacy of a justice-based democracy, not only as a form of government, or as one ideology amongst many, but as a historical necessity (at least in Western society). According to Kohlberg's theory, individual moral development represents the gradual cognitive appreciation of the full implications of liberal thought. Democracy is the system in which the practice of justice is most likely to develop, and in which the *idea* of justice is most likely to predominate. Much of Kohlberg's thinking about practical democracy he acknowledges to have been influenced by George Herbert Mead. Mead defined the successful practice of democracy individualistically, as the ability to absorb information from others, to listen before forming judgments and to take the role of the 'generalized other' as a precondition for action. Kohlberg has translated this into the 'ideal' Stage 6 situation of 'moral musical chairs' in which the judge role-takes the perspective of all interested parties in the situation. This also is consistent with Rawls' 'original position'.[4]

The critique of Kohlberg's liberal idealism take several forms. The first of these is addressed not only to Kohlberg, but to cognitive-developmental theory in general. This is the *cult of progressivism*, or the perfectibility of the human being; this concept owes much to the philosophy of Dewey. Central to American liberalism is the notion that government *and* education *and* individual cognitive development are all moving towards *improvement*. Sullivan argues that the popularity of Kohlberg's theory in the United States is at least in part due to the fact that his theory is consistent with the dominant cultural ethos of progression towards moral perfectibility, particularly as he also stresses the concepts of justice, rights and humanitarianism enshrined in the Constitution and therefore close to the hearts of American liberals.[5] And indeed, liberals in the early 1970s were on the whole pleased with the findings that the radical young, although somewhat of a nuisance, were nevertheless showing a high level of moral reasoning and humanitarian concern. Adelson argued:

> We do like to think of our young as possessing exemplary moral vision; it speaks so well of them and especially well of ourselves. What has not been sufficiently understood is that the moralism of the [student] Movement draws upon and continues the cursed American habit of pursuing moral uplift in the realm of politics.[6]

The second objection to Kohlberg's particular expression of liberalism is that he *ignores structural aspects of the social system*. Some critics regard his theory as a rather dangerous perpetration of the liberal myth of individual efficacy in making moral and political change. Reid and Yanarella, for example, argue that moral education packages and practices are relatively easy to derive from Kohlberg's method, and they are apparently effective in making people mouth democratic sentiments. But such piecemeal educational efforts do little to disturb the existing social system, and indeed shore it up. Individual ethical reform, and even local grass-roots democracy, do not, they argue, begin to tackle the fundamentally structural problems of American society; it is an illusion that making people 'better' in the sense of more morally critical has any effect on social change.[7]

The third objection is that Kohlberg's theory has *too narrow an ideological base*. This criticism has several forms. The most common is that the claim that moral developmental stages are universal ignores the very different social and political conditions even *within* Western societies, but particularly outside the West. Although the adolescent in a different culture may be able to respond to the Heinz dilemma, it is by no means certain that the issues of rights and justice are necessarily *central* to her thinking, nor that these issues correspond to what is most salient in the social system in which the individual lives. Many societies do not have social institutions which reify the world-view of post-Stage 3 thought; the dominant mode of social organization is the community, rather than society at large. Indeed, this may be an explanation for the general failure to find post-Stage 3 thinking outside the West. In contrast, in Israel there exists a sub-culture which quite explicitly practises and preaches collectivist socialism and democratic procedure; kibbutz respondents consistently score *higher* than their age-mates in the US on moral reasoning measures.[8]

The objection therefore is that the themes of justice and democracy, as emphasized in Kohlberg's formulation of the moral stages, are neither universal values, nor more particularly are they universally practised. The emphasis on justice and democracy ignores the possibility that other values and other forms of social and political praxis may exist, and be reflected in different kinds of thinking. Harré, for example, has argued that in many societies personal morality is based on the maintenance of honour rather than on the negotiation of contracts or rights. Even *within* American culture, Gilligan has argued that women tend to operate with a morality based on responsibility and mutuality rather than on rights and justice.[9] Other critics have argued that the development of increasing abstraction and articulation may itself be culturally determined; educational practice in advanced industrial societies encourages a move from the concrete to the abstract. Quite apart from its status as a dominant cultural value, justice lends itself to formalism and ultra-rational analysis, and may for that reason be particularly attractive in cultures which value formalistic procedures of thought.[10]

A fourth objection is that Kohlberg is *caught in a liberal paradox*. Part of the problem is inherent in the philosophy of liberalism, part comes from Kohlberg's attempts to link liberalism to development of individual thought. According to Fishkin, the paradox of liberalism is that it contains within it an uneasy tension between *relativism* and *absolutism*.[11] In practice, both are inconsistent with liberalism. The absolutist view, that one position may provide the ultimate ethical or political solution, is inconsistent with the idea that there should be individual liberty to choose between many points of view, and it is also inconsistent with the idea of continual change and improvement. Relativism is inconsistent with liberalism because it may imply subjectivism and arbitrariness; true liberalism requires that there be *objective* criteria for the acceptance of ethical or political positions, but these criteria may legitimate more than one position. The paradox of Kohlberg's position arises from the progressivist assumptions behind the developmental sequence; progressivism implies a goal, a *telos*. Kohlberg's theory accords justice a special status, explicitly associated with democracy, and furthermore he argues that because all Stage 6 thinkers would accept a common set of principles based on justice and democracy, and would all argue from Rawls' 'original position', they must come to a common conclusion.

The final criticisms which I will consider come from the *critical theory perspective*. Broadly, these criticisms argue that neither individual ideological development nor dominant political ideologies such as democracy or liberalism can be looked at separately from the social and historical conditions in which they occur. So the individual does not invent or construct her world in isolation, as a consequence of self-reflection. Instead, the individual's developing conceptualization is in a *dialectical relationship* with the available social representations, dominant ideologies and paradigms of common explanation.[12] These ideas themselves reflect the cultural and historical context. Kohlberg's theory itself is a product of the liberal tradition in which he lives and works.

In summary, the underlying theme of all the criticisms of Kohlberg's implicit and explicit political perspective is that he espouses the liberal position uncritically and does not consider any other possible perspective. The faults of his theory are the faults of this position; too much weight given to the individual as an effective political agent, too little appreciation of historical, cultural and economic factors in social change, and too great an emphasis on the analysis of *individual* behaviour. One major manifestation of this is the failure to make a distinction between democratic interaction at the interpersonal level, and democratic relations between the social group and the state.

In principle, I would accept that most of these criticisms are valid. At the very least, Kohlberg's working definition of democracy is located firmly within the framework of North American commonsense ideals and values, which reflect a different history even from that of European democracy. However, my defence of Kohlberg's contribution to political psychology is that by making his liberal position explicit, and by trying to make explicit parallels between individual development and political ideology, he has made a very important contribution to a number of debates.

First, he has demonstrated the vacuity of 'value-free' psychology of development; his affirmation that his theory reflects his own liberalism is a part of this, but his detailed analysis of a *particular form* of moral liberalism has effectively made his theory a case-history in the more general debate about psychological theories as cultural and historical products. Secondly, the application of his theory to current political and social issues has provided valuable data for the study of relations between cultural belief systems, political theory and moral rhetoric. Thirdly, the work of his critics has begun to piece together the relationship between moral development processes and the social processes involved in the development of political thought, in particular through the study of discourse and communicative action. Amongst his own research group, the work on just communities, 'moral atmosphere' and work democracy marks a shift from individualistic developmental psychology to a social psychological examination of moral and political interaction in small groups.[13]

In the remainder of this chapter I will consider how different kinds of empirical work on the relationship between moral development and politics elaborate some of these issues. The work which demonstrates a relationship between political ideology, action and moral thinking illustrates the overlap between cognitive explanations of moral and of political events, and between moral and political rhetorics. Work on the development of political thought shows parallels between the structure of thinking on political and social issues, and thinking on moral issues. The work on the 'just community' focuses first on discourse and communication, and secondly, it illustrates the micro-political context in which young people learn about conflicts of interest and power relations. Finally, in the last section I will look at the ways in which moral development research has enlarged our understanding of the transmission of cultural and political norms.

MORAL STAGE AND POLITICAL THOUGHT AND ACTION

One of the first reports of a clear relationship between political behaviour and moral stage was by Haan, Smith and Block; they studied the Free Speech Movement Sit-in at Berkeley in 1964.[14] Concurrently, Kohlberg and his associates were beginning to report a relationship between moral stage and the way in which the longitudinal sample were thinking about political issues—particularly the Vietnam War and Draft.[15] In the following few years there were many studies of student activism. A consistent picture emerged from these studies; activism, and support for radical political positions in general, was associated either with Stage 2 *or* with postconventional reasoning. The conclusion drawn from these studies—at least by those who popularized them—was that the activists were liberal gilded youth; they perceived the political in terms of the moral, and had the courage of their convictions to act upon the moral imperative. In reality, of course, the picture was more complicated.[16]

There are two kinds of question one can ask about the relationships between moral development and activism. The first is: 'who are the activists?'; the second is: 'what correlates with moral stage?' There are obvious differences in methodology and interpretation, and in choice of dependent and independent variables, depending on which question is asked. Questions about the characteristics of activists imply a *typological* model; the activist is a different kind of person from the non-activist. The question presupposes a search for a constellation of differentiating attributes. Questions about the correlates of moral stages assume developmental change; when a person moves from the present stage of moral reasoning to the next, she will change in other ways also. In other words, attributes are presumed to correlate with the *stage* rather than the *person*. Most of the campus activist studies were implicitly typological.

The studies of protest took several forms. Some research focused on behaviour specifically—on action and protest. Other studies looked at political beliefs. (Many of course covered both.) A third type of study looked at broader social, economic and political ideology; the *content* of what people believed rather than the labels they endorsed.

Direct action, in the form of demonstrations, sit-ins, marches and so forth was widespread fifteen years ago on campuses throughout the world, but it was by no means directed to a single issue. According to Fendrich and Tarleau: 'During the nineteen sixties hundreds of thousands of black and white students became involved as the direct action and rights protests mushroomed. Later, segments of the movement redirected their demands to ending the Vietnam War, reforming universities, stopping environmental pollution and a host of local issues.' *Pace* liberal democracy, this was a dangerous game: 'For their efforts, students were killed, beaten, tear-gassed, arrested, suspended from school and generally harassed as they used the tactics of political confrontation to reform or radically change major institutional sectors of the United States.'[17] The goals of protesters were heterogeneous; their common theme was the belief that certain *means* were legitimate, appropriate and effective.

Whatever the limitations of Haan, Smith and Block's study (and it has been criticized on many counts) it did at least try to obtain a reasonable sample of activists and a reasonable control group. It still remains the richest study of student politics and moral reasoning. It was an early example of campus protest; in 1964 direct action was still relatively unusual and associated mainly with civil rights and race issues. Haan's 'activists' were (1) those students who had been *arrested* at the *FMS* sit-in at Berkeley and (2) a group from San Francisco State College who belonged to organizations which *supported* direct action. The 'control' group were non-activist students from a variety of organizations at colleges in the Bay Area. Fifty-four per cent produced written moral reasoning protocols which could be assigned to a 'pure' stage. The relationship between activism and moral stage was very clear; 48 per cent of the activists were operating with Stage 5 or 6 thought, compared with only 23 per cent of the remainder; 41 per cent of activists were operating with Stage 3 or 4 thought, compared with 73 per cent of the rest.[18]

Other studies of activism and moral stage were conducted by Fishkin, Keniston and Mackinnon, Fontana and Noel, and Leming. Fishkin *et al.*'s study took place at the time of the Kent State incident, perhaps the peak of political consciousness and radical enthusiasm. Their study measured endorsement of slogans proposing, respectively, violent action, peaceful radicalism and conservatism. They found that support for 'violent' slogans correlated strongly only with Stage 2 reasoning; Stage 4 reasoners significantly *rejected* violent slogans.[19] In a study of students, faculty and administrators at Yale, Fontana and Noel defined activism broadly, including attending meetings, working for political candidates, serving on committees, soliciting support and distributing literature as well as forms of protest. They found that activism correlated with moral stage differently according to role; activist and non-activist students did not differ much in moral stage, faculty activists however used more Stage 5 and 6, and less Stage 2, reasoning than non-activitists.[20]

Leming, studying high school students, also identified two kinds of activism, community involvement in pressure groups and participation in a specific demonstration on school premises about the invasion of Cambodia; the latter resulted in temporary suspension from school. He found that Stage 5 reasoners were likely to be activists in either community or direct action, Stage 4 reasoners were not direct action supporters, Stage 3 reasoners were not differentiated, and Stage 2 reasoners were more likely to be involved in community action.[21]

These studies tend to confirm:

1 the rejection of direct action by Stage 4 reasoners;
2 the high involvement by postconventional reasoners with action in general, but the wide variation in definition of 'activism' is an important caveat to any generalizations.

Conservatism was unfashionable during this period: even the most 'conservative' students were quite liberal. However, Fontana and Noel found that Stage 4 reasoning correlated with Right orientation, and Left orientation correlated with Stage 2, 5 and 6 reasoning. Haan *et al.* also found that Stage 2, 5 and 6 reasoning correlated with radical political ideology. In Fishkin *et al.*'s study of slogan endorsement, Stage 4 thinkers rejected radical slogans and endorsed conservative slogans; conservative slogans were rejected by Stage 5 and 6 thinkers. Alker and Poppen measured ideology using Tomkins' measure of humanism *versus* normativism. They found a clear relationship between humanism and principled moral thought. Sullivan and Quarter studied only Stage 4 and postconventional reasoners, and their degree of political radicalism, in the context of parochial University of

Toronto issues; they found a monotonic relationship between radicalism and moral thought.[22]

Latterly, Left-wing radicalism has gone out of fashion; three recent studies in Europe show a definite shift to the Right. But the same kind of overall relationship between political beliefs and moral stage remains. Lind *et al.* studied 18-year-old West Germans. He used scales of humanism, egalitarianism, democratization and participation. His questionnaire measure of moral reasoning taps structural relations between stage items. The more 'democratic' their orientation, the more respondents endorsed higher-stage items on the moral scale. In a similar study with British youth, Weinreich-Haste found a clear relationship between endorsement of high-stage items and rejection of lower-stage items, and support for the Labour rather than the Conservative party. High-stage endorsement was also associated with support for liberal social policies. Emler, Renwick and Malone used Rest's DIT in a study of Scottish undergraduates; they found that endorsement of Stage 4 reasons was associated with Right-wing orientation, and endorsement of principled reasons with a Left-wing orientation.[23]

The pattern which emerges from these studies is consistent; it appears even in different political climates, and whether the measures of moral development are open-ended or by the endorsement of questionnaire items. *Prima facie*, Kohlberg's argument that moral development reflects the development of a liberal ideology is confirmed by these studies. But a number of caveats are in order; the strong evidence is for a relationship between the *production* of Stage 4 moral thought and the *endorsement* of conservative beliefs and actions, and the *production* of principled moral thought and the *endorsement* of liberal beliefs and actions. The political ideology correlates of the earlier stages of thought are more problematic. This is an important gap because a high proportion of respondents do not produce Stage 4 or higher reasoning, so the 'strong' relationship only applies to a proportion of respondents.

As it stands, the main questions which the data raise concern the interpretation of the relationship between a *type* of ideology and a *developmental stage* of moral reasoning. Because Stage 3 thinkers are not more conservative than Stage 4 thinkers, as far as we can see from the data, we must perhaps conclude that Stage 4 represents some kind of consolidation of conservatism, possibly consequent upon the increasing appreciation of the wider social implications of order and social institutions. But what happens next? Do individuals become less conservative as they progress in their moral thinking? In which case we would have to conclude that conservatism is a morally less 'mature' form of reasoning. The evidence is sketchy; some of the longitudinal data, and some of the data on the effects of political ordeal-by-fire, indicate that for *some* people this may be true, but it is unlikely to be universally the case.

Further evidence that the arguments of Stage 4 are *perceived* as conservative and postconventional arguments are *perceived* as liberal is provided by Emler and his associates. They tested this in two studies; in the first they asked respondents to complete the DIT firstly as themselves, secondly, as if they were of an extreme Left or of an extreme Right political orientation. They found that (1) Left-wingers showed greater endorsement of principled items than Right-wingers; (2) 'fake' Left-wing scores were higher than 'fake' Right-wing scores; and (3) faking produced more extreme scores than did answering 'as oneself', *except* that

Left-wingers' faking Left produced a *lower* P score. The reverse was true of the pattern for Stage 4 endorsement, but the polarization of scores in the faking condition was even greater. In a second study they asked respondents to identify the politics of responses supposedly 'written' by Stage 4 or Stage 5 respondents, and found that the Stage 4 responses were perceived as Right-wing, the Stage 5 as Left-wing.[24]

These findings confirm an overlap between ideology and stage content, and cast some doubts on the efficacy of questionnaire methods of measuring moral stage. In a study designed to extend Emler's hypothesis, Weinreich-Haste, Adams and Clay asked respondents to *produce* 'fake' Left- or Right-wing responses to a moral dilemma. We found that individuals 'faking Left' were no more likely than individuals 'faking Right' to produce higher scores on their 'fake' responses than on their 'real' responses, *but* that overall there was a tendency for 'Left' responses—real or fake—to be scored somewhat higher than 'Right' responses.[25]

These studies confirm a relationship between political ideology and moral stage, but its exact nature remains unclear. In the rest of this chapter I will look at other features of political development and the effects of political experience which illuminate some of the process of moral and political development.

DEVELOPMENT OF POLITICAL UNDERSTANDING

Studies of the development of political thought are not concerned with the origin of different ideological positions but with the growth of understanding of social, political and economic institutions. In the previous section I reviewed research on the *endorsement* of particular political *positions*; in this section, the material is primarily the *production* of political *cognitions*.

Adelson *et al.* studied the concepts of community and law amongst adolescents aged 11 to 18. They found a progression from *concrete* thought, focusing on individuals and present concerns, towards a more *abstract and integrated* general understanding of the social system, in which there was a focus on the community rather than on the individual.[26] As the thinking of the individual develops, she becomes less authoritarian, more able to realize that rule and law are modifiable, and more appreciative of the beneficial, as opposed to the restrictive, functions of social institutions. Connell studied 5- to 16-year-olds and identified four phases of political thought; intuitive, primitive realism, construction of a political order, and ideological thought. Furth and McConville presented a series of issues to adolescents in which the interests of different groups conflicted, or in which there was a conflict between individual interests and those of the community. They noted a shift from a 'no compromise' response to a recognition of alternative perspectives and the possibility of realistic compromise. Their study also showed progression from personalistic views of society to a more societal view and a recognition of community functions and responsibility.[27]

In a ten-nation study, Torney *et al.* identified five levels in political thinking;

1 vague inarticulate notions with emergent images of one or two institutions such as the police;
2 primarily the harmonizing values and process; a 'sheltered' view;

3   intermediate stage of growing awareness of social conflict, economic forces and multiple institutional roles;
4   understanding of the cohesive and divisive functions of many institutions, and overlap between institutional functions;
5   scepticism, general contempt for institutions, lack of belief in their efficacy, emphasis on discordant functions, unfairness and class bias.

These latter are interesting; like the other studies they show positive growth towards a more sophisticated conception of democracy, but they also indicate some negative aspects of increasing understanding of conflict and inequality.[28]

Several other studies have found very similar patterns of conceptual progression through adolescence. To my knowledge, no studies have looked at the correlation between moral stage and political stage, but some have found a relationship between the development of formal operations and the development of a 'societal' perspective. None of these studies makes formal claims for structured wholes in the description of the stages, but there is remarkable consistency in the general pattern of progressive cognitive change. All find movement from a personal, individualistic, authoritarian and controlling view of the world, through a period in which the individual has worked out some concrete functional understanding of norms, codes and procedures for regulating and explaining interpersonal relations, to an ultimate conception of social structure and the capacity to apply general principles and meta-perspectives to the situation.[29]

Two studies however do make a *conceptual* link between social and moral cognition. Tapp and Kohlberg studied the development of legal reasoning, and identified three levels: authoritarian control and fiat; rules and laws as normative means of control and guidance; and perception of the social utility of laws and of the rational principles underlying lawmaking. Tapp argues for a close connection between legal and moral thought: 'These concepts [obligation, authority and justice] intimately related to the institution of law and legal process, are also core aspects in moral thought. This correspondence suggests a consistency in moral and legal development. The law is the central human rule system, albeit the most venerable and specialized institutionalized expression of rule-or norm-guided behaviour, to which basic moral categories may apply.'

Torney studied children's conceptions of social welfare and justice: such issues as slavery, enforced residence, voting opportunity and economic privation. She explicitly commented on the interconnectedness of political and moral thinking: 'Faced with human rights issues, young people refer them to the social institutions. Moral justice appears to be closely tied to policy in the minds of young people.'[30]

These studies show a clear parallel between the structural changes which occur in the development of political thinking, and the stage structure of moral thinking. One of the main underlying themes in the development of moral thought is the growing understanding of the social system and of relations between the individual and the structure of social institutions; the difference between Stage 3 and Stage 4 moral thought, for example, is the shift from a generalized aggregate of the experiential 'community' to an appreciation of the abstract concept, 'society'.[31] Although the work in political concept development is as yet less rigorous than that in the moral domain, it is apparent that similar qualitative differences in cognition mark the transitions in political development.

There are a number of ways of interpreting the similarity. The first is that there is common underlying growth in cognitive ability; logical operations, and their social-cognitive manifestation as 'social perspective-taking', are cognitive processes applied to both domains.

A second explanation is in terms of the common *content* of justice, as expressed by Tapp and Kohlberg, by Candee, and to some degree by Torney, in the quotations presented earlier. According to this explanation, both moral and political reasoning are concerned with *justice*, and in both domains of development we are witnessing the gradual unfolding of justice-in-liberal-democracy. This of course raises again all the questions about the role of justice as the central theme of development which were discussed in the first section.

Another interpretation, however, is that the two fields of research are picking up the same phenomenon, namely the development of a broad conception of the social world, a set of schema for making sense of relations between persons and between the individual and social institutions. Elsewhere I have described this as the individual's 'implicit social theory'.[32] The implicit social theory is primarily *descriptive*; it reflects the way that the individual understands things *to be*; there *are* policeman, there *are* rules and conventions, there *are* forms of legal redress for injustices, there *are* normative methods of dealing with conflict. Both political and moral thought are *prescriptive* as well as descriptive; one generates an 'ought' statement from how one believes things *should* be, but that 'ought' also depends on how one believes things *actually* to be. By focusing only on prescriptive statements in developing the coding system, Kohlberg has made the descriptive underpinnings implicit, apparent only at the level of the structure of reasoning. According to the model of a common implicit social theory, the actual manifestation of prescriptive reasoning depends on the kind of questions asked; if the issue is couched in moral terms, the language of moral prescription is invoked, if in political terms, then political rhetoric emerges.

THE MICRO-POLITICAL CONTEXT AND MORAL DEVELOPMENT

So far I have considered the correlates of moral stage, and material which illustrates the structural changes in the development of individual reasoning. While this chapter is not concerned with the issues of growth and transition, in the work on stage transition and on the conditions which stimulate processes of moral growth, we find important material on what I shall term the 'micro-political context'.

There are two ways of looking at the process of moral development. One may focus on *individual* thought, and how it becomes restructured as a consequence of *cognitive disequilibrium*. According to this approach, external events or experiences are *catalysts* in creating constructive disturbance in the structure of current thought. This might be termed the 'developmental psychology' approach. It is characteristic of the early work of Turiel, Blatt and others; they sought the intervening variables in moral transition, looking at the effect of classroom 'Socratic discussion', or of major life events, on individual cognitive structures.[33] Alternatively one may focus on social processes, the actual social context in which disequilibrium takes place. This might be termed the 'social psychology' approach, and is characteristic of the later work on the 'just community' and 'moral atmosphere'. These studies looked at the interaction between people in an environment which was explicitly a self-governing participatory democracy; they focused on the ways in which *discussion* of moral issues changed over time within the group. Although the change in *individual* reasoning was an important variable in these studies, they were much more studies of a community in action.

One explanation of the development of political consciousness is that it arises from the child's experience of social interaction, and later from her experience of dealing—at first or second hand—with institutions. She learns at first hand how to deal with power relations and negotiations at the interpersonal level, and she learns also the nature of power structures in the school and the family. At second hand she learns about the relations between the social group to which her family belongs and the world of employers, bureaucrats and the police. Extensive sociological research, particularly in Britain, has looked at the 'hidden curriculum' of power relations in the school and the social world which the child inhabits. However, very little attention has been paid to the thinking of individual children; the analysis has focused primarily on sociological processes and the reproduction of power and class relations.[34]

Kohlberg's shift to looking at just communities rather than only at individual reasoning is a natural extension of the influence of Dewey and Mead, and their belief in the dominant role of participatory democracy in the development of ideas of justice. Practical participatory democracy has an important role in North American cultural and political history; the 'town meeting' had a real role in local government within folk, if not living, memory. The emphasis on participatory democracy in American life is not merely an echo of the ideals of the Constitution; it is a powerful myth even in the days of hierarchical corporations and dollar-rich presidential campaigns. Participatory democracy becomes equated with representational democracy. In Europe the long tradition of caste- or class-based power has provided little role, even at local level, for any equivalent of the 'town meeting'. The history of democracy in Europe has largely been the development—sometimes slow, sometimes swift and bloody—of representational democracy; the right to the ballot box rather than the right to negotiated consensus rising from the grass-roots. Kohlberg acknowledges the importance to his thinking of the 'town meeting' model. However, the specific impetus to creating just communities with participatory democracy was his realization that institutions have an 'implicit stage'. This is reflected in the structure of authority relations, the normative ways of interacting, the mechanisms by which members of the institution have to operate in order to manipulate the situation to their own advantage. So the authoritarian regime of a traditional prison, for example, embodies a Stage 1 or Stage 2 world; at most the prisoners are constrained to a Stage 2 instrumental relativism in their attempt to circumvent the system. Such an environment, Kohlberg argues, provides no opportunity for the individual to develop more complex thinking.[35]

Over a period of years, Kohlberg and his associates were involved in setting up a number of 'just communities' in prisons and schools. Though most of them had a fairly brief life of a few years (Kohlberg has described them as 'a successful operation in which the patient died'), they provided rich material on the micropolitical environment. The purpose of a just community is to provide an environment in which 'justice' is practised in the form of participatory democracy; everyone is involved equally in the decision-making process. The 'implicit stage' of such a community is 4 or 5. In the case of the prisons, the just communities were formed by a volunteer group of prisoners and staff, who reorganized their roles under the direction of the researchers and set up regular community meetings for the discussion of policy and grievances. In the case of the schools, students and staff spent a proportion of the school week in the 'alternative' school environment, which included some lessons and community meetings.[36]

The structure of relationships within the just community *embodies* Stage 4 or 5 reasoning, but that does not imply that the reasoning which went on in discourse within the community was at that level, or even that the aim was for everyone to reach that level. At the beginning of the life of the school just communities, the pupils were mostly operating with Stage 2 or 3 reasoning and the staff with Stage 3 and 4 reasoning. The purpose of a just community is to provide (1) a *norm* of participatory democracy and self-government, and (2) the opportunity for members to encounter situations in which the consequences of their decisions and actions become apparent to them. Initially, the dominant Stage 2 mode of self-interest was apparent in discussions; members showed little conception of either community obligations or community interests. Over time, the concept of community became increasingly salient in discussions.[37]

As micro-political environments, just communities have the following characteristics:

1 they involve the individual in taking responsibility for her decision-making processes in a group situation;
2 they provide first-hand experience of political and conceptual conflict and confrontation with others in the group; this exposes the members to alternative perspectives on the issues, and encourages discourse skills;
3 they provide experience of conflict between the group's desires and intentions and the power structure of the outside world; for example, attempts to legislate within the communities about the use of drugs, or attendance in class, were constrained by the legal responsibilities of the teachers and the school;
4 they provide a situation in which the group develops its own normative definition of 'appropriate' behaviour, values, goals, methods of interaction and power relations within the group.

Kohlberg and his associates—notably Higgins, Power and Reimer[38]—developed measures to identify some of the characteristics of just community interaction. Their measures define the group's 'moral atmosphere' and the development of a 'collective norm'. 'Moral atmosphere' means the shared values of the group (as expressed as a consensual norm in group discussion), the extent to which the group is operating as a community in its discussions and shared actions, and the moral stage structure of the shared perceptions held by the group. 'Collective norms' are the values-in-practice concerning community-oriented behaviour, and they develop during the group's lifetime. Collective norms concern what is done, not what the group thinks ought to be done. Reimer and Power postulate eight phases in the development of collective norms, which are divided into four main periods: collective norm *proposal*, collective norm *acceptance*, collective norm *expectation*, and collective norm *enforcement*. Classical social psychology of small group behaviour describes many of these phenomena: the difference is that Kohlberg's associates incorporate individual cognition, social communication and discourse, action and reflection on action into their analysis. In addition, the method incorporates measures of group and individual cognitive restructuring.

These studies provide insight into the role of the community as the crucible of political development. The norms which emerged concerned power relations between individuals and between the community and the wider world, and the maintenance of the community as a functioning unit. The 'meta-norm' of both prison and school communities was *survival*; it was clear that the experience was valued, enjoyable, and seen to have a number of pay-offs. Power and Reimer identified collective norms of property (concerning stealing), attendance at class, racial integration and drug use. The first two developed to a high degree; the norm of racial integration became 'expected' but never 'enforced', and the issue of marijuana use remained problematic. All aspects of norm development were associated with conflict; changes in shared perceptions were gradual and there were clashes between interest groups within the community. In the case of property and attendance norms, once the idea of community responsibility was consensually established, the collective norms consolidated. In the case of racial integration, however, the issue was that a high proportion of the pupils (and one staff member) were black; there were differences in style and values between the black and white groups, and this caused difficulty in creating a unified community loyalty. The virtual failure to establish a collective norm about drug use is explained by Reimer and Power as due to lack of consensus about the deleterious effects *to the community* of drug use. Indeed, at that time it was a tenet of the adolescent subculture that marijuana facilitated interaction, and good interaction was highly valued within the community.

Although the reports of just communities tend to concentrate on the benefits and effectiveness of participatory democracy, researchers did acknowledge the limitations of 'equality' amongst students or prisoners, and staff, in decision-making, and also the constraints arising from the power of the wider institution to close down the experiment if it did not conform to acceptable standards. The issues of escaping (for prisoners), attendance (for students) and drug use for both, placed the staff in a compromised position in which they had to invoke the threat of external sanctions. In addition, the school staff had the advantage of superior age and level of moral reasoning.

A strong criticism of the prison community democracy comes from Feldman.[39] He analyzed tapes of the community meetings in the prison experiments. He argues that, in practice, very few decisions were made in the group discussions, and decision-making was constrained by the knowledge that any decisions had to be acceptable to prison authorities. As far as the prison authorities were concerned, the effectiveness of the experiment was measured in terms of how far the community was *self-sanctioning*, so in order to fulfil the meta-norm of survival, the groups operated to maintain the appearance of being self-sanctioning.

Feldman argues that, contrary to Kohlberg's model, the discussions rarely focused on issues of justice and fairness; at least in the women's prison, the most salient issue was the maintenance of emotional warmth between staff and inmates, which was seen as the primary benefit of the community. But perhaps most sweeping is Feldman's criticism of Kohlberg's 'naive' equation of justice and democracy. In the prison community, he argues, there were no checks and balances against the tyranny of the majority, especially in sanctioning fellow inmates. Traditional hierarchical authority, he argues, was replaced by peer conformity pressure, a situation exacerbated by the fact that the deviant acts of individuals could cause the termination of the experiment if the prison authorities chose to act.

As before, I argue that the criticisms serve to highlight *political* processes in what was ostensibly a *moral education* experiment. In the just community, reflecting explicitly upon the process of decision-making is an essential part of the interaction and communication process: this also brings out into the open political processes which are implicit in any group. First, the group confronts power conflicts within itself, and develops ways of handling or manipulating them. Secondly, the limitations of democracy become sharply apparent when pre-existing group loyalties and identities intrude on the situation, or when the limits of effective power are set by a stronger external institutions. This is the nature of the real world; it is clear that this lesson was learnt within the just community, as well as lessons in interpersonal democratic interaction.

Not all just communities are artifically created: the kibbutz is an established collectivist system, and Kohlberg, Snarey and Reimer have investigated moral reasoning development longitudinally amongst kibbutznik youth. As we have already noted, kibbutzniks score higher on moral reasoning measures than their US age-mates. But a particularly interesting aspect of this study concerned the development of a group of city-born adolescents who were educated within the kibbutz system. They had therefore experienced a *change* in their life-style and values, in some ways comparable to the members of the school just communities in the United States. These adolescents came from economically disadvantaged backgrounds, and from Arab countries; they therefore had different cultural roots from the kibbutz-born youth whose parents and grandparents had emigrated to Israel from Western cultures. Kohlberg, Snarey and Reimer do not report sufficient data about interactions or individual reasoning to facilitate the kind of analysis discussed earlier, but they do report individual moral reasoning changes, which are a measure of the effectiveness of the community in promoting individual moral growth. The city-born adolescents started off with lower-stage scores than the kibbutz-born peers, but by the final interview they had virtually caught up with them; the city-born youth gained an average of 79 mms points over the period, the kibbutz-born 61 points.[40]

The effect of experiencing a challenging micro-political environment is clearly to alter consciousness and create disequilibrium in individual thought structure. This is also described in some of the studies of activist youth. Haan compared level of moral reasoning on 'hypothetical' (Kohlberg) dilemmas with moral reasoning on the 'real-life' moral-political issue of the Free Speech Movement sit-in.[41] She found that higher-stage students *who were activists* reasoned at a higher stage on the real-life situation than on the hypothetical dilemmas, whereas higher-stage students who were *supporters, but not activists*, showed higher-stage reasoning on the *hypothetical* dilemmas. There was no difference between hypothetical and actual reasoning amongst neutral or opposed-to-FSM students. However, *lower-stage* reasoners tended to reason at a higher stage on the real-life situation whether they were supporters of FSM or not. This finding strongly suggests that significant first-hand political experience is a growth-inducing—or at least a décalage-inducing—process. But why the difference between higher- and lower-stage thinkers? One possibility is the degree of surprise and shock: for higher-stage reasoners, who have some conception of social change and the structure of society, political engagement or disturbance is within their frame of reference. So for them it is *personal* engagement that induces décalage. However, for more conventional and concrete reasoners, merely *witnessing* disruptive events would be significant experience in itself, for it disturbs their normative assumptions about social order and social control that such events should occur at all.

In another study, Haan looked at the effects of Peace Corps experience.[42] A sample of Peace Corps trainees was part of the original FSM study. Compared to other students, female trainees were relatively conservative and tended to demonstrate a conventional level of moral reasoning. Male trainees had a high level of moral reasoning and were not so conservative. The effect of Peace Corps service was to increase moral reasoning scores—especially amongst women—and to increase political liberalism. Both sexes also altered their self-descriptions, in particular abandoning their former conventionally sex-stereotyped self-images.

THE TRANSMISSION OF POLITICAL NORMS

We have established that the individual is active, not passive, in making sense of her moral and political world, and that first-hand experience of explicit political process and moral conflict is a powerful learning situation. But all this takes place within a broader cultural context; ultimately, both the structure of individual political cognition, and the norms for negotiating interpersonal conflicts, are mediators of the political socialization process.

In this final section I will explore the relationship between cultural factors and individuals' political development. There are a number of salient points in this:

1   the individual does not exist in a cultural vacuum; she is not free to construct *ab initio* an explanation of the social and political world. Pre-existing 'theories', explanations and ideologies abound in the culture into which she is born;
2   by virtue of her parentage, locality and socio-economic status she will be socialized within a fairly narrow range of values and beliefs, but there exists also a wider range that she may come into contact with through education, peer contacts, etc. These are still culture-bound, however; the European child is much more likely to come into contact with socialism than the North American child;
3   the individual's cognitive structures are in *dialectical relation* with these external culturally-defined conditions. She does not wholly construct her own implicit theory, nor does she merely absorb the external world wholesale and passively; the nature of her interpretation of the external world itself depends upon the limitations of her existing cognitive structures.

First let us consider the effect of parents and family. Most studies of political socialization show a fairly close parallel between the political views of parent and offspring. Some studies also show a relationship between parental politics and offspring's moral stage. The (somewhat limited) evidence suggests that this relationship arises from the way that parental *behaviour* conveys values and expectations. For example, Hoffman and Salzstein demonstrated the effect of parental practices on the moral response style in young adults; *inductive* child-rearing methods produced the most reason-oriented offspring. Holstein looked at the relationship between parental moral stage, child's moral stage and parental behaviour in interactive discussion with the child. She found that principled-level parents encouraged the child's participation in discussion more than did conventional-level parents, and that the children of principled parents were more likely than the children of conventional-level parents to have reached conventional level reasoning.[43]

Left-wing offspring report more conflict with their parents even when the actual reported *degree* of difference in beliefs between parents and offspring is not large. Kraut and Lewis' Left-wing student respondents reported family conflicts about independence, domestic responsibilities, and career plans, as well as on political issues. Haan *et al.*'s radical, postconventional respondents reported conflict with their parents, though little difference in their beliefs: in contrast, Stage 4 conservatives perceived practically no conflict between their own views and those of their parents. Given the *prima facie* lack of a real difference in political views within Left-wing families, one conclusion which could be drawn is that not only do Left-wing parents pass on certain political values and beliefs, but they also value—and encourage—dissent. The child growing up in a Left-wing household learns to value, and be adept at, confrontational discourse, and to question received assumptions.[44]

The effect of subcultural norms is illustrated by the kibbutz studies. Kibbutz adolescents consistently scored higher on moral reasoning measures than did their age-mates in the United States or Turkey. One explanation of this is that the kibbutz is an ongoing 'just community', continually stimulating reflection upon political and moral processes. Another dimension is the dominant socialistic ethos of the kibbutz system; the explanations of social institutions, the implicit social theory, is based on collectivism rather than individualism. In the Kohlberg, Snarey and Reimer study, higher-stage respondents very explicitly referred to the ideology of the kibbutz as a democratic, collectivist community. 'Kibbutzniks typically brought much more of a communal emphasis to solving the dilemmas than did North Americans.' They explicitly referred to a 'socialist utopia'; for North Americans the just society is an *ideal*, for the kibbutzniks the democratic ideal exists already. The authors say: 'for some young adult kibbutzniks the very concept of "kibbutz" is based on the idea of commitment, a social contract, between all the members who share a consensus regarding the equal social rights and the equal democratic participation responsibilities of all persons.'[45]

This represents the operation *in action* of a dominant social rhetoric; the young kibbutzniks are exposed to a set of social explanations, expected forms of interaction and values about social and political life, which are *ideals* rather than *practice* in North America. Similarly but to a lesser extent, in Britain the existence of a welfare state means that certain forms of collectivist thinking are part of the stock-in-trade, or social representations, of everyone irrespective of their moral stage; even Stage 2 reasoners think there should be a National Health Service to help Heinz's wife.

These findings illustrate the importance of *action*, and the *practical experience* of operating within a particular context and set of norms (whether at the level of the family, the community or the social representations of society at large), in the development of political cognition. But they also raise questions about Kohlberg's conception of the ontogenesis of liberal democracy. It is clear from the theory of moral development that the higher stages of thought reflect a more complex view of society; it is also specifically demonstrated in the work on the development of political understanding that progression is from an individualistic conceptualization of the world to a conceptualization which focuses on societal and institutional structures. The kibbutz data do clearly indicate that experience of collectivist *rhetoric and social representations within society*, and collectivist *action at the level of the community*, are reflected in the moral and political cognitions of developing youth.

There are important cross-cultural differences in the extent to which collectivism is the dominant rhetoric. Studies which illustrate this were performed in Britain, Australia and the United States by Feather and Furnham.[46] They investigated the explanations offered for poverty and unemployment, distinguishing between 'individualistic' explanations which blame individuals or groups for misfortune—lack of effort, fecklessness etc—and 'societal' explanations which lay the blame at the door of social policy or the structure of society. On these measures, North Americans rate as more individualistic than Europeans or Australians.

Even though these and other Western societies subscribe to a broadly similar 'liberal' ideology, therefore, there is a considerable difference in (1) the explanations of inequality—and by implication, the cure, and (2) the actual operation of liberal democracy within the institutions of society. An important distinction is between whether the higher, more collectivist, or 'just' stages are reflected in the institutions of society, or whether they exist only as shared ideals. The United States is not a particularly just society, so the individual who expresses Stage 5 reasoning reflects the formulation of an *ideal* world, the *extrapolation* of culturally available principles. It is *post-normative* in the sense that the world of Stage 5 principles does not exist, but the *principles* are normative, derived from the Constitution and a history of democratic ideals. In other societies certain aspects of justice and democracy which in the United States are ideal norms, are practical norms; as I have indicated, these include the social contract world of the kibbutz, and the welfare state of some European countries. Longitudinal data exist only for Israeli society: I would predict that in 'socialist' societies the pattern of collectivist rhetoric and developmental progression would tend to approximate more to the Israeli than to the United States pattern.

The foregoing describes broad cultural differences, and their effect on individual development, but as we have seen, there are powerful *subcultural* effects as manifested in the difference in reasoning between individuals reared as conservatives, and individuals reared as liberals. Furnham, and Lewis, have demonstrated that in Britain, Conservative and Labour supporters differ in their attributions of the causes of poverty and unemployment, with Conservatives endorsing more individualistic explanations.[47] Weinreich-Haste, Cotgrove and Duff found a similar pattern in the explanation of unemployment and in the explanations of the origins of social order, and they also found that moral stage, as measured by the endorsement of high stage and the rejection of low stage statements, correlated with individualistic *versus* societal explanations.[48]

So if we adopt the position that prevailing normative explanations and implicit theories are an important source of how the growing individual comes to make sense of the world, then we can argue that the child who grows up in a liberal household or subculture will have greater access to collectivist explanations, and explanations which focus on social institutions, than the child who grows up in a conservative environment. It will therefore be *easier* for her to use these assumptive explanations as a basis for thinking.

These findings and interpretations indicate a *plurality* within liberal democracy, different assumptions about how to implement justice and different ways of dealing with the continuing paradox of liberty and equality. I will now return to another issue of the plurality of rhetorics, and the enduring critique that Kohlberg places too much emphasis on justice as the dominant theme of moral and political development. There are two pieces of research which illustrate the limitations of a monolithic definition of morality as justice-based, and which also illustrate clearly the effects of subcultural norms on rhetoric.

In a study of hippies, a self-consciously 'anti-establishment' subculture, Haan, Stroud and Holstein found an ideology which emphasized communality and love, *and* which specifically rejected abstraction and objectification. This is a counter-normative ideology, not only because of the expressed values but because the norms of liberal democracy—as mirrored in Kohlberg's stages—imply cognitive progression and increasing generalization and abstraction. Haan scored the hippies as Stage 3 thinkers.[49] More extensive and more problematic for Kohlberg's theory is Gilligan's work on the 'different voice' of women's moral thought. According to Gilligan, *males* do tend to think in terms of rights and obligations, in accordance with Kohlberg's model. Males have implicit models of social relations in which there are conflicts between rights, a situation which is resolved by formulating balances and equity-producing contracts. For *females*, Gilligan argues, the implicit model of social relations is based on mutuality and interpersonal attachment and responsibility. So women, she argues, do not reason in terms of rights but in terms of responsibilities; they do not weigh up the relative claims of Heinz and the chemist but suggest negotiation and persuasion so that their common responsibility to Heinz's wife can be met.[50]

Gilligan argues that these sex differences originate in the different childhood experience of women and men. Family roles, as well as the cultural stereotypes and expectations, direct the little girl towards responsibility and mutuality; the sexes grow up with a *different set of norms* about how to make sense of the social world, and emerge with a different dominant rhetoric of social relations. Her position is consistent with certain expressions of feminism that argue that women have a particular role to play in peace movements and the promotion of non-violence.[51] Whether or not Gilligan is right to identify the two pieces of morality as *sex-linked*, her work is of great importance in underlining the limitations of a monolithic interpretation of the rhetoric of liberal democracy based on rights and justice.

CONCLUSION

Kohlberg made his own connections between moral and political development when he asserted that the development of moral reasoning reflected the ontogenesis of liberal democracy and the conception of justice. Supporters endorsed his position because it confirmed a common American ideal that history reflected progress towards moral improvement within the individual and the state, and because in the optimistic mood of the Kennedy era it seemed that all kinds of social reform were possible, and the ideals of the Constitution might at last be realized. The Age of Aquarius was dawning. Even the subsequent disillusionments—the moral crises of My Lai and Watergate, the slow realization that the revolution was not at hand, and the political inertia consequent upon economic recession and conservative backlash—did not erode the optimism because it was obvious that the protesters and objectors (those on the side of the angels) were demonstrating the kind of thinking, and the level of reasoning, consistent with the model.[52]

The critics attacked the parochialism of Kohlberg's assertion—especially when he claimed its universality; liberalism is not a universal value, democracy is not practised, even nominally, across wide sections of the globe, and the oppressed and deprived even in the United States have no reason to believe in a just world. They attacked the narrow assumptions of the theory—that justice was the dominant or superordinate virtue, and that democracy (and, by implication, morality) was expressed most fully in a certain kind of socialistic liberalism, placing even good libertarian conservatives a poor second. They attacked his lack of attention to the role of historical and economic factors, not only in the conditions of the political situation at any point in time, but also in the kind of ideas which gain currency and fire people's hearts. Generally, they accused him of being a politically naive idealist.

From the perspective of the conservative eighties, caught in economic recession, there still appears to be right on both sides. The research data, whatever the limitations, do demonstrate a consistent relationship between certain kinds of political thinking and level of moral reasoning. Even more, they demonstrate a relationship between moral reasoning and political *commitment*. These findings need to be explained, and as yet they have not been. There is no *a priori* reason why conservative ideology is necessarily inconsistent with the *structure* of Stage 5 thought; sophisticated understanding of social institutions and the possibility of going beyond the social system as presently constituted, which are the conceptual substrates of Stage 5 thinking, are not lacking in the writings of conservative thinkers. What is clearly needed is a more subtle analysis of the development of political and moral thought, to disentangle the real nature of the relationship.

It is difficult (for a liberal) to see the present time as a continuation of the inexorable march of progress, and it is obvious that the critics are right in their identification of the limitations of Kohlberg's unitary view. At best, it can be said that his conception of the overlap between the moral and political probably does apply to the educated middle-class youth in a country where the dominant rhetoric is one of democracy, rights and social contract. The critics who argue that Kohlberg ignores the kind of consciousness which would arise in another political milieu (for example, in a Marxist state) may be right, but in the absence of such data, it can be said that he presents a reasonable map of the transmission of liberal-democratic consciousness to the élite members of a society whom such a consciousness serves reasonably well.

In this chapter I have also tried to show that Kohlberg's departure from the traditional methodology of cognitive-developmental psychology has far-reaching implications for a *rapprochement* between the individualism of developmental psychology and its emphasis on what goes on inside the individual head, and social psychological and sociological approaches. The latter tend to see the immediate situation, or the broad social context, as the determinants of individual thought, particularly in the domain of political development. They generally ignore the developmental dimension, in particular allowing no space for the concept that individuals at different stages of cognitive development might interpret the situation differently. The work on just communities, and the other work by followers of Kohlberg on the processes of discourse and communication, may lead eventually to a significant breakthrough in understanding the dialectical relationship between individual and social constructions of meaning. Kohlberg's own dialogue with critical theorists, in particular Habermas, is a vital part of this theoretical development, which regrettably there has not been space to do justice to in this chapter.[53]

NOTES

1 Kohlberg (1971, 1980a, 1981)
2 Kohlberg (1980a), p. 64.
3 Candee (1974), p. 621.
4 Kohlberg (1973, 1980a); Rawls (1971).
5 Sullivan (1977a, 1977b).
6 Adelson (1971a).
7 Reid and Yanarella (1980).
8 Simpson (1974); Kitwood (1983); Kohlberg, Snarey and Reimer (1984); and see Vine in this volume, Ch. 27.
9 Harré (1979, 1983); Gilligan (1983); Weinreich-Haste (1984b).
10 Buck-Morss (1975); Braun and Baribeau (1978).
11 Fishkin (1980, 1984).
12 Buck-Morss (1975); Braun and Baribeau (1978); Habermas (1979); Youniss (1983); Chilton (1983).
13 Mosher (1980); Wasserman (1980); Power (1980); Reimer and Power (1980); Higgins (1984).
14 Haan, Smith and Block (1968).
15 Kohlberg and Kramer (1969).
16 Adelson (1971a); Kenston (1968).
17 Fendrich and Tarleau (1973); p. 245.
18 One of the problems of the Haan *et al.* study, which in fact applies to all the early studies, was the coding of Stage 2 and Stage 6 reasoning. In the longitudinal study, Kohlberg discovered what at first he thought was 'regression to Stage 2', after the development of Stage 4 understanding of social order and institutions. The regression was manifested by an extreme relativism and apparent instrumentalist view, which looked like Stage 2 thinking. However, it became clear eventually that this was a décalage consequent upon people realizing the limitations of the ordered world of Stage 4 thought, and was followed in time by movement to Stage 5. The later coding methods, which focused more on structure than content of reasoning, accommodated this transitional phase. In fact when the Haan *et al.* data were recoded by Kohlberg and Candee, Stage 2 reasoning disappeared, and most Stage 6 reasoning was reclassified as Stage 5. The effect of this was to reveal a *monotonic* relationship between activism and moral stage: however, most of the early data on politics and moral reasoning have not been recoded. Kohlberg and Candee (1984).
19 Fishkin, Keniston and Mackinnon (1973).
20 Fontana and Noel (1973).
21 Leming (1974).
22 Alker and Poppen (1973); Sullivan and Quarter (1972).
23 Lind, Sandberger and Bargel (1981/82); Emler, Renwick and Malone (1983); Weinreich-Haste (1984a); Rest (1979).
24 Emler (1983); Emler, Renwick and Malone (1983); Reicher and Emler (1985).
25 Weinreich-Haste, Adams and Clay.
26 Adelson and O'Neil (1966); Adelson, Green and O'Neil (1969); Adelson (1971b).
27 Connell (1971); Furth and McConville (1981).
28 Torney, Oppenheim and Farnen (1975); Torney-Purta (1981).

29 Easton and Dennis (1969); Stradling and Zureik (1973); Merelman and McCabe (1974); Mussen, Sullivan and Eisenberg-Berg (1977).
30 Tapp and Kohlberg (1971), pp. 65–6; Torney-Purta (1983), p. 296.
31 Colby *et al.*, (1985).
32 Weinreich-Haste (1983, 1984a).
33 Turiel (1966); Blatt and Kohlberg (1975).
34 See, for example, Rutter *et al.* (1979); Willis (1977); Tyler (1977).
35 Kohlberg (1972, 1975, 1978, 1979, 1980b).
36 See Mosher (1980) and Fenton (1976) for collection of papers.
37 Higgins (1980); Kohlberg (1980b).
38 Power (1980); Reimer and Power (1980); Higgins (1984).
39 Feldman (1980).
40 Kohlberg, Snarey and Reimer (1984).
41 Haan (1975).
42 Haan (1974).
43 Hoffman and Salzstein (1967); Hoffman (1973); Holstein (1972).
44 Haan, Smith and Block (1968); Kraut and Lewis (1975).
45 Kohlberg, Snarey and Reimer (1984).
46 Feather (1974); Furnham (1982a, 1982b, 1983).
47 Furnham (1982a, 1982b, 1983); Lewis (1981).
48 Cotgrove and Weinreich-Haste (1982); Weinreich-Haste (1984a).
49 Haan, Stroud and Holstein (1973).
50 Gilligan (1983).
51 This argument is the rationale of the longstanding, women-only protest at the Greenham Common Airbase in England, which has deliberately affirmed a 'female rhetoric' in its behaviour, symbols and organization.
52 Candee (1975); Kohlberg and Scharf (1972).
53 Habermas (1979); Kohlberg, Levine and Hewer (1983).

REFERENCES

Adelson, J. (1971a) 'Inventing the young', *Commentary*, 51, pp. 43–8.
Adelson, J. (1971b) 'Political imagination of the young adolescent', *Daedalus*, Fall, pp. 1013–49.
Adelson, J. and O'Neil, R. (1966) 'The growth of political ideas in adolescence; The sense of community', *Journal of Personality and Social Psychology*, 4, pp. 295–306.
Adelson, J., Green, B. and O'Neil, R. (1969) 'Growth of the idea of law in adolescence', *Developmental Psychology*, 1, pp. 327–32.
Alker, H. H. and Poppen, P. J. (1973) 'Personality and ideology in university students', *Journal of Personality*, 41, pp. 653–71.
Blatt, M. M. and Kohlberg, L. (1975) 'The effects of classroom moral discussion upon children's level of moral judgment', *Journal of Moral Education*, 4, pp. 129–61.
Braun, C. M. J. and Baribeau, J. M. C. (1978) 'Subjective idealism in Kohlberg's theory of moral development', *Human Development*, 21, pp. 289–301.
Buck-Morss, S. (1975) 'Socio-economic bias in Piaget's theory and its implications for cross-cultural studies', *Human Development*, 18, pp. 35–49.
Candee, D. (1974) 'Ego developmental aspects of new Left ideology', *Journal of Personality and Social Psychology*, 30, pp. 620–30.
Candee, D. (1975) 'The moral psychology of Watergate', *Journal of Social Issues*, 31, pp. 183–92.
Chilton, S. (1983) 'Political development; Theoretical problems and a theoretical reconstruction', Unpublished manuscript, University of New Mexico.
Colby, A., Kohlberg, L., Gibbs, J., Candee, D., Speicher-Dubin, B., Kauffman, K., Hewer, A. and Power, C. (1985) *Measurement of Moral Judgment: A Manual*, New York, Cambridge University Press.
Connell, R. W. (1971) *The Child's Construction of Politics*, Carlton, Victoria, Melbourne University Press.
Cotgrove, S. F. and Weinreich-Haste, H. E. (1982) 'Career choice with special reference to engineering', End of Grant Report, Social Science Research Council.

Easton, D. and Dennis, J. (1969) *Children in the Political System; Origins of Political Legitimacy*, New York, McGraw-Hill.

Emler, N. (1983) 'Morality and politics', in Weinreich-Haste, H. and Locke, D. (Eds.), *Morality in the Making: Judgment, Action and Social Context*, Chichester, Wiley.

Emler, N., Renwick, S. and Malone, B. (1983) 'The relationship between moral reasoning and political orientation', *Journal of Personality and Social Psychology*, 45, pp. 1073–80.

Feather, N. T. (1974) 'Explanations of poverty in Australian and American samples: The person, society or fate?' *Australian Journal of Psychology*, 26, pp. 199–216.

Feldman, R. E. (1980) 'The promotion of moral development in prisons and schools', in Wilson, R. W. and Schochet, G. J. (Eds.), *Moral Development and Politics*, New York, Praeger.

Fendrich, J. M. and Tarleau, A. T. (1973) 'Marching to a different drummer: Occupational and political correlates of former student activists', *Social Forces*, 52, pp. 245–53.

Fenton, E. (Ed.) (1976) 'Cognitive-development approach to moral education', *Social Education*, 40 (4 whole).

Fishkin, J., (1980) 'Relativism, liberalism and moral development', in Wilson, R. W. and Schochet, G. J. (Eds.), *Moral Development and Politics*, New York, Praeger.

Fishkin, J. (1984) *Beyond Subjective Morality*, New Haven, Conn., Yale University Press.

Fishkin, J., Keniston, K. and Mackinnon, C. (1973) 'Moral reasoning and political ideology', *Journal of Personality and Social Psychology*, 27, pp. 109–19.

Fontana, A. F. and Noel, N. (1973) 'Moral reasoning in the university', *Journal of Personality and Social Psychology*, 27, pp. 419–29.

Furnham, A. (1982a) 'Explanations for unemployment in Britain', *European Journal of Social Psychology*, 12, pp. 335–52.

Furnham, A. (1982b) 'The perception of poverty among adolescents', *Journal of Adolescence*, 5, pp. 135–47.

Furnham, A. (1983) 'Attributions for affluence', *Personality and Individual Differences*, 4, pp. 31–40.

Furth, H. and McConville, K. (1981) 'Political compromise: The developmental task of societal understanding in adolescence', *Social Thought*, 7, pp. 22–34.

Gilligan, C. (1983) *In a Different Voice*, Cambridge, Mass., Harvard University Press.

Haan, N. (1974) 'Changes in young adults after Peace Corps experiences: Political-social views, moral reasoning and perceptions of self and parents,' *Journal of Youth and Adolescence*, 3, pp. 177–94.

Haan, N. (1975) 'Hypothetical and actual moral reasoning in a situation of civil disobedience', *Journal of Personality and Social Psychology*, 32, pp. 255–70.

Haan, N., Smith, M. B. and Block, J. (1968) 'Moral reasoning of young adults', *Journal of Personality and Social Psychology*, 10, pp. 183–201.

Haan, N., Stroud, J. and Holstein, C. (1973) 'Moral and ego stages in relationship to ego processes: A study of hippies', *Journal of Personality*, 41, pp. 596–613.

Habermas, J. (1979) *Communication and the Evolution of Society*, Trans McCarthy, T. London, Heinemann.

Harré, R. (1979) *Social Being*, Oxford, Basil Blackwell.

Harré, R. (1983) *Personal Being*, Oxford, Basil Blackwell.

Higgins, A. (1980) 'Research and measurement issues in moral education interventions', in Mosher, R. (Ed.), *Moral Education: A First Generation of Research*, New York, Praeger.

Higgins, A., Power, C. and Kohlberg, L. (1984) 'The relationship of moral atmosphere to judgments of responsibility', in Kurtines, W. M. and Gewirtz, J. L. (Eds.), *Morality, Moral Behaviour and Moral Development*, New York, Wiley.

Hoffman, M. L. (1973) 'Childrearing practices and moral development: Generalisations from empirical research', *Child Development*, 34, pp. 295–318.

Hoffman, M. L. and Salzstein, H. D. (1967) 'Parent discipline and the child's moral development', *Journal of Personality and Social Psychology*, 5, pp. 45–7.

Holstein, C. (1972) 'The relation of children's moral judgment level to that of their parents and to communication patterns in the family', in Smart, R. and Smart, M. (Eds.), *Readings in Child Development*, New York, Macmillan.

Keniston, K. (1968) *Young Radicals*, New York, Harcourt, Brace, Jovanovich.

Kitwood, T. (1983) '"Personal Identity" and Personal Integrity', in Weinreich-Haste, H. and Locke, D. (Eds.), *Morality in the Making: Judgment, Action and Social Context*, Chichester, Wiley.

Kohlberg, L. (1971) 'From is to ought: How to commit the naturalistic fallacy and get away with it in the study of moral development', in Mischel, T. (Ed.), *Cognitive Development and Epistemology*, New York, Academic Press.

Kohlberg, L. (1973) 'The claim to moral adequacy of a highest stage of moral judgment', *Journal of Philosophy*, 70, pp. 630–46.

Kohlberg, L. (1978) 'The moral atmosphere of the school', in Scharf, P. (Ed.), *Readings in Moral Education*, Minneapolis, Minn., Winston Press.

Kohlberg, L. (1979) 'Explaining the moral atmosphere of institutions: A bridge between moral judgment and moral action', Heinz Werner Memorial Lecture, Clark University, Worcester, Mass.

Kohlberg, L. (1980a) 'The future of liberalism as the dominant ideology of the West', in Wilson, R. W. and Schochet, G. J. (Eds.), *Moral Development and Politics*, New York, Praeger.

Kohlberg, L. (1980b) 'High school democracy and educating for a just society', in Mosher, R. (Ed.), *Moral Education: A First Generation of Research*, New York, Praeger.

Kohlberg, L. (1981) *The Philosophy of Moral Development: Moral Stages and the Idea of Justice*. Vol. I: *Essays on Moral Development Vol I: The Philosophy of Moral Dev.: Moral Stages and the item of Justics*, San Francisco, Harper and Row.

Kohlberg, L. and Candee, D. (1984) 'The relationship of moral judgment to moral action', in Kurtines, W. M. and Gewirtz, J. L. (Eds.), *Morality, Moral Behaviour and Moral Development*, New York, Wiley.

Kohlberg, L. and Kramer, R. (1969) 'Continuities and discontinuities in childhood and adult moral development', *Human Development*, 12, pp. 93–120.

Kohlberg, L. and Scharf, P. (1972) 'Bureaucratic violence and conventional moral thinking', *American Journal of Orthopsychiatry*.

Kohlberg, L., Hickey, J. and Scharf, P. (1972) 'The justice structure of the prison: A theory and intervention', *The Prison Journal*, 51, pp. 3–14.

Kohlberg, L., Kauffman, K., Scharf, P. and Hickey, J. (1975) 'The just community approach to corrections; A theory', *Journal of Moral Education*, 4, pp. 243–60.

Kohlberg, L., Levine, C. and Hewer, A (1983) 'Moral stages: A current formulation and a response to critics', *Contributions to Human Development 10*, Basel, S. Karger.

Kohlberg, L., Snarey, J. and Reimer, J. (1984) 'Cultural universality of moral judgment stages: A longitudinal study of Israel', in Kohlberg, L. *Essays on Moral Development Vol II: The Psychology of Moral Development*, San Francisco, Harper and Row.

Kraut, R. E. and Lewis, S. H. (1975) 'Alternative models of family influence on student political ideology', *Journal of Personality and Social Psychology*, 31, pp. 791–80.

Leming, J. S. (1974) 'Moral reasoning, sense of control, and social political activism amongst adolescents', *Adolescence*, 9, pp. 507–28.

Lewis, A. (1981) 'Attributions and politics', *Personality and Individual Differences*, 2, pp. 1–4.

Lind, G., Sandberger, J-U, and Bargel, T. (1981/82) 'Moral judgment, ego-strength and democratic orientation', *Political Psychology*, 2, pp. 70–110.

Merelman, R. M. and McCabe, A. E. (1974) 'Evolving orientations towards policy choice in adolescence', *American Journal of Political Science*, pp. 665–80.

Mosher, R. (Ed.) (1980) *Moral Education: A First Generation of Research*, New York, Praeger.

Mussen, P., Sullivan, L. B. and Eisenberg-Berg, N. (1977) 'Changes in political-economic attitudes during adolescence', *Journal of Genetic Psychology*, 130, pp. 69–76.

Power, C. (1980) 'Evaluating just communities: Towards a method for assessing the moral atmosphere of the school', in Kuhmerker, L., Mentkowski, M. and Erickson, V. L. (Eds.), *Evaluating Moral Development*, Schenectady, Character Research Press.

Rawls, J. (1971) *Theory of Justice*, Cambridge, Mass., Harvard University Press.

Reicher, S. and Emler, N. (1985) 'Moral orientation as a cue to political identity,' *Political Psychology*, 5, pp. 543–52.

Reid, H. G. and Yanarella, E. J. (1980) 'The tyranny of the categorical: On Kohlberg and the politics of moral development', in Wilson, R. W. and Schochet, G. J. (Eds.), *Moral Development and Politics*, New York, Praeger.

Reimer, J. and Power, C. (1980) 'Educating for democratic community: Some unresolved dilemmas', in Mosher, R. (Ed.), *Moral Education: A First Generation of Research*, New York, Praeger.

Rest, J. (1979) *Development in Judging Moral Issues*, Minneapolis, Minn., University of Minnesota Press.

Rutter, M., Maughan, B., Mortimore, P. and Ouston, J. (1979) *Fifteen Thousand Hours*, Harmondsworth, Penguin.

Simpson, E. L. (1974) 'Moral development research: A case-study of scientific cultural bias', *Human Development*, 17, pp. 81–106.

Stradling, R. and Zureik, E. T. (1973) 'Emergence of political thought among young Englishmen: A conflict perspective', *Political Studies*, 21, pp. 285–300.

Sullivan, E. V. (1977a) 'A study of Kohlberg's structural theory of moral development: A critique of liberal science ideology', *Human Development*, 20, pp. 352–76.

Sullivan, E. V. (1977b) 'Kohlberg's structuralism; A critical appraisal', *O.I.S.E. Monograph*, 15.

Sullivan, E. V. and Quarter, J. (1972) 'Psychological correlates on certain postconventional moral types; A perspective on hybrid types', *Journal of Personality*, 40, pp. 149–61.

Torney, J., Oppenheim, A. N. and Farnen, R. (1975) *Civic Education in Ten Nations*, New York, Wiley.

Torney-Purta J. (1981) 'Children's social cognition', *Teaching Political Science*, 8, pp. 297–318.

Torney-Purta J. (1983) 'The development of views about the role of social institutions in redressing inequality and promoting human rights', in Leahy, R. (Ed.), *The Child's Construction of Inequality*, New York, Academic Press.

Turiel, E. (1966) 'An experimental test of the sequentiality of developmental stages in the child's moral judgments', *Journal of Personality and Social Psychology*, 3, pp. 611–18.

Tyler, W. (1977) *The Sociology of Educational Inequality*, London, Methuen.

Wasserman, E. (1980) 'An alternative high school based on Kohlberg's just community approach', in Mosher, R. (Ed.), *Moral Education: A First Generation of Research*, New York, Praeger.

Weinreich-Haste, H. E. (1983) 'Social and moral cognition', in Weinreich-Haste, H. and Locke, D. (Eds.), *Morality in the Making: Judgment, Action and Social Context*, Chichester, Wiley.

Weinreich-Haste, H. E. (1984a) 'Political, moral and social reasoning', in Regenbogen, A. (Ed.), *Moral und Politik-Soziales Bewusstsein als Lernprozess*, Cologne, Paul Rugenstein Verlag.

Weinreich-Haste, H. E. (1984b) 'Morality, social meaning and rhetoric', in Kurtines, W. M. and Gewirtz, J. L. (Eds.), *Morality, Moral Behaviour and Moral Development*, New York, Wiley.

Weinreich-Haste, H. E., Adams, C. and Clay, A. (1985) 'Trying to be morally Right—or morally Left: The relationship between political orientation and moral reasoning'. Paper presented to the International Society of Political Psychology, 8th Annual Meeting, Washington, DC.

Willis, P. (1977) *Learning to Labour*, Farnborough, Saxon House.

Youniss, J. (1981) 'Moral development through a theory of social construction: An analysis', *Merrill-Palmer Quarterly*, 27, pp. 385–403.

23. The Genesis of Moral Domination*

JOHN M. BROUGHTON

The extensive work of Lawrence Kohlberg and his associates represents a major contribution to the field of psychology. As I have tried to show on different occasions (Broughton, 1978a, 1978b, 1978c, 1983a), most of the scientific and ethical criticisms levelled against the cognitive-developmental theory of moral stages are mistaken. There is something fundamentally wrong with the theory, nevertheless. This fault originates in the particular political metaphysics underlying the theory. Historically speaking, Kohlberg has inherited the limitations, distortions and mystifications inherent in the liberal democratic worldview, including both its political philosophy of the social life and its political psychology of subjectivity.

Chief among the misapprehensions of liberalism is the idea that knowledge and politics have separate spheres of operation. In fact, all reason and understanding are political in the most fundamental sense of that word (Wood, 1972; Fay, 1975; Unger, 1975; Foucault, 1980). The liberal tends to assimilate the political to the moral, and will even admit that science is not 'value-free'. But politics cannot be identified with the implied arbitrariness of 'values', nor can it be reduced to ethics. One result of this is that moral stage theory cannot be judged solely on the basis of its *moral* precepts. Its political stance, implicit and disguised as it may be, must be given interpretation and have its adequacy examined.

When this critical task is undertaken, what emerges is that the theory of moral stage development is unwittingly conducting itself politically with respect to precisely those structures and phenomena that it so sedulously avoids dealing with: the state, bureaucracy, authority, power, social control, ideology, alienation, exploitation, legitimation and domination. Furthermore, on account of its psycho-

---

*My thanks to Lawrence Kohlberg for what I have learned from him.

logical nature, the theory unwittingly captures the subjective side of the *polis*, the silent strife conducted in the inner world, the conflicting experience of living under liberal democracy.

Our inquiry starts with an examination of what moral stage theory proposes and presupposes about the objective political world, in particular its adherence to the liberal view of civil society and its inclination toward neo-Darwinian social evolutionism.

Then, our attention will turn inward, to the way in which moral stage theory constructs the private life of the psyche, unintentionally both concealing and revealing its profoundly political quality. Here we shall see what the tacit psychology of liberalism consists of.

Our very first task, however, is to ask what exactly 'liberalism' is.

LIBERALISM

Liberalism is a tradition of ideological thinking and writing, on the one hand, and a tradition of state organization, on the other. It is not only a system of concepts but also a kind of social life. Liberalism is admittedly polymorphous (Dworkin, 1978), but its various forms possess certain common features. These features can be summarized under the three major principles of the Newtonian universe: Balance, Spontaneous Generation and Circulation, and the Realization of Universal Order (Manning, 1976), as these are applied to public and private life. The most pervasive metaphor grounding individuality and freedom is that of the rational conduct of economic life.

A   Balance within Society, among Individuals, and between Individuals and the Social Order

1   Although it evolves, the social order is essentially stable in nature.
2   The individual is prior to society; society is an aggregation of individuals. Compared to the irreducible sovereignty of the individual person, society has a somewhat artificial character.
3   Society is to be understood as essentially civil society, a society of interpersonal transactions, rather than as a state.
4   There must be voluntary acceptance of rights and obligations by individuals in order to promote the interrelatedness that sustains civil society. Morality should not be enforced through the criminal law.
5   Freedom is to be equated with 'independence' or 'autonomy'. It derives from security from interference. It is instrumental to the stability of the social order.

B   Spontaneous Generation and Circulation as the Basis of Freedom and Progress

1   Individuals are ends in themselves.
2   All individuals are equally free to participate in public life.
3   The individual is spontaneously independent, i.e., internally motivated

toward autonomy and responsibility. Freedom is to be equated with the unfettered capacity of an individual to make the best of himself through development of the autonomous and responsible self.

4   All obligations are underpinned by moral obligations and all human relationships are sustained by moral will.

5   Coercion of any kind is consequently unnecessary and undesirable. State control therefore stands in opposition to human nature. It is freedom alone that allows a society to increase its resources.

6   Oppression leads to a proneness to revolutionary overthrow, and thence to dictatorship.

7   Conformism is equally tyrannical. The social formation of a 'mass' is to be avoided. The right to dissent and the rights of minorities must therefore be upheld.

8   The fundamental unit of social activity is the free formation of contracts. Freedom and validity of contract require that neither party be helpless relative to the other.

9   Progress is natural. It has its own laws that are revealed by the scientific study of man and his environment. The accordance of the will of the people with these laws ensures the continuation of progress.

10   The basis of the forward movement of society is the natural capacity of individuals for intelligent and imaginative thinking and discovery.

11   Man's institutions exhibit progress insofar as they show a perfectly symmetrical chronology moving toward a stable and harmonious functioning (the unification of the concepts of duration and perfection).

12   Increase in freedom is the only true measure of progress.

13   Progressive change is by definition gradual and piecemeal. The human condition cannot be altered fundamentally by any organized assault on imperfection. Social wrongs are not the result of impersonal forces. The battle against injustice and deprivation is the personal responsibility of each individual.

14   Therefore, any form of organized opposition to, rejection of, or separation from the social aggregate is wrong.

C   The Realization of Universal Order

1   Human nature is universally the same.

2   Democratic institutions emerge whenever a society attains an appropriate level of development. Tribal and feudal societies are stages in the development of civil society.

3   It is the responsibility of governors and leaders to provide the conditions for the emergence of the next step.

4   For this reason, it is natural that governance and leadership always rest in the hands of that class which is most intelligent, informed and actively inquisitive. This class will be the most exemplary in its autonomy and responsibility.

5   Therefore, the future of society lies in education. Education also leads to the breakdown of class and caste differences, further disseminating and potentiating progress.

From these premises, one can see that liberalism comprises a broad worldview, a social metaphysics that pivots on a specific interpretation of what human nature and social order are. However, the philosophical tenets of liberalism are policy-laden. As one can see from their meritocratic direction and point of culmination, 'liberalism is a ruling consciousness as well as a metaphysical theory' (Unger, 1975, pp. 24–5). Central to the vision of governance is a pervasive confidence in scientific knowledge, conceived in enlightenment terms as the subjection of nature to human will. Liberalism places its trust in the perfectibility of individual and social life through mastery over the natural order obtained via an understanding and control of the laws and principles of its progressive functioning. Understanding and control are united in the conceptualization of reason as the systematic choice of efficient and productive means to given ends. This leads quite naturally to a confidence in bureaucratically organized systems of management and authority as the functional solution to the regulation of the social order, 'bureaucracy as the characteristic institution that is the visible face of liberalism's hidden modes of consciousness and order' (*ibid.*, p. 20). The faith in institutional organization and bureaucratic mediation leads to a struggle between the commitment to impersonal rules as the foundation of society and the experience of dependence and domination.

LIBERALISM IN MORAL DEVELOPMENT THEORY

It is hardly necessary to demonstrate how most if not all of these characteristics of liberalism are also features of Kohlberg's moral development theory. In his article, 'The Future of Liberalism as the Dominant Ideology of the Western World' (1981/1977), Kohlberg explicitly locates his theory in the tradition of liberal thought that can be traced from Locke via Bentham and Mill to Dewey, the latter being the proximal forebear of Kohlberg's own liberalism. He repeats his commitment to this tradition in his recent 'Response to Critics' (Kohlberg, Levine and Hewer, 1983; p. 117). As Reid and Yanarella (1977) suggest, he elaborates the Kantian ethical and psychological aspects of liberalism.

Kohlberg admits that in placing himself directly in the line of descent of classical liberal thought, he is backing the odds-on favourite. Thus, he refers to liberalism as 'the dominant ideology of the past two centuries in the West' (1981, p. 231), and confidently predicts that it 'will not be replaced by a new ideology of the West but will continue to be its dominant ideology for the next century' (*ibid.*, p. 233). He describes its central precepts as follows:

> From a structural point of view, liberalism is first of all a doctrine of social reform, of progressive or constitutional social change. Central to it are moral principles of justice, where justice is defined in terms of individual rights, all of which revolve around liberty. These principles of justice are usually defined and justified through a social contract theory. The theory of social contract may be viewed as a set of premises about fact; notions that law and society did emerge from a contract of people living in a state of nature (*ibid.*, p. 232).

Kohlberg appropriates a phrase of Unger's, stating that 'liberalism is a way of thinking'. As such, just like any other cognitive structure, it undergoes developmental transformations. 'Liberalism is still evolving or developing as a dominant ideology of the West' (*ibid.*, p. 233). According to him, it has recently taken a qualitative step forward, apparently in response to 'the questioning of classical liberal doctrines that occurred in the 1960s and 1970s' (*ibid.*, pp. 227–8). However, unlike stages in cognitive development, this step does not involve a new form of thought. In the cognitive-developmental tradition, each qualitative reorganization makes the form of the previous stage into the content of the new stage. However, in the evolution of Western thought, says Kohlberg, the most recent discrete step forward is 'a new "stage" in the development of liberal thought' (*ibid.*). This 'stage' is embodied in the harmonious unity of liberal moral philosophers and liberal legislators or policy-makers (*ibid.*, p. 242).

Kohlberg appears to suggest that this step is the cultural equivalent of the individual's progress from Stage 5 to Stage 6 of moral judgment (*ibid.*, pp. 227 and 241). But he stipulates that 'the new "stage"' is only an advancement to a higher level of the *already existing dominant form of thinking*, without subordination of that thinking as content within a qualitatively new structure.[1]

Kohlberg fails to demonstrate how the qualitative superiority of this new cultural form that liberalism is taking in the 1970s and 1980s qualifies it for the title of 'stage'. However, he does tell us that the new ultra-liberal thinking has been captured best, and perhaps only, in the work of John Rawls (1958, 1971). Kohlberg claims that the 'state of nature' in which the social contract is arrived at is most adequately represented by Rawls' notion of 'the original position'. Briefly, this concept presents the ideal ethical viewpoint as a prior-to-society perspective, such that one deliberates the social contract as a virtual being—a spirit, so to speak, that is yet to be embodied as a particular person in specific circumstances. Thus, the 'original position' is a putative situation in which 'each person is under a "veil of ignorance" as to the position he or she will have in the society' (Kohlberg, 1981, p. 232).[2]

According to Rawls' argument, the two principles that necessarily would be given precedence under such a state of nature are those of liberty and equality. These are, of course, the classical precepts of political ethics within liberalism. However, with Rawls, Kohlberg contends that they are more than this.

> [These] principles of liberty and equality are not just the principles of Western liberalism, but would be chosen by rational people, acting under a veil of ignorance, as they worked toward development of a contract that would maximize their individual values in any society (*ibid.*).

There is thus a felicitous convergence of what it means to be a rational person and what it means to think in line with the Western liberal tradition.

SOCIAL EVOLUTIONISM IN MORAL DEVELOPMENT THEORY

For liberalism, society is logically posterior to individuality. Similarly, for Kohlberg, the individual constructs his or her moral world privately and independently (Emler, 1983).[3] Moral dilemmas are a function of conflicts of individual private interests. The ideal ethical agency for the resolution of such conflicts is the individual in the 'prior-to-society' mode. Societies function only in terms of the individuals that constitute them. Thus, 'the progress of a socio-political system formally at a certain stage or level is contingent on the moral level of the majority of members of the system' (Kohlberg, 1981, p. 238).

Given the privileged status of individuality in the liberal approach to morality, it should come as no surprise that in that approach society itself tends to be viewed as a macrocosmic individual. The individuality that societies possess is modelled upon that which persons possess. Thus, as one might expect, individual societies develop just like individual people. As indicated in the last quotation, each societal system is at a certain stage in a developmental sequence, that stage being determined by the moral developmental stage of the individual members of that society.

Central to the vision of liberalism is this parallel progress of individual and society. 'A faith in progress is a core of the liberal tradition' (Kohlberg, *ibid.*, p. 233).[4] Kohlberg admits that progress is 'agonizingly slow', but insists that nevertheless there is a 'relatively consistent trend toward greater justice, civil rights, and racial equality (which) is one of the many historical indicators of the directionality of a democratic system' (*ibid.*, pp. 238–9). Liberalism construes this progressive trend in terms of a gradual step by step movement.

> The liberal faith is . . . that under conditions of open exposure to information and communication and of a degree of control by the individuals over their actions and the ensuing consequences, basic changes in both individuals and societies tend to be in a forward direction in a series of steps or stages moving toward greater justice in terms of equity or recognition of universal human rights (*ibid.*, p. 233).

Kohlberg argues that this liberal 'faith' is a rational one that is factually grounded. 'Historical and cross-cultural evidence supports the notion of a long-range moral evolutionary trend on the societal level' (*ibid.*). This scientific claim is rooted in an appeal to a survey of ethnographic and historical data on societal stages of moral evolution carried out by Hobhouse at the turn of the century (Hobhouse, 1906, 1924; Nisbet, 1980).[5] For confirmation of Hobhouse's claims, he appeals to the thesis of an undergraduate, Elfenbein (1973), who examined some ethnographic materials in the Harvard Human Relations Area Files. Kohlberg interprets Hobhouse's work as demonstrating that ethical systems undergo developmental transformations in parallel with increases in the level of 'socio-technological complexity'. At times, especially in his frequent recourse to the hyphenated term 'socio-moral evolution', he seems to be suggesting that the social and the moral are tied, both being carried along together in the broad sweep of evolutionary advance. Elsewhere, he seems to be intimating a quasi-causal relationship: 'Increased socio-political complexity poses new problems for members of a society which give an impetus to growth of a new stage to cope with these problems' (Kohlberg, Levine and Hewer, 1983, p. 107). The switching between 'socio-technological', 'socio-moral' and 'socio-political', and the lack of clarity about whether the hyphens represent formal or causal relationships, not to mention an unusual error in the text,[6] indicate a certain confusion around this issue.[7]

Kohlberg seizes upon the traditional assumption of late nineteenth century anthropologists, handed down via twentieth century systems theorists and sociobiologists, that societies or cultures can be ranked according to 'their degree of evolutionary advancement, as indicated by level of societal differentiation, political integration and economic productivity' (Kohlberg, 1981, p. 234). This is certainly a bold move, and one which none of his cognitive-developmental colleagues have been willing to make with him. In fact, one of the more notable among them, William Damon, has explicitly dissociated himself from it, arguing that developmental concepts cannot be used to construct cultural taxonomies (Damon, 1977, pp. 10–13).

It should be noted that Kohlberg does not mean to evaluate the relative moral *worth* of cultures that he, Hobhouse or Elfenbein rank in evolutionary order. 'Moral principles ... prescribe universal human obligations; they are not scales for evaluating collective entities' (1971, p. 160; 1981, p. 111). 'A deontic judgment is one thing and an aretaic judgment of the moral worthiness of persons or cultures is another' (Kohlberg, Levine and Hewer, 1983, p. 107). 'We do not understand how a "moral ranking" of cultures could either be done or be scientifically useful' (*ibid.*, p. 114).

Nevertheless, this locution should not be interpreted to mean that *no* comparative evaluation of cultures is embodied in an evolutionary ranking. The meta-theoretical commitments of cognitive-developmental theory require that genesis represent increased organization and adaptation which, in this case, must be taken to imply that the moral structures of the 'more evolved' cultures are more ethically adequate than those of the 'less evolved' ones. Moreover, the distinction of 'deontic' from 'aretaic' distracts us from the more important question: since only one set of stages is proposed, and this is generalized from the individual psychological realm to the anthropological domain, is it not the case that the morals of relatively undeveloped cultures are implicitly being characterized in the same terms as the morals of modern Western children? Since Kohlberg does not refute recapitulationism or social Darwinism, he leaves moral development theory perilously close to them, ignoring a century of reasoned critical opposition (see, for example, Hofstadter, 1944; Chase, 1975; Sahlins, 1976; Caplan, 1978). Furthermore, as Buck-Morss (1975) suggests, the liberal commitment to providing principles for a 'ruling consciousness' does implicitly prescribe that Western states should express the superiority of their more 'evolved' moralities by encouraging less fortunate states to approximate gradually to the Western ideal. Here, the liberal concerns with moral education and internationalism converge. It is hard to see how cultural evolutionism of the type that Kohlberg favours could *not* lead to a species of cultural paternalism, despite the 'deontic versus aretaic' caveat.

MORAL EVOLUTION AS RATIONALIZATION

A salient anomaly in Kohlberg's argument is that he fails to distinguish 'structure' and 'content' in the realm of the development of cultures or societies. He assumes that inferences about cultural or societal development can be made from ethnographic data gathered with pre-structuralist anthropological methods that Kohlberg himself would have to characterize as confounding structure with content.[8] The difficulty of making this distinction in the realm of cultural history may help us to understand why the criteria proposed for evaluating the relative development of cultures or societies *are not rational ones*. At least, they are not rational in the same sense as the criteria that the cognitive-developmental approach specifies in the domain of psychological development. Rather, they are the functionalist criteria of systems-theoretical orientations, the criteria of bureaucratic 'rationalization' (cf. Habermas, 1975a). It is organizational *complexity*, economic *productivity* and political *integration* that determine a level as 'higher' or 'more developed'. This is the embryological growth language of functional differentiation and integration, as appropriated by management science. It is a language singularly lacking in any criterion of reason that specifies a prescriptive ideal for what societies *should be like*. Moral development theory here exhibits an unjustified slide from a principled philosophy of reason into an unprincipled conformity to the political sociology of rationalization. If, as Kohlberg, Levine and Hewer suggest, moral development in societies is a response to the problems of increased complexity, then even the supposed structural integrity of the ethical domain would appear to be contaminated with the pre-rational imperatives of economic expansion and bureaucratization. We are reminded of what Unger alerted us to: 'bureaucracy as the characteristic institution that is the visible face of liberalism's hidden modes of consciousness and order' (1975, p. 20).

History repeats itself: Kohlberg again commits the naturalistic fallacy and gets away with it. The 'is' of observed directions in societal and cultural change is quietly turned into an 'ought', a covert substitution that parallels the assumption implicit in the title of his 1981/1977 paper, the assumption that liberalism must be the highest stage (perhaps even the final one?) of Western development merely because it is the ideology that is 'dominant'. This 'ought' is given the appearance of necessity and inevitability by grounding it in the supposedly 'natural' course of evolution.[9] History, in its political, economic and sociological aspects, is reduced to biology.

Small wonder, then, that Kohlberg fails to reconstruct cultural transformations historically. Pleading that historical studies are 'immensely difficult to carry out' (1981, p. 237), he prefers inferences based chiefly upon observed cross-cultural differences. One may see such a leap of faith as courageous. Any decent anthropologist or historian, however, would face the prospect of such a jump with face pale and legs a-trembling. This disregard for history, rooted in a failure to understand what history is, is characteristic of the liberal tradition, and is particularly marked in both its structuralist and cognitive-developmental interpretations.[10] It can be seen most clearly in Kohlberg's psychological progenitors, Baldwin and Piaget (Broughton, 1981a, 1981b).

Kohlberg prefers to logicize historical explanation. Thus, he goes so far as to say that any argument about ideas or practices that draws on their historical origins is illogical, because it commits the 'genetic fallacy' (Kohlberg, Levine and Hewer, 1983, p. 117). He insists repeatedly that moral development theory must be evaluated not on the grounds of its ideological roots, but on the basis of its accordance with fact (Kohlberg, 1982; Kohlberg, Levine and Hewer, 1983, pp. 115 and 118). However, this dichotomy is itself an instance of the erroneous assumption that liberalism typically makes about the relationship of concepts to observations. Unger (1975) identifies this false assumption as the 'liberal antinomy of theory and fact'. This assumption brings with it a false opposition of science to ideology (Mannheim, 1936; Gabel, 1975), what I have called 'the ideology of ideology' (Broughton, 1976, 1981c).

Nevertheless, even on the basis of fact, Kohlberg's social evolutionist thesis encounters difficulties. His assumption that the liberal vision of justice is the natural accompaniment to modern forms of social and technological development flies in the face of the fact that there are many socially and technologically complex societies, integrated politically, that do not subscribe to or promote liberal ideology. Furthermore, if modernization, bureaucratization and technological development were so important, presumably one would be bound to the corollary that recent 'advances' in high technology modes and social relations of production in the West would have brought with them inevitable increments in ethical advancement. But an examination of the recent history of the United States and Great Britain, for example, would appear to provide compelling reasons to doubt such a predicted association (see, for example, Nairn, 1983; Veroff *et al.*, 1980; Lewis, 1984).

Kohlberg's assumption that justice evolves in parallel with social-institutional complexity of organization also flies in the face of some of his own research findings. For example, in his investigations into the 'moral atmosphere' of prisons, he and his colleagues have identified in developmental terms what the critical eye of sociologists and historians noticed long ago: the complex degree of organizational differentiation and politically stable integration in modern institutions by no means guarantees the regulation of those social structures by principles of justice, or even by advanced social conventions. Where even legitimate power and authority focus on sequestering, surveillance and discipline of populations, it is typically the case that the lowest levels of ethicality are engendered. Similar consequences of modernization and rationalization have been documented thoroughly for those most democratic institutions of care-giving, the hospital and the asylum (Goffman, 1961; Foucault, 1973b, 1975; Castel, Castel and Lovell, 1982), and for those institutions of knowledge so crucial to liberals' utopian vision, the schools (Apple, 1970; Bowles and Gintis, 1976; Bernstein, 1977; Willis, 1977; Giroux, 1981).

The liberal vision appears to be blind to the substantial evidence that it is precisely the increase in organizational complexity in administrative structures that fosters domination (Berger, Berger and Kellner, 1973; Adorno, 1978). What early liberalism was not able to foresee was that the state's 'caring' for its citizens entails the production of new forms of social control (Lasch, 1977; Ingleby, 1980; Kovel, 1981). To demonstrate that development is possible through manipulative interventions in the processes of administrative structures cannot and should not be used to draw attention away from the fact that the 'natural' and 'necessary' process of societal evolution gave rise in a systematic way to these degenerate modes of producing and maintaining injustice. In much the same way, the 'natural' evolution of the nation state has created the conditions of possibility of nuclear warfare (Kovel, 1983; Broughton and Zahaykevich, 1982). Innovation is no protection against evil, and illegitimate authority cannot hide behind bureaucratic rationality.

LIBERAL BLINDNESS TO SOCIAL CONTROL

It is characteristic of social science theories cast in the liberal mould that they ignore the ambiguity of the management functions of the state that combine expressions of increasingly benevolent concern for welfare with ever more powerful techniques of social control. 'Control' is not part of the liberal optic because its image of coercion is modelled on the Newtonian concept of 'force', as exerted more or less directly by one body upon another. Indirect coercion, action at a distance, is somehow an invisible, impossible political relationship. Besides direct coercion of individuals by government representatives, the only other constrictions on freedom comprehensible are the forced agreement between a dependent and an independent individual and the pressure of conformity—a 'force' exerted on an individual by the 'mass'. Through the principles of individualism, free contract and meritocratic promotion, these three forms of direct coercion are thought to be precluded.

The net effect is that liberalism substitutes social psychology for political sociology. It reduces the state to face-to-face civil society (see Laslett, 1956). This reduction is captured in and naturalized by the symbolic interactionist offshoot of liberal social theory (Lichtman, 1970; Roberts, 1977; Silver, 1979; Broughton, 1981a, 1985c). When society is conceived as individuals in interaction, our perception of social organization is biased toward a 'bottom up' model of ascending social construction through collective discussions and agreements. This distracts attention from the 'top down' descent of social regulation through vested authority. Liberalism speaks not of the state or its supreme authority, but of the 'social order' or the 'social aggregate', as though multiple transactions and contracts among equals generated all of social and cultural reality. A more critical perspective reveals that part and parcel of what it means for authority to rationalize itself lies in making itself more or less invisible (Harris, 1985). Authority camouflaged is authority secreted from inspection. The gaze comes to rest, instead, upon the veil of the 'social aggregate' as the source and location of order and disorder. In consequence, political authority, veiled from sight, is never obliged to justify itself or its mode of functioning (Sennett, 1981). It not only needs no recognition but also requires that it not be recognized.

As we saw at the outset, the liberal worldview does not crystallize its metaphysic around relationships of authority and control. Rather, it prefers to ground its premises on a faith in the spontaneous tendency toward autonomy and responsibility of the developing individual. The legitimacy of the governing elite is already rooted firmly in developmental principles of educated leadership. By definition, governance is identified with the active and imaginative example of the most free, most knowledgeable and most responsible. The possibility that the collective actions of such individuals could be any less in merit than their individual developmental attainments is beyond comprehension. Equally beyond comprehension is the possibility that the stable integration of interpersonal transactions within civil society might be compatible with the emergence of different and more pernicious laws of functioning at a level of organization above and beyond that echelon.

Liberalism has no ambivalence toward the state because it identifies the organization and authority of the state with the functioning of the constitutional system itself. The latter exists as unquestioned and unquestionable ideal, as the perfect self-correcting mechanism. It defines due process and therefore cannot but obey it. It acts as the standard in relation to which departures in the conduct of imperfectly developed individuals can be identified. This faith in the infallibility of the post-conventional ideal simultaneously embodies the liberal disdain for mass democracy and a profound suspicion of human nature in general:

> The American constitutional system, of course, was never assumed to require that most members of society think and act in terms of liberal moral principles. Rather, the system was designed to ensure that political and legal decisions compatible with liberal principles would emerge from the constitutional democratic process itself. The Constitution was an integration of liberal moral principles with a carefully suspicious sociology and psychology that attempted to consider all the abuses of power to which Stage 2 instrumental egoistic human nature was liable (Kohlberg, 1981, p. 238).

An unfortunate consequence of this particular interpretation of democracy is that it tends to encourage a sceptical orientation to dissent. In Kohlberg's words, 'Socio-moral progress, however, will always be accompanied by temporary waves of reaction as long as the majority of the society is conventional' (*ibid.*, p. 239). Once one has adopted the liberal assumption that advances in technology, differentiation in institutional structure, and stability of political order are necessarily evidence of progress, it follows that any opposition (especially organized or 'mass' opposition) to such progress is retrograde. Liberal developmental psychologists are handy at this point because they can attribute 'temporary waves of reaction' to the incomplete development of the protestors.[11] For example, the 'conventionality' of protestors, as viewed from the perspective of moral development theory, can be adduced as a reason for not taking the protest seriously. Moral education would be the prescribed cure. At this particular margin, liberal respect for dissent shades into repressive tolerance.

Tolerance is repressive also to the extent that it rigidly resists alternative perspectives or 'ideologies', instead insisting upon an assimilation of all difference to its own master framework. Insofar as moral development theory does not dismiss protest, it clasps it to its bosom. Where repressive tolerance gives way, friendly smothering takes over:

> There is also in both adults and adolescents a widespread questioning of democracy, or of our fundamental political structure, as an agency of social progress. Our form of government, and the nation itself, is seen not only as the preserver of human rights but also as a system in conflict with the rights and needs of minorities within the country, of others abroad, and of the natural environment. This is a questioning, I believe, of the inadequacies of the dominant Stage 5 liberal ideology of our constitutional democracy to resolve world moral problems, not a questioning of its inadequacies as an institutional system compared to some other possible system (Kohlberg, 1981, p. 241).

These selections illustrate well the subtleties of liberalism, the paternalistic form implicit in the arrangement of its democratic content. Liberalism has always encountered difficulties with authenticity (Berman, 1980). To the extent that a degree of inauthenticity is concealed by the liberal appeal to freedom and equality, indirect authoritarianism is tolerated and even legitimized. When one unilaterally assimilates all possibilities of difference to the single dominant ideology to which one subscribes, one engages in an act of covert control, and at the same time reveals a certain investment in both exerting control and denying power.

LIBERAL VIOLENCE TO SUBJECTIVITY

It would be a mistake to suppose that the political dimension of a psychological theory is confined to that theory's assumptions about what societal structures and phenomena are or ought to be. Although the psychological nature of moral development theory is obvious, this very quality carries its own specific political import. The psychologization of liberalism represents a phase in the history of ideology that is of major significance. Liberal developmental psychology tends to supply an added justification for the liberal structuring of society since it suggests that such structuring is in harmony with the natural construction of mind itself. This is particularly important for a worldview that stresses the unified emergence of individual autonomy and social progress.

From a more critical standpoint, the psychologization of liberalism can be seen as an ideological response to the increasing psychologization of society and culture that accompanies and is required by the ascendancy of bureaucratic order (Lasch, 1977). Making liberalism seem natural by locating liberal principles in the processes of psychological development can be interpreted as an attempt to distract attention from the contradictions of traditional liberalism by direct appeal to scientific facts. Kohlberg is wrong to think that his critics must dispute the facts documented by moral development research. Rather, they can be accepted and interpreted as evidence of how deeply ingrained political socialization into liberalism has become. What the developmental psychology of liberal morality suggests is that liberalism itself has become interiorized to the extent that it is now experienced as 'second nature'.

A considerable price has to be paid in order to squeeze the subjective world into a shape compatible with an objective world constructed in the liberal image. The cost is a thoroughgoing objectification and alienation of subjectivity.[12] We shall focus on two key terms of objectification, 'interest' and 'role'.

The concept of 'interest'

Even objectifying systems have to posit a subjective element to be objectified, the particularity upon which the vigorous activities of abstraction are to be visited. For liberalism in general, this element is *desire*, what used to be called 'impulse',[13] that part of the self which remains when rational understanding is subtracted. The 'antinomy of reason and desire' is the central feature of all liberal psychologies (Unger, 1975, pp. 38–41). It is visible also in the methodological opposition of description to evaluation, mentioned above.

In the cognitive-developmental approach to morality, the favoured term is 'interest'. It is supposedly the structure of interests and their relationships of symbolic interaction and exchange that develop. Morally immature individuals exhibit only a degenerate form of interest. They merely *want*, experiencing life in terms of simple need or pragmatic wish. With development, this primitive desire undergoes a double objectification, visited upon its substance and form respectively.[14] On the one hand, its specificity is rationalized. The concrete wish is reduced in stature to a mere *content* within a structural form. Its meaning is passively received from the formal context. Its essential *arbitrariness* (Unger, 1975, pp. 42–6) is made evident and neutralized. On the other hand, the form of desire becomes generalized. Desire acquires a more mature configuration, turning into, first, shared need erected as convention, and then rational, universalizable interest or right.

In both the narrowing and broadening transformations of desire, moral development theory subscribes to its virtual eclipse. The theory presents a view of desire as spontaneously tending to give up its 'egocentric' need orientation and turn into an aspect of the cognitive faculty. On the one hand, desire subordinates itself as content, reinforcing the subordination of lower stages to higher ones. On the other hand, it gives up its individuality, specificity and conative quality to the pure rationality of 'interest'. In either case, the pleasure of satisfying desire yields to duty.

This 'mature' interest is deceptive. At Stage 6, when one judges from the 'original position', the 'veil of ignorance' is in the first person subjunctive case—it is ignorance with respect to *who one might be*. The conflicting interests weighed in

any moral dilemma are first-person *self*-interests. The liberal tradition is systematically committed to a reduction of interest to self-interest (Benjamin, 1985), and
refuses to tolerate any other interpretation of what interest is. Only private ends
are conceivable. Rather than accepting the reality of otherness, the Stage 6
idealization of moral and social life reduces it to a recursive reduplication of the
self. This is why it cannot rid itself of the 'suspicious sociology and psychology that
attempted to consider all the abuses of power to which Stage 2 instrumental egoistic
human nature was liable' (Kohlberg's statement quoted above on p. 372).

Interest itself is not universalized in development; only self-interest is.
Although self-interests may be rearranged as elements in more and more complex
systems, the form of interest itself appears to resist development. It remains
stunted at a preconventional level (Habermas, 1978; Eckensberger and Reinshagen,
1978). Despite the appearance of a rational evolution, subjectivity retains its
first-person case, its conative coefficient of desiring impulsivity.

Small wonder, then, that for the liberal the notion of *conflicting interests*
becomes definitive of the moral sphere. Kohlberg, for example, defines morality in
terms of dilemmas posed by a conflict of interests. This is a problem-centred
definition. Covertly, it presses upon us an unwitting and unquestioning acceptance
of the naturalness of interests coming into conflict. We are enjoined to adopt the
bureaucratic 'problem-solving' attitude, accepting the conflict as given and trying to
resolve it. Intent on being intelligent, we prevent ourselves from disputing the
naturalness of the conflict and inquiring into the social (or even philosophical)
conditions under which such a difference was created and made problematic in the
first place. In Kohlberg's view, to offer such dispute would be only to succumb once
again to the 'genetic fallacy' that confuses the way things are with where they have
come from.

It is only in the liberal individualist tradition that interests are seen as naturally
in contest with one another. In other traditions, for example, the socialist one, the
emphasis is on understanding and if possible remedying those features of the social
context that have produced the conditions of possibility of the conflict. According
to such views, individual interests are not necessarily in competition with each
other, or with collective interests. The ideal envisaged instead is the 'natural' one in
which the good of each is identical with the good of all.

An alternative developmental psychology based on such a radically different
assumption would presumably describe how interests themselves undergo developmental transformation, transcending the form of privatized, conflict-generating
self-interest. Such transcendence would incorporate the dawn of awareness that
'interest' must be recontextualized in relation to what the subjective life of concrete
needs and desires means to specific subjects, and that these subjects experience the
pleasure of satisfying their desires in communicative and affiliative relations to
specific others.

The concept of 'role-taking'

In liberalism, the reduction of subjectivity to self-interest is paralleled by the
reduction of mutual human communication, understanding and recognition to
relations between roles. In classical liberalism, constructed in the context of early

free enterprise capitalism, transactions of individuals take place in terms of ascriptive social roles. It is to occupants of these roles that rights and obligations most frequently pertain. Obtaining social recognition as an autonomous individual is usually dependent upon the fulfilment of role-related duties as husband, father, doctor, tailor, judge, etc. (Unger, 1975, pp. 59–62). Liberal social science has shown how, through socializing experiences, these role activities may even become part of the individual's personality (Parsons and Bales, 1955).

The acknowledgment of responsible role performance may give the individual a sense of independence. However, this is only an impression of autonomy rather than a genuine freedom, because the roles occupied are relatively external to the self. 'Role' itself implies a socially necessary deindividuation; one individual can be substituted for another in the same role. Consequently, a network of role-related enterprises, however rationally and responsibly maintained, is insufficient to sustain any coherent unity of self other than that of a public 'persona' (Winnicott, 1965; Helmer, 1970; McClintock, 1979). This holds true even when one shifts from the conventional notion of societal role to the 'postconventional' Kantian perspective, as in the case of Mead or Kohlberg. Even Kohlberg himself has expressed doubt about the sufficiency of role-taking opportunities as means to developmental advance beyond his Stage 4. 'To be principled in moral judgment is not just to cognitively "see" principles ... To see a basis for commitment ... seems to require more than the vicarious experiences of role-taking' (Kohlberg, 1973b, pp. 194–5).[15]

Sociologists and historians are generally in agreement that the transactional matrix of modern, consumption-based bureaucratic societies exacerbates the split of public from private, posing a qualitatively escalated problem for the maintenance of personal identity and freedom.[16] In Riesman's terms, the recent historical emergence of this matrix has replaced the enterprising self-made individualist with the 'other-directed' personality. Moreover, the 'other' in question is less a concrete self than an objectified role-self, defined in terms of criteria functional for the maintenance and progress of civil order (Riesman, 1950). The consequence of such reciprocal objectification is a 'struggle for recognition among individuals without selves' (Unger, 1975, p. 25). Even 'self-interest' is not the interest of a fully unified, autonomous self. Under these conditions, social relatedness comes to resemble reciprocal attempts at mastery over the other. As Hegel (1910) described, this mastery posits the independence of the individual ego as requiring recognition by the other, combined with negation of the other as subject (Benjamin, 1980; Sennett, 1981).

It is this kind of strife that role-taking achieves. It objectifies the other's subjective need, desire or interest, alienates it from the other's experiential life-world with its biographically specific meaning, and incorporates it as content into the formal moral computations taking place within the ego's cognitive structure. As Hegel pointed out, this is not true social relatedness, but an attempt to make the other serviceable. It resembles the way in which we attempt to dominate nature through labour. Such transactions impoverish both participants and reinforce the split between public and private that severs the true self from the role self.[17] Furthermore, role-taking cannot be the basis of justice because it functions to eliminate that communication and expression of needs and desires on which mutual understanding is based; it is anti-dialogue (Habermas, 1975b).[18]

The invocation of role-taking as the psychological act crucial to social understanding and moral justice is problematic in several ways. First, no-one has thought to demonstrate that 'taking the role' of another is either sufficient or necessary for understanding the other's moral situation or needs and interests. It is certainly not sufficient because, even if identification with the other were possible through role-taking, there would still remain the problem of self-interpretation: no-one knows immediately their own psychological state or moral situation (Habermas, 1971). Moreover, there is a long and respectable tradition of hermeneutic theory that argues against the assumption that one can or does understand the other by some sort of identification with them or 'taking their point of view' (Merleau-Ponty, 1964). In fact, such identification begs the question since it already presupposes the grounds for similarity between the interpreter and the person interpreted (Baldwin, 1906).

Role-taking is not only insufficient for knowing or understanding the other, it is also unnecessary. We learn about the psychological and moral reality-for-the-other through direct communication with the other (Turiel, 1976). In so doing, we relate as simple self to the other, rather than as self-in-role-of-other.

Liberal psychology characteristically operates with an 'unreflective view of mind' (Unger, 1975, pp. 36–8). Role-taking is illustrative of that view since, under the description given it in moral development theory, it is not a reflective process. No explanation is given of how the role-taker asserts or even knows that the self in the role of the other is identical with the self that was not in the role of the other prior to the act of taking the other's role, or the self that is not in the role of the other after that act. Without that quality of reflectivity, it makes no sense to speak of moral *judgment* rather than, say, moral computation (cf. Blasi and Hoeffel, 1974; Broughton, 1977).[19] Such a non-reflective, non-judgmental computation can be conducted without any real knowledge, on the basis of mere information. Consequently, the computation would be even within the capacities of a computer (Blasi, 1983). Within the microelectronic matrix of an information-processing device, lived meaning disappears. The intentionality of a perspective, including whose perspective it is and who is taking it, is lost (Dreyfus, 1979). Computers do not and cannot know what the question 'Who?' means. This is why the totally abstract and impersonal concepts of 'perspective' and 'role', indeterminate as to subject or agent, are so adaptive in the informational environment.

Role-taking allows no relationship between selves. It impoverishes communication to the point where it is little more than information exchange between mutually external others. What the subjectivities of these mutually external individuals are, or whether they even have subjectivity, remain unknown and unknowable in such an exchange. It is the structures of role-taking that possess the properties of reversible exchange, and the individuals that are objects of that exchange. The structure dominates the selves to the point that they no longer enter it at all as knowing, willing or communicating subjects. To this extent, the alienation of self and other that occurs in the moral-cognitive transaction is not freely chosen or freely enacted. It is 'alienation' in the most pejorative sense (Geyer and Schweitzer, 1981). Appeal to the 'active' nature of the subject cannot mitigate this alienation. Even an activity of self-subordination is not a freely willed action (Broughton, 1985a, 1985b).

This alienation, in some sense quite immoral, is intrinsic to any moral psychology that imports the scientist equation of knowledge with method and of understanding with conformity to the conventions of correct procedure. Kohlberg

(1973) has admitted, and Blasi (1975) has demonstrated, that role-taking can never transcend a conventional level. Even the supposedly postconventional level of role-taking is still conventional. The conventions at this ultimate level are 'superior' in the sense that they are meta-conventions, or conventions about conventions. 'Postconventionality' claims dominance over conventionality only on the grounds that it is more 'adaptive' and 'organized'. It claims that these advantages accrue from having rationally reconstructed conventional reasoning at a meta-systematic level of moral methodology. The 'original position' is a technology for rationalizing the deployment of psychological technique. However, there is no reason to suppose that conventions about conventions or methods for the management of methods are any more true or moral than first-level conventions or methods (Broughton, 1974, 1984c). The added layer of stratification and its self-concealment through subtle ideological mystification may, indeed, render it more false and more immoral.

Subordination of self or other to the conventions of method impoverishes human relatedness. Human relationships are thereby stripped of their immediate and more distant historical context and so lose any personal meaning. In the operational vision of cognitive psychology, they are reduced to instantaneous transactions. The moral life is reduced to a kind of instrumental 'networking'; personal engagement is reduced to a set of moral 'cruising' skills.

The liberal model of economic technique, albeit revamped within the high technology context of information exchange, confounds what human relationships ought to be with the way that—under the constraints of the modern world—they are unfortunately turning out. Promiscuous instrumental transactions are methodical attempts to alienate self and other from self and other, thereby preserving isolation on the personal level and individualism on the ideological level. Anaesthetized 'interaction' of mutually external others is substituted for genuine discursive relatedness of expressive selves, and elevated to a norm governing social life. The system imperatives substitute for the lost sensuous reality of human experience the surrogate gratification of power over others that appears to reside in the authority of 'the moral'.

CONCLUSION

Ensuring the survival and continued dominance of the liberal system is Kohlberg's self-professed political aim. The moral stage theory, especially at its top end, is an expression of Kohlberg's awareness that traditional liberal thinking has its problems, and of his desire to solve them. However, he has proceeded on the assumption that these problems can be solved within liberalism. The 'troubleshooting' approach exhibited in his definition of morality in terms of 'conflicts of interest' is extended to liberalism as a whole. He acts on the faith that there is a technical or methodological cure for liberalism's ills. This cure requires no fundamental questioning of liberal principles. On the contrary, its purpose is to fortify and rejuvenate them.

The attempted cure claims to achieve the desired repair by grounding the liberal principles of individualism and progress in a 'natural' development revealed by the science of psychology. In addition, it is claimed that the same developmental hierarchy applies to the evolution of societies. The culmination of progress posited in both domains is interpersonal role exchange, as seen in Stage 6 reversible and prescriptive role-taking or in the transactional matrix of capitalist civil society.

Moral stage theory thereby achieves a simultaneous psychologization and depoliticization of liberalism and its problems. Attention is drawn away from liberalism as a 'ruling consciousness', as a system of social policy, as a political apparatus for the practice of governing, managing and controlling society, and as a form of nationalism ordering the global relationships of states. Liberalism is reduced to a 'liberal ideology' that is based on scientific fact and can be improved, perhaps even perfected, by developmental and social psychologists. Ideology itself is given a rational basis, so that the less rational competing ideologies can be subordinated to the dominant form. Once established as supremely reasonable, liberal ideology's historical function of legitimizing entrenched authority is simultaneously concealed and rendered inconceivable.

When the fullness of individual and collective experience is psychologized and depoliticized within the constrained social metaphysics of liberalism, most of what we would like to and need to understand is displaced:

> In place of the history of individual or collective endeavour—insight, speech, action, resistance—one finds the inexorable march of evolutionary progress.
> In place of judgment and dissent, democratic compliance.
> In place of public participation, the privatized activity of problem-solving.
> In place of respect for and understanding of tradition, the obsolescence and replacement of the cultural heritage.
> In place of the development of humanity, a hierarchical system for upgrading technical skills for interpersonal management.
> In place of a subjectively important life history with its salient familial experiences, a mind bent on erasing its memory, step by step.
> In place of race, class and gender, the anonymous cognitive monad.
> In place of sexuality, sensuousness and the aesthetic, the disembodied neutral intellect.
> In place of motivated, desiring subjectivity, a calculus of self-interests.
> In place of love and loss, cool, impartial knowledge that is always a gain.
> In place of pleasure and pain, the advance of rational mastery.
> In place of attachment with significant others, universal affiliation.
> In place of fantasy, play or dreams, the structures of thought.
> In place of the unconscious, the conscious.
> In place of meaning, truth.
> In place of the development of the self, the equilibration and adaptation of the cognitive system.
> Instead of the fostering of kinship, authenticity and community, the principle of individual moral meritocracy, administered by a professional educational bureaucracy of psychological specialists.

None of this is to be blamed on stupidity or deviousness. The desire for reparation of our individual and collective condition is in itself of noble intent. But the possibilities of a humane life need constant nurturance. And when the desire for social improvement yields to fascination with the complex and challenging task of totalizing a rational system, we are diverted from the simpler and less charismatic task of giving life.

Should we help Kohlberg steal the drug that will cure the fatal illness of his beloved liberalism? Or should we instead begin to try to feel the pain of all that loss we drag along, the dying self and other half-buried in the shadow of modern liberal democracy, which it seems still unable to admit to consciousness?

NOTES

1 In a recent response to Schweder's (1982) critique of his liberalism, Kohlberg (1982) has briefly dismissed this departure from the basic principles of cognitive-developmental meta-theory by arguing that the liberalism of Stage 6 is confined to the latter's compatibility with 'moral-political liberal ideological *content*' (p. 935, original emphasis). However, he nowhere shows how the *form* of Stage 6 can be untied from this liberal content, demonstrating that Stage 6 is not itself an essentially liberal construction. In fact, were he to do so, it would contradict his claim to be resolving the classical liberal Stage 5 problems through developmental-evolutionary advance to a higher stage *within liberalism*.

2 This complex metaphysical resolution to the problems of liberal meta-ethics has been expounded at length and in an interesting manner by Kohlberg (1973a/1981) and Boyd (1980).

3 As Kohlberg, Levine and Hewer (1983, p. 164) have pointed out, in retort to Habermas' criticisms, interaction is a central part of moral development theory, its method and its practical application. However, this interaction is one occurring between individuals who in theory, method and practice are sharply demarcated, both cognitively and morally (Broughton, 1982). As Waterman (1981) has argued at length, the concept of 'interaction' is essential to individualism. Thus, 'interactionism' is in no way either a departure from individualism or a qualification upon it. As pointed out by Emler (1983), Kohlberg's 'just community' approach in penal and educational institutions in no way represents an alteration of the moral development approach's commitment to the fundamental liberal postulate of individualism. If anything, studies of individuals in communities, groups, classrooms or dialogic interactions serve only to re-emphasize the principles of individualistic psychology by demonstrating their viability in situations supposedly biased toward the predominance of collective, communal and sociological phenomena.

   Thus, by claiming that liberalism and moral development theory see morality as independently and privately constructed by each individual, I do not mean that such individuals seal themselves off from others, or that they are not dependent upon interaction with others. Rather, I mean that morality itself is constructed *individualistically* and *privatistically*, such that all interindividual and public experiences serve instrumentally to aid in the individual's own construction of his or her own moral structures. Similarly, conflicting interests may be deliberated and mediated in the public sphere, but this does nothing to ameliorate their fundamentally, definitively private nature. In fact, as we shall see below, the very possibility of such conflicts of interest arising in the first place turns out to be premised upon that private form.

4 This vision of progress is contained also in Kant's notion of the 'ideal of humanity':

> The highest purpose of nature, which is the development of all the capacities which can be achieved by mankind is attainable only in society, and more specifically in the society with the greatest freedom. Hence, such a society is one in which there is mutual opposition among the members, together with the most exact definition of freedom and the fixing of its limits so that it may be consistent with the freedom of others. Nature demands that humanity should itself achieve its goal like all its other destined goals. Thus, a society in which freedom under external law is bound up with the greatest possible degree with irrestistible power, i.e., a perfectly just civic constitution, is the highest problem nature assigns to the human race; because nature can achieve her other purposes for mankind only upon the solution and completion of this assignment (1963, p. 16).

For further discussion of Kant's relationship to 'progress', see Adorno (1983–4).

5 Social evolutionists, from Spencer via Hobhouse to Kohlberg, are not evolutionary theorists, strictly speaking. They abandon the major principles of the concept of 'naturalized time' that was the heart of Darwin's revolutionary contribution. In fact, they abandon them in precisely the manner that Darwin warned against. The result is a kind of regression to the pre-evolutionary taxonomic approach of Linnaeus, a 'spatialized' concept of time (Fabian, 1983; cf. Foucault, 1973a).

6 In the very same sentence on page 107, Kohlberg makes an erroneous page reference to his own work (Kohlberg, 1981, 'p. 227'). This would not seem so peculiar were it not for the fact that the article in question is a retort to a criticism by Schweder (1982) in which Kohlberg starts by sternly rebuking Schweder for misreferencing this very same work!

7 It should also be noted that Kohlberg and his colleagues consistently fail to distinguish 'culture' from 'society'. It is not clear when they are talking about one rather than the other, since they use the terms interchangeably. But neither is this common practice in the social sciences nor should it be (Bauman, 1973), since a consistent differentiation between the two is essential if a social theory is to capture the important and variable relationships between social structure (including stratification, institutional organization and division of labour) and culture (traditions, myths, rituals, worldviews, and other symbolic forms and means of cultural transmission).

8 As someone who has worked with the materials in the Human Relations Area Files, I believe that I can testify strongly to the overwhelming difficulty of trying to impose upon those data the structuralist distinction that was so foreign to the ethnographers who reported them and the social scientists who assembled them.

9 The term 'evolution' unfortunately has become a last refuge for those wishing to invoke the image of some process necessarily good. It has the absoluteness of a process for the evaluation of which there exist no criteria except those generated by evolutionary theory itself. If nothing else, surely the spectre of nuclear annihilation calls into question this appeal to the necessary approbation of evolution, and perhaps even calls into question the very meaning of the word 'evolution' itself (cf. Broughton, 1984a).

10 It seems as one grows older,
   That the past has another pattern, and ceases to be a mere sequence—
   Or even development: the latter a partial fallacy
   Encouraged by superficial notions of evolution,
   Which becomes, in the popular mind, a means of disowning the past.
                                                      T. S. Eliot, *The Four Quartets*

11 A classic, and disturbing, example of such an attempt to impugn the 'maturity' of political protestors is Feuer's (1969) diatribe against the anti-war movement. Less well known but equally controversial attempts to undermine the credibility of youth activism in the late 1960s and early 1970s are the attacks mounted by Lorenz (1972) and Parsons (Parsons and Platt, 1970).

12 The necessity of objectifying subjectivity occasioned by the assumptive framework of the cognitive-developmental approach has been documented in detail by Blasi (1976), Morelli (1978), and also by myself (Broughton, 1981b).

13 It is interesting that the early liberal psychologies talked mostly of 'impulse' (for example, Hobhouse, 1913; Dewey, 1922). With the modernization of liberal psychology, the term appears to have disappeared in favour of the less conative and more consciously cognitive 'affect' (Ingleby, 1983). The transformation of the antinomy of reason and desire into the couplet of cognition and affect is regrettable in a number of ways, some of which are discussed in the proceedings of the Jean Piaget Memorial Conference (Broughton, Leadbeater and Amsel, 1981).

14 The duality of substance and form is a basic assumption of liberal psychology (Unger, 1975, p. 35). Out of this dichotomy arises the false inference that universality is to be obtained only through abstraction from particularity (Broughton, 1985b).

15 However, Kohlberg sought an account of 'personal experiences' and 'identity' within the liberal tradition, in the work of Erikson. In consequence, he was unable to formulate any alternative position from which the deindividuated 'vicariousness' of roles could be reintegrated in concrete subjects (Broughton, 1983b).

16 For a summary of this literature as it bears on theories of human development, see my recent review of self-psychology (Broughton, 1985c). A helpful sociological review is provided by Bensman and Lilienfeld (1979).

17 On the 'divided self' that results, see my response to R. D. Laing (Broughton, 1981d).

18 Kohlberg has misunderstood Habermas' critique. Kohlberg rejects Habermas' criticism that moral development theory is 'monological' rather than 'dialogical' on the grounds that (1) moral education research has employed dialogues between individuals, and (2) Stage 6 subscribes to reversible role-taking, 'moral musical chairs' (Kohlberg, Levine and Hewer, 1983, p. 164). However, verbal interaction between individuals need not imply true dialogue. As I have pointed out, the moral education research creates the conditions for role-functional cognitive exchanges, not meaningful conversation between selves (Broughton, 1982). Interaction alone cannot elevate a monological orientation to the level of a dialogical one [cf. Note 3]. Kohlberg has simply failed to grasp

Habermas' distinction between true moral *discourse* and the more mechanical interpersonal interaction (Habermas, 1979; McCarthy, 1973). As for the 'moral musical chairs' or reversible Stage 6 role-taking, it is quintessentially monological, as I have tried to demonstrate here in my consideration of the concept of 'interest' in moral development theory. (It may not be a coincidence that 'musical chairs' is a game that exhibits graphically all the features of competitive individualism, with only a single, triumphant moral agent surviving at the end!)

19 Hampshire (1978) has called such reasoning 'rational computational morality' and has examined several of its deficits.

REFERENCES

Adorno, T. W. (1978) 'Culture and administration', *Telos*, 37, pp. 93–111.

Adorno, T. W. (1983–4) 'Progress', *Philosophical Forum*, 15, 1–2, pp. 55–70.

Apple, M. (1970) *Ideology and Curriculum*, London, Routledge and Kegan Paul.

Baldwin, J. M. (1906) *Thought and Things*, Vol. 1, London, Swn Sonnenschein.

Bauman, Z. (1973) *Culture as Praxis*, London, Routledge and Kegan Paul.

Benjamin, J. (1980) 'The bonds of love: Rational violence and erotic domination', *Feminist Studies*, 6, 1, pp. 144–74.

Benjamin, J. (1985) 'The decline of the Oedipus complex', in Broughton, J. M. (Ed.), *Critical Developmental Theory*, New York, Plenum.

Bensman, J. and Lilienfeld, R. (1979) *Between Public and Private*, New York, Free Press.

Berger, P., Berger, B. and Kellner, H.-F. (1973) *The Homeless Mind*, New York, Random House.

Berman, M. (1980) *The Politics of Authenticity*, New York, Atheneum.

Bernstein, B. (1977) *Class, Codes and Control*, Vol. 3, London, Routledge and Kegan Paul.

Blasi, A. (1975) 'Role-taking and the development of social cognition', Paper presented at the annual meeting of the American Psychological Association, Chicago, August.

Blasi, A. (1976) 'The concept of personality in developmental theory', in Loevinger, J., *Ego Development*, San Francisco, Jossey-Bass.

Blasi, A. (1983) 'The self and cognition', in Lee, B. and Noam, G. G. (Eds.), *Developmental Approaches to the Self*, New York, Plenum.

Blasi, A. and Hoeffel, E. C. (1974) 'Adolescence and formal operations', *Human Development*, 17, pp. 344–63.

Bowles, S. and Gintis, H. (1976) *Schooling in Capitalist America*, New York, Basic.

Boyd, D. (1980) 'The Rawls connection', in Munsey, B. (Ed.), *Moral Development, Moral Education and Kohlberg*, Birmingham, Ala., Religious Education Press.

Broughton, J. M. (1974) 'The development of natural epistemology in the years 10–26', Unpublished doctoral dissertation, Harvard University.

Broughton, J. M. (1976) Review of J. Gabel's 'False Consciousness', in *Telos*, 29, pp. 223–38.

Broughton, J. M. (1977) ' "Beyond formal operations": Theoretical thought in adolescence', *Teachers College Record*, 79, 1, pp. 87–98.

Broughton, J. M. (1978a) 'The cognitive developmental approach to morality: A reply to Kurtines and Greif', *Journal of Moral Education*, 7, 2, pp. 81–96.

Broughton, J. M. (1978b) 'Criticism and moral development theory', *Journal Supplement Abstract Services*, 8.

Broughton, J. M. (1978c) 'Dialectics and moral development ideology', in Scharf, P. (Ed.), *Readings in Moral Education*, New York, Winston.

Broughton, J. M. (1981a) 'The genetic psychology of James Mark Baldwin', *American Psychologist*, 36, 4, pp. 396–407.

Broughton, J. M. (1981b) 'Piaget's developmental structuralism, IV: Knowledge without a self and without history', *Human Development*, 24, 5, pp. 325–50.

Broughton, J. M. (1981c) 'Piaget's developmental structuralism, V: Ideology-critique and the possibility of a critical developmental psychology', *Human Development*, 24, 6, pp. 390–411.

Broughton, J. M. (1981d) 'The "divided self" in adolescence', *Human Development*, 24, 1, pp. 13–24.

Broughton, J. M. (1982) 'Cognitive interaction and the development of sociality: A commentary on Damon and Killen', *Merrill-Palmer Quarterly*, 28, 3, pp. 369–78.

Broughton, J. M. (1983a) 'Women's rationality and men's virtues', *Social Research*, 50, 3, pp. 597–624.

Broughton, J. M. (1983b) 'The cognitive developmental theory of adolescent self and identity', in Lee, B. and Noam, G. G. (Eds.), *Developmental Approaches to the Self*, New York, Plenum.

Broughton, J. M. (1984a) 'The psychological basis of nuclear war', *Forum International*, 3, pp. 73–106.

Broughton, J. M. (1985c) 'The history, psychology and ideology of the self', in Larsen, K. (Ed.), *Psychology and Ideology*, Norwood, N.J., Ablex.

Broughton, J. M. (1985a) 'Computers and children: Education or political socialization?' in Sloan, D. (Ed) *Microcomputers in the Classroom: Critical Perspectives*, New York, Teachers College Press.

Broughton, J. M. (1984b) 'Not beyond formal operations but beyond Piaget', in Commons, M., Richards, F. and Armon, C. (Eds.), *Beyond Formal Operations*, New York, Praeger.

Broughton, J. M. (1985b) 'The political psychology of faith', in Wheeler, B. (Ed.), *James Fowler's Faith Development Theory*, Birmingham, Ala., Religious Education Press.

Broughton, J. M., Leadbeater, B. and Amsel, F. (1981) 'Reflections on Piaget', *Teachers College Record*, 83, 2, pp. 151–218.

Broughton, J. M. and Zahaykevich, M. K. (1982) 'The peace movement threat', *Teachers College Record*, 84, 1, pp. 152–73 (reprinted in Sloan, D. (Ed.), *Education for Peace*, New York, Teachers College Press, 1983).

Buck-Morss, S. (1975) 'The socio-economic bias in Piaget's theory and its implications for cross-cultural study', *Human Development*, 18, pp. 35–49.

Caplan, A. L. (1978) *The Sociobiology Debate*, New York, Harper.

Castel, R., Castel, F. and Lovell A. (1982) *The Psychiatric Society*, New York, Columbia University Press.

Chase, A. (1975) *The Legacy of Malthus*, New York, A. Knopf.

Damon, W. (1977) *The Social World of the Child*, San Francisco, Jossey-Bass.

Dewey, J. (1922) *Human Nature and Conduct*, New York, Holt.

Dreyfus, H. (1979) *What Computers Can't Do*, 2nd edn., New York, Harper and Row.

Dworkin, R. (1978) 'Liberalism', in Hampshire, S. (Ed.), *Public and Private Morality*, Cambridge, Cambridge University Press.

Eckensberger, L. and Reinshagen, H. (1978) 'Parallels within Kohlberg's stage sequence', Paper presented at the Colloquium on Moral Development, Max Planck Institute, Starnberg, West Germany, June.

Elfenbein, D. (1973) 'Moral stages in social evolution', Unpublished bachelor's thesis, Harvard University.

Emler, N. (1983) 'Morality and politics: The ideological dimension in the theory of moral development', in Weinreich-Haste, H. and Locke, D. (Eds.), *Morality in the Making*, New York, Wiley.

Fabian, J. (1983) *Time and the Other*, New York, Columbia University Press.

Fay, B. (1975) *Social Theory and Political Practice*, London, Allen and Unwin.

Feuer, L. (1969) *The Conflict of Generations*, New York, Basic.

Foucault, M. (1973a) *The Order of Things*, New York, Random House.

Foucault, M. (1973b) *Madness and Civilisation*, New York, Random House.

Foucault, M. (1975) *The Birth of the Clinic*, New York, Random House.

Foucault, M. (1980) *Power/Knowledge*, New York, Pantheon.

Gabel, J. (1975) *False Consciousness*, Oxford, Blackwell.

Geyer, R. F. and Schweitzer, D. (1981) *Alienation*, London, Routledge and Kegan Paul.

Giroux, H. (1981) *Ideology, Culture and the Process of Schooling*, Philadelphia, Penn., Temple University Press.

Goffman, E. (1961) *Asylums*, New York, Anchor.

Habermas, J. (1971) *Knowledge and Human Interests*, Boston, Mass., Beacon.

Habermas, J. (1975a) *Legitimation Crisis*, Boston, Mass., Beacon.

Habermas, J. (1975b) 'Moral development and ego identity', *Telos*, 24, pp. 41–55.

Habermas, J. (1978) 'Justice and reciprocity', Paper presented at the Colloquium on Moral Development, Max Planck Institute, Starnberg, West Germany, June.

Habermas, J. (1979) *Communication and the Evolution of Society*, Boston, Mass., Beacon.

Hampshire, S. (1978) 'Morality and pessimism', in Hampshire, S. (Ed.), *Public and Private Morality*, Cambridge, Cambridge University Press.

Harris, A. (1985) 'The rationalization of infancy', in Broughton, J. M. (Ed.), *Critical Developmental Theory*, New York, Plenum.

Hegel, G. W. F. (1910) *The Phenomenology of Mind*, London, Macmillan.

Helmer, J. (1970) 'The face of the man without qualities', *Social Research*, 37, 4, pp. 547–79.

Hobhouse, L. T. (1906) *Morals in Evolution*, New York, Holt.

Hobhouse, L. T. (1913) *Development and Purpose*, London, Macmillan.

Hobhouse, L. T. (1924) *Social Development*, London, Allen and Unwin.

Hofstadter, R. (1944) *Social Darwinism in American Thought*, Boston, Mass., Beacon.

Ingleby, D. (1980) *Critical Psychiatry*, New York, Pantheon.

Ingleby, D. (1983) 'Freud and Piaget: The phoney war', *New Ideas in Psychology*, 1, 2, pp. 123–44.

Kant, I. (1963) 'Idea for a universal history from a cosmopolitan point of view', *On History*, New York, Bobbs Merrill.

Kohlberg, L. (1971) 'From is to ought: How to commit the naturalistic fallacy and get away with it in the study of moral development', in T. Mischel (Ed.), *Cognitive Development and Genetic Epistemology*, New York, Academic.

Kohlberg, L. (1973a) 'The claim to adequacy of a highest stage of moral judgment', *Journal of Philosophy*, 18, pp. 630–46 (reprinted in Kohlberg, L., *Essays on Moral Development*, Vol. 1: The Philosophy of Moral Development, New York, Harper).

Kohlberg, L. (1973b) 'Continuities in childhood and adult development revisited', in Baltes, P. and Schaie, W. K. (Eds.), *Lifespan Developmental Psychology: Personality and Socialization*, New York, Academic.

Kohlberg, L. (1981) 'The future of liberalism as the dominant ideology of the Western world', in Kohlberg, L., *Essays on Moral Development*, Vol. 1: The Philosophy of Moral Development, New York, Harper (originally (1977) in *Proceedings of the Annenberg Conference on the Future of the West*, University of Southern California, Los Angeles, Centre for the Study of American Experience).

Kohlberg, L. (1982) 'Moral development does not mean liberalism as destiny: A reply to Schweder', *Contemporary Psychology*, 27, pp. 935–40.

Kohlberg, L., Levine, C. and Hewer, A. (1983) *Moral Stages: A Current Formulation and a Response to Critics*, Basel, Karger.

Kovel, J. (1981) *The Age of Desire*, New York, Pantheon.

Kovel, J. (1983) *Against the State of Nuclear War*, London, Pan.

Lasch, C. (1977) *Haven in a Heartless World*, New York, Harper.

Laslett, P. (1956) 'The face to face society', in Laslett, P. (Ed.), *Philosophy, Politics and Society*, Oxford, Blackwell.

Lewis, A. (1984) 'A profound contempt', *New York Times*, 15 June, p. 26.

Lichtman, R. (1970) 'Symbolic interactionism and social reality', *Berkeley Journal of Sociology*, 15, pp. 75–94.

Lorenz, K. (1972) 'The enmity between generations and its probable ethological causes,' in Piers, M. W. (Ed.), *Play and Development*, New York, Norton.

McCarthy, T. A. (1973) 'A theory of communicative competence', in *Philosophy of the Social Sciences*, 3, pp. 135–56.

McClintock, R. (1979) 'The dynamics of decline: Why education can no longer be liberal', *Phi Delta Kappan*, May, pp. 636–40.

Mannheim, K. (1936) *Ideology and Utopia*, New York, International Library in Philosophy, Psychology and Scientific Method.

Manning, D. J. (1976) *Liberalism*, New York, St Martins.

Merleau-Ponty, M. (1964) 'The child's relations with others', in Merleau-Ponty, M., *The Primacy of Perception*, Evanston, Northwestern University Press.

Morelli, F. (1978) 'The sixth stage of moral development', *Journal of Moral Education*, 7, 2, pp. 97–108.

Nairn, T. (1983) *The Break Up of Britain*, 2nd ed., London, New Left Books.

Nisbet, R. (1980) *History of the Idea of Progress*, New York, Basic.

Parsons, T. and Bales, R. F. (1955) *Family: Socialization and Interaction Process*, Glencoe, Free Press.

Parsons, T. and Platt, G. (1970) 'Age, social structure and socialization in higher education', *Sociology of Education*, 43, pp. 1–37.

Rawls, J. (1958) 'Justice as fairness', *Philosophical Review*, 67, pp. 164–94.

Rawls, J. (1971) *A Theory of Justice*, Cambridge, Mass., Harvard University Press.

Reid, H. G. and Yanarella, E. J. (1977) 'Critical political theory and moral development: Kohlberg, Hampden-Turner and Habermas', *Theory and Society*, 4, 4, pp. 505–42.

Riesman, D. (1950) *The Lonely Crowd*, New Haven, Conn., Yale University Press.

Roberts, B. (1977) 'George Herbert Mead: The theory and practice of his social philosophy', *Ideology and Consciousness*, 2, pp. 81–106.

Sahlins, M. (1976) *The Use and Abuse of Biology*, Ann Arbor, Mich., University of Michigan Press.

Schweder, R. (1982) Review of Lawrence Kohlberg's 'Essays in Moral Development, Vol. 1', in *Contemporary Psychology*, June, pp. 421–4.

Sennett, R. (1981) *Authority*, New York, Vintage.

Silver, A. (1979) 'Small worlds and the great society: The social production of moral order', Paper presented at the annual meeting of the American Sociological Association, Boston.

Turiel, F. (1976) 'Social convention and the development of societal concepts', Paper presented at the Western Regional Conference of the Society for Research in Child Development, Emeryville, Calif., April.

Unger, R. M. (1975) *Knowledge and Politics*, New York, Free Press.

Veroff, J., Depner, C., Kulka, R. and Douvan E. (1980) 'Comparison of American motives, 1957 versus 1976', *Journal of Personality and Social Psychology*, 39, 6, pp. 1249–62.

Waterman, A. (1981) 'Individualism and interdependence', *American Psychologist*, 36, 7, pp. 762–73.

Willis, P. (1977) *Learning to Labour*, London, Saxon House.

Winnicott, D. W. (1965) 'Ego distortion in terms of "true" and "false" self', in Winnicott, D. W. *The Maturational Processes and the Facilitating Environment*, New York, International Universities Press.

Wood, E. M. (1972) *Mind and Politics*, Berkeley, University of California Press.

Interchange

WEINREICH-HASTE REPLIES TO BROUGHTON

The main thrust of Broughton's chapter is that Kohlberg is trapped in the ideology of liberalism. Consequently Kohlberg's dominant values are rationality and justice—but particularly it permeates his view of the relationship between knowledge and politics (that they are inseparable) and between individual thought and social processes (that they are microcosmic and macrocosmic versions of the same thing). Broughton's analysis of Kohlberg's ideological position is thorough and accurate, but I will argue that it ignores some important aspects of Kohlberg as a *psychological* theorist. Kohlberg may, according to Broughton, be lacking in a sense of history, and like all liberals, ignorant of political sociology, but Broughton does not really address the ways in which these deficiencies affect Kohlberg's direct and indirect contributions to political psychology. He has attacked Kohlberg's *meta-theory*, his assumptions about progressivism and the perfectibility of the human being through education and the experience of democracy, rather than his *theory*.

I want to argue two things: that Broughton is actually wrong in some of his interpretations of Kohlberg's research findings, even if accurate about his general theory, and that Broughton's criticisms may apply to Kohlberg's effort to claim universalizability for his theory of liberal *morality*, but do not necessarily undermine the value of the theory as an account of political socialization within a particular culture where liberalism is the dominant political paradigm.

Broughton's specific criticism of the sequence of stages of moral reasoning is that they reflect the progress of liberal solutions to conflict. The liberal perspective is that politics is about the conflict of interests; therefore what the stages of moral (and therefore political) reasoning represent are increasingly sophisticated ways of resolving conflicts of interests. This means progressive sophistication in identifying the nature of conflicting interests, in understanding the perspectives of those whose interests differ, and in arriving at increasingly complex forms of contract to balance the conflicts. In contrast, Broughton argues that a socialist perspective on development would lead to a greater *integration* of interests, and a commitment to *changing* the system rather than to patching it up in ever more sophisticated ways.

Here we have a paradox; there is some disjunction between the interpretation of Kohlberg's *theory*, and the *evidence* which has arisen from research within the theoretical tradition, and quoted by Kohlberg as central data in the extension of the theory. Broughton derives this model of liberal conflict resolution mainly from the developmental theory of role-taking; it follows from progressive development of role-taking and perspective-taking through the stages, that conflict resolution becomes more sophisticated, that the game of moral (and presumably political) musical chairs gets more complicated. But against this we must consider the evidence of the way that postconventional moral reasoners actually view the world. It seems clear from the evidence of both political action and political ideology, as reviewed in my chapter, that postconventional reasoners do not only consider conflict resolution through the balancing of interests, but do in fact recognize that the system needs transformation.

Broughton is right in arguing that an increasingly complex society does not necessarily produce greater democracy, and that Kohlberg is on shaky ground with his claims for social evolution. But the evidence is reasonably good that *experience* of a complex social system is a necessary condition for the development of individual thought. This evidence comes not only from the sketchy and very tentative conclusions from cross-cultural studies, but more strongly from the detailed studies of individual responses to situations in which conflicts within the social structure, and the complexity of the social system, are experienced at first hand by the individual. Most explicitly, this comes from the just community studies, but the material on crisis situations and confrontational experiences tends to confirm these findings.

What Broughton's critique omits is a differentiation between Kohlberg's more sweeping claims of universalizability, and his very important contribution to understanding political development *within* a liberal society which shares his own historical perspective and values. The traditional approaches to political socialization have either taken a very broad view of economic and social factors and effectively argued that individual thought and political values and explanations are determined by such factors; or they have concentrated on the individual in relation to family influences, on individual psychodynamics or specific child-rearing methods, largely ignoring the role of wider social conditions. Both approaches are deterministic and non-dialectical. The strength of Kohlberg's position is that it provides a framework for looking at the dialectical relationship between individual and society, particularly *because* it is a case history of liberalism. By arguing that social systems and dominant paradigms of social thought have stage structure, he has made it possible to look at individual moral and political development in *interaction* with the conceptual environment in which the individual is developing.

To spell this out briefly, let us consider what a 'Stage 4 society' would look like. It is not a society in which all institutions operate in terms of Stage 4 principles, nor one in which the majority of people have reached Stage 4 reasoning. It is, however, a society in which at least *some* people formulate principles of social organization and the regulation of interpersonal interaction in terms of a level of complexity commensurate with Stage 4 thinking. In such a society, some at least of the explanations of social and moral processes available to the growing individual, through educational material, the media and what might be termed 'general social representations' have Stage 4 structure. But only a *proportion* of such socially available meaning will be Stage 4; a whole range of levels of complexity will be represented. A study by a British undergraduate illustrates this: Richard Tuffin looked at media representations of a debate about a mercy-killing involving a handicapped child. He analyzed editorial leaders and the correspondence columns of a range of newspapers from tabloids to the 'quality' press. He found that the 'quality press' (*The Times, The Guardian*) were more likely to have higher-stage arguments in their leaders and correspondence columns than were the tabloids.

The conclusion I want to draw from this for the present argument is that the growing (and the adult) individual has easy access to arguments at several different stages. She therefore has the options of: (1) attending to the arguments concurrent with her present stage of reasoning; (2) reinterpreting higher-stage arguments in terms of her present stage of reasoning; or (3) constructing individual meaning on the basis of her current stage of reasoning—but even this will not happen in isolation from the available social meaning and social representations within her culture. So the individual's current conceptual stage *sets limits* on what she can understand, but within the cultural milieu there are a number of social representations which she can harness in making sense of her world.

The link between social and individual meaning has not been made explicitly by Kohlberg, but it is my contention that the dominant paradigm of liberalism which his theory reflects is a case study of this relationship. His stages of reasoning are not, I would argue, simply a highly selected set of moral and political principles reflecting his own idiosyncratic preoccupations, but a developmental sequence of liberal thought within a culture in which this way of thinking is highly valued, highly salient and in some forms highly developed. His theory demonstrates, or can be seen to demonstrate, a model of political development which does not imply the simple transmission of ideas from generation to generation, but which analyzes the interaction between cultural beliefs and individual thought.

Finally, a problem with Broughton's critique, but also a problem with Kohlberg's theory, is that both are trying to *prescribe*. Kohlberg holds a brief for liberalism, as well as arguing that liberalism is a social evolutionary inevitability. Broughton's prescription is for socialism and a collectivist rather than individualist view of the social system. Both are in their way idealistic, and therefore go beyond merely *describing* either the spectrum of political thinking available within American culture, or the way that social change may come about at a time of political upheaval. Kohlberg's is a North American perspective, Broughton's a European; perhaps now greater attention needs to be paid to cultural *differences* in the social representations of political and social issues, rather than attempts made to create universalizable and idealistic prescriptions; then perhaps the potential value of the cognitive-developmental perspective as a dialectical model of political development can be realized.

BROUGHTON REPLIES TO WEINREICH-HASTE

In Weinreich-Haste's thoughtful, informed and illuminating advocacy of Kohlberg's theory, I find two major issues that I should like to remark upon: the psychological research on the relationship of morality to politics, and the ideology critiques of moral stage theory.

My judgment of the research literature on moral development and political attitudes and behaviour is that it conforms closely to the pattern that would be expected given my critical analysis of liberal psychology. Most noticeably, moral developmentalists appear to embrace wholeheartedly the traditional liberal social science approach to political life. The realm of politics is *psychologized*, being reduced to a set of cognitive exercises. It is *subjectivized* as a mere matter of 'rhetorics'. It is *relativized* as a mere competition between 'ideologies'. (These are arranged along a polar 'Left/Right' dimension, lumping liberals and radicals together at the 'Left' end.) Political advocacy is *trivialized* by studies showing how superficial 'espoused' ideologies are, and how individuals switch preferences according to the dictates of shifting tastes or 'fashions'. The arbitrary and evanescent quality of political commitments is accentuated by focusing on youth, those most ambivalent, inconsistent and mercurial of animals. Last but not least, the realm of politics is *individualized*, distracting us from the existence of political discourses and political movements, and the historical meaning of resistance to the illegitimate authority of the state engendered by such discourses and movements.

By so diminishing the political, the domain of the moral—governed by a meritocratic, prescriptive and legislative civil system—elevates itself to a position of primacy. It establishes its political domination by depoliticizing the political process and erecting in its place a system of power and authority disguised as a psychologically stable structure of justice.

By exploiting the assumption of perfectible, autonomous rationality, moral development theory dismisses desire and defence as mere irrationalities, thereby denying the heavily documented psychodynamic dimension of political authority. Moral domination depends upon a theory of genesis that precludes the possibility of people actively pursuing domination in the interests of their own intrapsychic economy. Hence, the moral educators of the 'just communities' were blind to the conformism and submissiveness to system imperatives that they fostered in the members of their democratic 'peer regulated' groups.

Weinreich-Haste's chapter admits some of the shortcomings of the moral stage theory, but overall argues for its robustness. According to her, it is possible to admit a certain validity to the ideology critiques of the theory but still go on to take at face value all the uncritical social science studies relating this theory to political phenomena. In so doing, she is correct in fact but not in principle. In fact, the critiques that she cites (e.g., by Simpson, Sullivan, Gilligan and Emler) do not undermine the Kohlbergian endeavour because they are formulated *within* liberalism. They adopt the traditional liberal assumptions about the dualistic oppositions between science and ideology, objectivity and subjectivity, reason and desire. They appeal to the fact that Kohlberg's theory is embedded in liberalism without demonstrating what is *wrong* with liberalism. They aim only to 'debunk', focusing narrowly on Kohlberg and how his psychological theory is derivative in relation to the liberal tradition, rather than focusing more broadly on liberal thought and how it constitutes an illusory worldview. In consequence, they threaten to pull the rug out from under their own feet as well as from under Kohlberg's. They are subject to the very same criticism that they visit upon his theory: that what they claim to be true is compromised or even invalidated by their own ideological 'biases'. In addition, the critiques are unable to deal with the fact that when one examines Kohlberg's *findings*, they do not appear to possess any of the characteristics of mere illusion.

In principle, however, Weinreich-Haste is incorrect. The Kohlbergian paradigm is not as robust as she indicates. Because of its completely uncritical posture with regard to liberal orthodoxy, the cognitive-developmental theory of morality is, in principle, completely vulnerable to any critique—whether philosophical, historical or political—that validly identifies and explains liberalism as a system of ideological distortion and that simultaneously frees itself from the distorting assumptions of that system.

By exposing the relativistic liberal view of ideology and adopting a more critical perspective on the individual and collective relationship of objectivity to subjectivity, my chapter attempted to demonstrate that vulnerability. I suggested that the political dimension of Kohlberg's theory lies deeper than social scientists have assumed. The task of political analysis is not an empirical one of interpreting the research findings on the relationship of moral stages to political commitments. Rather, it is the critical one of examining both the relatively explicit political nature of Kohlberg's attempt to promote and upgrade liberalism and the relatively implicit political nature of his attempt to naturalize and psychologize liberalism.

Neither of these would be reprehensible if it were not for the fact that the liberal worldview systematically conceals the real nature of the workings of authority and power, both outside and inside the individual. A careful interpretation reveals the extent and subtlety of ideological mystification permitted by a liberal psychology of naturally conflicting 'interests' and exchanging 'roles'. By an unobtrusive conversion of the descriptive into the prescriptive, moral stage theory recommends to us in the guise of healthy 'development' a process of political socialization. Our development as 'rational' beings requires the sacrifice of accepting as inevitable a form of life characterized by tragically sophisticated alienation, oppression and domination.

Such a critical rereading of this example of liberal social science does not dismiss the empirical findings as meaningless or illusory. Rather, it understands them as an unwittingly instructive documentation of how, within democracy, new generations come to experience as natural growth the interiorization of ideological mystification. Seen in this new light, Kohlberg's liberal psychology offers a detailed and accurate description of the production of democratic personalities. Once it is understood that the liberal commitments of democracy infringe upon essential qualities of human freedom, understanding and authentic selfhood, then theories like Kohlberg's could be used to suggest ways in which a truly 'moral' education might set about dismantling the authoritarianism implicit in democratic personality. A critical demystifying vision of human development could then be brought to bear instead, in the interests of individual and collective emancipation.

Part XIII: Theological Epistemology

24. Contributions of Kohlberg's Theory to Theological Epistemology

MARY MARKS WILCOX

This chapter presents a picture of the contribution of Kohlberg's theory of moral development to the field of theological epistemology. I describe some ongoing explorations into relationships between the two. The focus is not on any one theological tradition but rather on epistemology as it is applied to the task of theologizing. Working with me in this research venture at Iliff School of Theology are Dr H. Edward Everding, Jr., Professor of New Testament and Vice-President and Dean of Academic Affairs, and Dr Clarence H. Snelling, Jr., Professor of Teaching Ministries.

Joseph Reimer, who has looked at developmental theory from the perspective of Jewish theology, has suggested that it can be seen as 'a kind of philosophic or reflective storytelling, a contemporary *midrash* ... a storyline as a way of depicting human characters.'[1] This dimension has come alive for us at Iliff through the scoring process. Scoring is often a struggle, combining times of rigorous discipline with periods of reflection. Yet through this process we have found that invariably structure takes shape and meaning emerges. Frustration is replaced by excitement, awe and a sense of tremendous privilege, the privilege of a brief glimpse into another person's developmental story. This we find to be the essence of working with developmental theory.

It seems unfortunate that structure must be reduced to a stage score because in that action the meaning and mystery behind the score are often obscured or obliterated. Yet the score is essential for purposes of research. Maintaining this tension between the two is an integral part of the intent of this chapter.

BACKGROUND OF THE RESEARCH

Theology can be defined as a discipline devoted to the critical study of the beliefs of religious traditions and communities. From the viewpoint of epistemology, the task is then understood to be the exploration of how we determine the nature of religious knowledge and decide among competing claims. In other words, how do we validate that which we believe to be true?

My interest in the relationship between Kohlberg's theory and theological epistemology was sparked in the early 1970s by four unpublished papers. The first was the section on 'Organization of the Issues into Systems' in Kohlberg's *Issue Scoring Guide*.[2] Of particular significance was the description of dyadic and triadic systems. The dyadic system refers to two-way relationships between individuals. At Stage 2 this relationship is instrumental; at Stage 3 it involves mutuality and has intrinsic value in and of itself. The triadic system, which undergirds Stage 4, is differentiated from the dyadic in that each person is 'self-consciously oriented to the *system* in which he has a role, and sees the need of that system.'[3]

The three other papers[4] all contain descriptions of social perspective, a concept which picked up and added to the dimensions of the systems. Social perspective was described by Kohlberg in published form in 1976.[5] In this article, Kohlberg states: '... there is a more general structural construct which underlies *both* role taking and moral judgment. This is the concept of sociomoral perspective, which refers to the point of view the individual takes in defining both social facts and sociomoral values, or oughts.'[6] Kohlberg goes on to describe the social perspective for each level and stage of moral judgment. Here is a brief summary:

I Concrete individual perspective
    Stage 1 Egocentric point of view
    Stage 2 Concrete individualistic perspective
II Member-of-society perspective
    Stage 3 Perspective of the individual in relationships with other individuals
    Stage 4 Differentiates societal point of view from interpersonal agreement or motives
III Prior-to-society perspective
    Stage 5 Prior to society perspective
    Stage 6 Perspective of a moral point of view from which social arrangements derive.[7]

These insights led to the first research in developmental theory at the Iliff School of Theology. We explored the possibility that one's structure of reasoning, especially as understood through the concept of underlying systems, might be strongly influential in how one interpreted the Bible. We found clear correlations between moral reasoning stage and the structure of the interpretations of biblical texts. This research was reported in a paper in 1975[8] and contributed to the content of a book.[9]

In our research at Iliff we have made extensive use of social perspective, expanding it to include other factors. However, we have focused primarily on what we call 'community/society,' picking up a major element of Kohlberg's social perspective. We have also generalized to the idea of 'interpretive style' which includes but is not limited to social perspective.

In 1977 we embarked on a six-year longitudinal study of students at the Iliff School of Theology. Our primary intention was to explore a theory of instruction,[10] but within this purpose we included an explicit epistemological dimension, using the model of William G. Perry, Jr.[11] in dialogue with Kohlberg's moral judgment interviews. The rest of this chapter will focus on this project and the relationships we have discovered between moral reasoning and issues of theological epistemology.

The reader is reminded of our basic orientation toward this work: cognitive structural developmental theory is seen as one more story in our human attempts to understand ourselves. No one tale ever tells it all, but each story gives us some additional insight into what it means to be human.

DESCRIPTION OF THE RESEARCH PROJECT

Subjects: students at the Iliff School of Theology. A random sample of students has been interviewed at entrance and again upon graduation. A random sample of other graduating students plus student members of the research team are given the same exiting interview. Total number of subjects: 188; 82 women and 106 men, including a small number of ethnic/racial minorities and foreign students. Number interviewed two or more times: 81. Total interviews: 280. (Eight additional exiting interviews are now in process.)
Dates: started in fall of 1977. Final interviews now being done.
Setting: Iliff is a United Methodist seminary with a student body of theological diversity which includes a broad spectrum of Protestant, Roman Catholic, Jewish, Mormon and peace traditions, as well as students with no religious affiliation.
Results: Since the research is continuing into 1984, no final results are available.
Methodology: All interviews include the three moral dilemmas of Kohlberg's Form A. In addition, first interviews focus on structures of authority and truth; second interviews on professional self-understanding, especially in relation to community/society structures.

SOME RESULTS RELATED TO THEOLOGICAL EPISTEMOLOGY

In this report I will concentrate on three major areas: (1) what is truth and how it is determined, (2) relationship between community/society and professional self-understanding in the ministry, and (3) the function of the shaping vision.

What is true?

In the first interview, we have asked two questions of significance in terms of theological epistemology: *Is your understanding of the Bible true? Are other people's understandings of the Bible true?* We used the categories of William G. Perry, Jr.[12] to rank the responses to these questions, and then explored correlations between them and the moral maturity scores of the subjects for the moral dilemmas. Following are definitions for those of Perry's categories which have been most critical to our work:

Basic Duality/Absolutes: Assumption of dualistic structure of world taken for granted, unexamined ... Absolute defined as 'the established order; the Truth, conceived to be the creation and possession of the Deity, or simply to exist, as in a Platonic world of its own; the Ultimate Criterion, in respect to which all propositions and acts are either right or wrong.'

Multiplicity: 'A plurality of "answers", points of view, or evaluations, with reference to similar topics or problems. This plurality is perceived as an aggregate of discretes without internal structure or external relation, in the sense, "Anyone has a right to his own opinion", with implications that no judgments among opinions can be made.'

Relativism: 'A plurality of points of view, interpretations, frames of reference, value systems and contingencies in which the structural properties of contexts and forms allow of various sorts of analysis, comparison and evaluation.'

Commitment: 'An affirmation of personal values or choice in Relativism. A conscious act or realization of identity and responsibility. A process of orientation of self in a relative world. The word Commitment (capital C) is reserved for this integrative, affirmative function, as distinct from ... commitment to an unquestioned or unexamined belief, plan, or value....'[13]

So far, our analysis has concentrated on the transition between Kohlberg Stages 3 and 4, particularly at the Kohlberg Moral Maturity Score of 350 which seems to correlate with the Perry 'flip', or transition from multiplicity to relativism. Apparently underlying this 'flip' is the shift from dyadic to triadic structure described by Kohlberg. Below are examples from our interviews accompanied by brief definitions adapted from Perry's scheme.

> QUESTION: DO YOU FEEL THAT YOUR UNDERSTANDING OF THE BIBLE IS TRUE?
> *Student A.* 'Yes, I feel that I have reached what God wants me to know.'
> Truth is absolute, right or wrong, unexamined, derived from external authority.
> Kohlberg Moral Maturity Score: 307; Perry general category: Basic Duality.
> *Student B.* 'Yes, my understanding is good for me. But if someone else feels differently, it's not my job to say that is right or wrong. It's whatever he feels, whatever he gets out of it.'
> Truth can be different for different people until it interferes with 'my' truth. The only criterion for deciding among competing truth claims is 'what feels right' to the individual. Truth is derived from external authority. There is an absolute truth 'out there' somewhere, but we cannot always find out what it is.
> MMS: 318; Perry: Multiplicity.
> *Student C.* 'I don't feel that there is any one true way. I can see that the Bible can be interpreted in different ways, and that within certain brackets, within certain confines, they all can be valid.'
> Ideas are 'valid' rather than 'true'. Validity is determined by the use of analysis, rational criteria and consistency. Thus, authority begins to be internalized. Shift to triadic structure.
> MMS: 382; Perry: Relativism.
> *Student D.* 'A word that sticks out in that statement is "true". It is true for me at this time and place in my life, for my understandings of how things are. I think that this understanding is within tolerable limits of the understanding of

the Christian community at large of what the Bible is and how it functions. But there is not any one true understanding. My life changes and the community's changes. But right now that is where it is and I have to act on it.'

'Truth' is that to which one is committed at a particular moment in life. It has been chosen consciously and integrated from among many choices and by use of different kinds of criteria. Commitment is made in the expectation that it may change and grow. Authority is internalized, yet considers external sources of authority.

MMS: 482; Perry; Commitment.

We have tested the correlations in the following manner. For the past two years the members of the research team, trained in both Perry and Kohlberg scoring procedures, have been given copies of responses to the questions about the truth of the Bible. These responses are from interviews that have global moral reasoning scores falling within Kohlberg's Stages 3 to 4(3). The team members are asked to classify each response according to whether it is part of an interview which has been scored below or above an MMS of 350. Thus far, all responses have been identified correctly. In addition, some team members have been able to consistently estimate the MMS within a few points. We have not yet pursued this procedure in a disciplined way for Stage 4 and above, but have found no reason to think that there will not be similar correlations.

In summary, this research gives a tentative answer (in terms of stage structure) to the epistemological question: How do we validate that which we believe to be true? For Stage 3, truth is validated by absolutes. For Stage 3(4), it is through the criterion of 'how one feels about it'. For Stage 4(3), it is through critical analysis, rational criteria and logic, and the test of consistency.

Self-understanding by the professional in the church

This focus was pursued through the use of the following case study prepared by Everding and Dr Dana W. Wilbanks, Professor of Christian Ethics at Iliff, with questions designed to elicit different issues and factors. It is a part of the interview given to all graduating subjects.

Case Study

You are a member of the Board of Ministry of a denomination whose polity or law includes the ordination of women. The Board is meeting to decide on the ordination of Charles J. It has been determined that in general Charles meets the standards of fitness and competence for ministry. However, in discussions with Charles, a major issue has surfaced that raises in the minds of some members of the Board an obstacle to his ordination.

Charles has expressed his belief that the church is wrong in ordaining women to the Christian ministry. He believes this practice is contrary to his understanding of the Bible. In response to questions, Charles indicates that he would serve with women who were ordained and he would not seek to prevent the ordination of women, but he could not in conscience vote for the ordination of women or participate in the ordination of women. Some members of the Board believe Charles' view so violates the church's understanding of ministry that he should not be ordained.

Questions:

1 Should the Board of Ministry ordain Charles? Why?
2 Charles is making his decision out of conscience. Should this fact enter into the decision of the Board? Why?
3 Thinking in terms of the church, what would be the best reasons justifying a decision to ordain Charles? Not to ordain Charles? Why?
4 What is the purpose or function of church polity or law? Why?
5 In this situation there is a conflict between the authority of church and civil law on the one hand, and the authority of biblical interpretation on the other hand. Where do you think the final authority should lie? Why?
6 What do you think is the most important thing a minister should be concerned about in his/her responsibility to the institutional church?
7 Thinking in terms of society, what would be the best reasons to ordain Charles? Not to ordain Charles?

The following quotations from the interviews are excerpts which deal with the factor of community/society. They are grouped here according to stages.

Responses
Stage 3-3(4)

> YES. 'The church has a ministry to Charles . . . so we don't cut him off from his growth . . . there are other things people do I don't agree with . . . the loving response to Charles is to accept him.'
> NO. 'I can see him having problems so far as women in the church . . . women in leadership roles . . . I think he is going to have to work that out.'

Stage 4(3)-4

> YES. 'Because of his credentials . . . he has met the standards of fitness and competency for ministry . . . he has done all the things the church asked him to do . . . all it says is that he disagrees with one issue.'
> NO. 'It is stated that his denomination's polity includes the ordination of women . . . this is an important part of his denomination . . . church government is a framework in which people are better able to function in the community.'

Stage 5

> YES. 'For two reasons: the theological question of grace becomes, "where do we say yes or no to a person on what they believe?" If I demand the right to think or believe the way I do, then I have to give that right to others . . . Also, a question of civil rights . . . the constitutional freedom to think or believe the way he happens to think . . . The purpose of church polity would be to help all of us as individuals and as a collective move in the direction of the Kingdom of God.'
> NO. 'Any institution not only has the right but needs to define what it is as an institution . . . particularly when it is the kind of institution where people contract into it. I think Charles has a perfect right to disagree, but I would question trying to buy into an institution you don't agree with. When his decision of conscience deprives others of a basic right, then the institution is responsible to set limits. Church polity . . . implements in the life of the community what the church stands for.'

The Stage 3-3(4) responses demonstrate characteristics of dyadic structure, the social perspective of the individual in relationships with other individuals, and no indications of a more complex understanding of community/society. The Stage 4(3)-4 demonstrates triadic structure and the differentiation of the interpersonal point of view from the societal. 'Takes point of view of the system that defines roles and rules. Considers individual relations in terms of place in the system.'[14] Stage 5 responses demonstrate an understanding of Kohlberg's 'prior to society' or institution principles and polity as a mechanism for shaping an ideal society or institution. Examples from the Stage 4 to 5 transition are not included because we have so far done little analysis in that range. We have found very few discrepancies between score on moral judgment interviews and concepts of community/society, but a major emphasis in our continuing analysis will be an exploration of these.

In this section of our research, the validation of that which one believes to be true about the church and professional roles in the institutional church again seems to correlate very closely with Kohlberg's stages of moral reasoning and Perry's epistemological categories. One of the conclusions to be drawn is that stage structure is a vital factor in shaping concepts of the church.

In a closely related issue, we have in the past two years included the following question: Should an avowed homosexual be ordained? In June 1982 we received the first twenty-five transcribed responses. Estimated MMS's of these correlated very closely with those of the moral judgment interviews.

Following are excerpts from two interviews which offer contrasting responses to the question: Should an avowed homosexual be ordained?

The first response is from an interview with an MMS of 346 and a global score of 3(4).

> I don't think that should have anything to do with it . . . I don't think that is an important point, of what it means to be ordained. That is kind of a minor characteristic. . . . If they do molest children sexually, homosexuals or heterosexuals, that would be my question, that would determine.

The second response is from an interview scored at an MMS of 493, global score of 5.

> In the ideal church . . . there would be the notion of empowerment of all persons for the ministry of and to the community through the structures of the church. . . . Anytime we elevate our particular viewpoint we run the risk of golden idols and our culture has a long and bloody history of denying the integrity of homosexual persons, denying worth and dignity of homosexual persons. . . . The process of dialogue with scripture would be my rationale and the possibilities of a new creation . . . new reality . . . new way of knowing God . . . to be an advocate on behalf of inclusiveness.

These two quotations again add dimension to Kohlberg and Perry categories. The first emphasizes the personal and interpersonal aspects consistent with multiplicity and the dyadic structure. The second is in sharp contrast to the first in that it gathers together many issues and factors. The triadic structure is evident, and it adds the dimension of a vision for the church which was also found in the Stage 5 responses to the Charles J. case study. Again we see relationships between stage structure and images of the church.

The shaping vision and the epistemological question

Our research has been predicated on the assumption that descriptions of moral reasoning are the tip of the iceberg, revealing only in part the complex structures of human reasoning that lie below the surface. Our first clues to this fuller dimension came through Kohlberg's postulation of entry systems, and Kohlberg's and Rest's descriptions of social perspective, mentioned earlier. We have pursued social perspective and the clearly epistemological model of Perry, exploring correlations between moral reasoning descriptions and theological concepts. Our partial results thus far seem to confirm the existence of cognitive structures that extend to domains other than moral reasoning, including the epistemological task of how to validate that which one believes to be true.

Another dimension of Kohlberg's theory which has captured our imaginations is that of 'the shaping vision', a term I have applied to Stage 5/6 descriptions of the different issues. We find this appropriate to theological concepts. It is our contention that these visions carry the potential for shaping the values and lives of individuals and of communities, whether secular or religious. For example, Kohlberg describes justice in Stage 6 terms, and suggests that the Constitution of the United States incorporates this justice through Stage 5 principles of equal rights. These Stage 5 principles are concretized through laws which are designed to structure the life of the nation in ways ensuring (as much as law can do) that the communities/societies embody the shaping vision of justice.

Many theological traditions attempt to shape the values and beliefs of the religious community through various types of statements such as 'confessions of faith' and 'articles of faith'. These can be perceived as 'shaping visions' for those communities. It is my impression that they tend to emphasize ideological content. One exception is Part II of *The Book of Discipline* of the United Methodist Church where the section on 'Doctrinal Guidelines in the United Methodist Church' raises the following question:

> Since our present existing and established standards of doctrine ... are not to be construed literally and juridically, then by what methods can our doctrinal reflection and construction be most fruitful and fulfilling?[15] [The answer is to be found] in terms of our free inquiry within the boundaries defined by four main sources and guidelines for Christian theology: Scripture, tradition, experience, reason.... Interpreted with appropriate flexibility and self-discipline, they may instruct us as we carry forward our never-ending tasks of theologizing....[16]

The four guidelines are amplified in separate sections. From the section on 'reason':

> Christian doctrines which are developed from Scripture, tradition, and 'experience' must be submitted to critical analysis so that they may commend themselves to thoughtful persons as valid. This means that they must avoid self-contradiction and take due account of scientific and empirical knowledge.... No claims are made for reason's autonomy or omnicompetence, but it does provide tests of cogency and credibility. When submitting doctrinal formulations to critical and objectively rational analysis, our proper intention is to enhance their clarity and verifiability.[17]

Note here the close correlation between the concepts in this paragraph and the description of Perry's 'relativism', which we have equated with Kohlberg's Stage 4(3). This section on 'reason' is then set within a context which seems to employ an integrative epistemological approach exhibiting some elements of Kohlberg's Stage 5 and Perry's category of 'Commitment'.

In discussion with United Methodists, I have found a popular interpretation of these materials to be: 'Methodists can believe anything they want to.' In other words, the folklore seems to be based in Perry's 'multiplicity', Kohlberg's Stage 3(4). This orientation appears to be a dominant one also in secular society in the United States, in which complexities are often reduced to 'whatever people feel is right'. This is not surprising in a culture in which the structure of reasoning of many adults is Stage 3-3(4). (For example, slightly over half of a random sample of students starting graduate work at Iliff between 1977 and 1980 were scored at Stage 3-3(4).)

Some introspection by religious communities in terms of theological epistemology could be enlightening and challenging. The opportunities and obstacles associated with this task are illuminated by the knowledge that stage structure appears to be highly significant in shaping the individual's interpretation of the images, concepts, values and beliefs transmitted by the religious community.

IN CONCLUSION

Kohlberg's theory has been criticized for such divergent reasons as its philosophical and theological assumptions, its limited scope, the male bias of its longitudinal sample, its individualistic (as opposed to communal) emphasis and its methodology. It is not the purpose of this paper to defend the model against valid critique. Rather, it is to present a picture of the enormous potential which lies within the moral reasoning story, even with its limitations. My concern is that this potential has been too often obscured by the various critiques, and that the forest has not been visible because of the trees.

I would suggest that Kohlberg himself has not emphasized adequately the social perspective aspect in order to bring it the attention which I am convinced it deserves. In this article, therefore, I have attempted to expand on the possibilities for a stronger focus on social perspective as well as a more serious union with the epistemological work of Perry. The story of human development in moral reasoning is but one window into a much fuller story of what it means to be human.

I conclude with a true story about a student and one small facet of her developmental journey. This is the kind of insight which breathes life into a theory, and which raises more questions than it brings answers, reminding us that we never have the final word.

Leslie (not her real name) was interviewed when she entered Iliff. The moral maturity score of her interview was 373. She was interviewed again shortly before graduation, and this time the MMS was 380. She continued studies at Iliff, enrolling in the course in developmental theory. In her final paper for that course she wrote a critique of developmental theory in which she included the following paragraph:

> There is a point beyond which growth results in rejection and alienation. On my personal odyssey I learned to camouflage my growth in acceptable ways. The camouflaging takes energy and leaves me feeling less open than I'd like to be. This class has provided me with a mirror so at least I know what it is I've been hiding. It is disconcerting to find that ways of thinking which had been hidden for years and labeled weird/unacceptable are suddenly labeled O.K. But it is terribly disappointing to realize that the Land Beyond Stage 4 ≃ Utopia, the Promised Land—is not a land flowing with milk and honey, but is rather a familiar, intriguing and very, very lonely place, a sort of Secret Garden whose fruits cannot be shared because my most careful attempts have met with blank looks and the utter rejection of total silence.

Leslie was re-interviewed shortly after she wrote this, a few months after her second interview. This time her MMS was 460.

In this poignant essay moral reasoning is intertwined with other strands: feelings, experiences, personality and religious images. These are woven together to create a tapestry of this woman's life, which is brought to consciousness in her story.

In this article I have tried to describe the context of our research as a movement from mystery, to analysis, to mystery and wonder. Kohlberg's model contributed the initial impetus for our work and continues to provide essential foundations in social perspective and moral reasoning scoring procedure. It has opened windows into fresh insights in theological epistemology.

NOTES

1 Reimer, J. (1983) 'Beyond justice', in Joy, D. (Ed.), *Moral Development Foundations*, Nashville, Tenn., Abingdon Press, pp. 64–5.
2 Kohlberg, L. (n.d.) *Issue Scoring Guide*, (unpublished), pp. 26–39.
3 *Ibid.*, p. 33.
4 Kegan, R. 'Constructions of community', an earlier form of this paper was presented to the 1973 Fall Conference of the Society for the Scientific Study of Religion, San Francisco; Kohlberg, L., Kauffman, K., Scharf, P. and Hickey, J. (1974) *The Just Community Approach to Corrections: A Manual*, Moral Education Research Foundation, pp. 12–22; Rest, J. R. (n.d.) 'The hierarchical nature of moral judgment: A study of patterns of comprehension and preference of moral stages', (unpublished), Section II.
5 Kohlberg, L. (1976) 'Moral stages and moralization: The cognitive-developmental approach', in Lickona, T. (Ed.) *Moral Development and Behavior: Theory, Research, and Social Issues*, New York, Holt, Rinehart and Winston, pp. 31–53.
6 *Ibid.*, p. 33.
7 *Ibid.*, pp. 34–5.
8 Everding, H. E. and Wilcox, M. (1975) 'Report of a research project on implications of Kohlberg's theory of moral reasoning for biblical interpretation', presented at the annual meeting of the Association of Professors and Researchers in Religious Education, November.
9 Wilcox, M. (1979) *Developmental Journey*, Nashville, Tenn., Abingdon Press.
10 Everding, H. E., Snelling, C. H. and Wilcox, M. M. (1976), 'Toward a theory of instruction for religious education', presented at the annual meeting of the Association of Professors and Researchers in Religious Education.
11 Perry, W. G. (1960) *Forms of Intellectual and Ethical Development in the College Years*, New York, Holt, Rinehart and Winston.
12 *Ibid.*
13 *Ibid.*, pullout chart in back of book.
14 Kohlberg, L. (1976) *op. cit.*, p. 35.
15 The United Methodist Church (1972) *Doctorine and Doctrinal Statements, Part 2 of The Book of Discipline*, p. 35.
16 *Ibid.*
17 *Ibid.*, p. 38.

25. Some Critical Adaptations for Judaeo-Christian Communities

DONALD JOY

Cognitive-structural theory grounded in the research of Piaget reported in *The Moral Judgment of the Child*[1] did not quickly make its way into religious education. Goldman's experimental studies of children's perceptions of religious material in the public schools of England were a major application of Piaget's findings.[2] It was not until Sholl's graduate thesis was reflected in 'The contributions of Lawrence Kohlberg to religious education',[3] that American religious education looked seriously at structural development. My own research[4] was rooted in Piaget's conception of 'subjective responsibility', and was published within a year of Sholl's article in *Religious Education*.

Today religious educators are virtually all aware of structural development and of efforts to appropriate it to their work. For many, their awareness is indicated only by the briefest knowledge of 'Kohlberg stages'. Others have weighed Piaget and Kohlberg research and theory and rejected it entirely. Still others have offered critiques on and modified both Piaget and Kohlberg, and continue to rely on cognitive structural developmental theory as a source in creating and sustaining ministries of religious education.

In this chapter I wish to summarize the critical responses of representative researchers and theologians to the work of Lawrence Kohlberg. These will include Dykstra, Moran, Gilligan and Vitz. Elsewhere I have edited a symposium in which Reimer, Chazan, Philibert, Rowen, Schmidt, Moore and Sholl have set down their responses to Kohlberg and have indicated how they carry forward their work building on structural development research and theory.[5]

Following that summary, I will suggest some unique foundational contributions for religious education which lie embedded in structural development research. Over against this agenda for the future modifications of religious education research and theory, I will then place my non-negotiable foundational concerns and charges against Kohlberg's work. These concerns revolve around (1) what is moral reasoning? (2) the 'naturalistic fallacy', and (3) who is the 'reasoner', a subject, an object, or an agent?

REPRESENTATIVE CRITICS OF LAWRENCE KOHLBERG

Dykstra, chiefly in *Vision and Character: A Christian Educator's Alternative to Kohlberg*,[6] rejects Kohlberg's work. He does so on the grounds that it is not enough for moral psychology to 'investigate the development of cognitive structures'.[7] Dykstra insists that Kohlberg has carved out too much territory and that he cannot deliver the goods because 'moral growth is not developmental'. Furthermore, Dykstra concludes, religious faith and belief have been collapsed into human psychological structures which are incapable of adequately dealing with issues of transcendence.[8] Elsewhere Dykstra chronicles Kohlberg's failure to deal honestly with human sinfulness.[9] The Dykstra 'alternative' to Kohlberg is 'cognitive-experiential'.[10] He labels it thus because 'it involves the attempt to know and perceive, and because it is concerned with experience'.[11] Dykstra sees the cognitive as consisting of 'conceiving, imagining, reflecting, and judging'.[12] 'Experience' consists of doing, performing, and 'causing to happen'. Dykstra criticizes Kohlberg for his theological/philosophical presuppositions, but lays on Kohlberg the burden of his own philosophical demands: that Kohlberg abandon his empirical studies and generate a full-blown theory of moral philosophy. Dykstra does not hesitate to invent a speculative theory based on theological/philosophical work easily accomplished in his office.

Moran, in *Religious Education Development*, cuts loose from Kohlberg on several grounds: (1) Kohlberg is not as seriously grounded in Piaget as he claims to be; (2) he arbitrarily separates religion and morality, seeing religion rooted in morality, but not the other way around; (3) Kohlberg equivocates: on the one hand he says a core of values exists which is universal; on the other hand he advocates moral relativism in specific cases; (4) Kohlberg's stage system virtually eliminates the first six years of life as belonging to his moral system, thus undercutting both Piaget's work on moral development and the religious tradition by which the early years are prized for the cultivating of honesty and integrity in all relationships.[13] Moran then evaluates the work of Dykstra, then that of Fowler, both of whom he regards as set over against Piaget, Kohlberg and 'moral development'. Finally, Moran offers grammars of religious development and of educational development, closing with his own theory of religious education development. Here, as with Dykstra, we encounter yet another religious education specialist who ventures to formulate a theory without first verifying and validating the foundational perceptions upon which the theory rests. It is one thing to criticize an empiricist; it is quite another to imagine that Kohlberg can be supplanted by theological/philosophical speculation or by fusing a collage of parts from other people's experimental work without replicating and expanding the base.

Gilligan, *In Another Voice: Women's Conceptions of Self and Morality*, reports her own research. She did clinical interviews with women contemplating abortions. Her findings led her to challenge Kohlberg, her colleague/mentor on two grounds:

(1) the research of Kohlberg dating back to the University of Chicago experiment has been mostly with boys and men; (2) women, it appears, organize moral reasoning around a core of attachment/affection rather than around issues clustered around justice.[14] Unlike the theological/philosophical evaluation and speculative alternatives of Dykstra and Moran, the Gilligan data urge an expansion of moral development value structures, and they assume the importance of continuing empirical verification and validation.

Vitz, Associate Professor of Psychology at New York University, mounts a massive attack on Kohlberg's theory in 'Christian Perspectives on Moral Education: From Kohlberg to Christ'.[15] Vitz doubts whether Kohlberg's stages exist, and he marshalls evidence against Kohlberg by citing Kohlberg's own internal revision of his theory across the last twenty years. Then, with incisive flair, Vitz moves in to destroy with a series of critiques. (1) The empirical critique: the stage scale has not been standardized; moral development scores do not predict moral action; the data offered to support the idea of invariant stage sequence reveal 'no clear support'. (2) The rational critique: cognitive moral reasoning is competent apart from specific moral content to the reasoning; Kohlberg's system is profoundly relativistic; Kohlberg's 'Stage 6' is Kohlberg's own canonizing of a preferred way of doing moral reasoning. (3) The ideological critique: this is levelled not only against Kohlberg, but against social psychology as a whole, and indeed against all social science. 'It is,' Vitz says, 'part of the now rapidly growing awareness within social science that there is no neutral or objective theory, nor is such theory in principle even possible.'[16] The critique charges Kohlberg with (1) rationalism, no concern with the will or with affect; (2) individualism, all resources are within the person, hence the self, not a transcendent Source, is primary; (3) liberalism, the assumption that all reality is in transition toward undefined and relativistic ends; and finally, (4) atheism, most consistently visible in Kohlberg's scoring manual where any transcendent affection or value is categorically locked in at Stages 3 or 4, even though the value is otherwise clearly within Kohlberg's highest principled expressions. Vitz joins Dykstra and Moran in offering his own synthetic/speculative model in the theological/philosophical tradition. In the section of his paper entitled 'Toward a Christian Model of Moral Development', Vitz disclaims that he is willing only 'to sketch out some basic principles and concepts which any such theory would ... have to include.'[17]

Vitz calls his present proposal 'essentially an innate phenomenological model in terms of the origin of moral affect and cognition.'[18] So his theses are: (1) morality is acquired; (2) morality is mostly learned; (3) moral action depends upon the will. Looked at theologically, Vitz sees his model resting upon seven axioms: (1) the assumption of revelation; (2) the principle of love; (3) Christ as the model; (4) following Christ derives from loving him; (5) prayer is central to the development of love; (6) the Christian moral life helps to create the Christian virtues whose foundation is humility and whose flowering is love; (7) Christian morality requires Christian behaviour.[19] Here again is a theological/philosophical collage which deserves to be verified. It is perhaps striking that one researcher tending his protocols and computers could provoke such creativity on the part of religious educators, none of whom seems to be on the way to testing hypotheses against the real world of how people actually develop and how they experience moral sensitization.

CONSTRUCTS ROOTED IN COGNITIVE STRUCTURAL DEVELOPMENT

Every language contains terms for expressing ideas and metaphors of reality which differ from those in other languages. We encounter a similar phenomenon when we examine research and theory. Terms are coined or appropriated and invested with technical meanings which are essential to convey a description of that which must be described. No religious educator dare approach the agenda of our times armed with a single research theory. Whether Kohlberg is worth salvaging may be less important than whether we are wise enough to appropriate the constructs essential to describe what structuralists have been observing in human development. Here I want to comment briefly on three of the crucially valuable terms: adaptation, hierarchical integration, and perspectivism. Elsewhere I have elaborated on the unique empirical underscoring of the Hebraic construct of 'justice' as I identified 'common ground' with Kohlberg.[20]

Adaptation

To the extent that Kohlberg is rooted in Piaget, he brings forward the observation that the person is not trapped in the environment as a victim. Behaviourism places dominant weight on the environment as the shaper of the person. Psychodynamic theory places that dominant weight on early environment and family. Structuralism holds that the person impacts the environment and that each is changed; the result is a high view of the freedom of persons to respond to external events and environments in ways that enhance self-worth and predict diversity. Both behaviourism and psychodynamic theories tend toward determinism; structuralism offers us, with the adaptation process, a way of describing freedom and unpredictability. Adaptation consists of two alternating modes: assimilation of new content into existing structure in such a way that the present structure shapes the content, distorting it. However, given a cycle of assimilation, accommodation follows when the previous structure collapses with the impact of the assimilated content and the living person constructs 'a bigger box' to house the now fermented and expanding content. Assimilation and accommodation taken together constitute the adaptation process, sometimes called the equilibration process by Piaget.

Hierarchical integration

Every theory which takes into account the developmental changes which occur must find terms to describe what happens to earlier experience when it meets current and future experience. Erikson in his psychodynamic 'eight stages of growth' theory coins the term 'epigenetic' to describe how a person who is confronted by the polarities of 'identity versus identity diffusion' will move ahead into the 'intimacy crisis' with built-in predictions about its resolution. The 'seeds' of each solution are to be found planted in the solution of the previous crisis, hence 'epi-genetic' (embedded in the genes). There is a sense in which a 'bad start' seeds each future planting. Maslow, in a similar hierarchy of human needs, sees each of the early needs as so consuming the person's attention that no need will emerge into the person's consciousness until the previous, more primary, need has been fully met. He uses 'prepotency' to stress the urgency of primary needs. Structural language gets at quite a different phenomenon: hierarchical integration suggests that the person is both constantly changing and constantly transforming the past and all past experience into a new construction. Childhood is never lost and must be transformed in order for adolescent, adult and mature life to be whole and healthy. Repentance, then, is not denying previous guilt, but owning it, 'coming home' to it and allowing grace to transform it into the maturity of present honesty and integrity.

Perspectivism

Piaget's discovery that young children cannot imagine any perspective different from their own demanded a label. He called it egocentricism. By this he meant nothing negative or immoral, only the naive confusion of the self with the non-self and the belief that there is only one way of viewing reality. At the maturer end of the continuum lies perspectivism—the ability to take the perspective of persons, to feel what they feel, hear what they hear and to make judgments based on that objective, external ground: the self viewing the self from a non-self perspective.

These pieces of language are inherited from cognitive-structural development. Our path to life and ministry will no doubt be both easier and richer if we do not abandon them.

SOME FOUNDATIONAL FLAWS IN KOHLBERG'S WORK

I come now to the critical analysis of what I have called my non-negotiable concerns and charges against Kohlberg's research and theory. These judgments are made within the structural arena and in some cases lay demands upon that emerging system. The judgments are also made from my own partial/imperfect perspective— as one human agent toward another. Structural development is not an 'endangered species', and Kohlberg is making a significant contribution to its richness. These non-negotiable concerns and charges represent another structuralist's dream that structural development might reconstruct itself in the late twentieth century and serve all humanity more effectively than it will be able to do in its present form.

What is moral development?

When Piaget discovered the core of moral reasoning and its movement from 'objective' to 'subjective' responsibility, he saw it organizing spontaneously around issues of 'justice'.[21] Critics who neglect to trace Kohlberg back to that Piagetian source rarely show sensitivity in evaluating Kohlberg's preoccupation with justice.[22] Those who examine Piaget's 'Cooperation and the Idea of Justice',[23] on the other hand, find there an almost complete spectrum of justice. That justice construct is significantly richer than traditional Greek or other Western systems, but matches Hebraic understandings of righteousness and justice in amazing ways.[24] If Kohlberg had been faithful to the Piagetian structures of justice and had protected his work from his own political biases, his research and theory might not have so quickly fallen into obvious distortions of 'what is moral?'. The notion that justice when applied as the principle of wholeness or completion of all things brings about the perfect realization of all human ends in harmonious accord with one another is an elegant one. With that understanding, justice is a type of relational network which must be developed and maintained so that all interpersonal relationships may go on in an orderly way. Justice is thus not something that one gets or keeps as a personal possession; instead, it characterizes all of a person's ways and relationships.

Justice, however, is not a one-directional, hierarchically motivated system. Piaget reported aspects of its negative or mirror image, but regarded the lack of advancing justice only as a retardation of the one-directional, upward-moving system. Yet one has only to live in the present world for about five minutes to find that injustice is as easy to chronicle in the morning news as is justice. Isaiah cautioned: 'If you cease to pervert justice, to point the accusing finger and lay false charges, if you feed the hungry from your own plenty and satisfy the needs of the wretched, then your light will rise like dawn out of darkness and your dusk will be like noonday' (58:9–10). A full-spectrum justice must run all the way from morality through immorality.

I have little concern that moral theologians, ethicists and philosophers nibble away at Kohlberg because his definition of moral development does not put forward a complete and viable system of morality, universally applicable. By definition of his task, he never claimed to be doing so. But I am terrified at the myopic presupposition that moral development is inevitably linked to vertical progress through advancing stages of increasingly sensitive justice perspectives. The opportunities abound in which to test hypotheses about the downside of moral reasoning. Since each of us is capable of fantasizing enormous evil as well as enormous good, the possibilities which lie even with the limited sphere of 'hypothetical moral reasoning' are as close as Heinz or Faust under the negative magnet of Mephistopheles. Even more useful studies might chronicle famous or ordinary trajectories into immorality and destructive patterning of moral choice. Gilligan has opened the Harvard doors to the use of Piagetian clinical interviews with persons facing real, not hypothetical, moral choices.

Nor am I particularly concerned with the possible narrowness of justice as the core of morality. Kohlberg may be wrong. My students consistently leap to criticize him because the core is not 'love'. But the core of morality is continually open to expansion as new empirical evidence emerges. Again, Gilligan's study of women facing the abortion choice seems to suggest that women, at least, may organize moral choices around issues of attachment more than around issues of justice. Heschel's elaborations on justice suggest that the Hebraic notion of justice may indeed be more intrinsic to the divine nature than any other characteristic.[25] And Kohlberg nicely places love within justice.[26] If moral theologians and philosophers are impatient with Kohlberg for holding justice as the core of morality, then it would be courageous for them either to (1) suggest a way of expanding the conception of morality in empirically verifiable ways, or to (2) go on about their business of doing speculative and non-verifiable systematizing of the epistemologies of morality.

While I was not trained as a moral philosopher or moral theologian, still I sense an obligation as an educator and evangelist[27] to contribute to Kohlberg's work by suggesting ways of expanding the conception of morality consistent with his kind of investigation. I find the entire structural development base useful in enlarging my understanding of historical and biblical material. In the Matthean record of Jesus' 'Sermon on the Mount', for example, the 'beatitudes' unfold in a hierarchically integrative trajectory:

```
            8 Advocates of 1, 2, 3
          7 Peacemakers
        6 Pure in heart
      5 Merciful
    4 Righteous/just
  3 Meek/abused
2 Mourners/grieving
1 Poor
```

One way of searching for the 'mirror image' of morality might be to look for descending lists. Another would be to infer the negative side of the trajectory from the gradients on the positive side which is put forward. An interesting inversion occurs when we infer from the eight beatitudes, since the first three appear to be negative. This will require what appear to be positive conditions for the first three of the potentially negative set:

```
1 Wealth
  2 Ecstasy
    3 Exaltation
      4 Confrontation/demands for rights
        5 Exploitation
          6 Conspiracy/evil imagination
          7 Anarchy
          8 Terror
```

We would hypothesize that both the beauty set 1, 2 and 3, and the ugly set 1, 2 and 3 are contained in a primal matrix of both original sin and original grace. If so, we might expect that there is no guarantee of upward or downward progression in any sort of 'epigenetic' or 'prepotency' sense. In Jesus' words in Matthew 5, it is striking that the first three are unilateral statements requiring no action or no response, suggesting that the condition itself demands the full energy of the person at that time.[28] Items 4 and 5 are oriented toward reciprocal action in a community setting—what Piaget calls 'heteronomy'. So in a thoroughly 'adaptive' sense, the person engages destiny deliberately in a corporate milieu. In the positive trajectory the mid-section, then, appears to correspond easily with theological categories of justification and community participation. In the negative trajectory the descending egomania moves further toward ultimate absolute isolation and in the mid-section establishes true moral guilt and culpability; sin is now defined in terms of those choices and actions which are destructive to persons, self and others. The final three, 6, 7 and 8, appear to be analogical to Kohlberg's Level C on the upper projection: all are motivated out of internal holiness expressed by increasingly effective living on behalf of the highest values known among humans in community. Theologically, the flowering of social and community holiness, inward sanctification of which reorganizes the affective centre of human motivation, and the targeted affection denoted by *agape* love are consistent with the final three. The negative trio, in predictable contrast, moves the potential of human destructiveness into a cosmic crescendo. The trajectory has apparently moved from original sin into culpable sin, and finally into unpardonable sin—calling evil good and good evil, hence is hopelessly abandoned to the eternal pursuit of destruction which leads to the ultimate isolation: isolation in the tomb of 'self'. The elegant contrast of the higher trajectory is its movement toward relationship and toward intimacy through shared life, pain and the lifelong pursuit of righteousness and mercy. Thus original grace is followed by justifying grace and sanctifying grace, all leading to the ultimate intimacy: to 'know as we are known'.

I have wanted, here, to caution all of us that Kohlberg has not followed Piaget's first evidence about the mirror side of justice. It may be assumed by the non-religious philosophical and educational community that any such negative trajectory of destructive injustice or non-love is important only to the religious community. Such constructs as 'original sin', for example, may be thought to be only the esoteric concerns of historians and theologians. The fact is, all of us are living in the context of depravity and are endangered by human destructiveness every waking moment. If we do not generate ways of thinking and dealing with non-grace-filled aspects of the human community, and do it quickly, we may not long have opportunity to exist as humans. At the same time, I have here underscored the potentially useful way with which structural development provides us of thinking about morality and moral reasoning. These concerns have led me both to warn and to encourage in this discussion about the future of our understanding about the core of morality and the patterning in moral reasoning.

The 'naturalistic fallacy'

Kohlberg thinks of himself as an objective, unbiased researcher and theorist. It has not occurred to him that, as Toynbee once quipped, 'Every person has a theology, and one is never more at the mercy of that theology then when one denies that it exists.' Perhaps the nearest Kohlberg ever comes to admitting his bias is in his claim that he has committed the naturalistic fallacy and got away with it. In that confession, Kohlberg defines the 'fallacy' as 'that of asserting that any conception of what moral judgment ought to be must rest on an adequate conception of what it is.' He continues: 'By this we mean first that any conception of what adequate or ideal moral judgment should be rests on an adequate definition of what moral judgment is in the minds of men.'[29] I wish in this discussion to explore both some obvious risks taken in indulging the fantasy of the naturalistic fallacy and to trace the history of the philosophical distortion and deformity which have given us the phenomenon of naturalism and the naturalistic fallacy. I will trace that history in the hope that we may, in our generation, find a way to return human history to a holistic way of looking at the universe, including ourselves and our moral options.

The risks of inferring from what is, what ought to be, seem to me to be obvious. (1) Taking humans as they are as the norm for evaluating humans as they ought to become makes two errors: one, assuming health and vitality is irreducibly omnipresent to establish the norm; and two, assuming that existence itself is the credential for value and survival. (2) Any 'drift', whether upward or downward, has the effect of changing the norms by which human direction and destiny are programmed.

I wish to suggest that Kohlberg does not, in fact, practise the naturalistic fallacy in his research or in his theory. It is evident in reading Kohlberg that a 'phantom' human morality exists. Its pinnacle seems to be represented by Rawls' *A Theory of Justice*, which Kohlberg regards as 'the newest great book of the liberal tradition'. Kohlberg espouses it partly because it 'systematically justifies' his Stage 6. Rawls holds, for example, that persons who truly apply the Golden Rule, will not be distracted by their own preferences or the natural human tendency to put one's own interests ahead of corporate or other person's interests. The principles one will put forward, then, will be truly fair or just. Kohlberg illustrates Rawls' construct of justice by showing how it would process the issue of capital punishment. Eventually capital punishment would be negated as an option in the judgment of a Stage 6 person, because one of the perspectives the person would take would be that of the person convicted and sentenced to die. At that point the perspective would inform the judging person with the issue of what it would be like to face death. The judger would then conclude that since the condemned criminal wishes to live, the death penalty is not just. But such a fantasy sort of justice value would not hold up in the face of the smallest offence: sleeping in instead of going to classes, flunking out for not studying, for example. The 'most mature' judgment would be to suspend any consequence, since from the perspective of the offender, there is a preference for no consequence. I cite this instance simply to illustrate that Kohlberg either (1) has a morally flabby image of the universal principle of justice in human relationships and responsibilities, or (2) he is willing to throw the human race back to the stone age, in which every person does that which instrumentally satisfies the self, and those who could act for the group are obligated to indulge criminals by thinking flabbily about their danger to the general community. What I suspect is that Kohlberg is in touch with an inner vision of justice which is increasingly known to him, but which is largely out of his reach. Piaget empirically studied that inner vision as it is expressed in cognitive judgments. Kohlberg, with significantly less care, arbitrarily defines justice to match his vision of justice in his own current partial understanding of it. We are confronted with a dilemma of how to break with the naturalistic fallacy. We might choose to create a mythology of the ideal morality, constructed from the collective vision. Since such an inner vision seems to be universally present in humans we could do worse: we could continue to reflexively resort to the naturalistic fallacy. But we might choose to embrace an objectively defined, historically documented structure of justice and adopt it, however tentatively, as the global ideal by which to compare our empirical findings along the way.

We are prevented, however, from appropriating 'revelation' in the Judaeo-Christian sense largely by significant moments of error in the history of human thought. I will offer a rough chronicle of some of those moments of error, but I do so only in the hope that by evaluating long swatches of human history we may discover ways to correct the trajectory through which we move.

My basic premise is that the quality of human existence is directly proportional to the balance that we are able to maintain between (1) the material concrete reality as measured by human sensations and (2) the affective subjective reality as known by human intuitions. The first is commonly called the 'phenomenal' domain and the second the 'noumenal'.

Philosophers who share my concern for healing the breach between the phenomenal and the noumenal tend to lay the original blame at the feet of Descartes. The Cartesian error, expressed in the famous assertion, 'I think, therefore I am', leads to the abandonment of the non-material aspect of human reality and to regarding one's material existence as both the highest good and the only mode of existence. Polanyi[30] and Gill[31] are both working to close this part of the Cartesian gap.

Bassett points to Augustine who, he says, constructed the 'Augustinian bypass' around the affective, noumenal vision.[32] Augustine's response to the aspiration to Christian holiness, nicely integrated in the earlier church fathers, is delayed following Augustine to 'the next life'. The grim realities of human existence evoke Augustine's splitting away of inward holiness on the basis that 'what is', namely human failure to perform, 'is what ought to be', and we will have to wait until another time and place for being made perfect in love and justice. The Augustinian and Cartesian errors have in common the lopping off of that softer, affective dimension of human reality. What remains is cognition, and the hard concrete material reality.

Ellul pushes the curtain even further back and lays the blame at the feet of the serpent and of Cain. 'Yea, hath God said, . . .' was the first wedge between fact and faith. And Cain's turning toward the 'city', Ellul sees as a deliberate blocking off of affect in favour of building technology.[33]

Hampden-Turner describes Descartes' motive as 'probably reverential' when he separates 'mind from body, subject from object, knower from known in a lethal split which has yet to heal.'[34] Descartes regarded the Roman church as the proper guardian of the soul and wished, no doubt, to escape the wrath of the Pope for tampering in 'spiritual matters'. The operating field for science was *res extensa*— objects located in material space. *Res cogitans*, the domain of thought, belonged in private space, and was known only inwardly and in conversation with God. So Hampden-Turner documents this major moment of error, with considerable fault resting on the religious side for inviting the dichotomy of science and faith. But, he proceeds, the avalanche had only begun. Before long the 'mind' was subjected to the same scrutiny as the *res extensa*. A materialistic and mechanistic view of humanity was now established and science was flourishing—albeit as a systematic examination of only partial reality.[35]

Calvin, heavily influenced by the Cartesian error and losing trust in the Roman church, set out to systematize theology. Calvinism established a bi-polar universe in which persons are subjects, the Bible is object and thought about the religious realm is Christianity. Doctrine is all-important; affect is untrustworthy and dangerous. Hampden-Turner sees Calvinism as the necessary precursor of 'modern doctrines of scientism, positivism, and behaviourism'. What is more, those doctrines have borrowed from Calvinism 'even its most objectionable characteristic, a devastating lack of self-awareness'.[36]

Bassett notes that a thin line of survivors avoided the Augustinian bypass. They include Francis of Assisi, Bernard of Clairvaux, Count Zinzendorf and John Wesley.[37] Hampden-Turner cites the contrast between the two lines of descent by labelling the Cartesian distortion 'Puritan, atomistic individualism', and the more holistic alternative 'Anglo-Catholic organicism'.[38] Outler, in a lecture on John Wesley, posed the question, 'How do you explain the fact that it seems never to have crossed John Wesley's mind to construct and publish a systematic theology, large or small, and that every attempt to transform Wesley's ways of teaching doctrine into some system of doctrine has lost something vital in the process?'[39]

I furnish this historical summary in the belief that moral development research and theory is unwittingly resting on the one-eyed distortion commonly associated with Descartes. My final concern is intrinsically continuous with the review of the origin of naturalism and the omniscience attending it, which by obliterating self-awareness invents the 'naturalistic fallacy'.

Who is the reasoner: subject, object, or agent?

Macmurray, in his Gifford Lectures of 1953 and 1954, places the focus upon philosophical aspects of naturalistic individualism.[40] He traces the decline of religious influence and of religious practice. He notes that 'ideals of sanctity or holiness ... begin to seem incomprehensible or even comical. Success will tend to become the criterion of rightness, and there will spread through society a temper which is extraverted, pragmatic and merely objective, for which all problems are soluble by better organization.'[41] The root of these and other problems lies in the fact that 'modern philosophy is characteristically egocentric'. By this he means that it takes the self as its starting point—not God, nor the world, nor society. What is even more tragic is that the self is an individual in isolation, always an 'I' and never a 'we' or a 'thou'. In short, the self is the subject, and it acts on all material reality: the object. But since the self is also composed of elements and existing in material reality, the only way of knowing the self is through the same 'object' examination the self uses on the non-self. 'Substance' is the product of the self thinking about objects. The relation between the subject and object determines what is substantive. 'The objective is valid: the subjective is unreal, illusory or imaginary.'[42]

Modern philosophy broke down when it attempted to understand the self by using an analogy of the material world—the world of substantial objects. The 'spontaneity of inner self-determination and directed development' characteristic of humans was not reducible to object status in material terms nor trustworthy in subjective status. The 'key-concept is not substance but organism.' Macmurray sees 'the organism ... as a harmonious balancing of differences ... a tension of opposites ... a dynamic equilibrium of functions maintained through a progressive differentiation of elements within the whole.'[43] The self can no longer be conceived of as subject and as 'knower', but must be regarded as 'agent'. This agent moves only in relationship, never in isolation: traditional distinctions between subject and object must be abandoned in contemplating human considerations. We are also obligated, Macmurray insists, to 'abandon the traditional individualism or egocentricity of our philosophy. We must introduce the second person ... and do our thinking from the standpoint ... of the "you and I".'[44]

CONCLUSION

In this chapter I have reviewed a sample of critiques of the work of Lawrence Kohlberg and have responded to the main lines of their concerns. I have then affirmed three constructs which have been our legacy from the larger structural development field of study. Finally, I have set down three non-negotiable concerns which constitute an immediate agenda for those of us who have a stake in structural development and the empirically verifiable research/theory approach represented by Kohlberg. I am optimistic in the prediction that the minimal but radical adjustments called for here can be made within the lifetimes of both Kohlberg and myself. Should that fail, the future too belongs to us.

NOTES

1 Piaget, J. (1932) *The Moral Judgment of the Child*, trans. Gebain, New York, Collier Books, 1962.
2 Goldman, R. (1964) *Religious Thinking from Childhood to Adolescence*, New York, Seabury Press.
3 Sholl, D. (1971) 'The contributions of Lawrence Kohlberg to religious and moral education', *Religious Education*, 66, 5.
4 Joy, D. (1969) *Value-Oriented Instruction in the Church and in the Home*, Bloomington, Ind., Indiana University.
5 Joy, D. (Ed.) (1983) *Moral Development Foundations: Judeo-Christian Alternatives to Piaget/ Kohlberg*, Nashville, Tenn., Abingdon Press.
6 Dykstra, C. (1981) *Vision and Character: A Christian Educator's Alternative to Kohlberg*, New York. Paulist Press.
7 *Ibid.*, p. 61.
8 *Ibid.*, pp. 26–7.
9 Dykstra, C. (1983) 'What are people like? An alternative to Kohlberg's view', in Joy, (Ed.), *Moral Development Foundations: Judeo-Christian Alternatives to Piaget/Kohlberg*, *op. cit.*, pp. 153 ff.
10 Dykstra (1981) *op. cit.*, p. 175.
11 *Ibid.*
12 *Ibid.*, p. 176.
13 Moran, G. (1983) *Religious Education Development: Images for the Future*, Minneapolis, Minn., Winston Press, pp. 65–85.
14 Gilligan, C. (1982) *In a Different Voice: Psychological Theory in Women's Development*, Cambridge, Mass., Harvard University Press.
15 Vitz, P. (1982) 'Christian perspectives on moral education: From Kohlberg to Christ,' paper delivered at Ann Arbor, Michigan. See also his 'Christian moral values and dominant psychological theories: The case of Kohlberg', in Williams, P. (Ed.), (1981) *Christian Faith in a Neo-Pagan Society*, Scranton, Northeast.
16 Vitz (1982) *op. cit.*, p. 14.
17 *Ibid.*, p. 23.
18 *Ibid.*, p. 29.
19 *Ibid.*, pp. 27–40.
20 Joy (1983) *op. cit.*, pp. 49–58.
21 Piaget (1932) *op. cit.*, Ch. 2, 'Adult Constraint and Moral Realism'.
22 See Kohlberg, L. 'The primacy of justice', in his 'Stages of Moral Development', in Beck, C. *et al.* (Eds.) (1971) *Moral Education: Interdisciplinary Approaches*, Toronto, University of Toronto Press, pp. 62–6.
23 Piaget (1932), *op. cit.*, Ch. 3.
24 Joy (1983), *op. cit.*, pp. 26–34.
25 Heschel, A. (1962) *The Prophets*, Vol. I, New York, Harper and Brothers. See esp. Ch. 7, 'Justice'.
26 Kohlberg, L. in Beck (1971), *op. cit.*
27 Joy, D. (1983) 'The formation of an Evangelist', in Mayr, M., *Modern Masters of Religious Education*, Birmingham, Ala., Religious Education Press, Ch. 9.
28 The beatitudes came alive to me developmentally/hierarchically, when, in 1982, my son and pastor, the Reverend John M. Joy, posed a question early in his Sunday morning sermon: 'Is it any wonder that the victims of poverty, grief, and abuse are not in church on Sunday morning? Yet Jesus tells us explicitly that they are covered "carte blanche" by God's prevenient grace. The reciprocal conditions requiring our action do not begin until the fourth beatitude.'
29 Kohlberg, L. (1971) 'From is to ought: How to commit the naturalistic fallacy and get away with it,'

in Mischel, T. (Ed.), *Cognitive Development and Epistemology*, New York, Academic Press, pp. 151–284.

30 Polanyi, M. (1958) *Personal Knowledge*, Chicago; Ill., University of Chicago Press.

31 Gill J. (1971) *The Possibility of Religious Knowledge*, Grand Rapids, Mich., Eerdmans Publishing Company.

32 The ideas cited to Paul Bassett derive from a lectureship on the campus of Asbury Theological Seminary in the fall of 1982. They are adapted from the manuscript of *The Historical Path of the Doctrine of Entire Sanctification*, in press (1983) at Kansas City, Beacon Hill Press.

33 Ellul, J. (1970) *The Meaning of the City*, Grand Rapids; Mich., Eerdmans Publishing Company, pp. 1–9.

34 Hampden-Turner, C. (1981) *Maps of the Mind*, New York, Macmillan Publishing Company, p. 30.

35 *Ibid.*, pp. 30–3.

36 *Ibid.*, p. 36.

37 Bassett (1982), *op. cit.*

38 Hampden-Turner (1981), *op. cit.*, pp. 34–5.

39 Outler, A. *Repentance and Justification*, Wilmore, Ken., Asbury Theological Seminary Media Center, Tape 82BB3, 13 July 1982.

40 Macmurray, J. (1957) *The Self as Agent*, New York, Harper and Brothers. The second of the series of Gifford Lectures is (1961) *Persons in Relation*, New York, Harper and Brothers.

41 Macmurray (1957) *op. cit.*, p. 31.

42 *Ibid.*, p. 32.

43 *Ibid.*, p. 33.

44 *Ibid.*, p. 38.

Interchange

WILCOX REPLIES TO JOY

Joy has approached the general issue of theological epistemology from a somewhat different perspective than the one which I have taken. Whereas I focus on the general task of theologizing, he emphasizes Kohlberg's contributions to religious education and suggests modifications. In addition he responds to several critical charges against Kohlberg's work, and outlines 'non-negotiable foundational concerns and charges against Kohlberg's work.' His summary sentence indicates his generally positive assessment of Kohlberg's work, as does his defence of Kohlberg against the cited critics. Thus, inasmuch as I find our two approaches complementary rather than in conflict, my intent in this response is to introduce some different perspectives on some of the issues he raises.

I concur with much that Joy has to say in reply to the critiques formulated by Dykstra, Moran and Vitz. I would emphasize more strongly that many such criticisms fail to distinguish between Kohlberg's empirical data and his philosophical assumptions, and go on to reject his entire model on the basis of criteria which are appropriate only for the evaluation of his philosophy. They also tend to reveal a lack of understanding of the complexity of scientific method. The realization by Vitz that there is no 'neutral or objective theory' in social science (nor, may I add, in physical science) does not negate the validity of all research.

In regard to Gilligan's work, I am less enthusiastic than is Joy. Her present research grows out of her conviction that women score at lower stages of moral reasoning than men and that this is because Kohlberg's scoring instrument is biased in favour of a male mode of thinking quite different from that of women. Her statement that women's scores are lower is not supported by the extensive research of James Rest at the University of Minnesota nor by our research at Iliff. Rest has written that in the use of his Defining Issues Test of moral judgment: 'In 20 out of 22 studies, there are no significant sex differences.'[1] In the research at Iliff, the mean moral maturity score of entering women students is 359, and that of men is 357. These data suggest either that the difference between men's and women's moral reasoning is not as pronounced as Gilligan describes, or that Kohlberg's scoring instrument is not as biased toward males as she maintains. If the former is the case, this reduces the credibility of her major thesis. If the latter is true, it clearly removes the charge against Kohlberg that his model describes male reasoning only.

Joy objects to Kohlberg's concept of Stage 6 justice as it relates to capital punishment. I would suggest that Kohlberg's approach to this issue can be separated into two distinct sections. The first part consists of a discussion of his philosophical assumptions, summarized in the following statements:

... a reversible or fair (equilibrated) resolution is one whereby everyone whose interests are at stake 'is given his due' according to some principle that everyone judges to be morally valid, given that each person is not egoistic but is willing to take a moral point of view; that is, to consider his own claims impartially and to put himself in the shoes of the others.[2]

[The] attitude of respect for human dignity, for individual people as ends rather than means ... is systematically elaborated into a general concept of justice (at Stage 6).[3]

The second part of Kohlberg's approach comprises a lengthy attempt to apply this Stage 6 philosophy to decision-making about capital punishment. Joy aptly characterizes this application as 'a justice in which every person does that which instrumentally satisfies the self.' Kohlberg seems to reduce his Stage 6 concept to a mathematical formula which limits the rich possibilities inherent in his original image of justice. I suggest that the focus be less on Kohlberg's interpretation and more on the potential contributions of the Stage 6 philosophical vision to theological epistemology.

Joy deplores the dichotomizing of the phenomenal and the noumenal, and I share this view. I believe that developmental theory offers some insights toward understanding the persistence of this 'either/or' orientation. One of the characteristics at Stage 4 is the tendency to dichotomize and to perceive as either right or wrong those complex ideas and ideologies which conflict with one another. Stage 5, on the other hand, approaches such conflicts through the use of a dialectical process of decision-making, weighing data, searching for new information and relevant universal principles, and coming to tentatively committed conclusions.

Joy refers to John Wesley as one example of a person among a 'thin line of survivors (who) avoided the Augustinian bypass', in other words, an 'either/or' orientation. He then quotes Outler to the effect that 'every attempt to transform Wesley's ways of teaching doctrine into some system of doctrine has lost something vital in the process.' It is perhaps more than coincidental that Wesley authored the four guidelines of the United Methodist Church mentioned in my chapter, and that that religious tradition is one that has (officially, at least) transcended ideology in its way of doing theology. Wesley's theology may well be an example of how Stage 5 reasoning overcomes some of the problems of Stage 4.

In conclusion, I am not able to take serious issue with Joy's chapter. We seem to be in agreement that Kohlberg has made substantial contributions to theological epistemology, and that no-one has yet reached the final word.

NOTES

1 Rest, J. R. (January 1981), written communication.
2 Kohlberg, L. with Elfenbein, D. 'Capital punishment, moral development, and the constitution', in Kohlberg, L. (1981) *The Philosophy of Moral Development*, San Francisco, Harper and Row, p. 280.
3 *Ibid.*, p. 281.
4 *Ibid.*, p. 279.

JOY REPLIES TO WILCOX

I have watched the Iliff School of Theology work in moral development now for more than ten years. So, it was with a lot of pleasure that I read Wilcox's report on their longitudinal study with theology students. My admiration for their painstaking and thorough methodology is offset by a concern that the presuppositions are deformed. The Wilcox chapter documents those deformities.

Kohlberg's upper stages are the least reliable. When presuppositions are deformed, you can build three or four storeys on a tilted foundation, but five and six are likely to fall into the street. Then, when you look more carefully, you can often detect the tilt further down. When any of us blows the whistle on Kohlberg for thinking 'what is is what ought to be' we can be dismissed as feebleminded, of course. But the death of whole civilizations and the imminent danger to our own makes it plausible that Kohlberg, Wilcox and company will do themselves and all of us a favour to *read their own data* more carefully. What are those absolutely universal values which their empiricism identifies across cultures? How then dare they *confuse the values of contemporary popular culture* with their measures of 'structure' and retain their integrity as researchers?

Kohlberg's inability to distinguish between 'the value of human life' and community values of safety and order, and his blind reliance on Rawls' subjective reasoning on the matter illustrates in a thimble how unwittingly he has bought into a value embraced by modern popular culture and confused it with structure. So the scoring guidelines consistently exalt the compromises which favour life at the expense of the common good.

Nowhere has Kohlberg bothered to trace the 'death penalty', for example, in stone age cultures to ask, 'What is the universal value which requires death for crimes which today's popular culture regards as trivial?' That homework might begin to deliver moral development research from its hopeless lock-in on the deformities of values which we consume with our breakfast cereal and the six o'clock news every day. Instead, we are led to believe that moral development research consists of looking for the most sophisticated articulations which justify 'what is', since 'what is is what ought to be.' Moral development epistemology would be helped along if all of us would look for a taxonomic approach to examining issues.

The experimental work at Iliff which examines the moral issue of ordaining an 'avowed homosexual' is an amazing case which illustrates the need for a full spectrum taxonomy if there is to be any possibility that reasoning can be done as 'agent' and not consistently confused with 'object' or 'subject'. For example, let us assume that 'avowed homosexual' refers to a person who both expresses sexual attraction and current sexual practice with a member of the same sex. We will help the respondents if we consider also the ordination eligibility of a person who expresses sexual attraction but has never consummated a genital relationship. Let us then pose a third homosexual category by which one expresses both sexual attraction and previous genital relationships, but has taken an oath of celibacy for the self and makes a covenant with the ordaining community to live in genital celibacy. We then at least move toward an epistemology of moral reasoning on a troublesome issue in the popular culture. We will not have achieved the distancing necessary in an 'agent' relationship until we unscramble the empirical data from wide cross-cultural taboos against homosexual contact.

It is not difficult to imagine where we are headed if 'moral development research' finds itself in the service of popular culture and its values. Incest between consenting relatives may then be articulated in 'Stage 6 language'. Extra-marital genital contact whether heterosexual or homosexual is easily justified in the highest-sounding categories. Abortion as the fail-safe back-up for birth control, and unrestricted premarital genital contact are so deeply engrained in the popular culture that the moral development researchers themselves live and move within their murky waters. One of them quipped to me at Niantic Prison many years ago, 'We are lucky we didn't get married. If we had, without living together for these last six years, I'm sure we would have been divorced by now.'

It remains to be seen whether the primary moral development research base can correct itself from its own myopia and the entrapment in the present popular values. The discipline is liable to the charge of relativism, given this failure to attend to the unmoveable set of primary values which both Piaget and Kohlberg have identified, but to which Kohlberg and now Wilcox do not attend. None of us will live long enough to gain the 'agent' perspective by ourselves. But through empirical research which goes in search of the moral roots which sustain human communities, we have the tools and the means for sticking by the stuff which makes us distinctly human. If we refuse to take that rugged path, we are doomed, I suspect, and perhaps soon, to pay for our myopia by falling over the edge of history into the scrap-heap of dead civilizations.

Part XIV: Cross-Cultural Morality

26. Cross-Cultural Research on Kohlberg's Stages: The Basis for Consensus

CAROLYN POPE EDWARDS

When Lawrence Kohlberg (1969, 1971a) claimed that his moral stages were culturally universal, he ensured that a storm of controversy would greet his theory. He then intensified the controversy by further claiming that preliterate or semiliterate village peoples would generally fall behind other cultural groups in their rate and terminal point of development due to a relative lack of 'role-taking opportunities' in their daily lives.

Moral values are known to vary so greatly from culture to culture that a universal, invariant sequence in development or moral judgment is a provocative claim. Furthermore, to characterize the difference between the moral judgment of people in traditional face-to-face societies versus modern, complex, national states as a difference in 'adequacy' of moral judging (Kohlberg, 1971a) seems to violate norms of inter-cultural respect and ethical relativism.

Kohlberg's statements have been met by many theoretical statements attempting to refute aspects of his conclusions or assumptions about cultural universality (see, for example, Bloom, 1977; Buck-Morss, 1975; Edwards, 1975, 1982; Shweder, 1982a; Simpson, 1974; Sullivan, 1977). Equally of importance, the theoretical controversy has stimulated much empirical research intended, at least in part, to test the cross-cultural claims. Cross-cultural research is the only empirical strategy that can actually establish or discount the universalizability of the theory, and for that reason it has been actively pursued. This paper will review the status and current progress of comparative studies of moral judgment. I will attempt to show why the work as a whole can be considered productive, tending toward increased rather than diminished understanding of the moral reasoning of humankind. I will answer each of the following, pivotal questions below with a 'Yes, but ...' argument. Finally, I will try to show how, as comparative research has proceeded to become increasingly elaborated in theoretical intent and sophisticated in design and methods of analysis, it has quietly established its position as a viable

419

field of research. Controversy remains, of course, but it is a fruitful one, and there is a solid core of issues upon which we can reach reasonable consensus.

Questions Central to Establishing the Universality of Kohlberg Moral Stages

1   Is the dilemma interview method a valid way of eliciting the moral judgments of people in other cultures?
2   Is the standard scoring system appropriate and valid for cross-cultural use?
3   Is cognitive-developmental theory useful for understanding psychological development in comparative cultural perspective?

THE VALIDITY OF THE INTERVIEW METHOD

For the moral dilemma methodology to be considered valid for either a particular research study or comparative research in general requires three things. First, the specific dilemmas used in research must be 'real' to the particular people involved, that is, they must raise issues and pit values important to the respondents. This criterion requires either development of new dilemmas appropriate to particular cultural contexts or adequate adaptation of Kohlberg's Standard Interview. Secondly, dilemmas and probing questions must be well translated into respondents' native language, and respondents' answers must be translated without distortion back into the language of scoring. Thirdly, the interview methodology itself must be adequate to the sensitive task of eliciting respondents' 'best', 'highest', and most 'reflective' reasoning about morality (Edwards, 1981). The third criterion is the most subtle and difficult to determine, but it is absolutely critical to the success of the cross-cultural endeavour.

Research to date is uneven in quality according to the first criterion, but recent research can surely be judged generally more satisfactory. Most researchers have opted to adapt Kohlberg's standard stories rather than to create entirely new dilemmas, in order to take advantage of standard scoring systems. This practice assumes that standard stories (if adequately modified in details to fit the local setting) present real and relevant dilemmas to people everywhere because they share certain universal moral concerns, such as affectional, property and authority issues. Such an assumption seems to me a fair one, with a notable exception. True hunter-gatherer societies do not contain headmen or chiefs; nor do they contain formal courts or governing institutions. People in these societies would not be expected to make sense of problems pitting 'law' and 'life', or 'authority' and 'conscience'.

Regarding the first criterion, we can feel most confident about research conducted by investigators who are thoroughly familiar with the cultures studied. We can expect such researchers to have the best sense that the dilemmas used are relevant and adequately adapted. The early research studies (especially Grimley, 1973; Kohlberg, 1969; Saadatmand, 1972) are flawed by serious weakness in terms of trying to cover too much ground (four or five cultural settings each) with little or no ethnographic description provided for each sample and its moral values. In contrast, many of the recent researchers have focused in depth on their own society or cultural group (e.g., Lutz Eckensberger, Germany; Jean-Marc Samson, French-speaking Canada; Y. H. Chern, S. W. Cheng and T. Lei, Taiwan; Muhammed Maqsud, Nigeria; Bindu Parikh, India). In other cases, researchers have gained thorough familiarity of the cultures they studied. For example, Sara Harkness lived as an anthropologist for three years in Western Kenya, and John Snarey provides detailed ethnographic description of the Israeli kibbutz where he based his work. Although these researchers have not generally commented on how well dilemmas have seemed to 'work' in their studies, when they do, their comments have been generally positive. For example, Harkness, Edwards and Super (1981) say, 'All of the men readily accepted this task and became quite involved in giving their judgments' (p. 598).

Only a few researchers have experimented with creating entirely new dilemmas. I found (Edwards, 1975, 1978) that Kenyans were intensely interested and provoked by a new dilemma, called Daniel and the School Fees. However, I did not systematically compare subjects' level of responses to the new versus standard stories. Charles White and colleagues (1978) found in pilot work in the Bahamas that there were no stage differences in response to their new versus the standard dilemmas, so they did not pursue its use. By far the most original approach has been taken by Benjamin Lee (1973, 1976). Lee, an American of Chinese descent, departed completely from the standard stories and developed a series of 'filiality' stories to study moral reasoning in Taiwan. Filiality is a core Chinese value, of course, and Lee reports (personal communication) that subjects, especially those of the older generation, scored higher on filiality than standard stories, because 'fairness' was not an important issue for them. Lee's research illustrates how broadening the interview base to issues outside the core concerns of Westerners can enrich, not undermine, the structural approach to moral development. Further work, in my opinion, should involve quantitative and qualitative comparison of people's responses to original versus standard dilemmas. Such an approach would fully and adequately meet criterion one and lead to an improvement or elaboration of the theory.

Criterion two concerns adequacy of translation. Only one set of German researchers has taken the notable step of translating not only dilemmas but also the scoring manual into another language (Eckensberger, Eckensberger and Reinshagen, 1975–6). Most other researchers have translated the dilemmas into subjects' native language, then translated answers back into English for scoring. Their procedures have probably met at least minimal standards, especially when investigators, such as Jean-Marc Samson, are bilingual, with their first language the target non-English language. They have considered carefully problems of translating ethical terminology. For example, Parikh (1980) states, 'The first 10 translations were checked by a professor of English and a native of Gujarat. A list was made of those words for which it was difficult to get equivalents in English and this list was then discussed with a professor of Gujarati and another of English' (p. 1033).

However, translation is a fascinating subject in its own right that deserves closer inspection and analysis. No researcher, for example, has yet compared responses to a dilemma as translated by several different people, or compared moral maturity scores given to the same interview as translated into English by several different translators. Past researchers, quite rightly perhaps, have been more interested in simply taking the initial step of seeing whether moral judgment scores distribute themselves in a predictable or reasonable way over a target sample of people.

Criterion three concerns whether the interview method is able to elicit the very best and most mature reasoning about moral problems in cultures other than our own. This is an extremely difficult question, and common to research on cognition and social cognition in general, not just Kohlbergian research. The crux of the problem revolves around those groups who seem to show least high-stage reasoning. Findings from a large number of studies (reviewed in Edwards, 1981, 1982) have indicated that moral judgment Stage 5, and perhaps even full-Stage 4, are not found in interviews with preliterate or semiliterate adults who live in relatively 'traditional', small-scale societies, such as isolated peasant or tribal communities. Are these stages really missing, or are the results an artifact of testing bias? There are, in my opinion, good theoretical grounds for thinking that Stage 3 may be the stage at which the judgment of village adults stabilizes. The underlying structure of Stage 3 corresponds well to the social and moral order of a society based on face-to-face relations and a relatively high level of normative consensus (Edwards, 1975, 1981, 1982; Nisan and Kohlberg, 1982). However, it is still important to consider carefully the fundamental problems that exist with eliciting moral reasoning by asking people to reflect upon moral dilemmas.

The moral dilemma interview is best seen as a way to elicit a particular part of people's moral thinking, their 'conscious reflections' rather than intuitive or implicit knowledge about morality (cf. Pool, Shweder and Much, 1983). The interview stimulates people to explain their justifications and to self-reflectively volunteer criteria for decision-making. Do adults in all types of societies have this capacity? 'Yes', we can answer, considering the fact that adults in a wide range of cultural groups studied so far seem to enjoy dilemma discussions. They find it congenial to play the role of what Kenyans called the 'moral elder' and formulate their wisest, most considered opinion about posed, hypothetical problems.

Richard Brandt, a philosopher who many years ago studied Hopi ethical systems, similarly concluded that ethical principles are probably culturally universal. He inferred that 'wrong' had a true ethical meaning to the Hopi: 'If I were normal, impartial, and fully informed, I should feel obligated not to perform X' (Brandt, 1954, p. 109). Although Brandt had to piece together his picture of the Hopi's implicit principles from rather brief answers to formal dilemmas supplemented by many related remarks in other conversations, he believed that his results make 'a highly unfavorable beginning for any person who thinks the "moral" concepts of primitive peoples are quite different from, and vastly more simple and less elevated than our own' (p. 98).

Nevertheless, Kohlberg's highest stages are consistently missing in the interviews from certain groups, and this may relate to the level of formal discourse required for them. John Gibbs (1977, 1979; Gibbs and Widaman, 1982) has put forward the case that Stages 5 and 6 of Kohlberg's system are different from Stages 1 to 4. While Stages 1 to 4 are genuine developmental stages, Gibbs feels that Stages 5 and 6 are something else—namely, 'second-order' thinking about morality, 'meta-ethical reflections' on the decision-criteria constructed at an earlier stage—a kind of thinking made possible primarily by higher education. Gibbs, a close collaborator of Kohlberg, proposes to constructively revise the system by re-labelling Stages 1 and 2 as 'immature', Stages 3 and 4 as fully 'mature', and Stages 5 and 6 as a 'theory-defining level of discourse'. In a somewhat similar vein, Eckensberger and Reinshagen of Germany (1977, 1981), on the basis of theoretical analysis and their reading of the comparative literature, have suggested that Stages

1 to 3 are the basic developmental structures. Stages 4, 4/5 and 5, they speculate, represent horizontal *decalages* of the first three structures into less obvious content areas (social systems rather than concrete others).

Both of these sets of suggestions are very important from a comparative perspective. Although many adults in all societies seem able to step into the 'moral elder' role (Stage 3 or 4) in reflecting upon moral problems, they are not equally able to assume the 'moral theorist' role, as required for Stages 5 and 6. As anthropologist Richard Shweder (1982b) has said, 'Children and most adults in most cultures are not very good at spontaneously articulating the distinctions, ideas, and concepts underlying their sense of morality. Most people do not know how to talk like a moral philosopher' (pp. 58–9). While every cultural environment is indeed 'packed with implicit messages about what is of importance, what is of value, who counts as a person' (Shweder, 1982b, p. 56; also see Read, 1955), nevertheless most people in traditional societies may not be able to discourse at the 'theory-defining level' about what they know and think (Horton, 1968). Still, if critics are correct that the first 3 or 4 stages are the core developmental ones, then we can comfortably conclude that the moral dilemma method has shown itself surprisingly congenial to a wide variety of cultural groups with social systems at very different levels of political and economic complexity.

THE VALIDITY OF THE SCORING SYSTEM

The standard scoring system depends upon the theoretical notion that basic, universal moral judgment structures can be differentiated from highly variable, culturally-specific contents. Cross-cultural data, therefore, should 'fit' the scoring system. Problems can arise from two types of data: (1) data which seem to match most closely the criterion statements of one stage (e.g., Stage 2), but which really seem to flow from the social perspective or underlying structure of another stage (e.g., Stage 3); and (2) data which are 'unscorable', i.e., do not match any of the standard scoring categories. Insofar as empirical data present a serious challenge to either of these two varieties, they suggest that the scoring system is invalid or at least in need of revision.

Finding *any* anomalies, however, is not necessarily bad news for the theory. The scoring system is regarded by cognitive-developmental researchers as a living being, and new data that suggest ways to improve the scoring system can represent good news. The task of constructing and revising scoring categories that adequately distinguish form from content has been a continual one. Hard-to-score data are actually helpful if they suggest concrete ways to improve the scoring system.

Past researchers have reported that their cross-cultural data are generally readily scorable. Inter-rater reliabilities, where determined, have achieved acceptable standards of agreement. Researchers have commonly presented illustrative material to show how the reasoning of their target group had culturally-typical contents yet revealed an easily recognizable underlying structure. Most data labelled as 'unscorable', especially from child subjects, consisted merely of brief 'yes' or 'no' statements, or responses that were too incomplete to reveal their underlying stage (but for an exception, see Tomlinson, 1983).

Recently, however, researchers have begun to report upon and critically examine hard-to-score data from adult subjects and to suggest that these data are problematical. All of these scoring problems refer to ambiguities in Stages 3, 4 and 5. For example, Snarey (1982) and Snarey, Reimer and Kohlberg (1984) analyze difficult-to-score reasoning by Israeli kibbutz respondents. They describe how some subjects blind-scored as Stage 4 or 4/5 were determined by a 'culturally sensitive' scorer to be Stage 5. They conclude that the scoring manual needs to be 'fleshed out with culturally indigenous examples', especially at the higher stages (Snarey, 1982, p. 317). Cheng and Lei (1981) provide examples of Taiwanese reasoning that they thought difficult-to-score: some of the material seemed to be either transitional between 3 and 4, or between 4 and 5, but the categories and distinctions provided in the scoring manual did not allow accurate determination. They concluded, 'More clear delineation of the structure of the stages and better designed probing questions seem to be in need' (p. 16).

In research in Kenya, I too found several examples of hard-to-score interviews. While most of the interviews were readily scored, the most difficult ones were long and complete but arguably either Stage 3 or 4. These were interviews with mature adults who had not attended formal schooling beyond the primary grades. The men were 'community moral leaders', that is, respected elders often called to advise at hearings between local disputants.

To illustrate the way that interviews reflecting a non-Western frame of values and perspective upon society can be difficult to score—and to add to the growing literature seeking to elaborate constructively the scoring system—let me present two examples. The excerpts raise the fundamental question of whether Stage 4 merely requires a rough appreciation of society's need for institutionalized roles, or whether it requires a full-blown understanding of the organizational aspects of a social structure and the operation of a legal system (paraphrase of Cheng and Lei, 1981, p. 16). What the Kenyan elders have is a clear and elaborated vision of fair and reasonable rules for running a prosperous extended family, based on 'unity', 'respect', and 'understanding', key Kenyan traditional values.

From an interview with a Kikuyu man, age 53, with three years of schooling (Edwards, 1975; dilemma is Daniel and the School Fees):

> *Question:* In general, should a grown-up son obey all of his parents' wishes? Why, or why not?
>
> *Answer:* The parents should not authorize Daniel to educate his brother's son. They should only advise him. Daniel has a home to look after since he left his parents, and it's a complete house with one person as head, not two. So he should not obey his parents but should consider their advices.
>
> *Question:* Is it more important for Daniel to maintain harmonious relations with his wife, or with his brother and parents? Why?
>
> *Answer:* Once one is married, we say in Kikuyu society that, 'He is out of his parents' hands. . . .' The husband will be the Chairman and the wife the Treasurer, and as such she will control the resources. That is why Daniel's wife wants [to use the family money] to put her son in school.
>
> *Question:* Would you condemn Daniel if he just moved away to the city and did not help his brother's son?
>
> *Answer:* We cannot condemn Daniel . . . because it's right. He can only carry with him one home, not two. He can offer help if he can in other ways. If we draw a picture like this, we see that there are different generations being founded. Daniel is now very far from Kamau [his older brother who put Daniel himself through school] . . . .

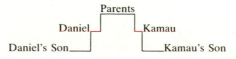

From an interview with a Kipsigis man, age 55, unschooled (Harkness, Edwards and Super, 1981; dilemma is adaptation of Joe story).

> *Question:* Should James refuse to give his father the money?
> *Answer:* If his father is a squanderer, then he shouldn't be given. But if he keeps it well, the father is like a bank, and he should keep it.
> *Question:* Should the father always direct the son?
> *Answer:* For the son to refuse to take his father's advice shows that he is not well cared for . . . But when you [a father] convince him [your son] by telling him, 'Do this sort of thing because this will earn us our living. You didn't do it this time, but do it next time,' then the child will comply since you did not command (shout at) him . . . and so both of you will be in good unity and understanding of each other.
> *Question:* Which is worse, for a father to break his promise or for a son?
> *Answer:* [If the father breaks his word] it will cause hatred because the son will be angry, saying, 'I wanted to follow my own intentions, but my father cheated: he permitted me and then refused me. Now I don't want to hear more of his words. He can't love me and is unable to protect me.' So it is bad. [However], the one for the son is worse. Imagine a child disobeying my own words, is he really normal? . . . Rules are mine and I want him to follow, e.g. 'Do this thing to earn you a living', as I did follow my father's rules also . . . Father's bad deeds are revealed when he does not care for his children . . . That man is like a drunkard whose children do not sleep at home because he drives them away when not sober. The man does not have rules which work and so it is bad. But if he has good functioning rules, he is able to keep his family. The maize will be growing because of his good work. Then it is clear that his family is well looked after. . . .

In conclusion, there seems a clear consensus that the scoring system has provided a useful tool for analyzing cross-cultural data. However, subtle distinctions between the higher stages need to be further clarified, and form and content need to be further differentiated to broaden definitions of stages or levels beyond Stage 3.

THE USEFULNESS OF THE THEORY FOR EXPLAINING HUMAN DEVELOPMENT

As explained in the earlier sections of this paper, recent years have seen the accumulation of many studies focused on groups other than the dominant majority culture of the USA. These studies allow us to consider our final question, whether cognitive-developmental theory has proven useful for understanding individual development within or between cultural groups.

The *within* question is surely less controversial and includes two parts. First, do the central claims of the theory about development (especially invariance of sequence) hold up in cross-cultural studies? Second, do specific examinations of moral judgment in relationship to experiential or background variables lead to increased understanding of the processes facilitating development? We cannot examine each of these questions in detail, but we can indicate the general shape of an answer.

In my recent survey, I found the following studies focused on groups from outside the mainstream US culture (also see review in Snarey, 1982):

The Americas
    USA   Alaskan Eskimo (Saxe, 1970)
              Puerto Rican (Pacheco-Maldonado, 1972)

Canada   Germanic Hutterite (Saadatmand, 1972)
　　　　　French (Marchand-Jodoin and Samson, 1982; Samson, 1983)
　　　　　English (Sullivan, 1975; Sullivan and Beck, 1975; Sullivan,
　　　　　　McCullough and Stager, 1979; Sullivan and Quarter, 1972)
Bahamas   (White, 1975, 1977; White, Bushnell and Regnemer, 1978)
Guatemala   (Saadatmand, 1972)
Honduras   (Gorsuch and Barnes, 1973)
Mexico   (Kohlberg, 1969)

Asia
India   (Parikh, 1975, 1980; Saraswathi, Saxena and Sundaresan, 1977)
Iran   (Saadatmand, 1972)
Israel   Kohlberg, with Bar Yam, 1971b; Snarey, 1982; Snarey, Reimer
　　　　and Kohlberg, 1984)
Hong Kong   (Grimley, 1973, 1974)
Japan   (Grimley, 1973, 1974)
Taiwan   (Cheng and Lei, 1981; Chern, 1978; Kohlberg, 1969; Lee, 1973,
　　　　1976)
Thailand   (Batt, 1974, 1975)
Turkey   (Nisan and Kohlberg, 1982; Turiel, Edwards and Kohlberg,
　　　　1978)

Africa
Kenya   (Edwards, 1974, 1975, 1978; Harkness, Edwards and Super,
　　　　1981)
Nigeria   (Maqsud, 1976, 1977a, 1977b, 1979, 1982)
Zambia   (Grimley, 1973, 1974)

Europe
France   (O'Connor, 1974, 1980)
Finland   (Helkama, 1981)
Germany   (Eckensberger, 1983; Gielen, 1982; Villenave and Eckensber-
　　　　ger, 1982)
Great Britain   (Grimley, 1973, 1974; O'Connor, 1974, 1980; Simon and
　　　　　Ward, 1973; Simpson and Graham, 1971; Tomlinson,
　　　　　1983; Weinreich, 1977)

Australia and Oceania
New Zealand   (Moir, 1974)

Two types of societies still represent critical missing cases: (1) foraging (hunter-gatherer) societies, which lack social classes or hierarchy and also formal political and legal institutions; and (2) societies such as those of Eastern Europe, USSR, and Peoples' Republic of China, which are complex nation-states but based on non-capitalist economies. A further serious weakness of the literature is that the only longitudinal cases in the above list are from the Bahamas, French Canada, Israel, Great Britain and Turkey. The great majority of studies are cross-sectional, due to the enormous expense and difficulty of conducting longitudinal work.

The proposition of invariant sequence requires that stage development be stepwise and progressive, with stage regressions and stage skippings no greater than expected by chance (measurement error). All of the cross-sectional studies have found average moral maturity and/or upper-stage-range to increase with age during the childhood and adolescent years (with the exception of the Hutterite sample). No studies have found any 'missing' stages between the lowest and highest stages present in a sample. Furthermore, the longitudinal studies (with the probable exception of Tomlinson's, 1983, British sample) have supported these conclusions by indicating no significant amounts of stage regression over time. Thus, while the available data cannot positively demonstrate invariant sequence, taken together they strongly suggest that development change is generally gradual and positive throughout the childhood and adolescent years, in a wide variety of cultural groups.

Most investigators, naturally, conducted their research with broader questions in mind than merely invariant sequence. Taking advantage of the natural range of variation in social life worldwide, they have been able to gain increased leverage on understanding experiential influences. For example, a number of researchers from the list above have been able to show that the following experiential factors relate positively to moral judgment. (*Note:* the dates of the studies are provided only when necessary for the reader):

socioeconomic status (Grimley; Kohlberg with Bar Yam; Nisan and Kohlberg; Simpson and Graham; Turiel *et al.*);

residential factors, e.g., living in city or village, or city versus kibbutz (Gorsuch and Barnes; Nisan and Kohlberg; Snarey; Turiel *et al.*);

educational level (Batt; Edwards, 1975);

school experiences (Edwards, 1978; Maqsud, all studies; Marchand-Jodoin and Samson; Sullivan, 1975; Sullivan and Beck);

parental discipline, warmth or identification (Parikh; Saadatmand; Simpson and Graham).

These studies taken together converge to suggest that moral judgment level is stimulated by at least three general types of experiences, that increase: (1) an individual's contact with a *diversity of personal or cultural values*; (2) an individual's ability to *reason in formal or school-like ways* about moral issues; and (3) an individual's tendency to *take as one's reference group a complex society*. The research allows a general consensus that conditions that lead to development in one group are comparable to conditions that lead to development in other groups.

Finally, we return to the issue with which this paper opened: how valid is Kohlberg's theory for comparing moral development (and moral adequacy) *between* people of different cultural groups?

Even on this controversial issue a certain consensus may be achievable. It is noteworthy that in response to criticism, Kohlberg has revised his own earlier position. He now states (in Kohlberg, Levine and Hewer, 1983):

> We do not believe that the comparison of one culture to another in terms of moral development is a theoretically useful strategy for the growth of scientific knowledge.... It is difficult to understand what a valid concept of 'comparative moral worth of culture' might be, but in any case such a concept could not be established on the basis of a comparison of means on our moral judgment assessment scale. There is no direct way in which group averages can be translated into statements of the relative moral worth of groups (p. 113).

In other words, cross-cultural differences have nothing to do after all with the relative moral worth or adequacy of moral judging. Moral judgment stages, from a cross-cultural point of view, are simply not achievements for which higher is necessarily better. Rather, Kohlberg's theory and methods offer just one useful way to study developmental growth in wisdom or 'conscious reflectiveness' in moral decision-making. Certainly they do not begin to encompass all that we would like to know in terms of understanding how human beings across the spectrum of world cultures develop in the capacity to make moral choices. Nevertheless, Kohlberg's theory and methods have surely generated a productive line of comparative research that has become more sophisticated, multidimensional and theoretically lively over time.

REFERENCES

Batt, H. W. (1974) 'Obligation and decision in Thai administration: From patrimonial to rational-legal bureaucracy'. Unpublished doctoral dissertation, State University of New York at Albany.

Batt, H. W. (1975) 'Thai conceptions of justice on Kohlberg's moral development scale', Unpublished manuscript, Department of Political Science, State University of New York at Albany.

Bloom, A. H. (1977) 'Two dimensions of moral reasoning: Social principledness and social humanism in cross-cultural perspective', *The Journal of Social Psychology*, 101, pp. 29–44.

Brandt, R. B. (1954) *Hopi Ethics*, Chicago, Ill., University of Chicago Press, [Midway Reprint, 1974].

Buck-Morss, S. (1975) 'Socio-economic bias in Piaget's theory and its implications for cross-cultural studies', *Human Development*, 18, pp. 35–49.

Cheng, S. W. and Lei, T. (1981) 'Performance of Taiwanese students on Kohlberg's moral judgment inventory', Unpublished manuscript, National Taiwan University.

Chern, Y. H. (1978) 'Moral judgment development in Chinese [Taiwanese] adolescents', *Journal of Education*, Kuashung Normal College Press.

Colby, A., Kohlberg, L., Gibbs, J. and Lieberman, M. (1983) 'A longitudinal study of moral judgment', *Monographs of the Society for Research in Child Development*, 48, Serial No. 200.

Eckensberger, L. H. (1981) 'On a structural model of the development of stages of moral development', in L. Oppenheimer (Ed.), *Action Theoretical Approaches to (Developmental) Psychology*, Proceedings of the Symposium: Action Theory and Developmental Psychology, Amsterdam.

Eckensberger, L. H. (1983) 'Research on moral development', *German Journal of Psychology*, 7, pp. 195–244.

Eckensberger, L. H. and Reinshagen, H. (1977) 'Cross-cultural research as a touchstone for Kohlberg's stage theory of moral development', Paper presented to the biennial conference of the ISSBD, Pavia, Italy.

Eckensberger, L. H., Eckensberger, U.S. and Reinshagen, H. (1975–6) 'Kohlberg's Interview zum moralischen Urteil Teil I–Teil IV', *Arbeiten der Fachrichtung Psychologie*, 31–34, Universitaet des Saarlandes.

Edwards, C. P. (1974) 'The effect of experience on moral development: Results from Kenya', Doctoral dissertation, Harvard Graduate School of Education, Ann Arbor, Mich., University Microfilms, 1975, 75–16860.

Edwards, C. P. (1975) 'Societal complexity and moral development: A Kenyan study', *Ethos*, 3, pp. 505–27.

Edwards, C. P. (1978) 'Social experience and moral judgment in Kenyan young adults', *Journal of Genetic Psychology*, 133, pp. 19–29.

Edwards, C. P. (1981) 'The comparative study of the development of moral judgment and reasoning', in R. H. Munroe, R. L. Munroe and B. B. Whiting, *Handbook of Cross-Cultural Human Development*, New York, Garland Press.

Edwards, C. P. (1982) 'Moral development in comparative cultural perspective', in D. Wagner and H. Stevenson (Eds.), *Cultural Perspectives on Child Development*, San Francisco, W. H. Freeman.

Gibbs, J. C. (1977) 'Kohlberg's stages of moral judgment: A constructive critique', *Harvard Educational Review*, 47, pp. 43–61.

Gibbs, J. C. (1979) 'Kohlberg's moral stage theory: A Piagetian revision', *Human Development*, 22, pp. 89–112.

Gibbs, J. C. and Widaman, K. F., with A. Colby (1982) *Social Intelligence: Measuring the Development of Sociomoral Reflection*, Englewood Cliffs, N.J., Prentice-Hall.

Gielen, U. P. (1985) 'Moral reasoning in radical and non-radical German students', *Behavior Science Research*, (in press).

Gorsuch, R. L. and Barnes, M. L. (1973) 'Stages of ethical reasoning and moral norms of Carib youths', *Journal of Cross-Cultural Psychology*, 4, pp. 283–301.

Grimley, L. (1973) 'A cross-cultural study of moral development', Unpublished doctoral dissertation, Kent State University.

Grimley, L. (1974) 'Moral development in different nations', *School Psychology Digest*, 3, pp. 43–51.

Harkness, S., Edwards, C. P. and Super, C. M. (1981) 'Social roles and moral reasoning: A case study in a rural African community', *Developmental Psychology*, 17, pp. 595–603.

Helkama, K. (1981) 'Toward a cognitive-developmental theory of attribution of responsibility', Unpublished doctoral dissertation, Helsinki University.

Horton, R. (1968) 'Neo-Tylorianism: Sound sense or sinister prejudice?' *Man*, 3, pp. 625–34.

Kohlberg, L. (1969) 'Stage and sequence: The cognitive-developmental approach to socialization', in D. Goslin (Ed.), *Handbook of Socialization*, New York, Rand McNally, pp. 347–480.

Kohlberg, L. (1971a) 'From is to ought: How to commit the naturalistic fallacy and get away with it in the study of moral development', in T. Mischel (Ed.), *Cognitive Development and Epistemology*, New York, Academic Press, pp. 23–92.

Kohlberg, L., with Bar-Yam, M. (1971b) 'Cognitive-developmental theory and the practice of collective education', in M. Wolins and M. Gottesman (Eds.), *Group Care: An Israeli Approach*, New York, Gordon and Breach, pp. 342–79.

Kohlberg, L., Levine, C. and Hewer, A. (1983) *Moral Stages: A Current Formulation and a Response to Critics*, New York, Karger, Contributions to Human Development, Vol. 10.

Lee, B. (1973) 'A cognitive-developmental approach to filiality development', Unpublished master's dissertation, Committee on Human Development, University of Chicago.

Lee, B. (1976) 'Fairness and filiality: A cross-cultural cultural account', Paper presented at the annual meeting of the American Anthropological Association, Washington, D. C., November.

Maqsud, M. (1976) 'The effects of different educational environments on moral development of Nigerian children belonging to various tribes', Unpublished doctoral dissertation, University of London.

Maqsud, M. (1977a) 'The influence of social heterogeneity and sentimental credibility on moral judgments of Nigerian Muslim adolescents', *Journal of Cross-Cultural Psychology*, 8, pp. 113–22.

Maqsud, M. (1977b) 'Moral reasoning of Nigerian and Pakistani Muslim adolescents', *Journal of Moral Education*, 7, pp. 40–9.

Maqsud, M. (1979) 'Cultural influences on transition in the development of moral reasoning in Nigerian boys', *The Journal of Social Psychology*, 108, pp. 151–9.

Maqsud, M. (1982) 'Effects of Nigerian children's group discussion on their moral progression', *Journal of Moral Education*, 11, 3.

Marchand-Jodoin, L. and Samson, J. M. (1982) 'Kohlberg's theory applied to the moral and sexual development of adults', *Journal of Moral Education*, 11, pp. 247–58.

Moir, D. J. (1974) 'Egocentrism and the emergence of conventional morality in preadolescent girls', *Child Development*, 45, pp. 299–304.

Nisan, M. and Kohlberg, L. (1982) 'Universality and variation in moral judgment: A longitudinal and cross-sectional study in Turkey', *Child Development*, 53, pp. 865–76.

O'Connor, R. E. (1974) 'Political activism and moral reasoning: Political and apolitical students in Great Britain and France', *British Journal of Political Science*, 4, pp. 53–78.

O'Connor, R. E. (1980) 'Parental sources and political consequences of levels of moral reasoning among European university students', in R. W. Wilson and G. J. Schochet (Eds.), *Moral Development and Politics*, New York, Praeger.

Pacheco-Maldonado, A. (1972) 'A cognitive-developmental study of moral judgments in Puerto Rican children', Unpublished doctoral dissertation, University of New York at Albany.

Parikh, B. (1975) 'Moral judgment development and its relation to family environmental factors in Indian and American urban upper-middle class families', Unpublished doctoral dissertation, Department of Special Education, Boston University.

Parikh, B. (1980) 'Development of moral judgment and its relation to family environmental factors in Indian and American families', *Child Development*, 51, pp. 1030–9.

Pool, D. L., Shweder, R. A. and Much, N. C. (1983) 'Culture as a cognitive system: Differentiated rule understandings in children and other savages', in E. T. Higgins, D. N. Ruble and W. W. Hartup, *Social Cognition and Social Development: A Sociocultural Perspective*, New York, Cambridge University Press.

Read, K. E. (1955) 'Morality and the concept of the person among the Gahuku-Gama', *Oceania*, 25, pp. 233–82.

Saadatmand, B. (1972) 'Cross-cultural investigation of the influences of parents, culture, and age on the moral reasoning of children', Unpublished dictoral dissertation, Brigham Young University.

Samson, J. M. (1983) 'Sexual and general moral reasoning of French Canadian adolescents', Paper presented at the annual meeting of the society for Cross-Cultural Research, Washington, D.C., February.

Saraswathi, T. S., Saxena, K. and Sundaresan, J. (1977) 'Development of moral judgment in Indian children between ages eight to twelve years', in Y. H. Poortinga (Ed.), *Basic Problems in Cross-Cultural Psychology*, Amsterdam, Sweets and Zeitlinger, pp. 168–77.

Saxe, G. (1970) 'The development of moral judgment: A cross-cultural study of Kalskagagmuit Eskimos', Unpublished manuscript, University of California, Berkeley.

Shweder, R. A. (1982a) 'Liberalism as destiny', *Contemporary Psychology*, 27, pp. 421–4.

Shweder, R. A. (1982b) 'Beyond self-constructed knowledge: The study of culture and morality', *Merrill-Palmer Quarterly*, 28, pp. 41–69.

Simon, A. and Ward, L. O. (1973) 'Variables influencing pupils' responses on the Kohlberg schema of moral development', *Journal of Moral Education*, 2, pp. 283–6.

Simpson, A. L. and Graham, D. (1971) 'The development of moral judgment, emotion, and behavior in British adolescents', Unpublished manuscript, University of Durham.

Simpson, E. L. (1974) 'Moral development research: A case study of scientific cultural bias', *Human Development*, 17, pp. 81–106.

Snarey, J. R. (1982) 'The social and moral development of kibbutz founders and sabras: A cross-sectional and longitudinal cross-cultural study', Unpublished doctoral dissertation, Graduate School of Education, Harvard University.

Snarey, J. R., Reimer, J. and Kohlberg, L. (1985) 'The development of social-moral reasoning among kibbutz adolescents: A longitudinal cross-cultural study', *Developmental Psychology*, 21 (1), pp. 3–17.

Sullivan, E. V. (1977) 'A study of Kohlberg's structural theory of moral development. A critique of liberal social science ideology', *Human Development*, 20, pp. 352–76.

Sullivan, E. V., with Beck, C., Joy, M. and Pagliuso, S. (1975) *Moral Learning: Some Findings, Issues, and Questions*, New York, Paulist Press.

Sullivan, E. V. and Beck, C. M. (1975) 'Moral education in a Canadian setting', *Phi Delta Kappan*, 56, pp. 697–701.

Sullivan, E. V. and Quarter, J. (1972) 'Psychological correlates of certain postconventional moral types: A perspective on hybrid types', *Journal of Personality*, 40, pp. 149–61.

Sullivan, E. V., McCullough, G. and Stager, M. A. (1970) 'A developmental study of the relationship between conceptual, ego, and moral development', *Child Development*, 41, pp. 399–411.

Tomlinson, P. (1983) 'Six years in the moral lives of some British adolescents', Paper presented to the psychology section of the Annual Meeting of the British Association for the Advancement of Science, University of Sussex, August.

Turiel, E., Edwards, C. P. and Kohlberg, L. (1978) 'Moral development in Turkish children, adolescents, and young adults', *Journal of Cross-cultural Psychology*, 9, pp. 75–86.

Villenave-Cremer, S. and Eckensberger, L. H. (1982) 'On the role of affective processes in moral judgment performances', Paper presented to the International Symposium on Moral Education, Fribourg, Switzerland, August-September.

Weinreich, H. (1977) 'Some consequences of replicating Kohlberg's original moral development study on a British sample', *Journal of Moral Education*, 7, pp. 32–9.

White, C. B. (1975) 'Moral development in Bahamian school children: A cross-cultural examination of Kohlberg's stages of moral reasoning', *Developmental Psychology*, 11, pp. 535–6.

White, C. B. (1977) 'Moral reasoning in Bahamian and United States elders: Cross-national comparison of Kohlberg's theory of moral development', Unpublished manuscript, University of Texas at Dallas.

White, C. B., Bushnell, N. and Regnemer, J. L. (1978) 'Moral development in Bahamian school children: A three-year examination of Kohlberg's stages of moral development', *Developmental Psychology*, 14, pp. 58–65.

27. Moral Maturity in Socio-Cultural Perspective: Are Kohlberg's Stages Universal?

IAN VINE

Cognitive-developmental analyses of ontogenetic processes characteristically stress the 'psychic unity' of humankind, in contrast to both empiricists' *tabula rasa* views and those nativist accounts which emphasize genetically specified individual differences. In avoiding the extremes of biological and environmental determinism, Piagetian 'genetic epistemology' has considerable appeal—so long as it can succeed in showing that self-constructed mental systems do control human action, and develop through dialectically creative interactions between the environment and an actively adapting human agent seeking to make sense of experience (e.g., Piaget, 1972).

The biggest challenge for the theory is to explain how the process of self-creation of mental structures can take forms which are in essence humanly universal, despite superficially substantial cultural, subcultural, familial and idiosyncratic variations in the raw materials with which our environments provide us. In this chapter I shall take for granted that in principle this challenge can be met, and thus confront the search for structural universals in moral thinking on its own terms. Although Piaget (1932) pioneered this endeavour, it has been Kohlberg and his group who have extended, formalized and tested cognitive-developmental moral theory on a significant scale—paying particular attention to predictions about uniformity and variability in development. Originally he proposed a unique and invariant, step-wise sequence of stages in moral reasoning, through which any individual should in principle pass, eventually attaining the capacity for fully equilibrated, principled thought, capable of generating ethically 'correct' resolutions of the most fundamental kinds of moral dilemmas. The principles embodied in the fully rational, cognitive-operational structures of Stage 6 thought would be formally ideal and impartially objective ones of universal justice and respect for individual rights (Kohlberg, 1969, 1971).

Kohlberg was well aware that individuals, groups and whole societies may not

431

in fact share these cardinal values or act in accord with them. He insisted that many variations concerned criteria for personal virtue, or the specific content of moral norms, rather than the structure of moral argument; and he sought to specify his stages, and to score responses to the dilemmas in his Moral Judgment Interview (MJI), in ways which would overcome confounding factors. But he also acknowledged that early cross-cultural research with the MJI did suggest that not only was the modal age for any particular stage-transition variable—so was the ceiling-level attained in adulthood. This was explained in terms of variations in the availability of the experiences necessary to stimulate development by creating moral conflicts which demanded more equilibrated reasoning for their resolution.

Inevitably, Kohlberg's theory attracted criticism on several counts—empirical, theoretical and moral-philosophical. In particular, because it saw Stage 6 as more 'morally adequate' as well as formally more advanced than others, and as embodying specific substantive principles as its moral priorities, its 'ethical objectivism' seemed highly partisan. By taking the rationalistic, individualistic, 'liberal-democratic' values of the white, male, American intellectual as distinctively mature, it was open to the charge of ideological and ethnocentric bias, arising from a failure to see moral judgment in a sufficiently broad socio-cultural context or to appreciate non-formalist ethical philosophies (e.g., Weinreich-Haste and Locke, 1983).

In response to such critiques, Kohlberg has progressively revised both the theory and the scoring criteria for identifying an individual's moral stage. Some changes have certainly reduced the force of earlier objections, while others have merely introduced new ambiguities and problems, or do not appear to meet the critics' points. Now that Stage 6 is apparently so rare that scoring criteria cannot be safely provided, and that development is held to continue well into adulthood, old data that have not been properly re-scored are of little value. Likewise the claim that Stage 6 is more 'morally adequate' has been distinguished from the theory of development, in which the stage now figures only as an hypothetical ideal. Whether these changes in any way undermine the rationale of the theory as a whole remains to be explored. Such issues are more properly the province of other chapters in this volume, and cannot be pursued here—although some general problems with the theory and evidence will need to be alluded to in the present context (cf. Vine, 1983a).

In the following discussion I shall rely almost exclusively upon recent Kohlbergian writings which embody the theoretical revisions, and on research using the current 'standard issue' scoring procedures (Colby, 1978; Kohlberg, 1976; Kohlberg et al., 1977; Kohlberg, Levine and Hewer, 1983a).[1] I shall also identify stages by reference to the most differentiated, thirteen-category system whenever appropriate, since most subjects predominantly make use of two adjacent stages of reasoning, one 'major' and one 'minor' (e.g., Stage 3(4)), according to Colby et al. (1983). I shall not refer to the A and B substage distinction, since so little research using this has so far been reported.

THE POSTULATE OF UNIVERSALITY

By any standard the claim that some central aspects of moral development are found universally is a remarkably bold one. If what I shall call the *universality postulate* can be adequately operationalized and confirmed through intra-cultural and cross-cultural research, it will undoubtedly constitute a powerful source of support for the cognitive-developmental theory as a whole. If the stages of moral reasoning are in fact defined and scored in ways independent of their normative 'content', and do truly reflect operational structures, then the theory must predict that persons will progress developmentally through the same stage sequence, without stage-skipping or regression, irrespective of the particular moral ideology of their cultural background. Although most data, particularly relating to the higher stages, have come from predominantly middle-class, white, American males, MJI responses are supposed to yield an unbiased measure of a subject's structural capacities. Thus any failure to find the relevant empirical patterns in other cultures and subcultures may bring into question the basic postulates of cognitive-developmental moral theory.

However, significant limitations upon what Kohlberg's particular moral universality postulate entails must be noted before proceeding to consider the evidence itself. It is explicitly restricted to a description of the formal cognitive properties of moral reasoning and judgments; and because Kohlberg sees the core of rational morality as a set of abstract principles for dealing with the just resolution of conflicts of individuals' interests, it is essentially a theory of justice-reasoning (Kohlberg, 1971, 1981; Kohlberg *et al.*, 1983a). (The relationships between a 'justice and rights ethic' and an 'ethic of caring and welfare' will be discussed briefly in a later section.) But the theory also makes development through the stages contingent upon the attainment of certain social role-taking capacities which cannot readily be developed without appropriate kinds of social experience (Kohlberg, 1976). Thus cultural background is expected to influence not just substantive moral values and the integrity with which judgments are in fact acted upon; it should affect the age norms for any particular transition between stages, and the stage-ceiling reached in adulthood.

This means that the universality being claimed is only for a dispositional capacity to develop through the stage sequence providing that one's social environment offers relevant 'affordances' or opportunities for growth. So long as the ordinal sequence is not violated, strict uniformity of cultures in their typical patterning of stages need not be predicted. This important restriction upon the universality postulate of course makes for considerable complexities when assessing the evidence for it or against it. Various kinds of criteria have been proposed as appropriate to demonstrating psycho-social universals of differing types (Brislin, 1983; Lonner, 1980; Van de Vijver and Poortinga, 1982). For Kohlberg's theory the purported universals are systematic (involving structurally linked features of responses to a range of moral problems), and sequential (involving invariant temporal transformations of operational structures). Thus the appropriate method of inquiry must involve longitudinal study, using a representative range of dilemmas and rather careful probing of subjects' reasons for their moral judgments to each of these. In principle the 'clinical' interview method of MJI administration can meet these criteria, and reveal the dynamic patterns in question.

Some caution is nevertheless required with quantitative comparisons of 'global' stage scores (GSSs), or the weighted 'moral maturity' scores (MMSs) often presented to take account of any spread of responses across more than one stage. (Typically the products of the stage number and the proportion of responses at that stage are summed.) Van de Vijver and Poortinga (1982) note that 'scalar equivalence' or 'strict' universality of measured constructs can rarely be demon-strated, as the same metric and scale-origin must apply to data from all cultures. Even to test for 'functionally equivalent' or 'weak' universals, which only require an ordinal level of measurement, construct-validity of the measure must be demon-strated in each culture. If the 'culture-alien' use of Kohlberg's instrument outside the USA is not to introduce ethnocentrically biased scores, a high degree of 'convergent construct-validity' is undoubtedly demanded (Irvine and Carroll, 1980)—and certainly not all cross-cultural reports have considered this issue in any detail.

The psychometric properties attributable to MJI scores are somewhat con-troversial (Broughton, 1978; Kurtines and Greif, 1974); but it seems unwise to regard GSSs as better than ordinal measures. This is adequate for evaluating the hypothesis of step-wise stage progression by longitudinal testing; but it necessitates great caution in making cross-sectional and especially cross-cultural comparisons of the means and distributions of scores at a given age. It would be excessively conservative to object to all inferences drawn from comparisons of groups' profiles—say, where means differ by a full stage or more; but it is equally clear that small quantitative differences between MMS averages are essentially not interpret-able, particularly in the cross-cultural context where some degree of quantitative incommensurability of scores is practically inevitable.

Unfortunately, even well-conducted longitudinal research with the MJI faces problems in deciding what would count as strong evidence for Kohlberg's theory. The universality postulate must predict that all persons whose general cognitive development has not been handicapped by organismic abnormalities will have a dispositional capacity to develop the judgmental competence appropriate to each stage in turn—given the relevant kinds of stimulation. Since no theory of something so complex as moral reasoning is likely to succeed in specifying *all* the determining factors, we should perhaps not be disturbed by the occasional finding of a deviant individual or culture that does not follow the stage sequence perfectly. The problem is that if, as appears to be the case, whole social classes and societies are deprived of the stimulation required to reach the higher stages, then the claim that their members *could* have attained them in the right circumstances is counter-factual. Even if all data are compatible with the ideal stage sequence, a failure to find full progression to Stage 5 in a wide range of cultures must leave the status of the higher stages in doubt. If a culture's mature adults reach a relatively invariant ceiling below Stage 5, that finding is open to several possible explanations.

The solution to this difficulty is clear in principle. If persons from specifiably deprived backgrounds can be provided with the relevant stimulation subsequently, and they then complete the stage progression, the theory may be given powerful support. But in practice large-scale social engineering within other cultures for the sake of testing theories is clearly not feasible, even if it were morally defensible. More limited 'training' studies of the kind appropriate for assessing hypotheses about dispositional capacities in general can be of some value (Brislin, 1983); but the use of these in moral development research requires caution when what is sought is actually self-initiated transformation of underlying structures, rather than rote learning of responses. If small-scale social interventions like group discussion of moral dilemmas are to produce real structural changes, individuals probably need to be on the verge of a change already; and in this case only small shifts can readily be brought about. The final possibility involves the study of migrants who actually change residence to cultures where the conditions facilitating full develop-ment are available. Here we may reasonably expect that if the universality postulate is true they will progress through the full sequence, at least in some cases. The snag here is that they may at the same time internalize the particular ideology of the test's home culture; so such evidence may not fully remove the possibility that the test is ethnocentrically biased. Nevertheless, in not seeking evidence from migrants, Kohlbergians have overlooked a distinctive source of support for the universality postulate.

To conclude this section brief reference must be made to the several potential sources of bias which may be attributable to MJI administration and scoring in 'test-alien' cultures. Methodological difficulties in cross-cultural work generally are well-documented (e.g., Triandis and Berry, 1980); and although bias can be minimized it can probably never be eliminated fully from any testing instrument. The various pitfalls of interviewing in unfamiliar cultures that can produce mislead-ing answers (Pareek and Rao, 1980), the problems of translating questions and responses (Brislin, 1980), and particularly the lack of stimulus equivalence or the incongruent functioning of the constructs being tapped (Irvine and Carroll, 1980), may all introduce errors that go undetected. There are also particular problems of representative sampling within alien cultures, and of the need to sample cultures themselves sufficiently widely to maximize relevant variances; and there is the general problem of balancing 'emic' and 'etic' research perspectives (Berry, 1980). In the case of the MJI in particular, we may say that the etic concern to tap a universal human competence using standard dilemmas may be subverted if there is insufficient emic sensitivity to how a culture's members may be unaccustomed to deploying that competence in artificial testing situations, or may define and interpret the situation and its stimuli in unpredicted and etically inappropriate ways.

This catalogue of difficulties has not been invoked in order to deny the possibility of establishing Kohlberg's universality postulate within reasonable confidence-limits, but only as a reminder of the obstacles to be surmounted. Great care is needed in adapting an instrument so subtle as the MJI for valid use in test-alien cultures. Even within its home culture, repeated refinement of the scoring methods has been necessary in seeking to separate formal aspects of reasoning from the substantive content of the norms which are brought to bear upon the dilemmas (Colby, 1978). It seems clear that translating and otherwise adapting dilemmas, interviewing and scoring responses, must all be done by persons intimately familiar with the culture being tested. As with other research on cognitive structures (Nyiti, 1982), it is probably essential to use probe-questions in a flexible way. For this reason, plus of course their restriction to literate cultures, it is doubtful whether simplified written versions of Kohlberg's test, like the Defining Issues Test (Rest, Davison and Robbins, 1978), can be validly used for cross-cultural comparisons.

Perhaps the major demand for a theory which stands accused of being biased in favour of a particular culture's values is that there should be 'hologeistic' or whole-world sampling of cultures before the universality postulate is pronounced as confirmed (Naroll, Michik and Naroll, 1980). We know that in pre-literate, small-scale, non-Westernized societies there is a strong reliance upon traditional values and informal conciliation procedures in resolving social conflicts of interest, as well as a tendency towards more collectivist ideologies and less hierarchical organization. Since the social conditions stimulating cognitive disequilibrium and subsequent stage progression remain relatively vague within Kohlberg's theory, it is clearly essential to study such cultures both intensively and fairly extensively—not just to test the universality postulate, but also to refine the theory as a whole.

CROSS-CULTURAL FINDINGS USING THE MJI

Kohlberg (1969) claimed support for the universality postulate from his briefly reported cross-sectional data, obtained at ages 10, 13 and 16 years from middle-class, urban boys in Taiwan and Mexico, and from their age-peers in 'isolated villages' in Turkey and Yucatan (Mexico). The results were interpreted as showing the similarity of the urban samples to American subjects, in that older boys made more use of higher stages and less use of lower ones—although Stage '5' responses were much higher by age 16 in the home culture of the test (roughly 30 per cent, versus 10 per cent in the alien cultures).[2] The villagers showed negligible signs of 'postconventional' reasoning by this age, and at least a third of responses were still 'preconventional' (Stages '1' and '2'). In the light of the later scoring revisions negligible weight can be attached to these data, as the earlier methods tend to over-score the higher stages.

Subsequently some dozens of studies in other cultures have been reported, mostly getting results compatible with the universality postulate. However, few of these have been carried out by researchers outside Kohlberg's own research group; most have only involved cross-sectional samples; and very few have used the current scoring procedures. Despite the paucity of data meeting all the relevant methodological requirements, Kohlberg continues to claim optimistically that there has been 'cross-cultural verification of the universality of stage sequence' (Kohlberg *et al.*, 1983a, p. 56), and that 'while moral behaviors or customs seem to vary from culture to culture, underneath these variations in custom there seem to be universal kinds of judging or valuing' (p. 123). As will become clear, although recent research findings are broadly compatible with the universality postulate, they in no sense constitute a sufficiently sensitive test of it. On a sceptical reading the very incomplete or indirect evidence for the universality of the developmental progression could be otherwise interpreted. Stage-score profiles based upon the use of the MJI in test-alien cultures are also basically compatible with the view that subjects may be responding to dilemmas which do not tap their own predominant moral concerns, in ways which are artificially constrained by aspects of the testing situation and are inappropriately assessed in abstraction from their local normative context. Thus testing may fail to do justice to the subjects' actual competence in moral reasoning, particularly of more abstract and 'principled' kinds.

Some critics have objected to the results of cross-cultural comparisons in similar terms (e.g., Baumrind, 1978; Simpson, 1974). Without assuming that such problems are insoluble, it is at least difficult to dispute one major objection brought by Simpson: 'If principled reasoning as defined by Kohlberg does not occur in some cultures, for whatever reason, then one third of the paradigm is missing and the assumption that, under different conditions, these stages *would* appear in these groups is not necessarily warranted. This is a researchable question, but one which has not been settled to date' (Simpson, 1974, p. 87). I shall argue that this remains true a decade later, and that the legitimate doubts extend down to the generalized 'conventional' reasoning of Stage 4—which may also be largely confined, in terms of scores from the MJI, to subjects exposed to Western values and related social systems.

Kohlberg *et al.* (1983a) respond to Simpson's critique at length, citing most of the currently relevant cross-cultural research. They claim: (1) that 'Stage 5 reasoning has been found in a fairly large number of such (non-Western) cultures (Parikh, 1980; Lei and Cheng, 1982; Nisan and Kohlberg, 1982; Grimley, 1974; and Edwards, 1978)'; (2) that Snarey's (1983) Israeli kibbutz study reveals 'the existence of Stage 5 reasoning that uses norms not included in our standard manual norm list', and which therefore does not presuppose a liberal-democratic ideology; (3) that 'longitudinal and cross-cultural data, scored with a scoring system developed since Simpson's article, does not show reversal and regression'; (4) that the failure of Nisan and Kohlberg, Snarey, and also Edwards (1981, 1982), to find Stages 4 or 5 'in small scale villages is not because these stages simply express Western values ... (but) because of their relatively simple degree of social-structural complexity and because their populations have little or no formal education' (Kohlberg *et al.*, 1983a, pp. 198–202). They do recognize, however, that evidence for progression through to the higher stages coming from longitudinal studies is at best still limited to subjects from the USA (especially the well-educated middle-class) and some Israeli and Turkish settings.

Some findings of the research cited deserve particular comment in the light of the potential sources of bias already alluded to.[3] Of special interest with regard to the appropriateness of Kohlberg's dilemmas for other cultures is that Parikh (1980, p. 1032) reported seeking to use four dilemmas 'adapted to Indian society'; yet even with an upper-middle-class sample she had to discard two 'because a number of subjects did not take a stand, finding the dilemmas too hypothetical for them.' The highest GSS in a cross-sectional sample of 15- to 16-year-olds was Stage 3(4) shown by one boy. Parents were also tested in each of the thirty-nine families. Of the four mothers reaching at least this level all had experience of working outside the home, and only one reached Stage 4(3). Fathers scored higher in general, yet only two were above Stage 4 and only one of these was predominantly at Stage 5.

Nisan and Kohlberg (1982) adapted six dilemmas for use in Turkey; and they report some longitudinal as well as cross-sectional data—although samples were mostly very small, and early testing had relied upon an interpreter. The highest GSS was in fact only Stage 4(5), reached by one urban, male adult, although another eight out of twenty showed appreciable use of Stage 4, as did two of sixteen from a rural village. Results were essentially compatible with the step-wise progression prediction—yet apparently five out of twenty-three subjects showed what might have been slight evidence of regression, at one time or another. The authors admit that the data do not necessarily support 'a strong claim of universality ... that the structures described by Kohlberg exhaust more or less the whole domain of morality in every culture', and that to exclude the possibility of more culture-specific forms of reasoning, especially at the principled level, 'would require≑in addition to an agreed-upon definition of the moral domain—the study of a broader sample of moral dilemmas, composed through cooperation with expert and sensitive informants from other cultures' (p. 874).

Snarey's longitudinal study of Israelis found much wider evidence of Stage 5 thought, particularly amongst kibbutz founders (Snarey, 1983)—surely a Westernized and atypical sample in any case—but to a lesser degree in younger kibbutzniks also. Kohlberg *et al.* (1983b) report results broadly comparable, for both males and females, to the American standardization study of Colby *et al.* (1983)—yet by early adulthood it appears that only three of sixty subjects had reached as high as Stage 4(5), presumably only after military training and education outside the kibbutz itself. Kohlberg *et al.* (1983b) actually admit that their scoring criteria are biased towards reasoning with an individualistic rather than collectivist content, since they claim that the formal competence of many subjects relying upon socialist norms was higher than could be scored using existing criteria in the manual (Kohlberg *et al.*, 1977). And the fact remains that despite wide evidence of Stage 4, none of these subjects could actually be scored as even predominantly Stage 5. (Likewise, only eight American subjects reached Stage 4(5) or above, and none scored better than Stage 5(4) by full adulthood.) It therefore appears that Kohlberg has not yet established definitively that *purely* postconventional reasoning is more than another idealization for any group so far studied.

Lei (1981) found that about one-third of forty-three Taiwanese college students aged 19 to 20 reached Stage 4 or higher, but only one of these attained predominantly Stage 5 reasoning. He also reports that their GSSs were sometimes under-scored because of a collectivist normative orientation. Amongst the other research cited by Kohlberg *et al.* (1983a), the inclusion of Grimley's (1974) cross-sectional studies in Hong Kong, Japan and Zambia is puzzling, since he could not have used the current scoring system to identify Stage '5' subjects; and Edwards (1978) did not find any in Kenya either. In reviewing her Kenyan researches she notes that 'Stage 4 as a predominant mode of moral reasoning is linked to educational experiences, leadership and occupational roles that promote a certain kind of conceptualization of society as a complex system' (Edwards, 1982, p. 273). In 'traditional' communities not even leaders reached Stage '4'; and even university students showed negligible signs of Stage '5' thought—again despite the use of the early and generous scoring method.

It should also be noted that little research using current criteria has tested subjects young enough to show much indication of Stage 1 moral reasoning; so strictly speaking the sequential nature of the lowest stages cannot yet be said to have been demonstrated convincingly. In this connection reference to one other longitudinal study in a test-alien culture deserves to be made, even though it used an earlier scoring method. White, Bushnell and Regnemer (1978) studied rural children in the Bahamas, and their results broadly supported the sequentiality of the first three stages. They found no subjects above Stage '3', even by age 17; but they did suggest that the culture's normative emphasis upon strict obedience might actively inhibit attainment of higher stages. Other researchers have made similar points; for example, Jaquette and Erkut (1975) explain low scores amongst Turkish villagers by reference to values of respect for authority and strong obligations to kin; but they doubt whether 'tradition oriented cultures necessarily function at qualitatively lower levels of operative thought' (pp. 90–1).

Apart from the evident problems arising from the necessarily imperfect nature of the attempt to exclude 'content' from the MJI and its scoring, thereby to assess the 'pure form' of moral reasoning, there is also some remaining doubt about possible stage regression in even the recent longitudinal research. Although the principal investigators reject this interpretation, because deviations from the ideal sequence are appreciably less than the test-retest ones attributed to measurement errors by Colby *et al.* (1983), Murphy and Gilligan (1980) claim to have found true regression amongst an American postconventional sample. Kohlberg *et al.* (1983a) rightly point to some problematic features of that study; but despite the fact that reversals were quantitatively small, on a strict reading of the Colby *et al.* findings it could be claimed that some twenty-eight of their own fifty-eight subjects showed some sign of stage reversals.

It is evident that the best evidence that Kohlberg can so far draw upon does *not* in fact give unequivocal support to the universality postulate. The most serious problem is undoubtedly the fact that even secondary use of Stage 5 reasoning has been found only amongst a few persons, coming from backgrounds likely to imbue them with much of the liberal-democratic moral ethos. Edwards (1981, 1982) shares the belief of Gibbs (1977) that postconventional stages are simply not 'hard' structural ones of a Piagetian kind; yet her own and other data actually raise the possibility that even fully equilibrated conventional reasoning is only found in cultures exposed to some Westernizing influences. Alternatively, it may exist elsewhere, but take forms which as yet are unsuited to Kohlbergian testing and scoring. In any case, the quantity of unimpeachable data is still pitifully small from an hologeistic perspective, with no studies at all from hunter-gatherer societies. Clearly the scoring revisions and the expense of longitudinal research partially excuse some of the deficits; but while they remain the universality postulate must still be in doubt.

As noted previously, some of the difficulties in establishing a universal, dispositional capacity to reach the higher stages, particularly for persons from relevantly deprived environments, might be overcome with 'training' research, especially involving migrants to Western cultures. Studies with American samples have predominantly supported the prediction that if the stages are 'hard' ones subjects will prefer, and be most stimulated to advance by exposure to, reasoning no more than a full stage above their current level (Kohlberg *et al.*, 1983a). A recent study by Walker (1982) using predominantly Stage 2 Canadian children casts some doubt upon this claim, as advances of around half-a-stage were equally facilitated by exposure to arguments one and two stages higher. Similar research was undertaken within Maqsud's (1979, 1982) studies of the Muslim culture of Nigerian Hausas. The first study suggested that jumps from Stage '2' to Stage '4' could be induced, contrary to Kohlbergian prediction. The second yielded data as predicted; but protocols were apparently not scored 'blind', and the older scoring methods were again employed.

On balance the research reviewed here probably favours Kohlberg's claims regarding at least the first three of his stages, and might plausibly hint at their validity for virtually all socio-cultural contexts. Even allowing for the flawed nature of much of the evidence, the higher stages also show some of the predicted features within some cultural milieus. But the possibility of systematic bias against non-Western modes of moral thought when using the existing MJI dilemmas and scoring methods is clear; and even whether *any* kinds of postconventional reasoning might meet the criteria for 'hard' structural stages remains in doubt. If the socio-political conditions and associated social experience favouring such reasoning do in fact happen to be confined to cultures or subcultures dominated by the Western liberal-democratic ideology, then it will be extremely hard to show that equilibration rather than indoctrination is the critical determinant of a principled commitment to an ethic of individual rights. Yet Kohlberg must be able to demonstrate this if the universality postulate is not to be diluted.

SOCIO-CULTURAL VARIABLES AND MORAL JUDGMENT

Kohlberg has made no secret of the fact that one of his major objectives has been to combat the several varieties of 'ethical relativism'—ethical doctrines which regard what is morally right, true or obligatory as a contingent matter localized to a particular time, place, situation, social group, or even individual conscience. Even in its most modest forms, relativism allows that the principles determining one's moral obligations can vary with socio-ecological circumstances, and thus precludes assuming that one particular set of principles must be objectively superior to any other set without dispute or qualification. In seeking to defend an 'objectivist' view of morality, with its prospect of rationally-based moral certainty and universal consensus regarding normative priorities, Kohlberg was naturally attracted to the 'formalist' philosophies of Kant, Hare, Rawls and others. Their conception of the nature of morality permits it to be abstracted from concrete psycho-social realities in ways which make it appear that there are criteria for judging the rightness of actions, or resolving social conflicts of interest, which *any* fully rational moral agent must accept.

The full moral maturity of Stage 6 is defined in the terms which Kohlberg sees as meeting these requirements uniquely and consistently. Judgments attain a 'pure' moral form by virtue of pre-empting considerations of personal prudence, the maximization of happiness, and so on, by embodying prescriptions which are universalizable to anyone in the relevant situation, and by being impartial, particularly in the sense that they depend upon an impersonal, idealized role-taking in assessing the justice of the claims of all parties involved. The substantive principles are 'deontological' ones concerning reciprocal rights and duties—the absolute right of each individual to be treated as morally equal in assessments of what is just, and the universal duty to respect the humanity, and thus the life and liberty, of all persons (irrespective of specific legal provisions). This abstracted, formal, moral ideal is seen as superior to those of lower stages by virtue of its power to generate judgments about any conflict of interests which one would regard as fair irrespective of which role one happened to be in personally, and thus upon which all rational moral agents would agree. Only by making individual rights and procedural justice into the core principles of morality can 'objective', universally valid normative standards be identified for judging conduct (Kohlberg, 1971, 1981).

I make no attempt to examine the philosophical persuasiveness of this characterization of, and defence of, an ethic of justice and rights as objectively preferable to others. Here I merely note that the coherence and consistency as well as the underlying assumptions of the arguments are contentious, and that whether a Piagetian, constructivist view of cognitive development can strictly predict that moral maturity should take a uniquely Stage 6 form is highly debatable (Vine, 1983a). The point I wish to emphasize is that Kohlberg's theory is explicitly grounded in meta-ethical principles which are 'necessary to begin the study of morality, which psychologists using the stage concept and measure must at least partially endorse' (Kohlberg *et al.*, 1983a, p. 110). He does admit that the empirical theory can be separated from the normative claim that 'justice is the *first* virtue of a person or of a society' (p. 163), or that 'morally valid forms of caring and community (ethic) presuppose prior conditions and judgments of justice' (p. 164). Yet he also acknowledges that these assumptions shaped the choice of MJI dilemmas, excluding any 'that were not frameable as rights conflicts' (p. 163). Likewise, although Kohlberg distinguishes the empirical theory of the universality of stage progression from his claim that 'there is a universalistically valid form of rational moral thought processes which all persons could articulate, assuming social and cultural conditions suitable to cognitive moral stage development' (p. 128), the stages are defined with this claim in mind. It is clear from the scoring manual that to qualify as a postconventional reasoner a subject must uphold a pre-eminent and universal right to life (Kohlberg *et al.*, 1977). Apart from the question of whether the particular dilemmas that Kohlberg uses really provide for rigorously ascertaining just how literally subjects would espouse this principle *irrespective* of social circumstances, there can be no doubt that the criteria of moral maturity are not purely formal and do measure it against a very specific moral ideology.

So long as the early scoring systems produced data suggesting that Stages 5 and 6 were reached in very diverse cultures, Kohlberg could hope to mask the partisan nature of his definitions of the higher stages. Already, as a responsible empirical scientist, he has been obliged to attenuate his claims for the unique developmental superiority of Stage 6 in the light of scoring revisions. But for all its 'hypothetical' status it clearly influences the scoring of lower stages, and reflects his underlying goal of finding psychological support for a universally valid, ahistorical, rationally binding set of moral principles. Procedural principles of justice as formal impartiality have at least a plausible claim to be rooted in cognitive structures of a kind intrinsic to mature formal-operational reasoning. If they appear to generate one particular substantive morality when fully developed, despite variability in the normative values into which individuals were first socialized, then there is a realistic hope for social progress towards a universal moral consensus.

It is surely for such reasons that Kohlberg must insist that all his stages are 'hard' Piagetian ones—with an invariant developmental order whereby 'structural wholes' emerging at higher levels transform and integrate lower ones while serving the same general function, and have their forms determined by the nature of 'socio-moral' cognitive operations rather than 'cultural factors' (Kohlberg *et al.*, 1983a). Gibbs (1977) and others have argued that the forms taken by postconventional moral reasoning are 'existentially' chosen, with Stage 5 involving detached meta-ethical reflection upon and abstract formalization of the concrete social reciprocity of Stage 2. Although his approach is similar, Eckensberger (1981) sees Stage 5 as structurally equivalent to Stage 3, with analogous parallels between Stages 1 and 4 and between Stages 2 and the transitional '4½'. But precisely because 'development to the higher soft stages is optional, not prescribed' (Kohlberg *et al.*, 1983a, p. 70), Kohlberg cannot accept such reformulations without opening the door to ethical relativism. Only intrinsic, formal, abstract features of operational reasoning itself, rather than prior contingencies of social loyalty, unconsciously absorbed cultural ideology, or personal existential choices, can hope to offer the prospect of a universally shared morality generating obligations and prescriptions which are also fully universalized across all moral agents.

Whatever sympathy one might have for Kohlberg's ideal of eliminating moral partisanship, moral disagreements, and radical moral uncertainties over effectively insoluble dilemmas, his progressively more elaborate attempts to protect the core of his theory seem unlikely to persuade either his philosophical or psychological critics. Only by making more modest claims is he likely to gain some consensus over the theory. It is quite plausible that there *are* 'hard' structural stages in moral development, including ones for reasoning about issues other than justice and individual rights. But it does not follow from this that they cover the full range of development within a domain—instead, 'soft' structures may be derived from earlier 'hard' ones in later life. Furthermore, even for the latter a less rigid view may be appropriate, especially with regard to how stages replace each other. Levine (1979) has argued against the strong 'displacement' view that earlier stage structures cease to be available at all when new ones emerge, and that stage mixtures in performance simply indicate that a person is in transition between stages. His own 'interactionist' view sees earlier structures as remaining available for use when functionally appropriate to a situation—thus how a person defines a given situational context determines the predominant mode of reasoning used.

Kohlberg *et al*. (1983a) seem to remain ambivalent on this proposal; but it can readily cope with otherwise awkward data on the dilemma-specificity and situational dependency of judgments. In the cross-cultural context a good example is provided by Turnbull's (1973) anthropological study of the Ik of Uganda. It seems clear that the practical morality of the culture when he studied it was little better than Kohlberg's Stage 1, and even its leaders showed little evidence of a higher competence. Yet there were hints that prior to being forced to relinquish their earlier hunter-gatherer life-style the Ik's norms had Stage 3 features, which some older individuals still could and did sometimes adhere to. A dispositional competence to attain Stage 3 justice-reasoning in favourable circumstances may well be humanly universal; but even then performance may often not reflect that competence.

Beyond Stage 3 the evidence for 'hard' stages is relatively poor in the light of cross-cultural findings. Stage 4 may be reliably reached by Euro-American adults of at least average intelligence who have some higher education, and by advantaged individuals in other cultures who have been exposed to Western values and social institutions. Stage 5 may be limited to highly advantaged individuals with appreciable experience of the personal benefits that liberal-democratic capitalist society offers to a fortunate minority, and with an educational background which highlights the moral rhetoric of equal opportunity and individual rights.

Kohlberg can claim that this assessment overstates the importance of social-organizational and ideological factors, and he can appeal especially to the high scores obtained by many Israeli kibbutzniks, committed to a collectivist and even socialist ideology (Kohlberg *et al*., 1983b). But this is far from being a persuasive example, since socialist kibbutzniks can hardly fail to be alert to pluralistic moral perspectives and to their own dependence upon both Israeli society at large and the capitalist system. It is also revealing that Bar-Yam, Kohlberg and Naame (1980, p. 356), commenting upon the high frequency of Stage '4' responses amongst their non-Arabic, middle-class, late-adolescent Israeli subjects, admit that a 'concern with national security and the need for unity' may have encouraged Stage 4 usage. In this connection it would be interesting to re-test Israeli Jews scored as Stage 5—on dilemmas involving the rights of Palestinian Arabs.

If he is to distinguish the effects of ideological factors from those which involve role-taking opportunities relating to education, class, leadership and other aspects of social participation, Kohlberg could begin with research within large, complex, stratified and relatively materially advanced collectivist societies, like the USSR. Although Garbarino and Bronfenbrenner (1976) used their own Moral Dilemma

Test, their findings comparing Eastern and Western industrial nations are of interest. Greater respect for adult authority than for peers' values was found in the former, correlating with those cultures' lower scores on a measure of 'socio-political pluralism'. Thus the authoritarian and monolithic nature of Soviet-style collectivism probably militates against development beyond Stage 3 for the average citizen. (At the same time, even if they would not score highly on the individual justice dilemmas, it is hardly credible that Eastern intellectuals committed to communism are not postconventional moral thinkers.) Unfortunately it is debatable whether 'developed' nations with a non-authoritarian but non-capitalist ideology, and a sufficiently pluralistic structure to provide on a wide scale the theoretical preconditions for principled justice-reasoning, currently exist at all as a better testing-ground for the theory.

In any case it is admitted that the scoring of MJI responses militates against those whose conception of justice itself is more collectivist, or who give greater moral weight to other values. The difficulty in getting appropriate and scorable responses to Kohlbergian dilemmas in some non-Western cultures reinforces this point. Indeed, it may be relevant even in Euro-American cultures; for Tomlinson (personal communication, 1983) has found many responses unscorable within his English longitudinal sample—and the debate regarding females' judgments and personally-involving 'real-life' dilemmas remains a live one (e.g., Gilligan, 1982). While Kohlberg *et al.* (1983a) do marshall data that speak against any extreme scoring biases, the problem cannot be ignored. For example, Dien (1982) argues that in traditional Chinese culture the influence of Confucianism is so strong that a 'dilemma' like the Form A number 1 story, involving parental demands for self-sacrifice by a child, would simply not be a dilemma, so potent is the duty of filial piety. Also the collectivist emphasis upon 'reconciliation rather than choice and commitment' is said to act against individualistic insistence upon absolute personal rights (p. 335). Both the forms which justice-reasoning takes and its priority relative to the *jen* value of caring concern or love would impede high scoring in non-Westernized Chinese subjects.

There is evidence that within non-Westernized cultures many adults can fail to show even fully equilibrated concrete-operational intelligence in some tests (e.g., Price-Williams, 1981). While this precondition of progress in moral reasoning may explain some Kohlbergian findings, here too there are similar possibilities of measurement biases. The extreme view that not just the tests but Piagetian theory itself is ideologically tainted has been argued forcefully in Marxist terms by Buck-Morss (1975), who sees the claim for the rational superiority of abstract thought as reflecting the logic of capitalist economics. Such critiques, like other examinations of Kohlberg's liberal-democratic ideology (Baumrind, 1978; Emler, 1983; Sullivan, 1977), are at least right to stress how a focus upon highly abstract reasoning obscures important issues about 'real-world' moral praxis.

Harkness, Edwards and Super (1981), in their study of Kipsigis villagers in Kenya, found that not even leaders typically gave responses above Stage '3'; but as Edwards (1982) emphasizes, their reasoning was quite adequately equilibrated for the nature of the moral disputes arising and demanding solution within their small, face-to-face, traditional communities. The functional adequacy of conventional reasoning in these contexts makes even the limited sense in which Kohlberg calls his higher stages more 'morally adequate' both ethnocentric and even offensive. It should in any case be remembered that postconventional moral rhetoric is by no means a strong predictor of just moral actions (Blasi, 1980; Wonderly and Kupfersmid, 1980). Western 'civilizing' influences have regularly ushered both exploitation and new forms of inhumanity into many stable, traditional cultures.

Kohlberg's explanations of slow stage progression and low ceilings hinge around his claim that the unifying structural concept of a stage is its 'socio-moral perspective' (Kohlberg, 1976), presupposing attainment of an appropriate stage of social role-taking competence (Selman, 1976.) These stages are themselves held to have Piagetian properties (Gurucharri and Selman, 1982). For Selman, the highest stage currently identified involves realizing that 'each self considers the shared point of view of the *generalized other* (the social system)' (Selman, 1976, p. 306), and that group consensus is important in sustaining roles and rules. This generates the normative Stage 4 morality of system-maintenance; but for postconventional morality Kohlberg has to assume an individual but universalized, supra-system perspective-taking. It is essentially through their effects upon role-taking that variables like social class, group membership, within-group roles, mobility and even formal education are seen as influencing the attainment of moral maturity. Unfortunately there are enough of these 'participation' factors to make it difficult to show that cultural ideology *per se* has an impact directly upon moral reasoning. Yet Krebs and Gillmore (1982) found that when general cognitive maturity was partialled out the correlation between role-taking and moral judgment was only .44. Although a *post-hoc* correction improved the relation, partial independence of the domains was still indicated. Since Kohlberg is so unspecific about other social factors, like the 'moral atmosphere' one experiences, it seems clear that culture-specific or subcultural values and institutional practices could be causally involved as well.

What Kohlberg's rationalist view of moral development leaves out is not just the sources of pro-social motivation in general, but people's concrete social loyalties to individuals and groups. Rather than seeing values of caring, responsibility and loyalty as presupposing that of individual justice, one must surely recognize that a genuine moral *commitment* to that value depends upon prior concern for others' welfare (Vine, 1983a). Morality, and especially justice-reasoning, has the important social function of extending our sympathies and sense of pro-social obligation when the conditions of social life demand it—that is, when social order would otherwise be seriously jeopardized. The complexities which functional perspectives introduce for the notion of moral maturity are too complex to consider properly here, but are succinctly outlined by Weinreich-Haste (in press). Only one implication will be given some consideration here—namely the social functions that a moral rhetoric pitched at the level of the higher moral stages can perform for particular interest-groups within society.

A FUNCTIONALIST MORAL SCENARIO

While personally rejecting some of Kohlberg's ethical philosophy and liberal-democratic ideology, and doubting whether even Stage 4 is a 'hard' one, I see his descriptive theory as having considerable heuristic value for illuminating the socio-political role which an individualistic rhetoric of justice and rights can play (cf. Habermas, 1979). Kohlberg (1971, 1981) has outlined an evolutionary model of societal development which closely parallels his ontogenetic theory; and these ideas have been developed at length by Chilton (1983). To conclude this chapter I shall offer a brief sketch of an alternative evolutionary scenario. Some of its more controversial aspects and underlying assumptions are partly treated elsewhere (Vine, 1982, 1983a, 1983b).

Humans are intrinsically social animals, so that to survive and thrive as individuals we must live interdependent lives within mutually supportive social networks. At the same time, sociobiological reasoning does suggest that we are naturally subject to egoistic, self-interested impulses which limit pro-social altruism and cooperativeness. Normative pressures and moral codes can be seen as social requirements which must be able to constrain individuals' motives and actions when these conflict with long-term personal prudence or the harmony and efficiency of the collectivity. At least in small, face-to-face societies, what is adaptive for the group also tends to be adaptive for the individual. For small social units of the kind within which our hunter-gatherer ancestors evolved biologically, primary social attachments would have largely sufficed to generate relatively indiscriminate mutual aid and caring concern amongst the group; and direct expressions of disapproval would restrain deviations from reciprocity, cooperation and support of the needy. With few opportunities for individuals to accumulate significant personal property or other sources of lasting social power, relationships were typically egalitarian. Strict reciprocity was more likely to be demanded in inter-group transactions; but generalized in-group loyalty and even inter-group cooperativeness could be based upon 'natural' and predominantly non-coercive experience and social control.

Since then various influences have combined to create larger and more complex societies, involving numerous situations where the direct supports for individual welfare and social fairness can fail, and systematic exploitation of individuals or groups becomes possible. The broad trend of social evolution has been to create potentially greater inequalities in individuals' contributions to and benefits from the common weal. The social scope of our moral loyalties has had to expand, to encompass individuals only known anonymously or in terms of group stereotypes, if social harmony is not to be jeopardized. Correspondingly stronger normative pressures have been required to support this extension of loyalties in opposition to self-interest and partisan personal attachments (Campbell, 1975), creating an 'expanding circle' (Singer, 1981) of persons to whom we are morally committed in some degree. The need for explicit norms of individual justice will tend to increase to the extent that mutual aid and caring are no longer guaranteed by face-to-face social processes. Power elites will increasingly control resources and their distribution, but also have control of information and coercive powers to enforce or induce particular values and norms—in the collective interest or more selfishly.

Seen in terms of the expanding circle concept, Stage 3 reasoning encompasses an appreciable horizontal *decalage*, from loyalty to one's primary group through to ethnocentric patriotism, which is formalized at Stage 4. The step from this to a 'speciesist' commitment to all of humanity (Stage 5) is still greater, and its rarity is unsurprising.[4] The temptation of leaders to exploit their power may sometimes be no greater than that of others; but because they are much less subject to normative constraints they are likely to do so in strongly hierarchical societies. Moral rhetoric can be a potent implement for this—especially when aided by the self-deception to which we are all readily subject (Vine, 1983c). Elites stand to gain if they can induce those they lead to overcome sectional loyalties and self-interest, and to be ready to make sacrifices for 'society' which disproportionately advantage elite groups—as in cases of successful conquest of other societies. It is highly functional for leaders to induce a fully extended Stage 3 morality and to discourage a postconventional morality which transcends ethnocentrism.

In 'advanced' contemporary societies elites are obliged to rely upon a bureaucracy and upon entrepreneurs and others who constitute a middle class which must be educated well and given some subsidiary powers. Their cooperation requires a more sophisticated Stage 4 loyalty, for they are in a position to know more of the exploitative nature and inequitability of aspects of the system. But the risk then is that when they grasp enough to recognize that others above them do not deserve their privileges, they will disaffect if they are not bought off or coerced subtly. Out of self-interest, *or* from genuinely collectivist commitments, some members of the middle class can be expected to discover a postconventional rhetoric of equal opportunity and individual rights, and to use it against the hegemony of the elite. It can be used for personal gain, with the aid of self-deception, without any genuine commitment. And it can force the elite to embody it in the letter of the law, even if it is in no sense generally applied in practice. They in turn can use it against those Stage 4 or 5 thinkers who might otherwise resist patriotic self-sacrifice, by highlighting abuses of the justice and rights ideal amongst groups—particularly other nation-states—they wish to interfere with.

The hollowness of so much Stage 5 rhetoric is thus to be expected, particularly as most of those who develop it will be vulnerable because they are relatively privileged, and do derive benefits from systematic exploitation of the lower classes at home and abroad. And leaders understand well that few people develop a full *commitment* to universal justice, or even to a universal right to life. If at best the majority of postconventional reasoners limits its circle of moral equals to the national boundary, then the appeal to real or spurious threats to 'national security' can normally be relied upon to prevent potential dissidents from pursuing their expressed principles vigorously. The whole issue of ethnocentrism is essentially missed with Kohlberg's dilemmas—yet it must be the acid test of the sincerity of the rights ideal, as it would be for postconventional welfare reasoning.

Of course the analysis offered here remains very crude, as well as pessimistic. I hope that it can carry at least enough conviction to show the necessity of taking the social systems perspective on morality seriously in a much broader way than Kohlbergians have hitherto done. At the very least it suggests that it must take a lot more than role-training, or the experience of 'just community' schooling, to make a serious impact upon world-wide patterns of moral reasoning and behavioural integrity (cf. Kupfersmid and Wonderly, 1982).

NOTES

1 For two important texts (Kohlberg *et al.*, 1977, 1983a) I have been obliged to rely upon draft manuscripts which may depart somewhat from the definitive publications. Likewise, I have not had access to all of the recent and unpublished Harvard research which Kohlberg cites in support of particular claims. Where reliance upon secondary sources has been unavoidable this is indicated.

2 Where stage numbers reported are based upon non-current scoring methods I indicate this by marking the numbers in quotation marks.
3 Of these reports the unpublished paper by Lei and Cheng (1982) was unavailable, but a related report by Lei (1981) was consulted instead; Grimley's (1974) and Snarey's (1983) doctoral dissertations could only be consulted as abstracts, but a report of Snarey's longitudinal study was accessible (Kohlberg, Snarey and Reimer, 1983b).
4 The theoretical arbitrariness of seeing the modern nation-state as a 'natural' social system from the moral point of view is another reason to doubt whether the formal moral structures of Stage 4 are really distinctive in 'hard' terms. A formalized 'system-maintenance' view might be developed for family loyalties prior to or even instead of a concrete Stage 3 patriotism. It also seems likely that it is the increasingly abstract nature of post-Stage 3 justice commitments that enables them to diverge from effectively stronger care and responsibility values that differentially favour those near and dear to oneself. Because Kohlberg's dilemmas do not adequately tap what might at the higher levels be independent stages of an 'ethic of care', one cannot know whether the two values develop in parallel, or whether whichever dominates tends to suppress the other. From the functional perspective the direction of domination is in any case likely to reflect whichever value one has derived most personal benefit from.

REFERENCES

Bar-Yam, M., Kohlberg, L. and Naame, A., (1980) 'Moral reasoning of students in different cultural, social, and educational settings', *American Journal of Education*, 88, pp. 345–62.

Baumrind, D. (1978) 'A dialectical materialist's perspective on knowing social reality', in Damon, W. (Ed.) *Moral Development*, San Francisco, Jossey-Bass, pp. 61–82.

Berry, J. W. (1980) 'Introduction to *Methodology*', in Triandis, H. C. and Berry, J. W. (Eds.), *Handbook of Cross-Cultural Psychology*, *Vol. 2: Methodology*, Boston, Allyn and Bacon, pp. 1–28.

Blasi, A. (1980) 'Bridging moral cognition and moral action: A critical review of the literature', *Psychological Bulletin*, 88, pp. 1–45.

Brislin, R. W. (1980) 'Translation and content analysis of oral and written material', in Triandis, H. C., and Berry, J. W. (Eds.), *Handbook of Cross-Cultural Psychology*, *Vol. 2: Methodology*, Boston, Allyn and Bacon, pp. 389–444.

Brislin, R. W. (1983) 'Cross-cultural research in psychology', *Annual Review of Psychology*, 34, pp. 363–400.

Broughton, J. (1978) 'The cognitive-developmental approach to morality: A reply to Kurtines and Greif', *Journal of Moral Education*, 7, pp. 81–96.

Buck-Morss, S. (1975) 'Socio-economic bias in Piaget's theory and its implications for cross-cultural studies', *Human Development*, 18, pp. 35–49.

Campbell, D. T. (1975) 'On the conflicts between biological and social evolution and between psychology and moral tradition', *American Psychologist*, 30, pp. 1103–26.

Chilton, S. (1983) 'Political development: Theoretical problems and a theoretical reconstruction', Sixth Annual Scientific Meeting of the International Society for Political Psychology, Oxford, 21 July. (Mimeo: Department of Government, New Mexico State University, Las Cruces, NM 88005, USA.)

Colby, A. (1978) 'Evolution of a moral-developmental theory', in Damon, W. (Ed.), *Moral Development*, San Francisco, Jossey-Bass, pp. 89–104.

Colby, A., Kohlberg, L., Gibbs, J. and Lieberman, M. (1983) 'A longitudinal study of moral judgment', *Monographs of the Society for Research in Child Development*, 48, 1–2, pp. 1–96.

Dien, D. S. (1982) 'A Chinese perspective on Kohlberg's theory of moral development', *Developmental Review*, 2, pp. 331–41.

Eckensberger, L. H. (1981) 'On a structural model of the development of stages of moral development', MOSAIC Interdisciplinary Colloquium on Problems of Morality, Liverpool, 31 March. (Mimeo: University of the Saarland, Saarbruecken, West Germany.)

Edwards, C. P. (1978) 'Social experience and moral judgment in Kenyan young adults', *Journal of Genetic Psychology*, 133, pp. 19–29.

Edwards, C. P. (1981) 'The comparative study of the development of moral judgment and reasoning', in

Munroe, R. H., Munroe, R. I. and Whiting, B. B. (Eds.), *Handbook of Cross-Cultural Human Development*, New York, Garland STPM Press, pp. 501–28.

Edwards, C. P. (1982) 'Moral development in comparative cultural perspective', in Wagner, D. A., and Stevenson, H. (Eds.), *Cultural Perspectives on Child Development*, San Francisco, W. H. Freeman, pp. 248–79.

Emler, N. (1983) 'Morality and politics: The ideological dimension in the theory of moral development', in Weinreich-Haste, H. and Locke, D. (Eds.), *Morality in the Making: Thought, Action, and the Social Context*, Chichester, John Wiley, pp. 47–71.

Garbarino, J. and Bronfenbrenner, U. (1976) 'The socialization of moral judgment and behaviour in cross-cultural perspective', in Lickona, T. (Ed.), *Moral Development and Behaviour: Theory, Research, and Social Issues*, New York, Holt, Rinehart and Winston, pp. 70–83.

Gibbs, J. C. (1977) 'Kohlberg's stages of moral judgment—a constructive critique', *Harvard Educational Review*, 47, pp. 43–61.

Gilligan, C. (1982) *In a Different Voice: Psychological Theory and Women's Development*, Cambridge, Mass., Harvard University Press.

Grimley, L. K. (1974) 'A cross-cultural study of moral development', *Dissertation Abstracts International*, 34, p. 3990A. (Doctoral dissertation, Kent State University, Ohio, 1973.)

Gurucharri, C. and Selman, R. L. (1982) 'The development of interpersonal understanding during childhood, preadolescence, and adolescence: A longitudinal follow-up study', *Child Development*, 53, pp. 924–7.

Habermas, J. (1979) *Communication and the Evolution of Society*, trans. McCarthy, T., London, Heinemann Educational Books.

Harkness, S., Edwards, C. P. and Super, C. M. (1981) 'Social roles and moral reasoning: A case study in a rural African community', *Developmental Psychology*, 17, pp. 595–603.

Irvine, S. H. and Carroll, W. K. (1980) 'Testing and assessment across cultures: Issues in methodology and theory', in Triandis, H. C. and Berry, J. W. (Eds.), *Handbook of Cross-Cultural Psychology*, Vol. 2: Methodology, Boston, Allyn and Bacon, pp. 181–244.

Jaquette, D. and Erkut, S. (1975) 'Operative and representational social thought: Some categories of social experience in the Turkish village', *Hacettape Bulletin of Social Sciences and Humanities*, 7, pp. 70–92.

Kohlberg, L. (1969) 'Stage and sequence: The cognitive-developmental approach to socialization', in Goslin, D. A. (Ed.), *Handbook of Socialization Theory and Research*, Chicago, Rand McNally, pp. 347–480.

Kohlberg, L. (1971) 'From is to ought: how to commit the naturalistic fallacy and get away with it in the study of moral development', in Mischel, T. (Ed.), *Cognitive Development and Epistemology*, New York, Academic Press, pp. 151–235.

Kohlberg, L. (1976) 'Moral stages and moralization: The cognitive-developmental approach', in Lickona, T. (Ed.), *Moral Development and Behavior: Theory, Research, and Social Issues*, New York, Holt, Rinehart and Winston, pp. 31–55.

Kohlberg, L. (1981) *Essays on Moral Development, Vol. 1: The Philosophy of Moral Development— Moral Stages and the Idea of Justice*, San Francisco, Harper and Row.

Kohlberg, L., Colby, A., Gibbs, J., Speicher-Dubin, B. and Power, C. (1977) *Assessing Moral Stages: A Manual*, preliminary edition. (Mimeo: Laboratory of Human Development, Harvard University, Cambridge, Mass. 02138, USA.)

Kohlberg, L., Levine, C. and Hewer, A. (1983a) *Moral Stages: The Current Formulation of Kohlberg's Theory and a Response to Critics*. (Mimeo: Laboratory of Human Development, Harvard University, Cambridge, Mass. 02138, USA. To be published by S. Karger, Basel.)

Kohlberg, L., Snarey, J. and Reimer, J. (1983b) 'Cultural universality of moral judgment stages: A longitudinal study in Israel'. (Mimeo: Laboratory of Human Development, Harvard University, Cambridge, Mass. 02138, USA.)

Krebs, D. and Gillmore, J. (1982) 'The relationship among the first stages of cognitive development, role-taking abilities, and moral development', *Child Development*, 53, pp. 877–86.

Kupfersmid, J. H. and Wonderly, D. M., (1982) 'Disequilibrium as a hypothetical construct in Kohlbergian moral development', *Child Study Journal*, 12, pp. 171–85.

Kurtines, W. and Greif, E. B. (1974) 'The development of moral thought: Review and evaluation of Kohlberg's approach', *Psychological Bulletin*, 81, pp. 453–70.

Lei, T., (1981) 'An empirical study of Kohlberg's theory and scoring system of moral judgment in Chinese society'. (Mimeo: Psychological Foundation, University of Minnesota, Minneapolis, MN 55404.)

Lei, T. and Cheng, S. W. (1982) 'An empirical study of Kohlberg's theory and moral judgment in Chinese society'. (Mimeo: Laboratory of Human Development, Harvard University, Cambridge, Mass. 02138, USA.)

Levine, C. G. (1979) 'Stage acquisition and stage use: An appraisal of stage displacement explanations of variation in moral reasoning', *Human Development*, 22, pp. 145–64.

Lonner, W. J. (1980) 'The search for psychological universals', in Triandis, H. C. and Lambert, W. W. (Eds.), *Handbook of Cross-Cultural Psychology*, Vol. 1: Perspectives, Boston, Allyn and Bacon, pp. 143–204.

Maqsud, M. (1979) 'Cultural influences on transition in the development of moral reasoning in Nigerian boys', *Journal of Social Psychology*, 108, pp. 151–9.

Maqsud, M. (1982) 'Effects of Nigerian children's group discussion on their moral progression', *Journal of Moral Education*, 11, pp. 181–7.

Murphy, J. M. and Gilligan, C. (1980) 'Moral development in late adolescence and adulthood: A critique and reconstruction of Kohlberg's theory', *Human Development*, 23, pp. 77–104.

Naroll, R., Michik, G. L. and Naroll, F. (1980) 'Holocultural research methods', in Triandis, H. C. and Berry, J. W. (Eds.), *Handbook of Cross-Cultural Psychology*, Vol. 2: Methodology, Boston, Allyn and Bacon, pp. 479–521.

Nisan, M. and Kohlberg, L. (1982) 'Universality and variation in moral judgment: A longitudinal and cross-sectional study in Turkey', *Child Development*, 53, pp. 865–76.

Nyiti, R. M. (1982) 'Validity of "cultural differences explanations" for cross-cultural variation in the rate of Piagetian cognitive development', in Wagner, D. A. and Stevenson, H. W. (Eds.), *Cultural Perspectives on Child Development*, San Francisco, W. H. Freeman, pp. 146–65.

Pareek, U. and Rao, T. V. (1980) 'Cross-cultural surveys and interviewing', in Triandis, H. C. and Berry, J. W. (Eds.), *Handbook of Cross-Cultural Psychology*, Vol. 2: Methodology, Boston, Allyn and Bacon, pp. 127–79.

Parikh, B. (1980) 'Development of moral judgment and its relation to family environmental factors in Indian and American families', *Child Development*, 51, pp. 1030–9.

Piaget, J. (1932) *The Moral Judgment of the Child*, trans. Gabain, M., London, Routledge and Kegan Paul.

Piaget, J. (1972) *The Principles of Genetic Epistemology*, trans. Mays, W., London, Routledge and Kegan Paul.

Price-Williams, D. (1981) 'Concrete and formal operations', in Munroe, R. H., Munroe, R. L. and Whiting, B. B. (Eds.), *Handbook of Cross-Cultural Human Development*, New York, Garland STPM Press, pp. 403–22.

Rest, J. R., Davison, M. L. and Robbins, S. (1978) 'Age trends in judging moral issues: A review of cross-sectional, longitudinal, and sequential studies of the Defining Issues Test', *Child Development*, 49, pp. 263–79.

Selman, R. L. (1976) 'Social-cognitive understanding: A guide to educational and clinical practice', in Lickona, T. (Ed.), *Moral Development and Behavior: Theory, Research, and Social Issues*, New York, Holt, Rinehart and Winston, pp. 299–316.

Simpson, E. L. (1974) 'Moral development research: A case study of scientific bias', *Human Development*, pp. 81–106.

Singer, P. (1981) *The Expanding Circle: Ethics and Sociobiology*, Oxford, Clarendon Press.

Snarey, J. R. (1983) 'The social and moral development of kibbutz founders and abras: A cross-sectional and longitudinal cross-cultural study', *Dissertation Abstracts International*, 43, p. 3416B. (Doctoral dissertation, Harvard University, Massachusetts, 1982.)

Sullivan, E. V. (1977) 'A study of Kohlberg's structural theory of moral development: A critique of liberal social science ideology', *Human Development*, 20, pp. 352–76.

Triandis, H. C. and Berry, J. W. (Eds.) (1980) *Handbook of Cross-Cultural Psychology*, Vol. 2: Methodology, Boston, Allyn and Bacon.

Turnbull, C. M. (1973) *The Mountain People*, London, Jonathan Cape.

Van de Vijver, F. J. R. and Poortinga, Y. H. (1982) 'Cross-cultural generalization and universality', *Journal of Cross-Cultural Psychology*, 13, pp. 387–408.

Vine, I. (1982) 'The cultural evolution of morality', Second MOSAIC Conference on Aspects of Morality, Winchester, 15 July. (Mimeo: Interdisciplinary Human Studies, University of Bradford, Bradford, BD7 1DP, England.)

Vine, I. (1983a) 'The nature of moral commitments', in Weinreich-Haste, H. and Locke, D. (Eds.), *Morality in the Making: Thought, Action, and the Social Context*, Chichester, John Wiley, pp. 19–45.

Vine, I. (1983b) 'Sociobiology and social psychology—rivalry or symbiosis? The explanation of altruism', *British Journal of Social Psychology*, 22, pp. 1–11.

Vine, I. (1983c) 'The human nature of self-deception', MOSAIC and Society for Applied Philosophy Joint Workshop on False Consciousness and Real Interests, Bradford, 3 December. (Mimeo: Interdisciplinary Human Studies, University of Bradford, Bradford, BD7 1DP, England.)

Walker, L. J. (1982) 'The sequentiality of Kohlberg's stages of moral development', *Child Development*, 53, pp. 1330–6.

Weinreich-Haste, H. (in press) 'Morality, social meaning and rhetoric: The social context of moral reasoning', in Gewirtz, J. and Kurtines, W. (Eds.), *Moral Development and Education*, New York, John Wiley.

Weinreich-Haste, H. and Locke, D. (Eds.) (1983) *Morality in the Making: Thought, Action and the Social Context*, Chichester, John Wiley.

White, C. B., Bushnell, N. and Regnemer, J. L. (1978) 'Moral development in Bahamian school children: A three-year examination of Kohlberg's stages of moral development', *Developmental Psychology*, 14, pp. 58–65.

Wonderly, D. M. and Kupfersmid, J. H. (1980) 'Promoting postconventional morality: The adequacy of Kohlberg's aim', *Adolescence*, 15, pp. 609–31.

Interchange

EDWARDS REPLIES TO VINE

Vine's critique of Kohlberg is a fairminded and sympathetic one, since Vine is willing to assume that, in principle, a culturally universal cognitive-developmental theory of morality can be created. In fact, Vine and I are in essential agreement on a number of points. Most importantly, we agree that some, but not yet enough, empirical evidence exists to support the cultural universality of 'hard' moral Stages, 1 to 3 or 4.

However, I believe Vine misinterprets the evidence when claiming that even Stage 4 requires exposure to Western values and/or Western socio-political influences. I have argued elsewhere that the societal perspective underlying Stage 4 is that of the complex, national state system, with formal legal, governmental and political institutions, social classes and hierarchy, 'distance between government and the governed', and clear separation of the office from the office-holder. I see no theoretical or empirical evidence to suggest that this national state need be Western (i.e., capitalist, or liberal democratic) in character. Vine contends that 'the authoritarian and monolithic nature of Soviet-style collectivism probably militates against development beyond Stage 3 for the average citizen.' But he may be oversimplifying the way that Soviet people understand morality and their society, which is, after all, highly bureaucratic and committed to standard procedures in law, government and the economy.

Furthermore, while Vine and I concur in our call for more, and more sophisticated, evidence from a broader range of societal types and concerning other core concerns than justice as fairness, nevertheless we differ on the strength of the record to date. Many studies have been done by now in many parts of the world, and none has presented evidence of something significantly awry with Kohlberg's conceptualization of Stage 1 to 3 (and perhaps 4). That in itself is a major achievement and establishes the strong plausibility of culturally universal moral judgment stages.

VINE REPLIES TO EDWARDS

Edwards and I are in total agreement as to the importance of cross-cultural research for the testing of Kohlberg's theory, and as to the difficulties and dangers in attempts to make valid comparisons across cultures using the MJI dilemmas and scoring criteria. We also concur regarding the important omissions so far from the

451

standpoint of representative sampling—especially the lack of research on persons from non-capitalist and unstratified societies. Finally, we are in complete agreement that Kohlberg has no warrant for regarding the higher stages as superior in terms of 'moral adequacy', since the functional utility of a particular mode of moral reasoning will depend upon the values and social organization of any particular society.

Where we differ in our assessments of how well Kohlbergian research has confirmed the universality postulate is largely evident within my own chapter. I am more sceptical about how well a few dilemmas dealing with only a few moral issues can hope to tap the whole domain of moral reasoning—particularly in cultures where the values of individual rights and justice may not be the predominant ones. Likewise, I doubt whether the present scoring criteria can avoid penalizing responses which reflect alternative moral priorities, since the dimension of moral maturity is still defined by reference to Kohlberg's own ethical stance and liberal-democratic ideology. Furthermore, I am more critical of much of the cross-cultural data which Edwards cites, particularly since data obtained with the older scoring systems cannot be trusted, at least regarding the ubiquity of the higher stages. Bearing this point in mind, it is noteworthy that Edwards too can doubt whether even Stage 4 is a 'hard' structural advance.

Another point upon which Edwards is silent is the poor quality of a number of the studies that 'support' Kohlberg. Even the most recent research reports sometimes omit information vital to evaluation of those studies or reveal their deficiencies. For example Marchand-Jodoin and Samson (1982) used only two of Kohlberg's dilemmas to assess the effects of group discussion upon the moral reasoning of their French-Canadian sample, and had no control group. Their samples were clearly too small for some of their attempted comparisons, and they claimed significance for small MMS differences which could clearly have arisen by chance. Although they appear to have relied upon the current scoring criteria they also purport to have found some Stage '6' responses. Research of this kind can scarcely qualify as empirical support for any theory.

Finally, although Edwards and I agree about the important effects which social experience has in mediating stage progression, I am not sure that we take quite the same view of its causal role. I see the theory as remaining resolutely individualistic and rationalistic in regarding cognitive equilibration and hypothetical role-taking as causally central in moral development, thereby subordinating social influence and motives involving affective commitments to the function of stimulating moral reflection. In contrast, I hypothesize that relatively passive accommodation to cultural ideology plays a significant role in shaping moral thought, and that actual social attachments and goals play a fundamental part in determining which moral issues become salient enough to stimulate relevant structural changes. As Perret-Clermont (1980) has shown, actual social interaction is important, even in stimulating development through Piaget's general intellectual stages. In fact it appears that the collective performance can be superior, even for more advanced individuals. Thus she can claim that: 'Rooted in biological structures, put to work by the individual, intelligence itself also appears to be, in essence, the fruit of the community' (p. 179). This is surely even more true for 'moral intelligence'.

There are complex and emergent properties of social life, which simply resist adequate explanation in terms of individual psychology alone. This is particularly so when one goes beyond dyadic interpersonal relationships and considers intragroup and inter-group processes which involve regarding another person as a stereotyped group-representative (Tajfel, 1982; Turner and Giles, 1981). Since the extension of the boundaries of the groups to which one experiences primary moral loyalties is so fundamental to the development of a more impartial morality, it must surely follow that the latter is primarily a collective attainment, which is difficult if not impossible to achieve by abstract moral reflection alone. Perhaps this is the key to the difference between hypothetical reasoning, which can generate high-flown moral rhetoric of an abstract kind, and genuine moral commitments to others, which are more closely reflected in behaviour, and typically much more modest. If the collective ideology of one's culture can provide the raw materials for one's abstract moral reasoning, I suggest that actual experiences of social reciprocity with others are critical in giving it motivational substance.

REFERENCES

Marchand-Jodoin, L. and Samson J.-M. (1982) 'Kohlberg's theory applied to the moral and sexual development of adults', *Journal of Moral Education*, 11, pp. 247–58.

Perret-Clermont, A.-N. (1980) *Social Interaction and Cognitive Development in Children*, trans. Sherrard, C., London, Academic Press.

Tajfel, H. (Ed.) (1982) *Social Identity and Intergroup Relations*, Cambridge, Cambridge University Press.

Turner, J. C. and Giles, H. (Eds.), (1981) *Intergroup Behaviour*, Oxford, Basil Blackwell.

Part XV: Moral Research Methodology

28. Moral Research Methodology[1]

JAMES R. REST

SCOPE OF THIS CHAPTER AND DELINEATION OF THE CONSTRUCT

The most fundamental part of any research methodology is the measurement of the constructs. This chapter focuses on the way Kohlberg and his associates measure moral judgment. Although other methodological issues are important in appraising Kohlberg's overall research programme (such as the way he relates moral judgment to behaviour and emotion, his cross-cultural research, his intervention studies, his research on cognitive prerequisites of moral judgment, etc.), and although other methodologies have been developed (for instance, research using the Defining Issues Test now totals over 500 studies—Rest, 1979, 1983, in preparation), for the sake of brevity, this chapter addresses only issues of measuring moral judgment, and only Kohlberg's methods.[2]

At the onset, the construct, moral judgment, needs to be delineated from moral development in general and from overall personality organization. Both supporters and critics of Kohlberg have treated the variable, moral judgment, at times as if it was the whole of moral psychology (and sometimes even more), thus expanding the interpretation of moral judgment scores beyond what the operations or data warrant. Strictly speaking, moral judgment refers to that aspect of the psychology of morality dealing with how a person judges which course of action in a social situation is morally right (or just, or morally most defensible). Moral judgment does not directly deal with a person's sensitivity to noticing that there is a moral dilemma in a particular situation—in tests of moral judgment, the moral dilemma is already precoded in the presentation of the stimulus material and the subject's task. Moral judgment does not directly deal with whether a person values moral goals over other goals and is motivated to be moral, nor with a person's persistence and implementation of moral goals, nor with actual behaviour to bring about a moral goal. A person may have very sophisticated ways of making moral judgments, yet may prize other goals more, may fail to follow through, or may not behave morally. Strictly speaking, moral judgment deals with the processes involved in defining one course of action as morally right in a given situation, regardless of the person's intent or performance in actually carrying out that course of action. It is, of course, a major interest of research to clarify what role moral judgment has in decision-making and behaviour, but the assessment of moral judgment cannot in itself inform us on these matters (see Rest, 1983, for further discussion of the major components of morality and the delineation of moral judgment *vis-à-vis* other processes). It is critical to keep in mind that moral judgment scores represent a specific process and not moral psychology in general and certainly not personality organization in general.

FOUR BASIC METHODOLOGICAL DECISIONS

There are four basic decisions that any researcher must make in devising a method for assessing moral judgment. There are reasonable options at each of these four decision-points, and there are trade-offs in taking any of the options. In this chapter we shall examine which options Kohlberg chose, and discuss the advantages and disadvantages of doing so. (1) The first decision concerns the source of data. Kohlberg has chosen to obtain information by presenting a small set of hypothetical moral dilemmas, then through a semi-structured interview asking subjects to explain and justify their solutions to these dilemmas. (2) The second decision concerns how the subjects' responses are to be classified or coded. Kohlberg and his associates have spent over a decade in developing their scoring system, and we shall examine the assumptions and operations of this scoring system. (3) Once material is coded, there are decisions about how to represent or index a subject's codes in a summary score. Kohlberg has used stage typing indices and the moral maturity score. (4) And lastly, a researcher must propose a validation strategy (what studies must be done and what results must be obtained in order to claim that the scores produced by one's assessment procedure are really measuring moral judgment). Kohlberg has relied on face validity, longitudinal change and internal consistency as the primary grounds for claiming validity for his assessment procedure.

The source of information

Let us now go through each one of the four basic decisions in more detail. Regarding Kohlberg's choice of information source, several subissues are noteworthy: (a) choosing *hypothetical* dilemmas rather than real-life dilemmas, (b) choosing the particular set of dilemmas that reflect only some aspects of the morality domain, (c) using a one-to-one semi-structured interview, asking subjects to explain verbally and justify their solutions. Much has been written recently to criticize the use of hypothetical dilemmas rather than ones from real life. The problem with hypothetical dilemmas is that they are contrived, artificial and out of the natural life-space of subjects, and hence what a person says in response to a hypothetical dilemma may be unrepresentative of the way the person actually thinks in real-life situations. The research evidence is sparse and inconsistent on the comparability in moral judgment scores of real-life with hypothetical dilemmas—for instance, Haan (1978) found a great discrepancy between the two, but Damon (1977) found comparability. Moreover, it should be pointed out that there are several advantages to using hypothetical dilemmas. By choosing situations that are novel for the subject, we may have a clearer picture of the generalizing tendencies of the subject rather than specific, situation-bound learning of the subject. For instance, if we ask a young boy about a situation that just occurred in his life last night, we are likely to hear the subject repeating verbalizations that his parents or other adults made at the time, not only the boy's own spontaneous thoughts. Researchers in other areas (e.g., language development, memory, prose comprehension) often use novel stimuli (comparable to hypothetical dilemmas) in order to minimize specific, idiosyncratic effects and maximize the study of general rule-based responses. In addition, hypothetical dilemmas have the virtue of being more standardized than the peculiarities of real-life dilemmas (for instance, my experience of cheating behaviour may be quite different in many aspects from your experience of cheating behaviour). If we then attempt to compare moral judgment responses from my real-life dilemma with moral judgment responses from your real-life dilemma, one cannot know how much of any differences in scores to attribute to different situations and how much to attribute to differences in the general cognitive processes in each subject. While there is always the problem of linking hypothetical thinking to real-life thinking, there is currently no compelling evidence that responses to real-life dilemmas are more highly correlated with behaviour than responses to hypothetical dilemmas are correlated with behaviour (and there is a large body of literature to document the modest but significant relation of hypothetical judgments with behaviour—see Blasi, 1980; Rest, 1979).

Table 1. *Summary of Hypothetical Dilemmas*

Form A

1   Should Heinz steal an over-priced drug in order to save his dying wife?
2   Should Heinz be punished for stealing?
3   Should a boy refuse to give his father the money that Joe had earned himself in order to go to camp?

Form B

1   Should a doctor commit euthanasia for a terminally-ill patient in pain who requests it?
2   Should the doctor be punished for committing euthanasia?
3   Should a girl tattle on her sister who lied to her mother after the mother had broken a promise?

   Table 1 summarizes the dilemmas currently used by Kohlberg, and this particular set of dilemmas cannot claim to represent the domain of all possible moral dilemmas. For instance, the Kohlberg dilemmas do not raise issues of the distribution of wealth, power, or opportunity (e.g., Should a baseball player earn more than a teacher? What is the justice of quota systems for hiring minorities? Should the wealthy be taxed more than the not-so-wealthy?) Some researchers are basing new lines of research on moral dilemmas that raise different issues than Kohlberg's standard set (e.g., Gilligan, 1977; Eisenberg-Berg, 1979; Iozzi, 1980). The general implication of this is that we cannot be sure of the generalizability of Kohlberg's characterizations of moral thinking until sufficient research has been carried out based on representative sampling of the moral domain. A major hindrance is that as yet we do not have a map of the moral domain (i.e., What are all the types of moral dilemmas possible?), and without a map of the domain, we cannot define a representative set of dilemmas.

Using a one-to-one interview is a very time-consuming format and very expensive if each interview is transcribed before coding. This, however, is solely an issue of practicality and not one of basic reliability and validity. Where an issue of reliability is relevant, however, is in the reactive effect of different interviewers upon the subject's responses. For instance, an interviewer who is perceived as encouraging and interested is likely to elicit more thoughtful responses than an interviewer who is perceived as hostile or condescending. Although inter-judge reliability in *scoring* the interview is habitually assessed, research on interviewer reactivity is virtually non-existent.

An even more serious problem in the information source used by Kohlberg is its reliance upon verbal expression. Unless a subject can explain and justify an idea, it is assumed that the subject does not have the idea. This assumes that all thought operations which are credited to a subject can be verbally articulated. Yet we know that many cognitive operations work 'behind the scenes' and cannot be verbalized or explained. For instance, a 4-year-old child has acquired much of the grammatical rules of his language, but is not able to explain the operations used in encoding and decoding sentences. On the other hand, it can be argued that the flexible clinical interview is the only means for adjusting for a subject's idiosyncratic understandings, and only if a subject can explain and justify a position can a researcher be confident that the subject really understands an idea (cf. Damon, 1977). Arguments for and against the interview method have been forthcoming for decades (Braine, 1959, 1962; Inhelder and Sinclair, 1969; Smedslund, 1963, 1969), and are certainly not settled yet. But by taking one side of this argument, Kohlberg is vulnerable to the opposing criticisms, the most important of which is that the Kohlberg assessment procedure can claim to deal only with a subject's verbalization of moral judgments, not necessarily with the implicit and tacit cognitive operations which may not be verbalized but be crucial in real-life decision-making.

Coding the subject's responses

The Kohlberg group's major research effort over the last decade has been to develop the scoring system. Why did this take so long and why did it seem so important? One set of reasons has to do with handling interview material. Free response data to open-ended dilemmas pose vexing problems in setting up a reliable scoring system. First, there is the problem of establishing a unit of analysis. In Kohlberg's 1958 work, two scoring systems were devised: one using the sentence or completed thought as the basic unit of analysis, the other global rating using all the subject's utterances to a dilemma as the unit of analysis. Both of these solutions had serious shortcomings. When using the sentence as the basic unit, stage scoring was too much influenced by concrete-word usage. Furthermore, a repeated idea was scored as many times as it was repeated. When the global-rating system was used, invariably the subject said some things that seemed at one stage, but other things that seemed at another stage. Therefore, because subjects did not give responses that completely fit the stage typology, there was the problem of knowing how to classify conflicting themes. A second problem with free-response data is that different subjects bring up different topics and touch on different aspects of the dilemma. For instance, in the Heinz dilemma, some subjects start out speaking of the druggist's property rights, other subjects pay attention to Heinz's marriage vows. Therefore, information from different subjects is not comparable, and we do not know whether to attribute this phenomenon to fleeting quirks of attention or to fundamental organizing structures. A third problem is in specifying how explicitly the subject must state an idea to be credited with 'having' it, or how 'clinically' it can be inferred. A fourth problem is in deciding what is 'content' (i.e., inconsequential features that are discarded in the analysis) and what is 'structure' (i.e., features at the level of abstraction that is the particular concern of the analysis). In other words, how formalistic, deep or abstract should the analysis be?

The Kohlberg group over the last decade has identified these problems, devised strategies for dealing with them, and tested and revised strategies in light of their workability. Their new scoring system is impressive, particularly for its methods of dealing with the problems inherent in scoring free-interview material. Indeed, even researchers concerned with interview material who have no interest in morality *per se* would be well advised to look at the new scoring system to see how it handles these methodological problems. While the scoring system is lengthy and forbidding, the rigour and detailed analysis of thinking provided by the scoring procedures is unparalleled. Although some critics (e.g., Gilligan, 1977) claim that moral judgments can be analyzed in terms of other features and categories besides the ones used by Kohlberg, I have not found any alternative scoring system that has the rigour, breadth or depth of the Kohlberg system, and by comparison these alternative systems remain rather empty claims and unfulfilled promises to date. What the Kohlberg group set out to do with the scoring system has been done exceedingly well. Only the slow, painstaking pace and numerous revisions detract from the dramatic accomplishment that the final version really is. The scoring system is the most outstanding research accomplishment of the Harvard group. Anyone who speaks about Kohlberg's programme but does not attempt to score some interview material with the new scoring system is like a mechanic who speaks about a car but does not bother to look under the hood of the car at the motor and transmission.

The old 1958 scoring system actually showed more than passable inter-judge agreement (Kohlberg, 1976), and produced data trends that are satisfactory by current journal standards (see Kohlberg's review of studies in 1969). Yet, from a theoretical point of view, the old system was loose, inelegant, *ad hoc* and lacked a clean conceptual architecture. The original impetus for revising the system was not to develop a standardized test or to provide an easier method of scoring; instead, the goal was to develop a method of logical analysis of people's moral thinking that captured its grammar, analogous to Chomsky's (1957) grammar of language. The hope was that the fundamental categories and logical operations of people's moral thinking could be described and that these descriptors would be valid for all dilemmas and for all kinds of spoken or written material, not just for responses to the Heinz story and company.

As a source of ideas about basic categories and descriptors, Kohlberg turned to academic moral philosophy. Philosophers distinguish different kinds of moral questions (e.g., Who has a responsibility to act in a given situation? Assuming responsibility, exactly what is a person obligated to do? If a person falls short of her obligation, how should she be treated?) Furthermore, philosophers differentiate principles of justification (justice, utility, prudence, perfection, etc.). And philosophers differentiate contexts in which a problem is set (law, affectional relations, property, punishment). The essential task of moral judgment research is to characterize the concepts, categories, assumptions, integrating strategies and prioritization rules that people employ in judging that one course of action is morally right in a situation with multiple courses of action available. The psychologist's task is to represent the implicit, operative, natural moral philosophies of people who are not professional moral philosophers. Kohlberg is original in attempting to use the basic distinctions, categories and integrating strategies of professional moral philosophers as the basic units of analysis in representing the natural terms of thinking of non-philosophers. Piaget's own preliminary venture into morality research (1932) did not attempt this, and the psychological approaches that were dominant when Kohlberg was starting out were innocent of the most preliminary distinctions of philosophers (such as distinguishing morality from conformity to group norms). Kohlberg's approach was similar to the use by psychologists of Chomsky's generative grammar as a tool for analyzing children's natural acquisition of language. Unfortunately, in the moral philosophy area, there was not a single system that one could use as a starting-point (like Chomsky's in linguistics), and so Kohlberg had to piece together strands from many moral philosophers.

In the early 1970s Kohlberg attempted to create a cross-classification system to all the major sets of philosophical distinctions in which any possible moral judgment could be located and related to all other possible moral judgments. In these scoring systems, ease of scoring and practicality were not major concerns, as evidenced by the fact that one system had over 2 million possible scoring categories. As might be imagined, the complications in this work are bewildering; in more recent years the emphasis has shifted from philosophical analysis to the more practical objective of devising a workable scoring system.

Another impetus to revise the scoring system was the occurrence of some disconfirming data. Using the 1958 system, Kohlberg and Kramer (1969) found some reversals in the developmental sequence of some subjects between the testing in high school and the testing in college. In high school some students had been scored at Stages 4 and 5, but as sophomores in college they were scored Stage 2. In other data some anomalies were found in subjects moving from Stage 4 back to Stage 3 or skipping from Stage 3 to Stage 5 (Kohlberg, 1976). These irregularities were a major challenge to Kohlberg's views about how development is supposed to take place if one talks about 'stages'. In one place Kohlberg declared, 'A stage sequence disregarded by a single child is no sequence' (1973b, p. 182). His strong views about the stage model of development required absolutely no anomalies, and his views on the stage concept in turn have had a tremendous impact on the way that he defines the features of analysis and the scoring system. Let us spend just a little time examining Kohlberg's stage model of development.

Kohlberg stresses the distinction between qualitative and quantitative analysis. Whereas trait psychology and most psychometric approaches view the person as an aggregate of quantitative dimensions (where each person has more or less of the various trait or dimension), the cognitive-developmental approach uses ideal-typological constructs that emphasize the patterning of behaviour rather than its quantitative descriptors (frequency, amplitude, intensity, latency, etc.). The qualitative/quantitative distinction in moral judgment research calls attention to the cognitive developmentalists' interest in identifying underlying patterns of thought—the various organizations of thinking that are called different stages. But Kohlberg goes further and assumes that the characterization of one specimen of material from a subject implies that the subject can be characterized generally as being at that stage—for instance, if a subject is scored Stage 4 on the Heinz dilemma, then the subject is 'at' Stage 4 generally. This assumes that only one organization of thinking is present at one time in a subject, discounting the possibility of multiple patterns or of different patterns manifested in response to different situations. Although Kohlberg's view is logically consistent with the qualitative/quantitative distinction, it is not required by the distinction and is an overextension of the initial interest in studying patterns of thinking. Back in the 1950s and 1960s structuralists were arguing with associationists that a subject's behaviour (or judgment) does not consist of aggregates of isolated S-R bonds but rather that behaviour is generated from general underlying cognitive structures that the subject calls forth from long-term memory in actively construing the situation and in organizing activity in accord with the situation. In order to argue for the structuralist's general view, Kohlberg embraced a 'hard' stage concept. He has made extremely bold claims about a subject's consistency in moral judgment stage: usage across situations; he believes that his six stages comprise a universal, invariant, irreversible, step-by-step sequence; that stages are structural wholes; and that trained scorers can reliably identify stages in all sorts of material. (Quotes from Kohlberg are cited in Rest, 1979, to document advocacy of these views.) Kohlberg finds it comfortable to talk about a person being 'in' a particular stage and he characterizes movement as going through each stage one step at a time in the prescribed order.

In the development of the scoring system, scoring criteria and scoring rules have been selected (or discarded) on the basis of how well the data conform to strict stage expectations (no reversals in longitudinal data, minimal stage mix, no stage skipping). Given the clash between his hard-line stage model and the disconfirming data, rather than soften his stage model, Kohlberg's response was to revise the scoring system, assuming that the fault must be in confusing content with structure. Consequently, the trend in scoring system revisions has been to purge more and more content from structure, that is, to key stage distinctions on progressively more abstract and formalistic descriptors. As Colby (1978, p. 91) puts it, 'We can view this history as a progressive differentiation of content from structure. Each major scoring change has involved an important redefinition of the content-structure distinction.'

Of course some differentiation of structure from content is necessary. For instance, a subject might respond to the Heinz dilemma by saying, 'Heinz shouldn't steal because it'd be against the law.' We would want to know how the subject regards the law—as simple fear of legal punishment, as concern for the social system, or as what. One must go beyond content concerns (life, law affiliation) to get to the underlying structure.

The recent scoring systems purge content from stage differentiations by holding content constant (Kohlberg, *et al.*, 1978). It does this by a four-tier classification system: the interview material for each dilemma is first separated into issues (two for each dilemma), then into norms (twelve possible for each issue), then into elements (seventeen possible for each norm), and only then is scored by stage. For instance, one subject said, 'Heinz shouldn't steal. If everyone went around breaking the law, things would be wild; stealing, murder. You couldn't live.' Because this response favours not stealing, it is classified under the law *issue*. It invokes a concern for the law as a reason for obeying the law, therefore the *norm* is law. The specific type of concern about the law has to do with group consequences, so it is classified as *element* II.9. Only after these classifications are made do we finally get to decide what stage it is. At this point, the scoring manual presents us with these choices:

> *Stage 3 scoring criteria:* 'One should obey the law because if everybody breaks the law there would be chaos, things would be wild, or everything would be topsy-turvy; *OR* because without laws immoral people would cause chaos.' (The response above is scored as an example of Stage 3 structure.) (Kohlberg *et al.*, 1978, Pt. 3, p. 96)

> *Stage 3/4 scoring criteria:* 'People should obey the law because otherwise laws will no longer be a guide to people; *OR* because otherwise a bad example or precedent will be set; *OR* because otherwise people will steal even if they don't really have to, will steal without thinking, or will think stealing is okay.' [*Example of a subject's response scored under this criteria:* 'Yes, I mean in general this type of precedent would be established for any kind of a want that somebody wants to satisfy. Just go ahead and rob or something like that, the results would be.' (Scored Stage 3/4—Law II.9)] (Kohlberg *et al.*, 1978, Pt. 3, p. 97)

> *Stage 4 scoring criteria:* 'People should obey the law because the law is essential if society or civilization is to survive; *OR* because the law is necessary for social organization, general social order, or smooth social functioning; *OR* because giving way to individual beliefs or values and decisions will cause disorganization.' [*Example:* 'If it's just, if it's necessary to preserve order. (Why do we need laws?) Well, I think without laws there would be chaos, there wouldn't be any order so to speak. I am talking about just laws now.' (Scored Stage 4—Law II.9.)] (Kohlberg *et al.*, 1978; Pt. 3, p. 107)

> *Stage 5 scoring criteria:* 'One should obey the law because if individuals are to live together in society, there must be some common agreement; *OR* because laws represent a necessary structure of social agreement.' [*Example:* 'Because it is so hard for people to live together unless there are some laws governing their actions. Not everybody is good certainly and we have to go by some code, so to speak, that we have to follow to make sure that everybody has their own individual rights.' (Scored Stage 5—Law II.17)] (Kohlberg *et al.*, 1978, Pt. 3, p. 117)

Notice that by the time we are able to score a response by stage, the distinctions have become exceedingly fine. (Admittedly I chose examples from the most difficult to distinguish points in the system.) The new scoring system purges content with a vengeance. In effect, the Kohlberg group contends that there is no developmental significance in whether a subject appeals to a husband's affection or to maintaining social order; what is important is the particular subvariety of social order the subject envisions (e.g., the subclassifications above) or what concept of affection the subject has (many subvarieties of this are also distinguished by stage). By the new system, a stage score would not reflect the difference between a response that appealed to a Stage 3 affectional concern from a response that appealed to a Stage 3 social-order concern. Variance in stage scores reflects the kind of distinctions embodied in the four examples above. One might ask, has something important been lost on the road to purging content? (See Rest, 1979, for further discussion.)

Indexing

A coding system is essentially a set of rules and procedures for converting interview material into the categories used for data analysis—i.e., for taking what a subject says in a particular passage and giving it a stage score. An entire interview produces many codes. Indexing is a procedure for deriving a general score from all these codes, integrating the information in some way so that the numbers produced reflect the developmental level of the subjects.

Many ways of indexing have been proposed by researchers: a subject's score is that stage that is used most (Kohlberg, 1958); a subject's score is the highest stage that is coded throughout the protocol (Damon, 1977); a subject's score is based on the extent to which the lower stages are rejected (Carroll and Rest, 1981); a subject's score is a continuous variable representing the weighted average of the extent of use of the various stages (Kohlberg's moral maturity quotient, 1958); and the DIT's P and D scores are also variants (Rest, 1979). Kohlberg's method of indexing in the new scoring system is essentially a two-step procedure: first, within a story, whenever different passages address the same issue (i.e., have the same issue-norm-element code) but have different stage scores, only the highest stage score is recorded (the 'upper stage inclusion rule'). And so the first step involving the recording of codes reflects a 'highest-stage' emphasis. However, in step two a 'predominant-stage rule' is used: a subject's overall score is based on that stage with the most codes. If most of the codes are scored at Stage 2, then the subject's score is 'Stage 2'. If a subject has 20 per cent or more codes scored at another stage (e.g., Stage 3), then the score is predominantly Stage 2, with Stage 3 minor stage (i.e., interpreted as a transition from Stage 2 to Stage 3). (Various weighting rules have been used from time to time, but the essential features of Kohlberg's indexing procedure are these two steps.)[3]

This indexing procedure is a reasonable one. However, allocating a stage number to a subject, we must not be led into assuming that there is a real entity such as a Stage 2 subject or a Stage 3 subject—as if a person had only one programme of thinking in his/her head at a time. This assumption is wrong because different dilemmas, different instructions to the subject, different response modes (rating statements rather than producing them) all affect what stage of thinking a subject will manifest. A subject is not 'in' a stage, but rather a subject manifests different organizations of thinking depending on the context and conditions of assessment. The question of assessment is, 'which organizations of thinking does a subject use in making moral judgments, to what extent, and under what conditions?' (See Rest, 1979, for further discussion.)

Secondly, the 'upper stage inclusion rule' entails that whenever a subject gives material that matches the scoring criteria at a lower stage, it is not recorded on the scoring sheet if elsewhere in the discussion of that dilemma the subject gives more elaborated material that is coded at a higher stage. For example, suppose that a subject started out discussing the Heinz dilemma with the response scored Stage 3 (above example), then later in the discussion the subject gave the response scored Stage 4. In this case, the lower-stage response would not be recorded at all and would not contribute to stage mixture. The theoretical justification for such a procedure is that higher-stage statements hierarchically include the lower-stage idea. Such scoring rules contribute to giving the Kohlberg measure good internal reliability and make sense as methods for inducing good inter-rater reliability.

Nevertheless, this procedure does not allow disconfirmation of the hard-stage model.

Any indexing procedure involves highlighting some information at the expense of other information, emphasizing some codes and de-emphasizing other codes. At this point in research good *a priori* arguments can be made for many indexing procedures, and developmental theory is not decisive for favouring stage-typing based on predominant use, or highest stage use, or averaging-composite indices, etc. The only reasonable strategy for choosing among indices is to try each one out empirically, and to see which procedure generates scores that best behave like the construct implies moral judgment scores should behave. In other words, to use one's data to calculate various indices, put them in competition with each other, and see which one produces better trends in the validity studies. To my knowledge, this has not yet been done in a systematic manner with Kohlberg's data (see Davison, Robbins and Swanson, 1978, for an example of testing various indices).

A validity strategy

What are the criteria for validating a measure of moral judgment? If there are two or more measures of moral judgment, what studies can be done to test which is the better measure?

Kohlberg's own discussions of the validity of his measure (e.g., 1976; Colby *et al.*, 1983) emphasize the stage properties of the construct (ordered sequence, structured wholeness—by which Kohlberg means internal consistency), reliability (inter-rater, test-retest, alternate forms), and face validity (information is collected by posing moral dilemmas and scoring involves a philosophical analysis of the person's reasoning). As we shall see in the next section, the studies on these aspects of the new scoring system are very impressive—indeed, the findings are without parallel in all social-cognitive development. For no other measurement procedure in the field have such strong confirmatory trends been reported.

There are, however, other implications of the construct, moral judgment, that are also testable and which are relevant to the question, do the scores from the test behave as they are supposed to? The aspects that Kohlberg chooses to emphasize are certainly central to the validation of a test of moral judgment, but they are theoretically incomplete and do not reflect the range of studies that are technically possible at this time and that are germane to building a case for the validity of the test. Validating a test of moral judgment is an incremental process of testing many implications of the construct with diverse methodology and cross-replications. Kohlberg has not set forth such a programme and has not laid out a more comprehensive listing of studies that bear on the validity of a test of moral judgment. Table 2 presents a list of validation studies and major questions that I think are relevant. (For examples of the type of studies, see Rest, 1979, 1983, in preparation.)

In this list of eighteen types of studies I have not included cross-cultural studies. I think it is possible that the basic organizational structures by which people make judgments of right and wrong may differ across cultural groups (just as the basic grammars of different languages differ) and yet that Kohlberg's descriptions of his six stages do describe the basic structures for most modern Westerners. Therefore, finding a culture that developed fundamentally different categories and

Table 2.	*List of Possible Validity Studies for a Test of Moral Judgment*

I	RELIABILITY
1. Inter-judge agreement (Can independent observers of a subject's responses agree on what the subject did?)
2. Test-retest stability (Is the score stable enough to allow a characterization of the subject for a period of time?)
3. Internal consistency (Is there sufficient trans-situational consistency across the situations sampled to warrant some generalization to non-test situations?)

II	COGNITIVE-DEVELOPMENT
   A	*Sequence* (Is there evidence of an order of development?)

4. Cross-sectional group comparisons, or 'criterion group validity' (Do presumed more-expert groups have higher scores than presumed less-expert groups?)
5. Longitudinal follow-up (In repeated testings of the same subjects over time, do test scores increase over periods of presumed development?)
6. Sequential analyses (Can cohort effects of cultural-historical change explain away age-related change?)
7. Internal structure (Do patterns of item intercorrelations and/or scaling studies indicate an ordering of items/responses in accord with the theoretical sequence?)

   B	*Cognitive nature* (Is there evidence that 'upward' change is due to increased cognitive capacity?)

8. Correlations (and 'prerequisiteness') of cognitive elements (Do Comprehension scores correlate with moral judgment? Do Comprehension scores increase as moral judgment increases? Are Formal Operation and/or Social perspective-taking prerequisites of moral judgment?)
9. Intervention studies designed to enhance cognitive development (Do experiences which theoretically should enhance development actually increase test scores?)
10. Intervention studies designed to demonstrate 'invulnerability' to 'faking' and other manipulations of 'non-essential' test taking sets

III	DISTINCTIVENESS (Do scores produced by the test reflect moral judgment rather than some other characteristic?)

11. 'Content' validity (Does the task imposed by the test and the scoring operations appear to be measuring moral judgment?)
12. Convergent-divergent pattern of correlations (Do scores from the test correlate more highly with other measures of moral judgment than with measures of theoretically dissimilar constructs?)
13. Selective responsivity to treatment specificity (Do test scores increase more in response to distinctively 'moral' stimulation than in response to 'non-moral' stimulation?)
14. Unique predictability in multiple-regression analyses (When predicting to some external criterion, e.g., school behaviour, political behaviour, do test scores add significant and unique variance to predictability beyond that accounted for by other likely variables—IQ, SES, attitudes, social desirability?)

IV	ROLE IN ACTUAL DECISION-MAKING (How do we know that the test's particular characterization of moral thinking represents the crucial process in the decision-making that is operative in real-life behaviour? Or do the scores represent defensive post-decisional rationalization, or do the scores represent characterizations of thinking that miss the critical features which are decisive in moral choice?)

15. Correlational studies of thinking in hypothetical moral dilemmas with thinking in real-life moral dilemmas
16. Studies linking moral judgment with actual behaviour (experimental measures or 'real-life' behaviour, including 'advocacy behaviour')
17. Studies which combine moral judgment scores with information from other related variables to increase predictability of behaviour
18. Manipulate moral judgment in order to change behaviour

---

integration strategies for moral problem-solving would not invalidate Kohlberg's test for our culture—hence I did not include cross-cultural studies as one of the validating studies. Nevertheless, cross-cultural studies are of tremendous importance and interest and so far Kohlberg's claim for cross-cultural universality seems to be supported more than disconfirmed (see reviews by Rest, 1983, and Snarey, Reimer and Kohlberg, in press).

What is beyond technical possibility now is to explain and predict with great accuracy how people live their lives morally. In order to do this, more is necessary than just knowing how they make moral judgments. Also involved are such processes as their moral sensitivity (how they encode social situations), their motivation to choose moral goals over other goals, their perseverence and ability to follow through on plans of action, etc. Theoretically, all these processes are involved and interact in complex ways in the production of a moral act (see Rest, 1983, 1984 for discussion). I think the strongest validation of a test of moral judgment will be in its contribution along with knowledge of other variables in jointly explaining and predicting ongoing, real-life moral behaviour.

SUMMARY OF VALIDATION RESEARCH

Recently the Kohlberg group published the results of using their new scoring procedure in a longitudinal study of more than twenty years (Colby *et al.*, 1983). The results are spectacular. Test-retest correlations were .96, .99 and .97 (using different data and different raters). Inter-rater correlations were .98, .96 and .92 for forms A, B and C respectively. Correlation between Form A and Form B was .95. On the longitudinal data of subjects tested at three- to four-year intervals over twenty years, fifty-six of fifty-eight subjects showed upward change, with *no* subjects skipping any stages; only 6 per cent of the 195 comparisons showed backward shifts between two particular testings. The internal consistency of scores is also impressive: between 67 and 72 per cent of the scores were at one stage and only 1 to 3 per cent of the scores were spread further than two adjacent stages; Cronbach's alpha was .92, .96 and .94 for Forms A, B and C respectively. Other studies by Gibbs and Widamon (1982),[4] Snarey, Reimer and Kohlberg (in press), Nisan and Kohlberg (1982), Walker (1980, 1983) and others provide replications and corroborations of the reliability, internal consistency and developmental ordering of Kohlberg's new scoring system. If one is not favourably impressed with these findings, it is difficult to know what would be impressive in all of social development literature.

Strong challenges have been made recently about Kohlberg's instrument and theory being sex-biased, favouring males and shortchanging females (e.g., Gilligan, 1977). Because Kohlberg's original norming sample and the longitudinal sample consisted entirely of males, it is understandable how a sex bias might have crept into the system. However, an extensive and careful review of the literature by Walker (in press) reveals that Kohlberg's scoring system does not show sex bias in more than seventy studies. The most recent studies using the latest scoring system also show no sex differences. And so a review of the literature does not support the claim that Kohlberg's test or theory is sex-biased, and Gilligan's characterization of female morality as separate and different from male morality confuses the distinctive processes of moral judgment with personality organization in general (see Thoma, in preparation, for meta-analyses on several thousand subjects).

Notwithstanding this positive appraisal of Kohlberg's new scoring system, several qualifications and future needs should be cited.

(1)   The system is a very coarse-grained description of development across the life-span, and not one sensitively attuned to precise, short-term developments. Even though the upward trends in the longitudinal studies are remarkably clear and consistent, nevertheless, the amount of change over twenty years is not great: most subjects moved up less than two full stages; one full stage shift (e.g., Stage 2 to Stage 3 or Stage 3 to Stage 4) takes on average 13.9 years. Most subjects start out around Stage 2 and end up around Stage 4.

(2)   With revisions in the stage definitions, the upper stages have become rare or non-existent. Stage 5 scoring even in older samples is extremely rare. Stage 6 is not a scoring possibility because the new scoring system does not describe it. Therefore the status of Stages 5 and 6 in Kohlberg's system is in some doubt. Perhaps the rare occurrence of the higher stages is due in part to the task characteristics of the interview and to the stringency of the scoring rules—a subject has to intrude a philosophical treatise in discussing Heinz-and-the-drug in order to be credited with the higher stages. This may underestimate higher-level thinking. Some support for this view comes from research using the DIT (a recognition test of moral judgment derived from Kohlberg's general approach) that finds indices based on Stages 5 and 6 the most useful indices. In any case, since the new scoring system has redefined many stage characteristics, Kohlberg needs to redo his theoretical characterization of the six stages (the accounts of 1971 and 1973a are now out of date), describing how all the characteristics of each stage form a unified organization, how each stage builds on the previous one and is a better conceptual tool for moral decision-making, and especially to describe theoretically the features of Stages 5 and 6 even if they are rare occurrences in the population at large.

(3)   With respect to stage consistency, it must be pointed out that the consistency of scores in Kohlberg's data is not a strong test of stage consistency in a person's moral thinking. Various scoring rules have been devised to weed out stage mixture, thus the procedure is biased toward stage consistency. Furthermore, the overwhelming majority of subjects even in Kohlberg's longitudinal sample are not pure types but show stage mixture. Therefore, given the coarse-grained nature of the system and the imperfect tests of stage consistency, one must be wary of how strong a claim can be made for the 'hard stage model' of development based on the longitudinal data (Colby *et al.*, 1983).

(4)   The new scoring system has been devised to generate scores that demonstrate stage-like properties: i.e., upward movement over time, negligible reversals, no stage skipping, high internal consistency, high reliability. However, the research in moral judgment is broadening now not solely to focus on characterizing the organizational forms of moral reasoning but also to study the role of moral judgment in decision-making and the regulation of behaviour. In a recent paper Kohlberg and Candee (1984) find that their stage scores based on the new scoring system are not the best predictors of behaviour. They talk about subjects who are scored at Stage 3 and Stage 4 by the new standard scoring system but who have intitutions and tacit, unverbalized apprehensions about Stage 5 ways of thinking. And it is these unarticulated, tacit understandings that govern actual decision-making and behaviour, not that which is verbalized and codable according

to the new scoring system. This raises some questions about the future of the new scoring system. Can a system based solely on verbalization really get at the governing structures of behaviour—structures which may not always be articulated and explainable? Is a scoring system designed to maximize stage-like properties necessarily the best strategy for identifying those features of thinking that are most crucial in governing decision-making and behaviour? At this point in the research enterprise these are open questions, because no one has much of a data base to proffer strong statements. Perhaps as we expand the characteristics of what we want moral judgment scores to do, we shall have to revise our notions about which features are important, and we may have to devise new ways of collecting information as well. But at this time it is clear that Kohlberg and his associates have succeeded grandly in what they originally set out to do.

NOTES

1 Portions of this chapter are adapted from Rest, J. R. (1983) 'Morality', in P. Mussen (Gen. Ed.), *Handbook of Child Psychology*, Vol. 3, 4th ed., New York, Wiley. Further discussion of many points can be found there. This chapter was supported in part by NIH Grant #RO1-MH38656.
2 Although I refer to 'Kohlberg's' methods, test and theory, I mean to include the many collaborators who have made major contributions, especially Dr Anne Colby, Dr John Gibbs, Dr Dan Candee and Dr Marcus Leibermann. Although I do not attempt to separate out the credits, Dr Kohlberg regularly cites their contributions to the Harvard group.
3 Kohlberg also describes a 'morality maturity score' which is a weighted average of stage usage, however, he regards this index as less preferable and therefore my focus is on his stage-typing index.
4 The Gibbs and Widamon studies use a slightly modified version of the Kohlberg test; however, it correlates .8 with the Kohlberg test and keys on the same features.

REFERENCES

Blasi, A. (1980) 'Bridging moral cognition and moral action: A critical review of the literature', *Psychological Bulletin*, 88, pp. 1–45.
Braine, M. D. S. (1959) 'The ontogeny of certain logical operations: Piaget's formulation examined by nonverbal methods', *Psychological Monographs*, 73, (5, Whole No. 475).
Braine, M. D. S. (1962) 'Piaget on reasoning: A methodological critique and alternative proposals', in W. Kessen and C. Kunlman (Eds.), *Thought in the Young Child, Monographs of the Society for Research in Child Development*, 27 (2, Whole No. 83).
Carroll, J. and Rest, J. R. (1981) 'Development in moral judgment as indicated by rejection of lower stage statements', *Journal of Research in Personality*, 15, pp. 538–44.
Chomsky, N. (1957) *Snytactic Structures*, The Hague, Mouton.
Colby, A. (1978) 'Developments in a theory', in W. Damon (Ed.), *New Directions for Child Development*, 2, San Francisco, Jossey-Bass, pp. 89–103.
Colby, A., Kohlberg, L., Gibbs, J. and Lieberman, M. (1983) 'A longitudinal study of moral judgment', *SRCD Monograph*, 48, 1–2, Serial No. 200.
Damon, W. (1977) *The Social World of the Child*, San Francisco, Jossey-Bass.
Davison, M. L., Robbins, S. and Swanson, D. (1978) 'Stage structure in objective moral judgments', *Developmental Psychology*, 14, 2, pp. 137–46.
Eisenberg-Berg, N. (1979) 'Relationship of prosocial moral reasoning to altruism, political liberalism, and intelligence', *Developmental Psychology*, 15, pp. 87–9.
Gibbs, J. C. and Widamon, K. F. (1982) *Social Intelligence: Measuring the Development of Sociomoral Reflection*, Englewood Cliffs, N.J., Prentice-Hall.

Gilligan, C. (1977) 'In a different voice: Women's conceptions of the self and of morality', *Harvard Educational Review*, 47, 4, pp. 481–517.

Haan, N. (1978) 'Two moralities in action contexts: Relationships to thought, ego regulation, and development', *Journal of Personality and Social Psychology*, 30, pp. 286–305.

Inhelder, B. and Sinclair, H. (1969) 'Learning cognitive structures', in P. H. Mussen, J. Langer and M. Covington (Eds.), *Trends and Issues in Developmental Psychology*, New York, Holt, Rinehart and Winston.

Iozzi, L. (1980) 'The environmental issues test', in L. Kuhmerker *et al.* (Eds.), *Evaluating Moral Development and Programs with a Value Dimension*, Schenectady, N.Y., Character Research Press.

Kohlberg, L. (1958) 'The development of modes of moral thinking and choice in the years 10 to 16', Unpublished doctoral dissertation, University of Chicago.

Kohlberg, L. (1969) 'Stage and sequence: The cognitive-developmental approach to socialization', in D. Goslin (Ed.), *Handbook of Socialization Theory and Research*, Chicago, Ill., Rand McNally, pp. 347–480.

Kohlberg, L. (1971) 'From is to ought: How to commit the naturalistic fallacy and get away with it in the study of moral development', in T. Mischel (Ed.), *Cognitive Development and Epistemology*, New York, Academic Press.

Kohlberg, L. (1973a) 'Continuities in childhood and adult moral development revisited', in P. B. Baltes and K. W. Schaie (Eds.), *Life-Span Developmental Psychology: Personality and Socialization*, New York, Academic Press.

Kohlberg, L. (1973b) 'The claim to moral adequacy of a highest stage of moral judgment', *Journal of Philosophy*, 40, pp. 630–46.

Kohlberg, L. (1976) 'Moral stages and moralization: The cognitive-developmental approach', in T. Lickona (Ed.), *Moral Development and Behaviour*, New York, Holt, Rinehart and Winston.

Kohlberg, L. and Candee, D. (1984) 'The relation of moral judgment to moral action', in W. Kurtines and J. Gewirtz (Eds.), *Morality and Moral Development*, New York, Wiley.

Kohlberg, L. and Kramer, R. (1969) 'Continuities and discontinuities in childhood moral development', *Human Development*, 12, pp. 93–120.

Kohlberg, L., Colby, A., Gibbs, J. and Speicher-Dubin, B. (1978) *Standard Form Scoring Manual*, Cambridge, Mass., Center for Moral Education, Harvard University.

Nisan, M. and Kohlberg, L. (1982) 'Universality and cross-cultural variation in moral development: A longitudinal and cross-sectional study in Turkey', *Child Development*, 53, pp. 865–76.

Piaget, J. (1932) *The Moral Judgment of the Child*, New York, Norton.

Rest, J. R. (1979) *Development in Judging Moral Issues*, Minneapolis, Minn., University of Minnesota Press.

Rest, J. R. (1983), 'Morality', in J. Flavell and E. Markman (Eds.), *Cognitive Development*, Vol. 4, in P. Mussen (Gen. Ed.), *Manual of Child Psychology*, New York, Wiley.

Rest, J. R. (1984) 'The major components of morality', in W. Kurtines and J. Gewirtz (Eds.), *Morality and Moral Development*, New York, Wiley.

Rest, J. R. (in preparation) 'Advances in morality research: Reviews', University of Minnesota.

Smedslund, J. (1963) 'Development of concrete transitivity of length in children', *Child Development*, 34, pp. 389–405.

Smedslund, J. (1969) 'Psychological diagnostics', *Psychological Bulletin*, 71, pp. 237–48.

Snarey, J. R. (1983) 'The cross-cultural universality of social-moral development: A critical review of Kohlbergian research', Unpublished manuscript, Harvard University.

Snarey, J. R., Reimer, J. and Kohlberg, L. (in press) 'The development of social-moral reasoning among Kibbutz adolescents: A longitudinal cross-cultural study', *Developmental Psychology*.

Thoma, S. (in preparation for publication) 'A review of sex differences in the Defining Issues Test', Unpublished manuscript, University of Minnesota.

Walker, L. J. (1980) 'Cognitive and perspective-taking prerequisites for moral development', *Child Development*, 51, pp. 131–9.

Walker, L. J. (1983 in press) 'Sex differences in the development of moral reasoning: A critical review of the literature', *Child Development*.

Walker, L. J., deVries, B. and Bichard, S. L. (in press) 'The hierarchical nature of stages of moral development'.

29. Kohlberg's Moral Judgment Interview: Is There a Need for Additional Research?

CHARLES EVANS

During the past two decades Lawrence Kohlberg and others have conducted extensive research in an effort to validate Kohlberg's theory of cognitive moral development. Much of this research has been conducted using the Moral Judgment Interview, or one of a variety of objective instruments based upon Kohlberg's theory and dilemmas that have been included in the Moral Judgment Interview. One of the most widely used objective instruments has been Rest's Defining Issues Test (Rest, 1974).

When interpreting the results of research, the reader must be aware of the instrument used, scoring procedures for the instrument, and how the instrument was used within the experimental or quasi-experimental design. In the case of Kohlberg's Moral Judgment Interview, several revisions have been made in the scoring procedures to address questions posed by critics. Even with changes made in the instrumentation, research results have raised questions regarding the validity of the theory as well as the instrument itself. Some of the questions raised in reference to the Moral Judgment Interview relate to the sample used to standardize the instrument; male characters serving as protagonists in the dilemmas and other biases against women; correlation of equivalent forms; and the ability of the instrument to distinguish actual stage development from pseudo-development.

In addition to questions related to the validity of the instrument itself, the use of the instrument can cause problems. If the research design calls for a pre- and post-test, what happens to the reliability? Does incidental learning occur as a result of exposure to the dilemmas contained in the instrument? And, can the interviewer influence the responses on the Moral Judgment Interview, oral version?

These and other concerns related to the validity, reliability, use and scoring of the Moral Judgment Interview will be addressed within this chapter. Most comments will be confined to the Moral Judgment Interview, as objective

471

instruments do not measure the same constructs. However, results of research which have used objective instruments will be used in support of given arguments.

VALIDITY

Since 1958 Kohlberg's theory has received praise and criticism alike. While much of the criticism has been directed at the validity of the theory, it is imperative that one look at the instrumentation used to measure moral stage development. As previously mentioned, the Moral Judgment Interview is one instrument that has been used to help validate the theory. From its inception with Kohlberg's original work (Kohlberg, 1958), this instrument has also received much criticism.

Evidence in support of the validity of the instrument is somewhat weak. Kurtines and Greif (1974) were unable to find evidence that the six stages by themselves had discriminate validity and predictive utility. Distinction among the last three stages was difficult, and very few studies had been conducted that included Stages 5 and 6. This lack of predictive validity was supported by a study where Stage 2 and 6 individuals reported similar behaviour but with different reasoning regarding political activism (Haan, Smith and Block, 1968). Evidence of construct validity was found to be lacking in a study by Ruma and Mosher (1967).

Since the publication of many of the critiques of the Moral Judgment Interview, similar to those above, the instrument and scoring procedures have been revised (Kohlberg, 1978). This revision was based upon data from a longitudinal study consisting of fifty-three subjects from the original study (Colby and Kohlberg, 1981). Efforts were made to answer criticisms, and the instrument was standardized.

One modification that has occurred in the instrument has been the removal of the criteria for assessing reasoning at Stage 6. This was done as none of the longitudinal sample seemed 'intuitively' to be Stage 6. Justification for this claim was an inadequacy on the part of the dilemmas to differentiate between Stage 5 and 6 (Colby and Kohlberg, 1981). However, by removing Stage 6 from the criteria for assessing moral reasoning, Kohlberg is seemingly rejecting aspects of his theory and the ultimate goal toward which the other stages are developing. In light of the findings of the longitudinal study, Kohlberg (1978) claims that Stage 6 is mainly a theoretical construct, which would be better interpreted as an elaboration of B substage of Stage 5.

This change also raises serious questions about the validity of the Moral Judgment Interview. Can the criteria for assessing Stage 6 reasoning be removed from the scoring manual based upon the fact that Stage 6 reasoning was not found in the longitudinal study, which consisted of fifty-three males from the original study? If the sample had been randomly selected and representative of the population, maybe the changes could be justified. However, an all-male sample is not representative of the population. As such, it is impossible to generalize the absence of Stage 6 reasoning.

An additional change in the instrument was made after a group of college sophomores appeared to regress to Stage 2 (Kohlberg and Kramer, 1969). However, after additional analysis of the data was conducted, an actual advance to Stage 4½ was found to have occurred (Kohlberg, 1973). What was originally thought to be a regression to Stage 2 was actually a questioning and rejection of previous commitment to conventional thought. With the addition of Stage 4½, the claim for validity of the concept 'invariant sequence' was supposedly upheld; however, regression has also been found in a study reported by Murphy and Gilligan (1980). Subjects participating in the study were Harvard-Radcliff undergraduates enrolled in a course on moral and political choice. Prior to starting the course in 1970, each of the fifty-three subjects, forty-two males and fourteen females, completed a written version of the Standard Moral Dilemmas, Form A or B. After the completion of the course they completed the alternate form. In 1973 twenty-six of the original group were interviewed with the structured interview. Use of the Issue Scoring Guide (Kohlberg, 1972) and protocols from twenty-two subjects who had responded to similar dilemmas in the first and third testing sessions resulted in regression being reported for six subjects. Each showed a regression of two-thirds of a stage or more, and all but one moved from postconventional to conventional.

The same protocols were also scored using the revised manual (Kohlberg *et al.*, 1978), as revisions had been made in light of the regression reported by Kohlberg and Kramer (1969). Even with the revised manual, six of the twenty subjects showed a regression, three of whom regressed two-thirds of a stage or more. Of the six, four regressed from the postconventional and two from the conventional.

The last analysis involved eighteen cases from the third and fourth interview, which was conducted orally in 1978. Of the eighteen cases, seven subjects showed regression, three of whom regressed two-thirds of a stage or more.

As in Kohlberg and Kramer's report (1969), all the subjects were in late adolescence, which questions the instrument's ability to assess adequately reasoning at the higher stages. Furthermore, Murphy and Gilligan (1980) suggest that the regression may have resulted from mistaking contextual relativizing for regression in the scoring process. Other factors that could have influenced the scores include knowledge of Kohlberg's theory, with the exception of the first session, and the use of alternate formats, written and oral.

Regardless of the possible causes for the regression in reasoning, its occurrence weakens Kohlberg's claim of validity. Based upon the nature of the instrument and what it is measuring, it would be assumed that construct validity scores would be available. However, Kohlberg does not feel that construct validity is appropriate, and contends that researchers should use research findings of invariant sequence as evidence of validity (Gibbs, 1979). However, incidence of regression hardly supports his contention.

Aside from the question of validity based upon a sample consisting of males, gender has provoked controversy regarding the protagonists within the hypothetical dilemmas. While the results of research are as yet inconclusive, some studies have found the gender of the protagonist to have an influence on the measurement of moral reasoning. Bussey and Maughan (1982) found that males scored significantly higher ($p < .001$) on male protagonist dilemmas than females on Form A of the Moral Judgment Interview. However, females did not score significantly higher on the female protagonist dilemmas, even though their scores did increase. Conversely, male scores dropped when the protagonist was a female. Similar results were reported by Freeman and Giebnik (1979), whereby both males and females made higher judgments to dilemmas with same-sex protagonists; however, the effect was only significant for females ($p < .005$). Subjects participating in the study were 11, 14 and 17 years of age, and the Objective Assessment of Moral Development Instrument was used to assess moral development. Conflicting results were reported by Orchowsky and Jenkins (1979), with subjects scoring higher on opposite-sex dilemmas used with the Defining Issues Test.

Additional criticism regarding the Moral Judgment Interview's bias against women has also been made. Evidence of a sexual bias has been reported by Murphy and Gilligan (1980), where males scored approximately one-half of a stage higher then females. Undergraduate college students served as subjects. Similar findings were reported by Schnurer (1976), with the reasoning of women being more pragmatic, stereotyped and immature. Male reasoning tended to be more vigorous, autonomous and independent.

While the above studies involved college-age subjects, adult males were found to reason at higher levels in a longitudinal study conducted by Holstein (1976). Using the Issue Scoring System (Kohlberg, 1972), males were found to be significantly higher than females on the first test ($p < .001$). Three years later the difference was not significant; however, the mean moral maturity scores (MMS) for the males were still higher. Holstein (1976) also interviewed the 13-year-old children of the adult subjects and was unable to find a significant difference. Again at age 16 the difference was not significant; however, there was a trend toward higher scores for the boys. All the subjects in Holstein's (1976) study were middle-class, intact families consisting of a father, mother and siblings.

Incidence whereby males have advanced beyond females in adulthood has also been reported by Kohlberg and Kramer (1969). Based upon their studies, only 6 per cent of the high school boys remained within Stage 3 once they reached adulthood. In contrast, Stage 3 seemed to be predominant for adult women.

While some of the bias might be a result of the socialization process, Gilligan (1977) sees the bias lying in the hierarchical sequence of the stages and criteria used within the various stages. As such, there has been a tendency for women to be categorized at Stage 3—the interpersonal concordance of 'good boy—nice girl' orientation. Criteria that categorize one as good—tact, gentleness and awareness of feeling—are also indicative of deficiency in moral development. However, this should not be interpreted to mean that women cannot reason beyond Stage 3. Without question, one's interpretation of a situation is based upon past experiences, and in the case of women their interpretations of hypothetical dilemmas have been based upon their reconstructing the dilemma in terms of real-life situations based upon the concept of conflicting responsibility. Therefore, the instrument may not account for actual adult experiences of moral conflict since it was standardized using a male sample.

Conflicting results have also appeared when the remoteness of the dilemma was a variable within a research study. Using the Objective Assessment of Moral Development, Freeman and Giebnik (1979) found that the highest judgments were found with those situations which were most remote and the lowest with those which were most familiar. Likewise, Leming (1974) found that subjects produced a lower stage of reasoning with dilemmas that were practical and dealt with common problems as opposed to hypothetical situations. Dissimilar findings have been reported by Bischoff (1977) and Bush (1981). Using treatment groups that were presented with dilemmas ranging from practical to classical, Bischoff (1977) was unable to find a significant difference between the groups. However, when Bush (1981) manipulated the dilemmas on the Defining Issues Test so as to increase empathy, males and females reasoned at higher levels then on the Defining Issues Test.

Although the research does not conclusively support or reject the importance of remoteness as a variable, it does raise a question regarding the importance of personal experience and points out the need for additional research. If one accepts the findings of Bush (1981), then one's psychosocial experience would be important, especially when designing dilemmas. Furthermore, Siegal (1980) has suggested that instruments which use hypothetical dilemmas might be inappropriate for younger subjects, due to the disparity between personal experience and the situation presented in the dilemma.

RELIABILITY

Aside from questions regarding the validity of the Moral Judgment Interview, the reliability of the instrument has also been criticized. While Kohlberg and his staff refer to the reliability coefficient as being within an acceptable range, their contention may be open to criticism. According to Guilford (1954), there are no 'hard and fast' rules as to what reliability scores should be; however, one would expect a coefficient of .80 or higher when using alternate forms of the instrument in an experimental design.

In a study reported by Evans (1982), a correlation coefficient of $r = .66$ was found when data from forty-four subjects taking Form A and B, written version, was analyzed. Subjects were high school juniors and seniors, and approximately half the group received Form A on the pre-test and Form B on the post-test, and *vice versa*. Such results raise the question as to whether Form A and B (Kohlberg *et al.*, 1978) are equivalent forms when given in the written version, especially since the subjects consistently scored higher on Form B than on Form A.

In addition to the low correlation, whereby one form only explained 44 per cent of the variance of the other form, a question of validity is raised. Based upon this finding, the two forms, Form A and Form B, are either non-equivalent forms and/or one or both of the forms are not valid measures of moral development when given in the written version.

Similar results were reported by Hayden and Pickar (1981), using the 1972 scoring procedures. Twenty-four seventh grade girls were given a written version of the Moral Judgment Interview, with half the subjects pre-tested on Form A and half on Form B. Forms were counter-balanced on the post-test. An analysis of the data from the protocols resulted in mean scores from the forms being significantly different ($p < .001$).

Further erosion of reliability can occur as a result of test-retest procedures and exposure to the same dilemmas over time. Although Kuhn (1976) contends that repeated testing with the same form does not significantly influence the subject's score, Guilford (1965) presents an opposite argument. According to Guilford, skills and knowledge gained during the first administration will affect the second performance, thus resulting in lower reliability. Likewise, Brandsford, Nitsch and Frank (1977) maintain that if one knows what one is supposed to do, it should facilitate the acquisition of learning and later performance. If such contentions are true and even if the learning is superficial, repeated exposure to the dilemmas could produce an inflated score.

Furthermore, such superficial learning could have a greater effect on assessment and moral development if the subjects had been exposed to Kohlberg's theory. While research has yet to answer this question, several studies have reported upward movement in subjects' moral reasoning after participating in a treatment that involved exposure to various aspects of Kohlberg's theory. Results from a study conducted by Small (1974) lend support to this idea. The hypothesis tested in Small's study was that college students who were trained to discriminate stages of moral judgment would advance in their stage of moral judgments. Subjects received the Moral Judgment Interview as a pre- and post-test, and results of a statistical analysis showed that the experimental group advanced 0.5 stages whereas the control group did not show any advance on the average. While no mention was made of instruction given in the theory *per se*, the subjects in the experimental group were provided with descriptions of the stages and given an opportunity to categorize statements by stages. The procedures used in the treatment raise the question as to whether knowledge of the theory was implicitly obtained during the course of the study.

In another study using college students as subjects, Justice (1977) reported change in stage development for those subjects receiving the treatment, which consisted of instruction on Kohlberg's theory, participation in moral dilemma solving, moral reasoning analysis and moral development case studies. Using Rest's Defining Issues Test, an analysis of the data indicated an increase in DIT P scores for the experimental group over the control group significant at ($p < .005$).

While explicitly part of one study (Justice, 1977) and not the other (Small, 1974), knowledge of the theory could have been a confounding variable accounting for part of the increase in moral judgment scores. This possibility that knowledge of the theory might influence the outcome of a study has also been suggested in studies by Napier (1979) and Evans (1982).

Aside from incidental learning and reduced reliability from retesting, Kavanagh (1977) and Turiel (1966) have reported a regression in post-test scores from pre-test scores. Although this regression might be attributed to a decline of interest, after exposure to the same or similar dilemmas, it further clouds the issue of stability over time.

USE OF THE MORAL JUDGMENT INTERVIEW

In addition to the questionable validity and reliability of the Moral Judgment Interview, consideration must be given to how the instrument is used. At present the instrument can be used in the written version, whereby the subjects respond to questions related to the standard dilemmas in a written format, or it can be used in the structured interview format. Although the structured interview was the original format, it is very time-consuming, and requires that the researcher have considerable practice is using the structured interview. The importance of the background training of the researcher has been demonstrated by Wilhelm (1977). By exposing pre-service teachers to different levels of training ranging from instruction in the knowledge of Kohlberg's theory to practice in using the target behaviour in moral discussions with children, Wilhelm (1977) found that those with the more extensive training elicited more reasoning responses from the subjects.

Furthermore, the researcher must avoid consciously or unconsciously cueing the subject as to what the correct answer should be. This is especially true when the researcher has knowledge of the stage that the subject is working toward (Aron, 1977), and is using probing techniques to help the subject achieve his or her goal.

Additional problems in using the interview format have been posed by Rest (1975), and include influence of verbal articulation, and insufficient information to score the interview. Rest (1976) contends that an individual can recognize and discriminate an idea before the idea can be spontaneously verbalized, when responding to a story dilemma. Consequently, an individual's moral judgment may be underestimated when assessed with the Moral Judgment Interview. Further contentions of the influence of verbal fluency and/or language have been put forth by Rubin and Trotter (1977), Locke (1979) and Moran and Joniak (1979). When undergraduates were exposed to reasoning which was written in an inflated manner, Moran and Joniak (1979) found that subjects preferred Stage 2 over Stage 4, which was written in a conversational manner ($p < .05$). The same subjects also viewed an inflated Stage 2 as smarter than a conversational Stage 4 ($p < .05$). However, when both Stages 2 and 4 were written in an inflated manner there was no preference for either. All subjects were pre-tested at Stage 3 according to the Moral Judgment Interview. Besides providing support for the influence of language, when exposed to a recognition format, Moran and Joniak's (1979) study further refutes the concept of invariant sequence and ultimately the validity of the theory.

Insufficient information poses problems, especially when the written format of the Moral Judgment Interview is being used. When individuals are left to complete the interview on their own, there is always the possibility of a superficial or incomplete response being provided. Such a response could result in the subject receiving a lower issue score or no score at all on a given issue. In some cases it may be impossible to assign a Moral Maturity Score (MMS). A case in point relates to the Heinz dilemma where a subject might write that Heinz would not steal the drug because it is against the law to steal. Unless the subject elaborates on what he means by 'against the law' he would be scored at Stage 1 on this response (Kohlberg *et al.*, 1978). Such problems should be reduced when the structured interview is used. However, as indicated by Rest (1976), the subject may not be able to verbalize his ideas even when present.

Another area of potential weakness relates to the scoring of the protocols, whether they were obtained from a written or oral format. As the scoring of responses is judgmental in nature, there is the potential for scorer bias. In order to lessen the subjectivity of the instrument, Kohlberg and his staff have developed manuals which are to be used in scoring the protocols. Also, there are basically two ways of scoring the protocols, global and detailed, and as both are used by researchers, it is difficult to relate the findings of one study to another. These shortcomings are further compounded by the fact that instruction on scoring procedures is available only from Kohlberg and his staff, and an extensive training period is required to be able to score the protocols correctly. Difficulties in learning to score have been found in a study by Arbuthnot (1979), where college-age subjects scored themselves significantly different from the researcher ($p < .001$) when using Form A of the Moral Judgment Interview.

The content of the subject's response has also been found to pose problems for individuals scoring the protocols. Researchers need to ignore the content of the responses and only judge the structure of the moral reasoning, which refers to the general characteristics of shape, pattern or organization of reasoning used while in the process of solving a dilemma (Kohlberg, 1969). However, Napier (1977) found that raters were very much influenced by the content. A manual has been developed to help reduce this problem, but it does not eliminate the need for extensive training in how to score protocols.

CORRELATION: MORAL JUDGMENT INTERVIEW AND DEFINING ISSUES TEST

Besides the Moral Judgment Interview, Rest's Defining Issues Test (1974) has probably been the most popular instrument used to assess moral development. Although the instrument is based upon Kohlberg's theory of cognitive moral development, it is not an equivalent instrument to the Moral Judgment Interview and does not measure the same constructs. While both instruments have been standardized, the Defining Issues Test is a recognition-type instrument while the Moral Judgment Interview requires that the subject produce a response. This difference accounts for more principled reasoning being measured by the DIT as recognition is an easier task than product (Rest, 1980).

Evidence rejecting the equivalency of the two instruments has been provided by several studies, including works by Rest. In a study reported by Rest *et al.* (1974), the correlation between the DIT and MJI was found to be r = .68. Page and Bode (1980) reported a correlation of r = .50, with the two instruments being significantly different (p < .001). In both studies the correlation coefficients are too low to consider the instruments equivalent forms. Fluctuations in scores will be reflected partially by the nature of the group participating in the study. Correlations will be much lower for homogeneous groups, which occur more frequently in research studies (Rest, 1980). Due to the lack of equivalency it would be extremely difficult to compare the DIT with the MJI, and researchers should avoid using both instruments in an experimental design where moral development is serving as the dependent variable.

CONCLUSION

As made evident by past research, numerous questions have been raised regarding the validity and reliability of the Moral Judgment Interview. Efforts have been made to answer these questions; however, research results are often conflicting. Such findings point out the need for continued research independent of that conducted by the Center for Moral Development. Otherwise, criticism will continually be made in reference to changes made in the scoring procedures, elimination of Stage 6 and the creation of Stage 4½.

Furthermore, additional studies need to be undertaken regarding the use of alternate forms in experimental settings. If various forms of the Moral Judgment Interview are not highly correlated when given in the written version, the validity of one or more of the forms is suspect. Likewise, there is a need for studies investigating the equivalency of the written and oral versions of the same form.

While the instrument is the same, the procedures under which it is administered are different. Also, additional consideration needs to be given to possible influences that the interviewer, knowledge of the theory, repeated exposure to the dilemmas and verbal fluency might have on the outcome of the study.

This need for additional research is underscored by the fact that questions have been raised regarding the absence of invariant sequence and the use of an all-male sample, both of which weaken claims of validity. It would seem only appropriate that longitudinal studies, using male and female pre-adolescents as subjects, be conducted to help answer these and other questions posed above. Furthermore, such studies should restrict themselves to using either the structured interview or the written version of the Moral Judgment Interview.

REFERENCES

Arbuthnot, J. (1979) 'Error in self-assessment of moral judgment stages', *Journal of Social Psychology*, 107, 2, pp. 289–90.

Bischoff, H. (1977) 'Adolescent moral judgment on classical contextual and practical moral dilemmas', Unpublished doctoral dissertation, University of Oregon.

Bransford, J. Nitsch, K. and Franks, J. (1977) 'Schooling and the facilitation of knowing', in Anderson, R. *et al.* (Eds.), *Schooling and the Acquisition of Knowledge*, Hillsdale, N.J., Lawrence Erlbaum Associates, pp. 31–55.

Bush, J. (1981) 'A comparison of the effect of Kohlberg dilemmas versus alternative dilemmas on the moral staging of adolescents', Unpublished doctoral dissertation, University of California.

Bussey, K. and Maughan B. (1982) 'Gender differences in moral reasoning', *Journal of Personality and Social Psychology*, 42, 4, pp. 701–6.

Colby, A and Kohlberg, L. (1981) 'Invariant sequence and internal consistency in moral judgment stages', ERIC Document Reproduction Service No. ED. 223-514.

Evans, C. (1982) 'Moral stage development and knowledge of Kohlberg's theory', *The Journal of Experimental Education*, 51, 1, pp. 14–17.

Freeman, S. and Giebnik, W. (1979) 'Moral judgment as a function of age, sex, and stimulus', *The Journal of Psychology*, 102, 1, pp. 43–7.

Gibbs, J. (1979) 'Personal conversation', Cambridge, Mass., Harvard University, 7 August.

Gilligan, C. (1977) 'In a different voice, women's conception of self and of morality', *Harvard Educational Review*, 47, 4, pp. 481–517.

Guilford, J. (1954) *Psychometric Methods*, New York, McGraw-Hill.

Guilford, J. (1965) *Fundamental Statistics in Psychology and Education*, 4th ed., New York, McGraw-Hill.

Haan, N., Smith, M. and Block, J. (1968) 'Moral reasoning of young adults: Political social behavior, family background, and personality correlates', *Journal of Personality and Social Psychology*, 10, 3, pp. 183–201.

Hayden, B. and Pickar, D. (1981) 'The impact of moral discussions on children's level of moral reasoning', *Journal of Moral Education*, 10, 2, pp. 131–4.

Holstein, C. (1976) 'Irreversible, stepwise sequence in the development of moral judgment: A longitudinal study of males and females', *Child Development*, 47, 1, pp. 51–61.

Justice, G. (1977) 'Facilitating principled moral reasoning in college students: A cognitive developmental approach', Unpublished doctoral dissertation, St Louis University.

Kavanagh, H. (1977) 'Moral education: Relevance, goals, and strategies', *Journal of Moral Education*, 6, 2, pp. 121–30.

Kohlberg, L. (1958) 'The development of modes of moral thinking and choices in years 10 to 16', Unpublished doctoral dissertation, University of Chicago.

Kohlberg, L. (1971) 'Stage and sequence: The cognitive-developmental approach to socialization', in Goslin, D. (Ed.), *Handbook of Socialization Theory and Research*, Chicago, Ill., Rand McNally, pp. 347–480.

Kohlberg, L. (1972) 'Issue Scoring Guide', Unpublished manuscript, Cambridge, Mass., Harvard University.

Kohlberg, L. (1973) 'Continuities in childhood and adult moral development revisited', in Baltes, P., and Schaie, K. (Eds.), *Life-Span Developmental Psychology: Personality and Socialization*, New York, Academic Press, pp. 180–204.

Kohlberg, L. (1978) 'Revisions in the theory and practice of moral development', in Damon, W. (Ed.), *Moral Development: New Directions for Child Development*, San Francisco, Jossey-Bass, pp. 83–7.

Kohlberg, L. Colby, A., Gibbs, J., Speicher-Dubin, B. and Power, C. (1978) 'Assessing moral stages: A manual', Unpublished manuscript, Cambridge, Mass., Harvard University.

Kohlberg, L. and Kramer, R. (1969) 'Continuities and discontinuities in childhood and adult moral development', *Human Development*, 12, 2, pp. 93–120.

Kuhn, D. (1976) 'Short-term longitudinal evidence for the sequentiality of Kohlberg's early stages of moral judgment', *Developmental Psychology*, 12, 2, pp. 162–6.

Kurtines, W. and Greif, E. (1974) 'The development of moral thought: Review and evaluation of Kohlberg's approach', *Psychological Bulletin*, 81, 8, pp. 453–70.

Leming, J. (1974) 'An empirical examination of key assumptions underlying the Kohlberg rationale for moral education', ERIC Document Reproduction Service No. ED 093-749.

Locke, D. (1979) 'Cognitive stages or developmental stages? A critique of Kohlberg's stage-structured theory of moral reasoning', *Journal of Moral Education*, 8, 3, pp. 168–81.

Moran, J. and Joniak, A. (1979) 'Effect of language on preference for responses to a moral dilemma', *Developmental Psychology*, 15, 3, pp. 337–8.

Murphy, J. and Gilligan, C. (1980) 'Moral development in late adolescence and adulthood: A critique and reconstruction of Kohlberg's theory', *Human Development*, 23, 2, pp. 77–104.

Napier, J. (1977) 'Content influence while stage scoring moral thought statements', *Educational and Psychological Measurement*, 37, 2, pp. 519–25.

Napier, J. (1979) 'Effects of knowledge of cognitive moral development and request to fake on defining issues test p-scores', *The Journal of Psychology*, 101, 1, pp. 45–52.

Orchowsky, S. and Jenkins, L. (1979) 'Sex biases in the measurement of moral judgment', *Psychological Reports*, 44, 3, p. 1040.

Page, R. and Bode, J. (1980) 'Comparison of measures of moral reasoning and development of a new objective measure', *Educational and Psychological Measurement*, 40, 2, pp. 317–29.

Rest, J. (1974) 'Manual for Defining Issues Test', Unpublished manuscript, Minneapolis, Minn., University of Minnesota.

Rest, J. (1975) 'New options in assessing moral judgment and criteria for evaluating validity', ERIC Document Reproduction Service No. ED 113-017.

Rest, J. (1976) 'New approaches in the assessment of moral judgment', in Lickona, T. (Ed.), *Moral Development and Behavior: Theory, Research and Social Issues*, New York, Holt, Rinehart and Winston, pp. 198–218.

Rest, J. (1980) 'Moral judgment research and the cognitive-developmental approach to moral education', *The Personnel and Guidance Journal*, 58, 9, pp. 602–5.

Rest, J., Cooper, D., Coder, R., Masanz, J. and Anderson, D. (1974) 'Judging the important issues in moral dilemmas—an objective measure of development', *Developmental Psychology*, 10, 4, pp. 491–501.

Rubin, K. and Trotter, K. (1977) 'Kohlberg's moral judgment scale: Some methodological considerations', *Developmental Psychology*, 13, 5, pp. 535–6.

Ruma, E. and Mosher, D. (1967) 'Relationship between moral judgment and guilt in delinquent boys', *Journal of Abnormal Psychology*, 72, 2, pp. 122–7.

Schnurer, G. (1976) 'Sex differences and personality variables in the moral reasoning of young adults', Unpublished doctoral dissertation, University of Pittsburg.

Siegal, M. (1980) 'Kohlberg versus Piaget: To what extent has one theory eclipsed the other?', *Merrill-Palmer Quarterly*, 26, 4, pp. 285–97.

Small, L. (1974) 'Effects of discrimination training on stage of moral development', *Personality and Social Psychology Bulletin*, 1, pp. 423–5.

Turiel, E. (1966) 'An experimental test of the sequentiality of developmental stages in the child's moral judgments', *Journal of Personality and Social Psychology*, 3, 6, pp. 611–18.

Wilhelm, F. (1977) 'The effects of extent of training on teacher discussion behaviors and children's moral reasoning development', Unpublished doctoral dissertation, State University of New York at Albany.

Interchange

REST REPLIES TO EVANS

Prominence such as Kohlberg's in a field of psychology brings its critics. This is as it should be: those theories and findings that claim our attention and that carry a certain degree of authority should be carefully scrutinized and critiqued. Evans has done us a service in providing a discussion of the criticisms made of the Kohlberg research approach and scoring system. If anyone ever entertained the notion that there is unanimous agreement and acceptance of Kohlberg's work, he/she should be convinced otherwise by Evans' chapter. However, several questions remain after citing the arguments of the critics: (1) Which criticisms are valid, in contrast to misunderstandings of Kohlberg's position? (2) Which criticisms were valid once but are no longer valid (because of recent changes or developments in Kohlbergian research)? (3) Which criticisms might logically be a potential problem but which have insufficient documentation to sustain the criticism? (4) Which criticisms are simple assertions of an alternative view and approach that may reflect different research priorities and interests, but that ultimately may be reconcilable with Kohlberg's work? (5) Given that there are bound to be some problems in any research area, on balance do they nullify the weight of evidence in support of the theory? In other words, are any of the problems 'fatal flaws'? (6) Which criticisms apply to other researchers who claim to be conducting 'Kohlbergian' research but whose standards of scholarship Kohlberg has no control over?

This volume as a whole is designed to provide much material for evaluating these questions. Here I will refer to some other sources that discuss some of these issues at length. While the Kurtines and Greif (1974) review continues to be cited in the literature as the final death verdict on Kohlberg's method and theory, their notion of what constitutes 'validity' is misconceived (see Broughton, 1978), their criticisms of the psychometric properties of the test are outdated (see Colby *et al.*, 1983; Snarey, Reimer and Kohlberg, in press; Nisan and Kohlberg, 1982), and the sequential ordering of the Kohlberg stages is as firmly established as anything in psychological research (see Rest, 1983). Also readers may be interested in reading the recent reappraisal of Kohlberg's theory by William Kurtines (Kurtines and Gewirtz, 1984). Regarding the charge of sex bias in the Kohlberg system, readers may be interested in several recent systematic, comprehensive reviews of the issue by Walker (1983) and Thoma (1984) that indicate that Gilligan's charge that women score lower on Kohlberg's test is simply not true as a general trend. Regarding the influence of verbal fluency on moral judgment assessment, one should be aware of the flaws in Moran and Joniak's study (1979) that nullify that study as serious grounds for explaining away the construct (see Rest, 1980).

I think that Evans is justified in pointing to serious problems in several cases: the contaminating of post-test results in intervention studies when the Kohlberg theory is taught as part of the intervention; the problem that production measures require verbal expressivenss in order for the subject to be credited with a cognitive structure; and the theoretical ambiguity in leaving Stage 6 undefined in the current scoring manual. Whether these problems constitute 'fatal flaws' or not cannot be resolved here.

Critics have had a constructive influence in the development of Kohlbergian theory and research. The many painstaking revisions of the scoring system have been motivated at least in part by critics, as has the increased effort at documenting claims and disseminating data in the usual channels. In the many publications that Kohlberg has recently published, I think one can see a responsiveness (not capitulation) to critics (for instance, see Kohlberg, Levine and Hewer, 1983).

REFERENCES

Broughton, J. (1978) 'The cognitive-developmental approach to morality: A reply to Kurtines and Greif', *Journal of Moral Education*, 7, pp. 81–96.

Colby, A., Kohlberg, L., Gibbs, J. and Lieberman, M. (1983) 'A longitudinal study of moral judgment', *Monographs of the Society for Child Development*.

Kohlberg, L., Levine, C. and Hewer, A. (1983) *Moral Stages: A Current Formulation and a Response to Critics*, Basel, S. Karger.

Kurtines, W. and Greif, E. (1974) 'The development of moral thought. Review and evaluation of Kohlberg's approach', *Psychological Bulletin*, 81, pp. 453–70.

Kurtines, W. and Gewirtz, J. (1984) *Morality, Moral Development, and Behavior*, New York, Wiley.

Moran, J. and Joniak, A. (1979) 'Effect of language on preference for responses to a moral dilemma', *Developmental Psychology*, 15, 3, pp. 337–8.

Nisan, M. and Kohlberg, L. (1982) 'Universality and variation in moral judgment: A longitudinal and cross-sectional study in Turkey', *Child Development*, 53, pp. 865–77.

Rest, J. (1980) 'Development in moral judgment research', *Developmental Psychology*, 16, pp. 251–6.

Rest, J. (1983) 'Morality', in J. Flavell and E. Markman (Eds.), Volume on Cognitive Development, in P. Mussen (Gen. Ed.), *Manual of Child Psychology*, New York, Wiley.

Snarey, J. R., Reimer, J. and Kohlberg, L. (1984, in press) 'The sociomoral development of kibbutz adolescents. A longitudinal cross-cultural study', *Development Psychology*.

Thoma, S. (1984) 'A review of sex differences in the Defining Issues Test', Unpublished manuscript, University of Minnesota, in preparation for publication.

Walker, L. J. (1983 in press) 'Sex differences in the development of moral reasoning: A critical review' *Child Development*.

EVANS REPLIES TO REST

Rest's manuscript provides a good historical overview of the development of Kohlberg's Moral Judgment Interview and pertinent methodological decisions related to the instrument. In identifying the points of discussion, he has indicated the strengths and weaknesses of each, which provides readers with a broad spectrum from which to develop their own perspectives. Along with the opposing points for each methodological decision, the reader is provided with a sound description of the construct, moral judgment. The inclusion of this narrative should reduce or eliminate misconceptions over how the concept relates to the measurement of moral judgment.

In addition, Rest's suggestions for possible validity studies should provide opportunities to those who are seriously interested in the assessment of moral judgment. However, in reviewing the suggestions, I feel that one issue needs to be included. Although Rest's discussion is based upon the use of the structured interview, the written format has been used in various studies. While this format can be administered with relative ease, there is a lack of evidence regarding its validity. If the written version is found to be a valid as well as reliable means for assessing moral judgment, opportunities for those who are interested in conducting research related to Kohlberg's theory would be greatly enhanced.

While I tend to agree with many of Rest's comments, there are several points of concern. One is the high correlations reported for the twenty-year longitudinal study conducted by Kohlberg's group. Although the scores are impressive and provide support for the validation for the instrument, there is a need for concurring research data obtained independently from the Kohlberg group. Until such data are available, the overall validity of the instrument is going to be suspect.

Another issue relates to changes that have been made in the scoring procedures, as a result of research findings. While one cannot disagree with making adjustment in procedures, questions have been raised regarding revisions being made so that scoring procedures fit the model. Such adjustments deny the possibility of weaknesses within the model. This is especially true when considering the concept invariant sequence. Although changes have been made in the scoring procedures to eliminate the occurrence of regression, such findings still appear in the literature. As invariant sequence is one of the cornerstones used for claims of validity its absence questions such claims.

Another possible weakness in the model appears when one considers the fact that the new scoring procedures do not provide for moral reasoning at Stage 6. This omission contradicts the intent of identifying scoring criteria and rules based upon confirmation to stage expectations. Furthermore, it will be hard to validate the theory with an instrument that does not provide a means of assessing moral judgment at each and every stage.

In discussing changes within the scoring procedures, Rest notes that the fundamental hope was to identify descriptions which would be valid for all dilemmas, whether they appear in the written or oral mode. While the statement is not definitive as to whether the goal has been reached, it would appear the goal has not been met. As such we are still faced with decisions related to the use of hypothetical or real-life dilemmas.

Overall, I find myself in agreement with many of the points discussed by Rest. This is especially true as he has identified areas of concern as well as positive aspects of the methodology. However, this could be disconcerting to some who are looking for a balance between the positive and negative aspects of methodology in the opposing chapters.

Part XVI: Concluding Chapter

30. A Current Statement on Some Theoretical Issues

LAWRENCE KOHLBERG

Constraints of time and space allow me to respond to only a few of the many interesting chapters and issues in this volume. Some chapters did not reach me in time to contribute to this section of the book, while others are too complex to respond to in a straightforward way within the page limits of this chapter. Accordingly I have attempted to focus upon a statement of my position on currently controversial issues in the psychological, philosophic and educational issues domains raised by the papers in this book. The book's schedule does not allow me to read the interchange between pairs of authors. I hope these interchanges will eliminate any need I might have to assess argumentatively the 'con' or critical chapters of the volume. I might add that except for Boyd and Carter, the chapters in this volume reflect no awareness of European, especially German, responses to my theory so that I include recent European views in this chapter.

RECENT UPDATE OF THE THEORY

At the time this book was planned it was hoped that all three volumes of my collected papers would be available to the authors. Unfortunately only the first volume (Kohlberg, 1981) was available to them with only part of the second volume (Kohlberg, 1984) available to them as Kohlberg, Levine and Hewer (1983), which some chapters' authors read and others did not. Much of my theoretical writing responded to in this volume was published in the early 1970s (Kohlberg, 1969, 1971, 1973).

My earlier writings, e.g., Kohlberg (1963, 1969), stressed moral stages as part of a general cognitive-developmental approach to an evolving unitary self oriented to a unitary social world. Kegan continues this holistic tradition, as Loevinger has long done and as Fowler does in the domain he calls faith development. Other writers, rather than presupposing holistic ego stages, have carved up both the self and the 'moral domain' into tighter subdomains. As Enright, Lapsley and Olson note: Selman's research on the domains of social perspective-taking and peer relations; Turiel's research on the domain of convention; Tapp's and Levine's research on the legal domain; Weinrich-Haste's research on the domain of political reasoning; Gilligan's research on the domain of personal care and response, etc. have emerged as independent research programmes from my earlier holistic cognitive-developmental research programme on morality.

With this proliferation of developmental research on the social-cognitive domain my Harvard colleagues and myself have thought our energy best employed in clarification of the foundations and validity of a more narrowly conceived moral domain, one, following Piaget, I conceived as the domain of justice judgments and reasoning. This work has meant (1) developing and validating a manual for scoring responses to hypothetical dilemmas through longitudinal and cross-cultural data; (2) examining the relation of hypothetical dilemma-based assessments of stages with moral action data; and (3) logically and philosophically attempting 'a rational reconstruction' of the ontogeny of moral stages. In these endeavours we 'pushed the limits' of the Piagetian structural approach to moral judgment and action with the thought that the many other developmental approaches to social cognition needed eventually to press these limits, though moral development with its philosophic and educational importance most clearly warranted the first effort to validate empirically the stage construct.

Central to our construction of a manual and analysis of longitudinal data has been our preoccupation with assessing 'hard' stages of justice reasoning, stages which in the moral domain would meet the criteria Piaget and Inhelder (1969) attribute to their logical stages, e.g., (a) qualitative distinctness; (b) culturally universal invariant sequence; (c) consistency or 'structured wholeness'; and (d) hierarchical integration. This research programme has entailed (1) making a clearer distinction between structure or *form* and content; and (2) a clearer distinction between operational *moral* or justice reasoning and social reasoning. The form-content distinction led us to define content in terms of what we thought to be culturally universal philosophic categories of norms and elements defined in Table 1 (from Kohlberg, 1984, Ch. 5).

It led us to define form in terms of sociomoral perspective defined in Table 2 (Kohlberg, 1976, 1984, Ch. 2).

Our focus on moral justice; our desire to tie justice or interpersonal operations to Piagetian theory of cognitive operations, and to define stages through the 'rational reconstruction of ontogenesis' as levels of perceived adequacy led us to define the stages in terms of increasingly reversible operations to resolve justice problems as defined in Table 3 (Kohlberg, 1984, Appendix A).

As we discuss later, we and others have most recently tried to make a rational reconstruction of our moral stages based on Habermas' (1984) theory of the development of communicative competence.

Table 1. *The Elements and Norms for Classifying Content*

THE ELEMENTS

I. *MODAL ELEMENTS*
   1. Obeying (consulting) persons or deity. Should obey, get consent (should consult, persuade).
   2. Blaming (approving). Should be blamed for, disapproved (should be approved).
   3. Retributing (exonerating). Should retribute against (should exonerate).
   4. Having a right (having no right).
   5. Having a duty (having no duty).

II. *VALUE ELEMENTS*
   A. *Egoistic Consequences*
      6. Good reputation (bad reputation).
      7. Seeking reward (avoiding punishment).

   B. *Utilitarian Consequences*
      8 Good individual consequences (bad individual consequences).
      9 Good group consequences (bad group consequences).

   C. *Ideal or Harmony-Serving Consequences*
      10. Upholding character.
      11. Upholding self-respect.
      12. Serving social ideal or harmony.
      13. Serving human dignity and autonomy.

   D. *Fairness*
      14. Balancing perspectives or role-taking.
      15. Reciprocity or positive desert.
      16. Maintaining equity and procedural fairness.
      17. Maintaining social contract or freely agreeing.

THE NORMS

1. Life	6.	Authority
a) Preservation	7.	Law
b) Quality/quantity	8.	Contract
2. Property	(9.	Civil Rights)
3. Truth	(10.	Religion)
4. Affiliation	11.	Conscience
(5. Erotic Love and Sex)	12.	Punishment

Source: Kohlberg (1984), Ch. 5.

Table 2. *The Six Moral Stages*

	Content of Stage		
Level and Stage	What Is Right	Reasons for Doing Right	Social Perspective of Stage
LEVEL I— PRECONVENTIONAL Stage 1—Heteronomous Morality	To avoid breaking rules backed by punishment, obedience of its own sake, and avoiding physical damage to persons and property.	Avoidance of punishment, and the superior power of authorities.	*Egocentric point of view.* Doesn't consider the interests of others or recognize that they differ from the actor's; doesn't relate two points of view. Actions are considered physically rather than in terms of psychological interests of others. Confusion of authority's perspective with one's own.
Stage 2—Individualism, Instrumental Purpose, and Exchange	Following rules only when it is to someone's immediate interest; acting to meet one's own interests and needs and letting others do the same. Right is also what's fair, what's an equal exchange, a deal, an agreement.	To serve one's own needs or interests in a world where you have to recognize that other people have their interests, too.	*Concrete individualistic perspective.* Aware that everybody has his own interest to pursue and these conflict, so that right is relative (in the concrete individualistic sense).
LEVEL II— CONVENTIONAL Stage 3—Mutual Interpersonal Expectations, Relationships, and Interpersonal Conformity	Living up to what is expected by people close to you or what people generally expect of people in your role as son, brother, friend, etc. "Being good" is important and means having good motives, showing concern about others. It also means keeping mutual relationships, such as trust, loyalty, respect and gratitude.	The need to be a good person in your own eyes and those of others. Your caring for others. Belief in the Golden Rule. Desire to maintain rules and authority which support stereotypical good behaviour.	*Perspective of the individual in relationships with other individuals.* Aware of shared feelings, agreements, and expectations which take primacy over individual interests. Relates points of view through the concrete Golden Rule, putting yourself in the other guy's shoes. Does not yet consider generalized system perspective.

Stage 4—Social System and Conscience	Fulfilling the actual duties to which you have agreed. Laws are to be upheld except in extreme cases where they conflict with other fixed social duties. Right is also contributing to society, the group, or institution.	To keep the institution going as a whole, to avoid the breakdown in the system 'if everyone did it,' or the imperative of conscience to meet one's defined obligations. (Easily confused with Stage 3 belief in rules and authority; see text.)	*Differentiates societal point of view from interpersonal agreement or motives.* Takes the point of view of the system that defines roles and rules. Considers individual relations in terms of place in the system.
LEVEL III—POST-CONVENTIONAL, or PRINCIPLED Stage 5—Social Contract or Utility and Individual Rights	Being aware that people hold a variety of values and opinions, that most values and rules are relative to your group. These relative rules should usually be upheld, however, in the interest of impartiality and because they are the social contract. Some nonrelative values and rights like *life* and *liberty*, however, must be upheld in any society and regardless of majority opinion.	A sense of obligation to law because of one's social contract to make and abide by laws for the welfare of all and for the protection of all people's rights. A feeling of contractual commitment, freely entered upon, to family, friendship, trust, and work obligations. Concern that laws and duties be based on rational calculation of overall utility, 'the greatest good for the greatest number.'	*Prior-society perspective.* Perspective of a rational individual aware of values and rights prior to social attachments and contracts. Integrates perspectives by formal mechanisms of agreement, contract, objective impartiality, and due process. Considers moral and legal points of view; recognizes that they sometimes conflict and finds it difficult to integrate them.
Stage 6—Universal Ethical Principles	Following self-chosen ethical principles. Particular laws or social agreements are usually valid because they rest on such principles. When laws violate these principles, one acts in accordance with the principle. Principles are universal principles of justice: the equality of human rights and respect for the dignity of human beings as individual persons.	The belief as a rational person in the validity of universal moral principles, and a sense of personal commitment to them.	*Perspective of a moral point of view* from which social arrangements derive. Perspective is that of any rational individual recognizing the nature of morality or the fact that persons are ends in themselves and must be treated as such.

Source: Kohlberg (1976, 1984).

Table 3.   *The Six Stages of Justice Judgment*

Our moral dilemmas address three problems of justice that have been identified in Aristotle's *Nicomachean Ethics*. The first problem is one of distributive justice; that is, the way in which society or a third party distributes 'honour, wealth, and other desirable assets of the community' (Aristotle, *Ethics*, 1130b). This is done in terms of such operations as equality, desert, or merit (i.e., reciprocity defined in terms of proportionality), and finally, equity in light of need or extenuating circumstances. The second type of justice problem is commutative justice, which focuses upon voluntary agreement, contract, and equal exchange. A third and closely related type of justice problem is the problem of corrective justice, which supplies corrective principle in private transactions which have been unequal or unfair and require restitution or compensation. In addition, corrective justice deals with crimes or torts violating the rights of an involuntary participant and in this sense requires restitution or retribution.

There is a fourth type of justice problem which is not independent of the three already mentioned. It is the problem of procedural justice, an aspect of justice which must be addressed in problems of distributive, commutative, and corrective justice. This problem of procedural justice, a concern more clearly distinguishable in high moral stage judgments, often represents the considerations which moral philosophers treat as validity checks on moral reasoning. These 'checks' are derived from a concern for balancing perspectives or making one's judgments reversible (i.e., employing the golden rule) and from a concern for making one's judgments universalizable (i.e., employing Kant's categorical imperative). The reversibility check asks, Would you judge this action as fair if you were in the other person's shoes? The universalizability check asks, Would you judge this action right if everyone were to do it? Procedural justice, which involves a special set of considerations at lower stages, becomes a solution to substantive justice problems of distribution and correction at Stage 6, where universalizability and reversibility constitute self-conscious validity checks on one's reasoning.

Before proceeding to our descriptions of the six stages, we wish to make a few comments about justice operations and that we understand them as developing into a grouped structure, in the Piagetian sense, by Stage 6.

In Chapter 3 we pointed out that there were four orientations to the justice problems reviewed above—that is, the norm-maintaining, utilitarian, perfectionistic, and fairness orientations. We also pointed out that justice operations were explicitly used in the fairness orientation, where they defined elements of fairness such as reciprocity, equality, equity, balancing perspectives, and so on. In contrast, we suggested that the justice operations were implicit in the use of elements of the other three justice orientations. Our stage descriptions will, accordingly, focus more directly on the fairness orientation, where the use of the justice operations is most clearly visible.

For us the justice operation of equality can be defined as (*a*) identical quantities of goods for all, or for all relevant, persons and/or (*b*) equal consideration of competing claims prior to distribution or adjudication and/or (*c*) assertion that all persons are equal as a justification for (*a*) and (*b*) (i.e., since all are of equal moral worth, then . . .). We define equity as an operation of compensation on equality; that is 'shades of inequality.' For example, an equity operation constructs a notion of unequal distribution in order to compensate for inequalities that may have existed prior to the situation or that are due to special circumstances within the situation. A contemporary example of the equity operation is the justification of 'reverse discrimination' with regard to affirmative action policy. We define a third justice operation, reciprocity, as an operation of distribution by exchange. Of course, what is considered just reciprocity varies by stage. However, in general terms reciprocity is an operation which exchanges merit or 'just deserts,' reward, or punishment in return for effort, virtue, talent, or deviance. At lower stages what is considered reciprocal and equal is often hard to distinguish since reciprocity implies some notion of equality in exchange. At Stage 6, however, reciprocity is distinguished from and derived from an explicit concern for equality or equity. Our fourth justice operation is prescriptive role-taking or balancing perspectives, an operation closely tied to the problem of procedural justice. At higher stages, prescriptive role-taking stems from the realization that one must (*a*) take into account the perspectives of others and (*b*) imaginatively change positions with others in such a way that one is satisfied with the outcome of the dilemma regardless of who one is (i.e., moral musical chairs or the validity check of reversibility mentioned already). At lower moral stages prescriptive role-taking is often closely tied to the other justice operations as well as to the respondent's sense of moral norms. For example, a question regarding upholding the norm of property is answered with the response: How would you feel if someone stole from you? While one can detect a prescriptive role-taking operation in a response such as this, it clearly does not take the form of a self-conscious validity check on justice reasoning as it does at Stage 6. The final operation which we identify is the operation of universalizability. This operation is closely tied to the operations of equality and equity, and it is expressed by the appeal, Is it right for anyone to do X? This statement implies a concern for equality and equity, and at the principled stages it is explicitly expressed as a self-conscious validity check on the conceptions of equality and equity which one has employed in moral reasoning.

We now offer the following stage descriptions. Each moral stage is reviewed by discussing stage-specific sociomoral perspectives on norms in general and upon the justice operations of equality, equity, reciprocity, prescriptive role-taking, and universalizability. Each stage description is then completed with examples of justice operations applied to the three justice problems of distributive, commutative, and corrective justice.

Stage 1: Heteronomous Morality

The perspective at Stage 1 is that of naive *moral realism*. That is, the moral significance of an action, its goodness or badness, is seen as a real, inherent, and unchanging quality of the act, just as color and mass are seen as inherent qualities of objects. This realism is reflected by an assumption that moral judgments are self-evident, requiring little or no justification beyond assigning labels or citing rules. For example, telling on your brother is wrong because it is 'tattling', breaking into the druggist's store is wrong because 'you're not supposed to steal'. Punishment is seen as important in that it is identified with a bad action rather than because the actor is attempting pragmatically to avoid negative consequences to him- or herself. Likewise, there is an absence of mediating concepts, such as deservingness or intentionality, through which the particular circumstances of the case alter its moral significance. Thus, moral rules and labels are applied in a literal, absolute manner and both distributive and retributive justice are characterized by strict equality rather than equity. Characteristics of persons that determine their authority, power, or moral worth tend to be physicalistic or categorical. For example, the father is the boss because he's bigger. You should steal to save a life if it is that of Betsy Ross, who made the flag. The perspective of moral realism represents a failure to differentiate multiple perspectives on dilemmas. This means that authority and subordinate, self and other, and other individuals in conflict or disagreement are assumed to share a single perception of the situation and of the morally appropriate response to it. Morality at Stage 1 is heteronomous in the Piagetian sense; that is, what makes something wrong is defined by the authority rather than by cooperation among equals.

Norms and Justice Operations

At Stage 1 *norms* are concrete rules which are not identified with the psychological perspective of, or expectations of, any individuals, including the self. Instead, norms are perceived categories of right and wrong behavior. These categories define types of actions and types of persons (e.g., thieves, good sons, important persons, etc.). *Equality* at Stage 1 is a notion of distribution by strict equalization to those who are classified within any one category of actor or person. Unequal distribution can be acceptable if to persons of a less valued category. *Reciprocity* is a notion of 'exchange' of goods or actions without regard for the psychological valuing of goods or actions by self or other. This exchange is balanced in terms of the idea of 'same for same' (i.e., Eskimos kill seals so seals should kill Eskimos). The operations of *equity* and *prescriptive role-taking* are absent at Stage 1 because of the egocentric, heteronomous nature of this stage of reasoning. Finally, at Stage 1 *universalizability* exists in the sense that a rule or norm is generalized and admits of no exceptions, with the possible exception of authorities who create and enforce the rule or norm. In formal terms, Stage 1 reasoning is characterized by the uncoordinated use of equality and reciprocity.

Distributive justice is guided by strict equality, and special considerations of need or deservingness are not taken into account. In cases where an authority is involved, distributive justice is guided by heteronomous obedience to or respect for authority. This is illustrated by the following response to Dilemma I:

Q.—Should Joe refuse to give his father the money?
A.—If his father told him to save the money up, I'd give it to him, because he's older than you and he's your father. Because he's older than him.

Corrective justice tends to be retributive and based on strict reciprocity. For example, 'The doctor should be given the death penalty (if he performs the mercy killing)—he killed the woman so they should kill him.' Again, moderating circumstances such as intention are not incorporated. Also characteristic of Stage 1 is the notion of immanent justice—that punishment necessarily follows as an automatic consequence of transgression. For example:

Q.—Why is it important to keep a promise?
A.—If you don't then you're a liar. You're not supposed to lie because you'll get pimples on your tongue.

Commutative justice, as already illustrated, is a matter of following externally defined rules: 'You should keep a promise because if you don't, you're a liar.' Avoidance of the punishment that would inevitably follow transgression is another reason to follow promise-keeping rules (as is also the case with other rules).

Stage 2; Individualistic, Instrumental Morality

Stage 2 is characterized by a concrete individualistic perspective. There is an awareness that each person has his or her own interests to pursue and that these may conflict. A moral relativity develops out of the understanding that different persons can have different, yet equally valid, justifications for their claims to justice. That is, there is a recognition of more than one perspective on a situation and a respect for the moral legitimacy of pursuing one's own interests. The morally right is relative to the particular situation and to the actor's perspective on the situation. Since each person's primary aim is to pursue his or her own interests, the perspective at Stage 2 is pragmatic—to maximize satisfaction of one's needs and desires while minimizing negative consequences to the self. The assumption that the other is also operating from this premise leads to an emphasis on instrumental exchange as a mechanism through which individuals can coordinate their actions for mutual benefit. Thus, the moral realism of Stage 1 is no longer in evidence. An important limitation of Stage 2 is that it fails to provide a means for deciding among conflicting claims, ordering or setting priorites on conflicting needs and interests.

Norms and Justice Operations

At Stage 2 *norms* are psychological expectations of individual selves. They are standards for regulating action which are thought to be satisfying to the needs or interests of individual selves. At this stage norms have no fixed values except insofar as they allow individuals to have expectations of one another which maintain a balance through exchange. The Stage 2 operation of *equality* recognizes the category 'persons' as all individuals, including the self, who have needs, desires, and so on that can be satisfied through one's own action and through the exchange of goods and actions with others. Categories of good and bad actions or actors have no inherent value at this stage except insofar as they represent an expectation of right that an individual would hold psychologically in terms of his or her interests or needs. The operation of *reciprocity* in this context defines a notion of concrete exchange of equal values or goods in serving the needs of self and other. The operations of equality and reciprocity are coordinated at Stage 2, as they are not at Stage 1. For example, at this stage one can reason that 'Joe should refuse to give his father the money because he worked for it and earned it, and if his father wants money, then he should earn it himself.' The Stage 2 operation of *equity* compensates by focusing on the needs, not the intentions, of actors. For example, it can be fair for the poor to steal because they *need* the food. The operation of *prescriptive role-taking* at this stage acknowledges the fact that the self would have needs as others do (e.g., 'If I were Heinz and needed the drug for my wife as he did, then I'd steal it'). While perspectives are balanced at this stage in the sense that self can understand the needs and actions of the other, they are not balanced in the sense of taking into account conflicts between perspectives. At Stage 2 the operation of *universalizability* is expressed in terms of a concern for limiting deviation from norms by naturally self-interested persons. Thus, it is a concern that if deviation from norms is allowed for one, then there could be deviation by many, and this could produce a state of affairs which would interfere with what is considered the fair pursuit of self-interest and fair exchange. An example of this type of concern can be seen in the following Stage 2 response: 'The judge should punish Heinz, because if he doesn't others may try to get away with stealing.'

Distributive justice involves coordinating considerations of equality and reciprocity, so that judgments take into account the claims of various persons and the demands of the specific situation. In addition to equality and reciprocity Stage 2 can use an equity operation to consider individual needs or intentions in the light of special or extenuating circumstances. The Stage 2 conception of equity is based on the reasonable pursuit of individual needs and interests, whereas at Stage 3, equity operations consider shared social norms as the basis of distribution.

The coordination of reciprocity with equality in distributive justice at Stage 2 is illustrated by the following response to Dilemma 1:

Q.—Should Joe refuse to give his father the money?
A.—He shouldn't give him the money, because he saved it and should use it however he wants. If his father wants to go fishing he should make his own money.

In this judgment, the reciprocal relation between working for money and being able to spend it is seen as applying equally to both father and son.

Corrective justice at Stage 2 can involve reference to individual needs or intentions as the basis for equity. For example, 'The doctor should not be given the death penalty for mercy-killing the woman, because she wanted to die, and he was just trying to put her out of her pain.' This represents the beginning of a recognition that one person can see the other's point of view and modify his or her own action in response. Another example is the following: 'The judge shouldn't punish the doctor, because the judge would think that if it was him who was sick he would want the doctor to kill him too.'

Commutative justice at Stage 2 is based on instrumental exchange which serves to coordinate in a simple way the needs and interest of individuals. For example, it is seen as important to keep promises to ensure that others will keep their promises to you and do nice things for you, or it is important in order to keep them from getting mad at you.

Stage 3: Interpersonally Normative Morality

At Stage 3 the separate perspectives of individuals are coordinated into a third person perspective, that of mutually trusting relationships among people, which is embodied in a set of shared moral norms according to which people are expected to live. These moral norms and expectations transcend or are generalized across particular persons and situations. Stage 3 norms can be distinguished from Stage 1 rules in that norms represent an integration of perspectives that have been recognized as separate, a coming to general social agreement on what constitutes a good role occupant, whereas the orientation to rules at Stage 1 represents a failure to differentiate individual perspectives. The primacy of shared norms at Stage 3 entails an emphasis on being a good, altruistic, or prosocial role occupant and on good or bad motives as indicative of general personal morality. This recognition of the importance of motives also distinguishes Stage 3 norms from Stage 1 rules. As a result of the socially shared perspective, the individual at Stage 3 is particularly concerned with maintaining interpersonal trust and social approval.

The justice operations of Stage 3 are most clearly represented in golden rule role-taking—Do unto others as you would have others do unto you. Logically, this involves the coordination of the inverse and reciprocal operations. It involves a second-order operation whereby a Stage 2 reciprocal exchange is subjected to evaluation by reference to a superordinate or shared norm against which its fairness can be judged. That is, reciprocal exchanges are not necessarily fair but must be negated or affirmed in relation to standards of morally good conduct that stand outside the reciprocal exchange.

Norms and Justice Operations

At Stage 3 *norms* are understood as expectations shared by persons in relationship. The purpose of norms is to maintain relationships and the loyalty, trust, and caring between persons in the relationship or group. Such relational norms are felt as obligatory. The Stage 3 operation of *reciprocity* constructs a conception of obligation as debt; the other has given a value or something valuable to the self, and the self cannot terminate this inequality by a simple one-to-one exchange but feels a sentiment of gratitude, loyalty, or duty to reciprocate. For example, when asked, 'Is it a duty for Heinz to steal?' Case 9 says: 'If I was Heinz, I would have stolen the drug for my wife. You can't put a price on love, no amount of gifts make love. You can't put a price on life either.' This respondent is asserting that relationships and obligation are not reducible to the Stage 2 notion of concrete equal exchange. When scored as Stage 2, Case 9 was asked, 'Should Heinz steal for a friend?' He replied, 'No, that's going too far. He could be in jail while his friend is alive and free. I don't think a friend would do that for him.' As the example of Case 9 suggests, Stage 3 reciprocity involves the notions of obligation, debt, and gratitude which allow one to understand reciprocity as going beyond concrete notions of equal exchange to maintaining relationship, mutuality of expectations, and sentiments of gratitude and obligation. Stage 3 reciprocity can also construct an idea of exchange whereby persons who are good or have worked hard are entitled to their just deserts or rewards (e.g. Heinz should steal if he doesn't love his wife, out of gratitude or appreciation). The operation of *equality* at this stage constructs a category of persons who are to be treated equally based on the notions of 'good role occupants' and 'persons with good motives'. The operation of *equity* at Stage 3 leads to the making of exceptions for those who deviate, based on the recognition of extenuating circumstance and upon empathy with good intentions. At this stage, the operations of reciprocity, equality, and equity can be expressed in a way that indicates that they are coordinated and linked to a prescriptive role-taking operation. The following response exemplifies this idea: 'It's all right for Heinz to steal the drug because the druggist is heartless in ignoring Heinz's wife's right to live.' Another example of this coordination of operations at Stage 3 can be seen in the following response: 'The judge should be lenient with Heinz because he has suffered enough and didn't want to steal.' The Stage 3 operation of *prescriptive role-taking* or balancing perspectives is the Golden Rule. There is a clear use of the Golden Rule for the first time at this stage. It is expressed as the idea that something is right or fair from one's point of view if one could accept it as right or fair from the other's point of view. Here the Golden Rule can be a positive prescription (e.g., 'You should help someone to save their life, because if you were them you would want that to be done for you') or it can be expressed as a limiting prescription in the sense that an expectation at odds with taking the other's viewpoint is not considered to be obligating (e.g., 'Joe should refuse to give his father the money because his father should not demand the money and should be concerned with how Joe feels'). An example of how the operation of *universalizability* is expressed at this stage can be seen in the following response: 'All people should obey the law because without laws immoral people would cause chaos.' At Stage 3 this operation of universalizability expresses a desire to limit deviation that would interfere with the actions and the realization of the intentions of morally motivated persons (i.e., those who are loyal, good, etc.). Thus, the chaos feared at Stage 3 is one that would interrupt a community of persons with good intentions.

Distributive justice at Stage 3 is based on the coordinated use of operations of equality, reciprocity, and equity. At Stage 3, the strict equality and literal reciprocity of Stage 2 is replaced and modified by reference to shared norms or motives. Thus, in addition to focusing on individual needs or interests, as at Stage 2, persons are now considered in terms of their goodness, badness, and deservingness. An example is provided by the following response to Dilemma III: 'That must be a pretty terrible druggist. A druggist is like a doctor; he's supposed to save people's lives.' Thus, the Stage 2 notion of reciprocity as 'he made the drug so he can do what he wants with it' is negated by reference to socially shared norms of a good druggist.

Corrective justice at Stage 3 also emphasizes the relevance of motives and whether or not the transgressor is living up to a shared conception of a good person. If so, punishment is not warranted:

Q.—Should the judge sentence Heinz?
A.—The judge should see why he did it and see his past record. Let him go free and give a warning.
Q.—Why?
A.—He did it from the fondness of his heart ... what most humans would do.

Commutative justice also involves the modification of reciprocity by reference to shared norms and deservingness. For example, while a young child might freely agree to trade his dollar for an adult's twenty-five-cent candy bar, at Stage 3 the fairness of this exchange would be denied on the ground that the adult knows better and should not take advantage of the child's ignorance. That is, at Stage 3 the adult should live up to a socially shared conception of his benevolent, protective role in relation to the child.

A similar idea is represented by the following response to Dilemma 1: 'Joe shouldn't give his father the money, because even though, as his parent, his father can demand the money, he shouldn't do it because that would be selfish and childish.'

Stage 4:   Social System Morality

At Stage 4 the individual takes the perspective of a generalized member of society. This perspective is based on a conception of the social system as a consistent set of codes and procedures that apply impartially to all members. The pursuit of individual interests is considered legitimate only when it is consistent with the maintenance of the sociomoral system as a whole. The informally shared norms of Stage 3 are systematized at Stage 4 in order to maintain impartiality and consistency. A social structure that includes formal institutions and social roles serves to mediate conflicting claims and promote the common good. That is, there is an awareness that there can be conflicts even between good role occupants. This realization makes it necessary to maintain a system of rules for resolving such conflicts. The perspective taken is generally that of a societal, legal, or religious system which has been codified into institutionalized laws and practices. Alternatively, the perspective may be that of some higher moral or religious law which is embodied in the individual's conscience and which may conflict with institutionalized law. In this case, internal conscience or moral law is equated with some system of divine or natural law. That is, moral judgments at Stage 4 are made in reference to institutions or systems—either legal and social institutions or moral and religious institutions and systems of belief.

Norms and Justice Operations

At Stage 4 *norms* promote cooperation or social contribution and act as regulations designed to avoid disagreement and disorder. *Equality* as an operation constructs the idea of 'equality before the law'; that is, persons are equal in the sense that the rights and obligations of each are defined by societal standards such that each counts as a citizen. For example, it is reasoned that 'you should obey a law even if you don't agree with it because a law is made by the majority of people and you have to consider what's good for the majority.' Examples of the *equity* operation at Stage 4 can be seen in the following responses:

'The judge should be lenient to Heinz in order to demonstrate that the law can be fair or humane.' In other words, equity at this stage makes exceptions to the general application of norms on the basis of the idea that societal standards may not be sufficiently sensitive to take into account certain individual circumstances or needs. This equity operation is different from the Stage 3 notion in the sense that it is the system and not a specific other that is recognized to be the agent responsible for exception making. The operation of *reciprocity* at this stage is articulated as a 'norm of reciprocity' linking the individual with the collectivity. There is a sense of duty, obligation, or debt to society incurred by the benefits received from living in or having membership in the institutions of society. Such an idea is expressed in the following response to Dilemma III: 'The druggist should have used his invention to benefit society,' and 'it is important to save another's life because people must have some sense of responsibility for others for the sake of society.' The operation of *prescriptive-role-taking* at Stage 4 achieves a balanced perspective between individual actions and societal standards, an idea expressed in the following response: 'Heinz should steal the drug but he should still see that it is wrong in society's eyes and that he'll have to be prepared to accept the consequences.' Finally, at this stage the operation of *universalizability* constructs the idea of limiting deviation for the sake of maintaining universalized attitudes of respect for law and the integrity of societal organization. This idea is expressed in the following response: 'One should obey the law because respect for the law will be destroyed if citizens feel they can break it just because they disagree with it.'

Distributive justice at Stage 4 is based upon the coordinated use of the three justice operations. However, at Stage 4 these operations are modified by a concern for impartiality, respect for social institutions (such as systems of authority and private property), and considerations of social merit and contribution to society. Generally, maintaining respect for property rights as a return for investment of efforts is considered to be central to social organization. On the other hand, property rights may also be seen as contingent upon demonstration of social responsibility. This is exemplified by the following response to Dilemma III:

Q.—Did the druggist have the right to charge that much?
A.—No, for him to make that much profit is ignoring his responsibility to people.

Corrective justice at Stage 4 centres on the notions of impartiality in application of the law and corrective action as protecting society through deterrence, by removing threats to society or by providing a means for the offender to 'pay his or her debt to society'. The importance of upholding impartiality or consistency reflects a concern about procedural justice which emerges as a central justice problem at Stage 4. This is illustrated by the following response to Dilemma III:

Q.—What would be the best reason for the judge to give him a sentence?
A.—Exceptions to the law cannot be given. This would lead to totally subjective decisions on the part of the law enforcers.

Commutative justice at Stage 4 is based on a recognition of the importance of contractual agreements for maintaining a smoothly functioning society or on the value of upholding one's moral character, integrity, or honour. For example:

Q.—Is it important to keep a promise to someone you don't know well?
A.—Yes. Perhaps even more so than keeping a promise to someone you know well. A man is often judged by his actions in such situations, and to be described as being a 'man of honour', or a 'man of integrity' is very fulfilling indeed.

Stage 5: Human Rights and Social Welfare Morality

The Stage 5 prior-to-society perspective is that of a rational moral agent aware of universalizable values and rights that anyone would choose to build into a moral society. The validity of actual laws and social systems can be evaluated in terms of the degree to which they preserve and protect these fundamental human rights and values. The social system is seen ideally as a contract freely entered into by each individual in order to preserve the rights and promote the welfare of all members. This is a 'society-creating' rather than a 'society-maintaining' perspective. Society is conceived of as based on social cooperation and agreement. Within the Stage 5 perspective, the primary focus may be either on rights or on social welfare. The former orientation emphasizes the point that some rights must be considered inviolable by the society. These rights cannot be abridged even through freely chosen contracts. Each person has an obligation to make moral choices that uphold these rights, even when they conflict with society's laws or codes. There is a concern for the protection of the rights of the minority that cannot be derived from the social system perspective of Stage 4. The social welfare orientation reflects a rule-utilitarian philosophy in which social institutions, rules, or laws are evaluated by reference to their long-term consequences for the welfare of each person or group in the society.

Norms and Justice Operations
At Stage 5 *norms* are defined as maximizing and protecting individual rights and welfare and are seen as being created among free persons through procedures of agreement. The *equality* operation at this stage recognizes the fundamental equal rights and equal worth of individuals as reflected in judgments about the ultimate value of human life and human liberty. At Stage 5 the *equity* operation reasserts equality claims when norms, laws, or procedures exist which are insensitive to, or prevent the realization of, basic human rights and respect for the value of human life. An example of such a view can be seen in the following response to Dilemma III: 'It may not be wrong to break a law where the function of it was not protecting rights, but was protecting infringements on them.' Unlike previous stages, where the 'target' of compensation for the equity operation was some notion of equality, at Stage 5 the target becomes the norms, laws, or procedures. This shift in perspective is a function of the fact that at Stage 5 equality notions of life and liberty are fundamental assumptions in reasoning and provide for the foundation of norms, whereas at earlier stages notions of equality are derived from norms, laws, and so on and are employed to justify them. The *reciprocity* operation at this stage constructs an idea of the exchange of concrete or symbolic equivalents between freely contracting individuals. In this notion, the key idea is free agreement into contract and not just the idea of the equivalence implied in exchange. At Stage 5 the *prescriptive role-taking* operation stresses the necessity of taking into account the viewpoint of each individual involved in a social situation; that is, each is seen as, and is to be counted as, an individual. This idea is expressed in the following response to Dilemma IV: 'The doctor should take the woman's point of view as to whether to live or not, out of respect for her own sense of dignity and autonomy.' An example of how equality, equity, and reciprocity are coordinated at Stage 5 can be seen in the following response concerning the issue of equal opportunity: 'Each should have an equal chance to make their contribution to society and reap the appropriate benefits, even if they have different starting points or are disadvantaged.' The operation of *universalizability* at this stage expresses a universalized regard for the value of human life and liberty. Moral norms or laws should be generalized or universalized for human beings living in any society.

The justice operations of *distributive justice* at Stage 5 are structured around respect for fundamental human rights and a rational hierarchy of rights and values, or around a process of social cooperation and agreement. The latter is exemplified in the following response to Dilemma III:

Q.—Last time we talked you mentioned something about a priori rights....
A.—... it revolves around what I was saying just now about rights that kind of go with being a human being, but really those rights have been defined by us as people, by agreements that we have reached through some kind of social process, and so I may be kind of backing off from the concept....

Corrective justice also focuses on human rights and/or social welfare, and retributive notions of punishment are given up. Capital punishment, for instance, is typically rejected as retributive. *Procedural justice*, including a concern for due process, is closely related to corrective justice at Stage 5. It is assumed that the practice of consistently applying due process will (in a reasonably just legal system) lead to more equity than will the practice of making each individual decision on an *ad hoc* basis. Corrective justice may also be oriented toward effecting social change through the judge's discretion in interpreting the law. For example, 'I can see the point of the judge trying to act as a reforming force in law by handing down a sentence which is so light as to effectively say the law itself is wrongly applied here.'

Commutative justice focuses on contract as a necessary form of social agreement, the foundation of human relationships. That is, making and being able to depend upon agreements is the basis for social relationships and a source of moral obligation: 'Society is interrelationships with other individuals. You would have no basis for that relationship if there were no trust or acting in good faith, so to speak.' As is true of distributive and corrective justice, commutative justice at Stage 5 may also focus on respect for the rights of the parties to an agreement. The importance of upholding contracts is seen as deriving from the fact that people warrant respect in their own right as individuals having intrinsic worth and dignity. Breaking an agreement is seen as a violation of the other's intrinsic dignity or value.

Stage 6: Morality of Universalizable, Reversible, and Prescriptive General Ethical Principle(s)
The sociomoral perspective of Stage 6 is that of 'the moral point of view,' a point of view which ideally all human beings should take toward one another as free and equal autonomous persons. This means

equal consideration of the claim or points of view of each person affected by the moral decision to be made. This prescriptive role-taking is governed by procedures designed to insure fairness, impartiality, or reversibility in role-taking. Procedures of this sort are formalized in various ways. One formalization is Rawl's original position of choosing under 'a veil of ignorance' in which the chooser does not know which person in a situation or society one is to be and must choose a principle or policy with which one could best live in any position including, especially, the position of the person(s) who would be most disadvantaged in the society. A second formalization is that of 'moral musical chairs,' a second order application of the Golden Rule. Not only is Heinz to take the point of view of the dying person, of the druggist, and of himself, but in doing so each person (druggist, dying person) is expected to take the point of view of the other in putting forward his claim and so modifying it. A third formalization is expressed through an emphasis on actual dialogue, as in what Habermas calls an ideal communication situation, the equivalent of internal dialogue as described by Kohlberg. A fourth, utilitarian, formalization by Harsanyi is that of considering preferences under the condition of having an equal probability of being any of those involved in a situation or a society. It is manifested in response to a dilemma by considering the point of view of each person involved and balancing these points of view. It is also manifested in explicit statements of the intrinsic worth, dignity, or equality of every human being, that is, in expressing the attitude of respect or care for persons as ends in themselves, not solely as means to achieving other values, no matter how lofty or desirable, such as the good of society or human survival and development. It is manifest in using the criterion of universalizability, that is, would I want anyone in my (or Heinz's) position to choose the way I do? It is manifest, fourth, in using one or more general principles to make a decision. General principles are distinct from either rules or rights, first, in being positive *pres*criptions rather than negative *pros*criptions (don't kill, don't steal or cheat), and second, in that they apply to all persons and situations. Respect for human dignity may imply sometimes breaking the rules or violating societally recognized rights (stealing the drug, giving a lethal dose of morphine at the request of a dying woman in pain). General principles at Stage 6 may be one or several. Single principles include the principle of justice or respect for human personality or dignity and the principle of utility or benevolence, that is, act so as to maximize the welfare of all individuals concerned, the attitude of universal human care or *agape*. Multiple principles of justice include the principle of maximum quality of life for each, maximum liberty compatible with the like liberty of others, equity or fairness in distribution of goods and respect. These principles may be expressed either in terms of the language of human rights (and reciprocal duties) or in the language of care and responsibility for human 'brothers and sisters'.

Operations and Principles

At Stage 6 the operations we have been discussing form a coordinated whole which constitutes a self-conscious structure for moral decision making. At Stage 5 law and moral norms are grounded on the operations of equality, equity, and so on. At Stage 6 these operations become self-conscious principles. Given this selfconsciousness of moral agency and decision making, the operations of prescriptive role-taking (i.e. balancing perspectives) and universalizability become operative principles as well as being validity checks on the reasons given for upholding moral laws or norms. Stage 6 is not so much 'based' on a new social perspective beyond Stage 5's notion of a prior-to-society perspective as it is on a *deliberate* use of the justice operations as principles to ensure that perspective when reasoning about moral dilemmas. These characteristics of Stage 6 reasoning require that Stage 6 raise dialogue to a principle, a principle of procedure or 'moral musical chairs.' Thus, while Stage 5 is grounded on the notion of fixed contract or agreement, Stage 6 is oriented to the process by which agreements or contracts are reached as well as to ensuring the fairness of the procedures which underlie such agreement. Underneath the fixed contract and agreement of Stage 5, designed to protect human rights, is the notion of the importance of maintaining human trust and community. At Stage 6 the notion of trust and community becomes the precondition for dialogue, human rights, and so on. (We should note that Stage 5 has difficulty balancing the notion of fixed contract with the underlying notions of trust and community, a problem that Stage 6 resolves through the operation of dialogue, a derivative of moral musical chairs.)

Distributive justice at Stage 6, in addition to the principle of equality, uses the principle of equity or fairness. At this stage equity does not include reference to special rewards for talent, merit, or achievement. These are largely seen as resulting from differences in genes or in educational and social opportunities which are morally arbitrary, or to unequal distribution by society. However, Stage 6 equity does include recognition of differential need, that is, the need to consider the position of the least advantaged. Where distribution of scarce basic goods must be unequal (e.g., issues of who should live in 'life-boat' dilemmas) a lottery approach is preferred to favouring the strong or the more socially useful.

Corrective justice is not retributive; while punishment through either incarceration or restitution is seen as necessary to protect the rights or welfare of potential or actual victims of crime through isolation or deterrence, it is not based upon inflicting suffering or death as 'repayment' for demerit or immorality. The offender is still seen as a human being with human dignity to be respected as far as this is compatible with justice principles. For example, the actions of Heinz stealing the drug or Dr. Jefferson performing euthanasia are seen to require no punishment, but they do require one to consider issues of procedural justice.

Commutative justice is based on the recognition of trust and mutual respect as the bases of contracts and promises. Promises are seen as the foundation of contracts. Promises presuppose and affirm a moral relationship between promisor and promisee. A violation of a promise is both a violation of trust and a violation of a relationship of mutual respect between promisor and promisee as autonomous persons of worth and dignity. It is the violation of a right awarded to the promisee in making the promise. Promises may be modified or violated only insofar as they maintain a moral relation of mutual respect or reversible role-taking; for example, one may break an appointment to serve the urgent need of a third party, a violation of promise which the promisee as a moral person would necessarily understand through ideal role-taking or 'moral musical chairs'. Violation of promises is not so much seen as a violation of the self's integrity (Stage 4) as it is seen as an issue of the integrity of the other and of the relationship.

Source: Kohlberg (1984), Appendix A.

PSYCHOLOGICAL ISSUES

Rest's chapter on our methodology and its results agrees with us that our method and data on the whole meet 'hard stage' criteria. He also points out the possible costs of maintaining (1) a very tight distinction between content and structure in defining moral stages, and (2) constructing a 'hard' or 'simple' stage model and manual in researching moral judgment. He points out that our delineating moral judgment development formally leaves open the possibility of missing variance relevant to moral action or to morality in the broader sense. He remarks, as we might, that it is rather surprising that rather remote hypothetical justice dilemmas pitting one socially approved norm against another relate in regular fashion at all to 'real-life' behaviour. My own rather complex theory as to why there are regular judgment-action relations and supporting data are reported in Kohlberg (1984, Ch. 7). Unfortunately Kutnick's chapter did not reach me in time for inclusion in my response, and since Straughan's chapter does not respond to my more recent statements on judgment and action I shall not elaborate on this issue. Straughan's major objection to my view is, however, well dealt with in Bailey's chapter on 'Kohlberg on Morality and Feeling'. Straughan argues that I confuse a justification or reason for moral action with a motive for moral action, giving reasons motivational force. Many readers of my earlier writings (Kohlberg, 1969, 1984, Ch. 1) were left with the belief that my moral stages were eventually expressions of a developmental hierarchy of motives. In this interpretation, preconventional judgments were motivated by, or expressed motives of, concern for extrinsic punishment and reward, conventional reasoning by affiliation, approval and respect-seeking, and postconventional judgments by motivations of conscience or moral self-judgment. In fact, however, I have avoided this emotivist view of the moral stage, I have claimed that in some sense there is a primary motivation 'to do the right thing' in the sociomoral world as Piaget assumed a primary adaptation a 'truth' motivation for the infant and child's actions toward the physical world. Even at Stages 1 and 2 perceived injustice is disequilibrating and action toward justice equilibrating. Punishment and reward are relevant to moral judgment because they are forms of justice as reciprocity between act and consequence and signs that an action is right or wrong (as decreed by powerful authority figures at Stage 1, and forms of reciprocity or exchange between equals at Stage 2). At the conventional level, social approval and respect are signs that one is acting rightly as decreed by group or dyadic mutual agreement or shared norms. Even at the preconventional and conventional levels, however, one is motivated by concerns for self-esteem for acting 'rightly', and by empathy and respect for others as persons, though not in the principled form of post-conventional morality.

Straughan has argued that I have confused reasons or justifications with motives in attempting to relate moral judgment to action. In terms of this question Bailey's chapter, 'Kohlberg on Morality and Feeling', is clarifying. As I claim in Kohlberg (1984, Ch. 7), and as Bailey clarifies, the question of the relation of judgment to action is not purely psychological, it is first a philosophic or meta-ethical question. For the 'formalist' meta-ethical philosophic position I hold, a necessary part of a moral action is guidance or justification by a moral reason, i.e., by a judgment of rational and autonomous obligation. Bailey also articulates the philosophic reasons why a description of an act as moral must take into account the judgment the actor uses to justify the act, especially to himself, and must stress the cognitive features of this judgment. This stress does not depend upon a Kantian metaphysical postulation of autonomy. As Bailey points out, moral judgments are typically accompanied by moral emotions, but emotions themselves do not present a sufficient condition for an act to be justified, which requires a moral reason for action contingent on a cognitive activity of judgment from what formalists called a 'moral point of view'. Doubtless, as Bailey points out, judgments affirming a moral point of view would not develop without emotions of sympathy and respect for other persons and their points of view, but these emotions are cognitively regulated in moral judgments which make claim to rationality and morality.

It is a philosophic claim or position that moral action ought to be cognitively steered or guided by moral judgment, but such a philosophic claim could carry little weight unless research psychology showed that it was empirically true, something demonstrated by reviews of Blasi (1980) and Kohlberg (1984, Ch. 7), of the relations of judgment stage to action, reviews indicating a monotonic increase of just action (or of consistency between justice or deontic judgments and actual action) by moral stage.

Bailey's chapter also helps put in perspective the basic issue in each of the chapters in this book, the issue of the scope of moral domain. The research programme of myself and my Harvard colleagues has moved from restricting the study of morality to the study of moral development to restricting it to the study of moral judgment (and its correspondence with action) to restricting it to the form or cognitive-structural stage of moral judgment as embodied in judgments of justice. Obviously these successive restrictions on the moral domain do not mean that this is the only way to define and psychologically research the moral domain. Rest (1984) has done a broad review of moral development research which includes content as well as structure, affect as well as cognition, 'soft' or complex stage models, like his own, as well as 'hard' or simple stages. Obviously the restricted range of the moral domain as we have now come to define it for our own theory or research programme does not imply that these restrictions should guide all fruitful moral psychology research. The moral domain is large and varied, and no one approach to its conceptualization and measurement will exhaust or explain the variance in it. Our major claim is that our theory or research programme is a progressive or content-enhancing one in Lakatos' (1978) sense, as explained by Enright, Lapsley and Olson in this volume and by Lapsley and Serlin (1985) at more length elsewhere. My examples of the 'progressive', content-enhancing nature of our research programme might be different from those used by them. For instance, it includes (1) revised stage definitions leading to clearer experimental as well as longitudinal findings by Walker (1980, 1982b); (2) the concepts of heteronomous and autonomous moral types; (3) differentiating judgments of justice and of responsibility from ego controls or attention-will; and (4) most important, the moral atmosphere or collective norms of institutions or groups as variables required to bridge the gap between judgment stage and action (Kohlberg, 1984, Chs. 3 and 7; Higgins, Power and Kohlberg, 1984). In addition to a predicted and confirmed straightforward monotonic link between stages and action (Kohlberg, 1984, Ch. 7), variables additional to justice stage enter into our research programme not because they are an eclectically defined independent set of psychological variables included to maximize the prediction of moral behaviour, but because each of them is related to a single theoretical perspective on moral development which attempts to integrate a mutually compatible psychology, philosophy and sociology in the service of moral education. In developing the theory, then, we have opted for an empirically and intuitively compelling Piagetian justice stage theory, sought gaps and problems in the application of the model and revised the theory and research methodology accordingly. The progressive circularity of our approach is discussed under our section on philosophy.

The issue of narrowness of domain raised by Rest is also raised more critically by Tomlinson who, in particular, critiques the interrelated narrowness of looking for hard stages, refining morality in terms of justice, and searching to define stages in a way amenable to ordering them normatively in terms of a rational reconstruction of ontogenesis. In discussing the limitedness of these interlocked assumptions, Tomlinson points to other researchers, work such as Turiel's on convention and Gilligan's on care and response. Both of these researchers have explicitly contrasted their constructs with the justice construct in order to enlarge the social cognitive domain rather than rejecting the distinctive definition of the justice domain. Tomlinson has undertaken to ask the question, 'How much (moral) valuing judgments can be explicitly subsumed under our justice stages?', finding that 50 per cent or less of standard interview responses are clearly stage scorable. It was for this reason that 'guess' scores were introduced into our scoring method for interviews which did not articulate clearly scorable material on each moral issue assessed. Much of the variability is due to variations in the dilemmas and to the interviewer's skill, but some of it is probably due to our manual's map of issues, norms, and elements failing to map the entire moral domain. Like Loevinger and Rest, Tomlinson reminds us 'there's more in moral development than is dreamt of in your philosophy.' But some philosophic definition of the moral domain is required as a starting-point for psychological or empirical study of moral development or morality becomes synonymous with all valuing. Since my thesis I have defined developing morality as involving 'a moral point of view' including not only Kant's or Hare's prescriptivity, universalizability and over-ridingness and its implication of judging and acting on principles, but also including impartiality or considering the good of everyone alike and reversibility, which is not quite the same as universalizability. The 'moral point of view' is somewhat broader than a concern for distributive, commutative and restorative justice, since it can centre on an attitude or principle of beneficence in situations without conflicting claims between two or more others and only involving the self and one other (Frankena, 1973, pp. 113–14). In the absence of justice questions, however, the moral may be relatively unproblematic and need not elicit reasoning or reasons, the object of our study. To attempt to include moral normative content without reasoning into the compass of data to be analyzed, or to include unconscious material, as Tomlinson suggests, would mean giving up on moral judgment development as a discrete focus of study. In the 1950s a good deal of moral research went on, based on analysis of reactions to projective-test stories, research guided by psychodynamic hypotheses. This approach led to contradictory and non-generalizable findings on various effects of various types of socialization, with little clarification of moral development itself (Kohlberg, 1963, 1964).

Our Harvard research programme is somewhat neutral or open to a variety of theories of the self and of motivation, though it is most compatible with the sort described by Kegan, which postulates a motivational system of primary adaptation, or of competence, effect and self-esteem motivation (Kohlberg, 1984, Ch. 1) rather than a model of needs and drives defined independently of cognitive structures. Kegan's stages of the self define levels of motivation which are broader than the moral but which are morally relevant in the fashion I described in talking about Straughan's and Bailey's chapters. Unpublished research by Jacquette shows those high in affiliation motivation are at least moral Stage 3, and those high in achievement motivation at least moral Stage 4. Unpublished research by Lasker and the Loevinger scoring manual show similar relations between affiliation motivation and Loevinger's Stage 3, and between achievement motivation and Loevinger's Stage 4.

Thus the central issue raised by both Kegan's chapter and Loevinger's chapter is the question as to whether moral development or moral stages, as assessed by our justice dilemmas and stages, represent a more general ego development or 'character' development domain looked at from a moral perspective, or whether there is a separable subdomain of social and self-development called 'moral judgment development'. Both Kegan and Loevinger take the more unitary or holistic view as opposed to my own view that moral judgment development is a distinct subdomain of social or ego development. Following the findings of relations between affiliation motivation and Stage 3 and 'conscience' or rule-governed achievement motivation and Stage 4, we stress that neither type of motivation is directly moral although both may be tapped by my moral dilemmas, e.g., 'Stage 3' affiliation in responding to the Heinz dilemma (centrally in terms of Heinz's affection for his wife) or Stage 4 in terms of issues of conscientious work by the druggist (or internal standards of achievement for a husband).

While I have speculated about the relations between moral decisions and the development of the self in a fashion consistent with Kegan's theory (Snarey, Kohlberg and Noam, 1983), my own work has concentrated not on a holistic conception of the self but on a 'rational moral subject' analogous to Piaget's 'rational epistemic subject' standing behind Piaget's genetic epistemology. On a theoretical level, our moral stages represent a 'rational reconstruction of ontogenesis', in which ontogenesis is defined by structure as distinct from content and competence as distinct from performance. This level of structural abstraction defines a logic of development which is somewhat neutral or open to a variety of theories of the development of the ego or self and of motivation, though it is perhaps most compatible with Kegan's.

The section on 'Ego Development' containing Kegan's and Loevinger's papers raising the question, 'Does research in the Kohlberg moral development paradigm enhance our understanding of ego development or development of the self?', is answered affirmatively by Kegan and negatively by Loevinger. I myself have not directly attempted to address this question nor to do serious research with regard to it. Kegan (1982) and somewhat before him Selman (1976, 1980) have postulated that beneath my stages of judgments of justice, there are more general levels of differentiation and coordination of social perspective-taking or of self-other relationship. The case examples in Kegan's chapter of Stage 2 and Stage 3 modes of defining self-other problems suggest the ways in which moral judgment structures may be extended to total self-other patterns going beyond morally prescriptive or justice questions.

Loevinger answers the question of the contribution of my moral stages to understanding of ego development in the negative for a variety of reasons. While for certain purposes I have pointed to philosophic modes or subdomains of the self or ego, the moral, the epistemological, the metaphysical-religious (Snarey, Kohlberg and Noam, 1983), like Loevinger I believe that there is a broad domain of ego development distinguishable from intelligence or cognitive development on the one side, and from psychosexual or 'drive' development on the other, and that moral development is one aspect or component of the ego domain (Kohlberg, 1984, Ch. 5). Attempting to sample the broad ego domain, Loevinger does not define distinctive moral stage items or distinctive moral stage criteria for scoring items. Just as we get a single general factor across our various moral dilemmas and issues (Colby and Kohlberg, 1984), Loevinger and Wessler (1970) get a single general factor across the sentence completions of her test, stage scored for ego development. I agree with Loevinger that there is a general domain of ego development, defined not by theory but by empirical consistency, that her test is a sensible and careful measure of this domain, and that our test of moral development is not, and does not purport to be, an assessment of the ego development domain. Much empirical work has recently been done demonstrating moderate to high correlations between the two tests. Noam (1984) reports correlation in the sixties between the two tests among adolescents. Loevinger (1976) and I (Kohlberg, 1984, Chs 1 and 5) have conceptually constructed rough parallels between each of our respective six stages. Because of different test methodologies and different scoring algorithms it is difficult to define clear conceptually and empirically valid relations between the two measures, or exact parallels between a particular Loevinger stage and a particular moral stage, though work is in progress attempting to do so (Lee, n.d.). While an extensive amount of research has been done on the relation between moral judgment and moral action (Blasi, 1980; Kohlberg, 1984, Ch. 7), it would be interesting to know whether some aspects of what is usually considered moral action are more closely related to Loevinger's ego stage test than to our moral stage measure. A complete theory of moral action and decision-making obviously requires a conception of the 'moral self', but a conception and measure of the development of the 'moral self' remains to be developed (Kohlberg, 1984, Ch. 7). Returning to the domain question, both Kegan and Loevinger question my partitioning of the ego development domain into subdomains of Piagetian cognitive stage, Selman's perspective-taking stage and moral stage. This division into subdomains represents a division of types of tasks (logico-mathematical and physical tasks, social prediction tasks and moral conflict resolution tasks), types of stage structures used for these tasks, and experiences of social interaction leading to development within each task area. As Lapsley, Enright and Olson also note, Walker (1980) and Walker and Richards (1979) have obtained clear empirical data that experimental change to the next moral stages occurs only in subjects having the parallel logical and social perspective-taking prerequisite of the next stage up. Loevinger questions my use of the term 'parallel structures' as implying that one set of structures is redundant if two sets are parallel. Perhaps I should have used the term 'partially isomorphic' with each later structure, e.g., the moral structures having additional structural elements to those of the logical and social perspective-taking structures which they include.

Perhaps the most fundamental disagreement between Loevinger and myself is that concerning the methodology of studying personality structures and their development. The very general methodological model Loevinger cites is E. Brunswick's probabilistic 'lens' model in which personality structures mediate probabilistic stimulus inputs and probabilistic response outputs. In this view 'pure' structures do not exist and the distinction between competence and performance is problematic. Loevinger's ogive rule is an effort to tap competence corresponding to our full probing of responses for competence. In our view our test forms A, B and C are samples of moral judgment and reasoning requiring careful and exact hermeneutic analysis similar to that used by a humanist in analyzing a particular text. This is what is done in the process of scoring moral dilemmas (Kohlberg, 1984, Chs 3 and 5; Colby and Kohlberg 1986, Ch. 1). This implies, as Habermas (1983) points out, that 'Only to the extent that the interpreter grasps the reasons that allow the author's utterance to appear as rational does he understand what the author could have meant.' This hermeneutic stance is related to our efforts to find a moral philosophic rationale for a later, more rational stage, and our view of the stage theory as a 'rational reconstruction of ontogenesis' (Kohlberg, 1984, Ch. 3), as Carter's chapter in this volume explicates. Our research programme is then linked to (1) a hermeneutic and exact interpretation of the stage of a moral judgment as having an inner logic, and (2) the hierarchy of stages as having a definite logic of hierarchy (though more than one theoretical rationale for the stage structures and their hierarchy may be elaborated). The scorer of a Stage 2 moral judgment must, apart from its content (norm and element), grasp the rationality of a Stage 2 judgment, e.g., of 'concrete payback', though he will not accept this rationality as ultimate. Our hermeneutic and reconstructive stance is part of our effort to define our stages as 'hard' Piagetian stages meeting the criteria of culturally invariant longitudinal sequence, structured wholeness and hierarchical integration of a lower stage into the next stage. As a result we eliminate structurally ambiguous responses. Loevinger (1979, p. 14) describes as an example of her test-construction method finding that many people respond to, 'What gets me into trouble . . . is my big mouth.'! She says, 'This is a popular response, and although someone of about any level might give it, on the average it is classed at the conformist stage.' In Loevinger's methodology this response would be a rather low probability sign of being a Stage 3 conformist in ego development. We would eliminate such structurally ambiguous responses as unscorable.

Loevinger (1979, p. 13) uses this example as indicating that:

Nothing is more characteristic of people than variability. What the psychometrician calls *subject unreliability*, what the Piagetian calls *decalage*, what the clinician calls *difficult cases*, are all aspects of what Egor Brunswick called the probabilistic texture of behavior. The same probabilistic texture of response permits researchers, such as Lawrence Kohlberg and me, when talking about the same people, and closely similar aspects of behavior to propose stage theories that contain irreconcilable differences. We are only two of many who have such stage theories, similar yet incapable of being collapsed into one. If any of us had a theory or conception that completely and closely fitted all cases, he would put all the others out of business. None of us will, not because there are no clever people trying, but because human variability guarantees that no theory will fit every case perfectly.

Loevinger's chapter in this volume points to examples in the Colby *et al.* (1983) data as indicating such subject variability or of 'the probabilistic texture of response'. One example is the fairly frequent occurrence of half-stage and occasionally whole-stage differences of subjects from one form of the dilemmas (e.g., Form A) to another form of the dilemmas (Form B). Part of this difference we attribute to *decalage*, i.e., to the fact that the Form B problems are more difficult than Form A dilemmas. In Piagetian terminology the Form B problems offer greater 'resistance' to the subject's higher-stage structure than Form A dilemmas. This represents a source of variation not due to variation in the subjects' stage structure, but variation due to the content of the stimulus problems themselves. This explanation is analogous to Piaget's explanation of conservation or class inclusion being attained earlier with some objects as opposed to others. As long as the order of difficulty is an order which is the same for all subjects, *decalage* effects are not attributable to the subject variability which Loevinger discusses. (In our study, difficulties were also compounded by the fact that different raters rated each form, a source of error additional to *decalage*, given relatively high but not perfect interjudge agreement in stage assignment.) Thus while we readily acknowledge measurement error or errors and ambiguities of interpretation, we do not believe interpretation is itself simply a reflection of probabilistic signs, as Loevinger assumes, but is rather a hermeneutic examination of an interview text, guided by an elaborate stage scoring manual holding content (Table 1) constant (Kohlberg, 1984, Ch. 5; Colby and Kohlberg, 1986). Further research will no doubt clarify the relation between Loevinger's 'soft stage' model and test our own, but the research results indicate, as Loevinger implicitly concedes, that our test has greater inter-judge reliability, greater test-retest reliability, greater inter-form reliability and greater construct validity if the 'hard stage' criteria of validity are used which I advocate, i.e., less longitudinal regression, less stage-skipping and greater across-item consistency (for us an issue on a dilemma is an item).

MORAL PHILOSOPHIC ISSUES: MORAL PHILOSOPHY, MORAL PSYCHOLOGY AND MORAL ANTHROPOLOGY

While the preceding section was called 'psychological issues', much of it dealt with chapter authors' views of the epistemology or philosophy of science of psychological theory or of the meta-ethical definition of the moral domain, rather than issues of empirical fact, with only Loevinger and Enright, Lapsley and Olson dealing with empirical results. We turn now from philosophical psychology to issues of moral philosophy and the relation between the two.

The central characteristic of my theory or research programme has been its interdisciplinary nature, using empirical psychological and anthropological data to make philosophic claims, and using philosophic assumptions to define and interpret psychological, anthropological and educational data. It is not only the effort to be interdisciplinary but the way in which I have attempted to be interdisciplinary, to relate philosophic assumptions and interpretations to empirical psychological and anthropological data, which has made my theory both a changing theory and one which is highly controversial. Boyd's chapter is central in this volume since it is a clear statement of the way in which I have tried to relate philosophic normative and analytic 'ought' propositions to empirical 'is' propositions in a progressive or content-enhancing theory or research programme. Staying within the 'is' domain of psychology, my way of relating theory to data has puzzled and annoyed many people because it attempts to be a circular but progressive spiral between theoretical propositions and empirical data. As noted by Lapsley and Serlin (1985) and Enright, Lapsley and Olson in this volume our notion of theory is Lakatos' (1978) view of a theory as a progressively spiralling research programme. In this interpretation a set of 'hard core' theoretical assumptions is surrounded by a 'protective belt' of empirical propositions and measurement methods which are revisable and are content-enhancing or provide new knowledge in a progressive research programme. We earlier described our empirical approach to studying moral judgment and action as attempting to proceed in this spiral fashion. Longitudinal data initially suggesting the falsity of the 'hard core' theoretical assumption of progressive invariant sequence led to a redefinition of stage definitions and scoring method with 'college sophomore regression to Stage 2' as a relativistic transition from conventional to postconventional morality (Kohlberg, 1984, Ch. 6). This in turn involved purifying the form-content distinction and defining high school response of 'regressors' as conventional but of an autonomous (as opposed to heteronomous) moral type or substage (Kohlberg, 1984, Appendix C; Colby and Kohlberg, 1986). This elaboration of the protective belt of the theory was 'content-enhancing' in that the definition of the autonomous substage or type helped explain the fact that some (the autonomous) conventional subjects acted like the postconventional subjects in three action studies where moral-type data were available (Kohlberg, 1984, Ch. 7). This in turn supported our 'hard core' equilibration theoretical assumption that there is a relationship of entailment or consisting between judgment and action linked to the degree of equilibration of judgment, defining greater equilibration or autonomy in terms of advance in both justice stage and moral type.

The 'spiral circularity' of theory and data I and my colleagues have used within psychology, I have also used in relating psychological data and theory and moral philosophical theory, a much more controversial endeavour. Boyd uses the metaphor of the two disciplines of moral philosophy and psychology as separated by a moat, 'Hume's law' or 'Moore's law pertaining to the danger of committing "the naturalistic fallacy"'. In this volume Siegel is the defender of the moat. For Siegel the naturalistic fallacy is the effort directly deductively to derive an ought judgment (or an ought theory or justification) from a factual or 'is' judgment (or an is theory or justification). Siegel thinks I commit the naturalistic fallacy because I claim that the developmentally later and developmentally higher stage is a more morally adequate way of making moral judgments. I do not do this by a direct deduction of a normative ought from a developmental psychology 'is'. As Boyd points out, the relationship of ought to is in my theory is not one of deriving or deducing an 'ought' from an 'is'. To such direct derivations or deductions as Siegel and Boyd point out, one can always ask the moral philosopher's 'open question'. To say postconventional or Stage 5 reasoning is more developed or evolved than conventional reasoning and is therefore better is to invite the open question, 'But why does being psychologically more evolved make it good or better?' In a similar way Skinner, who is a meta-ethical naturalist who derives an ought from an is, says (1971, p. 104), 'Good things are positive reinforcers. Physics and biology study things without references to their values, but the reinforcing effect of things is the province of behavioral sciences, which to the extent that it concerns itself with operant reinforcement, is a science of values. Things are good (positively reinforcing) because of the contingencies under which the species evolved.' Skinner's naturalism invites the open question, 'Why are reinforcers good or why ought we engage in the behaviour which leads to reinforcement?' As Carter's and Petrovich's chapters indicate, a response to the open question may eventually require an ethical and religious philosophy, my metaphorical Stage 7. Before that point is reached, however, there is a simpler answer which Boyd, Carter and I give. This is the constructivistic meta-ethical conception or answer given by Habermas (1983, 1984), Rawls (1980) and Boyd (1980) that moral or justice reasoning reasons and argumentation represent a human activity designed to produce consensus or agreement among persons with conflicting claims, under conditions where each person engaging in argumentation is recognized as a free and equal participant in such dialogue or argumentation. In the case of Rawls this consensus is the result of a hypothetical social contract on principles of social justice by rational persons in an original position under a 'veil of ignorance' designed to ensure 'pure procedural justice' or designed to ensure that each contractor will take a 'moral point of view'. From this original position Rawls derives the logically ordered principles of liberty and equity (modified equality from the point of view of the least advantaged) since in the 'original position' each must 'role-take' or put himself or herself in the position of any member of society including the least advantaged. In the case of Habermas (as Carter points out in his chapter) the constructive process is one of actual dialogue and role-taking of persons communicating with one another and attempting to argue for, or redeem, claims in an ideal universal communication situation without resort to authority, force or strategic manipulation to ensure agreement. In my conception of 'justice as reversibility' (Kohlberg, 1981, Ch. 5) this dialogue is carried on in an internal monologue by a moral judge through 'ideal role-taking' or 'moral musical chairs'. This general meta-ethical *constructivistic* view of moral reasoning and justification taken by Boyd, Carter and myself can be argued for apart from any claims about the ultimate adequacy of a hypothetical sixth stage of moral reasoning, which Locke critiques in his chapter. In this chapter I will limit my assumptions to those I have made about a postconventional fifth stage, leaving a defence of the existence and greater adequacy of a sixth stage to another place, the third volume of my collected essays (Kohlberg, 1986, in preparation). In the constructivism of Habermas (1983) and myself (Kohlberg, 1984, Ch. 3) moral philosophy is essentially a refinement of the natural activities of human beings as philosophers and communicators. Using more precise methods of argumentation than 'lay' philosophers, the methods of moral philosophy are primarily (1) the analysis of the meaning of moral language and concepts, meta-ethically clarifying the meaning of the terms 'moral' and 'moral development', and (2) the creation of normative theories or justifications of the ultimate rationality of moral beliefs or principles. As Boyd elaborates, I (Kohlberg, 1984, Ch. 3) accept a distinction made by Habermas (1983) between the 'performative' attitude of dialogic arguments of professional moral philosophers (or human beings as natural moral philosophers) and the 'objectivating' attitude of professional psychologists (or human beings as natural psychologists) trying empirically to describe and explain the moral judgment, actions and development of other human beings. The human being as philosopher is attempting to justify the rightness of moral judgments or principles. The human being as psychologist is attempting to establish the empirical truth of propositional explanations of moral judgment and action. As a result of this distinction I (Kohlberg, Levine and Hewer, 1983) followed Habermas (1983) in abandoning the ultimate identity or isomorphism of psychological explanations of why people move from stage to stage and of moral philosophic justifications of the greater adequacy of a later stage over its predecessor; an identity claim made in 'From Is to Ought' (Kohlberg, 1971, 1981, Ch. 4) and discussed clearly in Boyd's chapter in this volume. Instead I have retreated to what Habermas calls the 'complementarity thesis'. As Boyd elaborates, my earlier 'identity' or 'isomorphism' claim was not meant to say that the moral philosophic theory of stage adequacy and the moral psychological theory 'were broadly the same or identical', but rather to say that 'they were one and the same theory extended in different directions', an interpretation which Boyd elaborates in the metaphor of two different mirrors imaging a common object, moral judgment development.

Boyd then goes on to clarify the weaker 'complementarity thesis' which Habermas and I now would put forth, a thesis which depends upon the idea which Kohlberg, Levine and Hewer (1983) also accept from Habermas, the assumption that my theory is a 'rational reconstruction of moral ontogenesis'.

I shall briefly summarize by quoting Boyd's chapter's explanation of the complementarity hypothesis. He says,

> Habermas [1983, pp. 266–7] calls his interpretation [of Kohlberg's intent] the complementarity thesis, claiming that Kohlberg 'rightly insists' on this relationship of psychological and philosophical theories [Habermas says]:
>
> > 'This "complementarity thesis" states the case more adequately than the identity thesis does. The success of an empirical theory which can only be true or false may function as a check on the normative validity of hypothetically reconstructed moral intuitions. Kohlberg says, "The fact that our conception of the moral 'works' empirically is important for its philosophic adequacy." It is in this way that rational reconstructions can be put on trial or "tested," if "test" means an attempt to check whether pieces complementarily fit into the same pattern. In Kohlberg, the following is the clearest formulations: "Science, then, can test whether a philosopher's conception of morality phenomenologically fits the psychological facts." Science cannot go on to justify that conception of morality as what morality ought to be ...'

Boyd's chapter goes on to say:

> As Kohlberg now accepts the distinction between the two theses, 'identity' vs. 'complementarity', and clearly affirms the complementarity interpretation, it is important to try to elaborate more fully the nature of the connection being asserted.
>
> In order to clarify how within a developmental theory such as Kohlberg's psychology and philosophy might be 'complementary' (or how a psychological account of the 'is' of moral development might 'complement' a philosophical account of the 'ought' of moral judgment, and *vice versa*), it is necessary first to get a clearer picture of the nature of Kohlberg's empirical

methodology—why, in short, he refers to his theory (following Habermas) as a 'rational reconstruction of developmental progress'.... the essential point is that within Kohlberg's approach, empirical data are generated by one person (the interviewer) assuming an 'interpretive' or 'hermeneutical' stance *vis-à-vis* another person (the subject)—or at least this is the paradigmatic case underlying the approach. What this means is that the theoretical orientation of the interviewer's task is linked to that of interpretation, which 'rests on trying to come to agreement *with* another member of a speech-community who is *expressing his or her belief about something* in the world.

Boyd takes his point of departure from Kohlberg, Levine and Hewer (1983), who make the following points:

The first meaning of cognitive for us is that observations of others are made phenomenologically; i.e., by attempting to take the role of the other, to see things from his or her conscious viewpoint. Second, we mean by cognitive the fact that interviewing and scoring are acts of 'interpreting a text' around some shared philosophic categories of meaning. Insofar as each of us has been through the moral stages and has held the viewpoint of each stage, we should be able to put ourselves in the internal framework of a given stage. To understand others, to put oneself in the framework of others, is to be able to generate from their statements other statements that they can or do make from this framework, not because we are imposing upon them a framework to predict future speech acts but rather because we can organize the world as they do; i.e., for the moment we can share their meanings.

Boyd goes on to say:

Presented with a series of moral problems, or 'dilemmas', which invite the expressing and justifying of normative ought claims toward the solution of the problems, the subject is placed by the interviewer into what Habermas calls the 'performative attitude'. But, given the interpretive stance of the interviewer outlined above, to some extent the interviewer *must also* assume this performative attitude. The stages that result from an analysis of the data so generated are then structural descriptions of the 'pattern of connections within the subjects' meaning', or the 'set of relations and transformations', of the 'shared philosophic categories of meaning' identified as relevant by the end point of the stage sequence *performatively claimed by the interviewer....*

However, what Kohlberg now acknowledges more clearly in his acceptance of Habermas' characterization of the developmentalist's view of the 'is/ought' relationship as one of 'complementarity' is that, in order to give a full psychological explanation of the developmental progress through the stage sequence, the psychologist must adopt a perspective and utilize concepts and truthfulness checks which are 'external' to the interpretive stance which facilitates the reconstruction of qualitative changes in how the performative attitude in justice reasoning is manifested.... Habermas points out that the psychologist must at this point assume and be restricted to an 'objectivating' or 'third-person' attitude, one that seeks to explain the data in a way which meets the relevant standards of propositional truth claims. In Kohlberg's words,

> 'the psychological theory adds explanatory concepts in its explanation of ontogenesis, such as mechanisms of cognitive conflict, which are not reducible to the concepts of the normative philosophic theory.
>
>   Thus, the empirical verification of the psychological stage theory does not directly confirm the normative validity of theories of justice....'

In short, what this appears to me to leave room for is exactly the sort of difference between 'is' and 'ought' which preserves the 'critical leverage' of normative moral judgment.

What, then does the 'complementarity thesis' come down to? There seems to be two ways in which it might be cashed out. One of them, primarily negative, is that which both Kohlberg and Habermas seem to be adopting. Although this way has some plausibility for some degree of doubt, I believe it also could be interpreted as vitiating the difference between 'is' and 'ought' which we have just seen reaffirmed in Kohlberg. I will first examine this interpretation, and then, once again in the spirit of keeping the question open, I will briefly suggest a more positive interpretation which looks promising and avoids the problems.

First of all, as we have seen above ... Habermas states the strength of the complementarity thesis in a negative mode: 'The success of an empirical theory which can only be true or false may function as a *check* on the normative validity of hypothetically reconstructed moral intuitions'; i.e., 'rational reconstructions can be *put on trial* or *"tested"*.' . . . The problem here is that neither Kohlberg nor Habermas explains what is meant by phrases such as 'function as a check', 'put on trial or "tested",' or 'cast doubt on'. There are some senses which would perhaps yield a relatively unproblematic claim. Thus, to put it in Kohlberg's terms, if the 'doubt' that is 'cast on' one's sense of the rightness of a normative theory of justice is read as just '*some* doubt', rather than '*sufficient* doubt to reject', then the relationship suggested seems credible. That is, it would mean simply that one might be reasonably motivated to rethink one's normative position, to examine its justification even more carefully, if empirical data indicated that human subjects showed no indication of developing in that direction, but instead, offered at a mature level a form of judgment fundamentally at odds with one's own position. But this would seem to me to amount to a much weaker relationship between psychological fact and normative 'ought'-claims than is suggested by 'complementarity'. . . .

On the other hand, for 'sufficient' doubt, or for anything less than these 'extremely stringent "oughts"', the danger is that this negative formation of 'complementarity' runs the risk of cutting the ground out from under the 'critical leverage' which our concept of 'ought' supplies. If negative empirical results relevant to some aspect of the psychological theory (such as the failure of a predicted developmental change within specified natural or experimental conditions) were seen as fundamentally threatening to the normative validity of the moral theory, then 'ought'-claims lose their unique power. On the sense of the 'is/ought' distinction with which I have been working, 'ought'-claims function to 'cast doubt on' the legitimacy or acceptability of the facts of the case, not the other way around. . . .

How might the complementarity thesis be given a more positive interpretation which avoids this problem? What it requires, I believe, is going back to the interpretive stance of the developmental psychologist outlined above. . . . Assuming an interpretive stance, then, entails a mutual (both interviewer and subject) adopting of this performative attitude, and the stages of moral judgment are coherent, consistent, and relatively stable patterns which can be reconstructed through this method. However, a simple description of these different patterns so determined does not fully constitute a developmental theory such as Kohlberg's; rather, what is also required is an account of how they are hierarchically ordered and why people change from one to the next. Part of this task will involve making predictions about what will happen in a variety of conditions and then utilizing the appropriate scientific methodology to test those predictions for truth, procedures which, as we have already noted above, require restricting one's stance to an 'objectivating' or 'third-person' stance. However, it does not seem to me that *all* of this task can be so described; and thus, as I suggested above, Habermas may have overstated the case when he implies that the psychologist's orientation in this task of explanation is limited to *only* an objectivating attitude concerned with propositional truth alone.

The point is this: the developmental psychologist is required not only to 'interpret' how a person is making and evaluating 'ought'-claims, but also to 'interpret' why a person would *change* their way of making and evaluating 'ought'-claims and why this change is systematic in a particular direction. Why is there change from 'X' to 'Y', say from Stage 3 to Stage 4, and not *vice versa*? Explaining this kind of change cannot be done solely from an objectivating attitude; to do so would be to give up the unique strength that this theory starts with, namely, the view of the subject as a constructive moral agent. Rather, in asking the general question of 'why do/did . . . change from X to Y?', the psychologist must also assume mutuality with other subjects as a place holder in this question, thus also at the same time asking, 'why did I change from X to Y?' Thus part of a developmental psychological explanation of change *itself* requires the psychologist to adopt the performative attitude along with the subject, though now with regard to truth-claims rather than rightness-claims. . . . Thus the developmental psychologist must also ask, along with the subject, 'why ought I change from "X" to "Y"?' In order to *make sense* to humans as moral agents, the psychological explanation of moral development must include the performative examination of this 'ought' question. Conversely, in order to be grounded in psychological reality, the justifiable normative position must be compatible with a performative examination of the 'is'-questions of change which account for how such a normative position can be manifested in human subjects. Although the direction of the theoretical perspectives of psychology and philosophy cannot be reduced to each other, neither alone gives us a whole picture of the phenomenon in common, moral judgment. Yet *how* they can complement each other is suggested by the common factor of the assumption of the performative attitude with regard to the different kinds of questions that have to be asked of the human subject experiencing moral

development. It is, I believe, this bi-dimensional, correlative adoption of the performative
attitude by the developmental psychologist that best explains what lies behind the 'complementarity thesis' intended by Kohlberg. And it is also, finally, a rough blueprint for the work
of constructing a bridge across the 'is/ought' gap at the border between developmental
psychology and moral philosophy.

This bridge is implicit in Table 3, which represents both the normative and
psychological perspectives. While I agree with this conclusion of Boyd's chapter, I
think it needs further clarification. This is clarification of the idea that my
developmental theory is a hopefully progressive circle or spiral between moral
philosophic assumptions and arguments and empirical psychological propositions
and evidence. At the beginning of the study of the ontogenesis of moral judgment
and reasoning, I make certain meta-ethical assumptions, summarized in the
constructivistic notion cited earlier that the function of moral reasoning, judgment
and argumentation is to reach agreement where claims or interests conflict, most
especially where the conflict is between two or more persons (raising problems of
justice). In Kohlberg, Levine and Hewer (1983, p. 66, or Kohlberg, 1984, Ch. 3) I
list these assumptions as,

I) Value relevance of definitions of the moral and of moral development (as opposed to value
neutral definitions).
II) Phenomenological or hermeneutic definitions of morality and moral development imply moral
judgments (as opposed to simple behavioristic definitions of the moral).
III) Moral universality or 'methodological ethical non-relativism' (as opposed to 'cultural or
ethical (epistemological) moral relativism').
IV) Prescriptivism as the function of moral judgments (as opposed to descriptivism or simple
naturalistic views of the function of moral judgment).
V) Cognitivism or a central reasoning element of moral judgment (as opposed to emotivism).
VI) Formalism, the identification of a 'moral point of view' as defining what makes a judgment
moral or part of the moral domain.
VII) Principledness as the rule or (principled) governance of moral judgment, though not the
notion of judgment as direct or strict deduction from principles (as opposed to pure act theories
of judgment).
VIII) Constructivism (as opposed to either inductive empiricism or a priori absolutism as the
origin of moral judgments and principles).

These meta-ethical assumptions are to be justified by moral-philosophic
analysis and argument, prior to empirical inquiry. In fact Locke's and Carter's
chapters do not really dispute these claims on philosophic grounds, though they
make certain qualifications I will address later.

As Boyd points out, I start with the assumption that a certain amount of such
moral philosophizing is a prerequisite to the empirical study of moral development
and moral action. I start with a conception of morality derived from moral
philosophy and meta-ethics; the conceptions of morality as the 'moral point of
view' involving an effort at judging impartially, non-egoistically, making judgments
which are generalized or universalized or reversible, etc. (Frankena, 1973, p. 114).

Even at my conventional Stages 3 and 4 moral judgment to a considerable
extent can be characterized in this way. This philosophic assumption is associated
with the assumption of moral 'methodological non-relativism'. The philosophic
assumption of 'methodological' or ethical non-relativism leads to social science
propositions which can be empirically falsified, e.g., the proposition that moral
judgments have a universal component not relative to each culture. This means that
(1) the categories of moral judgment listed in Table 1 will be found in every culture,

and (2) the stages or at least the first three or four of them will be found in every culture. Edwards' chapter in this volume and the more extensive review of stage studies in forty-three cultures by Snarey (1985) show this to be the case. It might be added that the reviews of Snarey (1985) and Walker (1984) also indicate no sex differences in various cultures, when education and socioeconomic status, variables related to moral stage in both males and females, are controlled for. Thus Gilligan's (1982) thesis of the gender relativism of our justice stages, as well as the assumptions of anthropological relativists, cannot be said to falsify our thesis of the universality of our moral stages and our moral categories. As Carter's chapter as well as Boyd's elaborates, the only kinds of meta-ethical relativism clearly inconsistent either with my theory or with the data are radical forms of relativism, what Carter calls 'epistemological relativism', emotivism and scepticism, rather than 'perspectivistic' forms of relativism which recognize that any rational starting-point of moral principles and judgments is a human construction rather than an absolute. In any case, insofar as epistemological or ethical non-relativism was my starting meta-ethical assumption, it is one which could in part be falsified by empirical data and has not, we believe, been falsified. The empirical data reviewed by Edwards in this volume and by Snarey (1985) indicate the cultural universality of the norms and elements of Table 1 and at least the first four stages of moral judgment. We will return to this question of cultural and ethical universality in more depth after considering Habermas' view of it, and Locke's and Carter's views, but this brief discussion clearly shows how a meta-ethical philosophic theory of 'methodological non-relativism' can be supported or weakened by empirical anthropological or cross-cultural data, the implication of a 'complementarity' view of the relations between moral philosophic theory and psychological and anthropological data and their interpretation. Thus there are two central issues I believe relate moral philosophy to empirical psychology, the first that of ethical (or cultural) relativism, the second that of the greater adequacy of higher stages, especially the postconventional stages. For both issues, Boyd and I accept a strong form of Habermas' complementarity thesis about the relation of moral philosophy (meta-ethical universalism and normative-ethical questions of adequacy). To this latter issue we now turn.

What Siegel's chapter attacks, and Boyd's defends, is not so much my meta-ethical assumptions which are partially empirical via the complementarity thesis, but the normative ethical claims that each higher stage is a more adequate one. Siegel, defending the moat between normative moral philosophic theory or justification and psychological description and explanation (Hume's law or Moore's law that you cannot derive an 'ought' from an 'is'), goes so far as to say that the psychological study of moral development is useless for the definition of moral educational goals which can only be done by pure moral philosophy. Wilson takes a similar position to Siegel's in his chapter on my approach to moral education. For Wilson, the moral philosopher establishes what is rational or valid moral reasoning, and needs little or no help from the psychology of moral development to prescribe moral reasoning curricular goals though psychology may be used in the method of instruction to reach these goals. In contrast, Boyd and I defend the complementarity thesis between moral philosophy and psychology in the task of defining moral reasoning goals of education. This is because, in addition to the meta-ethical assumptions guiding the empirical study of ontogenesis, there have been normative ethical assumptions as to the nature of more 'rational' or more 'moral' judgment and reasoning. I have earlier (Kohlberg, 1981, Chs 4 and 5) stated these in terms of principles and normative moral theories of Stage 6, of which I have taken Rawl's theory as one example. In Kohlberg, Levine and Hewer (1983, or Kohlberg, 1984, Ch. 3) I have backed off from some claims about both the nature and adequacy of Stage 6, which have been critiqued by Locke and Carter (1980). For the purposes of this book it is sufficient to postulate the normative adequacy of Stage 5 as a basis for the rational reconstruction of ontogenesis. The normative adequacy of postconventional (Stage 5 or 6) reasoning is attested by all rule-utilitarian theorists from John Stuart Mill and Sidgewick to Brandt (1961) and R. M. Hare (1981). It is also attested to by all deontologists or theorists of justice as respect for persons and social contractarians from Kant to Rawls (1971) and Gewirth (1978). It is attested to also by those who combine both positions as does Frankena (1973). Finally, it is attested to by 'non-juridical' responsibility ethics such as those of John Dewey (1960), as Boyd (1979) clarifies in his 'Interpretation of Principled Morality'. It may also be attested to by moralities of *agape* or Christian love as long as these are not taken as 'obedience to divine command theories' but as a social ethic (Frankena, 1973, pp. 56–7). Insofar as these ethics address the justice dilemmas we have studied, all would be postconventional or Stage 5 (neglecting the possibility of a sixth stage). Other postconventional thinkers in the existentialist tradition, such as Kierkegaard or Nietzsche, would presumably not fit our conception of Stage 5 or 6 in proposing to go 'beyond the ethical into the religious', as did Kierkegaard, or 'beyond good and evil', as did an atheistic Nietzsche. It is at this point that their normative ethics are tied to meta-ethical assumptions different from those listed by Kohlberg, Levine and Hewer (1983), meta-ethical assumptions which I believe more recent analytic moral philosophy supports.

Given this broad range of postconventional moral philosophic justifications for Stage 5 (or 6), what is the meaning and value of the 'complementarity hypothesis' and of the idea of 'the rational reconstruction of ontogenesis' in the study of moral development? Let us start with the most purely philosophical and least psychological approach to 'rational reconstruction of ontogenesis', that of Rawls (1971). Rawls' theory in one sense 'follows Hume's law', and in another brings the natural intuitions of lay persons into his method. Rawls' method is clarified by an earlier essay by Boyd (1980). First, Boyd clarifies the common 'neo-Kantian' moral philosophic assumptions shared by Rawls (1971, 1980) and myself (Kohlberg, 1981, Ch. 4). He says (Boyd, 1980,[*] pp. 187–207):

> Both Kohlberg and Rawls approach moral questions through a focus on the concept of the right, that is, in terms of that aspect of morality dealing with (at least the potentiality of) interpersonal conflict and having an adjudicatory function. Conceptions of the good and ideals of human perfection are by no means unimportant for either Kohlberg or Rawls. But they do not constitute the essence of morality, nor adequately circumscribe the proper entry point into moral questions. For both, pursuit of the good and human perfection is subordinated as a concern to adjudicating *differences* among individuals on how the good and human perfection are to be defined, furthered, and distributed. One cannot understand this entry point unless one understands that they assume that individuals do and will differ in this way.
>
> In other words, both Kohlberg's and Rawls's theories start from the premise that no one view of the good can be taken as overriding. Choice of the good is seen as fundamentally subjective and pluralistic, and the moral point of view is seen as objectivity seeking, interperson-

---

[*]By kind permission of Professor Dwight Boyd and Religious Education Press, Alabama (MUNSEY, B. (Ed.) (1980) *Moral Development, Moral Education and Kohlberg.*).

al, and adjudicatory. They both start, I submit, from what Strawson has called a 'minimal interpretation of morality'. '. . . The problem of morality is justice, the problem of considering and choosing between the *claims* or rights of other persons. Stated otherwise, the sphere of morality is the sphere of duty or obligation. . . .' The dilemmas upon which Kohlberg's data-gathering procedure is based all exemplify this notion of morality as involving adjudication of competing claims or interests in an interpersonal context.

So far I have drawn the commonality between Kohlberg and Rawls in terms of narrowness of their foci and the deontological lens which tints what they see. What they see within these boundaries is justice, but their conception of justice is, paradoxically, far broader than many other philosophers'. It is clear, first of all, that both see justice as the central moral concept. Rawls describes 'justice as fairness' as trying to account for our intuitive convictions of the primacy of justice, as expressed most eloquently in the opening sentence of *A Theory of Justice*: 'Justice is the first virtue of social institutions, as truth is of systems of thought' (p. 3). And as we have already seen in the passages quoted above, Kohlberg sometimes simply identifies 'morality' with justice, arguing elsewhere that 'if the function of moral principles is to resolve conflicting claims, in some sense these principles must be principles of justice or fairness.' I doubt that many would disagree with this conclusion, given the premise. As John Orr has claimed:

'Persons who define morality as social rules will inevitably concern themselves with the origin and authority of those rules, and also with the more abstract principles in terms of which conflicts can be mediated. Ultimately the argument will be about the shape of justice. There is no other way to move.'

Although Kohlberg's variations are often puzzling, I think there is a core idea running through all of them. This core idea runs as follows. Justice is the general moral perspective through which competing claims of persons should be resolved. It is not simply an empty abstract formula requiring mechanistic application, but rather it identifies substantive ways of conceiving persons and their interactions in situations of competing interests. It is a perspective which does not dictate certain, final answers but rather structures a framework for a process of resolving conflicts (or potential conflicts) in a way acceptable to all parties. The central lines of this structure consist of an integration of two things: (i) a conception of persons as equal vis-à-vis their right to formulate their own ends and their agency as rule-following creatures, and (ii) a reciprocity of intention of persons to afford each other as much freedom as possible in furthering those ends. The motivational 'heart' of this structure is summarized in the attitude and principle of respect for persons—of recognizing and acknowledging the other as an equally unique subject of his or her own experience *including* the experience of myself and my ends, and of acting toward each other as if the other's interests and ends were my own.

It is one thing to string together a few nice-sounding phrases as expressing a 'core idea,' but quite another to flesh it out, showing not only what the parts mean and how they can be integrated, but also how the total conception coheres in a way which strengthens our basic intuitions and provides a plausible defense of them. I submit, however, that it is essentially this task which Rawls has tackled in *A Theory of Justice* and that his efforts are expressive of essentially the same core idea as that which I am suggesting makes the most sense of Kohlberg's various assertions.

First of all, it is clear that Rawls does not rest with the simple formal components of justice, but intends to offer a substantive conception of justice. Furthermore, as he says in many places throughout the book, it is the total picture which should be taken as his conception of justice: how the substantive parts fit together is to be understood as part of the conception, and its strength is to be tested by this rather than by the strength of any of the parts taken independently. It is also clear that equality in the sense suggested above is one of the essential parts of the overall conception:

'. . . the purpose of (the conditions which characterize the original position) is to represent equality between human beings as moral persons, as creatures having a conception of their good and capable of a sense of justice. The basis of equality is taken to be similarity in these two respects. Systems of ends are not ranked by value; and each man is presumed to have the requisite ability to understand and to act upon whatever principles are adopted.'

As noted above, Kohlberg seems to be more explicit than Rawls about the centrality of respect for persons in his conception of justice. Although sometimes it appears to be equated with justice, while other times it is *conjoined with* justice, respect for persons is consistently acknowledged by Kohlberg as the most basic principle of his most mature stage. However, nowhere does Kohlberg provide us with a systematic articulation of what he is referring to, beyond the identification of the principle as requiring that one 'treat each human being as an end in himself, as of ultimate worth'. I wish to claim, however, that *if* Kohlberg were to elaborate a more systematic articulation, it would be along the lines of that provided by Downie and Telfer.

The first point is that 'respect for persons as ends' can, according to Downie and Telfer, refer to both an attitude and a principle of action. And more importantly, they argue that the attitude is both logically and morally basic:

> 'The attitude is *logically* basic in that the principle has to be explained in terms of it, it is the principle which logically must be adopted (other things being equal) by someone who has the attitude of respect. But it is also *morally* basic in that it includes in its scope modes of feeling and thinking as well as of acting; and that which is morally fundamental is a total quality of life rather than a principle of acting in the narrow sense.'

I think this attitudinal side of respect for persons is what Kohlberg must be getting at when he characterizes a principle as a '*mode* of choosing,' or as a general guide to choice rather than a rule of action.' In this sense a Stage 6 conception of justice consists primarily of a way of *regarding* persons, which in turn entails a way of *treating* them according to certain principles of action. Failure to understand this attitudinal underpinning of Stage 6 has led, I suspect, to the many misinterpretations of Kohlberg as '*excessively rationalistic*'.

The second point important for the purposes of this paper consists of Downie and Telfer's analysis of the components of this attitude of respect for persons. They clearly identify two sides to this attitude, where Kohlberg is (mistakenly) thought to see only one. Downie and Telfer summarize:

> 'In so far as persons are thought of as self-determining agents who pursue objects of interest to themselves we respect them by showing active sympathy with them; in Kant's language, we make their ends our own. In so far as persons are thought of as rule-following we respect them by taking seriously the fact that the rules by which they guide their conduct constitute reasons which may apply both to them and to ourselves. In the attitude of respect we have, then, two necessary components: an attitude of active sympathy and a readiness at least to consider the applicability of other men's rules both to them and to ourselves. These two components are independently necessary and jointly sufficient to constitute the attitude of respect which it is fitting to direct at persons, conceived as rational wills.'

Indeed they go on to identify the whole attitude of respect for persons as the species of love known as *agape*. I think it is relatively clear that Kohlberg's conception of justice incorporates the second attitude of sympathy constituting respect for persons. In theoretical contexts it surfaces in his concern for universalizability and reversibility, and it lies at the heart of his developmentalism. However, I also want to claim that the attitude which Downie and Telfer identify as 'active sympathy' is equally integral to Kohlberg's conception of Stage 6 justice. The support for this claim is more indirect than that for the first because as far as I know Kohlberg never talks explicitly about an attitude of 'active sympathy,' but is equally integral to Kohlberg's conception of stage 6 justice. He comes very close to this occasionally when he discusses role-taking as a necessary component of moral judgment, and refers to a 'psychological unity of empathy and justice in moral role-taking.' Two additional points of direct support can also be noted. The first is that Downie and Telfer clearly see the attitude of active sympathy as an interpretation of the Kantian formulation of the categorical imperative to 'always treat another as an end in himself, never solely as a means'; and this is precisely that part of Kant to which Kohlberg refers us for a deeper understanding of his own views. If we assume this is a plausible interpretation of Kohlberg, how is it different from Rawls?

Rawls notes a possible objection to his theory that because the original position does not 'explicitly' include the notion of respect for persons his argument might be thought unsound. His answer is that although the principles of justice cannot be *derived* from the notion of respect for persons, the whole theory can be seen as giving more definite meaning to it:

> 'I believe . . . that while the principles of justice will be effective only if men have a sense of justice and do therefore respect one another, the notion of respect of the inherent worth

of persons is not a suitable basis for arriving at these principles. It is precisely these ideas that call for interpretation.... Once the conception of justice is on hand, however, the ideas of respect and of human dignity can be given a more definite meaning.... The theory of justice provides a rendering of these ideas but we cannot start out with them (pp. 585–586).'

However, it can be argued that although the two principles are not in any rigorous sense derived from respect for persons, this notion is assumed implicitly by Rawls as the very basis of the original position. Self respect is the most important primary good. It follows that under the veil of ignorance, respect for self is also indistinguishable from respect for 'other' persons. Respect for persons is in this sense at the heart of Rawls' theory, as well as of Kohlberg's. As Rawls says, 'the principles of justice manifest in the basic structure of society men's desire to treat one another not as a means but as ends in themselves' (p. 179). Dworkin has argued in a similar way that the fundamental concept which is assumed in the design and working of the original position is the 'abstract right to equal concern and respect.' He concludes:

> 'We may therefore say that justice as fairness rests on the assumption of a natural right of all men and women to equality of concern and respect, a right they possess not by virtue of birth or characteristic or merit or excellence but simply as human beings with the capacity to make plans and give justice.'

What makes respect the appropriate general attitude—and justice the main concern in situations of conflicting claims—is how the objects of that attitude are conceived. In short it is the characterization of persons as self-determining and rule-following agents that forms the most fundamental and pervasive link in the Kohlberg-Rawls connection. As Rawls puts it, 'Moral persons are defined as persons that have a conception of the good and a capacity for a sense of justice.'

First of all, that human beings are persons in the sense of individual, self-determining, and rule-following agents concerned with mutual respect is an assumption which differentiates Kohlberg's theory from other kinds of psychological theories and differentiates Rawls's theory from other kinds of philosophical theories. Kohlberg makes this assumption about his psychological subjects and then as a result is concerned with identifying the different patterns through which such subjects seek to understand interactions with others in the context of conditions of justice; by contrast, he does not concern himself with the way in which societies seek stability through the inculcation of fixed values into the consciousness of new members. Similarly, Rawls makes this assumption about the parties in the original position as a way of elaborating and legitimating our intuitions of the primacy of justice; in doing so he also seeks to contrast his theory with others, such as utilitarianism, which extend principles of choice appropriate for one person's conception of the good to questions concerning the regulation of associations of many persons (pp. 19, 28–29).

The second way in which Kohlberg and Rawls are linked is manifested as related to the first, but yet distinct. In the cases of Kohlberg and Rawls there is a healthy congruence between their normative anthropological assumptions and how they go about developing, testing, and validating their respective theories. For Kohlberg this congruence is perhaps reflected most prominently in what he has recently referred to as a 'boot-strapping' method of longitudinal interviews combined with an ongoing, theoretical interpretation of those interviews. The data which are elicited and interpreted are not predetermined, quantifiable choice responses, but rather, systematic attempts of one person trying through dialogue to understand the qualitative structure of how another person seeks to organize and make sense of certain aspects of a shared social world. Although Rawls is clearly engaged in the philosophical task of elaboration and justification of a theory of justice rather than in the scientific task of verification of a psychological theory about how a mature sense of justice develops, there is a similar kind of congruence between his deep theoretical assumptions about persons and the way he characterizes the interaction between his ideas and those of his readers. This is so seldom noticed that it is worth quoting here:

> '... If we should be able to characterize one (educated) person's sense of justice, we would have a good beginning toward a theory of justice. We may suppose that everyone has in himself the whole form of a moral conception. So for the purposes of this book, the views of the reader and the author are the only ones that count. The opinions of others are used only to clear our own heads (p. 50).'

I think Rawls should be taken seriously when he says that 'for the purposes of this book, the views of the reader and the author are the only ones that count.' It reflects, I believe, a radical expression of faith in philosophical method as a rational dialogue between two equal, self-determining, and rule-following agents. The second parallel is the constructivism of Rawls and Kohlberg. Speaking of Rawls, Dworkin says:

'One model of principles is that men discover them, as they discover laws of physics. The main instrument of discovery is a faculty of conscience which produces concrete intuitions of political morality in particular situations, like the intuition that slavery is wrong.... The second model is quite different. It treats intuitions of justice not as clues to the existence of independent principles, but rather as stipulated features of a general theory to be constructed, as if a sculptor set himself to carve the animal that best fits a pile of bones he happened to find together. This 'constructive' model does not assume, as the natural model does, that principles of justice have some fixed, objective existence, so that descriptions of these principles must be true or false in some standard way.... It makes the different, and in some ways more complex, assumption that men and women have a responsibility to fit the particular judgments on which they act into a coherent program of action, or, at least, that officials who exercise power over other men have that sort of responsibility.'

For our purposes here the essential point, if we accept Dworkin's claim about Rawls, is that the two models reflect different conceptions of persons insofar as they make claims of justice which impinge on others. As Dworkin notes,

'The natural model, we might say, looks at intuitions from the personal standpoint of the individual who holds them, and who takes them to be discrete observations of moral reality. The constructive model looks at these intuitions from a more public standpoint; it is a model that someone might propose for the governance of a community each of whose members has strong convictions that differ, though not too greatly, from the convictions of others.'

In the terms of this paper, it is the constructive model which conceives persons in such a way as to render mutual respect a viable, overriding attitude/principle. Persons are not thought of as independent, isolated 'rule followers,' with greater or lesser direct access to moral truth, but rather as rule-followers-in-relation who must construct and continually reconstruct through public dialogue the perspective from which rules governing their interaction have validity.

This is implied, first of all, on noting the understanding of conscience which is common to both Kohlberg and Rawls. Thus, contrary to what seems to be implied in the short descriptions on Stage 6, Kohlberg does not count reference to one's conscience as sufficient evidence for identifying the form of sound moral judgment.

'To count as post-conventional such ideas or terms (as 'conscience') must be used in such a way that it is clear that they have a foundation for a rational or moral individual whose commitment to a group or society is based on prior principles.'

Although this seems to me an awkward way of putting it, I think what Kohlberg is getting at here is, by implication, what Rawls notes very bluntly: 'A person's conscience is misguided when he seeks to impose on us conditions that violate the principles to which we would each consent in (the original position)' (pp. 518–519). In other words, the soundness of moral judgment does not reside in an individual's conscientious commitment or result from an infallible faculty of conscience which somehow 'discovers' moral truth in the form of abstract moral principles; rather it is something that is 'constructed' through an equilibrium with principles arrived at in a certain way.

For both Kohlberg and Rawls justice is the result of a dynamic, constructive decision procedure of a certain kind. Although there are some important differences with implications beyond the scope of this paper, the commonality which anchors these differences rests in a formally similar interpretation of how a conception of persons is embodied in decisions of justice. For Rawls this interpretation is reflected in the now familiar notion of the original position in which persons are thought of as deliberating about the choice of principles to regulate their interaction, a deliberation which is fair because it starts from a condition of 'equality between human beings as moral persons, as creatures having a conception of their good and capable of a sense of justice,' and procedurally 'excludes the knowledge of those contingencies which sets men at odds and allows them to be guided by their principles' (p. 19). For Kohlberg, this interpretation is reflected in his description of Stage 6 in terms of individuals seeking complete 'reversibility' of judgment through 'ideal role-taking' (or, more whimsically, 'moral musical chairs').

As Kohlberg suggests here the kind of equilibrium sought through justice is not the sort of thing that can be conceived from the point of view of persons in isolation (as the natural model would suggest). Rather, it is a provisional point of hypothetical agreement resulting from a way of entering moral argument and seeking fair adjudication of competing claims of persons, where persons are conceived as agents of mutual respect. If I am correct in this interpretation of Kohlberg, it is at this point that the Rawls connection is most clearly revealed and legitimated.

Boyd is saying that the principle of respect for persons which I have claimed as 'the principle' for ethical decision-making is the underlying presupposition of rational moral dialogue between persons differing as to what morality, the good and the right are. As I have come to believe, an adequate principle should not only prescribe a universalizable and general guide to moral action but also (1) state the presupposition of discourse in the face of disagreement in the application of the principle to a particular case or dilemma, and (2) state the presuppositions of discourse for justifying the principle itself. This is what Habermas (1982) attempts to do in his dialogue model of defining moral principles and attempting a rational reconstruction of my moral stages in terms of the types of dialogue of which a speaker is capable at a given stage. According to Habermas (1982), a Kantian respect for persons is a precondition for argument or dialogue among philosophers and in this sense it justifies itself as the ultimate moral principle.

In the case of Rawls the idea of a rational social contract begins in an original position in which each potential contractor implicitly acknowledges via the veil of ignorance the liberty and equality of all persons entering the social contract. This loosely corresponds to Habermas' notion that respect for persons is the implicit precondition of an ideal discourse or dialogue about morality.

Habermas' claim is that philosophers, or human beings as philosophers, must take the 'performative' attitude of dialogue, the understanding of the other's reasons and the relating of the other's reasons to one's own in a way which will reach or seek mutual consensus through acceptance of a convincing argument. The very process of moral philosophizing then ultimately presupposes mutual respect, the freedom and rationality of each participant in the dialogue. I shall cite some extracts from an unpublished paper by Habermas (1982)[*] to try to clarify his stance.

> I am going to defend a moral cognitivist position against moral scepticism.... Ever since Kant has claimed that human beings are endowed with a type of practical reason that enables them to solve moral problems in a similar way as they can solve theoretical problems, the plausibility of such a strong claim has been doubted. Empiricists of all brands have preferred to combine a universalistic position vis-à-vis science and knowledge in general, with a relativist position vis-à-vis moral values. Until recently this mixture of scientific cognitivism (or realism) and moral scepticism was a more or less obvious position to be taken—at least in the domain of analytical philosophy, and it was also an essential part of the professional background assumptions in the social sciences. This is to give just one example, still the starting point of Alasdair MacIntyre in his recent book "After Virtue". He accepts as a definite result of modern philosophy, and the process of enlightenment in general, what Horkheimer and Adorno once had stated as a critical verdict: 'Reason is calculative; it can access truths of fact and mathematical relations but nothing more. In the realm of practice it can speak only of means. About ends it must be silent.'

---

*By kind permission of Professor J. Habermas

This situation has been changing during the last ten to fifteen years.... It is a cognitivist or Kantian approach in practical philosophy that has been revived. Philosophers such as Rawls and Gewirth in the United States, Lorenzen and Apel in Germany, have again replaced metaethical analysis by plain normative ethics. We should not forget, however, the resistance which the present context of philosophical discussion, if not intellectual climate in general, puts up against any straight attempt to defend a cognitivist position in moral theory, that is in my case: to save Kantian intuitions in terms of an ethics of discourse.

Let me first develop the main thesis which is at stake in the controversy between the moral cognitivist and the moral sceptic.... If there is a rather unenlightened moral sceptic who would from scratch deny that moral judgments have any cognitive content whatsoever we would first have to engage in that kind of phenomenology of moral feelings for which P. F. Strawson's famous article "Freedom and Resentment" (London, 1974) is a good example. Strawson starts his analysis with every-day-repairs for injuries and offences, to which the person hurt reacts with resentment and indignation.... Resentment, and moral feelings in general, do have their proper place only in interactions where the participants are allowed to communicate with each other in *performative attitude*. The objectivating attitude of an observer, however, neutralizes the whole domain in which moral reactions are at all meaningful. This is Strawson's first point. Strawson makes another observation. Resentment and indignation are immediate 'personal' reactions in the sense that they are directed against some *particular person* who has *vulnerated* our integrity. But these reactions owe their distinct moral character not to the fact that the interpersonal relationship between these two individuals has been disturbed. What has been violated is a normative expectation, underlying this particular relationship, a behavioral expectation referring not only to *this* Ego and *that* Alter but to *all* the members of a social group, sometimes even to *everybody*.... It is this *impersonal* or intersubjective element which constitutes the claim of normative expectations and the corresponding obligation, to do what we ought to do. Resentment and indignation as well as shame and guilt, are internally or conceptually linked to the meaning of a normative claim, and to the possibility, that one explains why we are entitled to expect somebody else to act so and so—or why we feel obligated to act this way and not the other. That we ought to do something means—to have good reasons for doing it.

Strawson combined both of his observations. It is only from the perspective of a participant that we understand the network of moral feelings built into every-day-communication, and only from this inside-perspective can we also grasp the meaning of normative claims, that is of having or giving reasons for what one ought to do. If, however, the phrase 'ought to do something' in fact implies 'having good reasons for doing it,' then normative sentences should be capable of being true or false. If we trust this intuition which inevitably guides our common sense moral feelings, judgments and practices, then we have to admit that we, in some sense, cannot but believe in the objectivity of morals, and to believe in the objectivity of morals is to believe that some moral statements are true.

This then is the thesis of moral cognitivism; it is rejected by the moral sceptic who maintains that normative sentences are not capable of being either true or false.... The prevailing strategy of defending moral truth was at first some sort of moral intuitionism (G. E. Moore, Max Scheler, Nicolai Hartmann). It basically rests on the idea: if normative sentences like 'one should not lie' are capable of being true or false, then they should be analyzed according to the model of descriptive sentences. It is, however not too difficult to prove that in the case of normative sentences there is no equivalent for that set of rules which allow for the verification or falsification of simple descriptive sentences. The sceptic philosopher, of course, takes this failure of moral intuitionism as a corroboration for his suspicion that there cannot be any legitimate claim for moral truths. He would not deny the moral phenomena of every-day life, nor dispute the grammatical facts indicating that people think they could argue about moral questions and decide them rationally. He regards these intuitions, however, as mistakes or common-sense illusions which have to be explained. From the perspective of an observer who accepts what Strawson has called an objectivating attitude, the sceptic wants to disclose what we *really mean* when we say, we or they *ought* to do something.

For this purpose the sceptic assimilates normative sentences either to first person sentences which express emotions, wishes, preferences etc., or to imperatives. So, the *emotivist* or *imperative* approaches in ethics are attempts to *reduce the meaning of normative sentences to the meaning* of expressive sentences or imperatives, or of a combination of both: ' "This is good" means roughly the same as "I approve of this, do as well" ,' trying to capture by this equivalence both the *function* of the moral judgment as expressive of the speaker's attitude and the function of moral judgment as designed to influence the hearer's attitude.

These subjectivist approaches, however, make sense only on a premise which they share with their counterpart, moral intuitionism: if ought-sentences are at all linked with a claim to cognitive validity, this claim must be understood as propositional truth. It is this premise which I find questionable.

Confronted with this argument the sceptic can lift the debate to another level and point to the fact, that moral disputes are rarely ever settled, that basic moral problems are almost never solved. He may doubt that reasons do have the same problem solving capacity in moral discourse as they presumably have in theoretical argumentation. The first round of this discussion, therefore, ends with the question whether the cognitivist can offer some kind of rule or principle which allows us to achieve some sort of rationally motivated consensus in moral discourse.

The second round of our discussion focuses on whether we can provide a moral principle which, in moral discourse, might serve as an equivalent for the principle of induction which plays a prominent role in theoretical discourse. Since we cannot take recourse to any ultimate foundation in either case we need *bridging principles* which function as rules of argumentation. To make a long story brief let me just say that that all attempts to introduce some kind of moral principle can be understood as reformulations of the very intuition that Kant once has explicated in terms of his famous categorical imperative. Kant's moral principle demands the universalizability of modes of action or of maxims, or of the interests embodied by them. This principle is meant to grant the impartiality of moral judgment. Impartiality is that point of view which allows anybody to select exactly those norms which could find the qualified consent of all those involved and affected because they duly pay regard to their common interest (in view of the specific issue to be regulated). Because of the internal relationship between the *impartiality of moral judgments* and the *universalizability of moral norms* G. H. Mead has proposed for the categorical imperative the reading of an 'ideal role taking' which is demanded in 'universal discourse'. This principle forces everybody participating in moral discourse to take into account also the interests of everybody else. This principle can be stated in the following way: a valid norm has to satisfy the condition—that the consequences, intended or not, which will (probably) result from its *general* application for the interests of *every* individual affected would be consensually preferred by *all* of those involved.... Let us immediately move ahead to the sceptical objection that this kind of principle only expresses a moral point of view which is built into modern Western culture, so that it cannot make any claim to universality That is, what P. Taylor calls the *ethnocentric fallacy* of moral cognitivism.... If the moral cognitivist is honest he has to admit that moral theory, from Kant to Rawls, has no more to offer than a rational reconstruction of just those moral intuitions which we have, and which we meet in our every-day practice. It is this that Rawls means by his method of reflective equilibrium.... The third round of the discussion centres on attempts of giving a justification for the principle of morality, that is to explain on what conditions this principle can claim to be valid also for cultures different from ours. Let me state my goal in advance: I will defend the thesis that everybody who seriously enters into a rational discourse, thereby admits to inescapable pragmatic presuppostions the content of which entails relevant elements of the moral principle. To put it in a different way: everybody who attempts to refute the moral principle, stated above, will be caught in a performative contradiction to the very pragmatic presuppositions which he cannot escape once he seriously starts to argue at all.... The strategy of this form of argument is to accept the sceptical conclusion that these principles are not open to any proof, being presuppositions of reasoning rather than conclusions from it, but to go on to argue that commitment to them is rationally inescapable, because they must, logically, be assumed if one is to engage in a mode of thought essential to any rational human life. The claim is not exactly that the principles are *true*, but that their adoption is not a result of mere social convention of free personal decision: that a mistake is involved in repudiating them while continuing to use the form of thought and discourse in question.

A presuppositional justification of this type should prove that a subject, in raising and considering a certain range of questions, has to admit to certain presuppositions—and that there are no alternatives to this commitment until he is going to stop raising this type of questions. We will try to establish a moral principle which functions as a rule of argumentation and allows for reaching a rationally motivated consensus in particular moral discourses. On the *logico-semantic* level one might consider rules such as:
—everybody has to avoid contradictions

—everybody who attributes predicate F to an object 'x', has to be prepared to attribute the same predicate to any other object which is similar to 'x' in all relevant aspects.

It is hard to see, how one could derive a moral principle from this semantic type of rules. The same holds for strictly *procedural rules*. But there are also pragmatic presuppositions qualifying argumentations as a distinguished mode of discourse which, in view of the telos of reaching a rationally motivated consensus, has to meet rather demanding and improbable conditions: argumentation depends on a speech situation which is, from an insider's perspective, supposed to be more or less immune against repressions and inequalities of all kinds. On this pragmatic level one might consider as candidates the following rules:

1.   Every subject capable of speech and action is allowed to participate in rational discourse
2.1   Everybody is in principle allowed to question any statement
2.2   Everybody is in principle allowed to introduce any statement
2.3   Everybody is allowed to express, if relevant, his attitudes, needs and intentions
3.   No participant may be prevented, be it through external or internal constraint, from using his rights as specified under 1. and 2.

Rule 1 specifies the class of participants by including all subjects capable of speech and action. Rule 2 guarantees for all participants equal chances to contribute arguments and to have them seriously considered. Rule 3 defines conditions under which the right of universal access to, and the right of equal participation in discourses can become effective.... If anybody who enters rational discourse, must admit to pragmatic presuppositions, the content of which can be described in terms of the rules mentioned; and if, in addition, a normative claim (or an ought-claim) means that the corresponding norm regulate relevant social affairs in the common interest of those involved and affected; then everybody who seriously attempts to redeem a normative claim to validity has, by the very fact of entering into rational discourse, intuitively admitted to presuppositions with a specific normative content, and thereby also has implicitly recognized, as a rule of argumentation, a moral principle which can be stated in the form explicated above.

The argument against relativism and scepticism made by Habermas is similar in form, or is a 'rational reconstruction of', the process of development which we have found characteristic in our longitudinal subjects who go through a sceptical and relativistic phase on their way to postconventional (Stage 5) morality (Kohlberg, 1984, Ch. 6). At the heart of our subject's relativism is the idea that morality, conventionally understood, is a device for controlling and condemning the individual's free expression of his needs, interests and beliefs. Inherent in, or motivating their rejection of, all morality as relativistic is the implicit principle of individual liberty or of freedom of belief and action seen as limited by conventional morality. Underlying this ethical scepticism and relativism is the implicit 'principle' of liberty of conscience or of individual rights and liberty. Calling radical relativism 'Stage 4½' we find that with continued experience, this relativism is transformed into our fifth stage or recognition of individual rights of liberty, and of the need for a 'social contract' to govern social relations in a way which will recognize and protect individual rights. Habermas carries this 'rational reconstruction' one step further. He assumes that the ethical sceptic can go beyond a recognition of human rights and still remain a sceptic or relativist about any ultimate or formal moral principle. His argument is that once the relativistic moral philosopher enters a debate as to the shape of moral principles, he implicitly assumes the principles of an ideal communication interaction.

Habermas' argument against ethical scepticism and relativism, as well as my own (Kohlberg, 1981), leave uncertain the extent to which either he or I would accept certain forms of relativism. Carter contrasts what I have called 'radical relativism' and which he calls 'epistemological relativism' with 'perspectivism' or what has sometimes been called 'contextual relativism'. Basically two issues are involved. The first is raised by what Habermas and I (Kohlberg, 1984, Ch. 6) call decisionism, i.e., the question as to whether first principles of moral judgment are arbitrary. Weber, holding this position, claimed that an individual could choose an 'absolute ethic' (an ethic of motivation and principle) or 'a responsibility ethic' (an ethic of consequences), but that there were no rational grounds for choosing one over the other. In contemporary ethics the distinction is usually that between a utilitarian ethic and a deontological justice ethic. In my earlier writing I claimed that a deontological justice ethic was 'higher' or better than a utilitarian ethic. In attenuating the claim for Stage 6, I no longer take this position as one which could be clearly argued, in light of the formal similarities possible for each type of ethic. The second question is that of whether the principle(s) that Habermas, Rawls and I argue for are only necessary conditions for a moral solution or whether they are sufficient to define a unique solution to moral dilemmas on which rational moral agents could agree. This is the central issue raised by Locke's critique, which centres on the notion that 'justice as reversibility' or ideal role-taking does not yield any unique solution to complex moral dilemmas, which are contextually relative.

Locke's thinking is more carefully worked out in his paper, 'The Principle of Equal Interests' (Locke, 1981) than is the chapter in this volume, which consists of a mixture of criticisms rather than focusing on a single point. His earlier paper deals with two issues. The first is that of the status of what he calls 'the principle of equal interest' as a first principle of moral judgment. As he makes clear in that paper, this principle is that of reversibility, as I called it in my paper on 'Justice as Reversibility' (Kohlberg, 1981, Ch. 5). As he also makes clear, this principle is central to a full development of a utilitarian ethic, as well as to a deontological rights and justice ethic. As he also makes clear, it is not fully derivable from Hare's formalism, because (1) reversibility is distinct from universalizability, and (2) because reversibility requires some concept of rationality involved in the role exchange test, a concept of rationality or reasonableness which does not fully spring from the logical formal features of morality. Finally, he argues that while the 'principle of equal interest' or the 'principle of reversibility' is necessary for a consensual or moral solution to a dilemma, it is not sufficient for a universal or agreed upon solution of a dilemma, leaving the procedure subject to 'contextually relativistic' solutions. He concludes it is one of several moral principles, not *the* principle of morality. His argument is as follows (1981,[*] pp. 531ff):

> ... The Principle of Equal Interests (or PEI for short) bids us consider these interests impartially, allotting them no more, but also no less, weight merely because they happen to be our own interests or interests which we share. The aim, of course, is the maximum possible satisfaction of different people's interests: if we can discover which course of action satisfies more interests of more people or satisfies them to a greater degree, we will have discovered the correct solution to the conflict. But lacking a refertory calculus (from the Latin *'refert*,' meaning it matters, concerns, or is in one's interest), this can be difficult to determine with any exactitude. What we can do instead is imagine ourselves in the positive of the various parties to the conflict, with their interests in place of our own, and then combine their different points of view to arrive at that judgment which would give us more of what we would want, taking all those positions together, than any other. If we can do this correctly, it will then be the solution which does most to satisfy the different interests of the different parties to the actual situation. It will be the solution which most accords with the PEI.
>
> Clearly, a principle of this sort might find a place in any valid and acceptable system of morals. I am concerned, however, with attempts to elevate it into the supreme principle of morality, from which other, more particular moral rules and principles can be derived, and which

[*]By kind permission of Professor Don Locke and the Editor, *The Philosophical Review*, Cornell University, New York.

will not only solve the problems of practical morality (Singer, 1980) but also provide a source of rational argument, and ultimately of rational agreement, in ethics. This has recently been argued both by a philosopher, R. M. Hare (1976), and, less directly, by a psychologist, Lawrence Kohlberg (1963, 1979). Indeed, in ironic tribute to the Principle's importance and ubiquity, Hare refers to it as a version of Utilitarianism, which he clearly regards as taking precedence over considerations of justice, whereas Kohlberg prefers to speak of a principle of justice, which he explicitly describes as superior, both philosophically and psychologically, to any form of Utilitarianism. So although Hare himself dismisses the question as a terminological issue of no particular importance, I think it is worth indicating at the outset that the PEI is best regarded not as a form of Utilitarianism, not as a principle of justice, but as a distinctive approach to morality in its own right....

I begin with the question of what can be derived from Universal Prescriptivism alone. It is, Hare argues, a consequence of the very logic of moral language that you cannot sincerely and consistently make a moral judgment unless, first, you are prepared to accept the same moral judgment in any relevantly similar situation, including those which affect you personally differently (this is universalizability), and second, you are willing to act in accordance with that judgment yourself, should you ever be in some such relevantly similar situation (this is prescriptivity)....

It follows, then, that I cannot consistently assert a moral judgment unless I am prepared to act on it or have it acted on, should I be in the position of those to whom I am applying it: in Hare's celebrated example, I cannot sincerely and consistently assert that debtors ought to be imprisoned unless I am willing to be imprisoned myself, should I be a debtor. And this provides us, he believes, with a powerful weapon in moral argument: we simply ask people to imagine themselves in the position of those to whom they are applying their moral judgments and ask whether, supposing they were in that situation, they are still prepared to make the same judgment. If not, they stand convicted of inconsistency, insincerity, or both.

A device of this sort has been variously labelled sympathetic imagination, role-reversal, ideal role-taking and, more picturesquely, moral musical chairs.... But for all its familiarity among the folk-wisdoms of the world, the Golden Rule is subject to two major objections.

The first is that 'Do unto others as you would have them do unto you' is ambiguous between the claim that we ought to do as we would have others do unto us if we found ourselves in their position, but still with our own tastes and preferences, and the claim that we ought to do as we would have others do unto us if we actually were them, so to speak, with their tastes and preferences in place of our own.... So, as Hare's example of the trumpeter (who is only too willing to blow hot jazz unto others as he would have them blow hot jazz unto him) is intended to demonstrate, the crucial test is not 'How would you like it?' but 'How would you like it if you were them?': In other words, 'How do they like it?' But on this stronger interpretation the Golden Rule becomes quite unworkable: it makes it impossible for us to do anything to anybody which they would prefer us not to do. For that would mean we were doing unto them as we would not have them do unto us if we were them.

The second difficulty is that adhering to the Golden Rule in respect to one person may require us to break the Golden Rule in respect of another: doing unto one person as we would have him do unto us may involve our doing unto some other person as we would not have that person do unto us. The Golden Rule inevitably breaks down in those situations and there will be many, where the preferences of the different parties conflict with each other....

This, in effect, is Hare's solution to the problem of applying the Golden Rule to what he calls 'multilateral' situations: it is what I am calling the Principle of Equal Interests. It would, I think, be a mistake to say that the PEI follows from the Golden Rule—strictly, the two conflict with each other—but it is, at any rate, an elaboration or sophistication of the traditional formula.

Nevertheless, neither the Golden Rule nor the PEI follows from universalizability and prescriptivity as such, even if we add the role-reversal as well. Hare sometimes speaks as if the mere fact that someone would not want, or would be disinclined or sorry, to do something or to have it happen is a barrier to his sincerely and consistently asserting that it ought to be done....

There is, therefore, no conclusive argument to the PEI from Universal Prescriptivism alone. And in *Freedom and Reason*, at any rate, Hare is prepared to concede the point: it is possible to avoid the PEI, he implies, but only at a price, a price which most people will be unwilling to pay, the price of becoming what Hare terms a 'fanatic,' where a fanatic is just the sort of person we can hardly expect to convince by rational argument in the first place....

But it is not the only one. More recently, however, Hare has offered a more explicit argument for the PEI and against the idealist. If I understand it correctly it is not, as Hare suggests, an argument to the PEI from universalizability, prescriptivity, and role-reversal alone. It is based rather, on an appeal to prudence, or rational self-interest, on the part of the person making the moral judgment.... [For Hare] It is not universalizability and prescriptivity alone, but universalizability and prescriptivity combined with prudence, or rational self-interest, which generate the PEI. Indeed, Hare suggests, universalized self-interest is precisely what a liberal and tolerant morality consists in: 'it is when people step from the selfish pursuit of their own interests to the propagation of perverted ideals that they become really dangerous.' Not, of course, that self-interest as such can be the basis of morality, for the essential feature of morality is that it is universalizable, whereas self-interest is private and particular. But it is when we universalize self-interest, which we can do only by giving the same weight to other interests and desires that we give to our own, that we turn 'selfish prudential reasoning into moral reasoning'....

Our extended discussion of Hare has failed to find a convincing argument for the PEI. Nevertheless, there is another line of thought which may lie behind some of Hare's remarks, but which can be approached more directly by considering Lawrence Kohlberg's notion of justice as reversibility. Kohlberg himself does not formulate the PEI as I, and Hare, have formulated it. But it is towards the PEI, I shall suggest, that his arguments, properly understood, point....

Of Kohlberg's stages only the last two, Stages 5 and 6, provide distinctively moral—as opposed to merely prudential or social-conventional—judgments and reasoning. Stage 5 is a miscellany of Utilitarian, Natural Rights, and Social Contract theories. Stage 6 singles out a principle of justice, equality, or respect for persons as the highest form of moral thinking, inasmuch as it, and it alone, provides a means of resolving moral claims and conflicts, of solving moral problems and dilemmas. For what moves an individual from one stage to the next, Kohlberg suggests, are the moral cognitive conflicts which arise within, but cannot be solved within, that particular form of reasoning. Since no such conflicts arise at Stage 6 it is, accordingly, the stage than which there can be no higher.

I shall argue here that the principle appropriate to Stage 6 moral reasoning is in fact the PEI, though that is not the principle (or principles) which Kohlberg himself appears to adopt and utilize. But if Kohlberg's argument, as opposed to his conclusions, is correct, we will have what we are looking for: an argument for the PEI as the supreme—or fundamental, depending on your point of view—principle of a rational morality.

The crucial feature of moral judgments, for Kohlberg's purpose, is what he terms 'reversibility'. The term comes originally from Piaget who, typically, uses it in a bewildering variety of ways. But one sense in which moral judgments in particular might be said to be reversible is that they must be equally acceptable however they affect us personally, whatever our position in relation to them: 'we must be willing to live with our judgment or decision when we trade places with others in the situation being judged.' In short, a judgment is reversible if it can pass the test of role-reversal: what Kohlberg himself calls 'role-taking' or, more recently, 'moral musical chairs'.

But according to Kohlberg, whenever any moral problem or conflict arises, there will be one and only one judgment which is properly reversible in his sense. Indeed this must be so if Stage 6 reasoning is to be, as claimed, the highest stage of moral reasoning:

> Moral musical chairs means going around the circle of perspectives involved in a moral dilemma to test one's claim of right or duty until only the equilibrated or reversible claims survive. In 'non-moral' or competitive musical chairs there is only one 'winning person'. In moral musical chairs there is only one 'winning' chair which all other players recognize if they play the game, the chair of the person with the prior claim of justice.

At first sight the reference to a *prior* claim of justice may seem a slip on Kohlberg's part, since the point of moral musical chairs is, apparently, not to verify a prior claim of justice but to discover what that claim of justice might be. We shall see, however, that it is not.

As an example Kohlberg offers the case of a party of marines, who can escape only if one of their number goes back to blow up a bridge behind them, though whoever goes back will certainly be killed. Their chances of escape will be greater if this task is assigned to their demolition expert, but neither he nor anyone else volunteers. The question is whether the demolition expert should be ordered back or whether they should be ordered back, or whether they should choose someone by lot. Kohlberg's answer is that a lottery is the correct solution, apparently because it follows from Rawls's difference principle, in that it maximizes the prospects of the worst-off, in this case the demolition expert.

Yet this solution, however acceptable to Kohlberg personally, surely cannot be arrived at by the test of reversibility, by playing moral musical chairs. There is, in fact, no way of telling from the situation as described which moral judgment, if any, the marines are actually prepared to reverse—that might require a whole novel≏unless, of course, they are hand-picked to agree with Kohlberg. One marine might believe that they should stand or fall together, that it would be wrong to sacrifice any of their number for the good of the rest; and he will probably be willing to reverse his judgment, to accept it no matter whose position he imagines himself into. Another marine might believe, with Kohlberg, that it is right to sacrifice one life to save the others, but think that since everyone has an equal right to life they should, so far as possible, take an equal risk, and hence draw lots and he too should be willing to reverse his judgment, to accept it no matter whose position he imagines himself into. A third marine, however, might believe that they should follow whichever course of action is most likely to result in saving any lives, and therefore that the demolition expert should be ordered back; and he, too, might be willing to reverse his judgment, to accept it even if he were himself the demolition expert.

We have here three conflicting solutions to the problem, each one reversible, but reversible by different people. So far there is no single winning chair, no unique claim of justice. Kohlberg evidently assumes that if a judgment is acceptable no matter which position we imagine ourselves occupying, it will therefore be acceptable no matter who imagines himself in those positions. But this is not so. It is a merit of Hare's account that he recognizes, as Kohlberg does not, that different universalizers might be prepared to universalize or reverse different, conflicting judgments. Moreover it is clear that Kohlberg does not arrive at his preferred solution by the test of justice as reversibility. Instead he argues, in Rawlsian fashion, that a certain solution is rationally justified and then asserts that, once accepted, this solution is reversible—as indeed it must be to constitute a sincere and consistent moral judgment in the first place. It is no accident, therefore, that he refers to the *prior* claim of justice: the game of moral musical chairs is being used to test a solution independently arrived at, not as a way of providing that solution. Reversibility is, so far, only a necessary condition of justice, not a sufficient condition.

Nevertheless reversibility, properly understood, can provide us with a solution to the dilemma, a unique claim of justice, though not, unfortunately, the solution which Kohlberg favors. More accurately, there will be a solution of each case, but not always the same solution: it will depend on the particular group of marines. We can begin by noting that, so far, it has not been explained whether reversibility involves putting yourself in some-one else's position, but with your own attitudes and preferences, or putting yourself in their position with their attitudes and preferences. Either way there seems to be a problem: if the former, different people will be prepared to reverse different judgments; if the latter, no reversible judgment will be possible at all, given that our attitudes and preferences—and especially our moral opinions—differ to begin with. But in fact reversibility, in the sense appropriate to Stage 6 moral reasoning, is different from both of these....

So if we are to be true to the spirit of Kohlberg's argument we need a way of arriving at a single, mutually acceptable, meta-reversible judgment by means of role-reversal itself. We can do this by putting ourselves in someone else's position and taking account of his attitudes and preferences, but taking no more account of those attitudes and preferences when he put himself in anyone else's position. In other words, we all take the same account of each other's attitudes and preferences, including our own: we give everyone's attitudes and preferences the same weight, relative to how strongly they are held by the person concerned, regardless of whose they are. In short, we adopt the PEI.

Thus it is the PEI, not the Rawlsian difference principle, nor some (largely unspecified) principle of justice, equality, or respect for persons which in fact follows from Kohlberg's conception of justice as reversibility. The solution to any moral dilemma, as in the example of the marines, is provided by taking all the different attitudes and preferences, desires and interests into account, and then seeking the moral judgment which does most to satisfy those different interests. Which judgment that is will depend on the particular group: for each different group of marines with their different set of interests there will be a different balance of interests, and hence a different solution. But for each particular group there will be a unique claim of justice— though not, perhaps, a single winning chair, since it might not be a claim that any particular individual began with—one provided by the PEI....

It is, moreover, an argument which relies not on universalizability and prescriptivity, nor on role-reversal and reversibility as such, but on meta-reversibility, ideal role-taking, which seems a much stronger requirement. For the argument to hold we must be prepared not merely to accept our moral judgments if they were to apply to ourselves ('simple' role-reversal), and to accept them as applying to ourselves even in the imagined circumstances where we no longer accept them (universalizability); we must be prepared to accept them no matter who we are, no matter what our personal interests; that is, they must be judgments which everyone can accept. But what is the justification of this requirement? It can hardly be a consequence of the logic of moral discourse or the nature of moral reasoning as such....

But the assumption implicit in Kohlberg's psychological theory, and anticipated philosophically in Baier's *Moral Point of View*, is that the function of morality, of moral principles and moral reasoning, is to provide impartial, mutually acceptable solutions to conflicts of individual interest, solutions which all the parties can accept, whatever their original positions might be. Accordingly, Kohlberg's developmental progression through six stages of moral reasoning provides us with a step-by-step approach to the ultimate goal of mutually acceptable, meta-reversible moral judgments. Given this conception of morality, Stage 6 moral reasoning, in the form of the PEI, is indeed the highest possible stage: it is the stage at which we will find a single, mutually acceptable solution to the moral problem, a unique claim of justice.

In this statement of Locke, my (Kohlberg, 1981) principle of reversibility is restated as a principle of equal interest which would be acceptable to utilitarians as well as to those who start with respect for persons and agreement about justice. In the reconstruction of our moral stages represented by Table 3, concrete reciprocity at Stage 2 is replaced by ideal reciprocity, 'do as you would be done by', the Golden Rule. This is the structural core of Stage 3. In our analysis, the inadequacy of Stage 3 reversibility is represented by the fact that Stage 3 ideal reciprocity toward one person or group may conflict with ideal reciprocity toward another person or group. Solved at Stage 4 by impartial rules, at Stage 6 ideal reciprocity or reversibility is 'second order'. It says, 'Honour all claims which are themselves reversible, i.e., which are made in light of a validity check of ideal reciprocity with the competing claims of others.' The second problem raised by 'Stage 3' formulation of the Golden Rule, as Locke points out, is that it is unclear what attitudes I reverse in ideal role-reversal; I can't reverse all my own attitudes nor can I take on the actual attitude of another. In Kohlberg (1981) I proposed to resolve this difficulty by assuming Rawls' idea of reasonable self-interest or a maximin of one's values under a veil of ignorance.

This attempt to use Rawls' original position under the veil of ignorance turns out to be beset by many difficulties, when applied to interpersonal dilemma like the Korea dilemma. In particular it is not clear, as Locke points out, that the reversibility or second-order Golden Rule principle leads to a unique or single solution in the Korea or lifeboat dilemma he cites. In a situation like the Heinz dilemma, it yields a solution resolvable by Stage 5 reasoning; the druggist's claim to property is not a reversible claim, since a rationally self-interested druggist would, if he were to exchange roles with the dying woman, give up his claim to that part of his property which would cost a life. While this logic might be used to support the Korean expert's claim to risk his life only under the conditions of a lottery, it is not clear that this is the only way to interpret the principle of reversibility since, as Locke points out, it ignores the actual values of various actors as part of the role-reversal process. Obviously my interpretation of second order Golden Rule or ideal role-taking presupposed some solution to Locke's problems with the Golden Rule, the problem of whether to project your own preference value or interest in reversing role (like the hot jazz midnight trumpeter who would be pleased to have hot jazz blown back to him) or whether to accept the actual attitude of the neighbour wishing to sleep. This problem is one expression of the fact that Stage 3 Golden Rule role-taking is only partially reversible.

This is articulated as a problem for the Golden Rule as seen at what I would interpret as a higher stage than Stage 3, in response quoted by Gilligan and Lyons (1984). They say:

> Responding to an interview question which asked about how she might like to see herself in the future, the young woman, a high school junior, talks about how she would like 'to improve or expand on my compassion.' She goes on to say why:
>
> > With compassion, I'm sometimes not very understanding. I have a habit of putting myself in (another) person's place, which I found is not fair because I would do things differently and I think in a different way. And if they get angry, I would say, 'All right, how can I understand that? I will put myself in her place,' and I will say, 'I wouldn't get angry at that!' That doesn't help very much. (So) I would like to have more compassion towards them, to accept the way they feel really, and respect that.
>
> Thus discovering that an old way of understanding others, by putting herself in their place, was not 'fair', the young woman holds up for herself a new measure of her development: 'to improve or expand on my compassion ... to accept the way they feel really, and respect that.'

For this young woman Stage 3 role-reversal faces the problem noted by Locke, that her projections of herself into the other's place is not 'fair' since it does not correspond to the actual feelings of the other, which to understand and respect require that she be 'compassionate'. Gilligan and Lyons making a dichotomy between immediate response to feelings of the other (compassion) and role reversal (fairness). We would stress this young woman's orientation to respect for persons, the Kantian principle, as including both respect and what Boyd calls 'active sympathy'. As Boyd points out, my own notion of justice as fairness and that of Rawls is much broader than this usual conception of justice. Listening to the way this young woman uses the terms 'fairness' and 'respect for the feelings of others', we would stress the integration of 'cold justice' and 'compassion' involved in this young woman's notion of fairness as equal respect for the feelings of others.

We would agree with this developing young woman that a 'fair' or right response, based on respect for the feelings and dignity of others, requires an 'empathic' or 'compassionate' component. Returning to the slightly 'colder' and different standpoint of the 'rational' moral philosophers, elaborated by Locke, we would say that the solution to the problem he raises as to our claim for complete reversibility at Stage 6 rests on the assumption of a minimal notion of shared rationality formalized by Rawls as a 'thin theory of the good', i.e., that each individual wishes to maximize his own values, (whether selfish or altrustic) prior to reversing roles (in my case by meta-reversibility or musical chairs, in Rawls' case by entering the veil of ignorance). Intuitively we do this by thinking that the sleeping neighbour has the right to maximize his values and sleep, and the hot jazz trumpeter does not have the right to play jazz in a way which interferes with the sleep of his neighbour. The jazz player can maximize his values by reversing roles and playing jazz during the day, the sleeping neighbour cannot maximize his values by reversing roles and sleeping during the day and playing jazz at night. Usually this would be intuitively formulated by the Kantian notion that there is a perfect duty not to infringe on one's neighbour's liberty (to sleep) whereas there is not a perfect duty to play jazz even though it might be some sort of imperfect duty to develop one's own talents as a musiscain.

The same answer holds to the multilateral reversibility I have called 'moral musical chairs' on the Korea dilemma. Indeed as Locke points out, each marine may hold actually different values some being egoistic and thinking their own life of highest value, others being martyrs and thinking sacrificing their life for the group expresses the highest Christian value. My procedural assumption at Stage 6 makes the assumption that each actor is 'rational' in the sense of having a thin theory of the good. The martyr would prefer to have his ideal Christian values served by having a chance of continuing to stay alive to fulfil those values, the egoist would prefer to have a chance of living (through the lottery) than no chance of living at all. The common value which would be reversible under those conditions under a thin theory of the good would be an equal chance to life through the lottery, the one notion of the good which is shared or is reversible.

There are, however, problems with applying Rawls' notion of rationality as a thin theory of the good or equating an ideal moral role-taking as equivalent to the veil of ignorance, difficulties dealt with in another paper (Kohlberg, 1985a) responding to the critiques of my equating 'ideal' reversible role-taking with anything related to Rawls' theory of the original position. For this and other reasons, I have come to question that Stage 6 or reversibility raised to a principle necessarily provides a single or consensual answer to all dilemmas though, like Stage 5, it does lead to consensus on most of our dilemmas (Kohlberg, 1984, Ch. 7). In that sense I would accept a more contextual or what Carter calls perspectival relativity to principled morality, though not what he calls 'epistemological' or radical relativism.

In (Kohlberg, 1985a) we also try to show how each stage has a partial reversibility made more reversible by the next stage and made as fully reversible as possible by Stage 6, a sort of top (Stage 6) down rational reconstruction of the stages. This is explicated in Table 3 of this chapter.

Turning from my efforts to build on Rawls to my efforts to build on Habermas, if we follow Habermas' line, the process of reaching consensus most fully in postconventional morality, is not through an original position under the veil of ignorance, symbolized by drawing straws in the Korea dilemma, but through a dialogue among the participants based on the assumption of the principle of respect for persons in the Korea (or lifeboat) situation, a dialogue that respects the equal worth of each participant which could lead to a number of different outcomes.

For Habermas the justice structure analysis we have presented in Table 3 is 'monologic'. We all enter a moral situation with some monologic conception of rightness or justice, but the first moral effort is to reach agreement or consensus between the self and the various others involved through dialogue and communication. If consensus cannot be reached, then a decision must still be made by monologic methods and this may involve the use of coercion, like theft of the drug in the Heinz dilemma, if all else fails.

While I am not making definite claims about Stage 6, it may be noted that this is the approach taken by Joan, a woman whom we classified as Stage 6. Her response to the Heinz dilemma was as follows:

'NOW THE FIRST QUESTION IS, WHAT DO YOU SEE AS THE PROBLEM IN THIS SITUATION?'
    The problem for Heinz seems to be that his wife is dying and that he's caught in between obeying societal law of not stealing and committing a crime that would result in saving his wife's life. I would like to think that there's a conflict for the druggist as well. . . . There might also be a conflict for the woman. . . .

'WHY DO YOU THINK IT'S IMPORTANT TO TAKE INTO CONSIDERATION THE CONFLICTS FACING THE OTHER TWO CHARACTERS IN THE SITUATION?'

As soon as more than one person knows about a situation.... There's shared conflicts and the conflicts of each person sort of play off one another. And I think that the conflicts can be resolved to some extent by kind of pooling ... so that as soon as more than one person becomes aware of the conflict that there are automatically problems to be resolved by each, things to be considered by each; and each person then has the power to affect what happens in the conflict.

'SHOULD HEINZ STEAL THE DRUG?'

If I were Heinz, I, you know, would keep trying to talk with the druggist.... I have a hard time thinking of any decision as being static and it seems to me that dialogue is very important and a continuing dialogue in this kind of situation. But if it came to a point where nothing else could be done, I think that in consultation with his wife, if he and his wife decided that that would be an acceptable alternative for Heinz, then yes he should.

'WHY IS THAT IMPORTANT?'

Because I think that ultimately it comes down to a conflict of duties.... I don't think that Heinz should do anything that he wouldn't be willing to say that everyone should do. And breaking into a store and stealing, etcetera, is not an action that can be prescribed for humanity, for our societal group as a whole. On the other hand, I think Heinz, just by virtue of being a member of the human race, has an obligation, a duty to protect other people.... And when it gets down to a conflict between those two, I think that the protection of human life is more important.

'IF HEINZ DOESN'T LOVE HIS WIFE, SHOULD HE STEAL THE DRUG FOR HER?'

I don't think that he should steal it out of a sense of love. I think that Heinz should steal the drug, if it comes down to that far-reaching point, out of a sense of responsibility to preserve life, not out of love. I think responsibility, as I'm using it here, means a recognition of dignity, on the part of every living being, but I could narrow it down, if you like, to persons. And responsibility is really something that's entailed in that recognition. If we respect you as a creature with dignity and your own unique, special being, in recognizing that I won't intrude on you, I won't purposefully harm, you—there's this whole series of negatives that go along with being responsible and there's also some positives. And that's to recognize you as being unique, important and integral, in some sense, and to do what I can to preserve all that.

'SUPPOSE THE PERSON DYING IS NOT HIS WIFE BUT A STRANGER. SHOULD HEINZ STEAL THE DRUG FOR A STRANGER?'

Yes.

'LET ME ASK YOU THIS QUESTION: IN LOOKING AT THE ORIGINAL SITUATION OF HEINZ AND THE DRUG AND DECIDING WHETHER TO STEAL OR NOT, IS THERE ANY ONE CONSIDERATION THAT STANDS OUT IN YOUR MIND ABOVE ALL OTHERS, IN MAKING A DECISION OF THIS SORT?'

I would say that there are two things. The first thing is that no person has the right to make a decision that affects the dignity and integrity of another person without there being cooperative discussion among the people involved. Number one. The second thing is that, you know, in this very strange situation where it would come down to being, you know, the single person's decision (and I have trouble conceiving that as ever happening), then it comes down to preserving the dignity and integrity ... and for the reason of life usually is involved in that, of another person. So I guess I'm saying that, well ... I'm not saying that preserving life is *the* essential or ultimate thing. I think that preserving a person's dignity and integrity are the important things.

Her thinking, displayed at the end is centred on a single general principle, doing that which respects, preserves and enhances human dignity. This means, she tells us, first cooperative discussion before trying any other means of resolving conflicting claims. In this 'strange' Heinz situation where dialogue with the druggist fails, a monologic action should be taken based on preserving the dying wife's life, personhood and dignity.

Her thinking differs, first, from a more typical Stage 5 response in that it is oriented to a single general principle rather than a set of discrete rights and values like life and liberty. It differs, secondly, in that it involves a notion of equality of human worth. This single principle carries across dilemmas, she uses it in all dilemmas, not only in the Heinz dilemma. Thirdly, it arrives within its own justification, the press to dialogue to resolve the justice conflict.

A prototypical example of our fifth stage is Kenny, who responds to the Heinz dilemma as follows:

'WAS HEINZ RIGHT TO BREAK IN?'

I think he was justified in breaking in because there was a human life at stake. I think that transcends any right that the druggist had to the drug.

'DID THE DRUGGIST HAVE A RIGHT TO CHARGE THAT MUCH WHEN THERE WAS NO LAW SETTING A LIMIT?'

He has a legal right, but I don't think he had a moral right to do it. The profit was excessive, it was 10 times what he bought it for.

'IS IT THE HUSBAND'S DUTY OR OBLIGATION TO STEAL THE DRUG FOR HIS WIFE IF HE CAN GET IT NO OTHER WAY?'

Again, I think the fact that her life was in danger transcends any other standards you might use to judge his actions.

'SUPPOSE IT WAS SOMEONE DYING WHO WASN'T EVEN CLOSE. BUT THERE WAS NO ONE ELSE TO HELP HIM. WOULD IT BE RIGHT TO STEAL THE DRUG FOR SUCH A STRANGER?'

It's something he should do. In order to be consistent, yes, I would have to say. Something he should do again from a moral standpoint.

'WHAT IS THIS MORAL STANDPOINT?'

Well, I think every individual has a right to live and if there is a way of saving an individual I think an individual should be saved if he wants to be.

'WHAT DOES THE WORD MORALITY MEAN TO YOU?'

I think it is presuming or recognizing the right of the individual to do, well, basically it is recognizing the rights of other individuals, not interfering with those rights, act as fairly—it is going to sound corny, but as you would expect them to treat you, fairly, and honestly. I think it is basically to preserve the human being's right to existence, I think that is the most important. Secondly, the human being's right to do as he pleases, again without interfering with somebody else's rights.

Kenny considers maintaining life and liberty intrinsic or 'natural' rights transcending law and convention if these conflict. He sees recognition of these rights as representing the moral standpoint, a 'prior to society' moral point of view. This includes the right to liberty 'compatible with the like liberty of others'. This moral standpoint has implicitly the impartiality and reversibility of what Locke and Baier call the 'moral point of view', but it is not elevated to the level of a principle or an ideal method of consensus itself.

The immanence of 'Stage 6' reversibility in dialogic action led me to say (Kohlberg, 1981):

Let us look for a reversible solution in Charlene's dilemma. Charlene must choose between keeping a date with Joanne, an old friend, to counsel her about a problem. A new friend, Tina, has invited her to see a play at the same time.

Usually discussion of the dilemma with adults eventually leads to the conclusion that (1) it is a moral dilemma, and (2) the right action is for Charlene is keep her date with Joanne, the old friend.

The reasoning for such a conclusion may come from 'Stage 5': (1) keeping contract and promises as the foundation of social obligations and relations (with a rule-utilitarian rationale for contract) and (2) act-utilitarian considerations that the old friend's need to see her friend Charlene is greater than the new friend's needs.

Few would hesitate to think the right thing is to help the old friend with the need even if it entails breaking an appointment.

The whole use of utilitarian thinking is far-fetched because intuitively we would decide through 'moral musical chairs' and test our imaginative role taking with reality. If the prior date were made with the new friend Tina and the old friend Joanne had the urgent need, we would call up the new friend and explain. We would expect her to trade places with Joanne, the old friend, and, because her need was not as great, release her from the promise. Even if Charlene could not reach her until the last moment, we would expect Tina to understand.

If we reverse the situation and the new friend has the more urgent need and the date is made with the old friend, the situation is more difficult. This is because we don't know whether the old friend will understand and accept our reasons for breaking the date in order to counsel a new friend about college.

We expect, like Rawls, that envy should not be allowed to determine the fair solution. We also expect an old friend to role take the viewpoint of the new friend as well as vice versa. In the end, then, keeping a promise is a matter of reversible role-taking; testable through dialogue.

This centring on dialogue or dialogic action has led Habermas and his colleagues to a 'rational reconstruction' of our moral stages, based on dialogic or communicative action rather than monologic reasoning about justice dilemmas, a 'reconstruction' because it starts with a highest stage as dialogic and works down. At Stage 2, for instance, dialogue might be negotiation through exchange and compromise at Stage 3 through sharing perspectives on norms of caring and trust, etc.

We can clarify Habermas' approach to rational reconstruction by McCarthy's (1982,[*] p. 57) summary:

> The debate between Habermas and Gadamer which took place in the late 1960s and early 1970s came to a provisional close on Habermas's side with a series of promissory notes. While he agreed with Gadamer on the necessity for a *sinnverstehenden* access to social reality, he insisted nevertheless that the interpretation of meaningful phenomena need not, indeed can not, be restricted to the type of dialogic understanding characteristic of the hermeneutic approach. He held out instead the possibility of a theoretically grounded analysis of symbolically structured objects and events which, by drawing on systematically generalized empirical knowledge, would reduce the context-dependency of understanding and leave room for both quasi-causal explanation and critique. The types of theoretical-empirical knowledge in question, he suggested, included (i) a general theory of communication which would reconstruct the 'universal-pragmatic infrastructure' of speech and action; (ii) a general theory of socialization in the form of a theory of the acquisition of communicative competence; (iii) a theory of social systems which would make it possible to grasp objective meaning connections going beyond what is subjectively intended or expressly articulated in cultural traditions; and (iv) a theory of social evolution which would make possible a theoretical reconstruction of the historical situations of the interpreter (or critic) and his or her object.
>
> Philosophic hermeneutic stresses that the interpreter of social phenomena is a member of a life-world, that the interpreter too occupies a specific historical, social, cultural position from which he or she tries to come to terms with the beliefs and practices of others. The understanding achieved is, as a result, inexorably situation-bound, an understanding from a point of view that is on the same level as what is understood. There are, the argument goes, no privileged positions outside of or above history from which to view human life; there can be no interpreter without a language—in Wittgenstein's full-bodied sense of the term. And there is no such thing as *the* correct interpretation. 'Each time will have to understand ... in its own way.... One understands otherwise if one understands at all.' The interest behind hermeneutics is not an interest in bringing a certain object domain under theoretical control or submitting it to a critique of ideology; it is an interest in coming to an understanding through dialogue—with others in my culture, with alien cultures, with the past—about the common concerns of human life. The social inquirer is not, as may be mistakenly supposed, a neutral observer, explainer, predicter; nor is the inquirer a sovereign critic who may safely assume his or her own cognitive or moral superiority; the inquirer is, however virtually, a partner in dialogue, a participant rather than an observer or critic.

---

[*]By kind permission of Professor T. McCarthy, Macmillan Publishers, London and MIT Press, USA (Thompson, J. B. and Held, D. *Habermas Critical Debate*).

It was in part to oppose what he saw as the relativistic implications of this and related views that Habermas stressed the need for a theoretically grounded analysis of social phenomena. Recently the positivist emphasis on logic and mathematics, on universal laws and general theories, came increasingly under attack. A new front was forming along relativist versus universalist lines. Fundamental challenges to the idea of a critical theory of society no longer came solely from the direction of positivism; more and more they issued from the side of post-Heideggerian and post-Wittgensteinian versions of historicism and culturalism.

The strongly theoretical, universalist approach to social inquiry that Habermas wishes to defend does not rest on a rejection of the detranscendentalization of philosophy since Kant. On the contrary, a central theme of *Knowledge and Human Interests* was precisely the progressive radicalization of epistemology that led to the 'idea of a theory of knowledge as social theory'. Here and elsewhere Habermas traced the decline of the conception of the subject that had dominated modern philosophy from Descartes through to Kant.

But while Habermas fully endorses the decline and fall of the Cartesian ego, he does not regard relativism as its inevitable consequence. He holds that the conception of the subject that has replaced it is not *per se* incompatible with certain of the universalistic claims of transcendental philosophy—though these would clearly have to be reformulated in cooperation with the human sciences that have since taken that subject as their theme. He wants, in particular, to salvage by way of reconstruction Kant's claim that there are universal and unavoidable presuppositions of theoretical and practical reason, as well as his conception of *Mundigkeit*, autonomy and responsibility, as the essence of rational personality. But he also wants, thinking now more with Hegel, to present a reconstructed conception of the *Bidungsprozesse*, the self-formative processes of the individual and the species that have rational autonomy as their telos—a kind of systematic history of reason. Nor does he eschew the normative dimensions of this enterprise; quite the contrary, the universal scheme he espouses is both theoretical and moral-practical.

I shall focus on the general strategy of argumentation that Habermas is pursuing and the kinds of considerations to which he appeals for support, so as to make clearer both what the force of his argument would be if it were successful and the sorts of evidence that might count against it.

The Kantian aspect of Habermas's programme might be represented as an analogue to the question: how is experience possible in general? The corresponding question for Habermas would then read: 'How is understanding (among speaking and acting subjects) possible in general?' And just as Kant's analysis of the conditions of possibility of experience was at the same time an analysis of the possibility of the object of experience, Habermas's investigation of the 'general and unavoidable presuppositions of achieving understanding in language' is meant to elucidate the general structures of communicative social action itself. Having said this it is important to head off possible misunderstandings by immediately adding that Habermas explicitly distances himself from the claims and procedures of transcendental philosophy in the traditional sense. His project is empirical—not in the sense of the nomological sciences of nature but rather in the sense of the 'reconstructive' approaches that have been developed above all in linguistics and cognitive developmental psychology. As Habermas sees it, the basic idea behind this type of approach is that speaking and acting subjects know how to achieve, accomplish, perform, produce a variety of things without explicitly adverting to, or being able to give an explicit account of, the structures, rules, criteria, schemata on which their performances are based. The aim of rational reconstruction is precisely to render explicit the structures and rules underlying such 'practically mastered, pre-theoretical' know-how, the tacit knowledge that represents the subject's competence in a given domain. Thus it differs from hermeneutic understanding, which is primarily concerned with tracing semantic relations within the surface structure of a language or between those of different languages; its goal is not a paraphrase or a translation of an originally unclear meaning but an explicit knowledge of the 'deep' structures and rules, the mastery of which underlies the competence of a subject to generate meaningful symbolic configurations.

If the tacit, pre-theoretical knowledge that is to be reconstructed represents a universal know-how—and not merely that of a particular individual, group or culture—our task is the reconstruction of a 'species competence'. Such reconstructions can be compared in their scope and status with general theories (for example, of language or cognition). From another point of view, they can also be compared with Kant's transcendental logic. But the differences are critical here. Rational reconstructions of universal or species competences cannot make the strong *a prioristic* claims of the Kantian project. They are advanced in a hypothetical attitude and must be checked and revised in the light of the data, which are gathered *a posteriori* from the actual performances and considered appraisals of competent subjects. Any proposal must meet the empirical condition of conforming in a mass of crucial and clear cases to the intuitions of competent subjects, which function ultimately as the standard of accuracy.

Adopting this approach, Habermas advances a proposal for a universal or formal pragmatics, which is based on the idea that not only language (*langue*) but speech (*parole*) admits of rational reconstruction in universal terms, that 'communicative competence' has as universal a core as linguistic competence. The competence of the ideal speaker must be regarded as including not merely the ability to produce and understand grammatical sentences but also the ability to establish and understand those modes of communication and connections with the world through which speech becomes possible.

From this pragmatic point of view it becomes clear that communication necessarily (even if often only implicitly) involves the raising, recognizing and redeeming of 'validity-claims', claims to the truth of statements, to the sincerity or authenticity of self-presentations, and to the rightness of actions and norms of action.

To understand further Habermas' rational reconstruction of our moral stages, it will be helpful to summarize briefly the analysis of Keller and Reuss' (1984)* empirical construction of friendship stages, stages related to our first three stages, and of Selman's stages of friendship conceptions, in terms of Habermas' theory of communicative action. Their stages are based on answers to Selman's dilemma as to whether to keep an appointment with an old friend or go to the movie with a new friend. Keller and Reuss say:

> We take Selman's concept of perspective-taking to be central for the reconstruction of development of social cognitive competence. However, following Eckensberger and Silbereisen (1980) it should be reinterpreted in an action theoretical framework in order to disentangle structure and content of social cognition.
>
> In the following we shall outline how (a) levels of the interpretation of reality and (b) categories of a naive theory of action that constitute these levels are differentiated and co-ordinated in a specific developmental sequence. Within this theoretical framework two problems fall into place that have received major attention in social cognitive research: (1) the distinction between the two forms of action—action on physical objects and social interaction— and (2) the distinction between descriptive and prescriptive social cognition.
>
> The principle of justification implied by moral communication implies the potential consent of those affected by an action at the psychological level and requires the interacting subjects to achieve the solution of a dual task: *First*, to understand others as *concrete persons* with their background of particular life conditions and experiences, the changing circumstances, defined by a person's situation, needs, interests, problems, feelings, expectations, intentions and goals. *Second*, to take into account the *intersubjective* standards of rightness, which make certain intentions, goals, means, etc. acceptable in the light of shared knowledge of mutual action orientations. This shared knowledge is based on certain normative or quasi-normative in-variances of mutual action orientations.
>
> In the context of our empirical research knowledge of such relative *invariances of action* relates to three forms of certainties which regulate interaction: (a) *Regularities* of established patterns of action which give rise to mutual quasi-normative expectations at the level of concrete interpersonal action and tied to concrete and specific persons. In analogy to rules and norms such regularities serve to maintain generalized expectancies, which are upheld in spite of temporary violations. This feature, accounting for interpersonal invariance, is critically different from cognitive expectations referring to the physical world, where violation of expectations leads to

---

*By kind permission of Professor Monika Keller and publishers of *Human Development*. (Keller, M. et al. An Action—Theoretical Reconstruction of the Development of Social—Cognitive Competence, *Human Development*, 27, 211–20, Karger, Basel.

correction of error and to modification of knowledge. (b) Particular, *formal rules* (e.g. a promise given should not be broken) and the corresponding 'institutional facts'. While action oriented towards regularities is tied to specific persons and their relationships, rule oriented action is based on generalized expectancies independent of relationship to significant others. (c) Finally, regularities and formal rules guiding action can be integrated into systems of *norms of reciprocity*. For example, in a system of social interaction such as friendship mutually shared expectations of loyalty, trustworthiness and reliability are such norms of reciprocity. While formal rules refer to rather specified types of behavior, norms of reciprocity are rather general with regard to the behavior they call for. Their application always requires taking into account the context of the specific circumstances and life situation of another person. In other words: these circumstances may represent reasons to specify the validity claims attached to general expectancies.

Understanding the general (intersubjectively right) and the personal (subjective and particular) aspects of interaction requires the interacting subject to mediate between the shared patterns of expectation and the specific context of the situation. With the development of their social cognitive repertoire subjects engaging in intentional action characteristically experience a growing need to justify their actions and thus to apply their cognitive repertoire to negotiate mutual acceptance of intentions, motives, goals and consequences. Since the self can only be freed from this pressure through anticipation, i.e. through inner action, a process of structuring and restructuring progressively more complex knowledge systems is required to accomplish this task.

An important part of the actor's social knowledge system is the ability to anticipate the evaluation of actions and to construct strategies of justification, excuse and compensation in the case of violation of expectations. Structurally, the ability to regulate action in a form that is either competent or deficient with regard to the standards of communicative action depends on the selective function of social knowledge systems or naive theories of action. Similarly, the ability to coordinate single actions in a more or less complex sequence is a function of developmentally achieved knowledge systems. Systems of knowledge represent different levels of interpretation of social reality. They are characterized by a typical repertoire of naive action theoretical categories and give rise to typical strategies for the coordination of actions. The development of the ability to differentiate and coordinate perspectives (Mead, 1934; Selman, 1980) is a central component of the development of such knowledge systems.

A reinterpretation of perspective-taking in the framework of action theory requires an explication of those categories of a naive theory of action and their action-relevant relations which are constitutive for the differentiation and coordination of perspectives. These categories include the following:

a)   Representation of persons, relations and situations (typical vs. specific circumstances).

b)   Representation of internal states: needs, interests, expectations, feelings, motives, goals, means and consequences (intended vs. non-intended, short vs. long-term).

c)   Representation of social regularities; of rules and norms of reciprocity; of evaluative standards and principles and regulative strategies (excuses and justifications, compensations, discursive strategies).

Whenever an action is experienced as problematic or amenable to criticism, it has to be justified towards those concerned. Justifiability involves the analytical distinction between preference and '*preferability*'. While preference refers to action in descriptive terms, preferability refers to the condition of generalizability of action in prescriptive terms: preferability thus refers to the fact that responsible action is predicated, in principle, on the potential consent of those concerned, i.e. on the regulative principle of mutual acceptability or consensus. The necessity to (potentially) make accessible and justify action in all its aspects that can be experienced as problematic differentiates *communicative* from *instrumental* or *strategic* action (Habermas, 1984). In instrumental or strategic action intentions or goals are taken for granted. It is neither necessary to (potentially) make them accessible nor to justify them towards those concerned. This form of action has been characterized as '*goal-rational*', as action is regulated by goal adequacy (functionality) or by rules of prudence only. Rationality thus is reduced to the choice of adequate means given specific goals. While goal-rational action is regulated in a *monological* or pseudo-dialogical form, communicative action, in seeking the (potential) consent of those concerned by an action, is regulated in discursive, or *dialogical* forms.

In the following we shall present a developmental sequence of four different levels of interpretation of reality based on the categories of action outlined above. The data are derived from interviews about an everyday action dilemma occurring between friends, a slightly modified version of Selman's (1980) friendship dilemma. The main character of the story has promised his or her best friend to meet on a special day. Later the hero receives an invitation to a movie from a third child who has only recently moved to the neighborhood. This invitation happens to be at the same time he or she had promised to meet the old friend. A variety of additional psychological details are mentioned that complicate matters further, e.g. that the friend has problems he or she wants to talk about and that he or she does not like the new child.

In examining Keller and Reuss' reconstruction it is useful to remind the reader of Selman's own construction (Selman, 1976, p. 308) which is based on problem situations like the friendship story which Keller and Reuss take from Selman.

Table 4*. *Concepts of Friendship: The Resolution of Discord and Conflict between Two Individuals*

In exploring our subjects' ideas of friendship, we used the dilemma summarized earlier, in which the young protagonist must choose between a date with her old friend and one with a new friend. As with other dilemmas, questions and probes are first close to the story, then more general, and then touch upon subjects' personal experiences.

Conflict resolution, the issue discussed here, is not a process limited to the friendship relationship. It is a process, however, that plays a critical part in the maintenance of friendship and, depending upon how it is manifest, can play a progressive or regressive role in the development of the relationship itself. Within the domain of friendship, the issue of conflict resolution refers to children's and adults' ideas about how persons maintain friendships in the face of difficult situations, methods or procedures for rectifying discord and disagreement within a friendship, and notions of the kinds of conflicts that are seen as natural and expectable in a friendship.

As noted earlier, questions asked include the following:

1. What kinds of things do good friends sometimes fight or disagree about?
2. What are some good ways to settle fights, arguments, or disagreements with a friend?
3. Can friends have arguments and still be friends?

Following are the descriptions of concepts at each level.

LEVEL 0: MOMENTARY FRIENDSHIPS AND PHYSICAL SOLUTIONS TO CONFLICTS

At Level 0 children's suggestions for solutions to conflict between friends appear to be both momentary and physicalistic. Two consistent aspects or themes have been identified: conflict resolution through noninteraction and conflict resolution through direct physical intervention. In the former case, the child's reasoning about conflicts appears to be made without any reflective consideration of the psychological effects (feelings, motives, attitudes) of a given strategy upon *either* party. Two mechanisms are often articulated for dealing with conflict within this theme. The first is to simply suggest that one of the involved parties move to another activity ('Go play with another toy'). The second is to suggest a physical separation for a time ('Go away from her and come back later when you're not fighting'). It should be noted that despite the first impression given by such responses, young children coded at Level 0 do *not*, when their reasoning is probed, seem to see resolution through separation as a time to cool off and reflect on the problem (a Level 2 concept), but as a primitive 'out of sight-out of mind' solution. They believe that if two people do not interact physically, they cannot be in any conflict. Furthermore, conflict does not seem to be a disagreement of perspectives, but a case of one party not getting to *do* what it is (or act in the way) he or she wants because of some action on the part of the other party.

The second theme or aspect often mentioned as an alternative method for conflict resolution to physical withdrawal is physical force, or as one 5-year-old girl blithely said when asked what to do when two friends argue, 'Punch her out.'

---

*By kind permission of Professor Robert Selman

LEVEL 1:   ONE-WAY FRIENDSHIP AND UNRELATED SOLUTIONS TO CONFLICTS

Level 1 reasoning is reflected in responses that indicate a new understanding that the subjective or psychological effects of conflict are as important as the physical effects. However, the principle appears to apply only with respect to one of the individuals involved. Rather than viewing conflicts as between two subjective perspectives, children whose concepts are scored at this level appear to view conflicts as essentially a problem that is *felt* by one party and *caused* by the actions of the other. It is for this reason that we term these children's understanding of conflicts *one-way* or *unilateral*; their resolutions are also one-way.

Essentially, the child seems to be saying that what is important is to reduce the *psychological* effects of the conflict on the identified recipient by having the other party reverse the effects of the conflict-producing *activity*. Three strategies or themes for achieving this goal emerge at this stage. The first is negation of the problem action, thereby appeasing the offended friend's feelings ('Stop the fight and give him back what you took or take back what you called him'). A second and related suggestion is the performance of positive action that will return a person who is experiencing psychological discomfort back to a state of comfort or psychological calm ('Give him something nice that will make him feel better').

What is significant by omission in the suggestions of children whose responses are coded as Level 1 is any concern (or awareness) that the actor performing the rectifying actions needs to coordinate his or her action (objectivity) and intention (subjectivity). It is not so much a question of a child's not feeling it important to match words and actions, that is, to 'mean it'; it seems more a case of a child's exerting so much effort coordinating the *feelings* of one actor with the *actions* of the other that he or she does not have the conceptual 'energy' to think at the same time of coordinating the feelings and actions *within* each actor.

A third aspect of this level orientation is manifest in the tacit assumption that conflicts arise out of the negative actions of *one* of the two parties. The cause and locus of conflict is believed to be one actor's transgressions, not a coordinated mutual disagreement. Being focused on one individual as the cause of the other's discomfort, the subject also appears to assume that the seeds of resolution are also entirely in that party's hands.

HOW DO TWO FRIENDS MAKE UP IF THEY HAVE HAD A FIGHT?
Around our way the guy who started it just says he's sorry.
IS THAT ENOUGH?
Yup.

(8.3)

There are of course cases when in fact one person 'started it'. However, when the child can *only* conceive of a disagreement as started by *one* person, even when it in fact arises from honest disagreement we feel this represents a particular *social-cognitive* limitation that is typical of Level 1 conceptualizations.

LEVEL 2:   BILATERAL FRIENDSHIPS AND COOPERATIVE SOLUTIONS TO CONFLICTS

Advances in understanding coded as Level 2 reflect the subject's cognizance that both parties participate psychologically in a conflict, and so both parties must engage actively in its resolution. One aspect of this level of understanding is, therefore, that a satisfactory resolution of a conflict between friends requires an appeal to each person's sensibilities, each person's judgment.

HOW DO YOU SOLVE PROBLEMS WHEN FRIENDS DISAGREE?
Somebody wants to play one game and the other wants to play another game and you can settle it, but first we will play your game and then we will play my game.
WHY DOES THAT MAKE THINGS BETTER?
Then each person gets to do what they want.

(14:3)

CAN A PERSON STOP A FIGHT?
No. You've got to get both of them to agree.

(12:3)

The limitation of this belief appears to be in the child's assumption that each party can be satisfied independently of the other. Still lacking is a sense of truly *mutual* problem solving. This Level 2 belief that everything is fine as long as each is happy regardless of whether or not they come to a mutual consensus, indicates that the conflict is still not seen to originate within the relationship itself. Rather, some external circumstance or event is seen to be the cause of the disagreement and hence, its removal is the source of resolution.

A second aspect, an advance over concepts coded at the previous stage, is the child's belief that it is no longer sufficient to simply 'take back one's words' and the realization that in recanting, one must '*mean* what he or she says,' that is, must be sincere in his or her apologies rather than simply going through the motions.

HOW DO FIGHTS GET STARTED?
You will be playing and somebody will start to tease you or call you a name.
HOW DO YOU PATCH THINGS UP?
You make her take it back—you make sure she means it or you let her have it.

(10:1)

These excerpts also exemplify structural correspondences across domains. Recall that in the issue of self-awareness (domain of individuals).

Level 2 was characterized by a distinction in the child's mind between the *appearance* of outer manifestations (e.g., words) and the *truth* or reality of inner beliefs (e.g., feelings). For example, with this conception now in hand, the child is able to grasp not only that one should 'mean it,' but also a third aspect, that conflicts can arise when one party, in a moment of anger, says or does something he may not really mean. This is a more sympathetic interpretation of conflicts and their resolution.

CAN YOU BE FRIENDS WITH SOMEONE EVEN IF YOU HAVE FIGHTS?
Yes. If you have a fight and say I hate you and you brat, I hate you, I hate you, and if they really meant it, then it wouldn't be good, but if they didn't really mean it, and they really meant it at the time, except they didn't really mean it, then that's okay.
IF YOU HAVE THAT KIND OF FIGHT, HOW CAN YOU MAKE IT BETTER?
Well, if you say something and don't really mean it, they you have to mean it when you take it back.

(8:6)

Another aspect or strategy for resolving actual or potential conflicts which appears to require Level 2 perspective-taking understanding is the awareness that *psychological* space between 'warring factions' often needs to be provided if conflicts are to be resolved peacefully and positively.

IF YOU ARE HAVING TROUBLE WITH YOUR FRIEND, WHAT DO YOU DO?
Sometimes you got to get away for a while. Calm down a bit so you won't be so angry. Then get back and try to talk it out.

(14:1)

The kind of 'getting away' described by children coded as Level 2 is quite different from the 'forgetting as denial' suggested by younger children coded as Level 0. In the latter case 'out-of-sight' appeared to be equated with 'out-of-mind'. Here we infer that out-of-sight is seen as a way for mind to recollect its thoughts and feelings.

A fifth aspect or strategy, based upon what appears to be a reciprocal understanding of perspectives, is to appeal directly to the other's perspective, that is, to get the friend's okay.

SUPPOSE YOU WANT TO GO WITH THE NEW FRIEND AND YOU KNOW THE OLD FRIEND WILL BE ANGRY?
You go up and ask your old friend if it is okay with him. You try to get him to see why you want to go.

(12:6)

Here, getting the friend's okay really means presenting one's own point of view so as to convince the friend to change his or her point of view. As such, this is an important new strategy for conflict resolution.

However, in these last two cases, as with all the resolutions offered that are coded as Level 2, the reflective actions taken do not really rest on *mutual* agreement or coordination. There is an understanding that each party requires satisfaction, but not that each may care about or need to attend to the other's sense of how well the issue is resolved.

LEVEL 3:   STABILITY OF FRIENDSHIPS AND MUTUAL SOLUTIONS TO CONFLICTS

The core reorientation at Level 3 is the understanding that certain friendship conflicts reside within the relationship itself, in the interaction between the parties, rather than in external annoyances to each party individually. We will discuss five new aspects.

First, individuals whose responses are coded as Level 3 indicate a belief that resolutions cannot be arrived at solely through detente: *each* side must feel that *both* he or she and the other are truly satisfied with the resolution and would be satisfied if in the other's place.

> If you just settle up after a fight that is no good. You gotta really feel that you'd be happy the way things went if you were in your friend's shoes. You can just settle up with someone who is not a friend, but that's not what friendship is really about.
>
> (15:6)

> Alan and I had a problem, which movie to go to. So we try to decide but if one person gives in just for the other and is not really happy about what to do that's no good either. You both have to really agree.
>
> (14:8)

A second aspect is recognition that friendship conflicts may be due to conflicts of personality and a resolution made might be personality change.

> She doesn't like the new girl.
> WHY?
> Well, one is a show-off and the other is very shy.
> COULD THEY EVER BE FRIENDS?
> Well, only if one of them changed their personality. Shy people don't usually like show-offs.
>
> (13:8)

A third aspect is recognition that conflicts of a certain type may actually strengthen a relationship rather than weaken it. Subjects at Level 3 see true friendship as continuing through thick and thin. A fourth and related aspect or strategy is that conflicts should be 'talked out' or 'worked out'. Because one locus of conflict is seen as *between* persons, this 'working through' is understood to be a more difficult process than the expedient types of resolutions generally suggested as adequate at Level 2. Because the working through is seen as a commitment by both parties, there is the awareness at Level 3 that through this mutuality, conflict resolution may strengthen friendship bonds.

> IF YOU HAVE PROBLEMS WITH FRIENDS, WHAT IS THE BEST WAY TO WORK THEM OUT? IF YOU HAVE AN ARGUMENT?
> Usually we get into fights sometimes, he comes down my house and steals my bike out of the garage, or I steal his bike to pick at him or get at his nerves, usually I just call him up and tell him I am sorry, it always happens like that and then we just make up.
> SO A PERSON USUALLY SAYS IT IS THEIR FAULT?
> Sometimes they do. Sometimes it was their fault and you agree, and sometimes it was your fault and you agree. Sometimes it is easier to do that with a friend. They understand. Every friendship, you always fight and everything, about something.
> SO IS PART OF A DEEP FRIENDSHIP GOING THROUGH THESE FIGHTS?
> Yah, I guess so.
> IT SOUNDS CONTRADICTORY, A FRIEND IS SOMEONE YOU CAN HAVE FIGHTS WITH, WHY IS THAT?
> Because you show that you really like the kid and that you are friends. If you didn't have a fight with the kid, it means you do this, I do that. You all work together and things like that. Everybody disagrees with everybody about something. No one is perfect with each other.
>
> (14:1)

The fifth aspect of conflict resolution we identified at Level 3 is a distinction made between superficial conflict and deeper bonds. At Level 2 inner feelings and outer appearances are distinguished. At Level 3 there is a further recognition of the dichotomy between the immediate inner reaction during a period of conflict and the longer term affective relation that transcends these immediate feelings. The *bond itself* is seen as a source of healing, a means of conflict resolution between close friends.

> Like you have known your friend so long and you loved her so much, and then all of a sudden you are so mad at her you say, I could just kill you, and you still like each other, because you have

known each other for years and you have always been friends and you know in your mind you are going to be friends in a few seconds anyway.

(12:9)

The emphases of Level 3, then, appear to be on *active* interpersonal communication and sharing, and on verbal or mental rather than physical-action resolutions.

LEVEL 4:   AUTONOMOUS INTERDEPENDENCE AND SYMBOLIC ACTION AS A RESOLUTION TO CONFLICTS

If Level 3 understanding can be characterized as an interpersonal orientation based on a close-knit mutuality, Level 4 can be seen as a partial rejection of that mutuality when it precludes autonomous growth and development. At first, what we hear from subjects is the rejection of a perceived overdependence or overbonding in Level 3 relations. This move, in moderation, can be viewed as independence, but in its extreme is a counter-dependent position.

Then you come to the place where you almost depend on the other person and you're not an individual anymore. If you tell—like if she knows everything about you if you depend so much on the other person, I think it is egotistical.

(16—advanced placement student)

This independence, based on an understanding but partial rejection of mutuality, is itself subsequently tempered by the belief that total independence is as futile as total dependence.

No man is an island. I'm not saying you got to fuse with a friend and lose your identity all together. I'm just saying you got to rely on other people to some extent, so it might as well be a close friend who you trust and who you're in vibes with.
WHAT DO YOU MEAN, IN VIBES WITH?
Well, someone who understands you and you understand them without always having to say things all the time.

(24)

The idea of nonverbal communication, the idea of taking actions as *symbolic of the (repair of the) relationship* is one critical aspect of conflict resolution at Level 4.

WHAT IS THE BEST WAY FOR ARGUMENTS TO BE SETTLED BETWEEN GOOD FRIENDS?
Well, you could talk it out, but it usually fades itself out. It usually takes care of itself. You don't have to explain everything. You do certain things and each of you knows what it means. But if not, then talk it out.

(16)

The other particular aspect we identified in the reasoning of subjects coded at this level is the understanding that intrapsychic conflicts, that is, conflicts *within* a person, can be a factor in conflicts *between* that person and a friend.

Sometimes when a person's got problems of his own, he finds himself starting fights with all his friends. The best thing you can do is try to be understanding but don't get stepped on either.

(27)

You have to get yourself together if you expect to get along with others. A lot of relationships break up because one of the people is not really happy with himself. Of course, a good relationship like a good friendship is a good way for a person to find himself ... if he doesn't do things to alienate his friend first.
   One good way to straighten things out between friends is to understand how the problem may relate to problems the person has in general. For example, lots of people have problems with authority. If they start to see the friendship as an authority relation, there might be trouble. But to solve it they have to sort out their own feelings.

(34)

The first excerpt also demonstrates the balance between independence and dependence. Help, commit, but keep a sense of self, keep some distance.
   A third mode suggested for resolving conflicts between persons who are seen as capable of having everdeepening relations and commitments to one another is to 'keep the lines of communication open', to rely on established channels.

Friends are always having to deal with each other's problems, hurt feelings, slights, things like that. The only way to maintain the friendship is by keeping open lines of communication.

(34)

By this, the subjects seem to mean (*a*) keeping in touch with one's own deeper feelings; (*b*) keeping in touch with the more personal and sensitive concerns of the friends; and (*c*) establishing a mode or operating procedure for communicating these feelings back and forth with one another over time.

The Keller and Reuss levels include both descriptive and prescriptive components though the latter are stressed. An interpersonal morality of friendship is defined in the Keller and Reuss scheme in a way which is more specifically moral than is true for Selman. They say:

> Since the interpretation and solution of the dilemma involves clashes of interest as well as conflicts between norms, an adequate reconstruction of social cognitive competence involves both prescriptive and descriptive aspects.
>
> Each level represents a reorganization of the system of categories of which a naive theory of action is comprised. The levels are taken to form a hierarchical sequence.
>
> Description of the levels of socio-moral understanding exemplifies the differentiation and coordination of the categories of a naive theory of action. On the one hand it manifests growing awareness of others as concrete persons in particular circumstances as defined by their specific situations, relations, and internal states. On the other hand these descriptions show social knowledge to be increasingly structured by standards of moral rightness. Thus a person's actions, relations, and internal state are increasingly constructed and evaluated in the light of mutually shared standards of moral acceptability and legitimacy negotiated, in principle at least, in discourses among equals.

The levels are defined in Table 5.

In summary, the Keller and Reuss rational reconstruction of our first four stages in the interpersonal realm clarifies Habermas' theory of communicative action in which claims to rightness are 'redeemed' in dialogue aimed to reach consensus among equals.

Table 5*.

Level zero

At level zero no differentiation between the subjective perspectives of self and other has emerged. The situation is not yet interpreted in terms of conflicting claims, i.e. of self's needs and interests vs. other's (friend's) needs, interests or expectations. Self's mostly hedonistic perspective is attributed to other as well (friend wants to go to the movie as well). Therefore, no differentiation is possible between preferences and preferability in the sense of what would be right to do. The preferential behavior is not yet oriented towards the representation of alternative options, goals or action strategies. Action decisions are primarily oriented towards objects (movie, toys). They are not oriented towards intersubjective invariances and established action patterns in the context of an ongoing relationship (friendship). Persons are representatives of certain gratifying objects, and perceived in their instrumental function (offers made to the actor). Relations are not organized over time nor are they tied to specific persons, or specified by definite characteristics (such as old friendship, situation of new child). Actor may achieve a first differentiation of subjective perspectives with regard to the anticipation of various consequences of decisions for ego and alter: satisfaction of needs leads to positive, dissatisfaction to negative feelings. Thus, even if negative consequences of self's action decision for other can be anticipated (friend will feel bad if actor goes to movie), such understanding does not have a regulatory or modifying function for self's preferences concerning decisions, goals and means. Consequences are

*By kind permission of Professor Monika Keller

interpreted in terms of 'effects' for which the actor is not yet held responsible. Actions are not yet perceived as objects of justification and no necessity is felt to devise strategies of compensation for negative consequences for other. Strategic and communicative forms of action are not yet differentiated even in the most elementary form.

Level one

At this level a beginning differentiation between subjective-particular and intersubjectively 'right' perspectives emerges (actor should go to the friend). At this level subjective perspectives of self and other are differentiated in terms of specific needs, interests and expectations and can be perceived as conflicting (actor wants to go to the movie, friend wants actor to come). Expectations gain 'quasi-normative' status resulting, first, from ego's declaration of intent (actor said he or she would come). Second, they result from the relationship between self and other (actor and friend), a relationship interpreted in terms of the intersubjective invariance of action orientations. These are based on the given regularities of established patterns of action (they always meet and play together). Third, expectations may refer to the non-normative circumstances and the corresponding needs and feelings of the new child (new in town, alone). Therefore, a first differentiation between preference and preferability becomes possible. Preference relations are based on naive hedonistic criteria (which is more or less fun) and/or the 'quasi-obligatory' aspects of the situation (actor doesn't want to leave out one or the other). They take into account consequences of a decision for self and other. Consequences relate back to the self in terms of consequences of consequences (if actor does not go to friend, friend will never play with actor). The actor is construed as a person who knows about other's expectations towards him- or herself and about negative evaluations resulting from the violation of such expectations. Regularities in the context of the friendship can be seen as precursors of rules and therefore of moral claims. Their quasi-obligatory nature is evidenced by the fact that action orientations violating expectations that result from such regularities are subject to criticism and in need of justification (friend will ask actor where she has been). Justifications as well as strategies of regulation make use of simple material compensations (actor invites friend another time) as well as imperfect discourse strategies (hides action from friend). This strategy serves the function of avoiding negative consequences for the self.

Level two

At this level a clear distinction between subjective-particular perspectives and intersubjectively 'right' orientations of action is achieved. At the same time both dimensions are differentiated and elaborated. Action is no longer oriented only toward given regularities but also toward rules, i.e. toward normative expectations that self and other mutually accept as legitimate (actor has given a promise). Yet, these rules are still represented as isolated and abstract moral requirements. The differentiation between the descriptive and the prescriptive levels of social-cognitive reasoning—between 'is' and 'ought' (Kohlberg, 1969)—is presupposed by the ability to coordinate perspectives in a critical, self-reflective manner from a moral point of view (actor knows that friend will think he or she is a traitor). The distinction between given preference and preferability in a moral sense makes possible the interpretation of the situation as a conflict between 'desire and duty' (wants to go to a movie but has promised). The understanding of the 'inner world' of others gains a moral dimension, but the conflict is not yet understood as an 'inner conflict' of a moral self as is the case at the next level.

Preference behaviour now is based first on formal rules, i.e. on 'institutional facts'—such as having given a promise—and the normative expectations based on these facts. It is based second on interpersonal rules, i.e., on the regularities of established action patterns which gain quasi-normative character. Thus, the friendship relationship as such is taken to contain obligations that specify rules about how one should act towards a friend. Normative expectations are interpreted in abstract and general terms whose validity is claimed independently of the (concrete) persons, the circumstances and the specifying context which might restrict the validity claim of a norm (e.g., 'a promise must be kept'). This type of interpretation presupposes a social-cognitive generalization in a dual form: temporal and social-interpersonal, implying that the rule is valid always and for everyone.

Relations are seen as more exclusive and intimate (being best friends). At the same time, particular conditions of the relationship are taken into account (friends have their special day, friend does not like new child). Formal rules and the consequences of their violation are interpreted on the background of such a specifying interpretation of the situation. Consequences can also be constructed with regard to their longterm effects for the ongoing relationship (they will stop being friends). In the case of violation of obligations actor is aware that other (friend) morally evaluates his or her actions and ascribes certain personality attributes to him or her (e.g. being a traitor).

Level three

At this level the components of intersubjective rightness are further differentiated (preferability). Single rules and regularities are integrated into systems of norms of reciprocity basic to intimate relationships like friendship. The perspectives of self and other are tied to a role-bound understanding of how one generally acts and should act towards a friend. The norm of reciprocity and its derivatives such as dependability, reliability and trustworthiness constitutes the superordinate viewpoint guiding action in the context of an ongoing relationship. At the same time the moral point of view is elaborated. This leads to a view of an actor as having a strict obligation to orient action towards those norms (if she is a good friend she must go to her friend as promised, good friends must be able to trust each other). Obligations to the friend become part of an actor's self-evaluative system. Violating friendship norms would lead to a negative self-evaluation (he would feel guilty if he would let his best friend down, he would feel that he was a traitor, that he is not a trustworthy friend). A strict orientation towards these general norms also implies taking into account the particular circumstances of the friend's situation as well as that of the new child. Friend's specific needs and problems become dominant aspects for the structuring of action.

There is a clear distinction now between strategic and communicative action implying a differentiation between legitimate and illegitimate strategies of regulation. A justification of an action that violates reciprocity norms is generally avoided. In the case of problematic actions that are subject to criticism, actions tend to be regulated in dialogical form. Negotiation and communication between actors serve the function to achieve consensual interpretation and validation in the decision making process and to define mutually accepted reasons for action. In the case of violation of reciprocity norms self attempts to elicit other's assent by appealing to excuses and justifications of motives, circumstances and constraints (either the appeal of the offer made to the actor or the situation of the new child). Thus, self tries to restore the moral balance in order to ascertain the long-term existence of the relationship.

Hypothetical role switch serves the function to consider possible actions and reactions from the viewpoint of others (asking friend to take self's perspective or the perspective of the new child). This is the basis for a regulatory principle of universalization leading to the potential switch of the roles of actor, those concerned by an action and those judging the moral quality of an action.

It should be noted that the Habermas-influenced rational reconstruction of stages of friendships and interpersonal communication helps to extend the structural approach to include the 'non-Kantian' or non-justice defined aspects of sociomoral development in particularistic relations of special obligation (friendship) stressed by Gilligan (1982), Blum (1980) and Haan (1980). Kohlberg Levine and Hewer (1983) and Kohlberg (1984) interpreted Gilligan's care orientations as a moral orientation to particularistic relationships of kinship and friendship, and special-group membership (e.g., ethnic and religious) or to 'special obligations', to responsibilities where situational context and 'empathic' awareness of the psychology of the other and of self-awareness are more central than in our justice dilemmas, and take priority over generalized rules and rights. In this way, the Habermas project suggests an integration of our justice stages and the levels of care suggested by Gilligan and her colleagues.

To summarize, it is clear that Rawls, Habermas and myself all propose ideal procedures for reaching consensus in situations of moral conflict. For Rawls such a procedure is the 'original position under the veil of ignorance', for Habermas the rules for an ideal communication situation, for myself the procedure of moral musical chairs. All of these normative theories rely on Kant's original intuitions of the formal principle of universalizability and the substantive principle of respect for persons as central features of morality. None, however, rests on Kant's metaphysical assumptions about noumenal moral selves but assumes that moral principles are human constructions arising through human interaction and communication. Each is at least partly dependent on empirical psychological and anthropologic interpretation of data, on 'competent' moral judges or moral speakers, on 'the rational reconstruction of ontogenesis', and each presupposes a universalizing postconventional level of moral development. At this point this convergence is still uncertain and open to the criticisms of philosophers like Locke. For Carter, to ask either moral philosophy or moral psychology to do more in the way of reaching agreement on principles and their applications to concrete moral conflicts is an unreasonable expectation. To us it is still an open question as to what an integration of psychological enquiry and normative justification may do.

We have tried to indicate how minor variations in defining an ideal terminus of development (Habermas and ourselves) lead to somewhat different 'rational reconstructions' of earlier (i.e., preconventional and conventional stages) stages, but much further detailed conceptual work would have to be done to compare the adequacy of one rational reconstruction as opposed to another, an issue linked also to the possibility of arriving at a justifiable definition of a sixth stage.

EDUCATION

Unfortunately time and space prohibit my commenting on political and theological issues raised by my theory. Given these restrictions, I will also keep my remarks on education brief. Gordon's clarification of the various meanings of the term 'hidden curriculum' is helpful, though in our more recent work (Higgins, Power and Kohlberg, 1984) we have attempted to equate our concerns about the 'hidden curriculum' of the regular high school with its 'moral atmosphere'. 'Moral atmosphere' we identify with the governing moral norms of a school and its sense of solidarity, care or community. The most powerful norms are high in 'degree of collectiveness' and are shared among students and teachers alike. In the 'regular' high schools we studied there was little congruity between teacher and peer group norms on such issues as cheating or drug use, with peers actually holding 'counter-norms' of tolerance or support of drug use and cheating directly counter to the teachers' norms. These norms were hidden, in the sense that they were unshared by the teachers but implicitly supported by them. Peer counter-norms supporting cheating were in a sense natural consequences of the teachers' stress on norms of competitive achievement. Of more direct relevance to the general notion of moral atmosphere, in the regular school, even peer norms had a low 'degree of collectivity', i.e., they were not perceived as shared. In contrast, in the alternative democratic high schools we studied norms had a relatively high degree of collectiveness, i.e., they were perceived as consciously shared by the group or the community, the result of the fact that these norms were discussed in an open way and that there was an attempt to arrive at agreement on these norms through a democratic voting process. In this sense, then, the group norms of the traditional high school were relatively 'hidden' and unintended from the teacher's point of view. Further, they were not conceived of as moral in an explicit sense involving moral justification as was true in the democratic alternative schools.

Let me now turn to Leming's review of the practical difficulties of implementing developmental moral education in the public schools. Leming points to two basic reasons why teachers fail to persist in practising moral dilemma discussion after some training in it. The first is incongruity with self-conceptions of their role, the second is 'curricular press'. With regard to self-conception of role, teachers are used to thinking of themselves as classroom managers, not as moral educators, their philosophy need not be developmental. Our efforts, for which we cannot yet claim a great deal of success, to change teachers' role conceptions centre on a Harvard Summer Institute, which of course is preselected in the sense that teachers and administrators with an interest in moral education take it. In this summer institute an effort is made not only to discuss critically notions of development as the aim of education and democracy as the means of education, but to create a 'just community' atmosphere among participants and staff. This has led to at least one conspicuously successful implementation of the just community model, the Scarsdale alternative school which has been following the model since 1978 (Kohlberg, 1985b; Moral Education Forum, spring 1984). Two other alternative schools in New York city will also be trying the model.

Once started, a 'just community' alternative school provides many challenges and rewards for participating teachers. Teacher autonomy within a democratic framework and teacher colleagueship are powerful supports for teacher participants. These schools do require extra effort on the part of teachers with the possibility of burn-out. The sense of community, the 'school spirit', however, provides a powerful sense of satisfaction for teachers and students when things are going well.

As Leming points out, alternative schools can hardly represent a model for mainstream education. The theory points to a high school with small houses similar to the alternative schools and with representative democracy for overall school-work rules and policies (Power, 1985).

The continuing efforts of myself and my colleagues are based on the hope not that the idea involved will actually take hold in a large number of schools, but rather of keeping a model growing in which the compound of psychology, philosophy and educational practical wisdom called 'educational theory' can be tested. Leming's chapter accurately points out not only many of the practical difficulties involved in the implementation of a 'Kohlbergian' approach to moral education, but also the research challenges it poses.

Our major research efforts to date have been formatively to evaluate democratic alternative schools in terms of the growth of collective norms and a sense of community which does influence student action in areas like cheating, stealing, helping other students, etc. (Higgins, Power and Kohlberg, 1984). Our ethnographic method needs to be accompanied by 'hardline' data on these behaviours, relatively easy to get for a school or group though difficult to get for any individual student.

Leming also points to the ethical and political dilemmas resulting from the ethical requirement that the moral educator be open about the fact that he or she is doing moral education and being relatively open about the stage framework being used. In many cases, the very genuine difficulties Leming points to are not specific to 'Kohlbergian' moral education but are implicit in any theory and research-based approach to moral education, even when the theorist tries to move from practice to theory as much as from theory to practice (Kohlberg, 1984). Deliberate or rational moral education may be an idea whose time has not come, any more than it had in Socrates' and Plato's Athens or Dewey's America, but a programme of research discussed in previous sections of this chapter needs, I believe, to be steered by its implications for educational practice, whether or not it has wide-scale chances of implementation.

REFERENCES

Blasi, A. (1980) 'Bridging moral cognition and moral action: A critical review of the literature', *Psychological Bulletin*, 88, pp. 1–45.

Blum, L. (1980) *Friendship, Altruism and Morality*, London, Routledge and Kegan Paul.

Boyd, D. (1979) 'An interpretation of principled morality', *Journal of Moral Education*, 8, 2.

Boyd, D. (1980) 'The Rawls connection', in B. Munsey (Ed.), *Moral Development, Moral Education and Kohlberg*, Birmingham, Ala., Religious Education Press.

Brandt, R. B. (1961) *Value and Obligation: Systematic Readings in Ethics*, New York, Harcourt.

Carter, R. E. (1980) 'What is Lawrence Kohlberg doing?', *Journal of Moral Education*, 9, 2.

Colby, A. and Kohlberg, L. (Eds.) (1984) *The Measurement of Moral Judgment*, Vols. 1 and 2, New York, Cambridge University Press, in press.

Colby, A., Kohlberg, L., Gibbs, J. and Lieberman, M. (1983) 'A longitudinal study of moral judgment', Society for Research in Child Development: Monograph Series, Chicago.

Dewey, J. (1960) *The Theory of Moral Life*, New York, Holt, Rinehart and Winston.

Frankena, W. K. (1973) *Ethics*, Englewood, N.J., Prentice-Hall.

Gewirth, A. (1978) *Reason and Morality*, Chicago, Ill., University of Chicago Press.

Gilligan, C. (1982) *In a Different Voice: Psychological Theory and Women's Development*, Cambridge, Mass., Harvard University Press.

Gilligan, C. and Lyons (1984) 'The development of moral judgment in adolescent girls'. Unpublished research report Harvard Graduate School of Education.

Habermas, J. (1982) 'A universal ethic of communication and problems of ethical relativity and skepticism'. Paper presented at the International Symposium on Moral Education. Fribourg University, Switzerland.

Habermas, J. (1983) 'Interpretive social science vs. hermeneuticism', in N. Haan, R. Ballah, P. Rabinow and W. Sullivan (Eds.), *Social Science as Moral Inquiry*, New York, Columbia University Press.

Habermas, J. (1984) *A Theory of Communicative Action*, Boston, Mass., Beacon Press.

Hare, R. (1981) *Moral Thinking*, Oxford, Clarendon Press.

Higgins, A., Power, C. and Kohlberg, L. (1984) 'The relationship of moral atmosphere to judgments of responsibility', in W. Kurtines and J. Gewirtz (Eds.), *Morality, Moral Behavior and Moral Development*, New York, Wiley Interscience.

Kegan, R. (1981) 'A Neopiagetian approach to object relations', in B. Lee and G. Noam (Eds.), *The Self: Psychology, Psychoanalysis and Anthropology*, New York, Plenum.

Kegan, R. (1982) *The Evolving Self: Problem and Process in Human Development*, Cambridge, Mass., Harvard University Press.

Keller, M., and Reuss, S. (1984) 'An action-theoretical reconstruction of the development of social-cognitive competence', *Human Development*, 27, 211–220.

Kohlberg, L. (1963) 'Moral development and identification', in H. Stevenson (Ed.), *Child Psychology, 62nd Yearbook of the National Society for the Study of Education*, Chicago, Ill., University of Chicago Press.

Kohlberg, L. (1964) 'The development of moral character and ideology', in M. L. Hoffman (Ed.), *The Review of Child Development Research*, Vol. 1, New York, Russell Stage Foundation.

Kohlberg, L. (1969) 'Stage and sequence: The cognitive-developmental approach to socialization', in

D. A. Goslin (Ed.) *Handbook of Socialization on Theory and Research*, New York: Rand McNally.

Kohlberg, L. (1971) 'From *is* to *ought*: How to commit the naturalistic fallacy and get way with it in the study of moral development', in T. Mischel (Ed.) *Cognitive Development and Epistemology*: New York: Academic Press.

Kohlberg, L. (1973) 'Continuities in childhood and adult moral development revisited', in P. B. Baltes and K. W. Schaie (Ed.) *Life-Span Development Psychology: Personality and Socialization*, New York: Academic Press.

Kohlberg, L. (1976) 'Moral stages and moralization: the cognitive-developmental approach', in T. Lickona (Ed.) *Moral Development and Behaviour: Theory, Research and Social Issues*, New York: Holt, Rinehart and Winston.

Kohlberg, L. (1981) *The Philosophy of Moral Development: Moral Stages and the Idea of Justice*. San Francisco: Harper and Row Publishers, Volume 1.

Kohlberg, L. (1984) *The Psychology of Moral Development: Moral Stages and the Life Cycle*, San Francisco: Harper and Row Publishers, Volume 2.

Kohlberg, L. (1985a) 'The return of stage 6; its principle and its moral point of view'. Paper presented at Ringberg Gerreant Conference on Developmental Psychology and Moral Philosophy.

Kohlberg, L. (1985b) 'The Just Community in Theory and Practice'. In M. Berkowitz and F. Oser (Eds.) *Moral Education*, Hillside, N. J., Erlbaum.

Kohlberg, L. (1986) *Education and Moral Development: Moral Stages and Practice*, San Francisco: Harper and Row Publishers, Volume 3.

Kohlberg, L., Levine, C. and Hewer, A. (1983) 'Moral stages: A current formulation and a response to critics', *Contributions to Human Development 10*, Basel, S. Karger.

Lakatos, I. (1978) *The Methodology of Scientific Research Programs*, in J. Worral and G. Currie (Eds.), Cambridge, Cambridge University Press.

Lapsley, D. and Serlin, R. (1983) 'On the alleged degeneration of the Kohlbergian research program', Paper presented at the 1983 Society for Research in Child Development. (Obtainable from D. Lapsley, Department of Educational Psychology, University of Wisconsin, Madison, WI 53706.)

Lee, L. (n.d.) 'Relations between Kohlberg moral stages and Loevinger ego stages', Unpublished.

Locke, D. (1981) 'The principle of equal interest', *The Philosophical Review*, 90, 4, pp. 531–59.

Loevinger, J. (1976) *Ego Development. Conceptions and Theories*, San Francisco, Jossey-Bass.

Loevinger, J. (1979) 'Scientific ways in the study of ego development', *Heinz Werner Lecture Series*, Vol. 12, Worcester, Mass., Clark University Press.

Loevinger, J. and Wessler, R. (1970) *Measuring Ego Development*, Vol. 1, San Francisco, Jossey-Bass.

McCarthy, T. (1978) *The Critical Theory of Jurgen Habermas*, Cambridge, Mass., MIT Press.

McCarthy, T. (1982) 'Rationality and relativism', in J. Thompson and D. Held (Eds.), *Habermas: Critical Debates*, Cambridge, Mass., MIT Press.

Noam, G. (1984) 'Explorations in clinical-developmental psychology', Unpublished doctoral dissertation, Harvard University.

Piaget, J., and Inhelder, B. (1969) *The Psychology of the Child*. New York: Basic Books.

Power, C. (1985) 'Democracy in the Larger High School'. In M. Berkowitz and F. Oser (Eds.) *Moral Education*, Hillside, N. J., Erlbaum.

Rawls, J. (1971) *A Theory of Justice*, Cambridge, Mass., Harvard University Press.

Rawls, J. (1980) 'Kantian constructivism in moral theory', *Journal of Philosophy*, 87, pp. 525–72.

Rest, J. R. (1984) 'The major components of morality', in W. Kurtines and J. Gewirtz (Eds.) *Morality and Moral Development*, New York, Wiley.

Selman, R. (1976) 'The development of social-cognitive understanding: A guide to education and clinical practice', in T. Lickona (Ed.), *Moral Development and Behavior, Theory, Research and Social Issues*, New York, Holt, Rinehart and Winston.

Selman, R. (1980) *The Growth of Interpersonal Understanding*, New York, Academic Press.

Sidgwick, H. (1887) *Method of Ethics*, London, Macmillan.

Skinner, B. F. (1971) *Beyond Freedom and Dignity*, New York: Knopf.

Snarey, J. (1985) 'Cross-cultural studies of moral development: A critical review', *Psychological Bulletin*.

Snarey, J., Kohlberg, L. and Noam, G. (1983) 'Ego development and education: A structural perspective', *Developmental Review*, 3, pp. 303–38.

Walker, L. J. (1980) 'Cognitive and perspective-taking prerequisites for moral development', *Child Development*, 51, pp. 131–40.

Walker, L. J. (1984) 'Sex differences in the development of moral reasoning: A critical review of the literature', *Child Development*, 55, pp. 677–92.

Walker, L. J. (1982b) 'The sequentiality of Kohlberg's stages of moral development', *Child Development*, 53, pp. 1330–6.

Walker, L. J. (in press) 'The sequentiality of Kohlberg's stages of moral development', *Child Development*.

Walker, L. J. and Richards, B. S. (1979) 'Stimulating transitions in moral reasoning as a function of stage of cognitive development', *Developmental Psychology*, 15, pp. 95–103.

Author Index

Subject Index